LORD BYRON.

New York: Harper & Brothers, 1869

Lord Byron jugé par les témoins de sa Vie.

MY RECOLLECTIONS

OF

LORD BYRON;

AND

THOSE OF EYE-WITNESSES OF HIS LIFE.

"The long promised work of the
COUNTESS GUICCIOLI."—
Athenæum.

NEW YORK:

HARPER & BROTHERS, PUBLISHERS,

FRANKLIN SQUARE.

1869.

ADVERTISEMENT BY THE ENGLISH PUBLISHER.

THE Publisher of this Translation feels authorized to state, that it is the production of the celebrated COUNTESS GUICCIOLI.

RICHARD BENTLEY.

TO

THE AUTHOR OF THIS WORK,

THE

ENGLISH TRANSLATION

IS

Respectfully Dedicated

BY

HUBERT E. H. JERNINGHAM.

CONTENTS.

Lord Byron jugé par les Témoins de sa Vie.

MY RECOLLECTIONS, ETC.

INTRODUCTION.

"To know another man well, especially if he be a noted and illustrious character, is a great thing not to be despised."—SAINTE-BEUVE.

MANY years ago a celebrated writer, in speaking of Lord Byron, who had then been dead some years, said that so much had already been written upon him that the subject had almost become commonplace, but was far from being exhausted. This truth, indisputable when applied to Byron's genius, his works, and to his intellect, was then and still is equally positive when referring to his moral qualities. A subject as well as an object may become commonplace by the quantity, but nevertheless remain new and rare, owing to its quality. A subject can not be exhausted before it has been seen under every one of its various aspects, and appreciated in all its points. If much has been said of Lord Byron, has his truly noble character been fairly brought to light? Has he not, on the contrary, been judged rather as the author than the man, and have not the imaginary creations of his powerful mind been too much identified with reality? In the best biographies of his life do we not meet with many gaps which have to be filled up—nay, worse, gaps filled up with errors which have to be eradicated to make room for the truth? The object of this work is precisely to do away with these errors and to replace them by facts, and to dispel the shadows which fancy has raised around his name. For the old opinions we wish to substitute new appreciations, by weighing exactly the measure of truth which exists in the former; and by the logic of facts we wish to judge fairly so as to prevent posterity from being deceived. In doing this we do not pretend to give England any new information. For a long time, no doubt, error sprang from that country; but years and events have passed since that state of things existed. The liberal and tolerant spirit, enlightened by philosophy, which has spread all over liberal England, has also been reflected in the opinions formed of men, and has modified many pages of biography and history and made Englishmen feel how numerous were the wrongs of which they were guilty toward their illustrious countryman.

It is useless to speak of the national selfishness of England, and pretend that she only appreciates or rewards with her love and esteem such writers as flatter her pride or hide her defects from the eyes of foreigners. This may be true, generally speaking; but Lord Byron's patriotic feelings were of a very different cast. He thought it best to expose to the world at large the faults of his countrymen, in order to correct them. His patriotism was influenced by the superiority of the noble sentiments which actuated his life. Feeling as he did, that he was, above all, a member of the great human community, and declaring it openly; despising popularity, if it cost him the sacrifice of a truth which he deemed it useful and right to proclaim, and thus going against many of the passions, prejudices, and opinions of his countrymen, Byron certainly wounded many susceptibilities; and could we forget all he had to suffer at the hands of the English, we might almost say he was too severe in his judgments upon them. Notwithstanding, however, it is almost impossible to travel in England without meeting everywhere some token of homage paid to the memory of Byron. Scotland, who looks upon him almost as a son, is proud to show the several houses wherein he lived when a child, and preserves his name and memory with love and respect. To have seen him once, is a recollection of which one is proud. A particular charm encircles the places, mountains, rivers, and bridge of Don, of which he speaks, simply because he has mentioned them in his poems. A letter or any thing which has belonged to him is looked upon as a treasure.

At Harrow, the beloved residence of his youth, the growing generation bow with affectionate respect before the pyramid which has been erected to his memory by the love of a former youthful generation. At Cambridge, among all the monuments which recall the glories of the past, Lord Byron's statue commands the rest, and occupies the place of honor. The rooms which he had there are shown and reverenced as places which have harbored genius. In Parliament the same man who formerly, by unjust and unmerited criticisms of the youthful poet, decried his growing genius, and who was guilty of other wrongs against him, has made an act of reparation and of justice by expressing publicly his regret that a grudge of the dean in Byron's time had prevailed to prevent a monument being erected in Westminster Abbey to the memory of the poet. The pilgrimage to Newstead is looked upon as an intellectual feast, if not as a duty, by young Englishmen, and his genius is so much revered by them that they do not admit that he is equalled by any contemporary poet or likely to be surpassed by those who follow. No doubt, therefore, England now-a-days only prefers what formerly she used to exact from her poets. Moore's culpable timidities and Macaulay's declamatory exaggerations must, at least, be looked upon as weaknesses of character, which would have been disowned by themselves, had they lived long enough to witness the change in public opinion.

Although full justice has not yet been done to the noble character of the man, still partial justice has been rendered to Byron's memory by the summary dismissal of the numerous false writings which appeared and which tended to replace the truth by the creations of fancy, and to put into the mouth of the poet the thoughts of their authors and not his own, or to insult him by a magnanimous defense, the honor and glory of which was to redound entirely to the writers. It is necessary to observe, that if Byron was openly calumniated during his lifetime, he was not less so after his death by disguised slander, especially by that kind of absolution which in reality is one of the most odious forms of calumny, since it is the most hypocritical and most difficult to deal with, and least likely to be touched. But England has at last understood the truth and settled all such opinions.

To England, therefore, these pages, which contain the rectification of certain old opinions, will be useless. But can the same be said of other countries, and of France especially?

Even now-a-days, we read such fanciful appreciation of Byron's character that we could almost believe that the rumors and calumnies which came from England had never been refuted; and that extraordinary views expressed by Lamartine in beautiful verse are still entertained, and the question still asked, whether Byron was "a devil or an angel?" On reading such appreciations, it seems opportune to present those who admire genius and truth with a very humble but conscientious study of Byron's great mind.

Can it be objected, that the fact of the defense of a foreigner detracts from the interest of the reader? Can a genius be a stranger to man, and does not the earth seem too small to contain such exceptional beings?

Our civilization, which has almost suppressed every physical barrier that exists between the nations of the earth, has still further annihilated those of the intellect: so much so, that Shakspeare, Dante, Goethe, are as much revered in France as in their respective countries, notwithstanding the difference of the idioms in which they have written. The same will occur in respect to Lord Byron, whose name alone opposes every barrier, and against whom the difference of nationality can not form any obstacle. The language of genius is not of one country only, but appertains to humanity in general: and God Himself has implanted its rules in every heart.

This book is not a regular nor a methodical biography. Nor is it an apology; but rather a study, an analysis, the portrait of a great mind seen under all its aspects, with no other decided intention on the part of the writer than to tell the truth, and to rest upon indisputable facts and rely upon unimpeachable testimony.

The public now, it is said, can not bear eulogy, and cares only to know the weak points of great men. We do not believe this to be the case. It would be too severe a criticism of human nature in general, and of our times in particular. In any case, we can not accept the statement as correct, when applied to noble characters to whom we especially dedicate this work. It may be, the reader will find in our essay beauties which he had not yet observed, which have hitherto been disputed in the original, and which less sympathetic natures than ours might term complacent eulogies; but the fear of being blamed and of being unpopular shall not deter us from our intention of bringing them forth. No criticism can prevent our praising, when he deserves it, the man who never knew the weaknesses of jealousy, and who never failed to bestow eulogy upon every kind of talent without ever claiming any in return. In publishing the book we are, moreover, certain that what to-day may appear praise, to-morrow will be termed justice.

Lord Byron shone at a period when a school called Romantic was in progress of formation. That school wanted a type by which to mould its heroes, as a planet requires a sun to give it light. It took Byron as that type, and adorned him with all the qualities which pleased its fancy, but the time has more than arrived when it is necessary that truth should reveal him in his true light. My book is not likely to dispel every cloud, but a few shades only add to the lustre and brilliancy of a landscape.

LORD BYRON.

"Others form the man: I tell of him."—MONTAIGNE.

AT all times the world has been very unjust; and (who does not know it?) in the history of nations many an Aristides has paid with exile the price of his virtues and his popularity. Great men, great countries, whole nations, whole centuries, have had to bear up against injustice; and the truth is, that vice has so often taken the place of virtue, evil of good, and error of truth, some have been judged so severely and others so leniently, that, could the book of redress be written, not only would it be too voluminous, but it would also be too painful to peruse. Honest people would feel shame to see the judgments before which many a great mind has had to bend; and how often party spirit, either religious or political, moved by the basest passions—such as hatred, envy, rivalry, vengeance, fanaticism, intolerance, self-love—has been a pretext for disfiguring in the eyes of the public the greatest and noblest characters. It would then be seen how some censor (profiting by the breach which circumstances, or even a slight fault on the part of these great minds, may have made, and joining issue with other inferior judges of character) has often succeeded in throwing a shade on their glorious actions and in casting a slur upon their reputation, like those little insects which from their number actually succeed, notwithstanding their smallness, in darkening the rays of the sun. What is worse, however, is, that when history has once been erroneously written, and a hero has been put forward in colors which are not real, the public actually becomes accessory to the deception practiced upon it: for it becomes so enamored of the false type which has been held out to its admiration that it will not loosen its hold on it. Public opinion, once fixed, becomes a perfect despotism.

Never, perhaps, has this phenomenon shown itself more visibly and more remarkably than in the case of Lord Byron. Not only was he a victim of these obstinate prejudices, but in his case the annihilation of truth and the creation of an imaginary type have been possible only at the cost of common sense, and notwithstanding the most palpable contradictions. So that he has really proved to be one of the most curious instances of the levity with which human judgments are formed.

We have elsewhere described the various phases of this phenomenon, one of the principal causes of which has been the resolution to identify the poet with the first heroes of his poems. Such a mode of proceeding was as disloyal as it was contrary to all the received rules of literature. It was inspired by hatred and vengeance, adopted by an idle and frivolous public, and the result has proved to be something entirely opposed to the truth.

As long as such a whimsical creation was harmless, it amused Byron himself and his friends; but the day came when it ceased to be harmless without ceasing to be eccentric, and became to Byron a true robe of Nessus.

At his death the truth was demanded of his biographers; but the puppet which had been erected stood there, and amazed the good, while it served the malice of the wicked. His genius was analyzed, but no conscientious study of his character was made, and Byron, as man, remained an unknown personage.

Yet among his biographers there were men of upright and enlightened minds: they did not all seek to raise themselves at the cost of depreciating him, nor to gain popularity by sparing individuals at the expense of Lord Byron.

If among them many proved to be black sheep, there were several, on the other hand, who were sincere, and even kindly disposed. Yet not one did full justice to Byron, not one defended him as he deserved, not one explained his true character with the conscientious energy which in itself constitutes authority. We shall speak elsewhere of the causes which gave rise to this phenomenon. We shall mention the part which public opinion played in England when suddenly displeased with a poet who dared sound the deepest recesses of the human heart; and who as an artist and a psychologist was interested in watching the growth of every passion, and especially that of love, regardless of the conjugal felicity which that public wished him to respect. It began to fear that its enthusiasm for Lord Byron was a national crime, and by degrees became accessory to the calumnies which were heaped upon his noble character, on account of his supposed want of patriotism, and his refusal to be blind to the defects of the mother-country. We shall see how his biographers, preferring invention to strict adherence to the truth, compounded a Lord Byron such as not to be any longer recognizable, and to become even—especially in France—a caricature. Of all this we shall speak hereafter. We shall now rather point to the curious than to the unjust character of this fact, and notice the contradictions to which Byron's biographers have lent themselves.

All, or nearly all, have granted to him an infinity of virtues, and naturally fine qualities—such as sensitiveness, generosity, frankness, humility, charity, soberness, greatness of soul, force of wit, manly pride, and nobility of sentiment; but, at the same time, they do not sufficiently clear him of the faults which directly exclude the above-mentioned qualities. The moral man does not sufficiently appear in their writings: they do not sufficiently proclaim his character—one of the finest that was ever allied to a great intellect. Why? Are these virtues such that, like excellent and salutary substances, they become poisoned when placed in contact within the same crucible?

In this refusal to do justice there is contradiction; and as error exists where contradiction lies, it is precisely in that contradiction that we must seek the means of refuting error and assert the power of truth.

Nature always proceeds logically, and the effect is always in direct analogy with its cause. Even in the moral world the precise character of exact sciences must be found. If in a problem we meet with a contradiction, are we not certain that its solution has been badly worked out, and that we must begin it over again to find a true result? The same reasoning holds good for the moral spheres. When a judgment has been wrongly formed, that is, when there appears to be contradiction between various opinions, that judgment must be remodelled, the cause of the error must be looked for, truth must be separated from falsehood, and regard must be had to the law which obliges us to weigh impartially every assertion, and to discuss equally the ayes and noes. Let this be done for Lord Byron. Let us analyze facts, question the eye-witnesses of his life, and peruse his admirable and simply-written letters, wherein his soul has, so to say, photographed itself. Acts are unquestionably more significative than words; yet if we wish to inquire into his poetry, not by way of appreciating his genius (with which at present we have nothing to do), but the nature of the man, let us do so loyally. Let us not attribute to him the character which he lends to his heroes, nor the customs which he attributes to them, simply because here and there he has given to the one something of his manner, to the other some of his sentiments; or because he has harbored them, in the belief that hospitality can be extended to the wicked without the good suffering from it.

Let us first examine "Childe Harold,"—the poem which principally contributed to mystify the public, and commenced that despotic type of which we have already spoken.

Childe Harold does not tell his own story. His life is told by a poet. There are, therefore, two well-marked personages on the scene, perfectly distinct and different from one another. The first is the young nobleman in whom Byron intended to personify the precocious perversion of mind and soul of the age, and in general the blaséd existence of the young men of the day, of whom he had met many types at Cambridge, and on his first launch into society. The second is the minstrel who tells his story.

The heart of the former is closed to all joy and to all the finest impulses of the soul; whereas that of the other beats with delight at the prospect of all that is noble, great, good, and just in the world. Why identify the author rather with the one than with the other — with the former rather than with the latter? Why take from him his own sentiments, to give him those of his hero? That hero can not be called mysterious, since in his preface Byron tells us himself the moral object for which he has selected him. If Childe Harold personifies Lord Byron, who will personify the poet? That poet (and he is no other than Lord Byron) plays a far greater part than the hero. He is much oftener on the scene. In the greater part of the poem the minstrel alone speaks. In the ninety-three stanzas of which the first canto is composed, Harold is on the scene during nineteen stanzas only, while the poet speaks in his own name during the seventy-four other stanzas, displaying a beautiful soul under various aspects, and exhibiting no melancholy other than that inherent to all elevated poetry.

As for the second canto, it opens with a monologue of the minstrel, and Harold is forgotten until the sixteenth stanza. Then only does the melancholy hero appear, to disappear and reappear again for a few moments. But he rather seems to annoy the minstrel, who finishes at the seventy-third stanza by dismissing him altogether; and from that moment to the end of the canto the wretched and unamiable personage does not reappear. To whom, then, belong all the admirable sentiments and all the virtuous aspirations which we read of toward the end of the canto?—to whom, if not to the minstrel himself? that is, to Lord Byron. What poet has paid so noble a tribute to every virtue? Could that vigor and freshness of mind which breathe upon the lips of the poet, and which well belonged to him, suit the corrupted nature of Harold? If Byron dismisses his hero so often, it is because he experiences toward him the feelings of a logical moralist.

Why then identify Lord Byron with a personage he himself disowns as his prototype, both in his notes, in his preface, in his conversations; and who is proved by facts, by the poem itself, and by the poet's logical and moral reasoning, to be entirely different from his creation? It is true that Byron conceived the unfortunate idea of surrounding his hero by several incidents in his own existence, to place him in the social circle to which he himself belonged, and to give him a mother and a sister, a disappointed love, a Newstead Abbey like his own, and to make him travel where he had travelled, and experience the same adventures.

That is true, and such an act of imprudence can only be explained, by the confidence on which he relied that the identification could never have been thought of. At twenty-one conscience speaks louder than experience. But if we can justify the accusation of his having been imprudent, can we justify his having been calumniated?

Eight years after the publication of the second canto, Byron wrote the third; and here the pilgrim occasionally appears, but so changed that he seems to have been merged into the poet, and to form with him one person only. Childe Harold's sorrows are those of Lord Byron, but there no longer exists any trace of misanthropy or of satiety. His heart already beats with that of the poet for chaste and devoted affections, for all the most amiable, the most noble, and the most sublime of sentiments. He loves the flowers, the smiling and glorious, the charming and sublime aspect of nature.

> "Yet not insensible to all which here
> Awoke the jocund birds to early song
> In glens which might have made even exile dear;
> Though on his brow were graven lines austere,
> And tranquil sternness, which had ta'en the place
> Of feelings fiercer far but less severe,
> Joy was not always absent from his face,
> But o'er it in such scenes would steal with transient trace."

No longer, then, is satiety depicted upon the pilgrim's brow, but "lines austere;" and the poet seems so desirous of proving to us that Harold is metamorphosed, that when he expresses sentiments full of sympathy, humanity, and goodness, his horror for war and his dislike for the beauties of the Rhine, because—

> "A thousand battles have assail'd thy banks,"

he takes care to add—

> "Thus Harold inly said" . . . . . .

Harold, then, has ceased to be the weary *blasé* pilgrim of twenty-one, who in the first canto remains unmoved in presence of the attractions of Florence the beautiful, who inspired the poet with such different sentiments that in the midst even of a storm which threatens to swallow him up he actually finds strength enough to express his sentiments of real love for the lovely absent one—of a love, indeed, which is evidently returned. His heart, like the poet's, now beats with a pure love, and causes him to chant the absence of his friend in the most beautiful strain. Where is the old Harold? It would seem as if the poet, tired of a companion so disagreeable and so opposed to his tastes, and wishing to get rid of him but not knowing how, had first changed and moulded him to his own likeness by giving him his own sentiments, his own great heart, his own pains, his own affections, and, not finding the change natural, had dismissed him altogether. And so it appears, for after the fifty-fifth stanza of the third canto, Childe Harold disappears forever. Thus at the beginning of the fourth canto, which was published a year after, under the auspices of an Italian sky, the reader finds himself in the presence of the poet only. He meets in him a great and generous soul, but the victim of the most odious and unmerited persecution, who takes his revenge in forgiving the wrongs which are done to him, and who reserves all his energies to consecrate them to the love of that which is lovable, to the admiration of that which calls for it, and who at twenty-nine years of age is imbued with Christian and philosophical qualities, which his wearied hero could never have possessed.

Why then again have identified Byron with Childe Harold? For what reason? It strikes us, that the simplest notions of fairness require us at least to take into account the words of the author himself, and to listen to the protestations of a man who despised unmerited praise more than unjust reproof.

"A fictitious character," says Byron, "is introduced for the sake of giving some connection to the piece. . . . .

"It had been easy to varnish over his faults, to make him do more and express less, but he never was intended as an example, further than to show that early perversion of mind and morals leads to satiety of past pleasures and disappointment in new ones, and that even the beauties of nature and the stimulus of travel are lost on a soul so constituted, or rather misdirected.

"It has been suggested to me by friends, on whose opinions I set a high value, that in this fictitious character, 'Childe Harold,' I may incur the suspicion of having intended some real personage: this I beg leave once for all to disclaim—Harold is the child of imagination, for the purpose I have stated. In some very trivial particulars, and those merely local, there might be grounds for such a notion: but in the main points, I should hope, none whatever."

Warned by his friends of the danger which there was for him in being identified with his hero, he paused before publishing the poem. He had written it rather by way of recreation than for any other motive; and when Dallas expressed to him his great desire to see the work published, Byron told him how unwilling he was that it should appear in print, and thus wrote to him, after having given way to Dallas's wishes in the matter:—

"I must wish to avoid identifying Childe Harold's character with mine. If in certain passages it is believed that I wished to identify my hero with myself, believe that it is only in certain parts, and even then I shall not allow it. As for the manor of Childe Harold being an old monastic residence, I thought I might better describe what I have seen than what I invent. I would not for worlds be a man like my hero."

A year after, in writing to Moore on the occasion of dedicating his "Corsair" to him, after saying that not only had his heroes been criticised, but that he had almost been made responsible for their acts as if they were personal to himself, he adds:

"Those who know me are undeceived, and those who do not I have little interest in undeceiving. I have no particular desire that any but my acquaintance should think the author better than the beings of his imagining; but I can not help a little surprise, and perhaps amusement, at some odd critical exceptions in the present instance, when I see several bards in very reputable plight, and quite exempted from all participation in the faults of their heroes, who nevertheless might be found with little more morality than the Giaour; and perhaps—but no—I must admit Childe Harold to be a very repulsive personage, and as to his identity, those who like it must give him whatever *alias* they please."

And in order to embrace the whole of his life in these quotations, we will add what he said at Cephalonia, to Dr. Kennedy, shortly before his death:—

"I can not conceive why people will always mix up my own character and opinions, with those of the imaginary beings which, as a poet, I have the right and liberty to draw."

"They certainly do not spare your lordship in that respect," replied Kennedy; "and in 'Childe Harold,' 'Lara,' the

'Giaour,' and 'Don Juan,' they are too much disposed to think that you paint in many instances yourself, and that these characters are only the vehicles for the expression of your own sentiments and feelings."

"They do me great injustice," he replied, "and what was never before done to any poet. . . . But even in 'Don Juan' I have been misunderstood. I take a vicious and unprincipled character, and lead him through those ranks of society whose high external accomplishments cover and cloak internal and secret vices, and I paint the natural effects of such characters, and certainly they are not so highly colored as we find them in real life."

"This may be true," said Kennedy, "but the question is, what are your motives and object for painting nothing but scenes of vice and folly?"

"To remove the cloak which the manners and maxims of society," said his lordship, "throw over their secret sins, and show them to the world as they really are. You have not," added he, "been so much in high and noble life as I have been; but if you had fully entered into it, and seen what was going on, you would have felt convinced that it was time to unmask the specious hyprocrisy, and show it in its native colors!"

Kennedy having then remarked that the lower and middling classes of society never entertained the opinion that the highest classes exhibited models of piety and virtue, and were, indeed, disposed to believe them worse than they really were, Byron replied:—

"It is impossible you can believe the higher classes of society worse than they are in England, France, and Italy, for no language can sufficiently paint them."

"But still, my lord, granting this, how is your book calculated to improve them, and by what right, and under what title do you too come forward in this undertaking?"

"By the right," he replied, "which every one has who abhors vice united with hypocrisy. My plan is to lead Don Juan through various ranks of society and show that wherever you go vice is to be found."

The doctor then observed, that satire had never done any good, or converted one man from vice to virtue, and that while his satires were useless, they would call upon his head the disapproval both of the virtuous and the wicked.

"But it is strange," answered Byron, "that I should be attacked on all sides, not only from magazines and reviews, but also from the pulpit. They preach against me as an advocate of infidelity and immorality, and I have missed my mark sadly in having succeeded in pleasing nobody. That those whose vices I depicted and unmasked should cry out is natural, but that the friends of religion should do so is surprising: for you know," said he, smiling, "that I am assisting you in my own way as a poet, by endeavoring to convince people of their depravity; for it is a doctrine of yours—is it not?—that the human heart is corrupted; and therefore if I show that it is so in those ranks which assume the external marks of politeness and benevolence,—having had the best opportunities, and better than most poets, of observing it,—am I not doing an essential service to your cause, by first convincing them of their sins, and thus enabling you to throw in your doctrine with more effect?"

"All this is true," said Kennedy; "but you have not shown them what to do, however much you may have shown them what they are. You are like the surgeon who tears the bandages from the numerous wounds of his ulcerated patients, and, instead of giving fresh remedies, you expose them to the air and disgust of every bystander, who, laughing, exclaims, 'How filthy these fellows are!'"

"But I shall not be so bad as that," said Lord Byron; "*you shall see what a winding up I shall give to the story.*"

The end was to justify and give a moral to every thing. While reproving, however, this system of identification, which not only leads to error but also to calumny, can it, however, be denied that there was not some reason, if not to justify it, at least to explain it? To deny that there is, would, we think, be to commit another error. The nature of Lord Byron's genius, the circumstances of his life, the innate qualities of his heart and soul, were unquestionably aids to his detractors.

Upon the measure of the relations which existed between reality and fiction in his poems, and especially as applied to his own history, here are the words of Moore:—

"As the mathematician of old required but a spot to stand

upon, to be able, as he boasted, to move the world, so a certain degree of foundation in fact seemed necessary to Byron, before that lever which he knew how to apply to the world of the passions could be wielded by him. So small, however, was, in many instances, the connection with reality which satisfied him, that to aim at tracing through his stories these links with his own fate and fortunes, which were after all, perhaps, visible but to his own fancy, would be a task as uncertain as unsafe; and this remark applies not only to the 'Bride of Abydos,' but to the 'Corsair,' 'Lara,' and all the other beautiful fictions that followed, in which, though the emotions expressed by the poet may be in general regarded as vivid recollections of what had at different times agitated his own bosom, there are but little grounds, however he might himself occasionally encourage such a supposition, for connecting him personally with the groundwork or incidents of the stories."

To analyze the analogies and differences which existed between the personal character of Byron and that of the poet would form a very curious psychological study. It would be even an act of justice toward his memory, but one which would prove too long, and would ill suit these pages. Let us merely declare, that both analogies and differences have existed, and that if the same can not be said of him as has been said of men of less renown, "the poet is different from the man," it must be allowed that in Byron the two characters were associated without being coupled. This association did not exist between himself and the creatures of his fancy, but merely with the principal features of his poetry, their energy and sensitiveness. As to certain analogies between his heroes, or between them and himself, when they really exist, they should be pointed out; the duty of criticism being to discern and to point to the nature and limits of these analogies.

When Byron began his travels, his genius ever sought an outlet. Too young to have as yet much experience, he had only made known what were his tendencies.

The education of his genius began in his childhood, on the romantic banks of the Dee and on the shores of the ocean; in the midst of the Scottish firs, in the house of his mother, which was peopled with relics of the past; and at Newstead Abbey, situated in the heart of the romantic forest of Sherwood, which is surrounded by the ruins of the great Norman abbeys, and teems with traditional recollections of Robin Hood. The character of that sympathetic chief of the outlaws, who was a nobleman by birth, and who was always followed by the lovely Marian, dressed up as a page; his generosity, his courage, his cleverness, his mixture of virtue and vice, his pride, his buoyant and chivalrous nature, his death even, which was so touching, must, to our mind, have produced a powerful impression upon one who, like Byron, was gifted with as much heart as imagination. At least the poet's fancy, if not the acts of the man himself, must have been influenced by these early impressions; and, no doubt, Conrad, and other heroes of his early poems, must have sprung from the poet's recollections of the legendary stories in the midst of which he had been nursed. In any case, however, the impressions which he had received did not affect his nature.

He had, notwithstanding his youthful years, been able to show the measure, not the tendency of his genius, as well as his aversion for all that is artificial, superficial, insipid, and effeminate; and he had proved that the two great characteristics of his nature were energy and sensitiveness.

An education thus begun was to be continued and matured during his first voyage among scenes the most poetical and romantic in the world; in the glorious East, where there exists a perpetual contrast between the passionate nature of man and the soft hue of the heavens under the canopy of which he lives.

The manners, character, ideas, and singular passions of those races, which civilization has not yet tamed down; their energy, which often betrays itself in the perpetration of the greatest crimes, and as frequently in the practice of the finest qualities; and the life which Byron was forced to lead among them, all produced a great impression upon his mind, and became precious materials to help the development of his intellect. In the same way that, as it has been said, Salvator Rosa's encounters with bandits contributed to the development of his talent, so did the adventures of Lord Byron during this first journey contribute to form his particular taste. Had he always remained in the midst of extremely civilized nations, in which poetry and the great passions are lost, and the heart too often becomes cold, his mind might have developed itself in a less brilliant and original manner.

It was this extraordinary union of energy and sensitiveness in Byron which was to determine the choice of subjects. No doubt the desire to produce an effect had a part in the selection, especially at the dawn of his genius; and this would seem evident in the picture of satiated pleasure as represented by Childe Harold, and in the strange nature of Manfred. But this is only a portion of the reality. His principal qualities were the real arbiters in the selection of subjects which he made. God has not given to us all the same voice. The largest trees—the oaks—require the help of storms to make their voices heard, while the reed only needs the help of the summer breeze.

Byron's attention was ever directed to what was uncommon, either in nature or in the human heart; either in good or in evil, either in the ordinary course of things or beyond its limits. To the study of placid nature he preferred that of that soul which, though less well regulated, yet rises superior to fortune by its energy and will.

The spark which lit up his genius could not live in that goodness which constituted the groundwork of his nature, but in passion, called forth by the sight of great misfortunes, great faults, great crimes, in fact, by the sight of all which attracted or repelled him, which was most in harmony with his energetic character, or at greatest variance with his sensitive nature. One of the motives which actuated his mind was sympathy—the other, antipathy; which exercised over him the same kind of fascination which the bird feels whom the serpent's glance has fascinated, or like the unaccountable impulse which causes a man to throw himself down the precipice on the verge of which he stands.

The various aspects of nature exercised a similar influence over him. With his exquisite sense of their beauties, Byron no doubt often described the enchanting climates in the midst of which he placed the action of his poems; but his pen had always a manly action, with a mixture of grace and vigor in it quite inimitable. His descriptions, however, always appeared to be secondary objects in his mind, and rather constituted the frames which encircled the man whom he wished to depict.

One would say that the soft beauties of a landscape and the playful zephyrs which caress the crests of little waves were too effeminate subjects for him to dwell upon. His preferences evidently point to the savage side of nature, to the struggles between physical forces, to the sublimities of the tempest, and almost, I would say, to a certain disorganization of nature; provided, of course, all is restored to order the moment such a disorganization threatens the existence of beauty in art or in the moral world.

At that time, what Byron could not find in his real and historical subject, he took from another reality, which was himself,—that is, his own qualities, the circumstances of his life, his tastes; without ever inquiring whether Conrad's fear at the sight of the mysterious drop of blood on Gulnare's forehead was that of Byron, whether the Venetian renegade Alp could really experience the horror which Byron did at Constantinople at the sight of dogs feasting upon human carcasses; or whether the association of the qualities with which he idealized his heroes would not induce psychologists to accuse him of sinning against truth, of destroying the unity of a Corsair's nature.

In this Lord Byron confided in his powers. He felt that the love of truth, and of what is beautiful, was too strong in him ever to depart from or cause him to violate the essential rules of art; but he wished to remain a poet while trusting in reality.

When he went to the East, and found himself there in contact with outward circumstances so in harmony with the natural bent of his views, and in presence of men like Ali Pasha, of whose victims he could almost hear the moans and the screams "in the clime"

> "Where all save the spirit of man is divine;
> Where wild as the accents of lovers' farewell
> Are the hearts which they bear and the tales which they tell,"

he felt that he was at last in the land most likely to fire his natural genius, and to permit of his satisfying the imperious want which his observing mind constantly experienced of resting upon reality and upon truth. The terrible Ali Pasha of Yanina was especially the type which attracted his notice. "Ali Pasha," says Galt, "is at the bottom of all his Oriental heroes. His 'Corsair' is almost the history of Ali Pasha."

In the "Bride of Abydos" the old Giaffir is again Ali. As for "Lara," it is thought that Byron conceived him on being very strongly impressed by the sight of a nobleman who was accused of murder, and who was pointed out to him at the Cagliari theatre. "I always thought," says Galt, who was present on the occasion, "that this incident had a share in the conception of 'Lara,' so small are the germs which fructify genius." The "Giaour" is due to a personal adventure of Byron's, in which he played, as was his wont, a most energetic and generous part. The origin of "Manfred" lies in the midst of sublime Alpine scenery, where, on a rock, Byron discovered an inscription bearing the names of two brothers, one of whom had murdered the other at that spot. The history of Venice inspired him with Alp the renegade, who, disgusted with the unjust severities of his countrymen, turned Mohammedan and swore vengeance against the land of his birth.

It is, however, indispensable to remark, that in each of these characters there are two distinct realities. The one tries, by a display of too much energy, to overstep the limits of the natural; the other brings the subject back to its true proportions by idealizing it. The first is the result of the poet's observations of men and their customs, or of his study of history; the other, by the impossibility which he knows to exist in him of departing from the rules of art by pushing reality to the point of making of it a positive suffering. In the first case his heroes are like one another by their analogy in the use and abuse of strength; in the other they are like Byron, because he has almost instilled a portion of his own life into them, in order to idealize them.

Conrad is the real pirate of the Ægean Sea: independent, haughty, terrible in battle, full of energy and daring such as becomes the chief of corsairs, and such as Byron's study of the country where the action lies pointed out to him that such a man should be placed. But the poet describes himself when he makes Conrad, at the risk of his own life, save women from a harem, or shudder at the sight of a drop of blood on the brow of a lóvely maiden. The spot on Gulnare's forehead, while causing him to suspect some crime, banishes all her charms in his eyes, and inspires him with the greater horror from the fact that the love which she had sworn him probably inspired her with the foul act, to save his life and restore him to liberty. He accuses himself with having been the involuntary cause of it, and feels that his gratitude will be a torture; his former love for Gulnare an impossibility. We find Byron's own nature again in the ascetic rule of life to which Conrad has subjected himself, and in his passionate and ideal tenderness for Medora, whose love, in his eyes, surpasses all the happiness of this world, and whose death plunges him into irretrievable despair.

In the "Siege of Corinth," Alp is the real type of the historical Venetian renegade, who is incapable of forgiveness, and who makes use of all his energies to gratify his revenge. But he represents Byron when he speaks of the impressions which he felt under the starry canopy of heaven the night before the battle, when his imagination, taking him back to the happy, innocent days of his childhood, he contrasts them with the present, which for him is one of remorse, and when there glimmer still in his soul faint lights of humanity which make him turn away from the horrible sight of dogs devouring the dead bodies of men.

Byron speaks in his own person in the introduction of the "Giaour," which is replete with most exquisite beauty. In it he opens to the reader unexplored fields of delight, leads him through delicious countries where all is joy for the senses, where all recollections are a feast for the soul, and where his love of moral beauty is as strongly marked in his praise of olden Greece, as is his condemnation of modern degraded Greece. Byron speaks again in his own name when he puts invectives in the mouth of the Mussulman fisherman, and makes him curse so strongly the crime of the Giaour and the criminal himself, whose despair is the expiation of his crimes and the beautiful triumph of morality.

In the "Bride of Abydos" (where the terrible Ali again comes forward in the shape of the old Giaffir) the amiable and unfortunate Selim and the poet share the real sentiments of Byron. Byron is also himself when he adorns his heroine with every grace and perfection of body and soul, and also whenever it is necessary to idealize in order that a too rigorous imitation of reality may not offend either the laws of art or the feelings of the reader. As for "Don Juan," it is only fair to say that he in a measure deserved the persecution which it brought upon him. Yet, if we judge the poem with no preconceived severity, we shall find that, with the exception of certain passages where he went beyond the limits prescribed to satire, from his hatred of hypocrisy, and also at times as a revenge against his persecutors, the poem is charming. These passages he intended to suppress,* but death prevented him. This is greatly to be regretted, for otherwise "Don Juan" would have been the most charming satirical poem in existence, and especially had not the last four cantos, written in Greece, been destroyed. The scene lay in England, and the views expressed in them explained many things which can never now be known. In allowing such an act to be committed for the sake of sparing the feelings of some influential persons and national susceptibilities, Byron's friends failed in their duty to his memory, for the last four cantos gave the key to the previous ones, and justified them. From the moment Byron conceived "Don Juan" he steeled his heart against feeling; and he kept to his resolution not to give way to his natural goodness of disposition, wishing the poem to be a satire as well as an act of revenge. Here and there, however, his great soul pierces through, and shows itself in such a true light that Byron's portrait could be better drawn from passages of "Don Juan," than from any other of his poems.† We have sufficiently proved, we think, that the

* He often told and promised his friends at Genoa that he would alter the passages which are unjust and reprehensible, and that, before it was finished, "Don Juan" would become a chaste and irreproachable satire.

† "His manner was perhaps the more seductive,
Because he ne'er seemed anxious to seduce;
Nothing affected, studied, or constructive
Of coxcombry or conquest: no abuse
Of his attractions marr'd the fair perspective,
To indicate a Cupidon broke loose,
And seem to say, 'Resist us if you can'—
Which makes a dandy while it spoils a man.

uniform character of Byron's heroes, which has been blamed by the poet's enemies, was merely the reflection of the moral beauty which he drew from himself. It might almost be said that the qualities with which he had been gifted by Heaven conspired against him.

We have been led to dwell upon this phase of his literary career, at the risk even of tiring the patience of the reader, from the necessity which we believe exists to destroy the phantom of identification which has been invoked, and to explain the moral nature of Byron in its true light before analyzing the poet under other aspects. It is not in "Harold" or in "Conrad," nor in any of his Oriental poems, that we are likely to trace the moral character of Byron, for, although it would be easy to detach the author's sentiments from those of the personages of these poems, yet they might offer a pretext of blame to those who hate to look into a subject to discover the truth which does not appear at first sight. Nor is

---

XIII.

"Don Juan was without it;
In fact, his manner was his own alone:
Sincere he was—

XIV.

"By nature soft, his whole address held off
Suspicion: though not timid, his regard
Was such as rather seem'd to keep aloof,
To shield himself than put you on your guard.

XV.

"Serene, accomplish'd, cheerful, but not loud,
Insinuating without insinuation;
Observant of the foibles of the crowd,
Yet ne'er betraying this in conversation;
Proud with the proud, yet courteously proud,
So as to make them feel he knew his station
And theirs:—without a struggle for priority
He neither brook'd nor claim'd superiority.

XVI.

"That is with men: with women he was what
They pleased to make or take him for."—*Canto* XV.

LIV.

"There was the purest Platonism at bottom
Of all his feelings."—*Canto* X.

it in "Manfred"—the only one of his poems wherein, perhaps, reason may be said to be at fault, owing to the sickness under which his soul labored at the time when it was written, and to his diseased imagination, produced by solitude and unmerited grief. In his lyrical poems Byron's soul must be sought. There he speaks and sings in his own name, expresses his own sentiments, breathes his own thoughts; or, again, in his elegies and in his miscellaneous poems, in his dramas, in his mysteries, nay, even in his satires—the noble and courageous independence of which has never been surpassed by any satirist, ancient or modern—and generally in all the poems which he wrote in Italy, and which might almost be called his second form. In these poems no medium is any longer required between his soul and that of the reader. It is not possible any longer to make any mistake about him in these. The melancholy and the energy displayed in them can not serve any more to give him the mask of a Conrad, or of a Harold, or of a misanthrope, or of a haughty individual, but they place in relief what there is of tender, amiable, affectionate sublime in those chosen beings whom God occasionally sends upon earth to testify here below of the things above:—

"Per far di colassu fede fra noi."—PETRARCH.

Thus, in his elegy upon the death of Thyrzà, "far too beautiful," says Moore, "and too pure to have been inspired by a mortal being," what pathos, what sensitiveness! What charm in his sonnets to Guinevre! What soft melancholy, what profound and intimate knowledge of the immortality and spirituality of our soul, in his Hebrew melodies! "They seem as though they had been inspired by Isaiah and written by Shakspeare," says the Very Rev. Dr. Stanley, Dean of Westminster. What touching family affection in his domestic poems, and what generosity in the avowal of certain wrongs! What great and moral feeling pervade the two last cantos of "Childe Harold," melancholy though they be, like all things which are beautiful! How one feels that the pain they tell of has its origin in unmerited persecution, and how his intellect came to his aid, and enabled him to bear with calmness the uncertainties incident to our nature! What greatness of soul in the forgiveness of what to others would seem unpardonable! What love of humanity and of its rights! What hatred of injustice, tyranny, and oppression in the "Ode to Venice," in "The Lament of Tasso," in "The Prophecy of Dante," and in general in all his latter poems, even in the "Isle," a poem little known, which was written a short time before he left Genoa for Greece. Here, more than in any other of his poems, we see the admirable peace of mind which he had created for himself, and how far too high his great intellect soared to be any longer moved by the world's injustice.

Quotations from his poems would be impossible. How choose without regretting what has been discarded? They must be read; and those must be pitied who do not feel morally better after having read them.

This is precisely what has been least done up to the present time: people have been content with reading his early poems, and with seeking Byron in "Childe Harold" or in the heroes of his Oriental poems; which is about as just as to look for Shakspeare in Iago, Milton in Satan, Goethe in Mephistopheles, or Lamartine in the blasphemies of his ninth Meditation.

Thus French critics,—disposed to identify the man with the imaginary beings of his poems, and neglecting to seek him where they could have found him, relying upon judgments formed in England, and too often by people prejudiced against Byron,—have themselves adopted false views with respect to the author and his works. Thus, again, poetry—which without any preconceived teaching or any particular doctrine of its own, without transgressing the rules laid down by art, moved the soul, purified and elevated it, and taught it to despise the base and cowardly desires of nature, and excited in it the admiration of all that is noble and heroic,—was declared to be suspicious even in France, because too often it had proclaimed openly the truth where one would have wished truth to have been disguised. Many would fain have thought otherwise, but they preferred remaining silent, and to draw from that poetry the poetical riches of which they might be in want.

Our intention being to consecrate a chapter to the examination of the moral tendency of Byron's poetry, we will not now say more. We must add, however, that these views which had been so easily adopted in France were not those of the majority of right-thinking persons in England, although they dared not proclaim their opinions then as they can now.

I shall only quote the opinion of two Englishmen of great merit (Moore and Sir Egerton Brydges), who can neither one nor the other be suspected of partiality; the first, on account of his great fear of ever wounding the susceptibilities of his countrymen, the other by the independence and nobility of his character.

"How few are the pages in his poems," says Moore, "even if perused rapidly, which by their natural tendency toward virtue, or some splendid tribute to the greatness of God's works, or by an explosion of natural piety more touching than any homily, do not entitle him to be admitted in the purest temple of which Christianity may have the keep!"—*Moore*, vol. ii.

Sir Egerton Brydges, after having fully appreciated the poems of Lord Byron, says:—

"They give to the reader's best instincts an impulse which elevates, purifies, instructs, charms, and affords us the noblest and purest of joys."—*Sir E. Brydges*, vol. x. p. 141.

These quotations perhaps will be found too many, but are they not necessary? Is truth which can be so easily changed equally easy to re-establish? Are not a thousand words wanted to restore a reputation which a light word or, may be, slight malice has tarnished? If the author of these pages only expressed individual opinions without adducing any proof, that is to say, without accompanying them with the disinterested and enlightened testimonies of people who have known Byron personally, these volumes might gain in interest by being condensed in a shorter space.

But in shortening the road would the author attain the desired end? would the self-imposed task be fulfilled? would his or her own convictions become those of others? Should not authors sacrifice themselves to their subject in all works inspired by a devoted spirit? Shall it be said that oftentimes one has wished to prove what had already been conceded by every body? that the value of the proofs adduced is lessened by the fact that they are nearly all already known? In answer, and without noticing the words "nearly all," he might say that, as truth has several aspects, one may almost, without mentioning new facts, arrive at being what might be called the guide in the tour round the soul, and fathom its depth in search of the reality; just as when we have looked at all the sides of a picture, we return to it, in order to find in it fresh beauties which may have escaped our notice on a first inspection. There are certain souls, to fathom which it is absolutely necessary to employ a retrospective method; in the same way that the pictures, for instance, of Salvator Rosa enchant on close inspection of the great beauties which in some lights seem hid by a mass of clouds.

"One can hardly employ too many means," says Ste. Beuve, "to know a man; that is, to understand him to be something more than an intellectual being. As long as we have not asked ourselves a certain number of questions about such and such an author, and as long as they have not been satisfactorily answered, we are not sure of having completely made him out, even were such questions to be wholly irrelevant to the subjects upon which he has written.

"What did he think upon religious matters?

"How did the aspect of nature affect him?

"How did he behave in regard to women?

"How about money?

"What rules did he follow?

"What was his daily life? etc., etc.

"Finally, what was his peculiar vice and foible? Every man has one.

"Not one of these questions is unimportant in order to appreciate an author or his book, provided the book does not treat of pure mathematics; and especially if it is a literary work, that is to say, a book wherein there is something about every thing."*

Be this opinion of an eminent critic our rule and an encouragement to our efforts.

We are well aware that in France, now-a-days, writers do not like to use the same materials in describing a character as are used by other nations, and especially by England. A study of this kind in France must not be a judgment pro-

* Ste. Beuve, "Nouveaux Lundis," vol. iii. p. 28.

nounced upon the individual who is the object of it, and still less an inquiry. The qualities and defects of a man of genius do not constitute the principal business of the artist. Man is now rather examined as a work of art or as an object of science. When reason has made him out, and intellectual curiosity has been satisfied, the wish to understand him is not carried out further. The subject is abandoned, lest the reader may be tired.

This may be good reasoning in many cases; but in the present perhaps the best rule is "in medio tutissimus." When a good painting is spoilt by overpolish, to wash the polish off is not to restore it to its former appearance. To arrive at this last result, however, no pains should be spared; and upon this principle we must act with regard to Byron. In psychological studies the whole depends upon all the parts, and what may at first seem unimportant may prove to be the best confirmation of the thesis. To be stopped by details (I might almost say repetitions) would therefore be to exhibit a fear in adducing proof.

Can it be said that we have not sufficiently condemned? To add this interest to the volume would not have been a difficult task.

To attack is easier than to defend; but we should then have had to invent our facts, and, at the same time, to add romance to history.

The world, says a great moralist of our times, prefers a vice which amuses it rather than a virtue which bores it; but our respect for the reader convinces us that the adoption of such a means of arriving at success would forfeit their respect for us and be as repugnant to their sense of justice as to our own. As regards Byron, the means have more than once been employed, and with the more success by those who have united to their skill the charms of style.

But in claiming no talent, no power to interest, and in refusing to appear as an author from motives of pusillanimity, idleness, or self-love, is one less excusable for hiding the truth when one is acquainted with it?

If it is the duty of a man of honor and a Christian to come to the rescue of a victim to violence when it is in one's power, is it not incumbent upon one to raise a voice in the defense of those who can no longer resent an insult, when we know that they are wrongly accused? To be silent under such circumstances would be productive of remorse; and the remorse is greater when felt on the score of those whose genius constitutes the monopoly of the whole world, and forms part of the common treasure of humanity, which enjoins that it should be respected.

Is not their reputation a part of the inherited treasure? To allow such reputation to be outraged would, in our minds, be as culpable as to hide a portion of a treasure which is not our own.

"Truth," says Lamartine, "does not require style. Its light shines of itself; its appearance is its proof."

In publishing these pages, written conscientiously and scrupulously, we confide in the opinion expressed above in the magic language of the man who can create any prestige. If the reader finds these guarantees of truth sufficient, and deigns to accept our conscientious remarks with indulgence and kindness; if, after examining Byron's character under all its aspects, after repeating his words, recalling his acts, and speaking of his life—especially of that which he led in Italy—and mentioning the various impressions which he produced upon those who knew him personally, we are justified in the reader's opinion in having endeavored to clear the reality from all the clouds which imagination has gathered round the person of Byron, and in trying to earn for his memory a little sympathy by proclaiming the truth, in place of the antipathy which falsehood has hitherto obtained for him, our object will have been obtained.

To endeavor to restore Byron's reputation is the more necessary, since Moore himself, who is his best biographer, failed not only in his duty as a friend, but as the historian of the poet's life: for he knew the truth, and dared not proclaim it. Who, for instance, could better inform us of the cause which led to Byron's separation from his wife? And yet Moore chose to keep the matter secret.

Who was better acquainted with the conduct of Byron's colleagues at the time of his conjugal differences—with the curious proposals which were made to him by them to recover their good graces—with his refusal to regain them at such a cost—with the persecution to which he was, after that, subjected—with the names of the people who instigated a popular demonstration against him—with all the bad treatment which obliged him to quit England? And yet has Moore spoken of it?*

Who, better than Moore, could tell of the friends on whom Byron relied, and who at the time of his divorce sided with Lady Byron, and even went so far as to aggravate the case by falsely publishing reports of his having ill-treated Lady Byron and discharged loaded guns in order to frighten her?

Who was better acquainted with the fact that the last cantos of "Don Juan," written in Greece, had been destroyed in England, and that the journal which he kept after his departure from Genoa had been destroyed in Greece? Moore knew it very well, and did not reveal these facts, lest he should create enemies for himself. He actually went so far as to pretend that Byron never wrote any thing in Greece.†

* When the persecution to which Lord Byron was exposed by his separation had attained its greatest height, an influential person—not belonging to the peerage—came to visit him, and told him that, if he wished to see how far the folly of men went, he had only to give orders for having it shown that nothing said against him was true, but that then he must change politics and come over to the Tory party. Lord Byron replied that he would prefer death and all kinds of tortures to such meanness. Hereupon the person in question said that he must suffer the consequences, which would be heavy, since his colleagues were determined on his ruin, out of party spirit and political hatred. It was at this time that, going one day to the House, he was insulted by the populace, and even treated in it like an outlaw. No one spoke to him, nor approached to give any explanation of such a proceeding, except Lord Holland, who was always kind to him, and indeed to every one else. Others—such as the Duke of Sussex, Lord Minto, Lord Lansdowne and Lord Grey—would fain have acted in a like manner; but they suffered themselves to be influenced by his enemies, among whom more than one was animated by personal rancor because the young lord had laughed at them and shown up their incapacity.

Lord Byron, finding himself received in this way by his colleagues, pretended not to see it, and after a few moments quitted the House, never more to set foot within it.

† Lord Byron's mind, incapable of idleness, was constantly at work, even despite himself and amid pressing active occupations. During his stay in the Ionian Islands, Missolonghi, he wrote five cantos of Don Juan. The scene of the cantos that followed was laid first in England and then in Greece. The places chosen for the action naturally rendered these last cantos the most interesting, and, besides, they explained a host of things quite justifying them. They were taken to England with Lord Byron's other papers; but there they were probably considered not sufficiently respectful toward England, on which they formed a sort of satire too outspoken with regard to living personages, and doubtless it was deemed an act of patriotism to destroy them. And so the world was deprived of them.

Lord Byron had also kept a journal since the day of his departure from Genoa

Who better than Moore knew that Byron was not irreligious?—And yet he pretended that he was. And finally, Who was better aware that Byron's greatest aim was to be useful to humanity, and yet encouraged the belief that Byron's expedition to Greece was purely to satisfy the desire that people should speak of him as a superior man? In a few words, Moore has not made the best of Byron's qualities, has kept silence over many things which might have enhanced his character in public opinion; and wished, above all, to show the greatness of his poetical genius, which was never questioned. One would almost say that Moore did not like Byron to be too well spoken of: for whenever he praises, he ever accompanies the praise with a blame, a "but" or an "if;" and instead of openly contradicting accusations which he knew to be false, and honestly proclaiming the truth, he, too, preferred to excuse the poet's supposed shortcomings. Moore was wanting in courage. He was good, amiable, and clever; but weak, poor, and a lover of rank—where, naturally, he met with many political enemies of Byron. He, therefore, dared not then tell the truth, having too many interests to consider. Hence his concessions and his sluggishness in leaving the facts as they were; and in many cases, when it was a question between the departed Byron and one of his high detractors, the one sacrificed was the dead friend who could no longer defend himself. All such considerations for the living were wrongs toward the memory of Byron.

The gravest accusation, however, to which Moore is open is, that he did not preserve the Memoirs which Byron gave him on the sworn condition that nothing should prevent their publication. The promise thus given had restored peace to Byron's mind, so confident was he that it would be fulfilled. To have broken his word is a crime for which posterity will never forgive Moore. Can it be alleged, by way of excuse,

up to the time when illness made the pen drop from his hand. To it he had consigned his most intimate thoughts; and we may well imagine how full of interest it must have been, written amid all the emotions agitating his soul at that time. This journal was found among his papers by a personage of high standing in Greece, who was the first to inspect them, and who, seeing his own name and conduct mentioned in no flattering terms, destroyed them in order to hide from England the unvarnished truth told of himself. Count Gamba often speaks of this journal in the letters addressed at this period to his sister.

We leave the reader to make his own comments on these too regrettable facts.

that he gave extracts from it? But besides the authenticity of the extracts, which might be questioned, of what value can be a composition like Moore's in presence of Byron's very words? No one can pretend to be identified with such a mind as Byron's in the expression of his own feelings; and, least of all, a character like Moore's.

The "Memoirs," then, which were the justification of Byron's life; the last cantos, which were the justification of the poet and of the man; the journal, which showed his prudence and sagacity beyond his age, which by the simple relation of facts proved how he had got rid of all the imperfections of youth, and at last become the follower of wisdom, so much so that he would have been one of the most virtuous men in England—all have been lost to the world: they have descended with him into the tomb, and thus made room for the malice of his detractors. Hence the duty of not remaining silent on the subject of this highly-gifted man.

In restoring, however, facts to their true light, we do not pretend to make Byron appear always superior to humanity in his conduct as a man and a poet. Could he, with so sensitive and passionate a nature as his was, and living only that period when passions are strongest, have always acted as those who from age no longer are affected by them? If it is easy not to give way to our passions at seventy, is it equally so at twenty or at thirty?

Persecuted as he was, could Byron be expected to remain unmoved? If his passion for truth made him inexorable in some of his poems; if his passion for justice allowed his pen at times to go beyond the limits which it should have respected; if even at times he was unjust, because he had been too much injured and irritated,—he undoubtedly would have compensated for his involuntary and slight offenses, had he not been carried off so early.

As for the imperfection of these pages,—once we have dissipated error, and caused truth to be definitely received as regards Byron,—an abler pen can easily correct it, and do away with the numberless repetitions with which we are aware we shall be reproached. We could not do otherwise, as we wished to multiply proofs. Others, some day, will achieve what we have been unable to perform.

Our work is like the stream which falls from the mountain and is filled with ooze: its only merit is to swell the river into which it runs. But, sooner or later, a stronger current will purify it, and give clearness and brilliancy to it, without taking from it the merit of having increased the bulk of the waters.

Such as it is, we dedicate this humble work to the noble souls who worship truth. They will feel that we have been able to place them in a more intimate connection with another great mind, and thus we shall have gained our reward.

CHAPTER I.

LORD BYRON AND M. DE LAMARTINE.

To Count de ——.

Paris, 17th June, 1860.

MY DEAR COUNT,—Confiding in your willingness to oblige, I beg to ask a favor and your advice. I received, a short time ago, a prospectus of a subscription to be raised for a general addition of the works of M. de Lamartine. You are aware that when it is a question of showing my sympathy for M. de Lamartine I would never miss the opportunity of doing so; but on this occasion I see on the programme the promise of a Life of Lord Byron. Such an announcement must alarm the friends of that great man; for they remember too vividly the sixteenth number of the "Cours Littéraire" to subscribe hastily to a work when they have not more information than is therein given. You, who forget nothing, must probably remember the strange judgment of Byron formed by M. de Lamartine in that article. Identifying the man with the poet, and associating his great name with that of Heine on account of some rather hazardous lines in "Don Juan," and forgetting the license allowed to such poetry—an imitation of the Italian poets Berni, Ariosto, Pulci, Buratti—M. de Lamartine did not forget a few personal attacks upon himself, and called Byron the founder of the school for promoting satanic laughter, while he heaped upon him the most monstrous accusations. M. de Lamartine ventured to say of Byron things which even his greatest enemies never dared to utter at that time when in England it was the custom to revile him. Although the time has not yet come when Lord Byron's life should be written, since the true sources of collecting information respecting him are unattainable so long as the people live to whom his letters were addressed, still it is easy to perceive that the time has at length arrived when in

England the desire to do him justice and fairly to examine his merits is felt by the nation generally. Moore, Parry, Medwin, etc., have already attempted to make known the character of the man as distinct from that of the poet. They no longer sought to find in him a resemblance with Childe Harold, or the Corsair, or Manfred, or Don Juan, nor to judge of him by the conversations in which he sought to mystify those with whom he conversed; but they judged him by his acts and by his correspondence.

If so happy a reaction, however, is visible in England the same can not be said of France, where there being no time to read what is published elsewhere, an error is too soon embraced and ingrafted on the mind of the public as a consequence of a certain method which dispenses with all research. Hence the imaginary creation which has been called Byron, and which has been maintained in France notwithstanding its being wholly unacceptable as a portrait of the man, and totally different from the Byron known personally to some happy few who had the pleasure of beholding in him the handsomest, the most amiable of men, and the greatest genius whom God has created.

But M. de Lamartine, who wishes particularly to show the character of the man, instead of adding to the numerous proofs of courage and grandeur of mind which he has personally shown to the world—that of confessing that he has erred in his judgment of Byron — endeavors to study him only in his works. But in doing this, and even though a moral object may be found in each of Byron's works, it strikes us that M. de Lamartine would have done better to pursue this line in the analysis of the intellectual part of the man, and not the moral side.

"You err" (wrote Byron to Moore on the occasion of the latter saying that such a poem as the "Vision of Judgment" could not have been written in a desponding mood): "a man's poetry is a distinct faculty or soul, and has no more to do with the every-day individual than the inspiration of the Pythoness when removed from her tripod." To which Moore observes: "My remark has been hasty and inconsiderate, and Lord Byron's is the view borne out by all experience. Almost all the tragic and gloomy writers have been, in social life, mirthful persons. The author of the 'Night Thoughts' was a fellow of infinite jest; and of the pathetic Otway, Pope says, 'He! why, he would laugh all the day long; he would do nothing but laugh!'"

It is known that many licentious writers have led very regular and chaste lives; that many who have sung their success with women have not dared to declare their love to one woman; that all Sterne's sentiment was perfectly ideal, and proceeded always from the head and never from the heart; that Seneca's morality was no barrier to his practicing usury; and that, according to Plutarch, Demosthenes was a very questionable moralist in practice. Why, then, necessarily conclude that a moralist is a moral man, or a sarcastic satirist a deceitful one, or the man who describes scenes of blood and carnage a monster of cruelty? Does not Montaigne say of authors that they must be judged by their merits, and not by their morals, nor by that show of works which they exhibit to the world. Why, then, does M. Lamartine appreciate Byron according to his satirical works, when all those who knew him assert that his real character was very different to his literary one? He did not personify, but create his heroes; which are two very different things.

Like Salvator Rosa, who, the meekest of men in private life, could only find a vent to his talent by painting scenes of brigandage and horror, so did Byron's genius require to go down into the darkest recesses of the passions which generate remorse, crime, and heroism, to find that spark which fired his genius. But it must be owned, that even his great qualities were causes of the false judgment of the world upon him. Thus, in describing Childe Harold, he no doubt wished to paint a side of nature which had not yet been seen. At the scenes of despair, at the scenes of doubt which assail him, the poet assists rather as the historian than as the actor. And the same holds good for other poems, where he describes those peculiar diseases of the mind which great geniuses alone can comprehend, though they need not have experienced them. But it was the very life which he infused into his heroes that made it appear as if they could not personify any one but himself. And as to their faults, because he was wont to give them his qualities, it was argued, that since the latter were observable to be common to the author and the creations of his fancy, the faults of these must likewise be his. If only the faults, why not also the crimes? Thus it came that, caring little for their want of argument, Byron's enemies erected themselves into avengers of too much talent bestowed upon one single man.

Byron might have taken up his own defense, but did not care to do so, or did it carelessly in some letters written to intimate friends. To Moore he wrote:—"Like all imaginative men, I, of course, embody myself with the character while I draw it; but not a moment after the pen is from the paper." He always, however, begged that he might be judged by his acts; and a short time before he died at Missolonghi, after recommending Colonel Stanhope to desist from then pressing the necessity of giving liberty to the press, and from recommending the works of Bentham to a people who could not even read, Byron replied to the colonel's rather hasty remarks, "Judge me by my acts." This request he had often repeated, as his life was not one of those which fear the light of day. All in vain. His enemies were not satisfied with this means of putting an end to their calumnies.

Where does M. de Lamartine find the truth which he proposes to tell the world about Byron? Not surely among the writers whose biographies of Byron were either works of revenge or of speculation, and sometimes both. Not in the conversations which Byron had with several people, and on the credulity of whom he loved to speculate. It can not, therefore, be in the biographies of men who have written erroneously, and have not understood their subject; but in Moore, in Parry, in Count Gamba's works, and, may be, in a few others. I am, however, far from saying, that Moore has acted toward Lord Byron with all that friendly feeling which Byron recommended to him on asking him to write the Life of Sheridan, "without offending the living or insulting the dead." Quite the contrary. I take it that Moore has wholly disregarded his duties as a true friend, by publishing essentially private letters, by introducing into his books certain anecdotes which he might, if even they were true, have advantageously left out; and in failing, from fear of wounding living susceptibilities, to assert with energy that which he knew to be the real case with Byron. More than any one, Moore experienced the fatal influence which injures independence in aristocratic England. An Irishman by birth, and a commoner, Moore was flattered to find himself elevated by his talents to a position in aristocratic circles which he owed to his talents, but which he was loath to resign. The English aristocracy then formed a kind of clique whose wish it was to govern England on the condition that its secret of governing should not be revealed, and was furious with Byron, who was one of them, for revealing their weaknesses and upbraiding their pretensions. Moore wished to live among the statesmen and noblemen whose despotic views and bad policy Byron had openly condemned, and among those lovely islanders in whose number there might be found more Adelinas than Auroras, and to whom Byron had preferred foreign beauties. Moore, in short, wished to live with the literary men whom Byron had ridiculed in his satires, and among the high clergy, then as intolerant as they were hypocritical, and who, as Byron said, forgot Christ alone in their Christianity. Moore, whose necessity it had become to live among these open revilers and enemies of Byron, after allowing the memoirs of Byron to be burnt, because in them some of the above-named personages were unmasked, this Moore was weak enough not to proclaim energetically that Byron's character was as great as his genius, but to do so only timidly. By way of obtaining pardon even for this mite of justice to the friend who was gone, Moore actually condescended to associate himself with those who pleaded extenuating circumstances for Byron's temper, like Walter Scott and other poets. But truth comes out, nevertheless, in Moore; and in the perusal of Byron's truthful and simple letters we find him there displayed in all his admirable and unique worth as an intellectual and a moral man. We find him adorned with all the virtues which Heaven gave him at his birth; his real goodness, which neither injustice nor misfortune could alter; his generosity, which not only made him disbelieve in ingratitude, but actually incited him to render good for evil and obliged him to own that "he could not keep his resentments;" his gratitude for the little that is done for him; his sincerity; his openness of character; his greatness and disinterestedness. "His very failings were those of a sincere, a generous, and a noble mind," says a biographer who knew him well. His contempt for base actions; his love of equity; his passion for truth, which was carried almost to a hatred of cant and hypocrisy, were the immediate causes of his want of fairness in his opinion of himself and of his self-accusation of things most contrary to his nature.

So singular a trait in his character was by no means the result of eccentricity, but the result of an exceptional assembly of rare qualities which met for the first time in one man, and which, shining in the midst of a most corrupt society, constituted almost more an anomaly which became a real defect, hurtful, however, to himself only. His ideal of the beautiful magnified weaknesses into crimes, and physical failings into deformities. Thus it is that with the saints the slightest transgression of the laws appears at once in the light of mortal sin. St. Augustin calls the greediness of his youth a crime. The result of all this was that his very virtues mystified the world and caused it to believe that the faults which he attributed to himself were nothing in comparison of those which he really had.

Byron, however, was indignant at being so unfairly treated. He treated with contempt the men who calumniated him, and as if they were idiots. He can safely, therefore, be blamed for not urging enough his own defense. This, to my mind, constitutes his capital fault, unless one considers defects of character those changes of humor which rapidly passed from gayety to melancholy, or his pretended irritability, which was merely a slight disposition to be impatient. These were all the result of his poetical nature, added to the effects of early education and to those of certain family circumstances. It would be too hard and too unfair to attribute these slight weaknesses of character proper to great genius to a bad nature or to misanthropy.

Had Lord Byron not been impatient he must have been satisfied with his own condition and indifferent to that of others. In other words, he must have been an egotist, which he was not. He was gay by nature, and repeatedly showed it; but he had been sorely wounded by the injustice of men, and his marriage with Miss Milbank had undermined his peace and happiness. How, then, could he escape the occasional pangs of grief, and not betray outwardly the pain which devoured him inwardly. In such moments it was a relief to him to heave a sigh, or take up a pen to vent his grief in rhyme. His misanthropy was quite foreign to his nature. All those who knew him can bear testimony to the falseness of the accusation.

Moore, who knew him so well, and who always speaks the truth when no longer under the influences which at times overpower him, after speaking of the charm of Byron's manner when he saw him for the first time, ends by saying: "It may be asserted that never did there exist before, and it is most probable never will exist again, a combination of such vast mental power and surpassing genius, with so many others of those advantages and attractions by which the world is in general dazzled and captivated."

When, therefore, M. de Lamartine seeks the truth in Moore, Parry, and some other biographers respecting Byron, he will find that this eminently beautiful form was in harmony with the splendid intellect and moral qualities of the man. M. de Lamartine will see that Byron was a good and devoted son, a tender father and brother, a faithful friend, and indulgent master, beloved by all who ever knew him, and who was never accused, even by his enemies, of having tried to seduce an innocent young girl, or having disturbed the peace of conjugal bliss. He will behold his charity, which was universal and unbounded; a pride which never stooped to be subservient of those in power; a firm political faith; a contempt of public dignities, so far as they reflected glory upon himself; and such a spirit of humility that he was ever ready to blame himself and follow the advice of those whom he deemed to be animated by no hostile spirit against himself.

When M. de Lamartine sees all this, not merely written down as in these pages, but actually proved by facts and irrefutable testimonies, his loyal soul must revolt and wish to do justice to himself by rejecting his former opinions. He will understand that if he himself has been called a drinker of blood by the party whom he styles bigoted and composed of old men, Byron, too, may have been calumniated. Looking, then, at the great poet in his proper light, that is, in the plenitude of his rare qualities, and considering him under each of the circumstances of his life, M. de Lamartine will own that he had misunderstood that most admirable of characters, and grant that the "satanic laughter" of which he spoke was, on the contrary, the smile which was so beautiful that it might have lighted up by its magic soft rays the dark regions of Satan. His doubts being cleared away, M. de Lamartine will end by saying that Byron was an "angel, not a demon."

Byron's misfortune was to have been born in the England of those days. Do you remember his beautiful lines in the "Due Foscari?"—

> "He might have lived,
> So formed for gentle privacy of life,
> So loving, so beloved; the native of
> Another land, and who so bless'd and blessing
> As my poor Foscari? Nothing was wanting
> Unto his happiness and mine save not
> To be Venetian."

In writing these lines Byron must have thought of his own fate. He was scarcely British by origin, and very little so by his turn of mind, or by his tastes or by the nature of his genius. "My ancestors are not Saxon, they are Norman," he said; "and my blood is all meridian."

If, instead of being born in England then, he had come before the world when his star would have been hailed with the same love and regard that was granted to Dante in Italy, to Chateaubriand and Lamartine in France, or to Goethe in Germany, who would ever have blamed him for the slight errors which fell from his pen in "Don Juan,"—a poem written hastily and with carelessness, but of which it can be said, as Montesquieu said of the prettiest women, "their part has more gravity and importance than is generally thought." If the sense of the ridiculous is ever stronger among people whose appreciation of the beautiful is keenest, who more than Byron could have possessed it to a higher degree? Is it therefore to be marvelled at that, in order to make the truth he revealed accessible to all, and such whose minds had rusted in egotism and routine, he should have given to them a new and sarcastic form?

Had he been born anywhere but in the England of those days, he never would have been accused of mocking virtue because he claimed for it reality of character, and not that superficial form which he saw existed then in society. He believed it right to scorn the appearances of virtue put on only for the purpose of reaping its advantages. No one respected more than he did all that was really holy, virtuous, and respectable; but who could blame him for wishing to denounce hypocrisy? As for his supposed skepticism, and his expressions of despair, they may be classed with the misgivings of Job, of Pascal, of Lamartine, of Chateaubriand, and of other great minds, for whom the unknown world is a source of constant anxiety of thought, and whose cry of despair is rather a supplication to the Almighty that He would reveal himself more to their eyes. It must be borne in mind that the skepticism which some lines in his poems denounce is one of which the desponding nature calls more for our sympathy than our denunciations, since "we discover in the midst of these doubts," says Moore, "an innate piety which might have become tepid but never quite cold." His own words should be remembered when he writes, as a note to the two first cantos of "Childe Harold," that the spirit of the stanzas reflects grief and illness, more than an obstinate and mocking skepticism; and so they do. They do not embody any conclusions, but are only the expression of a passionate appeal to the Almighty to come to the rescue and proclaim the victory of faith.

Could any thing but a very ordinary event be seen in his separation from a wife who was in no way suited to him, and whose worth can be esteemed by the remark which she addressed to Byron some three weeks after her marriage: "When, my lord, do you intend to give up your habit of versifying?" And, alas! could he possibly be happy, born as he was in a country where party prejudices ran so high? where his first satire had created for him so many enemies? where some of his poems had roused political anger against him, and where his truth, his honesty, could not patiently bear with the hypocrisy of those who surrounded him, and where, in fact, he had had the misfortune to marry Miss Milbank?

The great minds whom God designs to be the apostles of truth on earth, make use for that purpose of the most efficacious means at their disposal. The universal genius of Byron allowed of his making use of every means to arrive at his end. He was able to be at once pathetic, comic, tragical, satirical, vehement, scoffing, bitter, and pleasant. This universality of talents, directed against Englishmen, was injurious to his peace of mind.

When Byron went to Italy his heart was broken down with real and not imaginary sorrows. These were not of that kind which create perfection, but were the result of an unheard-of persecution on account of a family difference in which he was much more the victim than the culprit.

He required to live in a milder climate, and a softer atmosphere to breathe in. He found both at Venice; and under their influence his mind took a new turn, which had remained undeveloped while in his own clouded country.

In the study of Italian literature he met with the Bernesque poetry, which is so lightly and elegantly sarcastic. He made the acquaintance of Buratti, the clever and charming satirist. He began, himself, to perceive the baseness of men, and found in an æsthetical mockery of human failings the most copious of the poetical currents of his mind. The more his friends and his enemies told him of the calumnies which were uttered against him, so much the more did Byron's contempt swell into disdain; and to this circumstance did "Beppo" and "Don Juan" owe their appearance.

The social condition of his country and the prevalent cant opened to him a field for reflection at Venice, where customs were so different and manners so tolerant. Seeing new horizons before him, he was more than ever disgusted at the judgments of those who calumniated him, and ended by believing it to be best to laugh at their silly efforts to ruin him. He then wrote "Beppo" and afterward "Don Juan."

He was mistaken, however, in believing that in England this new style of poetry would be liked. His jests and sarcasms were not understood by the greater portion of those against whom they were levelled. The nature of the Bernese poetry being essentially French, England could not, with its serious tendencies, like a production in which the moral purpose was artistically veiled. From that day forward a severance took place between Byron and his countrymen. What had enchanted the French displeased them, and Byron in vain translated the "Morgante" of Pulci, to show them what a priest could say in that style of poetry in a Catholic country. In vain did he write to his friends that "Don Juan" will be known by-and-by for what it is intended,—a satire on the abuses of the present state of society, and not a eulogy of vice. It may be now and then voluptuous: I can't help it. Ariosto is worse; Smollett ten times worse; Fielding no better. No girl will ever be seduced by reading 'Don Juan,'" etc.

But he was blamed just because he jested. To his ultramontane tone they would have preferred him to blaspheme in coarse Saxon.

One of the best of Byron's biographers asserts that he was a French mind lost on the borders of the Thames. Lord Byron had every kind of mind, and that is why he was equally French. But in addressing his countrymen, as such, he heaped a mountain of abuse upon his head.

With the most moral portion of the English public a violent satire would have had better chance of success. With the higher classes the work was read with avidity and pleasure. It was not owned, because there were too many reasons for condemning it; but it found its way under many a pillow, to prove to the country how virtue and patriotism were endangered by this production.

Murray made himself the echo of all this wrath, and Lord Byron, not able at times to contain his, wrote to him much to the following purpose—

"I intend to write my best work in Italian, and I am working at it. As for the opinion of the English, which you mention, let them know how much it is worth before they come and insult me by their condescension.

"I have not written for their pleasure; if they find theirs in the perusal of my works, it is because they wish it. I have never flattered their opinion or their pride, nor shall I ever do so. I have no intention either of writing books for women or to '*dilettar le femine e la plese.*' I have written merely from impulse and from passion, and not for their sweet voices. I know what their applause is worth; few writers have had more. They made of me a kind of popular idol without my ever wishing, and kicked me down from the pedestal upon which their caprice had raised me. But the idol did not break in the fall, and now they would raise it again, but they shall not." As soon as they saw that Byron was perfectly happy in Italy, and that their abuse did him but very little harm, they gave full vent to their rage.

They had shown how little they knew him when they identified him with his heroes; they found that they knew even less of him when he appeared to them in the reality of his character. Calumny followed upon calumny. Unable to find him at fault, they interpreted his words themselves, and gave them a different meaning. Every thing was figurative of some wickedness, and to the simplest expressions some vile intention was attributed.

They depreciated his works, in which are to be found such admirable and varied types of women characters, that they even surpass in beauty those of Shakspeare (Angiolina, Myrrha, Anna): they said that Faliero wanted interest, that Sardanapalus was a voluptuary; that Satan in "Cain" did not speak as a theologian (how could he?), that there were irreverent tendencies in his sacred dramas—and finally that his declaration—

"My altars are the mountains and the ocean,
Earth, air, stars,—all that springs from the great Whole,
Who hath produced, and will receive the soul,"

was hazardous, and almost that of an atheist. Atheist! he! who considered atheists fools.

On leaving Venice for Ravenna,* where he had spent a few months, only by way of distraction in the midst of his sor-

* Galt says, "It was in the course of the passage to the island of Zea, where he was put on shore, that one of the most emphatic incidents of his life occurred; an incident which throws a remarkable gleam into the springs and intricacies of his character, more perhaps than any thing which has yet been mentioned. One day, as he was walking the quarter-deck, he lifted an attaghan (it might be one of the midshipmen's weapons), and unsheathing it, said, contemplating the blade, '*I should like to know how a person feels after committing murder.*' By those who have inquiringly noticed the extraordinary cast of his metaphysical associations, this dagger scene must be regarded as both impressive and solemn; the wish to know how a man felt after committing murder does not imply any desire to perpetrate the crime. The feeling might be appreciated by experiencing any actual degree of guilt; for it is not the deed,—the sentiment which follows it makes the horror. But it is doing injustice to suppose the expression of such a wish dictated by desire. Lord Byron has been heard to express, in the eccentricity of conversation, wishes for a more intense knowledge of remorse than murder itself could give. There is, however, a wide and wild difference between the curiosity that prompts the wish to know the exactitude of any feel-

rows and serious occupations, he was accused of dissolute conduct; and the serious attachment which he had wished to avoid, but which had mastered his whole heart, and induced him to live an isolated life with the person he loved in a town of Romagna, far from all that could flatter his vanity and from all intercourse with his countrymen, was brought against him to show that he lived the life of an Epicurean, and brought misery into the heart of families.

All this, no doubt, might have again called for his contempt, but on his way from Ravenna to Pisa he wrote the outpourings of his mind in a poem, the last lines of which are:—

"Oh Fame! if I e'er took delight in thy praises,
'Twas less far the sake of thy high-sounding phrases,
Than to see the bright eyes of the dear one discover,
The thought that I was not unworthy to love her.

There chiefly I sought thee, *there* only I found thee;
Her glance was the best of the rays that surround thee;
When it sparkled o'er aught that was bright in my story,
I knew it was love, and I felt it was glory."

His heart was wounded by the persecutions to which those he loved were subjected. His thoughts were for his daughter, who was growing up in the midst of her father's enemies, and for his beloved sister who was praying for him. He contemplated in the future the time when he could show the moral and heroic power of his soul. He looked forward to the great deeds by which he was going to astonish them, and perhaps call for their admiration, instead of his writings, which had never reaped for him any thing but pain.

ing or idea, and the direful passions that instigate to guilty gratifications."—Galt, 152.

His curiosity was psychological and philosophical, that of a great artist wishing to explore the heart of man in its darkest depths.

On the eve of his departure from Rome he assisted at the execution of three assassins, remaining to the end, although this spectacle threw him into a perfect fever, causing such thirst and trembling that he could hardly hold up his opera-glass.

At Venice he preferred Madame Benzoni's conversation to that of Madame Albrizzi, because she was more thoroughly Venetian, and as such more fitted for the study he wished to make of national manners. He used to say that *every thing in the world ought to be seen once*, and it is to this idea that we must specially attribute some of the oddities so exaggerated and so much criticised during his short stay at Venice, for in reality he had none of these tastes.

Parry says, "Lord Byron had an insatiable curiosity, he was forever making questions and researches. He wished me to relate to him all the most trifling incidents of my life in America, Virginia, and Canada."—Parry, 180.

"If I live," he wrote to Moore, "you will see that I shall do something better than rhyming."

Truth however, when told by such men as Byron, and however ungraciously received, must guide in the end the steps of those who walk in its wake.

This has been the case with Byron's poetry. Its influence over the minds of Englishmen has been very salutary and great, and is one of the principal causes which brought on a reform of the rooted prejudices and opinions of the public in England, by the necessity under which it placed them of looking into the defects of the law and of the constitution, to which they had hitherto so crouchingly submitted. Since then the feeling of good-will toward other nations has materially increased in that great country.

Others have improved the way which Byron opened up for reform, and thanks to him England at his death began to lose her excessive susceptibility. She became accustomed to listen to the truth, and those who now proclaim it are not required to be exiled, or to suffer as Byron did up to the time of his death. His sufferings, no doubt, paved his way to everlasting glory, but his heroic death left him at the mercy of the enemies who survived him.

If ever a premature death was unfortunate, Byron's was; not only for him, because he was on the point of giving to the world the proof of those virtues which had been denied him, but also for humanity, by the loss of various treasures which will probably never be found again.

The epoch, however, of faint words and unbecoming silence has gone by even in England. Already one of the greatest men of England has claimed a monument in Westminster Abbey, which had been denied to his memory by the bigoted rancor of the man who was dean at the time of Byron's death, denied to that poet whom another great English statesman has called "a great writer, but a still greater man."

There remains a still more imperious duty to be fulfilled by those who have been able to appreciate his great qualities. That duty is to proclaim them and to prevent the further spread of falsehood and error as to his real character.

This is a very long letter, my dear count, but you know how long all letters must be which are intended to refute opinions and to rectify judgments. M. de Lamartine has the excellent habit of listening to your advice, and that is why I have had at heart to let you know the truth about Byron. The present work will adduce the proofs of the appreciations contained in this letter. I know that you do not require them, but also that the public does.

Pray accept, etc. ———.

CHAPTER II.

PORTRAIT OF LORD BYRON.

THE following letter was addressed to M. de Lamartine, who had asked the author of these pages to give him the "portrait physique" of Lord Byron.

MY DEAR MONSIEUR DE LAMARTINE,—

Being on the point of departure, I nevertheless wish to send you a few explanations which must serve as my apology. You have asked me to draw the portrait of Lord Byron, and I have promised you that I would do so. I now see that my promise was presumptuous. Every time I have endeavored to trace it, I have had to put down my pen, discouraged as I was by the fact of my always discovering too many obstacles between my reminiscences and the possibility of expressing them. My attempts appeared to me at times to be a profanation by the smallness of their character; at others, they bore the mark of an extreme enthusiasm, which, however, seemed to me very weak in its results and very ridiculous in its want of power. Images which are preserved in thought to a degree which may almost be considered supernatural, are susceptible of too much change during the short transit of the mind to the pen.

The Almighty has created beings of such harmonious and ideal beauty that they defy description or analysis. Such a one was Lord Byron. His wonderful beauty of expression has never been rendered either by the brush of the painter or the sculptor's chisel. It summed up in one magnificent type the highest expression of every possible kind of beauty. If his genius and his great heart could have chosen a human form by which they could have been well represented, they could not have chosen another! Genius shone in his very looks. All the effects and emotions of a great soul were therein reflected as well as those of an eminently good and generous heart, and indeed contrasts were visible which are scarcely ever united in one and the same person. His eyes seized and betrayed the sentiments which animated him, with a rapidity and transparency such as called forth from Sir Walter Scott the remark, that the fine head of his young rival "was like unto a beautiful alabaster vase lightened up by an interior lamp." To see him, was to understand thoroughly how really false were the calumnies spread about as to his character. The mass, by their obstinacy in identifying him with the imaginary types of his poems, and in judging him by a few eccentricities of early youth, as well as by various bold thoughts and expressions, had represented to themselves a factitious Byron, totally at variance with the real man. Calumnies, which unfortunately he passed over in disdainful silence, have circulated as acknowledged facts. Time has destroyed many, but it would not be correct to say that they have all entirely been destroyed. Lord Byron was silent, because he depended upon time to silence his calumniators. All those who saw him must have experienced the charm which surrounded him as a kind of sympathetic atmosphere, gaining all hearts to him. What can be said to those who never saw him? Tell them to look at the pictures of him which were painted by Saunders, by Phillips, by Holmes, or by Westall? All these, although the works of great artists, are full of faults. Saunders's picture represents him with thick lips, whereas his lips were harmoniously perfect: Holmes almost gives him a large instead of his well-proportioned and elegant head! In Phillips's picture the expression is one of haughtiness and affected dignity, never once visible to those who ever saw him.*

"These portraits," says Dallas, "will certainly present to the stranger and to posterity that which it is possible for the

* Among the bad portraits of Lord Byron spread over the world, there is one that surpasses all others in ugliness, which is often put up for sale, and which a mercantile spirit wishes to pass off for a good likeness; it was done by an American, Mr. West,—an excellent man, but a very bad painter. This portrait, which America requested to have taken, and which Lord Byron consented to sit for, was begun at Montenero, near Leghorn; but Lord Byron, being obliged to leave Montenero suddenly, could only give Mr. West two or three sittings. It was then finished from memory, and, far from being at all like Lord Byron, is a frightful caricature, which his family or friends ought to destroy.

brush to reproduce so far as the features are concerned, but the charm of speech and the grace of movement must be left to the imagination of those who have had no opportunity to observe them. No brush can paint these."

The picture of Byron by Westall is superior to the others, but does not come up to the original. As for the copies and engravings which have been taken from these pictures, and circulated, they are all exaggerated, and deserve the appellation of caricatures.

Can his portrait be found in the descriptions given by his biographers? But biographers seek far more to amuse and astonish, in order that their writings may be read, than to adhere to the simple truth.

It can not be denied, however, that in the portraits which several, such as Moore, Dallas, Sir Walter Scott, Disraeli in London, the Countess Albrizzi at Venice, Beyle (Stendhal) at Milan, Lady Blessington and Mrs. Shelley in Italy, have drawn of Lord Byron there is much truth, accompanied by certain qualifications which it is well to explain. I shall therefore give in their own words (preferring them to my own impressions) the unanimous testimony of those who saw him, be they friends or beings for whom he was indifferent. Here are Moore's words:—"Of his face, the beauty may be pronounced to have been of the highest order, as combining at once regularity of features with the most varied and interesting expression.

"His eyes, though of a light gray, were capable of all extremes of expression, from the most joyous hilarity to the deepest sadness, from the very sunshine of benevolence to the most concentrated scorn or rage. But it was in the mouth and chin that the great beauty as well as expression of his fine countenance lay.

"His head was remarkably small, so much so as to be rather out of proportion with his face. The forehead, though a little too narrow, was high, and appeared more so from his having his hair (to preserve it, as he said) shaved over the temples. Still the glossy dark-brown curls, clustering over his head, gave the finish to its beauty. When to this is added that his nose, though handsomely was rather thickly shaped, that his teeth were white and regular, and his complexion colorless, as good an idea perhaps as it is in the power of mere words to convey may be conceived of his features.

"In height he was, as he himself has informed us, five feet eight inches and a half, and to the length of his limbs he attributed his being such a good swimmer. His hands were very white, and, according to his own notions of the size of hands as indicating birth, aristocratically small."

"What I chiefly remember to have remarked," adds Moore, "when I was first introduced to him, was the gentleness of his voice and manners, the nobleness of his air, his beauty, and his marked kindness to myself. Being in mourning for his mother, the color as well of his dress, as of his glossy, curling and picturesque hair, gave more effect to the pure, spiritual paleness of his features, in the expression of which, when he spoke, there was a perpetual play of lively thought, though melancholy was their habitual character when in repose."

When Moore saw him again at Venice, some eight years after the first impressions which Byron's beauty had produced upon him in London (1812), he noted a change in the character of that beauty.

"He had grown fatter both in person and face, and the latter had most suffered by the change—having lost by the enlargement of the features some of that refined and spiritualized look that had in other times distinguished it. . . . . . He was still, however, eminently handsome, and in exchange for whatever his features might have lost of their high romantic character, they had become more fitted for the expression of that arch, waggish wisdom, that epicurean play of humor, which he had shown to be equally inherent in his various and prodigally gifted nature; while by the somewhat increased roundness of the contours the resemblance of his finely-formed mouth and chin to those of the Belvedere Apollo had become still more striking."*

Here are now the words of Lady B——, who saw him a few weeks only before his last departure for Greece. This lady had conceived a totally different idea of Byron. According to her, Byron would have appeared affected, *triste*, in accordance with certain portraits and certain types in his poems.

* Moore, vol. ii. p. 248.

But, if in order not to cause any jealousy among the living, she dared not reveal all her admiration, she at least suffered it to appear from time to time.

"There are moments," she says, "when Lord Byron's face is shadowed over with the pale cast of thought, and then his head might serve as a model for a sculptor or a painter to represent the ideal of poesy. His head is particularly well formed: his forehead is high, and powerfully indicative of his intellect: his eyes are full of expression: his nose is beautiful in profile, though a little thickly shaped. His eyebrows are perfectly drawn, but his mouth is perfection. Many pictures have been painted of him, but the excessive beauty of his lips escaped every painter and sculptor. In their ceaseless play they represented every motion, whether pale with anger, curled in disdain, smiling in triumph, or dimpled with archness and love."

This portrait can not be suspected of partiality; for, whether justly or not, she did not enjoy Lord Byron's sympathy, and knew it; she had also to forgive him various little circumstances which had wounded her "amour propre," and was obliged to measure her praise in order not to create any jealousy with certain people who surrounded him and who had some pretension to beauty.

Here is the portrait of him which another lady (the Comtesse Albrizzi of Venice) has drawn, notwithstanding her wounded pride at the refusal of Lord Byron to allow her to write a portrait of him and to continue her visits to him at Venice:—

"What serenity on his forehead! What beautiful auburn, silken, brilliant, and naturally curled hair! What variety of expression in his sky-blue eyes! His teeth were like pearls, his cheeks had the delicate tint of a pale rose; his neck, which was always bare, was of the purest white. His hands were real works of art. His whole frame was faultless, and many found rather a particular grace of manner than a fault in the slight undulation of his person on entering a room. This bending of the body was, however, so slight that the cause of it was hardly ever inquired into."

As I have mentioned the deformity of his foot, even before quoting other testimonies to his beauty, I shall tarry a while and speak of this defect, the only one in so pre-eminently favored a being. What was this defect, since all becomes illustrious in an illustrious man? Was it visible? Was it true that Lord Byron felt this imperfection so keenly? Here is the truth.

No defect existed in the formation of his limbs; his slight infirmity was nothing but the result of weakness of one of his ankles.

His habit of ever being on horseback had brought on the emaciation of his legs, as evinced by the post-mortem examination; besides which, the best proof of this has been lately given in an English newspaper much to the following effect:—

"Mrs. Wildman (the widow of the colonel who had bought Newstead) has lately given to the Naturalist Society of Nottingham several objects which had belonged to Lord Byron, and among others his boot and shoe trees. These trees are about nine inches long, narrow, and generally of a symmetrical form. They were accompanied by the following statement of Mr. Swift, bootmaker, who worked for his lordship from 1805 to 1807. Swift is still alive, and continues to reside at Southwell. His testimony as to the genuineness of the trees, and to the nature of Lord Byron's deformity, of which so many contradictory assertions have circulated, is as follows:—

"'William Swift, bootmaker at Southwell, Nottinghamshire, having had the honor of working for Lord Byron when residing at Southwell from 1805 to 1807, asserts that these were the trees upon which his lordship's boots and shoes were made, and that the last pair delivered was on the 10th of May, 1807. He, moreover, affirms that his lordship had not a club foot, as has been said, but that both his feet were equally well formed, one, however, being an inch and a half shorter than the other. The defect was not in the foot but in the ankle, which, being weak, caused the foot to turn out too much. To remedy this his lordship wore a very light and thin boot, which was tightly laced just under the sole, and, when a boy, he was made to wear a piece of iron with a joint at the ankle, which passed behind the leg and was tied behind the shoe. The calf of this leg was weaker than the other, and it was the left leg. (Signed) WILLIAM SWIFT.'"

This, then, is the extent of the defect of which so much has been said, and which has been called a deformity. As to its being visible, all those who knew him assert that it was so little evident that it was even impossible to discover in which of the legs or feet the fault existed. To the testimonies already quoted I must add another:—

"His defect," says Mr. Galt, "was scarcely visible. He had a way of walking which made it appear almost imperceptible, and indeed entirely so. I spent several days on board a ship with him without discovering this defect; and, in truth, so little perceptible was it that a doubt always existed in my mind whether it might not be the effect of a temporary accident rather than a natural defect."

All those who knew him being therefore agreed in this opinion, that of people who were not acquainted with him is of no value. But if, in the material appreciation of a defect, they have not been able to err, several have erred in their moral appreciation of the fact by pretending that Lord Byron, for imaginary reasons, was exceedingly sensible of this defect. This excessive sensibility was a pure invention on the part of his biographers. When he did experience it (which was never but to a very moderate extent), it was only because, physically speaking, he suffered from it. Under the sole of the weak foot he at times experienced a painful sensation, especially after long walks.

"Once, at Genoa," says Mme. G., "he walked down the hill of Albaro to the seaside with me, by a rugged and rough path. When we had reached the shore he was very well and lively. But it was an exceedingly hot day, and the return home fatigued him greatly. When home I told him I thought he looked ill. 'Yes,' said he, 'I suffer greatly from my foot; it can hardly be conceived how much I suffer at times from that pain,' and he continued to speak to me about this defect with great simplicity and indifference."

He used often even to laugh at it, so superior was he to that weakness. "Beware," said Count Gamba to him on one occasion while riding with him, and on reaching some dangerous spot, "beware of falling and breaking your neck." "I should decidedly not like it," said Byron; "but if this leg of which I don't make much use were to break, it would be the same to me, and perhaps then I should be able to procure myself a more useful one."

The sensitiveness, therefore, which he was said to experience, and which would have been childish in him, was in reality only the occasional experience of a physical pain which did not, however, affect his strength, nor the grace of his movements, in all those physical exerçises to which he was so much attached. It in no wise altered his good looks, and, as a proof of this, I shall again bring testimonies, giving first that of M. N., who was at Constantinople when Byron arrived there for the first time, and who thus describes him in a review which he wrote of him after Byron's death:—

"A stranger then entered the bazar. He wore a scarlet cloak, richly embroidered with gold in the style of an English aid-de-camp's dress uniform. He was attended by a janissary attached to the English Embassy and by a cicerone: he appeared to be about twenty-two. His features were of so exquisite a delicacy, that one might almost have given him a feminine appearance, but for the manly expression of his fine blue eyes. On entering the inner shop he took off his hat, and showed a head of curly auburn hair, which improved in no small degree the uncommon beauty of his face. The impression his whole appearance made upon my mind, was such that it has ever remained most deeply engraven on it; and although fifteen years have since gone by, the lapse of time has not in the least impaired the freshness of the recollection." Then, speaking of his manner, he goes on to say: "There was so irresistible an attraction in his manner, that only those who have been so fortunate as to be admitted to his intimacy can have felt its power."

Moore once asked Lady Holland whether she believed that Lady Byron had ever really loved Lord Byron. "Could it be otherwise?" replied Lady Holland. "Was it possible not to love so lovable a creature? I see him there now, surrounded as it were by that great light: oh, how handsome he was!"

One of the most difficult things to define was the color of his eyes. It was a mixture of blue, gray, and violet, and these various colors were each uppermost according to the thought which occupied his mind or his heart. "Tell me, dear," said the little Eliza to her sister, whose enthusiasm for Byron she shared, "tell me what is the color of his eyes?" "I can not say; I believe them to be dark," answered Miss Eliza, "but all I know is that they have quite a supernatural splendor." And one day, having looked at them with greater attention in order to ascertain their color, she said, "They are the finest eyes in the world, but not dark, as I had at first believed. Their hue is that of the eyes of Mary Stuart, and his long, black eye-lashes make them appear dark. Never did I before, nor ever again shall I, see such eyes! As for his hands, they are the most beautiful hands, for a man, I ever saw. His voice is a sweet melody."*

Sir Walter Scott was enchanted when he could dilate on the extraordinary beauty of Byron. One day, at Mr. Home Drummond's, he exclaimed :—"As for poets, I have seen the best that this country has produced, and although Burns had the finest eyes that can be imagined, I never thought that any man except Byron could give an artist the exact idea of a poet. His portraits do not do him the least justice; the varnish is there, but the ray of sunshine is wanting to light them up. The beauty of Byron," he added "is one which makes one dream."

Colonel Wildman, his colleague at Harrow, and his friend, was always wont to say, "Lord Byron is the only man among all those I have seen, who may be called, without restriction, a really handsome man."

Disraeli, in his novel entitled "Venetia," speaks thus of the beauty of Hubert (who is Lord Byron) when Venetia finds his portrait :—

"That being of supernatural beauty is her father. Young as he was, command and genius, the pride of noble passions, all the glory of a creative mind, seemed stamped upon his brow. With all his marvellous beauty he seemed a being born for greatness. . . . Its reality exceeded the wildest dreams of her romance, her brightest visions of grace and loveliness and genius seemed personified in this form. He was a man in the very spring of sunny youth and of radiant beauty. He was above the middle height, yet with a form that displayed

* Miss E. Smith.

exquisite grace. . . It was a countenanee of singular loveliness and power. The lips and the moulding of the chin resembled the eager and impassioned tenderness of the shape of Antinous; but instead of the effeminate sullenness of the eye, and the narrow smoothness of the forehead, shone an expression of profound and piercing thought. On each side of the clear and open brow descended, even to the shoulders, the clustering locks of golden hair; while the eyes large and yet deep, beamed with a spiritual energy, and shone like two wells of crystalline water that reflect the all-beholding heavens."

M. Beyle (Stendhal) writes to Mr. Swanton Belloc:—"It was in the autumn of the year 1816 that I met Lord Byron at the theatre of the Scala, at Milan, in the box of the Bremen Minister. I was struck with Lord Byron's eyes at the time when he was listening to a sestetto in Mayer's opera of "Elena." I never in my life saw any thing more beautiful or more expressive. Even now, when I think of the expression which a great painter should give to genius, I always have before me that magnificent head. I had a moment of enthusiasm." And further, he adds that one day he saw him listening to Monti while the latter was singing his first couplet in the "Mascheroniana." "I shall never forget," said he, "the divine expression of his look; it was the serene look of genius and power."

I might multiply these testimonies of people who have seen him, and fill many pages; their particular character is their uniform resemblance. This proves the soundness of the ground on which their truth is based. I will add one more testimony to the others, that of Mrs. Shelley, which is even nearer the truth, and condenses all the others:—"Lord Byron," said this distinguished woman, "was the first genius of his age and the handsomest of men."

In all these portraits there is much truth, but they are not sufficiently complete to give those who never saw him any but a faint idea of his smile, or of his mouth, which seemed to be not suited to material purposes, and to be purely intellectual and divine; of his eyes, which changed from one color to another according to the various emotions of his soul, but the habitual expression of which was that of an infinite and intense softness; of his sublime and noble brow; of his melodious voice, which attracted and captivated; and of that kind of supernatural light which seemed to surround him like a halo.

This inability on the part of artists and biographers to render exactly Byron's features and looks, is not to be wondered at, for although perfectly regular, his features derived their principal beauty from the life which his soul instilled into them. The emotions of his heart, the changes of his thoughts, appeared so variously upon his countenance, and gave the latter so changeable a cast, that it sufficed not for the artist who had to portray him, to gaze at and study him, as one generally does less gifted or elevated organizations. The reality was more likely to be well interpreted when it stood a prey to the various emotions of the soul; in his leisure hours, in the full enjoyment of life and love, he was satisfied with the knowledge that he was young, handsome, beloved, and admired. Then it was that his beauty became, as it were, radiant and brilliant like a ray of sunshine.

The time to see him was when, under the influence of genius, his soul was tormented with the desire of pouring out the numberless ideas and thoughts which flooded his mind: at such moments one scarcely dared approach him, awed, as it were, by the feeling of one's own nothingness in comparison with his greatness. Again, the time to see him was when, coming down from the high regions to which a moment before he had soared, he became once more the simple child adorned with goodness and every grace; taking an interest in all things, as if he were really a child. It was impossible then to refrain from the contemplation of this placid beauty, which, without taking away in the least from the admiration which it inspired, drew one toward him, and made him more accessible to one, and more familiar by lessening a little the distance which separated one from him. But, above all, he should have been seen during the last days of his stay in Italy, when his soul had to sustain the most cruel blows; when heroism got the better of his affections, of his worldly interests, and even of his love of ease and tranquillity; when his health, already shaken, appeared to fail him each day more and more, to the loss of his intellectual powers. Had one seen him then as we saw him, it would scarcely have been possible to paint him as he looked. Does not genius require genius to be its interpreter? Thorwaldsen alone has, in his marble bust of him, been able to blend the regular beauty of his features with the sublime expression of his countenance. Had the reader seen him, he would have exclaimed with Sir Walter Scott, "that no picture is like him."

Not only would he have observed in his handsome face the denial of all the absurd statements which had been made about him, but he would have noticed a soul greater even than the mind, and superior to the acts which he performed on this earth; he would have read in unmistakable characters, not only what he was,—a good man,—but the promise of a moral and intellectual perfection ever increasing. If this progressive march toward perfection was at one time arrested by the trials of his life, and by the consequences of undeserved sorrow, it was well proved by his whole conduct toward the end of his life, and in the last poems which he wrote. His poems from year to year assumed a more perfect beauty, and increased constantly, not only in the splendor of their conception, but also in the force of their expressions, and their moral tendency, visible especially in his dramas. In them will be found types surpassing in purity, in delicacy, in grandeur, in heroism, without ever being untrue to nature, all that ever was conceived by the best poets of England. Shakspeare, in all his master creations, has not conceived a more noble soul than that of Angiolina, or a more tender one than Marina's or even one more heroic than Myrrha's. As his genius became developed, his soul became purified and more perfect. But the Almighty, who does not allow perfection to be of this world, did not permit him to remain on earth, when once he had reached that point. He allowed him, however,—and this perhaps as a compensation for all the injuries which he had suffered,—to die in the prime of life a death worthy of him; the death of a virtuous man, of a hero, of a philosopher.

Excuse this long letter, for if I have ventured to speak to you at such length of the moral, and—may I say the word?—"physical" beauty of the illustrious Englishman, it is because one genius can appreciate another, and that, in speaking of so great a man as Lord Byron, there is no fear of tiring the listeners.

CHAPTER III.

FRENCH PORTRAIT.

"I see that the greater part of the men of my time endeavor to blemish the glory of the generous and fine actions of olden days by giving to them some vile interpretation, or by finding some vain cause or occasion which produced them—very clever, indeed! I shall use a similar license, and take the same trouble to endeavor to raise these great names."—MONTAIGNE, chap. "Glory."

THE portrait of Lord Byron, in a moral point of view, is still to be drawn. Many causes have conspired to make the task difficult, and the portrait unlike. Physically speaking, on account of his matchless beauty—mentally, owing to his genius—and morally, owing to the rare qualities of his soul, Lord Byron was certainly a phenomenon. The world agrees in this opinion; but is not yet agreed upon the nature and moral value of the phenomenon. But as all phenomena have, besides a primary and extraordinary cause, some secondary and accidental causes, which it is necessary to examine in order that they may be understood; so, to explain Byron's nature, we must not neglect to observe the causes which have contributed chiefly to the formation of his individuality.

His biographers have rather considered the results than the causes.

Even Moore, the best among them, if not, indeed, the only one who can claim the title of biographer, grants that the nature of Lord Byron and its operations were inexplicable, but does not give himself the trouble to understand them.

Here are his own words:—"So various indeed, and contradictory were his attributes, both moral and intellectual, that he may be pronounced to have been not one, but many: nor would it be any great exaggeration of the truth to say, that out of the mere partition of the properties of his single mind, a plurality of characters, all different and all vigorous, might have been furnished. It was this multiform aspect exhibited by him that led the world, during his short, wondrous career, to compare him with the medley host of personages, almost all differing from each other, which he playfully enumerates in one of his journals.

"The object of so many contradictory comparisons must probably be like something different from them all; but what *that* is, is more than I know, or any body else."

But, while merely explaining the extraordinary richness of this nature by the analysis of its results, by his changeable character, by the frankness which ever made his heart speak that which it felt, by his excessive sensitiveness, which made him the slave of momentary impressions, by his almost child-like delight and astonishment at things, Moore does not arrive at the true causes of the phenomenon. He registers, it is true, certain effects which become causes when they draw upon the head of Lord Byron certain false judgments, and open the door to every calumny.

Without adopting the system of the influence of races on mankind—which, if pushed to its extreme consequences, must lead to the disastrous and deplorable doctrine of fatalism, and would make of man a mere machine—it is, however, impossible to deny that races and their amalgamation do exercise a great influence over our species.

It is to this very influence of race, which was so evident in Lord Byron, that we attribute, in a measure, the exceptional nature of the great English poet.

As the reader knows, Lord Byron was descended, by his father, from the noble race of the Birons of France. His ancestors accompanied William the Conqueror to England, aided him in the conquest of that country, and distinguished themselves in the various fields of battle which ultimately led to the total subjugation of the island.

In his family, the sympathies of the original race always remained strong.

His father, a youthful and brilliant officer, was never happy except in France. He was very intimate with the Maréchal de Biron, who looked upon him as a connection. He even settled in Paris with his first wife, the Marchioness of Carmarthen. Soon after his second marriage, he brought his wife over to France, and it was in France that she conceived the future poet. When obliged to return to England to be confined, she was so far advanced in pregnancy that she could not reach London in time, but gave birth to Lord Byron at Dover. It was in France that Byron's father died at thirty-five years of age. Through his mother—a Scotch lady connected with the royal house of Stuart—he had Scotch blood in his veins.

The powerful influence exercised by the Norman Conquest, in the modification of all the old habits of Great Britain, and in making the English that which they now are, has descended as an heirloom to some old aristocratic families of the kingdom, where it discovers itself at different times in different individuals. Nowhere, perhaps, did this influence show itself more clearly than in the person of Lord Byron.

His duplicate or triplicate origin was already visible in the cast of his features. Without any analogy to the type of beauty belonging to the men of his country (a beauty seldom found apart from a kind of cold reserve), Lord Byron's beauty appeared to unite the energy of the western with the splendor and the mildness of the southern climes.

The influence of this mixture of races was equally visible in his moral and intellectual character.

He belonged to the Gallic race (modified by the Latin and Celtic elements) by his vivacity and mobility of character, as well as by his wit and his keen appreciation of the ridiculous, by those smiles and sarcasms which hide or discover a profound philosophy, by his perception of humor without malice, by all those amiable qualities which in the daily intercourse of life made of him a being of such irresistible attraction. He belonged to that race likewise by his great sensitiveness, by his expansive good-nature, by his politeness, by his tractableness, by his universal character which rendered every species of success easy to him; by his great generosity, by his love of glory, by his passion for honor, his intuitive perception of great deeds, by a courage which might have appeared rash, had it not been heroic, and which, in presence of the greatest perils and even of death, ever preserved for him that serenity of mind which allowed him to laugh, even at such times; by his energy, and also by his numerous mental and bodily requirements; and by his defects,—which were, a slight tendency to indiscretion, a want of prudence injurious to his interests, impatience, and a kind of intermittent and apparent fickleness.

He belonged to the western race by his vast intellect, by his practical common sense, which formed the basis of his intellect, and which never allowed him to divorce sublime conceptions from sound sense and good reason,—two qualities, in fact, which so governed his imagination as to make people say he had not any; by the depth of his feelings, the extent of his learning, his passion for independence, his contempt of death, his thirst for the infinite, and by that kind of melancholy which seemed to follow him into the midst of every pleasure. All these various elements, which belonged separately to individuals in France, in England, and in various countries, being united in Lord Byron, produced a kind of anomaly which startled systematic critics, and even honest biographers. The apparent contradiction of all these qualities caused his critics to lose their psychological compass in their estimate of his charming nature, and justice, together with truth, suffered by the result. Thus a portrait, drawn over and over again, still remains to be painted.

The most imaginary portrait, however, of Lord Byron, and certainly the least like him, is that which has general currency in France: not only has that portrait not been drawn from nature, not only is it a caricature, but it is also a calumny. Those who drew it took romance for history. They charged or exaggerated incidents in his life and peculiarities of his character; thus the harmony of the *tout ensemble* was lost. Ugliness and eccentricity, which amuse, succeeded beauty and truth, which are sometimes wearisome.

Those who knew and loved Lord Byron even more as a man than a genius (and, after all, these are those who knew him personally) suffer by this injustice done to him, and feel the absurdity of making so privileged a being act so whimsical a part, and one so contrary to his nature as well as to the reality of his life.

If this imaginary portrait, however, were more like those which his best biographers have drawn of him, justice to his memory would become so difficult a task as to be almost impossible. Happily it is not so; and those who would conscientiously consult Moore, Parry, and Gamba, must at least give up the idea that this admirable genius was the eccentric and unamiable being he has been represented. To reach this point would, perhaps, require a greater respect for truth.

Even in France there are many superior persons who, struck by the force of facts, have at times endeavored to seize certain features which might lead to the discovery of truth, and have attempted to show that Lord Byron's noble character and beauty of soul, as well as his genius, did honor to humanity. But their efforts have been vain in presence of the absurd and contradictory creation of fancy which has been styled "Lord Byron," and which with few modifications, continues to be called so to this day.

How has this occurred? what gave rise to it? ignorance, or carelessness? Both causes in France, added to revenge in England, which found its expression in cant,—a species of scourge which is becoming quite the fashion.

The first of these French biographers (I mean of those who have written upon and wished to characterize Lord Byron), without knowing the man they were writing about, set to work with a ready-made Byron. This, no doubt, they found to be an easier method to follow, and one of which the results must prove at least original. But where had they found, and from whose hands did they receive this ready-made poet, whose features they reproduced and offered to the world? Probably from a few lines, not without merit, of Lamartine, who by the aid of his rich imagination had identified Byron with the types which he had conceived for his Oriental poems, mixing up the whole with a heap of calumnies which had just been circulated about him.

Perhaps also from certain critics who believed in the statements of various calumniators, and who themselves had probably not had any better authority than a few articles in badly informed papers, or in newspapers politically opposed to Lord Byron. We all know, by what we see daily in France, how little we can trust the moderation of these, and the justice they render to their adversaries; what must it not have been in England at that time, when passions ran so high?—Perhaps also from the jealousy of dethroned rivals!—the echoes, perhaps, of the revenge of a woman equally distinguished by her rank and by her talent, but whose passion approached the boundaries of madness, or of the implacable hatred of a few fanatics who, substituting in the most shameless manner their worldly and sectarian interests for the Gospel, denounced him as an atheist because he himself had proclaimed them hypocrites. Finally, perhaps, from a host of absurd rumors, equally odious and vague, caused by his separation from his wife, and by the articles published in newspapers printed at Venice and at Milan.

For Byron's noble, simple, and sublime person was therefore substituted an imaginary being, formed out of these prejudices and these contradictory elements, too outrageous even to be believed, and by dint of sheer malice.

Thus enveloped in a dense atmosphere, which became an obstacle to the disclosure of truth as the clouds are to the rays of the sun, his image only appeared in fantastical outlines borrowed from "Conrad the Corsair," or "Childe Harold," or "Lara," or "Manfred," or indeed "Don Juan." Analogies were sought which do not exist, and to the poet were attributed the sentiments, and even the acts, of these imaginary beings, albeit without any of the great qualities which constituted his great and noble soul, and which he has not imparted to any of his poetical creations.

Upon him were heaped every possible and most contradictory accusation—of skepticism and pantheism, of deism and atheism, of superstition and enthusiasm, of irony and passion, of sensuality and ideality, of generosity and avarice. These went to form his portrait, presenting every contrast and every antagonism, which God Himself, the Father and Creator of all things, but also the Author of all harmony, could not have assembled in one and the same being unless He made of him a species of new Frankenstein, incapable of treading the ordinary paths of physical, moral, or intellectual, nay, of the most ordinary existence.

After thus producing such an eccentric character,—the more extraordinary that they entirely forgot to consult the true and most simple history of his life, where if some of the ordinary excusable faults of youth are to be found, "some remarkable qualities, however, must be noticed,"—these wonderful biographers exclaim, astonished as it were at their own conclusions :—"This is indeed a most singular, extraordinary, and not-to-be-defined being!"

I should think so: it is their own work, not the noble, amiable, and sublime mind, the work of God, and which he always exhibited in himself,

"Per far di colassà fede fra noi."—PETRARCH.

Happily, if to paint the portrait of Byron has become impossible, now that

"Poca terra è rimasto il suo belviso,"

it is easy to describe his moral character. His invisible form is, it is true, above, but a conscientious examination of his whole life will give us an idea of it. He knew this so well himself, that a few days before his death he begged, as a favor, of his friend Lord Harrington, then Colonel Stanhope, at Missolonghi, to judge him only by his deeds. "Judge me by my deeds."

All bombastic expressions, all systematic views should be discarded, and attention paid only to facts, in order to discover the fine intellectual figure of Lord Byron so completely lost sight of by his detractors.

Since the imaginary creations of his pen in moments of exalted passion should not be taken as the real manifestation of his character, the latter is to be found in his own deeds, and in the testimony of those who knew him personally. Herein shall we seek truth by which we are to deal with the fanciful statements which have too long been received as facts. Let us consider the opinions of those who by their authority have a right to portray him, while we study the various causes which have contributed to lead the public into errors which time has nearly consecrated, but which shall be corrected in France, and indeed in every country where passion and animosity have no interest in maintaining them.

"Public opinion," says M. Cousin, "has its errors, but these can not be of long duration." They lasted a long time, however, as regards Lord Byron; but, thanks to God, they will not be eternal. He depended upon this himself, for he once at Ravenna wrote these prophetic words in a memorandum:—

"Never mind the wicked, who have ever persecuted me

with the help of Lady Byron: triumphant justice will be done to me when the hand which writes this is as cold as the hearts that have wounded me."

In England, Lord Byron triumphed over many jealous enemies whom his first satire earned for him, no less than the rapid and wonderful rise of his genius, which, instead of appearing by degrees, burst forth at once, as it were, and towering over many established reputations. The prestige which he acquired was such that every obstacle was surmounted, and in one day he saw himself raised against his will, and without his having ever sought the honor, to the highest pinnacle of fashion and literary fame.

In a country where success is all, his enemies, and those who were jealous of his name, were obliged to fall back; but they did not give up their weapons nor their spite. One curious element was introduced in the national veneration for the poet. It was agreed that never had such an accumulation of various gifts been heaped upon the head of one man: he was to be revered and honored, but on one condition. He was to be a mysterious being whose genius should not transgress the boundaries of the East; who was to allow himself to be identified with the imaginary beings of his own fancy, however disagreeable, nay, even criminal they might be in reality. True, his personal conduct (at twenty-four) was to be above all human weakness; if not, he was to be treated, as certain superstitious votaries treat their idols if they do not obtain at once the miracles they ask for. His secret enemies perfidiously made use of these stupid demands of the public.

Insinuating and giving out at times one calumny after another, they always kept behind the scenes, resolved, however, to ruin him in the public esteem on the first opportunity, which they knew they would not have long to wait for from one so open, so passionate, so generous as Lord Byron. The greatest misfortune of his life—his marriage—gave them their opportunity. Then they came forth, threw down the mask which they had hitherto worn, to put on one more hideous still; overturned the statue from the pedestal upon which the public had raised it, and tried to mutilate its remains. But as the stuff of which it was made was a marble which could not be broken, they only defiled, insulted, and outlawed it.

Then it was that France made acquaintance with Lord Byron. She saw him first mysteriously enveloped in the romantic semblance of a Corsair, of a skeptical Harold, of a young lord who had despised and wounded his mother-country, from which he had almost been obliged to exile himself, in consequence of a series of eccentricities, faults, and—who knows?—of crimes, perhaps. Thus caught in a perfidious net, Lord Byron left England for Switzerland.

He found Shelley, whom he only knew by name, at Geneva, where he stopped. Shelley was another victim of English fanatical and intolerant opinions; but he, it may be allowed at least, had given cause for this by some reprehensible writings, in which he had declared himself an atheist. No allowance had been made for his youth, for he was only seventeen when he wrote "Queen Mab," and he found himself expelled not only from the university but also from his home, which was to him a real cause of sorrow and misfortune.

Between these two great minds there existed a wide gulf—that which exists between pantheism and spiritualism; but they had one great point of resemblance, their mutual passionate love for justice and humanity, their hatred of cant and hypocrisy, in fact, all the elevated sentiments of the moral and social man. With Lord Byron these noble dispositions of the heart and mind were naturally the consequence of his tastes and opinions, which were essentially spiritualistic. With Shelley, though in contradiction with his metaphysics, they were notwithstanding in harmony with the beautiful sentiments of his soul, which, when he was only twenty-three years of age, had already experienced the unkindness of man. Their respective souls, wounded and hurt by the perfidiousness and injustice of the world, felt themselves attracted to each other. A real friendship sprang up between them. They saw one another often, and it was in the conversations which they held together at this time that the seed was sown which shortly was to produce the works of genius which were to see the day at the foot of the Alps and under the blue sky of Italy.

Although Lord Byron's heart was mortally wounded, still no feeling of hatred could find its way into it. The sorrow which he felt, the painful knowledge which he had of cruel and perfidious wrongs done to him, the pain of finding out the timidity of character of his friends, and the recollection of the many ungrateful people of whom he was the victim, all and each of these sentiments found their echo in the "Prisoner of Chillon," in the third canto of "Childe Harold," in "Manfred," in the pathetic stanzas addressed to his sister, in the admirable and sublime monody on the death of Sheridan, and in the "Dream," which according to Moore, he must have written while shedding many bitter tears. According to the same authority, the latter poem is the most melancholy and pathetic history that ever came forth from human pen.

I shall not mention here the persecution to which Byron was subjected then, nor the ever-manly, dignified, but heart-rending words which it drew forth from the noble poet in the midst of his retired, studious, regular, and virtuous existence. I shall speak of it elsewhere; but I will say now that so unexampled, atrocious, and foolish was this persecution, that his enemies must have feared the awakening of the public conscience and the effects of a reaction, which might make them lose all the fruits of their victory, if they tarried in their efforts to prevent it. The most cruel among them was the poet laureate, in whose eyes Byron could have had but one defect—that of being superior to him. True, Byron had mentioned him in the famous satire which was the work of his youth; but he had most generously expiated his crime by confessing it, in buying up the fifth edition so as to annihilate it, and by declaring that he would have willingly suppressed even the memory of it. This noble action had gained for him the forgiveness and even the friendship of the most generous among them; but the revengful poet laureate was not, as Byron said, "of those who forgive."

This man arrived at Geneva, and at once set about his hateful work of revenge. This was all the easier on account of the spirit of cant which reigned in that country, and owing to the intimacy which he found to be existing between Byron and Shelley, for whom likewise he had conceived a malignant hatred. It must be said, however, that the laureate having to account for, among other works, his "Wat Tyler" (which had been pronounced to be an immoral book, and had been prohibited on that account), rather trusted to his hypocrisy to regain for him the former credit he enjoyed.

The intimacy between Byron and the spurned atheist Shelley presented a capital opportunity for this man to take his revenge. He circulated in Geneva all the false reports which had been current in London, and described Byron under the worst colors. Switzerland was at that time overrun by the English, whom the recently-signed Peace had attracted to the Continent. The laureate took the lead of those who tried to make the good but bigoted people of Geneva believe in all the tittle-tattle against Byron which was passed about in London, and actually attempted to make a scandal of his very presence in their town. When he passed in the streets they stopped to stare at him insolently, putting up their glasses to their eyes. They followed him in his rides; they reported that he was seducing all the girls in the "Rue Basse," and, in fact, although his life was perfectly virtuous, one would have said that his presence was a contagion. Having found in a travellers' register the name of Shelley, accompanied by the qualification of "atheist!" which Byron had amiably struck out with his pen, the laureate caught at this and gave out that the two friends had declared themselves to be atheists. He attributed their friendship to infamous motives; he spoke of incest and of other abominations, so odious that Byron's friends deemed it prudent not to speak to him a word of all this at the time. He only learned it at Venice later.*

* When political events obliged Count Gamba to quit Romagna, he thought at first of going with his family to take up his abode at Geneva.

Lord Byron, on learning this, through a letter from the Countess Guiccioli, who had rejoined her family at Florence, disapproved of their design, and begged Shelley—then on a visit to him at Ravenna—to express for him his disapprobation, and state the reasons of it. Shelley addressed the following letter in Italian to the countess, and the project was abandoned:—

"MADAM,—At the request of my friend, Lord Byron, I consider it my duty to offer you some considerations relative to the proposed journey to Geneva, so as to give you an idea of the undesirable results likely to follow. I flatter myself that you will accept this request of his, together with the motives leading me to acquiesce, as an excuse for the liberty taken by a total stranger. In acting thus, the sole object I have in view is my friend's peace of mind, and that of those in whom he is so deeply interested. I have no other motive, nor can entertain any other; and let it suffice, in proof of my perfect sincerity, to assure you that I also have suffered from an intolerant clergy at home, and from tyranny, and that I like your family, have met with persecution and calumny as my sole reward for love of country.

Loaded with this very creditable amount of falsehoods, most of which were believed in Geneva, the laureate returned

"Allow me, madam, to state the reasons for which it seems to me that Geneva would not be an appropriate residence for your family. Your circumstances offer some analogy with those existing between my family and Lord Byron in the summer of 1816. Our dwellings were close together; our mode of life was quiet and retired; it would be impossible to imagine an existence simpler than ours, less calculated to draw down the aspersions cast upon us.

"These calumnies were of the most unheard-of nature,—really too infamous to permit us to treat them with disdain. Both Genevans and English established at Geneva affirmed that we were leading a life of the most unblushing profligacy. They said that we had made a compact together for outraging all held most sacred in human society. Pardon me, madam, if I spare you the details. I will only say that *incest*, *atheism*, and many other things equally ridiculous or horrible, were imputed to us. The English newspapers were not slow in propagating the scandal, and the nation lent entire faith.

"Hardly any mode of annoying us was neglected. Persons living on the borders of the lake opposite Lord Byron's house made use of telescopes to spy out all his movements. An English lady fainted, or pretended to faint, with horror on seeing him enter a saloon. The most outrageous caricatures of him and his friends were circulated; and all this took place in the short period of three months.

"The effect of this, on Lord Byron's mind, was most unhappy. His natural gayety abandoned him almost entirely. A man must be more or less than a stoic to bear such injuries with patience.

"Do not flatter yourself, madam, with the idea, that because Englishmen acknowledge Lord Byron as the greatest poet of the day, they would therefore abstain from annoying him, and, as far as it depended on them, from persecuting him. Their admiration for his works is unwillingly extorted, and the pleasure they experience in reading them does not allay prejudice nor stop calumny.

"As to the Genevans, they would not disturb him, if there were not a colony of English established in the town,—persons who have carried with them a host of mean prejudices and hatred against all those who excel or avoid them; and as these causes would continue to exist, the same effects would doubtless follow.

"The English are about as numerous at Geneva as the natives, and their riches cause them to be sought after; for the Genevans, compared to their guests, are like valets, or, at best, like hotel-keepers, having let their whole town to foreigners.

"A circumstance, personally known to me, may afford proof of what is to be expected at Geneva. The only inhabitant on whose attachment and honor Lord Byron thought he had every reason to count, turned out one of those who invented the most infamous calumnies. A friend of mine, deceived by him, involuntarily unveiled all his wickedness to me, and I was therefore obliged to inform my friend of the hypocrisy and perversity we had discovered in this individual. You can not, madam, conceive the excessive violence with which Englishmen, of a certain class, detest those whose conduct and opinions are not exactly framed on the model of their own. This system of ideas forms a superstition unceasingly demanding victims, and unceasingly finding them. But, however strong theological hatred may be among them, it yields in intensity to social hatred. This system is quite the order of the day at Geneva; and, having once been brought into play for the disquiet of Lord Byron and his friends, I much fear that the same causes would soon produce the same effects, if the intended journey took place. Accustomed as you are, madam, to the gentler manners of Italy, you will scarcely be able to conceive to what a pitch this social hatred is carried in less favored to London to spread them in England, so as to prevent the effects of the beautiful and touching poems which were poured forth from the great and wounded soul of Byron, and which might have restored him to the esteem of all the honest and just minds of his country.

Meanwhile Lady C. L—— having failed to discover any one who would accept the reward she offered to the person who would take Byron's life, had recourse to another means of injuring him—to a kind of moral assassination—which she effected by the publication of her revengeful sentiments in the three volumes entitled "Glenarvon." Such a work might justify a biographer in passing it over with contempt without even mentioning it; but as enemies of Lord Byron have made capital out of this book,—as it found credence even with some superior minds, such as Goethe's—as the intimacy which prefaced this revenge caused great sensation all over England, and was a source of continual vexation and pain for Byron—it must not be passed over without comment, as Moore did to spare the susceptibility of living personages.

Lady C. L—— (afterward Lady M——) belonged to the high aristocracy of England. Young, clever, and fashionable, but a little eccentric, she had been married some years when she fell so desperately in love with Lord Byron that she braved every thing for him. It was not Byron who made the first advances, for his powers of seduction were only the attractions with which nature had endowed him. His person, his voice, his look,—all in him was irresistible. In presenting himself anywhere, he could very well say with Shakspeare, in "Othello,"—

"This only is the witchcraft I have used."

---

regions. I have been forced to pass through this hard experience, and to see all dearest to me entangled in inextricable slanders. My position bore some resemblance to that of your brother, and it is for that reason I hasten to write you, in order to spare you and your family the evil I so fatally experienced. I refrain from adding other reasons, and I pray you to excuse the freedom with which I have written, since it is dictated by sincerest motives, and justified by my friend's request. To him I leave the care of assuring you of my devotion to his interests, and to all those dear to him.

"Deign, madam, to accept the expression of my highest esteem.

"Your sincere and humble servant,

"PERCY B. SHELLEY.

"P.S.—You will forgive a barbarian, madam, for the bad Italian in which the honest sentiments of his letter are couched."

Lord Byron, who was then only twenty-three years of age, and not married, was flattered, and more than pleased, by this preference shown to him. Although Lady C. L——'s beauty was not particularly attractive to him, and although her character was exactly opposite to the ideal which he had formed of what woman's character should be, yet she contrived to interest him, to captivate him by the power of her love, and in a very short time to persuade him that he loved her.

This sort of love could not last. It was destined to end in a catastrophe. Lady L——'s jealousy was ridiculous. Dressed sometimes as a page, sometimes in another costume, she was wont to follow him by means of these disguises. She quarrelled and played the heroine, etc. Byron, who disliked quarrels of all kinds (and perhaps even the lady herself), besides being intimate with all her family, was too much the sufferer by this conduct not to endeavor to bring her back to a sense of reason and of her duty. He was indulging in the hope that he had succeeded in these endeavors when, at a ball given by Lady Heathcote, Lady L——, after vain efforts to attract Byron's attention, went up to him and asked him whether she might waltz. Byron replied, half-absently, that he saw no reason why she should not; upon which her pride and her passion became so excited that she seized hold of a knife, and feigned to commit suicide. The ball was at once at an end, and all London was soon filled with accounts of this incident. Lady L—— had scarcely recovered from the slight wound she had inflicted on herself, when she wrote to a young peer, and made him all kinds of extravagant promises, if he would consent to call out Byron and kill him. This, however, did not prevent her calling again upon Lord Byron, not, however, says Medwin, with the intention of blowing his brains out; as he was not at home, she wrote on one of his books

"Remember me."

On returning home, Byron read what she had written, and, filled with disgust and indignation, he wrote the famous lines

"Remember thee! Ay, doubt it not,"

and sent her back several of her letters sealed up. "Glenarvon" was her revenge. She painted Byron in fiendish colors, giving herself all the qualities he possessed, so as to appear an angel, and to him all the passions of the "Giaour," of the "Corsair," and of "Childe Harold," so that he might be taken for a demon.

In this novel, the result of revenge, truth asserts its rights, notwithstanding all the contradictions of which the book is full. Thus Lady L—— can not help depicting Byron under some of his real characteristics. She was asked, for instance, what she thought of him, when she met him for the first time after hearing of his great reputation, and she answers, while gazing at the soft loveliness of his smile,—

"What do I think? I think that never did the hand of God imprint upon a human form so lovely, so glorious an expression."

And further she adds:—

"Never did the sculptor's hand, in the sublimest product of his talent, imagine a form and a face so exquisite, so full of animation or so varied in expression. Can one see him without being moved? Oh! is there in the nature of woman the possibility of listening to him, without cherishing every word he utters? and having listened to him once, is it possible for any human heart ever to forget those accents which awaken every sentiment and calm every fear?"

Again:—

"Oh better far to have died than to see or listen to Glenarvon. When he smiled, his smile was like the light of heaven; his voice was more soothing from its softness than the softest music. In his manner there was such a charm, that it would have been vain to affect even to be offended by its sweetness."

But while she was obliged to obey the voice of passion and of truth, she took on the other hand as a motto to her novel that of the "Corsair," which even applied to the "Corsair" is not altogether just, for he was gifted with more than "one virtue:—"

> "He left a Corsair's name to other times,
> Link'd with one virtue and a thousand crimes."

It is, however, fair to add, that this revenge became the punishment of the heroine; she never again found any rest, struggled against a troubled mind, and never succeeded in forgetting her love. It is even said that, diseased in mind and body, she was one day walking along one of the alleys of her beautiful place, on the road to Newstead Abbey, when she saw a funeral procession coming up the road in the direction of Newstead. Having inquired whose funeral it was, and being told it was that of the great poet, whose mortal remains were being conveyed to their last resting-place, she fainted, and died a few days afterward. His name was the last word she uttered, and this she did with love and despair. In London, and wherever the authoress was known, the book had no success, but the case was different abroad and in the provinces.

Attracted as he always was toward all that is good, great, and sincere, Byron was wont to break the monotony of his retired life in the villa Diodati by frequent visits to Madame de Staël at her country-seat, "Coppet." She was the first who mentioned "Glenarvon" to him, and when Murray wrote to him on the subject, Byron simply replied,—

"Of Glenarvon, Madame de Staël told me (ten days ago at Coppet) marvellous and grievous things; but I have seen nothing of it but the motto, which promises amiably 'for us and for our tragedy' . . . 'a name to all succeeding,' etc. The generous moment selected for the publication is probably its kindest accompaniment, and, truth to say, the time *was* well chosen."*

"I have not even a guess at its contents," said he, and he really attached no importance to its publication. But a few days later he had a proof of the bad effect which its appearance had produced, for all this venom against him had so poisoned the mind of a poor old woman of sixty-three, an authoress, that on Lord Byron entering Madame de Staël's drawing-room one afternoon, she fainted, or feigned to do so. Poor soul! a writer of novels herself, and probably most partial to such reading, she had, no doubt, from the perusal of "Glenarvon" gleaned the idea that she had before her eyes that hideous monster of seduction and perpetrator of crimes who was therein depicted!

At last Lord Byron read this too famous novel, and wrote to Moore as follows on the subject:—

* Moore, vol. ii. p. 8.

"Madame de Staël lent me 'Glenarvon' last autumn. It seems to me that if the author had written the truth, and nothing but the truth, and the whole truth, the novel might not only have been more romantic but more amusing. As for the likeness, it can not be good, I did not sit long enough for it."

From Venice Byron wrote as follows to Murray, in consequence of a series of articles which appeared in Germany, where a serious view had been taken of the novel of "Glenarvon:"—

"An Italian translation of 'Glenarvon' was lately printed at Venice. The censor (Sgr. Petrolini) refused to sanction the publication till he had seen me on the subject. I told him that I did not recognize the slightest relation between that book and myself; but that, whatever opinions might be held on that subject, I would never prevent or oppose the publication of any book in any language, on my own private account, and desired him (against his inclination) to permit the poor translator to publish his labors. It is going forward in consequence. You may say this, with my compliments, to the author."*

Madame de Staël had a great affection for Lord Byron, but his detractors had found their way into her house.† Among these was a distinguished lawyer, who had never been injured by any speech or word of Lord Byron, but who, setting him-

* When that extravagant book "Glenarvon" appeared, Moore wrote a comic review on it, and sent the paper to Jeffrey, who thought it a good caricature, and wanted to publish it in the "Edinburgh Review." But the friends of the author of "Glenarvon" interfered to such purpose that Jeffrey gave up the idea of mentioning the novel at all, which was also approved by Lord Byron's friends as the best means of proving, by silence, the contempt such a book merited.

† Madame de Staël said one day at Coppet, with an air of mystery, "You are often seen at night, Lord Byron, in your bark upon the lake, accompanied by a white phantom." "Yes," answered he, "'tis my dog." Madame de Staël shook her head, not at all convinced that he kept such innocent company, for her head had been filled with fantastic tales and lies about him. In this instance, however, she was somewhat right; for the white phantom was not only his dog, but often Mrs. Shelley, and even sometimes a young woman intimate with her. This lady, with whom he had, and would have, nothing to do, was bent on running after him, although he did all in his power to avoid her. She succeeded sometimes in getting into the boat with the Shelleys, and thus made inquisitive people talk. But Lord Byron was very innocent in it all, and even victimized, for the *ennui* it caused him made him quit Switzerland and the Alps, he loved so well, before the season was even over.

self up as an amateur enemy of the poet, had, under an anonymous designation, been one of his bitterest detractors in the "Edinburgh Review," on the occásion of the publication of his early poems. This same lawyer endeavored to gain Madame de Staël over to his opinion of Byron's merit, probably on account of the very knowledge that he had of the harm he had done him; hatred, like nobility, has its obligations. But Madame de Staël, who, on reading "Farewell," was wont to say that she wished almost she had been as unfortunate as Lady Byron, was too elevated in mind and too noble in character to listen quietly to the abuse of Byron in which his enemies indulged. She, however, tried to induce Lord Byron to become reconciled to his wife, on the ground that one should never struggle against the current of public opinion. Madame de Staël actually succeeded in obtaining his permission to endeavor to effect this reconciliation; but the lawyer before mentioned used every argument to prevent her pursuing this project of mediation.

Lord Byron's biographers have told how Lady Byron received this proposal; which, after the way in which he had been treated, appears to have been, on the part of Byron, an act of almost superhuman generosity. Such an offer should have moved any being gifted with a heart and a soul. But I will not here speak of her refusal and of its consequences; all I wish to state is, that the calumnies put forward against him being too absurd for Byron to condescend to notice, assumed a degree of consistency which deceived the public, and even made dupes of superior men, who in their turn contributed to make dupes of others. At this time, then, when the war and the continental blockade were at an end, when each and every one came pouring on to the Continent, did the star of Byron begin to shine on the European horizon; but, instead of appearing as a sublime and bountiful star, it appeared surrounded by dark and ominous clouds.

Lamartine, who was then travelling in Switzerland, was able to find in this sad state of things materials for his fine poem "Meditation," and for doubts whether Byron was "an angel, or a demon," according to the manner in which he was viewed, be it as a poet or as a man; and, as if all this were not enough, a host of bad writings were attributed to his pen, which brought forth the following expressions in a letter to Murray, his publisher:—

"I had hoped that some other lie would have replaced and succeeded to the thousand and one falsehoods amassed during the winter. I can forgive all that is said of or against me, but not what I am made to say or sing under my own name. I have quite enough to answer for my own writings. It would be too much even for Job to bear what he has not said. I believe that the Arabian patriarch, when he wished his enemies had written a book, did not go so far as to be willing to sign his name on the first page."

But the public mind was so disposed to look at Byron in the light of a demon, as traced by Lamartine, that when some young scattered-brain youth published out of vanity, or perhaps for speculative motives, another monstrous invention, in the hope of passing it off as a work of Byron, he actually succeeded for some time in his object without being discovered.

"Strange destiny both of books and their authors!" exclaims the writer of the "Essai sur Lord Byron," published in 1823,—"an evidently apocryphal production, which was at once seen not to be genuine by all persons of taste, notwithstanding the forgery of the title, has contributed as much to make Byron known in France as have his best poems. A certain P—— had impudence enough to attribute indirectly to the noble lord himself the absurd and disgusting tale of the 'Vampire,' which Galignani, in Paris, hastened to publish as an acknowledged work of Byron. Upon this Lord Byron hastened to remonstrate with Messieurs Galignani; but unfortunately too late, and after the reputation of the book was already widespread. Our theatres appropriated the subject, and the story of Lord Ruthven swelled into two volumes which created some sensation."*

Goethe also believed the novels to be true stories, and was especially impressed with "Glenarvon."† It is reported that

* "Essai sur Lord Byron," p. 177.

† Lord Byron wrote to Moore in November, 1820:—

"Pray, where did you get hold of Goethe's 'Florentine' husband-killing story? Upon such matters, in general, I may say, with Beau Clinker, in reply to Erraud's wife:—

"'Oh, the villain, he hath murdered my poor Timothy!'

"*Clinker.*—'Damn your Timothy! I tell you, woman, your husband has murdered me—he has carried away my fine jubilee clothes.'"

he became jealous of Byron on the appearance of the poem of "Manfred." If he were not, it is at least certain that the pagan patriarch never could sympathize with the new generation of Christian geniuses.

On the 7th of June, however, of the year 1820, Byron writes as follows to Murray, from Ravenna:—

"Inclosed is something which will interest you, to wit, the opinion of the greatest man of Germany, perhaps of Europe, upon one of the great men of your advertisements (all 'famous hands,' as Jacob Tonson used to say of his ragamuffins)—in short, a critique of Goethe's upon 'Manfred.' There is the original, an English translation, and an Italian one; keep them all in your archives, for the opinions of such a man as Goethe, whether favorable or not, are always interesting; and this more so, as being favorable. His 'Faust' I never read, for I don't know German; but Matthew Monk Lewis, in 1816, at Geneva, translated most of it to me *vivâ voce*, and I was naturally much struck with it: but it was the 'Steinbach,' and the 'Yungfrau,' and something else, much more than 'Faustus,' that made me write 'Manfred.' The first scene, however, and that of 'Faustus' are very similar."

One can scarcely conceive how so great a mind as that of Goethe could have been duped by such mystifications. And yet this is what he wrote at that time in a German paper relative to Byron's "Manfred:"—

"We find in this tragedy the quintessence of the most astonishing talent borne to be its own tormentor. The character of Lord Byron's life and poetry hardly permits a just and equitable appreciation. He has often enough confessed what it is that torments him. He has repeatedly portrayed it, and scarcely any one feels compassion for this intolerable suffering over which he is ever laboriously ruminating. There are, properly speaking, two females whose phantoms forever haunt him, and which, in this piece also, perform principal parts, one under the name of Astarte, the other without form or actual presence, and merely a voice. Of the horrid occurrence which took place with the former the following is related. When a bold and enterprising young man, he won the affections of a Florentine lady. Her husband discovered the amour, and murdered his wife; but the murderer was the same night found dead in the street, and there was no one to whom any suspicion could be attached. Lord Byron removed from Florence, and these spirits haunted him all his life after.

"This romantic incident is rendered highly probable by innumerable allusions to it in his poems."

And Moore adds:—"The grave confidence with which the venerable critic traces the fancies of his brother poet to real persons and events, making no difficulty even of a double murder at Florence, to furnish grounds for his theory, affords an amusing instance of the disposition, so prevalent throughout Europe, to picture Byron as a man full of marvels and mysteries, as well in his life as his poetry. To these exaggerated or wholly false notions of him, the numerous fictions palmed upon the world, of his romantic tours and wonderful adventures in places he never saw, and with persons who never existed, have, no doubt, considerably contributed, and the consequence is, so utterly out of truth and nature are the representations of his life and character long current upon the Continent, that it may be questioned whether the real 'flesh and blood' hero of these pages (the social, practical-minded, and, with all his faults and eccentricities, English Lord Byron) may not, to the over-exalted imaginations of most of his foreign admirers, appear only an ordinary, unromantic, and prosaic personage."

Then, quoting some of the falsehoods which were spread everywhere about Byron, Moore says:—

"Of this kind are the accounts, filled with all sorts of circumstantial wonders, of his residence in the island of Mytilene; his voyages to Sicily, to Ithaca, with the Countess Guiccioli, etc. But the most absurd, perhaps, of all these fabrications are the stories told by Pouqueville, of the poet's religious conferences in the cell of Father Paul, at Athens; and the still more unconscionable fiction in which Rizo has indulged, in giving the details of a pretended theatrical scene, got up (according to this poetical historian) between Lord Byron and the Archbishop of Arta, at the tomb of Botzaris, at Missolonghi."

As the numerous causes which led to the false judgment of Byron's true character never ceased to exist during his lifetime, one consequence has been that those who never knew him have never been able to arrive at the truth of matters concerning him. The contrast which existed between the real and imaginary personage was such as to cause the greatest astonishment to all those who, having hitherto adopted the received notions about him, at last came to know him at Ravenna, at Pisa, at Genoa, and in Greece, up to the very last days of his life. But, before quoting some of these fortunate travellers, I must transcribe a few more passages from Moore:

"On my rejoining him in town this spring, I found the enthusiasm about his writings and himself, which I had left so prevalent, both in the world of literature and society, grown, if any thing, still more genuine and intense. In the immediate circle perhaps around him, familiarity of intercourse must have begun to produce its usual disenchanting effect."

"His own liveliness and unreserve, on a more intimate acquaintance, would not be long in dispelling that charm of poetic sadness, which to the eyes of distant observers hung about him; while the romantic notions, connected by some of his fair readers with those past and nameless loves alluded to in his poems, ran some risk of abatement from too near an acquaintance with the supposed objects of his fancy and fondness at present."

"But, whatever of its first romantic impression the personal character of the poet may, from such causes, have lost in the circle he most frequented, this disappointment of the imagination was far more than compensated by the frank, social, and engaging qualities, both of disposition and manner, which, on a nearer intercourse, he disclosed, as well as by that entire absence of any literary assumption or pedantry, which entitled him fully to the praise bestowed by Sprat upon Cowley—that few could ever discover he was a great poet by his discourse."

While thus by his friends, he was seen in his true colors, in his weakness and in his strength, to strangers, and such as were out of this immediate circle, the sternness of his imaginary personages were, by the greater number of them, supposed to belong, not only as regarded mind, but manners, to himself. So prevalent and persevering has been this notion, that, in some disquisitions on his character published since his death, and containing otherwise many just and striking views, we find, in the portrait drawn of him, such features as the following:—"Lord Byron had a stern, direct, severe mind: a sarcastic, disdainful, gloomy temper. He had no sympathy with a flippant cheerfulness: upon the surface was sourness, discontent, displeasure, ill-will. Of this sort of double aspect which he presented, the aspect in which he was viewed by the world and by his friends, he was himself fully aware; and it not only amused him, but indeed to a certain extent, flattered his pride."

"And if there was ever any tendency to derangement in his mental conformation, on this point alone could it be pronounced to have manifested itself. In the early part of my acquaintance with him, when he most gave way to this humor, I have known him more than once, as we have sat together after dinner, to fall seriously into this sort of dark and self-accusing mood, and throw out hints of his past life with an air of gloom and mystery designed evidently to awaken curiosity and interest . . . . It has sometimes occurred to me that the occult cause of his lady's separation from him, round which herself and her legal adviser have thrown such formidable mystery, may have been nothing more, after all, than some imposture of this kind, intended only to mystify and surprise, while it was taken in sober seriousness."

I have mentioned elsewhere how Moore, while justly appreciating the consequences of this youthful eccentricity,—of which later, but too late, Byron corrected himself,—does not equally appreciate the motives, or rather the principal motive, which gave rise to it. As, however, he judges rightly of the results, I shall continue to quote him for the reader's benefit.

"M. Galignani, having expressed a wish to be furnished with a short memoir of Lord Byron for the purpose of prefixing it to the French edition of his works, I had said jestingly, in a preceding letter to his lordship, that it would but be a fair satire on the disposition of the world to 'remonster his features' if he would write for the public, English as well as French, a sort of mock heroic account of himself, outdoing in horrors and wonders all that had been yet related or believed of him, and leaving even Goethe's story of the double murder at Florence far behind."

Lord Byron replied from Pisa, on the 12th of December,

1821:—"What you say about Galignani's two biographies is very amusing; and, if I were not lazy, I would certainly do what you desire. But I doubt my present stock of facetiousness—that is, of good serious humor—so as not to let the cat out of the bag. I wish you would undertake it. I will forgive and *indulge* you (like a pope) beforehand, for any thing ludicrous that might keep those fools in their own dear belief that a man is a *loup-garou.*

"I suppose I told you that the 'Giaour' story had actually some foundation in fact. . . I should not like marvels to rest upon any account of my own, and shall say nothing about it: . . The worst of any real adventures is that they involve living people."

He at last tired of always appearing in the guise of a corsair, or of a mysterious criminal, or of a hero of melodrama. These various disguises had afforded him too much pain, and one day he said to Mr. Medwin:—

"When Galignani thought of publishing a fresh edition of my works he wrote to Moore to ask him to give him some anecdotes respecting me: and we thought of composing a narrative filled with the most impossible and incredible adventures, to amuse the Parisians. But I reflected that there were already too many ready-made stories about me, to puzzle my brain to invent new ones."

Mr. Medwin adds:—

"The reader will laugh when he hears that one of my friends assured me that the lines of Thyrza, published with the first canto to 'Childe Harold,' were addressed by Byron to his bear! There is nothing too wicked to be invented by hatred, or believed by ignorance."

Moore often refers to the wonderful contrast which existed between the real and imaginary Byron. Thus, in speaking of his incredibly active and sublime genius at Venice, he says:—

"While thus at this period, more remarkably than at any other during his life, the unparalleled versatility of his genius was unfolding itself, those quick, chameleon-like changes of which his character, too, was capable, were, during the same time, most vividly and in strongest contrast, drawn out. To the world, and more especially to England,—the scene at once of his glories and his wrongs,—he presented himself in no other aspect than that of a stern, haughty misanthrope, self-banished from the fellowship of men, and most of all from that of Englishmen. . . . . ."

How totally all this differed from the Byron of the social hour, they who lived in familiar intercourse with him may be safely left to tell. The reputation which he had acquired for himself abroad, prevented numbers, of course, of his countrymen, whom he would most cordially have welcomed, from seeking his acquaintance. But as it was, no "English gentleman ever approached him, with the common forms of introduction, that did not come away at once surprised and charmed by the kind courtesy and facility of his manners, the unpretending play of his conversation, and, on a nearer intercourse, the frank youthful spirits, to the flow of which he gave way with such a zest as even to deceive some of those who best knew him into the impression that gayety was, after all, the true bent of his disposition."

I must confine myself to these quotations, as it is not in my power to reproduce all that Moore has said on the subject. His statements, however, prove two things:—

First, that Lord Byron, instead of being a dark and gloomy hero of romance, was a man full of amiability, goodness, grace, sociability, and liveliness. Of the impression produced upon all those who knew him in these combined qualities, I shall have occasion to speak hereafter.

Secondly, that since even after Byron's death the fantastical notions about him were entertained even by so impartial and so enlightened a person as Sir Edward Brydges, it is not surprising (nor should they be blamed for it) that Frenchmen, and all foreigners in general, and even a great portion of Englishmen, should have believed in this fallacy. There was no means at that time of clearing up the mystery, nor can one see in this belief, however exaggerated, especially in France and on the Continent, any spirit either of direct hostility, or even ill-will toward him. The error was exported from England, and upon it they reasoned, logically and oftentimes wittily. But surely those can not be absolved who still adhere to the old errors, after the true state of things had been disclosed at the poet's death in the writings of such biographers as Moore,

Parry, Medwin himself, Count Gamba, and others who knew Byron personally.

That a portion of the British public should maintain certain prejudices, and preserve a certain animosity against Byron, is not matter of astonishment to those who have at all studied the English character. The spirit of tolerance which exists in the laws, is far from pervading the habits of the people; cant is on the decrease, but not quite gone, and may still lead one to a very fair social position. There still live a host of enemies whom Byron had made during his lifetime, and the number of whom (owing to a bonâ fide treachery, by the indiscreet publication of a correspondence which was destined to be kept secret and in the dark), increased greatly after his death from the number of people whose pride he had therein wounded.

He may be liable to the punishment due to his having trespassed on certain exclusively English notions of virtue, as intimated in the condemnation of the *imaginary* immorality of some of his works. He may be accused, with some truth, of having been too severe toward several persons and things. But not one of these reasons has any *locus standi* in France,—a country which might claim a certain share in the honor of having been his mother-country. Besides having a French turn of mind in many respects, Byron, descended directly from a French stock, had been conceived in France, and had long lived in its neighborhood. If those, therefore, may be absolved who falsely appreciated Byron's character both before and immediately after his death, the same indulgence can not be extended to those who persist in their unjust conclusions. Such men were greatly to blame; for, in writing about Byron, they were bound in conscience to consult the biographers who had known him, and having neglected to do so, either from idleness or from party spirit, they failed in their duty as just and honorable men.

Before finishing this chapter, we must add to these pages, which were written many years ago, a few remarks suggested by the perusal of a recent work which has caused great sensation by the talent which pervades it, by its boldness, and original writing. I allude to the work of M. Taine upon English literature; therein he appreciates, in a manly, fine style, all the loftiness of Lord Byron's poetry, but always under the influence of a received, and not self-formed, opinion. He likewise deserves, by his appreciations and conclusions, the reproaches addressed to the other critics of the illustrious and calumniated poet. In this work, which is rather magnificent than solid, and which contains a whole psychological system, one note is ever uppermost,—that of disdain. Contempt, however, is not his object, but only his means. All must be sacrificed to the triumph of his opinions.

The glory of nations, great souls, great minds, their works, their deeds, all must serve to complement his victory. Bossuet, Newton, Dante, Shakspeare, Corneille, Byron, all have erred. If he despises them, if he blames them, it is only to show that they have not been able to discover the logical conclusions which M. Taine at last reveals to us,—conclusions which are to transform and change the soul as well as the understanding. This doctrine has hitherto been but a dream, and society has, up to the present time, walked in darkness.

This philosophical system is so beautifully set forth, that it can only be compared to a skeleton, upon which a profusion of lovely-scented flowers and precious jewels have been heaped, so that, notwithstanding the horror it inspires, one is unable to leave it.

Here, then, we find that M. Taine comes forth resolutely, by the help of a vigorous understanding and a surpassing talent, to review all that England has produced in a literary sense,—authors as well as their works. The type which he has conceived alone escapes his censure. This type must be the result of three primeval causes, viz., race, centre and time. History must prove its correctness. History and logic might in vain claim his indulgence on behalf of other types. He has conceived his system in his own mind, and, to establish it, facts and characters are made subservient to it; history's duty is to prove their correctness. Indulgence can be shown to one type only.

All he says is, however, so well said, that if he offended truth a little less, if he only spoke for beings in another planet, and above all, if, under these beautiful surroundings, one failed to notice the gloom of a heaven without God, the work would enchant one.

It must be allowed that the charms of truth are still to be preferred; we must therefore be allowed to say a few words about M. Taine's system. It can only be in one sense; not on account of any philosophical pretension, nor in the hope of restoring nature to its rights, however much we may grieve at seeing it reduced to a mere animal, nay, a vegetable, and alas! may be, a mineral system.

Many able pens will repeat the admirable words of one of the cleverest men of the day, who, in his criticism upon M. Taine's book, has so thoroughly examined how far a physiological method could be applied to the comprehension of moral and intellectual phenomena, and has shown to what fatal consequences such a method must lead. The analysis of the moral world, the study of souls and of talent, of doctrines and of characters, become in M. Taine's mind only a branch of zoology, and psychology ends by being only a part of natural history.

Many other able writers will echo the noble words of M. Caro, and will not fail to point out the numerous contradictions which exist between the work itself and history proper, between it and natural history, and, finally, between it and the author himself.

Thus, men who have never allowed that a thistle could produce a rose, will question also whether those young Englishmen, whom M. Taine depicts in such glowing colors,—"So active," says he, "just like harriers on the beat flaring the air in the midst of the hunt," can be transformed in a few years "into beings resembling animals good for slaughter, with appearances equally anxious, vacant, and stupid; gentlemen six feet high, with long and stout German bodies, issuing from their forests with savage-looking whiskers and rolling eyes of pale earthenware-blue color."

Such critics will question whether the "pale earthenware-blue eyes" of these ugly sires can possibly be those of the fathers of the candid-eyed girls, the fairest among the fair treasures of this earth, whom M. Taine describes in such exquisite terms:—

"Delightful creatures, whose freshness and innocence can not be conceived by those who have never seen them! full-blown flowers, of which a morning rose, with its delicious and delicate color, with its petals dipped in dew, can alone give an idea."

Critics will deny the possibility of the existence of such a phenomenon, so contrary to the laws of creation does it seem to be. Such airy-like forms can not be produced by such heavy brutes as he describes. Say what he likes, nature can not act in the manner indicated by M. Taine. Nature must ever follow the same track.

We, however, shall confine ourselves to oppose the real Lord Byron to the fanciful one of M. Taine; and we say that the portrait of the poet drawn by the latter is drawn systematically, in such a manner as to contribute to the general harmony of his work. But truth can not be subservient to systems. As M. Taine views Lord Byron from a false starting point, it follows that, of course, the whole portrait of him is equally unreal.

All the colors in his picture are too dark. What he says of the poet is not so false as it is exaggerated. This is a method peculiar to him. He decidedly perceives the real person, but exaggerates him, and thus fails to realize the original.

If the facts are not always entirely false, his conclusions, and the consequences suggested to him by them, are always eminently so.

When the facts seem ever so little to lend themselves to his reasoning, when the proportions of his victim allow of their being placed in the *bed of Procrustes*, the magnificent draperies of which do not hide the atrocious torture; then, indeed, does M. Taine respect history more or less; when this is not the case, his imagination supplies the deficiency. On this principle he gives us his details of Lord Byron's parents and of the poet's childhood.

He makes use of Lord Byron as an artist makes use of a machine: he places him in the position which he has chosen himself, gives him the gesture he pleases, and the expression he wishes. The portrait he shows us of him may be a little like Lord Byron; but a very distant likeness, one surrounded by a world of caprice of fancy and eccentricity which serve to make up a powerful picture. It is the effect of a well-posed manikin, with its very flexible articulations, all placed at the disposal of M. Taine's system. The features may be slightly those of Lord Byron, but the gestures and the general physiognomy are the clever creations of the artist.

This is how he proceeds, in order to obtain the triumph of his views:—

He selects some quarter of an hour from the life of a man, probably that during which he obeyed the impulses of nature, and judges his whole existence and character by this short space of time.

He takes from the author's career one page, perhaps that which he may have written in a moment of hallucination or of extreme passion; and by this single page he judges the author of ten volumes.

Take Lord Byron, for instance. With regard to his infancy, M. Taine takes care to set aside all that he knows to be admirable in the boy, and only notices one instance of energy, one fit of heroic passion, into which the unjust reprimand of a maid had driven him. The touching tears which the little Byron sheds when, in the midst of his playmates, he is informed that he has been raised to the dignity of a peer of the realm, are no sign to M. Taine of a character equally timid, sensitive, and good, but the result of pride. In this trait alone, M. Taine sees almost sufficient ground to lay thereon the foundations of his work, and to show us in the boy what the man was to be. A similar process is used in the examination of Byron as an author. He analyzes "Manfred," which is most decidedly a work of prodigious power, and all he says of it is certainly both true and worthy of his own great talent; but is it fair to say that the poet and the man are entirely revealed in this work, and to dismiss all the other creations of the poet, wherein milder qualities, such as feeling, tenderness, and goodness are revealed, and shine forth most prominently? "Manfred" is the cry of an ulcerated heart, still struggling, with all the energy of a most powerful soul, against the brutal decrees of a recent persecution. Lord Byron felt himself to be the victim of the relentless conduct of Lady Byron, and if his mind was not deranged, at least his soul was wounded and ill at ease, and it was this spirit that dictated "Manfred." Did he not clearly confess it himself? When he sent "Manfred" to Murray, did he not say that it was a drama as mad as the tragedy of "Lee Bedlam," in twenty-five acts, and a few comic scenes—his own being only in three acts?

Did he not write to Moore as follows?—

"I wrote a sort of mad drama for the sake of introducing the Alpine scenery. Almost all the *dramatis personæ* are spirits, ghosts, or magicians; and the scene is in the Alps and the other world, so you may suppose what a Bedlam tragedy it must be. . . . . The third act, like the Archbishop of Grenada's homily (which savored of the palsy), has the dregs of my fever, during which it was written. It must on no account be published in its present state. . . . . The speech of Manfred to the sun is the only part of this act I thought good myself; the rest is certainly as bad as bad can be, and I wonder what the devil possessed me."

But let Byron's ideas take a different turn, as the lovely blue Italian sky and the refreshing breezes from the Adriatic waters contribute to quicken his blood, and other tones will be heard, wherein no longer shall the excesses, but the beauties only of energy be discernible.

What does M. Taine say then? This new aspect does not, evidently, satisfy him! but what of that? He goes on to say that Byron's genius is falling off. If the poet takes advantage of a few moments of melancholy common to all poetical and feeling souls, M. Taine declares that the melancholy English nature is always associated with the epicurean. What is it to him, that England thinks differently? that in her opinion Lord Byron's grandest and noblest conceptions are the poems which he wrote in Italy, and even on the eve of his death? and that she finds his liveliness "too real and too ultramontane to suit her national tastes?" Nothing of this troubles M. Taine.

Is it quite fair to judge so powerful a mind, so great and yet so simple a being as Lord Byron, only by his "Manfred," or by some other passages of his works, and especially of "Don Juan?" Can his amiable, docile, tender, and feeling nature honestly be seen in the child of three years of age, who tears his clothes because his nurse has punished him unfairly? No; all that we see is what M. Taine wishes us to see for the purpose he has in view, that is, admiration of the Lord Byron he has conceived, and who is necessary to his cause,—a Byron only to be likened to a furious storm.

Wishing Byron to appear as the type of energy, M. Taine exhibits him to our eyes in the light of Satan defying all powers on earth and in heaven. The better to mould him to the form he has chosen, he begins by disfiguring him in the arms of his mother, whom with his father and his family he scruples not to calumniate. Storms having their origin in the rupture of the elements, and a violent character being, according to M. Taine, the result of several forces acting internally and mechanically; it follows that its primary cause is to be found in the disturbed moral condition of those who have given birth to him in the circumstances under which the child was born, and in the influence under which he has been brought up. Hence the necessity of supplementing from imagination the historical and logical facts which otherwise might be at fault.

As for Lord Byron's softness of manner, and as to that tenderness of character which was the bane of his existence,—as to his real and great goodness, which made him loved always and everywhere, and which caused such bitter tears to be shed at the news of his death,—these qualities are not to be sought in the strange, fanciful being who is styled Byron by M. Taine. These qualities would be out of place; they would be opposed to the idea upon which his entire system is founded. They must be merged in the energy and greatness of intellect of the poetical giant.

Unfortunately for M. Taine, facts speak too forcibly and too inopportunely against him. Not one of the causes which he mentions, not one of the conclusions which he draws in respect to Lord Byron's character as a poet, and as a mere mortal, are to be relied upon. He, who contends that he possesses preeminently the power of comprehending the man and the author, insists that Lord Byron was no exception to the rule, though his best biographer, Moore, most distinctly opposes this opinion:—

"In Lord Byron, however, this sort of pivot of character was almost wholly wanting. . . . So various indeed, and contradictory, were his attributes, both moral and intellectual, that he may be pronounced to have been not one, but many; nor would it be any great exaggeration of the truth to say that out of the mere partition of the properties of his single mind a plurality of characters, all different and all vigorous, might have been furnished."

On the other hand, M. Taine, who generally pays little attention to the opinion of others, gives as Lord Byron's predominant characteristic that which phrenologists denominate "*combativité*." Which of the two is likely to be right? If Moore is right, Lord Byron must have been almost wanting in consistency of character; if Taine is correct, then Byron was really of a most passionate nature. But as we have proved that Lord Byron was not inconsistent, as Moore declares, except in cases where this want of consistency did not interfere with his character as a man, and, on the other hand, that no one had a less combative disposition, we are forced to arrive at the conclusion that if Byron had one dominant passion, it was most decidedly not that of "*combativité*." It is impossible to deny that if in his early youth signs of resistance may have appeared in his character, yet these had so completely disappeared with the development of his intellect and of his moral sentiments that no one more than himself hated controversies and discussions of all kinds. In fact, no one was more obedient to the call of reason and of friendship; and his whole life is an illustration of it.

In order that Lord Byron should represent the English type, even if we adopt M. Taine's philosophy, he should have had a deal of Saxon blood in his veins. But this was not the case. It is the Norman blood which predominates. He may be said to have been almost borne in France, and to be of French extraction by his father, and of Scotch origin through his mother. The total absence of the Saxon element, which was so remarkable in him, was equally noticeable in his tastes, mind, sympathies, and inclinations.

He loved France very dearly, and Pouqueville tells a story, that when Ali Pasha had got over the fright caused by the announcement that a young traveller, named Byron (his name had been pronounced Bairon, which made the Pasha believe he was a Turk in disguise), wished to see him, he received the young lord very cordially. As he had just conquered Preveza from the French, Ali Pasha thought he should be pleasing the Englishman by announcing the fact to him. Byron replied—"But I am no enemy of France. Quite the contrary, I love France."

It might almost be said that he was quite the opposite of

what a Saxon should be. Lord Byron could not remain, and, actually, lived a very short time, in England. His habits were not English, nor his mode of living. Far from over-eating, as the English, according to M. Taine, are said to do, Byron did not eat enough. He was as sober as a monk. His favorite food was vegetables. His abstinence from meat dated from his youth. His body was little adapted to the material wants of his country. This remarkable sobriety was the effect of taste and principle, and was in no ways broken by excesses which might have acted as compensations. The excesses of which M. Taine speaks must have been at the utmost some slight deviations from the real Pythagorean abstinence which he had laid down as the rule of his life. Abroad, where he lived almost all his life, he had none of the habits of his countrymen. He lived everywhere as a cosmopolitan. All that his body craved for was cleanliness, and this only served to improve his health and the marvellous beauty with which God had gifted him.

Lord Byron was so little partial to the characteristic features and customs of the country in which he was born—" but where he would not die "—that the then so susceptible *amour-propre* of his countrymen reproached him with it as a most unpardonable fault.

It was not he who would have placed England and the English above all foreigners, and Frenchmen in particular; nor was it he who would have declared them to be the princes of the human race. Justice and truth forbade his committing himself to such statements in the name of national pride.

Are the animal rather than moral, and moral rather than intellectual instincts of energy and will, which M. Taine so much admires in the Saxon race, defects or qualities in his eyes? It is difficult to say, for one never knows when he is praising or when he is condemning. Judging by the very material causes from which he derives this energy,—namely, the constitution of the people, their climate, their frequent craving for food, their way of cooking the food they eat, their drinks, and all the consequences of these necessities visible in the absence of all sense of delicacy, of all appreciation of the fine arts, and the comprehension of philosophy,—he must evidently intend to depreciate them.

But as regards Lord Byron in particular, it is equally certain that he has no intention of depreciating him. For him alone he finds expressions of great admiration and real sympathy. He allows him to represent the whole nation, and to be the incarnation of the English character; but on one condition,—that of ruling it as its sovereign. Thanks to this supremacy, the poet escapes more or less the exigencies of M. Taine's theories.

M. Taine, however, is not subject to the weakness of enthusiasm. Judging, as he does, in the light of a lover of nature, both of the merits of virtue and of the demerits of vice, which to him are but fatal results of the constitution, the climate, and the soil—"in a like manner will sugar and vitriol"—why care about Lord Byron doing this or the other *rightly* or *wrongly* rather than any one else? Nature follows its necessary track, seeks its equilibrium, and ends by finding it.

What pleases him in Lord Byron, is the facility which is offered to him of proving the truth of this fatalist philosophy which appears at every page of his book.

No one more than Byron could serve the purpose of M. Taine, and become, as it were, the basis of his philosophical operations.

His powerful genius, his short but eventful existence, which did not give time for the cooling down of the ardor of youth, to harmonize it with the tempered dictates of mature age,—the universality of his mind, which can furnish arguments to every species of critics,—all contributed wonderfully to the realization of M. Taine's object.

Thus, thanks to the deceptive but generally received portrait which is said to be that of Lord Byron, and to his identification with the heroes of his poems, and in particular with "Manfred" and "Childe Harold," aided by the impossibility which the human mind finds in estimating moral subjects as it would a proposition of "Euclid," M. Taine has been able to make use of a great name, and to make a fine demonstration of his system, to call Byron the interpreter of the British genius, and his poetry the expression of the man himself.

In many respects, however, he has not been able to act in this way without violating historical facts. This is what I hope to point out in these pages, the object of which is to describe Byron as he was, and to substitute, without any derogation to his sublimity of character, the reality for the fiction created by M. Taine. To refute so brilliant and so powerful a writer, my only means is to proceed in this work with the help of positive proofs of the statements which I make, and by invoking unimpeachable testimonies. These alone constitute weighty arguments, since they all contribute to produce the same impression. In order that truth may be restored to history, I shall adopt a system diametrically opposed to that of M. Taine, or rather I shall abstain from all systems, and from all pretensions to literary merit, and confine myself entirely to facts and to reason.

The reader will judge whether I shall be able to accomplish this object; he will see how really unimportant are the causes which cast a shade upon the memory of Byron, and how careful one should be not to give credit too implicitly to the sincerity of that hypocritical praise which several of his biographers have bestowed upon him. They have, as it were, generally, taken a kind of pleasure in dwelling upon his age, his rank, and other extenuating circumstances, as a cover to their censure, just as if Byron ever required their forgiveness. In thus searching into the secrets of his heart, and analyzing his life, the reader will soon be obliged to admit, that if Byron, in common with others, had a few of the faults of youth, he in return had a host of virtues which belonged only to him. In short, if Byron is received in the light in which he was esteemed by those who knew him personally, he will still constitute one of the finest, most amiable, and grandest characters of his century. As for ourselves, in summing up the merits of this very humble, but very conscientious work, we can only repeat with delight the beautiful words in which Moore sums up his own estimate of Lord Byron's worth: "Should the effect of my humble labors be to clear away some of those mists that hung round my friend, and show him, in most respects, as worthy of love as he was, in all, of admiration, then will the chief and sole aim of this work have been accomplished."*

* Moore, vol. ii. p. 782.

CHAPTER IV.

LORD BYRON'S RELIGIOUS OPINIONS.

"When the triumph of a cause of such importance to humanity is in question, there never can be too many advocates. . . . . . But it is not enough to count up the votes; their value must, above all, be weighed."—SHERER.

THE struggles between heart and reason, in religious matters, began almost with Lord Byron's infancy. His desire of reconciling them was such, that, if unsuccessful, his mind was perplexed and restless. He was not, as it were, out of the cradle, when, in the midst of his childish play, the great problems of life already filled his youthful thoughts; and his good nurse May, who was wont to sing psalms to him when rocking him to sleep, had also to answer questions which showed the dangerous curiosity of his mind.

"Among the traits," says Moore, "which should be recorded of his earlier years, I should mention, that, according to the character given of him by his first nurse's husband, he was, when a mere child, 'particularly inquisitive and puzzling about religion.'"

At ten years of age, he was sent to school, at Dulwich, under the care of the Rev. Dr. Glennie, who, in the account given by him to Moore, and after speaking of the amiable qualities of Byron, adds: that "At that age he already possessed an intimate acquaintance with the historical facts in the Scriptures, and was particularly delighted when he could speak of them to him, especially on Sunday evenings after worship. He was wont then to reason upon all the facts contained in the Bible, with every appearance of faith in the doctrine which it teaches.

But while his heart was thus drawn toward its Creator, the power of his reason began imperiously to assert its rights. As long as he remained sheltered under his father's roof, under the eyes of his mother, and of young ecclesiastics who were his first teachers, and whose practice agreed with their teaching,—as long as his reason had not reached a certain degree of development,— he remained orthodox and pious. But when he went to college, and particularly when he was received at Cambridge, a vast field of contradictions opened before his observing and thinking mind. His reflections, together with the study of the great psychological questions, soon clouded his mind, and threw a shade over his orthodoxy. If Lord Byron, therefore, had really the misfortune to lose at an earlier age than ordinary children, the simple faith of his childhood, the fact is not to be wondered at. By the universality of his genius he added to the faculties which form the poet, those of an eminently logical and practical mind; and being precocious in all things, he was likewise so in his powers of reflection and reasoning. "Never," says Moore, "did Lord Byron lose sight of reality and of common practical sense; his genius, however high it soared, ever preserved upon earth a support of some kind."

His intellectual inquisitiveness was likewise, with him, a precocious passion, and circumstances stood so well in the way to serve this craving, that when fifteen years of age (incredible as it seems), he had already perused two thousand volumes, among which his powerful and vivid intellect had been able to weigh the contradictions of all the principal modern and ancient systems of philosophy. This thirst for knowledge (anomalous according to the rules of both school and college) was the more extraordinary that it existed in him together with a passionate love for boyish play, and the indulgence in all the bodily exercises, in which he excelled, and on which he prided himself. But as he stored his mind after the usual college hours, and apart from the influences of that routine discipline, which, with Milton, Pope, and almost all the great minds, he so cordially hated, the real progress of his intellect remained unobserved by his masters, and even by his fellow-students. This mistake, on the part of men little gifted with quickness of perception, was not shared by Disraeli, who could so justly appreciate genius; and of Byron he spoke as of a studious boy, who loved to hide this quality from his comrades, thinking it more amiable on his part to appear idle in their eyes.

While the young man thus strengthened his intellect by hard though irregular study, his meditative and impassioned nature, feeling in the highest degree the necessity of confirming its impressions, experienced more imperatively than a youth of fifteen generally does, the want of examining the traditional teachings which had been transmitted to him. Byron felt the necessity of inquiring on what irrevocable proofs the dogmas which he was called upon to believe were based. Holy writ, aided by the infallibility of the teachings of the Church, etc., were adduced as the proofs he required.

He was wont, therefore, to read with avidity a number of books treating on religious matters; and he perused them, both with artless ingenuity and in the hope of their strengthening his faith. But, could he truly find faith in their pages? Are not such books rather dangerous than otherwise for some minds?

"The truth is," says the author of the "Essays," "that a mind which has never entertained a doubt in revelation, may conceive some doubts by reading books written in its defense." And he adds elsewhere, in speaking of the writers of such controversial works, that "impatient of the least hesitation, they deny with anger the value of their adversary's arguments, and betray, in their way of getting over difficulties, a humor which injures the effects of their reasoning, and of the proofs they make use of to help their arguments." After reading several of these books, he must have found, as did the great Pitt, "that such readings provoke many more doubts than they dispel;" and, in fact, they rather disquieted and shook, than strengthened his faith. At the same time, he was alive to another striking contradiction. He noticed that the men who taught the doctrines, too often forgot to make these and their practice agree; and in losing his respect for his masters, he still further doubted the sincerity of their teaching. Thus, while remaining religiously inclined, he must have felt his faith becoming more and more shaken, and in the memorandum of his early days, after enumerating the books treating upon religious subjects which he had read, he says: "All very tedious. I hate books treating of religious subjects; although I adore and love God, freed from all absurd and blasphemous notions."

In this state of mind, of which one especially finds a proof in his earlier poems, the philosophy of Locke, which is that professed at Cambridge, and which he had already skimmed, as it were, together with other philosophical systems, became his study. It only added an enormous weight in the way of contradictions to the already heavy weight of doubt.

Could it be otherwise? Does not Locke teach that all ideas being the creation of the senses, the notion of God, unless aided by tradition, has no other basis but our senses and the sight of the external world? If this be not the doctrine professed by Locke, it is the reading which a logical mind may give to it.

He believes in God; yet the notion of God, as it appears from his philosophical teaching, is not that which is taught by Christian doctrine. According to him, God is not even proclaimed to be the Creator of the Universe. But even were He proclaimed such, what would be the result of this philosophical condescension, unless it be that God is distinct from the world? Would God possess then all those attributes which reason, independently of all philosophy, points to in the Divinity? Would power, goodness, infinite perfection be God's? Certainly not: as we are unable to know Him except through a world of imperfections, where good and evil, order and confusion, are mixed together, and not by the conception of the infinite, which alone can give us a true and perfect idea of God, it follows that God would be much superior to the world, but would not be absolute perfection.

After this depreciation of the Omnipotent, what says this philosophy of our soul? It does away altogether with one of the essential proofs of its spiritual nature, and thereby compromises the soul itself, declaring as it does, that "it is not unlikely that matter is capable of thought." But then of what necessity would the soul be, if the body can think? How hope for immortality, if that which thinks is subject to dissolution and to death?

As for our liberty, it would be annihilated as a consequence of such doctrines; for it is not supposed to derive its essence from the interior activity of the soul, but would seem to be limited to our power of moving. Yet we are hourly experiencing what our weakness is in comparison with the power of the laws of nature, which rule us in every sense and way. In making, therefore, all things derivable from sensations, Locke fell from one error into another, and nearly arrived at that point when duty and all principles of justice and morality might be altogether denied. Being himself, however, both good, honest, liberal, and Christian-minded, he could only save himself from the social wreck to which he exposed others, by stopping on the brink of the abyss which he had himself created, and by becoming in practice inconsistent with his speculative notions. His successors, such as Condillac and Cabanis, fell by following his system and by carrying it too far.

A doctrine which denies the right of discovering, or of explaining the religious truths which are the grounds of all moral teaching, and which allows tradition the privilege only of bestowing faith; a system of metaphysics, which can not avoid the dangers in which morality must perish, owing to its contradictions and its inconsistencies, must be perilous for all but those happily constituted minds for whom simple faith and submission are a part of their essence, who believe on hearsay and seek not to understand, but merely glance at the surface of the difficult and venturesome questions which are discussed before them, either because they feel their weakness, or because the light of revelation shines upon them so strongly as to make that of reason pale. For more logical minds, however, for such who are inquisitive, whose reason is both anxious and exacting, who want to understand before they believe, for whom the ties which linked them to tradition have been loosened, owing to their having reflected on a number of contradictions (the least of which, in the case of Lord Byron, was decidedly not that of seeing such a philosophy professed and adopted in a clerical university); for minds like these such doctrines must necessarily lead to atheism. Though Lord Byron's mind was one of these, he escaped the fearful results by a still greater effort of his reason, which made him reject the precepts of the sensualists, and comprehend their inconsistencies.

His protest against the doctrines of the sensualists is entered in his memorandum, where, after naming all the authors of the philosophical systems which he had read, and, coming to the head of that school, he exclaims from the bottom of his heart:

"Hobbes! I detest him!"

And notwithstanding the respect with which the good and great Locke must individually have inspired him, he evidently must have repudiated his precepts, inasmuch as they were not strong enough to uproot from his mind the religious truths which reason proclaims, nor prevent either his coming out of his philosophical struggle a firm believer in all the dogmas which are imperiously upheld to the human reason, or his proclaiming his belief in one God and Creator, in our free will, and in the immortality of the soul.

This glorious and noble victory of his mind and true religious tendencies at that time, is evinced in his "Prayer to Nature," written when he had not yet reached his eighteenth year. In this beautiful prayer, which his so-called orthodox friends succeeded in having cut out of the volume containing his earliest poems, we find both great power of contemplation and humility and confidence in prayer—a soul too near the Creator to doubt of His Omnipotence, but also too far from Him for his faith and confidence in the divine mercy not to be mixed up with a little fear; in fact, all the essential elements of a noble prayer which is not orthodox. Though written on the threshold of life, he might, with few modifications, have signed it on the eve of his death; when, still young, fate had spared him nothing, from the sweetest to the bitterest feelings, from every deserved pleasure to every undeserved pain.

THE PRAYER OF NATURE.

Father of Light! great God of Heaven!
Hear'st thou the accents of despair?
Can guilt like man's be e'er forgiven?
Can vice atone for crimes by prayer?

Father of Light, on thee I call!
Thou seest my soul is dark within;
Thou who canst mark the sparrow's fall,
Avert from me the death of sin.

No shrine I seek, to sects unknown;
Oh, point to me the path of truth!
Thy dread omnipotence I own;
Spare, yet amend, the faults of youth.

Let bigots rear a gloomy fane,
Let superstition hail the pile,
Let priests, to spread their sable reign,
With tales of mystic rites beguile.

Shall man confine his Maker's sway
To Gothic domes of mouldering stone?
Thy temple is the face of day;
Earth, ocean, heaven, thy boundless throne.

Shall man condemn his race to hell,
Unless they bend in pompous form?
Tell us that all, for one who fell,
Must perish in the mingling storm?

Shall each pretend to reach the skies,
Yet doom his brother to expire,
Whose soul a different hope supplies,
Or doctrines less severe inspire?

Shall these, by creeds they can't expound,
Prepare a fancied bliss or woe?
Shall reptiles, grovelling on the ground,
Their great Creator's purpose know?

Shall those who live for self alone,
Whose years float on in daily crime—
Shall they by faith for guilt atone,
And live beyond the bounds of Time?

Father! no prophet's laws I seek,—
Thy laws in Nature's works appear;—
I own myself corrupt and weak,
Yet will I pray, for thou wilt hear!

Thou, who canst guide the wandering star
Through trackless realms of æther's space;
Who calm'st the elemental war,
Whose hand from pole to pole I trace:

Thou, who in wisdom placed me here,
Who, when thou wilt, canst take me hence,
Ah! while I tread this earthly sphere,
Extend to me thy wide defense.

To Thee, my God, to thee I call!
Whatever weal or woe betide,
By thy command I rise or fall,
In thy protection I confide.

If, when this dust to dust's restored,
My soul shall float on airy wing,
How shall thy glorious name adored
Inspire her feeble voice to sing!

But, if this fleeting spirit share
With clay the grave's eternal bed,
While life yet throbs I raise my prayer,
Though doom'd no more to quit the dead.

To Thee I breathe my humble strain,
Grateful for all thy mercies past,
And hope, my God, to thee again
This erring life may fly at last.
December 29, 1806. [First published, 1830.]

As much may be said of another poem which he likewise wrote in his youth; when, very dangerously ill, and believing his last end to be near, he turned all his thoughts to the other world, and conceived the touching poem which ended in the lines:—

"Forget this world, my restless sprite;
Turn, turn thy thoughts to Heaven;
There must thou soon direct thy flight
If errors are forgiven."

But if Lord Byron did not adopt Locke's philosophy he at least paid the greatest tribute of regard to his goodness by following ever more closely his best precept, which is to the effect that to love truth for the sake of truth is an essential part of human perfection in this world, and the fertile soil on which is sown the seed of every virtue.

While his mind thus wavered between a thousand contradictory opinions, and, finding part of the truth only in every philosophical system which he examined, but not the whole truth—which was what his soul thirsted for; calling himself at times skeptic, because he hesitated in adhering to one school, in consequence of the numerous errors and inconsistencies common to all (the great school which has, to the honor of France, harmonized them all, was not yet open); but not losing sight of the great eternal truths of which he felt inwardly the proofs, he made the acquaintance of a young man who had just completed his university education with great success. This young man, who exercised a great influence over all his fellow-students, owing to his superior intellect, influenced Byron in a similar manner. Bold, logical, inflexible, he was not swayed by the dangers which the sensualistic teaching presented to all logical minds; dangers which had frightened the chief of that school himself, and who, in wishing to oppose them, had not been able to do so except by contradictions. This young man, by a noble inconsistency, drew back in presence of the moral conclusions of that metaphysical doctrine, but not without culling from the master's thoughts conclusions, such that they leave all that is spiritual and immortal without defense, together with all the legitimate inferences to be derived from the principles he taught, however impious or absurd.

Among the Germans he had likewise met with several bold doctrines; but, merely to speak here of the conclusions to which the school he belonged necessarily brought him, he arrived at those conclusions by a series of deductions from the study of those great questions, which experience always ends by referring either to reason or to revelation. Compelled by the tenets of that school, to solve all these problems by means of the sensations only, he was naturally led to the conclusion that no such thing existed as the spirituality of the soul, and hence, that it had neither the gift of immortality nor that of liberty, nor any principles of morality. Finally, obliged to seek in tradition the conviction that a God existed, and that He can only be perceived through a maze of imperfections, and not as reason conceives Him clearly and simply with all His necessary attributes of perfection, he was even led to the necessity of losing sight of a Creator altogether.

The fatal precipice, which this young student himself avoided by the practical conclusions by which he abided, Byron likewise escaped both by his conclusions and his theoretical notions. He even hated the name of atheist to that degree, that at Harrow he wished to fight his companion Lord Althorpe, because he had written the word atheist under Byron's name. This is so true that Sir Robert Dallas, of whose judgment no interpretation can ever be given without making allowances for the intolerant spirit and the exaggeration required by his notions of othodoxy and by his party prejudices, after regretting that Lord Byron should not have had a shield during his minority to protect him against his comrades, "proud, free-thinking, and acute sophists," as he calls them, adds that, if surprise must be expressed, it is not that Byron should have erred, but that he should have pierced the clouds which surrounded him, and have dispersed them by the sole rays of his genius.

So many struggles, however, so many contradictions, so many strains upon the mind, while leaving his heart untouched, could not but multiply the doubts which he conceived, and more or less modify his mind, and even give to it a tinge of skepticism.

When he left England for the first time, his mind was in this transitory, suffering state. The various countries which he visited, the various creeds with which he became acquainted, the intolerance of the one, the laxity in others in direct opposition to their superstitious and irrational practices; the truly touching piety which he found in the Greek monasteries (at Zytza and at Athens), in the midst of which and in the silence of whose cloisters, he loved to share the peace and even the austerities of a monkish life; his transition from the Western countries, where reason is placed above imagination, to the East, where the opposite is aimed at—all contributed to prevent what was vacillating in his mind from becoming settled. Meanwhile endless disappointments, bitter sorrows, and broken illusions contributed their share to the pain which his mind experienced at every stage of its philosophical inquiry, and contributed to give him, in the loneliness of his life, a tinge of misanthropy opposed to his natural character, which suggested the rather philosophical and generous than prudent conception of "Childe Harold's Pilgrimage," where he depicts his hero as intellectually imbued with philosophical doctrines which lead practical minds to skepticism and materialism! These doctrines resulted in causing "Childe Harold" to lose that traditional faith which gives peace to the soul by insuring conviction to the mind. The poet shows the impossibility of withdrawing himself from their disastrous results when arrived at the age when passions assert their rule, and when in a certain social position, they must be carried into practice. Nature not having gifted him with a sufficiently generous heart to check the disease of his mind, Childe Harold, *disgusted with the sins of his youth*, no longer seeks the road to virtue, but begins to experience with Solomon the vanity of human things, becomes a prey to satiety, ennui, and to insensiblity to both physical and moral worth.

Byron, who made the intellectual education of his day responsible for Childe Harold's faults, had conceived this character in his earliest days at Harrow. It was in any case, he said, a characteristic of the youth of those days, although idealized and drawn from his own imagination. His enemies and his rivals have endeavored to prove that he wished to describe in this poem the state of his own mind. They made capital out of a few historical and local circumstances, to give to their falsehood some appearance of truth. But only those who did not know him personally could be ignorant how improbable it was that any resemblance between the poet and his hero could be maintained.

Let us confine ourselves to the remark that Lord Byron, instead of personifying his hero, personifies no one but simply the poet. Let us add, besides, that in no case could Lord Byron be made responsible for the consequences of the doctrines of the materialists, as held by his hero. Not only because of his nature, which was totally opposed to them, but also and especially because of his tendencies, which were eminently and persistently those of a spiritualist, and which clung to him throughout his life even at the time when he was accused of skepticism. This was at the time when he wrote the second canto of "Childe Harold." Thoughts, little in unison with, if not entirely opposed to his intimate convictions, sprang from his sick heart to his head: his soul became dejected, and his copious tears so obscured his eyes as to veil from them for a time the existence of the Almighty, which he seemed to question; and he appeared to think that if the Cambridge philosophy was right in doubting the soul's spirituality, its immortality might be equally questioned. These doubts having been expressed in his own, and not in his hero's name, at the outset of the second canto of "Childe Harold," led to his being also accused of skepticism.

But if pain actually paralyzed for a time the elasticity of his mind, the latter very soon recovered its natural vigor and showed itself in all its glowing energy in the eighth and ninth stanzas, which are most delicate emanations from a beautiful soul. The first stanzas alone, however, continued to occupy the attention of some orthodox and over-scrupulous minds: poetry not necessarily being a mode of teaching philosophy. We must besides remark that the meaning of the lines is purely hypothetical. In *saying* that the soul might *not be immortal*, is it not saying much the same as was said by Locke in the words *the soul is perhaps spiritual?* Is not that perishable which is capable of dissolution according to the laws of the world? Lord Byron, though a stanch spiritualist at heart, derived his doubts from other much less exalted authorities. Believing implicitly in the omnipotence of the Creator, could he not modestly fear that God, who had made his soul out of nothing, might cause it to return to nothing? Might he not imagine that the contrary belief was rather the result of our wishes, of our pride, and of the importance which we love to attach to ourselves? Can the conviction of the existence of immortality, unless founded upon revelation, be any thing else but a hope or a sentiment? Pantheists alone find immortality to be the fatal consequence of their presumptuous doctrine. But what an immortality! One to be laughed at, as a philosopher of our days so well expresses it.

Accused of skepticism, Byron replied by explaining the meaning of his lines in a note which, at the instance of Mr. Dallas, he also consented to suppress with his habitual good-nature, and in which he endeavored to show that the spirit which pervaded the whole of the poem was rather one of discouragement and despair, than raillery at religion, and that, after all, the effect of religion upon the world had been less to make men love their equals than to excite the various sects to a hatred against one another, and thus give rise to those fanatical wars which have caused so much bloodshed and injured so deeply the cause which they were intended to defend.

In reading this note again, one can with difficulty make out what Dallas's objections were, and why he tried so hard to have it suppressed; for it savors much more of a spirit of toleration and charity than of skepticism. Lord Byron nevertheless withdrew it.

But this was not enough to satisfy the British straight-lacedness. As the accusations against his skepticism were on the increase daily, Mr. Gifford, for whose enlightened opinion Byron ever had great respect, advised him to be more prudent, whereupon Byron replied:—

"I will do as you advise in regard to religious matters. The best would perhaps be to avoid them altogether. Certainly the passages already published are rather too rigorously interpreted. I am no bigot of incredulity, and I did not expect that I should be accused of denying the existence of God, because I had expressed some doubts as to the immortality of the soul. . . . . After all, I believe my doubts to be but the effects of some mental illness."

It is clear from this letter, the tone of which is so honest and sincere, that if in the stanzas which his rivals blamed there was really more skepticism than can be gathered from the consideration of man's littleness and God's greatness, yet it was not his real conviction. Perhaps it was only a kind of cloud overhanging the mind, produced by the great grief which weighed on his heart. These sentiments, however, must have been really his own for some time longer. In his journal of 1813 he expresses himself thus:—

"My restlessness tells me I have something within that 'passeth show.' It is for him who made it to prolong that spark of celestial fire which illuminates yet burns this frail tenement. . . . . In the mean time I am grateful for some good, and tolerably patient under certain evils, *grace à Dieu et à mon bon tempérament.*"

But all this, as we have said, amounted to the opinion that an omnipotent God is the author of our soul, which is of a totally different nature to that of our body, and that the soul being spiritual and not subjected to the laws which rule the body, the soul must be immortal. That he who made it out of nothing can cause it to return to nothing. The orthodox doctrine does not teach, as pantheism does, that our soul can not perish. It gives it only an individual immortality.

Notwithstanding this, and indeed on account of it, he was accused of being an atheist, in a poem entitled "Anti-Byron." This poem was the work of a clever rival, who made himself the echo of a party. Murray hesitated to publish it, but Byron, who was always just, praised the poem, and advised its publication.

"If the author thinks that I have written poetry with such tendencies, he is quite right to contradict it."

But having done so much for others, this time, at least, he fulfilled a duty toward himself by adding:—

"The author is however wrong on one point; I am not in the least an atheist;" and ends by saying, "It is very odd; eight lines may have produced eight thousand, if we calculate what has been and may still be said on the subject."

He speaks of the same work to Moore, in the same tone of pleasantry:—

"Oh, by-the-by, I had nearly forgot. There is a long poem —an 'Anti-Byron'—coming out, to prove that I have formed a conspiracy to overthrow by rhyme all religion and government, and have already made great progress! It is not very scurrilous, but serious and ethereal. I never felt myself important till I saw and heard of my being such a little Voltaire as to induce such a production."

He therefore laughed at these accusations as too absurd. As for skepticism, he did not defend himself from a touch of it; for not only did he feel that the suspicious stanza could partly justify the belief, but also because there did exist in him a kind of religious skepticism which proceeded far more from meditation and observation than from a passion for it. Such a skepticism is in truth a sigh for conviction. A painful vision which appears to most reflective minds in a more or less indistinct and vague manner, but which appeared more forcibly to him, inasmuch as it sought to be expressed in words.

"He," says Montaigne, "who analyzes all the circumstances which have brought about matters, and all the consequences which have been derived from them, debars himself from having any choice, and remains skeptical."

This skepticism of Lord Byron, however, did not overstep the boundaries of permissible doubt, as prescribed by an intelligence desirous of improvement. This privilege he exercised; and one might say that he remained, as it were, suspended between heaven and earth, ever looking up toward heaven, from whence he felt that light must come in the end, —a light ever on the increase, which would daily steady him in the great principles which form the fundamental basis of truth,—one God the creator, the real immortality of our soul, our liberty and our responsibility before God.

Tired, however, of ever being the butt of the invectives of his enemies, and of the clergy, whom he had roughly handled in his writings, Lord Byron preferred remaining silent; and until his arrival in Switzerland he ceased making any allusions in his writings to any philosophical doubts which he may have entertained. The heroes which he selected for his Oriental poems were, moreover, too passionate to allow the mysterious voices from heaven to silence the cries from their heart. These celestial warnings, however, Byron never ceased to hear, although absorbed himself by various passions of a different kind; he was at that time almost surrounded by an idolizing public, and rocked in the cradle of success and popularity. This is but too visible whenever he ceases to talk the language of his heroes, and expresses merely his own ideas and his own personal feelings. It was at this time that he wrote those delicious "Hebrew Melodies," in which a belief in spirituality and immortality is everywhere manifest, and in which is to be found the moral indication, if not the metaphysical proof, of the working of his mind in a religious point of view, as he matured in years. Two of these Melodies especially, the third and the fifteenth, contain so positive a profession of faith in the spiritualist doctrines, and carry with them the mark of so elevated a Christian sentiment, that I can not forbear quoting them *in extenso.*

IF THAT HIGH WORLD.

I.

If that high world, which lies beyond
   Our own, surviving Love endears;
If there the cherish'd heart be fond,
   The eye the same, except in tears—
How welcome those untrodden spheres!
   How sweet this very hour to die!
To soar from earth and find all fears
   Lost in thy light—Eternity!

II.

It must be so: 'tis not for self
   That we so tremble on the brink;
And striving to o'erleap the gulf,
   Yet cling to Being's severing link.
Oh! in that future let us think
   To hold each heart the heart that shares;
With them the immortal waters drink,
   And soul in soul grow deathless theirs!

WHEN COLDNESS WRAPS THIS SUFFERING CLAY.

I.

When coldness wraps this suffering clay,
   Ah! whither strays the immortal mind?
It can not die, it can not stay,
   But leaves its darken'd dust behind.

Then, unembodied, doth it trace
  By steps each planet's heavenly way?
Or fill at once the realms of space,
  A thing of eyes, that all survey?

II.

Eternal, boundless, undecay'd,
  A thought unseen, but seeing all,
All, all in earth or skies display'd,
  Shall it survey, shall it recall:
Each fainter trace that memory holds
  So darkly of departed years,
In one broad glance the soul beholds,
  And all, that was, at once appears

III.

Before Creation peopled earth,
  Its eyes shall roll through chaos back;
And where the furthest heaven had birth,
  The spirit trace its rising track.
And where the future mars or makes,
  Its glance dilate o'er all to be,
While sun is quench'd or system breaks,
  Fix'd in his own eternity.

IV.

Above our Love, Hope, Hate, or Fear,
  It lives all passionless and pure:
An age shall fleet like earthly year;
  Its years as moments shall endure.
Away, away, without a wing,
  O'er all, through all, its thought shall fly,
A nameless and eternal thing,
  Forgetting what it was to die.

There is no passage in Plato, or in St. Augustin, or in Pascal, which can equal the sublimity of these stanzas.

It was in this painful state of mind that he spent the unfortunate year of his marriage. Having separated from his wife, he came to Geneva. Here, at the same hotel—Hôtel de Secheron—Shelley had also arrived, who some years previously had offered Byron a copy of his poem entitled "Queen Mab." Here they became acquainted. Although only twenty-three years of age, Shelley had already experienced much sorrow during his short existence. Born of rich and aristocratic parents, and who professed very religious and Tory principles, Shelley had been sent to Eton at thirteen. His character was most peculiar. He had none of the tastes of the young, could not stand scholastic discipline, despised every rule and regulation, and spent his time in writing novels.

F

He published two when fifteen years old only, which appeared to be far above what could be expected from a boy of his age, but which deserved censure from their immoral tone. Owing to the nature of his mind, and especially at a time when reading has much influence, Shelley had conceived a great taste for the books which were disapproved of at college. Consequently the doctrines of the materialist school, which were the most in fashion then both in France and in England, so poisoned his mind as to cause him to become an atheist, and to argue as such against several theologians. He even published a pamphlet, so exaggerated in tone that he entitled it, "On the Necessity of Atheism." To crown this folly, Shelley sent round to all the bishops a copy of this work, and signed it with his own name.

Brought before the authorities to answer the charge of this audacious act, he persisted in his doctrines, and was actually preparing an answer to the judges in the same sense, when he was expelled from the university.

For people who know England a little, it is easy to conceive what an impression such conduct must have produced on the part of the eldest son of a family like his, of Tory principles, belonging to the aristocracy, intimate with the prince regent, and stanch, orthodox and severe in their religious tenets. Expelled from college, he was likewise sent away from home; and when his indignant father consented to see him again, Shelley was treated with such coldness that he was enraged at being received as a stranger in the bosom of a family of which he was the eldest son. This was not all: even the young lady for whom Shelley had already conceived an affection, deemed it right to cast him off. Overwhelmed by all these but too well merited misfortunes, he took refuge in an inn, where he tried to poison himself.

As he was struggling between life and death, a young girl of fifteen, Miss Westbrook, took care of him. Believing himself to be past recovery, and having no other means of rewarding her attention except by marrying her, he did so, in the hope that after his death his family would provide for her. But it is not always so easy to die, and he did not die. His health, however, was completely broken, and all that remained to him besides was an ill-assorted marriage. After the Gretna

Green ceremony, Shelley went to reside in Edinburgh. His marriage so exasperated his father, that from that time he ceased to have any intercourse with him.

From Scotland Shelley went to Ireland, which was then in a very disturbed state. His metaphysics led him to conceive the most dangerous social theories. Conquered by a very real love of humanity, which he hoped to serve by the realization of his chimerical views, he even believed it to be his duty to make proselytes. While recommending the observance of peace, and of a spirit of moderation on the one hand, he, on the other, published pamphlets and spoke at meetings with a degree of talent which earned for him a certain amount of reputation, if not of fame. Then he was seized with a violent admiration for the English school called "Lockists," and devoted himself to poetry by way of giving a literary expression to his metaphysical reveries, and to his social theories. Thus he wrote "Queen Mab," a poem full of talent and imagination, but which is only the frame which encircles his most deplorable fancies. He sent a copy of it to all the noted literary men of England, and among them to Lord Byron, whose star had risen since the publication of "Childe Harold." Lord Byron declared, as may be seen in a note to the "Due Foscari," that the metaphysical portion of the poem was quite in opposition with his own opinions; but, with his usual impartiality and justice, he admired the poetry which is noticeable in this work, agreeing in this "with all those who are not blinded by bigotry and baseness of mind."

Shelley's marriage, contracted as it was under such strange auspices, was, of course, very unfortunate. By his acquaintance with Godwin, one of the greatest literary characters of his day, Shelley came to know Mary, his daughter, by his marriage with the celebrated Mrs. Woolstoncraft. Each fell in love with the other, but Shelley was not yet free to marry Miss Godwin. He separated from the wife he had chosen only from grateful motives, although he had two children by her, and he left England for the first time, where he had become the object of persecutions of all kinds, and of a hatred which at a later period culminated in taking away his right to the guardianship of his children.

Such was his position when Lord Byron arrived in Switzerland, and alighted at the Hôtel Secheron. To make acquaintance, therefore, with the author of "Queen Mab," and with the daughter of Godwin, for whom he entertained great regard, was a natural consequence on the part of the author of "Childe Harold."

Notwithstanding their difference of character, their diversity of taste, and their different habits, owing to the very opposite mode of living which they had followed, the two poets felt drawn to one another by that irresistible sympathy which springs up in the souls of two persecuted beings, however just that persecution may have been, as regards Shelley, but which was wholly unjust as regards Byron. Here we must allow Moore to speak:—

"The conversation of Shelley, from the extent of his poetic reading, and the strange, mystic speculations into which his systems of philosophy led him, was of a nature strongly to interest the attention of Lord Byron, and to turn him away from worldly associations and topics into more abstract and untrodden ways of thought. As far as contrast indeed is an enlivening ingredient of such intercourse, it would be difficult to find two persons more formed to whet each other's faculties by discussion, as on few points of common interest between them did their opinions agree: and that this difference had its root deep in the conformation of their respective minds, needs but a glance through the rich, glittering labyrinth of Shelley's pages to assure us.

"In Lord Byron, the real was never forgotten in the fanciful. However Imagination had placed her whole realm at his disposal, he was no less a man of this world than a ruler of hers: and, accordingly, through the airiest and most subtle creations of his brain, still the life-blood of truth and reality circulates. With Shelley it was far otherwise: his fancy was the medium through which he saw all things, his facts as well as his theories; and not only the greater part of his poetry, but the political and philosophical speculations in which he indulged, were all distilled through the same over-refining and unrealizing alembic. Having started as a teacher and reformer of the world, at an age when he could know nothing of the world but from fancy, the persecution he met with on the threshold of this boyish enterprise only confirmed him in his first paradoxical views of human ills, and their remedies. Instead of waiting to take lessons from those of greater experience, he with a courage, admirable, had it been but wisely directed, made war upon both. . . . With a mind, by nature, fervidly pious, he yet refused to acknowledge a Supreme Providence, and substituted some airy abstraction of 'Universal Love' in its place. An aristocrat by birth, and, as I understand, also in appearance and manners, he was yet a leveller in politics, and to such an utopian extent as to be the serious advocate of a community of goods. Though benevolent and generous to an extent that seemed to exclude all idea of selfishness, he yet scrupled not, in the pride of system, to disturb wantonly the faith of his fellow-men, and, without substituting any equivalent good in its place, to rob the wretched of a hope, which, even if false, would be better than all this world's best truths.

"Upon no point were the opposite tendencies of the two friends more observable than in their notions on philosophical subjects: Lord Byron being, with the great bulk of mankind, a believer in the existence of matter and evil, while Shelley so far refined upon the theory of Berkeley, as not only to resolve the whole of creation into spirit, but to add also to this immaterial system, some pervading principle, some abstract nonentity of love and beauty—of which, as a substitute at least for Deity—the philosophic bishop had never dreamed."

The difference existing between their philosophical doctrines was that which existed between the two most opposed systems of spiritualism and pantheism.

I said that Shelley, notwithstanding his originality of mind, was destined, through the mobility of his impressions, to be easily influenced by what he read. The study of Plato and of Spinoza had already given to his metaphysical views a different bent. But before his transition from atheism to a mystical pantheism, before finding God in all things, after having sought him in vain everywhere, before considering himself to be a fragment of a chosen existence, and before shutting himself up in a kind of mysticism which did actually absorb him at a later period, he confined himself to a positive worship of nature, which appeared to him then in the glorious shape of the mountains and lakes of Helvetia. Wordsworth was his oracle, and thus cultivating a poetry which deified nature, Shelley, in reality, remained at heart an atheist, and doubtless tried to imbue Byron with his enthusiasm and with his opinions.

Himself greatly delighted with the beauties of the scenery in the midst of which they lived, and, as he was wont to say in laughter, having received many large doses of Wordsworth from Shelley, Lord Byron wrote several stanzas in which the same enthusiasm may be met with, recorded in terms almost of adoration.

It was only a poetical form, however, a poetical illusion, which was succeeded by stanzas in which God himself as our creator, was loudly proclaimed. If in the seventy-second and following stanzas of the third canto, opinions were expressed which savored of pantheistic tendencies, they were at once followed by some such as these:—

> "All heaven and earth are still—though not in sleep,
> But breathless, as we grow when feeling most;
> And silent, as we stand in thought too deep:—
> All heaven and earth are still: from the high host
> Of stars to the lull'd lake and mountain-coast,
> All is concentred in a life intense,
> Where not a beam, nor air, nor leaf is lost,
> But hath a part of being, and a sense
> Of that which is of all *Creator* and *Defense*."

And again, on viewing the Alps, he writes the poem of "Manfred," in which his belief in a One God, and Creator, is expressed in sublime lines. His repugnance to atheism and to materialism is testified not only in his poetry, but also by his own actions.

On reaching Montauvert with his friend Hobhouse, and on the point of ascending Mont Blanc with him, he found Shelley's name in the register of the travellers, and under it the qualification of "atheist" written in Shelley's own hand. Lord Byron at once scratched it out. But on reading, a little below, a remark by another traveller, who had justly rebuked Shelley's folly, Byron added the words, "The appellation is well deserved."

He soon after left the Alps, and came to Italy, without his views, either philosophical or religious, being in the least altered by the seductions of "that serpent," as he jokingly denominated Shelley.

We shall now follow him, step by step, until the end of his life, and we shall see whether he will not show himself stanch in his adherence to great principles. Lord Byron had enough of systems, and was disgusted with their absurdity, their proud dogmatical views, and their intolerant spirit. Whenever the great questions of life and the dictates of the soul occupy his thoughts, either in the silence of the night or in the absence of passion, we shall see him set himself resolutely to the examination of his own conscience, for the purpose of arriving at truth and justice. The answers which his powerful reasoning suggested to him served to determine and confirm his faith in God.

On leaving Geneva, Lord Byron proceeded to Milan. "One day," says Mr. Stendhall, who knew Lord Byron at Milan, in 1817, and saw a great deal of him there, "some people alluded to a couplet from the 'Aminta' of Tasso, in which the poet appears to take credit to himself for being an unbeliever, and expresses it in the lines which may thus be translated:—

'Listen, oh my son, to the thunder as it rolls.
But what is it to us what Jupiter does up there?
Let us rejoice down here if betroubled above;
Let the common herd of mortals dread his blows:
And let the world go to ruin, I will only think
Of what pleases me; and if I become dust again,
I shall only be what I have already been.'

Lord Byron says that these lines were written under the influence of spleen. A belief in the existence of a superior Being was a necessity for the fiery and tender nature of Tasso. He was, besides, far too Platonic to try to reconcile such contrary opinions. When he wrote those lines, he probably was in want of a piece of bread and a mistress."

Lord Byron reached Venice, and there his most agreeable hours and days were spent with Padre Pasquale, in the convent of the Armenian priests.

He also wrote, at this time, the sublimely moral poem entitled "Manfred," in which he renders justice to the existence of God, to the free will of man, the abuse of which has resulted in the loss of "Manfred," and retraces, in splendid lines, all the duties incumbent upon man, together with the limits which he is not allowed to pass. The apparition of his lovely and young victim, the uncertainty of her happiness, which causes Manfred's greatest grief, and finally his supplication to her that he may know whether she is enjoying eternal bliss,

> . . . . . "That I do bear
> This punishment for both—that thou wilt be
> One of the blessed—. . . . ."

the whole bears the impress of a truly religious spirit.

He shortly afterward visited Rome, and finding himself in presence of St. Peter's, he again gave expression to his religious sentiments, in the admirable fourth canto of "Childe Harold," which Englishmen do not hesitate to acknowledge as the finest poem which ever came from mortal hands.

TO ST. PETER.

Stanza 153.

> * * * * * *
> "Christ's mighty shrine above his martyr's tomb!"

Stanza 154.

> "But thou, of temples old, or altars new,
> Standest alone, with nothing like to thee.
> * * * * * *
> Power, glory, strength, and beauty all are aisled
> In this eternal ark of worship undefiled."

From Venice he went on to Ravenna. The persecution to which he was subjected, on the ground of religion and morality, on account of the publication of the two first cantos of "Don Juan," was then at its height, and he was tormented in every possible way. It was useless for him to protest, in verse, in prose, by letter, or by words, against the accusation of his being an atheist and a skeptic. It was asserted that "Manfred" was the expression of his doubts upon the dispensation of Providence, and that his other poems, all more or less imbued with passion, had tendencies of an irreverent nature in respect to the Divinity. His two famous stanzas in "Childe Harold" were always held up to him by the innumerable army of hypocrites and wicked people who assailed him.

All were not hypocrites, however; some were his enemies in good faith, but were blinded by sectarian prejudices. Among these was an Irishman of the name of Mulock, author of a work entitled "Atheism Answered." Lord Byron one day at Ravenna received a paper from the editor of the "Bologna Telegraph," with extracts from this work, in which "there is a long eulogium of" his "poetry, and a great *compatimento* for" his "misery" on account of his being a skeptic and an unbeliever in Christ; "although," says Mr. Mulock, "his bold skepticism is far preferable to the pharisaical parodists of the religion of the Gospel, who preach and persecute with an equally intolerant spirit."

Lord Byron, writing that day to Murray, says:—

"I never could understand what they mean by accusing me of irreligion. They may, however, have it their own way. This gentleman seems to be my great admirer, so I take what he says in good part, as he evidently intends kindness, to which I can't accuse myself of being insensible."

In the evening he talked to and laughed a good deal with the Countess Guiccioli about this great *compatimento*,* treating it as a great oddity. A few months later, Moore having written to him about this same Mr. Mulock, and told him that that gentleman was giving lectures upon religion, Lord Byron, while riding with the young Count G—— in the forest of Ravenna, made his profession of faith, and finding his youthful companion not quite orthodox, said to him: "The nature of classical and philosophical studies generally paralyzes all logical minds, and that is why many young heads leave college unbelievers: you are even still more so, because you mix up your religious views with your political antipathies. As for me, in my early youth, when I left college, where I had to bow to very superior and stronger minds who themselves were under various evil influences of college and of youth, I was more than heterodox. Time and reflection have changed my mind upon these subjects, and I consider Atheism as a folly. As for Catholicism, so little is it objectionable to me, that I wish my daughter to be brought up in that religion, and some day to marry a Catholic. If Catholicism, after all, suggests difficulties of a nature which it is difficult for reason to get over, are these less great than those which Protestantism creates? Are not all the mysteries common to both creeds? Catholicism at least offers the consolation of Purgatory, of the Sacraments, of absolution and forgiveness; whereas Protestantism is barren of consolation for the soul."

* Sympathy.

This open profession of faith, expressed by such a man as Lord Byron, in a calm and dispassionate tone, produced a great impression upon the young count. It had been so much the fashion to consider him as irreligious, that one would say that even his friends were of the same opinion. Some time had elapsed since Byron had sent a translation from the Armenian of one of the Epistles of St. Paul, which Murray delayed in publishing. Rather annoyed by this delay, Byron wrote to him on the 9th of October, 1821, from Ravenna:—

"The Epistle of St. Paul, which I translated from the Armenian, for what reason have you kept it back, though you published that stuff which gave rise to the 'Vampire?' Is it because you are afraid to print any thing in opposition to the cant of the 'Quarterly' about Manicheism? Let me have a proof of that Epistle directly. I am a better Christian than those parsons of yours, though not paid for being so."

If Byron hated fanatical and persecuting clergymen, he, on the other hand, entertained great regard for priests of every denomination, when he knew that they exercised their functions without fanaticism and in a tolerant spirit. Among his dearest and earliest friends he placed two young clergymen,* both distinguished in their profession by their piety and their attainments. At Ravenna, his alms in favor of churches and monasteries were very liberal. If the organ were not in order, if the steeple wanted repairs, Lord Byron's pecuniary assistance was asked for, and he ever gave liberally though it was for the benefit of the Catholic community. He was always indignant at his writings, especially if connected with religion, being sent back to him by Murray with alterations to which he was no party. On one occasion he reproached him in the following terms:—

"In referring to the mistake in stanza 132, I take the opportunity to desire that in future, in all parts of my writings referring to religion, you will be more careful, and not forget that it is possible that in addressing the Deity a blunder may become a blasphemy: and I do not choose to suffer such infamous perversions of my words or of my intentions. I saw the canto by accident."

* The Rev. Mr. Hodgson and the Rev. Mr. Harness.

His dearest paternal care was the religious education to be given to his natural daughter, Allegra, who was with him at Ravenna. In writing to Mr. and Mrs. Hoppner, to give them tidings of his dear Allegra, whom he had sent to a convent in Romagna to be educated there, he declares that in presence of the political disquietude which reigned in the Romagna, he thought he could not do better than send his child to that convent. Here "she would receive a little instruction, and some notions of morality and the principles of religion."

Moore adds to this letter a note, which runs thus:—

"With such anxiety did he look to this essential part of his daughter's education, that notwithstanding the many advantages she was sure to derive from the kind and feminine superintendence of Mrs. Shelley, his apprehensions lest her feelings upon religious subjects might be disturbed by the conversation of Shelley himself prevented him from allowing her to remain under his friend's roof."

The Bible, as is well known, constituted his favorite reading. Often did he find in the magnificent poetry of the Bible matter for inspiration. His "Hebrew Melodies" prove it, and as for the Book of Job, he used to say that it was far too sublime for him even to attempt to translate it, as he would have wished. Toward the end of his stay at Ravenna, when his genius was most fertile and almost superhuman—(he wrote five dramas and many other admirable poems in fifteen months, that is to say, in less time than it requires to copy them)—two biblical subjects inspired his muse: "Cain," and "Heaven and Earth." Both were admirably suited to his pen. He naturally treated them as a philosopher, but without any preconceived notion of making any religious converts. His enemies nevertheless seized hold of these pieces, to incriminate him and impugn his religious belief. I have spoken elsewhere* of that truly scandalous persecution. I will only add here that Moore, timid as he usually was when he had to face an unpopularity which came from high quarters, and alarmed by all the cries proceeding from party spirit, wrote to approve the beauty of the poem in enthusiastic terms, but disapproved of the harm which some doubts expressed therein might produce. Byron replied:—

* Article on his Life in Italy and at Pisa.

"There is nothing against the immortality of the soul in 'Cain,' that I recollect. I hold no such opinions; but in a drama the first rebel and the first murderer must be made to talk according to his character."

And in another letter he says, with regard to the same subject:—

"With respect to religion, can I never convince you that I have no such opinions as the characters in that drama, which seem to have frightened every body? Yet they are nothing to the expressions in Goethe's 'Faust' (which are ten times hardier), and not a whit more bold than those of Milton's 'Satan.' My ideas of character may run away with me: like all imaginative men, I, of course, embody myself with the character while I draw it, but not a moment after the pen is from off the paper.

"I am no enemy to religion, but the contrary. As a proof, I am educating my natural daughter a strict Catholic in a convent of Romagna, for I think people can never have enough of religion, if they are to have any. I incline myself very much to the Catholic doctrines; but if I am to write a drama, I must make my characters speak as I conceive them likely to argue."

The sympathy of persons sincerely religious was extremely agreeable to him. A short time after he had left Ravenna for Pisa, a Mr. John Sheppard sent him a prayer he had found among the papers belonging to his young wife, whom he had lost some two years before. Lord Byron thanked him in a beautiful letter, in which he consoled the distressed husband by assuring him of his belief in immortality, and of his confidence that he would again see the worthy person whom himself he could not but admire, for her virtues and her pure and simple piety.

"I am obliged to you," he added, "for your good wishes, and more than obliged by the extract from the papers of the beloved object whose qualities you have so well described in a few words. I can assure you that all the fame which ever cheated humanity into higher notions of its own importance, would never weigh in my mind against the pure and pious interest which a virtuous being may be pleased to take in my welfare. In this point of view I would not exchange the prayers of the deceased in my behalf for the united glory of Homer, Cæsar, and Napoleon, could such be accumulated upon a living head. Do me at least the justice to suppose that

'Video meliora proboque,'

however the *deteriora sequor* may have been applied to my conduct. BYRON."

Not only did Lord Byron prevent his reason being influenced by the arguments of others, but even by the dictates of his own heart. Both his mind and his heart were perfectly independent of one another, nay, often took different directions. It was to him unquestionably painful to see such a division, but it was the fatal result of the excessive development of the powers of each. In the same letter to Mr. Sheppard which we have quoted, and which is full of gratitude for the prayers which the young wife had addressed to heaven to obtain his conversion, Byron adds:—

"A man's creed does not depend upon himself: who can say, 'I will believe this, that, or the other?' and, least of all, that which he least can comprehend."

Walter Scott once told him in London that he was convinced he would daily become more and more religious.

"What!" vehemently replied Lord Byron, "do you believe that I could become bigoted?"

"No," said Walter Scott, "I only think that the influence of some great mind might modify your religious views."

Galt says the same thing:—

"A mind like Byron's," says he, "was little susceptible of being impressed by the reasonings of ordinary men. Truth, in visiting him, must come accompanied by every kind of solemnity, and preceded by respect and reverence. A marked superiority, a recognized celebrity, were indispensable to command his sincere attention."

Without taking implicitly for granted the rather exaggerated opinion of Galt with respect to Lord Byron, we must allow that the great poet's attention could not be captivated by reasonings of a superficial kind, but could be influenced only by great learning, and powerful arguments which had conviction for their basis.

But he might have found at Pisa the great intellectual influence spoken of, for he found Shelley there. Seeing him every day, in the quiet intimacy which the delightful sojourn in Tuscany procured for them, it was easy for both to forget all the troubles of an agitated and political existence, and only to think about the world of spirits. Shelley had every opportunity for inculcating his doctrines, having, or rather being able to exercise, the most exclusive influence upon Byron's mind. Did he exercise that influence, and if he did not, for what reason?

We have said that Shelley, notwithstanding his original views, his extreme readiness to be impressed by every thing he heard and saw, was often the victim of his reading. He had read a great deal, and though since he had written the "Apology for Atheism" he had not changed his mind as to his metaphysical tenets, nevertheless the study of the German philosophy, and especially of Spinoza's, had produced on him a revolution of ideas. From a materialistic atheism, which denies the existence of God in every thing, he had gone over to a kind of mystic pantheism, which supposes God to be everywhere and in every thing. This species of pantheism is in reality but a disguised atheism, but which, in such a man as Shelley, appeared more in the actions of his life as a pervading devotion than an impious belief. Shelley ever adored all that is beautiful, true, and holy. From this it followed that his doctrines, far from appearing to be the result of pride, seemed, on the contrary, to be founded upon humility, sacrifice, and devotion to humanity. If the mystic pantheism of Spinoza could have found a living justification of its silly principles, and an excuse for its want of power, Shelley would have supplied both. The individuality, always more or less egotistical, which is prominent in the word *ego*, seemed positively to have ceased to exist with him: one would have said that he almost already felt himself absorbed in that universal and divine substance, which is the God of Spinoza. If in a century like ours such a philosophy as Eclecticism could return and become again a doctrinal institution, Shelley might have personified it. He had so sacrificed his individuality to chimeras of all kinds, that he appeared to consider himself a mere phenomenon, and to look upon the external world as mere fiction, in order that the impossible and never-to-be-found divinity of his dreams might occupy all the space.

He was perhaps the meekest, most generous, and the most modest of the creatures of the true God, whom he yet persistently refused to recognize as his Creator.

If, however, there was no impiety in his irreligion, no real pride, in his pride, there existed that weakness, if I may use the word, peculiar to a brain which can not grasp at reality, but adheres to a chimera as a basis for its arguments.

"His works," says Galt, "are soiled by the false judgments proceeding from a mind which made him look at every thing in a false light, and it must be allowed that that mind was either troubled or defective by nature."

If this opinion is too severe, it is, however, certain that Shelley had so exalted an imagination that his judgment suffered by it. As he is in his works, so was he in all the commonest actions of his life. A few anecdotes will serve to make him still better known.

Once, at Pisa, he went to see Count Gamba, who expected him, for some charitable purpose which they were to agree upon together. A violent storm burst forth suddenly, and the wind tore a tile from a roof, and caused it to fall on Shelley's head. The blow was very great, and his forehead was covered with blood. This, however, did not in the least prevent his proceeding on his way. When Count Gamba saw him in this state he was much alarmed, and asked him how it had occurred. Shelley replied quite calmly, passing his hand over his head, just as if he had forgotten all about it, that it was true that the wind had blown down a tile which had fallen on his head, but that he would be taken care of later upon his return home. Shelley was not rich, but whenever he went to his banker's it was necessary that no one should require his assistance, in order that the money which he had gone to fetch should come home untouched. As, on one occasion, he was returning from a visit to his banker's, some one at the door of his house asked for assistance. Shelley hastily got up the stairs, and throwing down his gold and notes on the floor, rushed suddenly away, crying out to Mrs. Shelley, "There, pick it all up." This the lady did as well as she could, for she was a woman of order, and as much attached to the reality of things as her husband was wanting in that particular.

I shall not multiply these characteristic instances of the man, but will only add that such incidents were by no means uncommon, nay, that they were matters of daily occurrence.

There was almost a kind of analogy in his life between him and Spinoza. Notwithstanding their great qualities and merits, both were hated and persecuted for sufficiently just motives, — society having the right of repudiating doctrines which tend to its destruction; but both were persecuted in undue and unfair proportions. Both had weak and sickly constitutions. Both had great and generous souls. Both endeavored to understand the laws which govern the destiny of the world, without ever being subject to their moral consequences, and both devoted themselves to be practically useful to their fellow-creatures—a contradiction which was the effect of their too generous minds.

In Shelley's heart the dominant wish was to see society entirely reorganized. The sight of human miseries and infirmities distressed him to the greatest degree; but, too modest himself to believe that he was called upon to take the initiative, and inaugurate a new era of good government and fresh laws for the benefit of humanity, he would have been pleased to see such a genius as Byron take the initiative in this undertaking. "He can be the regenerator of his country," wrote Shelley, speaking of Byron, in 1818, at Venice.

Shelley therefore did his best to influence Lord Byron. But the latter hated discussions: he could not bear entering into philosophical speculation at times when his soul craved the consolations of friendship and his mind a little rest. He was quite insensible to reasonings, which often appear sublime because they are clothed in words incomprehensible to those who have not sought to understand their meaning. But he made an exception in favor of Shelley. He knew that he could not shake his faith in a doctrine founded upon illusions, by his incredulity: but he listened to him with pleasure, not only on account of Shelley's good faith and sincerity of meaning, but also because he argued upon false data with such talent and originality that he was both interested and amused. But with all his great and noble qualities was it to be expected that Lord Byron would fall into the doctrines proffered by pantheists? Doctrines rejected by reason, which wound the heart, are opposed to the most imperative necessities of our nature, and only bring desolation to our minds.

Lord Byron had examined every kind and species of philosophy by the light of common sense, and by the instinct of his genius: the result had been to make him compassionate toward the vain weaknesses of the human understanding, and to convince him that all systems which have hypothesis as groundwork are illusions, and consequently likely to perish with their authors.

Pantheism in particular was odious to him, and he esteemed it to be the greatest of absurdities. He made no difference between the Pantheism "absolute," which mixes up that which is infinite with that which is finite, and that which struggles in vain to keep clear of Atheism.

In an age like ours, when the common tendency is of a materialistic character, such as almost to defy the power of man, mysticism has little or no *locus standi*. Shelley's opinions, on account of their appearance of spiritualism, were most likely of any to interest Byron; but, founded as they are upon fancy, could they please him? Could he possibly consent to lose his individuality, deny his own freedom of will, all responsibility of action, and hence all his privileges, his future existence, and all principles of morality? Could he possibly admit that the doctrine which prescribed these sacrifices was better than any other? Even with the best intentions, could any of the essential, moral, and holy principles of nature be introduced into such a system? Byron could not but condemn it, and he attributed all Shelley's views to the aberrations of a mind which is happier when it dreams than when it denies.

Here, then, was the cause of his being inaccessible to Shelley's arguments. He used sometimes to exclaim, "Why Shelley appears to me to be mad with his metaphysics." This he one day repeated to Count Gamba at Pisa, as Shelley walked out and he came in. "We have been discussing metaphysics," said he: "what trash in all these systems! Say what they will, mystery for mystery, I still find that of the Creation the most reasonable of any."

He made no disguise of the difficulties which he found in admitting the doctrine of a God, Creator of the world, and entirely distinct from it; but he added, "I prefer even that mystery to the contradictions by which other systems endeavor to replace it." He certainly found that in the mystery of Creation there existed the proof of the weakness of our minds, but he declared that pantheism had to explain absurdities far too evident for a logical mind to adopt its tenets. "They find," said he, "that reason is more easily satisfied with a system of unity like theirs, in which all is derived from one principle only: may be, but what do we ask of truth? why all our never-ceasing efforts in its pursuit? Is it merely that we may exercise the mind, and make truth the toy of our imagination? Impossible. At any rate it would be a secret to which, as yet, God has not given us any clue. But in doing this, in constantly placing the phenomena of creation before us without their causes or without ever explaining them, and at the same time instilling into our souls an insatiable thirst for truth, the Almighty has placed within us a voice which at times reminds us that He is preparing some surprise for us; and we trust that that surprise may be a happy one."

Poor Shelley lost his time with Byron. But, however much Byron objected to his doctrines, he had no similar objection to Shelley himself, for whom he professed a great respect and admiration. He grieved to find so noble an intellect the victim of hallucination which entirely blinded him to the perception of truth. Shelley, however, did not despair of succeeding in making Byron some day give up what he termed his philosophical errors, and his persistency earned for him the appellation of "serpent" which Byron gave him in jest. This persisteney, which at the same time indicates the merit of Byron's resistance, has often been mentioned by Shelley himself. Writing from Pisa to a friend in England, a very few days before his death, and alluding to a letter from Moore which Byron had shown him, and wherein "Cain" was attributed to the influence which he (Shelley) had evidently exercised over Byron, he said, "Pray assure Moore that in a philosophical point of view I have not the slightest influence over Byron; if I had, be sure I should use it for the purpose of uprooting his delusions and his errors. He had conceived 'Cain' many years ago, and he had already commenced writing it when I saw him last year at Ravenna. How happy I should be could I attribute to myself, even indirectly, a part in that immortal work!"

Moore wrote to Byron on the same subject a little later, and received the following reply:—"As for poor Shelley, who also frightens you and the world, he is, to my knowledge, the least egotistical and kindest of men. I know no one who has so sacrificed both fortune and sentiments for the good of others; as for his speculative opinions, we have none in common, nor do I wish to have any."

All the poems which he wrote at this time, and which admitted of his introducing the religious element either purposely or accidentally into them, prove one and all that his mind, as regards religion, was as we have shown it to be. This is particularly noticeable in his mystery called "Heaven and Earth;" but the same remark is applicable to others, such as the "Island," and even to some passages in "Don Juan." "Heaven and Earth" — a poem which appeared about this time, and which he styled "A Mystery"—is a biblical poem in which all the thoughts agree with the Book of Genesis, and "which was inspired," says Galt, "by a mind both serious and patriarchal, and is an echo of the oracles of Adam and of Melchisedec." In this work he exhibits as much veneration for scriptural theology as Milton himself. In the "Island," which he wrote at Genoa, there are passages which penetrate the soul with so religious a feeling, that Benjamin Constant, in reading it, and indignant at hearing Byron called an unbeliever, exclaimed in his work on religion, "I am assured that there are men who accuse Lord Byron of atheism and impiety. There is more religion in the twelve lines which I have quoted than in the past, present, and future writings of all his detractors put together."

Even in "Don Juan," in that admirable satire which, not being rightly understood, has given rise to so many calumnies, he says, after having spoken in the fifteenth canto of the moral greatness of various men, and among others of Socrates:—

"And thou, Diviner still,
Whose lot it is by man to be mistaken,
And thy pure creed made sanction of all ill?
Redeeming worlds to be by bigots shaken,
How was thy toil rewarded?"

At the end of this stanza he wrote the following note:—

"As it is necessary in these times to avoid ambiguity, I say that I mean by 'Diviner still,' Christ. If ever God was man—or man God—he was both. I never arraigned his creed, but the use or abuse made of it. Mr. Canning one day quoted Christianity to sanction negro slavery, and Mr. Wilberforce had little to say in reply. And was Christ crucified that black men might be scourged? If so, he had better been born a mulatto, to give both colors an equal chance of freedom, or at least salvation."

Notwithstanding these beautiful lines, which were equally professions of faith, England, instead of doing Byron justice, continued more than ever to persecute him.

Shortly afterward he embarked at Genoa for Greece, and halted at Cephalonia. He there made the acquaintance of a young Scotchman, named Kennedy, who was attached as doctor to the Greek army. Before taking to medicine this young man had studied law, with the intention of going to the Edinburgh bar. He was so deeply convinced of the truths of Christianity, and so familiar with its teaching, that he would fain have imparted his belief to every one he met. From his position he found himself among a host of young officers, mostly Scotch, and all more or less lax in their religious practices. Among these, however, he met with four who consented to listen to his explanation of the doctrines of Christianity. As their principal challenge was to show proofs that the Bible was of divine origin, he accepted the challenge in the hope of making some conversions.

One of these officers informed Lord Byron of this projected meeting, and Byron, from the interest which he always took in the subject which was to be their ground of discussion, expressed a wish to be present. "You know," said he, "that I am looked upon as a black sheep, and yet I am not as black as the world makes me out, nor worse than others,"—words, which, from the fact of his rarely doing himself justice, were noteworthy in his mouth.

Under such auspices, then, was Kennedy fortunate enough to open his discussion, and Lord Byron was present in company of the young Count Gamba and Dr. Bruno.

Mr. Kennedy has given a detailed account of this meeting, as also of his subsequent conversations with Lord Byron. We will mention some of them here, because they show Lord Byron's religious opinions in the latter portion of his life. Mr. Kennedy had made a condition that he should be allowed to speak, without being interrupted, but at various intervals, for twelve hours. This condition, was soon set aside, and then Lord Byron joined the conversation. After exciting admiration by his patient silence, he astounded every one as an interlocutor. If Kennedy was well versed in the Scriptures, Lord Byron was not less so, and even able to correct a misquotation from Holy Writ. The direct object ot the meeting was to prove that the Scriptures contained the genuine and direct revelation of God's will. Mr. Kennedy, however, becoming a little entangled in a series of quotations, which had not the force that was required to prove his statements, and, seeing that a little impatience betrayed itself among the audience, could not resist showing some tempeı, and accusing his hearers of ignorance. "Strange accusation, when applied to Lord Byron," says Galt. Lord Byron, who had come there to be interested, and to learn, did not notice the taunt of Mr. Kennedy, but merely remarked, "that all that can be desired is to be convinced of the truth of the Bible, as containing really the word of God; for if this is sincerely believed, it must follow, as a necessary consequence, that one must believe all the doctrines contained in it."

He then added, that in his youth he had been brought up by his mother in very strict religious principles; had read a large number of theological works, and that Barrow's writings had most pleased him; that he regularly went to church, that he was by no means an unbeliever who denied the Scriptures, and wished to grope in atheism; but, on the contrary, that all his wish was to increase his belief, as half-convictions made him wretched. He declared, however, that he could not thoroughly understand the Scriptures. He also added, that he entertained the highest respect for, and confidence in, those who believed conscientiously; but that he had met with many whose conduct differed from the principles they professed simply from interested motives, and esteemed the number of those who really believed in the Scriptures to be very small. He asked him about his opinion as to various writers against religion, and among others of Sir W. Hamilton, Bellamy, and Warburton, who pretend that the Jews had no notion of a future existence. He confessed that the sight of so much evil was a difficulty to him, which he could not explain, and which made him question the perfect goodness of the Creator. He dwelt upon this argument a long time, exhibiting as much tenderness of heart as force of reasoning. Kennedy's answers were weak, as must be those of one who denies the measure of evil, in order that he may not be compassionate toward it, and who promises a reward in after life to escape the necessity of its being bestowed in the present. In reply Lord Byron pointed to moral and physical evil which exists among savages, to whom Scripture is unknown, and who are bereft of all the means of becoming civilized people. Why are they deprived of these gifts of God? and what is to be the ultimate fate of Pagans? He quoted several objections made to our Lord by the apostles; mentioned prophecies which had never been fulfilled, and spoke of the consequences of religious wars. Kennedy replied with much ability, and even with a certain degree of eloquence, and prudently made use of the ordinary theological arguments. But to influence such a mind as Byron's more was required. In the search after truth, he looked for hard logic, and eloquence was not required by him. Fénélon could not have persuaded him; but Descartes might have influenced him. He preferred, in fact, in such arguments, the method of the geometrician to that of the artist; the one uses truth to arrive at truth, the other makes use of the beautiful only, to arrive at the same end.

The meeting lasted four hours, and created much sensation in the island, and every one agreed in praising Lord Byron's great knowledge of the Scriptures, joined to his moderation and modesty. Kennedy, however, a little irritated by the superiority granted to his adversary, did his best to dissipate the impression produced by it. He went so far as to reproach his friends for having allowed themselves to be blinded by the rank, the celebrity, and the prestige of Lord Byron. "His theological knowledge being," said he, "in reality quite ordinary and superficial." This meeting was the only one in which Lord Byron took a part, for he left Argostoli for Metaxata.

The meetings continued, however, for some time longer, and Kennedy showed a zeal which deserved to meet with better success. He brought before his audience with talent every possible reasoning in favor of orthodoxy; but his audience, composed of young men, were far too engrossed with worldly occupations to be caught by the ardor of their master's zeal. Disappointed at not seeing Lord Byron again among them, they all deserted Kennedy's lectures just at the time when he was going to speak of miracles and prophecies, the subject of all others upon which he had built his greatest hopes. Not only did they desert the hall, but actually overwhelmed the speaker with mockery. Some declared they would put off their conversion to a more advanced age; others actually maintained that they had less faith than before.

Meanwhile Kennedy, though disappointed in his religious enthusiasm on the one hand, received some consolation on the other, at the hands of Lord Byron, who had not forgotten him, and who often inquired after him though he had not been convinced by his arguments. Kennedy also had conceived a great liking for Byron. He admired in the poet all his graceful qualities and his unequalled talents. He wished, but dared not yet, visit Lord Byron. Meeting, however, Count Gamba at Argostoli on one occasion, and hearing from him that Byron was on the point of departure for Continental Greece, he resolved to pay him a visit, "as much," said he, "to show the respect which is due to such a man, as to satisfy one's own curiosity in seeing and hearing so distinguished a person."

Byron received him with his natural cordiality. He made him stay to dinner with him, and thus gave him the opportunity of entering into a long conversation. Kennedy, who never lost sight of his mission of proselytism, brought the conversation round to the object of his wishes, and prefaced his arguments by saying that he was prepared to talk upon the matter; but that he had no doubt lost his time, since it was not likely that his lordship would consider these subjects urgent at that moment. Byron smiled and replied, "It is true that at the present time I have not given that important subject all my attention, but I should nevertheless be curious to know the motives which not only have convinced you, as a man of sense and reflection, as you undoubtedly are, of the truth of religion, but also have induced you to profess Christianity with such zeal."

"If there had been men," said Kennedy, "who had rejected Christianity, there were greater men still who had accepted it; but to adopt a system merely because others have adopted it is not to act rationally, unless it is proved that the great minds which adopted it were mistaken."

"But I have not the slightest desire," answered Byron, "to reject a doctrine without having investigated it. Quite the contrary; I wish to believe, because I feel extremely unhappy in a state of uncertainty as to what I am to believe."

Kennedy having told him then that to obtain the grace of faith, he should pray humbly for it, Byron replied, that prayer does not consist in the act of kneeling or of repeating certain words in a solemn manner: "Devotion is the affection of the heart, and that I possess, for when I look at the marvels of creation I bow before the Majesty of Heaven, and when I experience the delights of life, health, and happiness, then my heart dilates in gratitude toward God for all His blessings."

"That is not sufficient," continued the doctor. "I should wish your lordship to read the Bible with the greatest attention, having prayed earnestly before that the Almighty may grant you the grace to understand it. For, however great your talents, the book will be a sealed letter to you unless the Holy Spirit inspires you."

"I read the Bible more than you think," said Byron. "I have a Bible which my sister, who is goodness itself, gave me, and I often peruse it."

He then went into his bedroom, and brought out a handsomely-bound pocket Bible which he showed the doctor. The latter advised his continuing to read it, but expressed his surprise that Byron should not have better understood it.

He looked out several passages in which it is enjoined that we should pray with humility if we wish to understand the truth of the Gospel; and where it is expressly said that no human wisdom can fathom these truths; but that God alone can reveal them to us, and enlighten our understanding; that we must not scrutinize His acts, but be submissive as children to His will; and that, as obedience through the sin of our first parents, and our own evil inclinations, has become for us a positive difficulty, we must change our hearts before we can obey or take pleasure in obeying the commandments of our Lord God; and, finally, that all, whatever the rank of each, are subject to the necessity of obedience.

Byron's occupations and ideas at that time were not quite in accordance with the nature of these holy words, but he received them with his usual kind and modest manner, because they came from one who was sincere. He only replied, that, as to the wickedness of the world, he was quite of his opinion, as he had found it in every class of society; but that the doctrines which he had put forth would oblige him to plunge into all the problems respecting the Old Testament and original sin, which many learned persons, as good Christians as Dr. Kennedy, did not hesitate to reject. He then showed the doctor, in answer to the latter's rather intolerant assertion of the omnipotence of the Bible, how conversant he was with the subject by quoting several Christian authors who thought differently. He quoted Bishop Watson, who, while professing Christianity, did not attribute such authority to the contents of the Bible. He also mentioned the Waldenses, who were such good Christians that they were called "the true Church of Christ," but who, nevertheless, looked upon the Bible as merely the history of the Jews. He then showed that the Book of Genesis was considered by many doctors of divinity as a mere symbol or allegory. He took up the defense of Gibbon against Kennedy's insinuation that the great historian had maliciously and intentionally kept back the truth; he quoted Warburton as a man whose ingenious theories have found much favor with many learned persons; finally, he proved to the doctor that, in any case, he could not himself be accused of ignorance of the subject.

This conversation afforded him the opportunity also of refuting the accusation brought against him by some of his numerous enemies; namely, that of having a tendency to the doctrines of Manicheism. Kennedy having said that the spirit of evil, as well as the angels, is subject to the will of God, Lord Byron replied,—

"If received in a literal sense, I find that it gives one a far higher notion of God's majesty, power, and wisdom, if we believe that the spirit of evil is really subject to the will of the Almighty, and is as easily controlled by Him as the elements follow the respective laws which He has made for them."

Byron could not bear any thing which took away from the greatness of the Divinity, and his words all tended to replace the Divinity in that incomprehensible space where He must be silently acknowledged and adored. Their conversation extended to other points of religious belief. While the doctor, taking the Bible to be the salvation of mankind, indulged in exaggerated and intolerant condemnation of the Catholic Church, which he called an abominable hierarchy not less to be regretted than Deism and Socinianism, Byron again displayed a spirit of toleration and moderation. Though he disapproved of the doctor's language, he did not contradict him, believing him to be sincere in his recriminations, but brought back the conversation to that point from which common sense should never depart. He deplored with him existing hypocrisies and superstitions, which he looked upon as the cause of the unbelief of many in the existence of God; but he added, that it was not confined to the Continent only, but likewise existed in England. Instead of resting his hopes upon the Bible, he said that he knew the Scriptures well enough "to be sure that if the spirit of meekness and goodness which the religion of the Gospel contains were put into practice by men, there would certainly be a marvellous change in this wicked world;" and he finished by saying, that as for himself he had, as a rule, ever respected those who believed conscientiously, whatever that belief might be; in the same manner as he detested from his heart hypocrites of all kinds, and especially hypocrites in religion.

He then changed the topic of conversation, and turned it to literature. All he said on that subject is so interesting that I reserve the record of it to another chapter. The doctor, however, soon resumed the former subject of their conversation, and, more in the spirit of a missionary than a philosopher, he went on to recommend the study of Christianity, which he said was summed up entirely in the Scriptures.

"But what will you have me do?" said Byron. "I do not reject the doctrines of Christianity, I only ask a few more proofs to profess them sincerely. I do not believe myself to be the vile Christian which many—to whom I have never done any harm, and many of whom do not even know me—strenuously assert that I am, and attack me violently in consequence."

The doctor insisted.

"But," said Byron, "you go too fast. There are many points still to be cleared up, and when these shall have been explained, I shall then examine what you tell me."

"What are those difficulties?" replied the doctor.

"If the subject is important, why delay its explanation? You have time; reason upon it; reflect. You have the means of disposing of the difficulty at your command."

"True," answered Byron, "but I am the slave of circumstances, and the sphere in which I live is not likely to make me consider the subject."

As the doctor became more urgent, Byron said—

"How will you have me begin?"

"Begin this very night to pray God that he may forgive you your sins, and may grant you grace to know the truth. If you pray, and read your Bible with purity of intention, the result must be that which we so ardently wish for."

"Well, yes," replied Byron, "I will certainly study these matters with attention."

"But your lordship must bear in mind, that you should not be discouraged, even were your doubts and difficulties to increase; for nothing can be understood without sufficient time and pains. You must weigh conscientiously each argument, and continue to pray to God, in whom at least you believe, to give you the necessary understanding."

"Why then," asked Byron, "increase the difficulties, when they are already so great?"

The doctor then took the mystery of the Trinity as an

example, and spoke of it as a man who has faith and accepts the mystery as a revealed dogma.

"It is not the province of man," said he, "to comprehend or analyze the nature of an existence which is entirely spiritual, such as that of the Divinity; but we must accept it, and believe in it, because it has been revealed to us, being fully convinced that man in his present state will never be able to fathom such mysteries."

He not only blamed those who wish to explain all things, but likewise the presumption of certain theologians in mixing up their own arguments with the revelations of Scripture in order to prove the unity in the Trinity, and who speculate upon the attributes of the Deity to ascertain the relative mode of existence of each of the three persons who compose the Trinity. "They must fall," he added, "or lead others to a similar end." Hence he concluded that mysteries should be believed in implicitly, as children believe fully what their parents tell them.

"I therefore advise your lordship," said he, "to put aside all difficult subjects,—such as the origin of sin, the fall of man, the nature of the Trinity, the mystery of predestination, etc.,—and to study Christianity not in books of theology, which, even the best, are all more or less imperfect, but in the careful examination of the Scriptures. By comparing each part of it, you will at last find a harmony so great in all its constituent parts, and so much wisdom in its entire whole, that you will no longer be able to doubt its divine origin, and hence that it contains the only means of salvation."

To so firm and enviable a faith, Byron replied as follows:—

"You recommend what is very difficult; for how is it possible for one who is acquainted with ecclesiastical history, as well as with the writings of the most renowned theologians, with all the difficult questions which have agitated the minds of the most learned, and who sees the divisions and sects which abound in Christianity, and the bitter language which is often used by the one against the other; how is it possible, I ask, for such a one not to inquire into the nature of the doctrines which have given rise to so much discussion?

One Council has pronounced against another; Popes have belied their predecessors, books have been written against other books, and sects have risen to replace other sects; the Pope has opposed the Protestants and the Protestants the Pope. We have heard of Arianism, Socinianism, Methodism, Quakerism, and numberless other sects. Why have these existed? It is a puzzle for the brain; and does it not, after all, seem safer to say 'Let us be neutral; let those fight who will, and when they have settled which is the best religion, then shall we also begin to study it?'

"I, however, like," he continued, "your way of thinking, in many respects; you make short work of decrees and councils, you reject all which is not in harmony with the Scriptures, you do not admit of theological works filled with Latin and Greek of both high and low church, you would even suppress many abuses which have crept into the Church, and you are right; but I question whether the Archbishop of Canterbury or the Scotch Presbyterians would consider you their ally.

"As for predestination, I do not believe as S—— and M—— do on that subject, but as you do; for it appears to me that I am influenced in a manner which I can not understand, and am led to do things which my will does not direct. If, as we all admit, there is a supreme Ruler of the universe, and if, as you say, He rules, over both good and bad spirits, then those actions which we perform against our will are likewise under His direction. I have never tried to sift this subject, but satisfied myself by believing that there is, in certain events, a predestination which depends upon the will of God."

The doctor replied, "that he had founded his belief upon his own grounds."

The doctor then touched upon the differences which existed in religious opinions, and expressed his regret at this, while showing, nevertheless, some indulgence for those Christain sects which do not attack the actual fundamental doctrines of Christianity. But he was intolerant as regards other sects, such as Arianism, Socinianism, and Swedenborgianism, of which he spoke almost with passion.

"You seem to hate the Socinians greatly," remarked Byron, "but is this charitable? Why exclude a Socinian, who believes honestly, from any hope of salvation? Does he not also found his belief upon the Bible? It is a religion which gains ground daily. Lady Byron is much in favor with its followers. We were wont to discuss religious matters together, and many of our misunderstandings have arisen from that. Yet, on the whole, I think her religion and mine were much alike."

Of course the doctor deplored the existence of such bold doctrines.

Lord Byron then spoke of Shelley:—

"I wish," he said, "you had known him, and that I might have got you both together. You remind me of him, not only in looks, but by your manner of speaking."

Besides physical appearance, it is easy to understand that there existed a great likeness between the two minds, different though their moral tendencies might have been. In both could be traced that degree of mysticism and expansiveness, which make the poet and the missionary. Byron praised the virtues of Shelley, and styled them Christian, and spoke mainly of his great benevolence of character, and of his generosity above his means.

"Certainly," replied the doctor, "such rare virtues are esteemed among Christians, but they can not be called Christian virtues, unless they spring from Christian principles: and in Shelley they were not so. His virtues might deserve human praise, they were no doubt pagan virtues; but they were nothing in the eyes of God, since God has declared that nothing pleases Him but that which springs from a good motive, especially the love of and belief in Christ, which was wanting in Shelley."

When Kennedy had characterized Shelley in even stronger terms, Byron said to him: "I see it is impossible to move your soul to any sympathy, or even to obtain from you in common justice a little indulgence for an unfortunate young man, gifted with a lofty mind and a fine imagination."

These remarks reveal the tolerant spirit of Lord Byron, but they also show how the best natures are spoiled by dogmatism.

The conversation had lasted several hours. Night was

coming on, and the doctor, carried away by his zeal, had forgotten the hour. His host, however, did nothing to remind him of it, and when Kennedy got up to take his leave, he said to Byron, after making excuses for remaining so long, "God having gifted you, my lord, with a mind which can grasp every subject, I am convinced that if your lordship would devote yourself to the study of religion, you would become one of its lights, the pride of your country, and the consolation of every honest person."

Lord Byron replied:—

"I certainly intend to study the matter, but you must give me a little time. You see that I have begun well: I listen to all you say. Don't you find that my arguments are more like your own than you would have thought?"

"Yes," answered the doctor, "and it gives me great pleasure. I have far better hopes of your lordship's conversion than of that of the young officers who listened to me without understanding the meaning of my words. You have shown greater patience and candor than I could have imagined you to be capable of; whereas they, on the contrary, exhibited so hardened a spirit that they appeared to look upon the subject as one which lent itself admirably to ridicule and laughter."

"You must allow," said Byron, "that in the times in which we are now living it is difficult to bestow attention to any serious religious matter. I think, however, I can promise to reflect even more on the subject than I have done hitherto, without, however, promising to adopt your orthodox views."

The doctor then asked him leave to present him with the work of B——, which he commended in high terms. Lord Byron said he would have great pleasure in reading it, and told the doctor that he should always be happy to see him, and at any time that he liked to come." "Should I be out when you come," he added, "take my books and read until my return."

On leaving Byron the doctor reflected over all that had taken place, and feared that his zeal had carried him too far —that his long conversation might have tired rather than interested Byron; but on the whole, he concluded by saying to himself, "It appears to me, that Byron never exhibited the least symptom of fatigue, but, on the contrary, continually showed great attention from beginning to end."

We have, perhaps, dwelt too much in our report of this conversation, but we wished to do so for several reasons. First, because it shows, better than a public debate, the real thoughts and feelings of Byron on religious matters, next, the real nature of his religious opinions, and finally we find, in Byron's conversation, virtues such as amiability, goodness, patience, delicacy, and toleration, which have not been sufficiently noticed.

The sympathy which Kennedy had conceived for Byron after the public meeting greatly increased after this first conversation. The candor and simplicity depicted on his handsome countenance, showed that his lofty intelligence could, better than any one else, grasp the theories of the doctor; and the latter felt that if he could not prevail in making Byron a believer in his own orthodox views, at least he could prepare the way for the acquirement of every virtue, and he resolved, therefore, to profit by the permission given him of often visiting Byron.

Meanwhile, the young officers continued their jokes, and pretended that Byron was laughing at the doctor, and making use of him in order to study Methodism, which he wished to introduce into his poem of "Don Juan." There is, however, a community of feeling between two frank natures, and Byron felt that the doctor's sincerity commanded respect, while the doctor, on the other hand, knew that Lord Byron was too earnest to condescend to a mockery of him.

"There was," says Kennedy, "nothing flighty in his manner with me, and nothing which showed any desire to laugh at religion."

When he returned to see Lord Byron, he found him more than ever preoccupied with his approaching departure for Continental Greece, and engrossed with a multitude of various occupations and visits. Byron, nevertheless, received him most graciously, and maintained that jovial humor which was one of his characteristics in conversation. Byron had reflected a good deal since his last interview with the doctor, but the direction which his thoughts had taken was not precisely that which the doctor had advised him to pursue. They did not agree with the tenets of the doctor's religion. The latter had not advised an unlimited use of one's reason, but, on the contrary, had recommended reliance on the traditional and orthodox teachings of the Church. To reason, however, constituted in Byron a positive necessity. He could not admit that God had given us the power of thought not to make use of it, and obliged us to believe that which in religion, as in other things, appears ridiculous to our reason and shocks our sense of justice. "It is useless to tell me," he said, somewhere in his memoranda, "that I am to believe and not to reason: you might just as well tell a man, 'Wake not, but sleep.' Then to be threatened with eternal sufferings and torments!—I can not help thinking that as many devils are created by the threat of eternal punishment, as numberless criminals are made by the severity of the penal laws."

Mysteries and dogmas, however, were not objectionable to Byron. This was shown in his conversation with Kennedy on the subject of the Trinity and of predestination. However little disposed he may have been to believe in mysteries, he nevertheless bowed in submission before their existence, and respected the faith which they inspire in minds more happily constituted than his own. His partial skepticism, or rather that in him which has been so denominated, was humble and modest in comparison to Montaigne's skepticism. Byron admitted that these were mysteries because the littleness of man and the greatness of God were ever present to him. He would have agreed with Newton in saying that "he was like a child playing on the beach with the waves which bathed the sands. The water with which he played was what he knew; what he ignored was the widespread ocean before him." Surrounded as we are by mysteries on all sides, he would have esteemed it presumption on his part to reject, in the name of science, all the mysteries of religion, when science itself has only to deal with phenomena. All is necessarily a mystery in its origin, and not to understand was no sufficient reason in the eyes of Byron to deny altogether the existence of matters relating to the Divinity. Could he reject religious dogmas under the pretext of not being able to understand them, when he admitted others

G 2

equally difficult of comprehension, although supported by logical proofs?

Among the mysteries of religion founded entirely upon revelation, there was one, however, which not only weighed upon his mind, but actually gave him positive pain. This was the dogma of eternal punishment, which he could not reconcile with the idea of an omnipotent Creator, as omnipotence implies perfect goodness and justice, of which the ideal has been implanted in our hearts. Here again his objections sprang from kindness of disposition.

After speaking a while on the subject of prayer, Byron said to Kennedy :—

"There is a book which I must show you," and, having chosen from a number of books on the table an octavo volume, entitled "Illustrations of the Moral Government of God, by E. Smith, M.D., London," he showed it to Kennedy, and asked him whether he knew of it. On Kennedy replying in the negative, Byron said that the author of the book proved that hell was not a place of eternal punishment.

"This is no new doctrine," replied Kennedy, "and I presume the author to be a Socinian, who, if consistent at all with his opinions, will sooner or later reject the Bible entirely, and avow himself to be what he really is already, namely, a Deist. Where did your lordship find the book?"

"It was sent to me from England," replied Byron, "to convert me, I suppose. The author's arguments are very powerful. They are taken from the Bible, and, while proving that the day will come when every intellectual being will enjoy the bliss of eternal happiness, he shows how impossible is the doctrine which pretends that sin and misery can exist eternally under the government of a God whose principle attributes are goodness and love."

"But," said Kennedy, "how does he then explain the existence of sin in the world for upward of 6000 years? That is equally inconsistent with the notion of perfect love and goodness as united in God."

"I can not admit the soundness of your argument," replied Byron; "for God may allow sin and misery to co-exist for a time, but His goodness must prevail in the end, and cause their existence to cease. At any rate it is better to believe that the infinite goodness of God, while allowing evil to exist as a means of our arriving at perfection, will show itself still greater some day when every intellectual being shall be purified and freed from the bondage of sin and misery."

As Kennedy persisted in arguing against the author's opinions, Lord Byron asked him "Why he was so desirous of proving the eternity of hell, since such a doctrine was most decidedly against the gentle and kind character of the teaching of Christ?" To other arguments on the same subject, Byron replied, that he could not determine as to the justice of their conclusions, but that he could not help thinking it would be very desirable to show that in the end all created beings must be happy, and therefore rather agreed with Mr. Smith than with the doctor.

As Lord Byron, however, had always allowed that man was free in thought and action, and therefore a responsible being made to justify the ends of Providence, he believed that Providence did give some sanction to the laws implanted in our natures. Sinners must be punished, but a merciful God must proportion punishments to the weakness of our natures, and Byron therefore inclined toward the Catholic belief in Purgatory, which agreed better with his own appreciation of the goodness and mercy of God.

Lord Byron's preference for Catholicism is well known. His first successes of oratory in the House of Lords were due to the cause of Catholicism in Ireland, which he defended; and when he wished his little daughter Allegra to be brought up in the Catholic faith, he wrote to Mr. Hoppner, British consul at Venice, who had always taken a lively interest in the child, to say that:—

"In the convent of Bagna-Cavallo she will at least have her education advanced, and her morals and religion cared for. . . . . It is, besides, my wish that she should be a Roman Catholic, which I look upon as the best religion, as it is assuredly the oldest of the various branches of Christianity."

This predilection for Catholicism was not the result of the poetry of that religion, or of the effect which its pomps and gorgeous ceremonies produced upon the imagination. They, no doubt, were not indifferent to a mind so easily impressed as his, but not sufficient to justify his preference; for

Byron, although a poet, never allowed his reason to be swayed by his imagination. He reasoned upon every subject. His objections proceeded as much from his mind as his heart. "Catholicism," he was wont say, "is the most ancient of worships; and as for our own heresy, it unquestionably had its origin in vice. With regard to those difficulties which baffle our understanding, are they more easily explained by Protestants than by Catholics?

"Catholicism, at least, is a consoling religion, and its belief in Purgatory conciliates the justice of the Almighty with His goodness. Why has Protestantism given up so human a belief? To intercede for and do good to beings whom we have loved here below, is to be not altogether separated from them."

"I often regretted," he said on one occasion at Pisa, "that I was not born a Catholic. Purgatory is a consoling doctrine. I am surprised that the Reformers gave it up, or that they did not at least substitute for it something equally consoling. It is," he remarked to Shelley, "a refinement of the doctrine of transmigration taught by your stupid philosophers."

It was, therefore, chiefly this doctrine, and his abhorrence of Calvin, which attracted Byron toward Catholicism. A comparison was made before him, on one occasion, between Catholicism and Protestantism. "What matters," said Byron, "that Protestantism has decreased the number of its obligations, and reduced its articles of faith? Both religions proceed from the same origin,—authority and examination. It matters little that the measures of either be different; but why does the Protestant deny to the Catholic the privilege, which he claims more than he uses, of free examination? Catholics also claim the right of proving the soundness of their belief, and, therefore, admit likewise the right of discussion and examination. As for authority, if the Catholic obeys the Church and considers it infallible, does not the Protestant do the same with the Bible? And while recognizing the authority of the Church on the one hand, on the other he claims a right to free examination, does he not incur the liability of being thought inconsistent? And, after all, is not the authority of the Church the better of the two? There seems to greater peace for the mind who confides in it, than in the belief in the authority of a book, where one must ever seek the way to salvation by becoming a theologian, as it were. And is it not fairer to have certain books, such, for instance, as the 'Apocalypse,' explained to us by the Church, than to have them expounded by people more or less well informed or prejudiced?"

Such were Byron's views, if not his very words. Before Byron left for Greece, Kennedy had several other conversations with him; but as the limits of this chapter do not allow of my entering into them, I will merely add that they all prove the great charm of Byron's mind, and the gentleness of his nature in dealing with persons of contrary opinions to his own, but who argued honestly and from conviction. So it came about that, although the most docile of the doctor's pupils, he refused to change his views concerning eternal punishment. During one of the last of Kennedy's visits to him, he found several young men with Lord Byron, and among these M. S——, and M. F——. The former, seated at one corner of the table, was explaining to Count Gamba certain views which were any thing but orthodox. Lord Byron turned to the doctor, and said:—

"Have you heard what S—— said? I assure you, he has not made one step toward conversion; he is worse than I am."

M. F—— having joined in the conversation, and said that there were many contradictions in the Scriptures, Byron replied:—

"This is saying too much: I am a sufficiently good believer not to discover any contradictions in the Scriptures which can not, upon reflection, be explained; what most troubles me is eternal punishment: I am not prepared to believe in so terrible a dogma, and this is my only difference with the doctor's views; but he will not allow that I am an orthodox Christian, unless I agree with him in that matter."

This was said half-seriously, half-jestingly, but in so amiable a manner, and in a tone which was so free from mockery, that even the austere doctor was fain to forgive him for entertaining such erroneous views.

When Byron left for Missolonghi, he carried away with him a real regard for Kennedy, notwithstanding their differences of opinion. Kennedy, on the other hand, had conceived for Byron the greatest liking, and, indeed, shows it in his book. His portrait of Lord Byron is so good, that we have thought it right to reproduce it, together with his general impressions in another chapter.

Byron's death plunged Kennedy into the deepest grief; and it was then that he gathered all his conversations which he had had with Lord Byron into one volume, which he published. But his friends, or so-called friends, showed themselves hostile to the publication. Some feared that he would exaggerate either Lord Byron's faith or want of it, and others, less disinterested, apprehended the revelation of some of their own views, which might fail to meet with the approval of the public at home. When, therefore, Kennedy applied to several of these who were at Missolonghi to know in what religious frame of mind Byron died, he met with rebukes of all kinds, and his credit was attacked by articles in newspapers, endeavoring to show that Byron had all along been laughing at the doctor. All these attacks might have influenced Kennedy's picture of Byron, but it will be seen that, with the exception of a few puritanical touches, the artist's picture is not unworthy of the original.

In the preface to his book, the doctor, not knowing whether he should make use of the conversation he had had with Byron to give a greater interest to his work, the object of which was to be of use to the public, answers his own objections in the following words :—

" If my doing so would injure his character or fame, there could not be a moment's hesitation in deciding on the baseness of the measure. But, as far as I can judge, a true statement of what occurred will place his lordship's character in a fairer light than he has himself done in many of his writings, or than can, perhaps, be done by a friendly biographer. The brightest parts of his life were those which he spent in Cephalonia and Missolonghi, and the fact of his wishing to hear Christianity explained by one, simply because he believed him to be sincere, confessing that he derived no happiness from his unsettled notions on religion, expressing a desire to be convinced, and his carrying with him religious books, and promising to give the subject a more attentive study than he had ever done, will throw a certain lustre over the darker side of his fame, . . . and deprive deists of the right of quoting him as a cool, deliberate rejecter of Christianity."

To these very significant declarations, coming as they do from so conscientious a believer as Kennedy, I shall add the testimony of a few persons who have been conspicuous by their hostility to Byron. Mr. Galt is one of these, and yet he says:—

"I am persuaded, nevertheless, that to class him among absolute infidels were to do injustice to his memory, and that he has suffered uncharitably in the opinion of the 'rigidly righteous,' who, because he had not attached himself to any particular sect or congregation, assumed that he was an adversary to religion. To claim for him any credit as a pious man would be absurd; but, to suppose he had not as deep an interest as other men 'in his soul's health and welfare,' was to impute to him a nature which can not exist."

And elsewhere, after showing, first, what Byron did not believe in; secondly, what he would have liked to believe, but which had not sufficient grounds to satisfy his reason; thirdly, what he did actually believe, Mr. Galt adds:—

"Whatever was the degree of Lord Byron's dubiety as to points of faith and doctrine, he could not be accused of gross ignorance, nor described as animated by any hostile feeling against religion."

The same biographer says elsewhere:—

"That Byron was deeply imbued with the essence of natural piety; that he often felt the power and being of a God thrilling in all his frame, and glowing in his bosom, I declare my thorough persuasion; and that he believed in some of the tenets and in the philosophy of Christianity, as they influence the spirit and conduct of men, I am as little disposed to doubt; especially if those portions of his works which only trench upon the subject, and which bear the impression of fervor and earnestness, may be admitted as evidence. But he was not a member of any particular church."

Medwin, who might be considered to be an authority,

before his vanity was wounded by the publication of writings wherein his good faith was questioned, and it was shown that Lord Byron had no great esteem for his talents, says,—

"It is difficult to judge, from the contradictory nature of his writings, what the religious opinions of Lord Byron were. But on the whole, if he were occasionally skeptical, yet his wavering never amounted to a disbelief in the divine Founder of Christianity. 'I always took great delight,' observed he, 'in the English Cathedral service. It can not fail to inspire every man who feels at all, with devotion. Notwithstanding which, Christianity is not the best source of inspiration for a poet. No poet should be tied down to a direct profession of faith. Metaphysics open a vast field. Nature and heterodoxy present to the poet's imagination fertile sources from which Christianity forbids him to draw; and he exemplified his meaning by a review of the works of Tasso and Milton.

"'Here is a little book somebody has sent me about Christianity," he said to Shelley and me, 'that has made me very uncomfortable. The reasoning seems to me very strong, the proofs are very staggering. I don't think you can answer it, Shelley; at least, I am sure I can't, and, what is more, I don't wish to do so.'"

Speaking of Gibbon, he says,—"L—— B—— thought the question set at rest in the 'History of the Decline and Fall,' but I am not so easily convinced. It is not a matter of volition to unbelieve. Who likes to own that he has been a fool all his life,—to unlearn all that he has been taught in his youth? Or can think that some of the best men that ever lived have been fools?" And again,—

"You believe in Plato's three principles, why not in the Trinity? One is not more mystical than the other. I don't know why I am considered an enemy to religion, and an unbeliever. I disowned the other day that I was of Shelley's school in metaphyics, though I admired his poetry."

"Although," says Lord Harrington, "Byron was no Christian, he was a firm believer in the existence of a God. It is, therefore, equally remote from truth to represent him as either an atheist or a Christian. He was, as he has often told me, a confirmed Deist." Further on, the same writer adds:—

"Byron always maintained that he was a skeptic, but he was not so at all. During a ride at Cephalonia, which lasted two or three hours almost without a pause, he began to talk about 'Cain' and his religious opinions, and he condemned all atheists, and maintained the principles of Deism." Mr. Finlay, who used to see Lord Byron in Greece, says, in a letter to his friend Lord Harrington:—

"Lord Byron liked exceedingly to converse upon religious topics, but I never once heard him openly profess to be a Deist."

These quotations are sufficiently numerous, and all point to the same conclusion, but I must quote the words of Gamba before I conclude this subject. He was, as it is known, the great friend of Byron, and alas! sacrificed his noble self, at the age of twenty-four, to the cause of Greece. To Kennedy's inquiries respecting Lord Byron's religious tendencies at Missolonghi, P. Gamba replied as follows:—

"My belief is that his religious opinions were not fixed. I mean, that he was not more inclined toward one than toward another of the Christian sects; but that his feelings were thoroughly religious, and that he entertained the highest respect for the doctrines of Christ, which he considered to be the source of virtue and of goodness. As for the incomprehensible mysteries of religion, his mind floated in doubts which he wished most earnestly to dispel, as they oppressed him, and that is why he never avoided a conversation on the subject, as you are well aware.

"I have often had an opportunity of observing him at times when the soul involuntarily expresses its most sincere convictions; in the midst of dangers, both at sea and on land; in the quiet contemplation of a calm and beautiful night, in the deepest solitude, etc.; and I remarked that his thoughts always were imbued with a religious sentiment. The first time I ever had a conversation with him on that subject was at Ravenna, my native place, a little more than four years ago. We were riding together in a pine wood, on a beautiful spring day, and all was conducive to religious meditation. 'How,' said he 'raising our eyes to heaven, or directing them to the earth, can we doubt of the existence of God? Or how, turning them inward, can we doubt that there is something within us more noble and more durable than the clay of which we are formed? Those who do not hear, or are unwilling to listen to those feelings, must necessarily be of a vile nature.' I answered him with all those reasons which the superficial philosophy of Helvetius, his disciples and his masters, have taught. He replied with very strong arguments and profound eloquence, and I perceived that obstinate contradiction on this subject, forcing him to reason upon it, gave him pain. This discourse made a deep impression on me.

"Many times, and in various circumstances, I have heard him confirm the same sentiments, and he always seemed to me to be deeply convinced of their truth. Last year, at Genoa, when we were preparing for our journey to Greece, he used to converse with me alone for two or three hours every evening, seated on the terrace of his palace in Albano, in the fine evenings of spring, whence there opened a magnificent view of that superb city and the adjoining sea. Our conversation turned almost always on Greece, for which we were so soon to depart, or on religious subjects. In various ways I heard him confirm the sentiments which I have already mentioned to you. 'Why, then,' said I to him, 'have you earned for yourself the name of impious, and enemy of all religious belief, from your writings?' He answered, 'They are not understood, and are wrongly interpreted by the malevolent. My object is only to combat hypocrisy, which I abhor in every thing, and particularly in religion, and which now unfortunately appears to me to be prevalent, . . . and for this alone do those to whom you allude wish to render me odious, and make me out to be an impious person, and a monster of incredulity.'

"For the Bible he had always a particular respect. It was his custom to have it always on his study table, particularly during these last months; and you well know how familiar it was to him, since he sometimes knew how to correct your inaccurate citations.

"Fletcher may have informed you about his happy state of mind in his last moments. He often repeated subjects from the Testament, and when, in his last moments, he had in vain attempted to make known his wishes with respect to his daughter, and others most dear to him in life, and when, on account of the wanderings of his mind, he could not succeed in making himself understood, Fletcher answered him, 'Nothing is nearer my heart than to execute your wishes; but, unfortunately, I have scarcely been able to comprehend half of them.' 'Is it possible?' he replied. 'Alas! it is too late. How unfortunate! Not my will, but the will of God be done.' There remained to him only a few intervals of reason and interruptions of delirium, the effect of determination of blood to the head.

"He often expressed to me the contempt which he felt for those called *esprits forts* (a set of ignorant egotists, incapable of any generous action, and hypocrites themselves), in their affected contempt of every faith.

"He professed a complete toleration, and a particular respect for every sincere conviction. He would have deemed it an unpardonable crime to detach any one persuaded of the truth from his belief, although it might be tinctured with absurdity, because he believed it could lead to no other end than to render him an infidel."

After so many proofs of Byron's religious tendencies, is it not right to ask, What was that skepticism of which so much has been said that it has been almost received as a fact by the world generally? Did he not believe in the necessity of religion? In a God, Creator of all things? In the spirituality, and therefore immortality, of the soul? In our liberty of action, and our moral responsibility? We have seen what others have said on each of these subjects; let us now see what he said himself upon the subject. But some will object, "Are you going to judge of his views from his poetry? Can one attach much importance to opinions expressed in verse? Do not poets often say that which they do not think, but which genius inspires them to write? Are such dictates to be considered as their own views?" Such objections may be valid, and we shall so far respect them, therefore, as to dismiss Lord Byron's poetry, and treat only of that which he has written in prose: we will not consider him when under the influence of inspiration and of genius, but when given up entirely to the silent examination of his conscience. What did his thorough good sense tell him about religion in general? The following note, in which he repels the stupid and wicked attacks of Southey, who called him a skeptic, will prove it:—

"One mode of worship yields to another, but there never will be a country without a worship of some sort. Some will instance France; but the Parisians alone, and a fanatical faction of them, maintained for a short time the absurd dogma of theophilanthropy. If the English Church is upset, it will be by the hands of its own sectaries, not by those of skeptics. People are too wise, too well informed, to submit to an impious unbelief. There may exist a few speculators without faith; but they are small in numbers, and their opinions, being without enthusiasm or appeal to the passions, can not make proselytes unless they are persecuted, that being the only means of augmenting any sects."

"'I am always,' he writes in his memorandum, 'most religious upon a sunshiny day, as if there were some association, some internal approach to greater light and purity and the kindler of this dark lantern of our existence.

"'The night had also a religious influence, and even more so when I viewed the moon and stars through Herschel's telescope, and saw that they were worlds.'"

And what thought Byron of the existence of God? "Supposing even," he says, "that man existed before God, even his higher pre-Adamite supposititious creation must have had an origin and a creator, for a creation is a more natural imagination than a fortuitous concourse of atoms; all things remount to a fountain, though they may flow to an ocean.

"If, according to some speculations, you could prove the world many thousand years older than the Mosaic chronology, or if you could get rid of Adam and Eve, and the apple, and serpent, still what is to be set up in their stead? or how is the difficulty removed? Things must have had a beginning, and what matters it when or how?"

If Byron did not question the existence of God, did he doubt the spirituality and immortality of the soul? Here are some of his answers:—

"What is poetry?" he asked himself in his memorandum,

and he replied—"The feeling of a former world and future." And further, in the same memorandum:—

"Of the immortality of the soul, it appears to me that there can be little doubt, if we attend to the action of the mind for a moment: it is in perpetual activity. I used to doubt it, but reflection has taught me better. The stoics Epictetus and Aurelius call the present state 'a soul which drags a carcass'—a heavy chain, to be sure, but all chains, being material, may be shaken off. How far our future life will be individual, or, rather, how far it will at all resemble our present existence, is another question; but that the mind is eternal, seems as probable as that the body is not so. Of course, I here venture upon the question without recurring to revelation, which, however, is at least as rational a solution of it as any other. A material resurrection seems strange and even absurd, except for purposes of punishment: and all punishment which is to revenge, rather than correct, must be morally wrong: and when the world is at an end, what moral or warning purpose can eternal tortures answer? Human passions have probably disfigured the Divine doctrines here; but the whole thing is inscrutable."

And again:—

"I have often been inclined to materialism in philosophy; but could never bear its introduction into Christianity, which appears to me essentially founded upon the soul. For this reason, Priestley's 'Christian Materialism' always struck me as deadly. Believe the resurrection of the body, if you will, but not without a soul. The deuce is in it, if after having had a soul (as, surely, the mind, or whatever you call it, is) in this world, we must part with it in the next, even for an immortal materiality; and I own my partiality for spirit."

It has already been seen that, in his early youth, he was intimately convinced of the immortality of his soul, by the fact of the existence of his conscience. But it is equally proved that, as his soul became more perfect, and rose more and more toward all that is great and virtuous, his conviction of the immortality of the soul became still more certain.

The beautiful words which he addressed to Mr. Parry, a few hours before his agony, confirm our assertions:—

"Eternity and space are before me; but on this subject,

thank God, I am happy and at ease. The thought of living eternally, of again reviving, is a great pleasure. Christianity is the purest and most liberal religion in the world; but the numerous teachers who are continually worrying mankind with their denunciations and their doctrines, are the greatest enemies of religion. I have read, with more attention than half of them, the Book of Christianity, and I admire the liberal and truly charitable principles which Christ has laid down. There are questions connected with this subject, which none but Almighty God can solve. Time and space, who can conceive? None but God: on Him I rely."

If he neither questioned the existence of God nor the spirituality and immortality of the soul, did he question our liberty of thought, and hence our moral responsibility?

To put such a question, is to misunderstand Byron completely. Who, more than Byron, ever believed in our right of judgment, and proclaimed that right more strenuously than he has, in prose and in verse? Let any one who has read "Manfred," say whether a poet ever developed such Christian and philosophical views with greater energy and power.

Did Lord Byron really question, in his poems, the infinite goodness of God, as he has been accused of doing? Did his doubts and perplexities of mind, caused by the terrible knowledge of the existence of evil, ever go beyond the limits of the doubts which beset the minds of intellectual men, when the light of faith fails to aid them in their philosophical researches after truth?

When he published his drama, " Cain, a Mystery," he was attacked by enemies in the most violent manner. They selected the arguments put into the mouth of Lucifer, and their influence upon Cain, to prove that this biblical poem was a blasphemous composition, and that its author was consequently deserving of being outlawed, as having attempted to question the supreme wisdom of God. But most certainly Lucifer speaks in the poem as Lucifer should speak, unless, indeed, the Evil Spirit ought to speak as a theologian, and the first assassin as a meek orthodox Christian? Byron gave them each the language logically most suited to their respective characters, as Milton did, without, however, incurring the accusation of impiety. It was argued that Byron ought, at least, to have introduced some one charged with the defense of the right doctrines. But was not the drama entitled a Mystery, and was not the title to be justified, as it were? Could he have done otherwise, even if he had wished it ever so much? What could Adam, or even God's angel, do better than remain silent in presence of the mental agony of Cain, and only advise his bowing to the incomprehensibility of the mystery? Again, if discussion was fruitful of results with Abel, must it be the same with Cain? Was Lord Byron to turn both these personages into theologians, ready to discuss any and every metaphysical question, and to explain the origin and effects of evil? Had they done so, it is not very likely they would have succeeded in persuading Cain of the solidity of their argument, or in dispelling the clouds which obscured his mind, and both calm his despair and satisfy so inquisitive a nature, influenced and mastered, as it was, by evil passions. If Lord Byron thought he could explain the existence of evil, he would not have entitled his poem "a Mystery." But, above all, Lord Byron did not wish to outstep the limits of reason to prove still more how powerless is reason, alone and unaided, in its endeavors to conciliate contradictory attributes. The drama was called a Mystery, and Byron wished it to remain such.

Were some of his biographers right in asserting that he had adopted Cuvier's system? But Cuvier never denied the existence of the Creator, as Moore seems to believe. On the contrary, he endeavored to show, even more forcibly, the admirable work of the Creation, in order to bring out still more in relief the perfection of its Creator.

In the end, however, Byron ceased to think the existence of evil to be so great an injustice to the infinite goodness of God, and expressed in his memorandum the opinion "that history and experience show that good and evil are counterbalanced on earth."

"Were I to begin life again," he said, in the same memorandum, "I don't think I would change any thing in mine." A proof that, without understanding why or wherefore, he felt our life on earth to be but the beginning of one which is to be continued in another sphere, under the rule of Him whose gentle hand can be traced in all things created. For the same reason he was reconciled to the injustice of mankind, believing this life to be a trial, and bearing it with noble courage and fortitude. This mental resignation, however, did not prevent his suffering bitterly in a moral sense. All pleasure became a pain to him at the sight of the sufferings of others. He declared on one occasion, at Cephalonia, that if every body was to be damned, and he alone to be saved, he would prefer being damned with the rest. This excess of generosity may have appeared eccentric, but can scarcely seem too exaggerated to those who knew him. Certain it is, that to witness the sufferings of others with resignation, appeared to him to be egotism, and to evince a coldheartedness, which would have been unpardonable in his eyes. Sometimes even the energy of his writings, dictated, as they were, by his great generosity of heart, appeared as the revolt of a noble nature against the miseries of humanity.

In such a frame of mind was he when he wrote " Cain, at Ravenna, in the midst of people who were for the most part unjustly proscribed, and in the midst of sufferings which he always tried to alleviate.

Did he deserve the appellation of skeptic, because he despised that vain philosophy which believes it can explain all things, even God's nature itself, by the sole force of reason? or because, while respecting the dogmas proclaimed by our reason and our conscience, he preferred to follow the principles of a philosophy that argues with diffidence, and humbly owns its inability to explain all things, and which caused him to exclaim in "Don Juan"—

> "For me, I know naught; nothing I deny,
> Admit, reject, contemn: and what know you,
> Except, perhaps, that you were born to die?"

But to whom were these lines addressed? To those metaphysicians, of course, whom he would also have denominated "men who know nothing, but who, among the truths which they ignore, ignore their own ignorance most,"—to those arrogant minds who wish to fathom even the ways which God has kept back from us, and who, in seeking to know the wherefore of all things in creation, are forced to give the name of explanation to mere comparisons.

Byron says, in "Don Juan,"—

> "Explain me your explanation."

He addressed himself finally, to all hypocrites and intolerant men; Byron has been called a skeptic, notwithstanding.

That a sincere and orthodox Catholic, who holds that the negation of a dogma constitutes skepticism, should have called Byron a skeptic because he questioned the doctrine of eternal punishment, is not to be wondered at; but what is matter of astonishment is, that the reproach was addressed to him by the writer of "Faust," and by the writer of "Elvire," and the "Meditations." Yet it is so; and if this psychological problem is not yet solved, let others do it,—we can not.

To sum up, we may declare, from what we have said, that as regards Lord Byron there has been a confusion of words, and that his skepticism has merely been a natural and inevitable situation in which certain minds who, as it were, are the victims of their own contradictory thoughts, are placed, notwithstanding their wish to believe. Faith, being a part of poetical feeling, could not but form a part likewise of Byron's nature, but there existed also in him a great tendency to weigh the merits of the opinions of others, and consequently the desire not to arrive too hastily at conclusions.

This combination of instinctive faith and a philosophical mind could not produce in him the belief in those things which did not appear to him to have been first submitted to the test of argument, and proved to be just by the convictions resulting from the test of reasoning to which they had been subjected. It produced, on the contrary, a species of expectant doubt, a state of mind awaiting some decisive explanation, to reject error and embrace the truth. His skepticism, therefore, may be said to have been the result of thought, not of passion.

In religion, however, it must be allowed that his skepticism never went so far as to cause him to deny its fundamental doctrines. These he proclaimed from heartfelt convictions, and his modest, humble, and manly skepticism may be said to have been that of great minds, and his failings, also, theirs. Is a day said to be stormy because a few clouds have obscured the rays of the sun?

Is it necessary to say any thing about what he doubted? In showing what he believed, the exception will be found unnecessary. He believed in a Creator, in a spiritual and consequently immortal soul, but which God can reduce to nothing, as He created it out of nothing. He believed in liberty of thought, in our responsibility, our privileges, our duties, and especially in the obligation of practicing the great precept which constitutes Christianity; namely, that of charity and devotion toward our neighbor, even to the sacrifice of our existence for his sake. He believed in every virtue, but his experience forbade his according faith to appearances, and trusting in fine phrases. He often found it wise and prudent to scrutinize the idol he was called upon to worship, but when once that idol had borne the test of scrutiny no worship was so sincere.

"Was he orthodox?" will again be asked. To such a question it may be justly answered, that if he did not entertain for all the doctrines revealed by the Scriptures that faith which he was called upon to possess, it was not for want of desiring so powerful an auxiliary to his reason. He felt that, however strong reason might be, it always retains a little wavering and anxious character; and, though essentially religious at heart, he could not master that blind faith required in matters which baffle the efforts of reason to prove their truth logically and definitively. This is to be accounted for by the conflict of his conscience and his philosophical turn of mind. Conviction, for him, was a difficult thing to attain. Hence for him the difficulty of saying "I believe," and hence the accusation of skepticism to which he became liable. He wanted proofs of a decisive character, and his doubts belonged to that school which made Bacon confess that a philosopher who can doubt, knows more than all the wise men together. Byron would never have contested absolutely the truth of any mystery, but have merely stated that, as long as the testimonies of its truth were hidden in obscurity, such a mystery must be liable to be questioned. He was wont to add, however, that the mysteries of religion did not appear to him less comprehensible than those of science and of reason.

As for miracles, how could he think them absurd and impossible, since he admitted the omnipotence of God? His mind was far too just not to understand that miracles surround us, even from the first origin of our race. He often asked himself, whether the first man could ever have been created a child? "Reason," says a great Christian philosopher, "does not require the aid ot the Book of Genesis to believe in that miracle."

One evening at Pisa, in the drawing-room of the Countess G——, where Byron was wont to spend all his evenings, a great discussion arose respecting a certain miracle which was said to have taken place at Lucca.

The miracle had been accompanied by several rather ludicrous circumstances, and of course laughter was not spared. Shelley, who never lost sight of his philosopher, treated miracles as deplorable superstitions. Lord Byron laughed at the absurdity of the history told, without any malice however. Madame G—— alone did not laugh. "Do you, then, believe in that miracle?" asked Byron. "I do not say I exactly believe in that miracle," she replied; "but I believe in miracles, since I believe in God and in His omnipotence; nor could I believe that God can be deprived of His liberty, when I feel that I have mine. Were I no longer to believe in miracles, it seems to me I should no longer believe in God, and that I should lose my faith."

Lord Byron stopped joking, and said—

"Well, after all, the philosophy of common sense is the truest and the best."

The conversation continued, in the jesting tone in which it had begun, and M. M——, an *esprit fort*, went so far as to condemn the supernatural in the name of the general and permanent laws which govern nature, and to look upon miracles as the legends of a by-gone age, and as errors which affect the ignorant. From what had gone before, he probably fancied that Byron was going to join issue with him. But there was often a wide gulf between the intimate thoughts of Byron and his expressions of them.

"We allow ourselves too often," he said, "to give way to a jocular mood, and to laugh at every thing, probably because God has granted us this faculty to compensate for the difficulty which we find in believing, in the same manner as playthings are given to children. But I really do not see why

God should be obliged to preserve in the universe the same order which He once established. To whom did He promise that He would never change it, either wholly or in part? Who knows whether some day He will not give the moon an oval or a square shape instead of a round one?"

This he said smiling, but added immediately after, in a serious tone:—

"Those who believe in a God, Creator of the universe, can not refuse their belief in the possibility of miracles, for they behold in God the first of all miracles."

Finally, Lord Byron determined himself the limits of what he deemed his necessary belief; and remained throughout life a stanch supporter of those opinions, but he never ceased to evince a tendency to steer clear of intolerance, which according to him only brought one back to total unbelief.

Let us not omit to add that, as he grew older, he saw better the arrogant weakness of those who screen themselves under the cover of science, and recognized more clearly each day the hand of the Creator in the works of nature.

"Did Lord Byron pray?" is another objection which will be made.

We have already seen what he thought of prayer; we have shown that his poems often took the form of a prayer, and we have read with admiration various passages containing some most sublime lines which completely answer those who accused him of want of religion, while they exhibit the expansion of his soul toward God.

We also know with what feelings of respect he approached places devoted to a religious life, and what charms he found in the ceremonies of the Church. All this is proof enough, it would seem; but, in any case, we must add that if his prayers were not those advised by Kennedy, they were at least the prayers of a great soul which soars upward to bow before its Creator. "Outward ceremonies," says Fénélon, "are only tokens of that essential point, the religion of the soul, and Byron's prayer was rather a thanksgiving than a request."—"In the eyes of God," says some one, "a good action is worth more than a prayer."

Such was his mode of communing with God even in his

early youth, but especially in his last moments, which were so sublime. Can one doubt, that at that solemn moment his greatest desire was to be allowed to live? He had still to reap all the fruits of his sacrifices. His harvest was only just beginning to ripen. By dint of heroism, he was at last becoming known. He was young, scarcely thirty-six years of age, handsome, rich. Rank and genius were his. He was beloved by many, notwithstanding a host of jealous rivals; and yet, on the point of losing all these advantages, what was his prayer? Was it egotistical or presumptous? was it to solicit a miracle in his favor? No, his last words were those of noble resignation. "Let Thy holy will, my God, be done, and not mine!" and then absorbed, as it were, in the infinity of God's goodness, and, confiding entirely in God's mercy, he begged that he might be left alone to sleep quietly and peacefully into eternity. On the very day which brought to us the hope of our immortality, he would awake in the bosom of God.

CHAPTER V.

CHILDHOOD AND YOUTH OF LORD BYRON.

ALL Byron's biographers (at least all those who knew him) have borne testimony to his great goodness, but they have not dwelt sufficiently upon this principal feature in his character. Biographers generally wish to produce an effect. But goodness is not a sufficiently noticeable quality to be dilated upon; it would not repay ambition or curiosity. It is a quality mostly attributed to the saints, and a biographer prefers dilating upon the defects of his hero, upon some adventure or scandal—means by which it is easy, with a spark of cleverness, to make a monster of a saint: for, alas! the most rooted convictions are often sacrificed for the sake of amusing a reader who is difficult to please, and of satisfying an editor.

Lord Byron's goodness, however, was so exceptional, and contrasted so strongly with the qualities attributed to him by those who only knew him by repute, that, in making an exception of him, astonishment, at the very least, might have been the result. If we look at him conscientiously in every act of his life, in his letters, and in his poetry, we must sympathize particularly with him. We find that his goodness shines as prominently as does his genius, and we feel that it can bear any test at any epoch of, alas! his too short existence. As, however, I do not purpose here to write his biography, I shall confine myself merely to a few instances, and will give only a few proofs taken from his early life. To no one can the words of Alfieri be better applied than to Byron:—"He is the continuation of the child"—an idea which has been expressed even more elegantly of late by Disraeli, in his "Literary Characters:"—

"As the sun is seen best at its rising and its setting, so men's native dispositions are clearly perceived while they are children, and when they are dying."

LORD BYRON'S CHILDHOOD.

Of those who have written Byron's life, the best disposed among them have not sufficiently noticed his admirable perfection of character when a child, as revealed to us by sundry anecdotes and by his own poems, entitled "Hours of Idleness:"—

"There was in his disposition," says Moore, "as appears from the concurrent testimony of nurses, tutors, and all who were employed about him, a mixture of affectionate sweetness and playfulness, by which it was impossible not to be attached, and which rendered him then, as in his riper years, easily manageable by those who loved and understood him sufficiently to be at once gentle and firm enough for the task. The female attendant whom he had taken the most fancy to was the youngest of two sisters, named Mary Gray, and she had succeeded in gaining an influence over his mind against which he very rarely rebelled."

By an accident which occurred at the time of his birth one of his feet was twisted out of its natural position, and, to restore the limb to shape, expedients were used under the direction of the celebrated Dr. Hunter. Mary Gray, to whom fell the task of putting on the bandages at bed-time, used to sing him to sleep, or tell him Scotch ballads and legends, in which he delighted, or teach him psalms, and thus lighten his pain. Mary Gray was a very pious woman, and she unquestionably inspired Byron with that love of the Scriptures which he preserved to his last day. She only parted from Byron when he was placed at school at Dulwich, in 1800. The child loved her as she loved him. He gave her his watch, and, later, sent her his portrait. Both these treasures were given to Dr. Ewing (an enthusiast of Byron, who had collected the dying words of Mary Gray, which were all for the child she had nursed), by her grateful husband.

The same gratitude was shown by Byron to Mary Gray's sister, who had been his first nursery governess. He wrote to her after he had left Scotland, to ask news of her, and to announce with delight that he could now put on an ordinary shoe—an event, he said, which he had greatly looked forward to, and which he was sure it would give her pleasure to hear.

Before going to school at Aberdeen, Byron had two tutors, Ross and Paterson, both young, intelligent, and amiable ecclesiastics, for whom he always entertained a pleasing and affectionate remembrance.

At seven years of age he went to the Aberdeen Grammar School, and the general impression which he left there, as evinced by the testimony of several of his colleagues who are still living, was, says Moore, "that he was quick, courageous, passionate, to a remarkable degree venturous and fearless, but affectionate and companionable.

"He was most anxious to distinguish himself among his school-fellows by prowess in all sports and exercises, but, though quick when he could be persuaded to attend, he was in general very low in his class, nor seemed ambitious of being promoted higher."

The anecdotes told of him at this time all prove his fine nature, and show the goodness and greatness of soul which characterized him up to his last day.

All the qualities which are to shine in the man will be found already marked in the child. On one occasion he was taken to see a piece at the Edinburgh theatre, in which one of the actors pretends that the moon is the sun. The child, notwithstanding his timidity, was shocked by this insult to his understanding, rose from his seat, and cried out, "I assure you, my dear sir, that it is the moon." Here, again, we can trace that love of truth which in after life made him so courageous in its proclamation at any cost.

When, at Aberdeen, he was, on one occasion, styled Dominus Byron in the school-room, by way of announcing to him his accession to the title, the child began to cry. Can not these tears be explained by the mixture of pleasure and pain which he must have felt at that moment—pleasure at becoming a peer, and distress at not being able to share this pleasure with his comrades? Are they not a prelude of the sacrifice of himself which he afterward made by actually placing himself in the wrong, in order that at the time of his greatest triumph his rivals might not be too jealous of him?

On one occasion, as he was riding with a friend, they arrived at the bridge of Balgounie, on the river Dee, and, remembering suddenly the old ballad which threatens with death the man who passes the bridge first on a pony, Byron stopped his comrade, and requested to be allowed to pass first; because if the ballad said true, and that one of them must die, it was better, said he, that it should be him, rather than his friend, because he had only a mother to mourn his loss, whereas his friend had a father and a mother, and the pain of his death would fall upon two persons instead of upon one. Another illustration of that heroic generosity of character of which Byron's life offers so many instances.

On another occasion he saw a poor woman coming out of a bookseller's shop, distressed and mortified at not having enough to buy herself the Bible she wanted. The child ran after her, brought her back, made her a present of the desired book, and, in doing so, obeyed that same craving of the heart to do good which placed him all his life at the service of others. These instances will suffice at present.

On his accession to the title, as heir to his great uncle, he left Scotland, and was taken to see Newstead Abbey, his future residence. He spent the winter at Nottingham, the most important of the towns round Newstead. His mother, who was blindly fond of him, could not bear to see any physical defect in him, however slight. She confided him to a quack doctor named Lavender, who promised to cure him, while his studies were continued under the direction of a Mr. Rogers. The treatment which he had to undergo being both painful and tedious, furnishes us with the opportunity of admiring his strength of mind. Mr. Rogers, who had conceived a great liking for the child, noticed on one occasion that he was suffering. "Pray do not notice it," said Byron, "you will see that I shall behave in such a way that you will not perceive it." Notwithstanding his own want of skill, Mr. Lavender might, perhaps, have cured the child. But Byron, who had no faith in him, always found fault with every thing he did, and played tricks upon him.

At last his mother agreed with Lord Carlisle, who was his guardian, to take him to London, to be better educated and taken care of. He was sent to Mr. Glennie's school at Dulwich, and his foot was to be attended to by the famous Dr. Baillie. For the first time, then, did Byron leave the home where he had been rather spoiled than neglected.

Dr. Glennie at once took a great fancy to him, made him sleep in his own study, and watched with an equal care the progress of his studies and the cure of his foot. This latter task was no easy one, owing to the restlessness of the child, who would join in all the gymnastic exercises suitable to his age, whereas absolute repose was prescribed for him. Dr. Glennie says, however, that, once back in the study-room, Byron's docility was equal to his vivacity. He had been instructed according to the mode of teaching adopted at Aberdeen, and had to retrace his steps, owing to the difference of teaching prescribed in English schools.

"I found him enter upon his tasks," says Dr. Glennie, "with alacrity and success. He was playful, good-humored, and beloved by his companions. His reading in history and poetry was far beyond the usual standard of his age, and in my study he found, among other works, a set of our poets — from Chaucer to Churchill — which, I am almost tempted to say, he had more than once perused from beginning to end. He showed at this age an intimate acquaintance with the historical parts of the Holy Scriptures, upon which he seemed delighted to converse with me, and reasoned upon the facts contained in the sacred volume with every appearance of belief in the divine truths which they unfold. That the impressions thus imbibed in his boyhood had, notwithstanding the irregularities of his after life, sunk deep into his mind, will appear, I think, to every impartial reader of his works, and I never have been able to divest myself of the persuasion, that he must have found it difficult to violate the better principles early instilled into him."

He remained two years with Dr. Glennie, during which time he does not appear to have made great progress in his studies, owing to the too frequent amusements procured for him by his over-fond mother. But though Mr. and Mrs. Glennie saw the child very seldom after he left them, they always remained much attached to him, and followed his career with much interest, owing to the fine qualities which they had loved and admired in him as a child.

At thirteen years old he went to Harrow, the head master of which school was Dr. Drury, who at once conceived a great fancy for the boy, and remained attached to him all his life. He thus expresses himself with regard to Byron:—

"A degree of shyness hung about him for some time. His manner and temper soon convinced me that he might be led by a silken string, rather than by a cable. On that principle I acted."

To Lord Carlisle's inquiries about Byron, Drury replied:— "He has talents, my lord, which will add lustre to his rank."

After having been his master he remained his friend, and shortly before his death, Byron declared that, of all the masters and friends he ever had, the best was Dr. Drury, for whom he should entertain as much regard as he would have done for his own father.

Now that we have passed in review both his tutors and his servants; that we have seen them all, without exception, beloved by the child as they loved him, we must take a glance at his college life, and see how he came to possess such charms of manner and of character. In the youth will appear those great qualities which began in the child, and will shine in the man. On one occasion he prevented his comrades from setting fire to the school, by appealing to their filial love, and pointing to the names of their parents on the walls which they wished to destroy. He thus saved the school.

"When Lord Byron and Mr. Peel were at Harrow together," says Moore, "a tyrant some few years older, whose name was N——, claimed a right to fag little Peel, which claim Peel resisted. His resistance was vain, and N—— not only subdued him, but determined also to punish the refractory slave by inflicting a bastinado on the inner fleshy side of the boy's right arm. While the stripes were succeeding each other, and poor Peel was writhing under them, Byron saw and felt for the misery of his friend; and, although he knew he was not strong enough to fight N—— with any hope of success, and that it was dangerous even to approach him, he advanced to the scene of action, and, with a flush of rage, tears in his eyes, and a voice trembling between terror and indignation, asked very humbly if N—— would be pleased to tell him how many stripes he meant to inflict? 'Why,' returned the executioner, 'you little rascal, what is that to you?' 'Because, if you please,' said Byron, holding out his arm, 'I would take half.' There is a mixture of simplicity and magnanimity in this little trait which is truly heroic."

At fifteen Byron was still at Harrow. A certain Mr. Peel ordered his fag, Lord Gort, to make him some toast for tea. The little fag did not do it well, and as a punishment had a red-hot iron applied to the palm of his hand. The child cried, and the masters requested that he should name the author of such cruelty. He did not, however, as the expulsion of Peel might have resulted from the avowal.

Byron, highly pleased with this courageous act, went up to Lord Gort and said, "You are a brave fellow, and, if you like it, I shall take you as my fag, and you will not have to suffer any more ill-treatment."

"I became his fag," says Lord Gort, "and was very fortunate in obtaining so good a master, and one who constantly gave me presents as he did.

"When he gave dinners he always recommended his fag to partake of all the delicacies which he had ordered for his guests."

At all times Byron's greatest pleasure was to make people happy, and his conduct to his fags showed the kind heart with which through life he acted toward his subordinates.

His favorite fag at Harrow was the Duke of Dorset. How much he loved him can be seen in the beautiful lines which he addressed to the duke on leaving Harrow, and which reveal his noble heart:—

TO THE DUKE OF DORSET.

Dorset! whose early steps with mine have stray'd,
Exploring every path of Ida's glade;
Whom still affection taught me to defend,
And made me less a tyrant than a friend,
Though the harsh custom of our youthful band
Bade *thee* obey, and gave *me* to command;
Thee, on whose head a few short years will shower
The gift of riches and the pride of power;
E'en now a name illustrious is thine own,
Renown'd in rank, nor far beneath the throne.
Yet, Dorset, let not this seduce thy soul
To shun fair science, or evade control,
Though passive tutors, fearful to dispraise
The titled child, whose future breath may raise,
View ducal errors with indulgent eyes,
And wink at faults they tremble to chastise.

When youthful parasites, who bend the knee
To wealth, their golden idol, not to thee—
And even in simple boyhood's opening dawn
Some slaves are found to flatter and to fawn—
When these declare, "that pomp alone should wait
On one by birth predestined to be great;
That books were only meant for drudging fools,
That gallant spirits scorn the common rules;"
Believe them not;—they point the path to shame,
And seek to blast the honors of thy name.
Turn to the few in Ida's early throng,
Whose souls disdain not to condemn the wrong;
Or if, amid the comrades of thy youth,
None dare to raise the sterner voice of truth,
Ask thine own heart; 'twill bid thee, boy, forbear;
For *well* I know that virtue lingers there.

Yes! I have mark'd thee many a passing day,
But now new scenes invite me far away;
Yes! I have mark'd within that generous mind
A soul, if well matured, to bless mankind.
Ah! though myself by nature haughty, wild,
Whom Indiscretion hail'd her favorite child;
Though every error stamps me for her own,
And dooms my fall, I fain would fall alone;
Though my proud heart no precept now can tame,
I love the virtues which I can not claim.

'Tis not enough, with other sons of power,
To gleam the lambent meteor of an hour;
To swell some peerage page in feeble pride,
With long-drawn names that grace no page beside;
Then share with titled crowds the common lot—
In life just gazed at, in the grave forgot;
While naught divides thee from the vulgar dead,
Except the dull cold stone that hides thy head,
The mouldering 'scutcheon, or the herald's roll,
That well-emblazon'd but neglected scroll,
Where lords, unhonor'd, in the tomb may find
One spot, to leave a worthless name behind.
There sleep, unnoticed as the gloomy vaults
That veil their dust, their follies, and their faults,
A race, with old armorial lists o'erspread,
In records destined never to be read.
Fain would I view thee, with prophetic eyes,
Exalted more among the good and wise,
A glorious and a long career pursue,
As first in rank, the first in talent too:
Spurn every vice, each little meanness shun;
Not Fortune's minion, but her noblest son.

Turn to the annals of a former day;
Bright are the deeds thine earlier sires display.
One, though a courtier, lived a man of worth,
And call'd, proud boast! the British drama forth.

Another view, not less renown'd for wit;
Alike for courts, and camps, or senates fit;
Bold in the field, and favor'd by the Nine;
In every splendid part ordain'd to shine;
Far, far distinguish'd from the glittering throng,
The pride of princes, and the boast of song.
Such were thy fathers, thus preserve their name;
Not heir to titles only, but to fame.
The hour draws nigh, a few brief days will close,
To me, this little scene of joys and woes;
Each knell of Time now warns me to resign
Shades where Hope, Peace, and Friendship all were mine:
Hope, that could vary like the rainbow's hue,
And gild their pinions as the moments flew;
Peace, that reflection never frown'd away,
By dreams of ill to cloud some future day;
Friendship, whose truth let childhood only tell;
Alas! they love not long, who love so well.
To these adieu! nor let me linger o'er
Scenes hail'd, as exiles hail their native shore,
Receding slowly through the dark-blue deep,
Beheld by eyes that mourn, yet can not weep.
Dorset, farewell! I will not ask one part
Of sad remembrance in so young a heart;
The coming morrow from thy youthful mind
Will sweep my name, nor leave a trace behind.
And yet, perhaps, in some maturer year,
Since chance has thrown us in the self-same sphere,
Since the same Senate, nay, the same debate,
May one day claim our suffrage for the State,
We hence may meet, and pass each other by,
With faint regard, or cold and distant eye.

For me, in future, neither friend nor foe,
A stranger to thyself, thy weal or woe,
With thee no more again I hope to trace
The recollection of our early race;
No more, as once, in social hours rejoice,
Or hear, unless in crowds, thy well-known voice:
Still, if the wishes of a heart untaught
To veil those feelings which perchance it ought,
If these—but let me cease the lengthen'd strain,—
Oh! if these wishes are not breathed in vain,
The guardian seraph who directs thy fate
Will leave thee glorious, as he found thee great.

It was especially at Harrow that Byron contracted those friendships which were like cravings of his heart, and which, although partaking of a passionate character, had nevertheless none of the instability which is the characteristic of passion.

The death of some of his friends, and the coldness of others, caused him the greatest grief, and broke up the illusions of youth, exchanging them for that misanthropy discernible in some of his poems, though contrary to his real character.

For those, on the other hand, who were spared, and remained faithful to him, Byron preserved through life the warmest affection and the tenderest regard; the principal feature of his nature being the unchanging character of his sentiments.

Although he showed at an early age his disposition to a poetical turn of mind, by the force of his feelings and by his meditative wanderings—in Scotland among the mountains and on the sea-shore at Cheltenham;—by his rapturous admiration of the setting sun, as well as by the delight which he took in the legends told him by his nurses, and the emotions which he experienced to a degree which made him lose all appetite, all rest, and all peace of mind; yet no one would have believed at that time that a gigantic poetical genius lay dormant in so active a nature. Soon, however, did his soul light up his intelligence, and obliged him to have recourse to his pen to pour out his feelings. From that moment his genius spread its roots in his heart, and Harrow became his paradise owing to the affection which he met with there.

It was at Harrow that he wrote, between his fourteenth and eighteenth year, the "Hours of Idleness, by a Minor," of which he had printed at the request of his friends, a few copies for private circulation only. These modest poems did not, however, escape the brutal attacks of critics. Mackenzie, however, a man of talent himself, soon discovered that at the bottom of these poems there lay the roots of a great poetical genius. The "Hours of Idleness" are a treasure of intellectual and psychological gleanings. They showed man as God created him, and before his noble soul, depressed by the insolence of his enemies and the troubles of life, endeavored to escape the eyes of the world, or at least of those who could not or would not understand him.

The noblest instincts of human nature shine so conspicuously in the pages of this little volume, that we thank God that he created such a noble mind, while we feel indignant toward those who could not appreciate it. But to understand him better he must reveal himself, and we shall therefore quote a few of his own sayings as a boy. His first grief brought forth his first poem. A young cousin of his died, and of her death he spoke to this effect in his memorandum:—

"My first recourse to poetry was due to my passion for my cousin Margaret Parker. She was, without doubt, one of the most beautiful and ethereal beings I ever knew. I have forgotten the lines, but never shall I forget her. I was twelve years of age, and she was older than myself by nearly a year. I loved her so passionately, that I could neither sleep, nor get rest, or eat when thinking of her. She died of consumption, and it was at Harrow that I heard both of her illness and of her death."

Then it was that Byron wrote his first elegy, which he characterizes as "very dull;" but it is interesting as his first poetical essay, and as the first cry of pain uttered by a child who vents his grief in verse, and reveals in it the goodness of his heart and the power of his great mind. On a calm and dark night he goes to her tomb and strews it with flowers; then, speaking of her virtues, exclaims:—

"But wherefore weep? Her matchless spirit soars
Beyond where splendid shines the orb of day;
And weeping angels lead her to those bowers
Where endless pleasures virtue's deeds repay.

"And shall presumptuous mortals Heaven arraign,
And, madly, godlike Providence accuse?
Ah, no! far fly from me attempts so vain;—
I'll ne'er submission to my God refuse.

"Yet is remembrance of those virtues dear,
Yet fresh the memory of that beauteous face,
Still they call forth my warm affection's tear,
Still in my heart retain their wonted place." 1802.

So beautiful a mind, and one so little understood, reveals itself more and more in each poem of this first collection; and on this account, rather than because of its poetical merits, are the "Hours of Idleness" interesting to the psychological biographer of Byron. "Whoever," says Sainte-Beuve, "has not watched a youthful talent at its outset, will never form for himself a perfect and really true appreciation of it."

Moore adds: "It is but justice to remark that the early verses of Lord Byron give but little promise of those dazzling miracles of poesy with which he afterward astonished and enchanted the world, however distinguished they are by tenderness and grace.

"There is, indeed, one point of view in which these productions are deeply and intrinsically interesting; as faithful reflections of his character at that period of life, they enable us to judge of what he was before any influences were brought to bear upon him, and so in them we find him pictured exactly such as each anecdote of his boyish days exhibits him—proud, daring, and passionate—resentful of slight or injustice, but still more so in the cause of others than in his own; and yet, with all this vehemence, docile and placable at the least touch of a hand authorized by love to guide him. The affectionateness, indeed, of his disposition, traceable as it is through every page of this volume, is yet but faintly done justice to even by himself; his whole youth being from earliest childhood a series of the most passionate attachments, of those overflowings of the soul, both in friendship and love, which are still more rarely responded to than felt, and which, when checked or sent back upon the heart, are sure to turn into bitterness."

While his soul expanded with the first rays of love which dawned upon it, friendship too began to assert its influence over him. But in continuing to observe in him the effects of incipient love, let us remark that, while such precocious impressions are only with others the natural development of physical instincts, they were, in Byron, also, the expression of a soul that expands, of an amiability, of a tenderness ever on the increase. Though sensible to physical beauty as he always was through life, his principal attraction, however, was in that beauty which expresses the beauty of the soul, without which condition no physical perfection commanded his attention. We have seen what an ethereal creature Miss Margaret Parker was. Miss Chaworth succeeded her in Byron's affections, and was his second, if not third love if we notice his youthful passion at nine years of age for Mary Duff. But his third love was the occasion of great pain to him. Miss Chaworth was heiress to the grounds and property of Annesley, which were in the immediate neighborhood of Newstead. Notwithstanding, however, the enmity which had existed between the two families for a long time, on account of a duel which had resulted in the death of Miss Chaworth's grandfather, Byron was received most cordially at Annesley. Mrs. Chaworth thought that a marriage between her daughter and Byron might perhaps some day efface the memory of the feud that had existed between their respective families. Byron therefore found his school-boy advances encouraged by both mother and daughter, and his imagination naturally was kindled. The result was that Byron fell desperately in love with Miss Chaworth; but he was only fifteen years old, and yet an awkward schoolboy, with none of that splendid and attractive beauty for which he was afterward distinguished. Miss Chaworth was three years older, and unfortunately her heart was already engaged to the man who, to her misfortune, she married the year after. She therefore looked upon Byron as a mere child, as a younger brother, and his love almost amused her. She, however, not only gave him a ring, her portrait, and some of her hair, but actually carried on a secret correspondence with him. These were the faults for which she afterward had to suffer so bitterly. Such a union, however, with so great a difference of age, would not have been natural. It could only be a dream; but I shall speak elsewhere* of the nature of this attachment, which had its effect upon Byron, in order to show the beauty of his soul under another aspect. I can only add here that he had attributed every virtue to this girl whom he afterward styled frivolous and deceitful.

On his return to Harrow this love and his passionate friendships divided his heart. But when the following vacation came, his dream vanished. Miss Chaworth was engaged to another, and on his return to Harrow he vainly tried to forget her who had deceived and wounded him. Like other young men, he devoted his time during the Harrow or Cambridge vacations to paying his respects and offering his regards to numerous belles, whose names appear variously in his poems as Emma, Caroline, Helen, and Mary. Moore believes them to have been imaginary loves. A slight acquaintance with the liberty enjoyed by young men at English universities would lead one to believe these loves to have been

* See chapter upon Generosity.

any thing but unreal. This can be the more readily believed, as Byron always sought in reality the objects which he afterward idealized. He always required some earthly support, though the slightest, as Moore observes, in speaking of the charming lines with which his love for Miss Chaworth inspired him, at the time when the recollection of it made him compare his misfortune in marrying Miss Milbank, with the happier lot which might have been his had he married Miss Chaworth. Whether these loves were real or not, however, it must be borne in mind that Byron deemed all physical beauty to be nothing if unaccompanied by moral beauty. Thus, in speaking of a vain young girl, he exclaims:—

"One who is thus from nature vain,
I pity, but I can not love."

And to Miss N. N——, who was exquisitely beautiful, but in whose eyes earthly passion shone too powerfully, he says:—

"Oh, did those eyes, instead of fire,
With bright but mild affection shine,
Though they might kindle less desire,
Love, more than mortal, would be thine.
For thou art form'd so heavenly fair,
Howe'er those orbs may wildly beam,
We must admire, but still despair;
That fatal glance forbids esteem."

In a letter to Miss Pigot, which he wrote from Cambridge, he says:—

"Saw a girl at St. Mary's the image of Ann ——; thought it was her—all in the wrong—the lady stared, so did I—I blushed, so did *not* the lady—sad thing—wish women had more modesty."

On awaking from his dream, and on finding that the jewels with which he had believed Mary's nature to be adorned were of his own creation, he sought his consolation in friendship. His heart, which was essentially a loving one, could not be consoled except by love, and Harrow, to use his own expressions, became a paradise to him. In tracing the picture of Tasso's infancy he has drawn a picture of himself:—

"From my very birth
My soul was drunk with love, which did pervade
And mingle with whate'er I saw on earth:
Of objects all inanimate I made
Idols, and out of wild and lonely flowers,

And rocks, whereby they grew, a paradise
Where I did lay me down within the shade
Of waving trees, and dreamed uncounted hours,
Though I was chid for wandering. . . . ."

This sentiment of friendship, which is always more powerful in England than on the Continent, owing to the system of education which takes children away from their parents at an early age, was keenly developed in Byron, whose affectionate disposition wanted something to make up for the privation of a father's and a brother's love. In his pure and passionate heart friendship and love became mixed: his love partook of the purity of friendship, and his friendships of all the ardor of love.

But to return to his fourteenth year. While expressing in verse his love for his cousin, he expressed at the same time in poetry the strong friendship he had conceived, even before going to Harrow, for a boy who had been his companion.

This boy, who had a most amiable, good, and virtuous disposition, was the son of one of his tenants at Newstead. Aristocratic prejudices ran high in England, and this friendship of Byron for a commoner was sure to call forth the raillery of some of his companions. Notwithstanding this, Byron, at twelve years and a half old, replied in these terms to the mockery of others:—

To E——.

Let Folly smile to view the names
  Of thee and me in friendship twined;
Yet Virtue will have greater claims
  To love, than rank with vice combined.

And though unequal is thy fate,
  Since title deck'd my higher birth!
Yet envy not this gaudy state;
  Thine is the pride of modest worth.

Our souls at least congenial meet,
  Nor can thy lot my rank disgrace;
Our intercourse is not less sweet,
  Since worth of rank supplies the place.

What noble views in a child of twelve! How well one feels that, whatever may be his fate, such a nature will never lose its independence, nor allow prejudice to carry it beyond the limits of honor and of justice, and that its device will always be, "*Fais ce que dois, advienne que pourra.*" "I do what I ought, come what may."

At thirteen he wrote some lines in which he seemed to have a kind of presentiment of the glory that awaited him, and, at any rate, in which he displayed his resolve to deserve it:—

A FRAGMENT.

When to their airy hall, my fathers' voice
Shall call my spirit, joyful in their choice;
When, poised upon the gale, my form shall ride,
Or, dark in mist, descend the mountain's side;
Oh! may my shade behold no sculptured urns
To mark the spot where earth to earth returns!
No lengthen'd scroll, no praise-encumber'd stone;
My epitaph shall be my name alone:
If *that* with honor fail to crown my clay,
Oh! may no other fame my deeds repay!
That, only *that*, shall single out the spot;
By that remember'd, or with that forgot.

Again, at thirteen, a visit to Newstead inspired him with the following beautiful lines:—

ON LEAVING NEWSTEAD ABBEY.

"Why dost thou build the hall, son of the winged days? Thou lookest from thy tower to-day; yet a few years, and the blast of the desert comes, it howls in thy empty court." —OSSIAN.

Through thy battlements, Newstead, the hollow winds whistle;
Thou, the hall of my fathers, art gone to decay:
In thy once smiling garden, the hemlock and thistle
Have choked up the rose which late bloom'd in the way.

Of the mail-cover'd Barons, who proudly to battle
Led their vassals from Europe to Palestine's plain,
The escutcheon and shield, which with every blast rattle,
Are the only sad vestiges now that remain.

No more doth old Robert, with harp-stringing numbers,
Raise a flame in the breast foı the war-laurell'd wreath
Near Askalon's towers John of Horistan slumbers,
Unnerved is the hand of his minstrel by death.

Paul and Hubert, too, sleep in the valley of Cressy;
For the safety of Edward and England they fell:
My fathers! the tears of your country redress ye;
How you fought, how you died, still her annals can tell.

On Marston, with Rupert, 'gainst traitors contending,*
Four brothers enrich'd with their blood the bleak field;
For the rights of a monarch their country defending,
Till death their attachment to royalty seal'd.

* Marston Moor, where the adherents of Charles I. were defeated. Prince Rupert, son of the Elector Palatine, and nephew to Charles I. He afterward commanded the fleet in the reign of Charles II.

Shades of heroes, farewell! your descendant departing
 From the seat of his ancestors, bids you adieu!
Abroad, or at home, your remembrance imparting
 New courage, he'll think upon glory and you.

Though a tear dim his eye at this sad separation,
 'Tis nature, not fear, that excites his regret;
Far distant he goes, with the same emulation,
 The fame of his fathers he ne'er can forget.

That fame and that memory still will he cherish;
 He vows that he ne'er will disgrace your renown:
Like you will he live, or like you will he perish:
 When decay'd, may he mingle his dust with your own!

When only fourteen his tenant friend dies, and Byron wrote his epitaph, in which, even at that early age (thirteen and a half), he particularly mentions his friend's virtues:—

EPITAPH ON A FRIEND.

"'Ἀστὴρ πρὶν μὲν ἔλαμπες ἐνὶ ζωοῖσιν ἑῷος."—LAERTIUS.

Oh, Friend! forever loved, forever dear!
What fruitless tears have bathed thy honor'd bier!
What sighs re-echo'd to thy parting breath,
While thou wast struggling in the pangs of death!
Could tears retard the tyrant in his course;
Could sighs avert his dart's relentless force;
Could youth and virtue claim a short delay,
Or beauty charm the spectre from his prey;
Thou still hadst lived to bless my aching sight,
Thy comrade's honor and thy friend's delight.
If yet thy gentle spirit hover nigh
The spot where now thy mouldering ashes lie,
Here wilt thou read, recorded on my heart,
A grief too deep to trust the sculptor's art.
No marble marks thy couch of lowly sleep,
But living statues there are seen to weep;
Affliction's semblance bends not o'er thy tomb,
Affliction's self deplores thy youthful doom.
What though thy sire lament his failing line,
A father's sorrows can not equal mine!
Though none, like thee, his dying hour will cheer,
Yet other offspring soothe his anguish here:
But who with me shall hold thy former place?
Thine image, what new friendship can efface?
Ah, none!—a father's tears will cease to flow,
Time will assuage an infant brother's woe;
To all, save one, is consolation known,
While solitary friendship sighs alone.

Other friends succeeded his earliest one and consoled him for his loss. At Harrow, those he loved best were Wingfield, Tattersall, Clare, Delaware, and Long.

His great heart sought to express in verse what it felt for each of them. But it is observable that what touched him most was the excellence of the qualities both of the mind and soul of those he loved. To prove this I shall quote in part a poem which he wrote shortly after leaving Harrow for Cambridge, entitled "Childish Recollections." After giving a picture of his life at Harrow in the midst of his companions, and after describing very freshly and vividly the scene when he was chosen Captain of the School, he exclaims:—

"Dear honest race! though now we meet no more,
One last long look on what we were before—
Our first kind greetings, and our last adieu—
Drew tears from eyes unused to weep with you.
Through splendid circles, fashion's gaudy world,
Where folly's glaring standard waves unfurl'd,
I plunged to drown in noise my fond regret,
And all I sought or hoped was to forget.
Vain wish! if chance some well-remember'd face,
Some old companion of my early race,
Advanced to claim his friend with honest joy,
My eyes, my heart, proclaim'd me still a boy;
The glittering scene, the fluttering groups around,
Were quite forgotten when my friend was found;
The smiles of beauty—(for, alas! I've known
What 'tis to bend before Love's mighty throne)—
The smiles of beauty, though those smiles were dear,
Could hardly charm me, when that friend was near;
My thoughts bewilder'd in the fond surprise,
The woods of Ida danced before my eyes;
I saw the sprightly wand'rers pour along,
I saw and join'd again the joyous throng;
Panting, again I traced her lofty grove,
And friendship's feelings triumph'd over love."

After deploring his fate:—

"Stern Death forbade my orphan youth to share
The tender guidance of a father's care.
* * * * * *
"What brother springs a brother's love to seek?
What sister's gentle kiss has prest my cheek?
* * * * * *
"Thus must I cling to some endearing hand,
And none more dear than Ida's social band:"—

he goes on to name his dearest comrades, giving them each a fictitious name. Alonzo is Wingfield; Davus, Tattersall; Lycus, Lord Clare: Euryalus, Lord Delaware; and Cleon, Long:—

"Alonzo! best and dearest of my friends,
Thy name ennobles him who thus commends:
From this fond tribute thou canst gain no praise:
The praise is his who now that tribute pays.
Oh! in the promise of thy early youth,
If hope anticipate the words of truth,
Some loftier bard shall sing thy glorious name,
To build his own upon thy deathless fame.
Friend of my heart, and foremost of the list
Of those with whom I lived supremely blest,
Oft have we drain'd the font of ancient lore;
Though drinking deeply, thirsting still the more.
Yet, when confinement's lingering hour was done,
Our sports, our studies, and our souls were one:
Together we impell'd the flying ball;
Together waited in our tutor's hall;
Together join'd in cricket's manly toil,
Or shared the produce of the river's spoil;
Or, plunging from the green declining shore,
Our pliant limbs the buoyant billows bore;
In every element, unchanged, the same,
All, all that brother's should be, but the name.

Nor yet are you forgot, my jocund boy!
Davus, the harbinger of childish joy;
Forever foremost in the ranks of fun,
The laughing herald of the harmless pun;
Yet with a breast of such materials made—
Anxious to please, of pleasing half afraid;
Candid and liberal, with a heart of steel
In danger's path, though not untaught to feel.
Still I remember, in the factious strife,
The rustic's musket aim'd against my life:
High poised in air the massy weapon hung,
A cry of horror burst from every tongue;
While I, in combat with another foe,
Fought on, unconscious of th' impending blow;
Your arm, brave boy, arrested his career—
Forward you sprung, insensible to fear;
Disarm'd and baffled by your conquering hand,
The grovelling savage roll'd upon the sand:
An act like this, can simple thanks repay?
Or all the labors of a grateful lay?
Oh no! whene'er my breast forgets the deed,
That instant, Davus, it deserves to bleed.

"Lycus! on me thy claims are justly great:
Thy milder virtues could my muse relate,
To thee alone, unrivall'd, would belong
The feeble efforts of my lengthen'd song.
Well canst thou boast, to lead in senates fit,
A Spartan firmness with Athenian wit:
Though yet in embryo these perfections shine,
Lycus! thy father's fame will soon be thine.
Where learning nurtures the superior mind,
What may we hope from genius thus refin'd!

When time at length matures thy growing years,
How wilt thou tower above thy fellow-peers!
Prudence and sense, a spirit bold and free,
With honor's soul, united, beam in thee.

"Shall fair Euryalus pass by unsung?
From ancient lineage, not unworthy sprung:
What though one sad dissension bade us part?
That name is yet embalm'd within my heart;
Yet at the mention does that heart rebound,
And palpitate, responsive to the sound.
Envy dissolved our ties, and not our will:
We once were friends,—I'll think we are so still,
A form unmatch'd in nature's partial mould,
A heart untainted, we in thee behold:
Yet not the senate's thunder thou shalt wield,
Nor seek for glory in the tented field;
To minds of ruder texture these be given—
Thy soul shall nearer soar its native heaven.
Haply, in polish'd courts might be thy seat,
But that thy tongue could never forge deceit:
The courtier's supple bow and sneering smile,
The flow of compliment, the slippery wile,
Would make that breast with indignation burn,
And all the glittering snares to tempt thee spurn.
Domestic happiness will stamp thy fate;
Sacred to love, unclouded e'er by hate;
The world admire thee, and thy friends adore;
Ambition's slave alone would toil for more.

"Now last, but nearest, of the social band,
See honest, open, generous Cleon stand;
With scarce one speck to cloud the pleasing scene,
No vice degrades that purest soul serene.
On the same day our studious race begun,
On the same day our studious race was run;
Thus side by side we pass'd our first career,
Thus side by side we strove for many a year;
At last concluded our scholastic life,
We neither conquer'd in the classic strife:
As speakers, each supports an equal name,*
And crowds allow to both a partial fame:
To soothe a youthful rival's early pride,
Though Cleon's candor would the palm divide,
Yet candor's self compels me now to own
Justice awards it to my friend alone.

"Oh! friends regretted, scenes forever dear,
Remembrance hails you with her warmest tear!
Drooping, she bends o'er pensive Fancy's urn,
To trace the hours which never can return;
Yet with the retrospection loves to dwell,
And soothe the sorrows of her last farewell!

* This alludes to the public speeches delivered at the school where the author was educated.

Yet greets the triumph of my boyish mind,
As infant laurels round my head were twined,
When Probus' praise repaid my lyric song,
Or placed me higher in the studious throng;
Or when my first harangue received applause,
His sage instruction the primeval cause,
What gratitude to him my soul possest,
While hope of dawning honors fill'd my breast!
For all my humble fame, to him alone
The praise is due, who made that fame my own.
Oh! could I soar above these feeble lays,
These young effusions of my early days,
To him my muse her noblest strain would give:
The song might perish, but the theme might live.
Yet why for him the needless verse essay?
His honored name requires no vain display:
By every son of grateful Ida blest,
It finds an echo in each youthful breast;
A fame beyond the glories of the proud,
Or all the plaudits of the venal crowd.

"Ida! not yet exhausted is the theme,
Nor closed the progress of my youthful dream.
How many a friend deserves the grateful strain!
What scenes of childhood still unsung remain!
Yet let me hush this echo of the past,
This parting song, the dearest and the last;
And brood in secret o'er those hours of joy,
To me a silent and a sweet employ,
While, future hope and fear alike unknown,
I think with pleasure on the past alone;
Yes, to the past alone my heart confine,
And chase the phantom of what once was mine.

"Ida! still o'er thy hills in joy preside,
And proudly steer through time's eventful tide;
Still may thy blooming sons thy name revere,
Smile in thy bower, but quit thee with a tear,—
That tear, perhaps, the fondest which will flow
O'er their last scene of happiness below.
Tell me, ye hoary few, who glide along,
The feeble veterans of some former throng,
Whose friends, like autumn leaves by tempests whirl'd,
Are swept forever from this busy world;
Revolve the fleeting moments of your youth,
While Care as yet withheld her venom'd tooth;
Say if remembrance days like these endears
Beyond the rapture of succeeding years?
Say, can ambition's fever'd dream bestow
So sweet a balm to soothe your hours of woe?
Can treasures, hoarded for some thankless son,
Can royal smiles, or wreaths by slaughter won,
Can stars or ermine, man's maturer toys
(For glittering bawbles are not left to boys),
Recall one scene so much beloved to view
As those where Youth her garland twined for you?

Ah, no! amid the gloomy calm of age
You turn with faltering hand life's varied page;
Peruse the record of your days on earth,
Unsullied only where it marks your birth;
Still lingering pause above each checker'd leaf,
And blot with tears the sable lines of grief;
When Passion o'er the theme her mantle threw,
Or weeping Virtue sigh'd a faint adieu;
But bless the scroll which fairer words adorn,
Traced by the rosy finger of the morn;
When Friendship bow'd before the shrine of Truth,
And Love, without his pinion, smiled on youth."

On leaving Harrow and his best friends, Byron felt that he was saying adieu to youth and to its pleasures, and he was as yet unable to replace these by the feasts of the mind. This filled his heart with regret in addition to the sorrows which he experienced by those reflections upon existence which are common to all poetical natures. The cold discipline of Cambridge fell like ice upon his warm nature. He fell ill, and, by way of seeking a relief to the oppression of his mind, he wrote the above transcribed poem.

Harrow is called Ida, as his friends are denominated by fictitious names. To the college itself, and to the recollections which it brought back to his memory of physical and mental suffering, he addresses himself:—

"Ida! blest spot, where Science holds her reign,
How joyous once I join'd thy youthful train!
Bright in idea gleams thy lofty spire,
Again I mingle with thy playful quire.
* * * * * *
My wonted haunts, my scenes of joy and woe,
Each early boyish friend, or youthful foe;
Our feuds dissolved, but not my friendship past,
I bless the former, and forgive the last."

The same kind, affectionate disposition can be traced in all his other poems, together with those well-inculcated notions of God's justice, wisdom, and mercy, of toleration and forgiveness, of hatred of falsehood and contempt of prejudices, which never abandoned him throughout his life.

I really pity those who could read "The Tear" without being touched by its simple, plaintive style, written in the tenderest strain, or "L'Amitié est l'Amour sans Ailes," or the lines to the Duke of Dorset on leaving Harrow, or the "Prayer of Nature," or his stanzas to Lord Clare, to Lord

Delaware, to Edward Long, or his generous forgiveness of Miss Chaworth; or, again, his lines on believing that he was going to die, his answer to a poem called "The Common Lot," his reply to Dr. Beecher, and, finally, his address to a companion whose conduct obliged him to withdraw his friendship:—

"What friend for thee, howe'er inclined,
Will deign to own a kindred care?
Who will debase his manly mind,
For friendship every fool may share?

"In time forbear; amid the throng
No more so base a thing be seen;
No more so idly pass along;
Be something, any thing, but—mean."

Since our object is to show in these effusions of a youthful mind, its natural beauty, and not that genius which is shortly to be developed by contact with the troubles and pains of this life, it may not be irrelevant to our subject to give in parts, if not entirely, some of the poems which he wrote at this time:—

THE TEAR.

"O lachrymarum fons, tenero sacros
Ducentium ortus ex animo; quater
Felix! in imo qui scatentem
Pectore te, pia Nympha, sensit."—GRAY.

When Friendship or Love our sympathies move,
When truth in a glance should appear,
The lips may beguile with a dimple or smile,
But the test of affection's a Tear.

Too oft is a smile but the hypocrite's wile,
To mask detestation or fear;
Give me the soft sigh, while the soul-telling eye
Is dimm'd for a time with a Tear.

Mild Charity's glow, to us mortals below,
Shows the soul from barbarity clear;
Compassion will melt where this virtue is felt,
And its dew is diffused in a Tear.

The man doom'd to sail with the blast of the gale,
Through billows Atlantic to steer,
As he bends o'er the wave which may soon be his grave,
The green sparkles bright with a Tear.

The soldier braves death for a fanciful wreath
In glory's romantic career;
But he raises the foe when in battle laid low,
And bathes every wound with a Tear.

If with high-bounding pride he return to his bride,
  Renouncing the gore-crimson'd spear,
All his toils are repaid, when, embracing the maid,
  From her eyelid he kisses the Tear.

Sweet scene of my youth! seat of Friendship and Truth,*
  Where love chased each fast-fleeting year,
Loth to leave thee, I mourn'd, for a last look I turn'd,
  But thy spire was scarce seen through a Tear.

Though my vows I can pour to my Mary no more,
  My Mary to love once so dear,
In the shade of her bower I remember the hour
  She rewarded those vows with a Tear.

By another possest, she may live ever blest!
  Her name still my heart must revere:
With a sigh I resign what I once thought was mine,
  And forgive her deceit with a Tear.

Ye friends of my heart, ere from you I depart,
  This hope to my breast is most near:
If again we shall meet in this rural retreat,
  May we meet as we part, with a Tear.

When my soul wings her flight to the regions of night,
  And my corse shall recline on its bier,
As ye pass by the tomb where my ashes consume,
  Oh! moisten their dust with a Tear.

May no marble bestow the splendor of woe,
  Which the children of vanity rear;
No fiction of fame shall blazon my name,
  All I ask—all I wish—is a Tear.

L'AMITIÉ EST L'AMOUR SANS AILES.

Why should my anxious breast repine,
  Because my youth is fled?
Days of delight may still be mine;
  Affection is not dead.
In tracing back the years of youth,
One firm record, one lasting truth,
  Celestial consolation brings;
Bear it, ye breezes, to the seat,
Where first my heart responsive beat,
  "Friendship is Love without his wings!"

Through few, but deeply checker'd years,
  What moments have been mine!
Now half-obscured by clouds of tears,
  Now bright in rays divine;

---

* Harrow.

Howe'er my future doom be cast,
My soul enraptured with the past,
  To one idea fondly clings;
Friendship! that thought is all thine own,
Worth worlds of bliss, that thought alone—
  "Friendship is Love without his wings!"

Where yonder yew-trees lightly wave
  Their branches on the gale,
Unheeded heaves a simple grave,
  Which tells the common tale;
Round this unconscious schoolboys stray,
Till the dull knell of childish play
  From yonder studious mansion rings;
But here when'er my footsteps move,
My silent tears too plainly prove
  "Friendship is Love without his wings!"

Oh, Love! before thy glowing shrine
  My early vows were paid;
My hopes, my dreams, my heart was thine,
  But these are now decay'd;
For thine are pinions like the wind,
No trace of thee remains behind,
  Except, alas! thy jealous stings.
Away, away! delusive power,
Thou shalt not haunt my coming hour;
  Unless, indeed, without thy wings.

Seat of my youth! thy distant spire
  Recalls each scene of joy;
My bosom glows with former fire,
  In mind again a boy.
Thy grove of elms, thy verdant hill
Thy every path delights me still,
  Each flower a double fragrance flings;
Again, as once, in converse gay,
Each dear associate seems to say,
  "Friendship is Love without his wings!"

My Lycus! wherefore dost thou weep?
  Thy falling tears restrain;
Affection for a time may sleep,
  But, oh! 'twill wake again.
Think, think, my friend, when next we meet,
Our long-wish'd interview, how sweet!
  From this my hope of rapture springs;
While youthful hearts thus fondly swell,
Absence, my friend, can only tell,
  "Friendship is Love without his wings!"

In one, and one alone deceived,
  Did I my error mourn?
No—from oppressive bonds relieved,
  I left the wretch to scorn.

I turn'd to those my childhood knew,
With feelings warm, with bosoms true,
  Twined with my heart's according strings;
And till those vital chords shall break,
For none but these my breast shall wake
  Friendship, the power deprived of wings!

Ye few! my soul, my life is yours,
  My memory and my hope;
Your worth a lasting love insures,
  Unfetter'd in its scope;
From smooth deceit and terror sprung
With aspect fair and honey'd tongue,
  Let Adulation wait on kings;
With joy elate, by snares beset,
We, we, my friends, can ne'er forget
  "Friendship is Love without his wings!"

Fictions and dreams inspire the bard
  Who rolls the epic song;
Friendship and truth be my reward—
  To me no bays belong;
If laurell'd Fame but dwells with lies,
Me the enchantress ever flies,
  Whose heart and not whose fancy sings;
Simple and young, I dare not feign;
Mine be the rude yet heartfelt strain,
  "Friendship is Love without his wings!"

December, 1806.

These early poems are well characterized by the impression which they produced upon Sir Robert Dallas, a man of taste and talent, who, though a bigot and a prey to prejudices of all kinds, hastened, nevertheless, after reading them, to compliment the author in the following words:—"Your poems are not only beautiful as compositions, but they also denote an honorable and upright heart, and one prone to virtue."

This eulogium is well deserved, and I pity those who could read the "Hours of Idleness" without liking their youthful writer. If we had space enough, we fain would follow the young man from Cambridge to the mysterious Abbey of Newstead, where he loved to invite his friends and institute with them a monastery of which he proclaimed himself the Abbot—an amusement really most innocent in itself, and which bigotry and folly alone could consider reprehensible. With what pleasure he would show that in the monastery of Newstead its abbot lived the simplest and most austere existence,—"a life of study," as Washington Irving describes it, from what he heard Nanna Smyth say of it some years after Byron's death. How delighted we should be to follow him in his first travels in search of experience of life, and when his genius revealed itself in that light which was shortly to make him the idol of the public and the hatred of the envious. We could show him to have been always the same kind-hearted man, by whom severity and injustice were never had recourse to except against himself, and whose melancholy was too often the result of broken illusions and disappointments. His simple and noble character, having always before it an ideal perfection, perpetually by comparison, thought itself at fault; and the world, who could not comprehend the exquisite delicacy of his mind, took for granted the reputation he gave himself, and made him a martyr till heaven should give him time to become a saint.

CHAPTER VI.

THE FRIENDSHIPS OF LORD BYRON.

THE extraordinary part which friendship played in Lord Byron's life is another proof of his goodness. His friendships may be divided into two categories: the friendships of his heart, and those of his mind. To the first class belong those which he made at Harrow and in his early Cambridge days, while his later acquaintances at the University matured into friends of the second category. These had great influence over his mind. The names of those of the first category who were dearest to him, and who were alive when he left Harrow for Cambridge (for he had lost some very intimate friends while still at Harrow, and among these Curzon), were—

WINGFIELD.	CLARE.
DELAWARE.	LONG.
TATTERSALL.	EDDLESTON.

HARNESS.

I will say a word of each, so as to show that Byron in the selection of his friends was guided instinctively by the qualities of those he loved.

WINGFIELD.

The Hon. John Wingfield, of the Coldstream Guards, was a brother of Richard, fourth Viscount Powerscourt, and died of fever at Coimbra, on the 14th of May, 1811, in his 20th year.

"Of all beings on earth," says Byron, "I was perhaps at one time more attached to poor Wingfield than to any. I knew him during the best part of his life and the happiest portion of mine."

When he heard of the death of this beloved companion of

his youth, he added the two following stanzas to the first canto of "Childe Harold:"

XCI.

"And thou, my friend!—since unavailing woe
Bursts from my heart, and mingles with the strain—
Had the sword laid thee with the mighty low,
Pride might forbid e'en Friendship to complain:
But thus unlaurell'd to descend in vain,
By all forgotten, save the lonely breast,
And mix unbleeding with the boasted slain,
While Glory crowns so many a meaner crest!
What hadst thou done, to sink so peacefully to rest?

XCII.

"Oh, known the earliest, and esteem'd the most!
Dear to a heart where naught was left so dear!
Though to my hopeless days forever lost,
In dreams deny me not to see thee here!
And Morn in secret shall renew the tear
Of Consciousness awaking to her woes,
And Fancy hover o'er thy bloodless bier,
Till my frail frame return to whence it rose,
And mourn'd and mourner lie united in repose."

Writing to Dallas on the 7th of August, 1812, he says, "Wingfield was among my best and dearest friends; one of the very few I can never regret to have loved." And on the 7th of September, speaking of the death of Matthews, in whom he said he had lost a friend and a guide, he wrote to Dallas to say: "In Wingfield I have lost a friend only; but one I could have wished to precede in his long journey."

TATTERSALL (DAVUS).

The Rev. John Cecil Tattersall, B.A., of Christ Church, Oxford, died on the 8th of October, 1812, aged 24.

"His knowledge," says a writer in the "Gentleman's Magazine," "was extensive and deep; his affections were sincere and great. By his extreme aversion to hypocrisy, he was so far from assuming the appearance of virtue, that most of his good qualities remained hidden, while he was most anxious to reveal the slightest fault into which he had fallen. He was a stanch friend, and a stranger to all enmity; he behaved loyally to men when alive, and died full of confidence and trust in God."

DELAWARE (EURYALUS).

George John, fifth Earl of Delaware, born in October, 1791, succeeded to his father in July, 1795.

Lord Byron wrote from Harrow on the 25th of October, 1804:—

"I am very comfortable here; my friends are not numerous, but choice. Among the first of these I place Delaware, who is very amiable, and my great friend. He is younger than I am, but is gifted with the finest character. He is the most intelligent creature on earth, and is besides particularly good-looking, which is a charm in women's eyes."

In consequence of a misunderstanding, or rather of a false accusation,—of which I shall speak elsewhere, in order to show the generosity of Lord Byron's character,—a coolness took place in their friendship. A charming piece in the "Hours of Idleness" alludes to it, and shows well the nature of his mind. I will only quote the seventh stanza:—

"You knew that my soul, that my heart, my existence,
If danger demanded, were wholly your own;
You knew me unalter'd by years or by distance,
Devoted to love and to friendship alone."

CLARE (LYCUS).

John Fitzgibbon, second Earl of Clare, succeeded to his father in 1802; was twelve years Chancellor of Ireland, and, later, Governor of Bombay.

Lord Byron wrote of him at Ravenna:—

"I never hear the name of Clare without my heart beating even now, and I am writing in 1821, with all the feelings of 1803, 4, 5, and *ad infinitum*."

He had kept all the letters of his early friends, and among these is one of Lord Clare's, in which the energy of his mind appears even through the language of the child. At the bottom of this letter and in Byron's hand, is a note written years after, showing his tender and amiable feelings:—

"This letter was written at Harrow by Lord Clare, then, and I trust ever, my beloved friend. When we were both students, he sent it to me in my study, in consequence of a brief childish misunderstanding, the only one we ever had. I keep this note only to show him, and laugh with him at the remembrance of the insignificance of our first and last quarrel. BYRON."

Besides mentioning Lord Clare in "Childish Recollections," his "Hours of Idleness" contain another poem addressed to him, which begins thus:—

TO THE EARL OF CLARE.

"Tu semper amoris
Sis memor, et cari comitis ne abscedat imago."—VAL. FLAC.

Friend of my youth! when young we roved,
Like striplings, mutually beloved,
With friendship's purest glow,
The bliss which winged those rosy hours
Was such as pleasure seldom showers
On mortals here below.

The recollection seems alone
Dearer than all the joys I've known,
When distant far from you:
Though pain, 'tis still a pleasing pain,
To trace those days and hours again,
And sigh again, adieu!

* * * * * *

Our souls, my friend! which once supplied
One wish, nor breathed a thought beside,
Now flow in different channels:
Disdaining humbler rural sports,
'Tis yours to mix in polish'd courts,
And shine in fashion's annals:

* * * * * *

I think I said 'twould be your fate
To add one star to royal state:—
May regal smiles attend you!
And should a noble monarch reign,
You will not seek his smiles in vain,
If worth can recommend you.

Yet since in danger courts abound,
Where specious rivals glitter round,
From snares may saints preserve you;
And grant your love or friendship ne'er
From any claim a kindred care,
But those who best deserve you!

Not for a moment may you stray
From truth's secure, unerring way!

May no delights decoy!
O'er roses may your footsteps move,
Your smiles be ever smiles of love,
Your tears be tears of joy!

Oh! if you wish that happiness
Your coming days and years may bless,
And virtues crown your brow;
Be still, as you were wont to be,
Spotless as you've been known to me,—
Be still as you are now.

And though some trifling share of praise,
To cheer my last declining days,
To me were doubly dear,
While blessing your beloved name,
I'd waive at once a *poet's* fame,
To prove a *prophet* here.

In 1821, as he was going to Pisa, Byron met his old and dear friend Clare on the route to Bologna, and speaks of their meeting in the following terms:—

"'There is a strange coincidence sometimes in the little things of this world, Sancho,' says Sterne, in a letter (if I mistake not), and so I have often found it. At page 128, article 91, of this collection, I had alluded to my friend Lord Clare in terms such as my feelings suggested. About a week or two afterward I met him on the road between Imola and Bologna, after an interval of seven or eight years. He was abroad in 1814, and came home just as I set out in 1816.

"This meeting annihilated for a moment all the years between the present time and the days of Harrow. It was a new and inexplicable feeling, like rising from the grave, to me. Clare, too, was much agitated—more in appearance than I was myself; for I could feel his heart beat to his fingers' ends, unless, indeed, it was the pulse of my own which made me think so. He told me, that I should find a note from him left at Bologna. I did. We were obliged to part for our different journeys—he for Rome, I for Pisa—but with the promise to meet again in the spring. We were but five minutes together, and on the public road; but I hardly recollect an hour of my existence which could be weighed against those few minutes. . . . Of all I have ever known he has always been the least altered in every thing from the excellent qualities and kind affections which attached me to him so strongly at school. I should hardly have thought it possible for society to leave a being with so little of the leaven of bad passions.

"I do not speak from personal experience only, but from all I have ever heard of him from others during absence and distance."

"My greatest friend, Lord Clare, is at Rome," he wrote to Moore from Pisa, in March, 1822: "we met on the road, and our meeting was quite sentimental—really pathetic on both sides. I have always loved him better than any male thing in the world."

In June Lord Clare came to visit Byron, and on the 8th of that month Byron wrote to Moore:—

"A few days ago my earliest and dearest friend, Lord Clare, came over from Geneva on purpose to see me before he returned to England. As I have always loved him, since I was thirteen at Harrow, better than any male thing in the world, I need hardly say what a melancholy pleasure it was to see him for a day only; for he was obliged to resume his journey immediately."

On another occasion he told Medwin that there is no pleasure in existence like that of meeting an early friend.

"Lord Clare's visit," says Madame G——, "gave Byron the greatest joy. The last day they spent together at Leghorn was most melancholy. Byron had a kind of presentiment that he should never see his friend again, and in speaking of him, for a long time after, his eyes always filled with tears."

LONG (CLEON).

Edward Long was with Lord Byron at Harrow and at Cambridge. He entered the Guards, and distinguished himself in the expedition to Copenhagen. As he was on his way to join the army in the Peninsula, in 1809, the ship in which he sailed was run down by another vessel, and Long was drowned with several others.

Long's friendship contributed to render Byron's stay at Cambridge bearable after his beloved Harrow days.

"Long," says Lord Byron, "was one of those good and amiable creatures who live but a short time. He had talents and qualities far too rare not to make him very much regretted." He depicts him as a lively companion, with an occasional strange touch of melancholy. One would have said he anticipated, as it were, the fate which awaited him.

The letter which he wrote to Byron, on leaving the University to enter the Guards, was so full of sadness that it contrasted strangely with his habitual humor.

"His manners," says Lord Byron, "were amiable and gentle, and he had a great disposition to look at the comical side of things. He was a musician, and played on several instruments, especially the flute and the violincello. We spent our evenings with music, but I was only a listener. Our principal beverage consisted in soda-water. During the day we rode, swam, walked, and read together; but we only spent one summer with each other."

On his leaving Cambridge, Byron addressed to him the following lines :—

TO EDWARD NOEL LONG, ESQ.

"Nil ego contulerim jocundo sanus amico."—HORACE.

Dear Long, in this sequester'd scene,
  While all around in slumber lie,
The joyous days which ours have been
  Come rolling fresh on Fancy's eye ;
Thus if amid the gathering storm,
While clouds the darken'd noon deform,
Yon heaven assumes a varied glow,
I hail the sky's celestial bow,
Which spreads the sign of future peace,
And bids the war of tempests cease.
Ah! though the present brings but pain,
I think those days may come again;
Or if, in melancholy mood,
Some lurking envious fear intrude,
To check my bosom's fondest thought,
  And interrupt the golden dream,
I crush the fiend with malice fraught,
  And still indulge my wonted theme.
Although we ne'er again can trace
  In Granta's vale the pedant's lore;
Nor through the groves of Ida chase
  Our raptured visions as before,
Though Youth has flown on rosy pinion,
And Manhood claims his stern dominion,
Age will not every hope destroy,
But yield some hours of sober joy.

  Yes, I will hope that Time's broad wing
Will shed around some dews of spring:

But if his scythe must sweep the flowers
Which bloom among the fairy bowers,
Where smiling youth delights to dwell,
And hearts with early rapture swell;
If frowning age, with cold control,
Confines the current of the soul,
Congeals the tear of Pity's eye,
Or checks the sympathetic sigh,
Or hears unmoved misfortune's groan,
And bids me feel for self alone;
Oh, may my bosom never learn
To soothe its wonted heedless flow,
Still, still despise the censor stern,
But ne'er forget another's woe.
Yes, as you knew me in the days
O'er which Remembrance yet delays,
Still may I rove, untutor'd, wild,
And even in age at heart a child.

Though now on airy visions borne,
To you my soul is still the same.
Oft has it been my fate to mourn,
And all my former joys are tame.
But hence! ye hours of sable hue!
Your frowns are gone, my sorrows o'er:
By every bliss my childhood knew,
I'll think upon your shade no more.
Thus, when the whirlwind's rage is past,
And caves their sullen roar inclose,
We heed no more the wintry blast,
When lull'd by zephyr to repose.

Long's death was the cause of great grief to Lord Byron.

"Long's father," said he, "has written to ask me to write his son's epitaph. I promised to do it, but I never had the strength to finish it."

I will add that Mr. Wathen having gone to visit Lord Byron at Ravenna, and having told him that he knew Long, Byron henceforth treated him with the utmost cordiality. He spoke of Long and of his amiable qualities, until he could no longer hide his tears.

In the month of October, 1805, Lord Byron left Harrow for Trinity College, Cambridge, and in 1821 he thus described himself, and his own feelings on leaving his beloved Ida for a new scene of life:—

"When I went to college it was for me a most painful event. I left Harrow against my wish, and so took it to heart, that before I left I never slept for counting the days which I had still to spend there. In the second place, I wished to go to Oxford and not to Cambridge; and, in the third place, I found myself so isolated in this new world, that my mind was perfectly depressed by it.

"Not that my companions were not sociable: quite the contrary; they were particularly lively, hospitable, rich, noble, and much more gay than myself. I mixed, dined, and supped with them; but, I don't know why, the most painful and galling sensation of life was that of feeling I was no longer a child."

His grief was such that he fell ill, and it was during that illness that he wrote and partly dictated the poem "Recollections of Childhood," in which he mentions and describes all his dear comrades of Harrow, with that particular charm of expression and thought which the heart alone can inspire.

It was again under the same impression that he wrote the most melancholy lines in the "Hours of Idleness," where the regret of the past delightful days of his childhood, spent at his dear Ida, ever comes prominently forward.

"I would I were a careless child,"

he exclaims in one poem, and finishes the same by the lines,—

"Oh that to me the wings were given
Which bear the turtle to her nest!
Then would I cleave the vault of Heaven
To flee away, and be at rest."

Life at Harrow appears to have been for him then the ideal of happiness. At times the distant view of the village and college of Harrow, inspires his muse, at others a visit to the college itself, and an hour spent under the shade of an elm in the church-yard. His whole soul is so revealed in these two poems, that I can not forbear quoting them *in extenso*:—

ON A DISTANT VIEW OF THE VILLAGE AND SCHOOL OF HARROW-ON-THE-HILL.

"Oh! mihi præteritos referat si Jupiter annos."—VIRGIL.

Ye scenes of my childhood, whose loved recollection
Embitters the present, compared with the past;
Where science first dawn'd on the powers of reflection,
And friendships were form'd, too romantic to last;

Where fancy yet joys to trace the resemblance
 Of comrades, in friendship and mischief allied,
How welcome to me your ne'er-fading remembrance,
 Which rests in the bosom, though hope is denied!

Again I revisit the hills where we sported,
 The streams where we swam, and the fields where we fought;
The school where, loud warn'd by the bell, we resorted,
 To pore o'er the precepts by pedagogues taught.

Again I behold where for hours I have ponder'd,
 As reclining, at eve, on yon tombstone I lay;
Or round the steep brow of the church-yard I wander'd,
 To catch the last gleam of the sun's setting ray.

I once more view the room, with spectators surrounded,
 Where, as Zanga, I trod on Alonzo o'erthrown;
While, to swell my young pride, such applauses resounded,
 I fancied that Mossop himself was outshown.*

Or, as Lear, I pour'd forth the deep imprecation,
 By my daughters of kingdom and reason deprived;
Till, fired by loud plaudits and self-adulation,
 I regarded myself as a Garrick revived.

Ye dreams of my boyhood, how much I regret you!
 Unfaded your memory dwells in my breast;
Though sad and deserted, I ne'er can forget you.
 Your pleasures may still be in fancy possest.

To Ida full oft may remembrance restore me,
 While fate shall the shades of the future unroll!
Since darkness o'ershadows the prospect before me,
 More dear is the beam of the past to my soul!

But if, through the course of the years which await me,
 Some new scene of pleasure should open to view,
I will say, while with rapture the thought shall elate me,
 "Oh! such were the days which my infancy knew!"

LINES WRITTEN BENEATH AN ELM IN THE CHURCH-YARD OF HARROW.

Spot of my youth! whose hoary branches sigh,
Swept by the breeze that fans thy cloudless sky;
Where now alone I muse, who oft have trod,
With those I loved, thy soft and verdant sod;
With those who, scatter'd far, perchance deplore,
Like me, the happy scenes they knew before:
Oh! as I trace again thy winding hill,
Mine eyes admire, my heart adores thee still,

---

* Mossop, a contemporary of Garrick, famous for his performance of Zanga.

Thou drooping Elm! beneath whose boughs I lay,
And frequent mused the twilight hours away;
Where, as they once were wont, my limbs recline,
But ah! without the thoughts which then were mine:
How do thy branches, moaning to the blast,
Invite the bosom to recall the past,
And seem to whisper, as they gently swell,
"Take, while thou canst, a lingering, last farewell!"

When fate shall chill, at length, this fever'd breast,
And calm its cares and passions into rest,
Oft have I thought, 'twould soothe my dying hour—
If aught may soothe when life resigns her power—
To know some humble grave, some narrow cell,
Would hide my bosom where it loved to dwell.
With this fond dream, methinks, 'twere sweet to die—
And here it linger'd, here my heart might lie;
Here might I sleep where all my hopes arose;
Scene of my youth, and couch of my repose;
Forever stretch'd beneath this mantling shade,
Press'd by the turf where once my childhood play'd;
Wrapt by the soil that veils the spot I loved,
Mix'd with the earth o'er which my footsteps moved;
Blest by the tongues that charm'd my youthful ear,
Mourn'd by the few my soul acknowledged here;
Deplored by those in early days allied,
And unremember'd by the world beside.

"But although he may for a time," says Moore, "have experienced this kind of moral atomy, it was not in his nature to be long without attaching himself to somebody, and the friendship which he conceived for Eddleston—a man younger than himself, and not at all of his rank in society—even surpassed in ardor all the other attachments of his youth."

EDDLESTON

was one of the choristers at Cambridge. His talent for music attracted Byron's attention. When he lost the society of Long, who had been his sole comfort at Cambridge, he took very much to the company of young Eddleston. One feels how much he was attached to him, on reading those lines in which he thanks Eddleston for a cornelian heart he had sent him:—

THE CORNELIAN.

No specious splendor of this stone
  Endears it to my memory ever;
With lustre only once it shone,
  And blushes modest as the giver.

Some, who can sneer at friendship's ties,
   Have for my weakness oft reproved me;
Yet still the simple gift I prize,
   For I am sure the giver loved me.

He offer'd it with downcast look,
   As fearful that I might refuse it;
I told him, when the gift I took,
   My only fear should be to lose it.

When Eddleston left college, Lord Byron wrote to Miss Pigott a letter full of regret at having lost his youthful friend, and thanking her for having taken an interest in him.

"During the whole time we were at Cambridge together," says Byron, "we saw each other every day, summer and winter, and never once found a moment of *ennui*, but parted each day with greater regret. I trust," he added, at the end of his letter, "that you will some day see us together; that is the being I esteem most, though I love several others."

But in the year 1811 Eddleston died of consumption; and Lord Byron wrote to Miss Pigott's mother, to beg of her to return the cornelian heart which he had intrusted to her care, because it had "now acquired a value which he wished it had never had;" the original donor having died at the age of twenty-one, a few months before, and being "the sixth in the space of four months of a series of friends and relations whom he had lost since May."

The cornelian heart was restored, and Byron was informed that he had only intrusted it, but not given it to Miss Pigott. It was on learning of Eddleston's death that Byron added the touching ninth stanza to the second canto of "Childe Harold."

After speaking of the hope of meeting again in a celestial abode, those whom he loved on earth, and all those who taught the truth, he exclaims,—

"There, thou!—whose love and life together fled,
Have left me here to love and live in vain—
Twined with my heart, and can I deem thee dead
When busy Memory flashes on my brain?
Well—I will dream that we may meet again,
And woo the vision to my vacant breast:
If aught of young Remembrance then remain,
Be as it may Futurity's behest,
For me 'twere bliss enough to know thy spirit blest!"

Among the children younger than himself of whom he established himself the protector, one of those he loved best was his fag William Harness.

HARNESS.

The Rev. William Harness is the author of the work entitled the "Relations between Christianity and Happiness, by one of the oldest and most esteemed friends of Lord Byron."

Harness was four years younger than Byron, and one of the earliest friends he made at Harrow. Lord Byron had not been long at the school, and had not yet formed any friendship with other boys, when he saw a boy, "still lame from an accident of his childhood, and but just recovered from a severe illness, bullied by a boy much older and stronger than himself." Byron interfered and took his part.

"We both seem perfectly to recollect," says he, "with a mixture of pleasure and regret, the hours we once passed together; and I assure you, most sincerely, they are numbered among the happiest of my brief chronicle of enjoyment. I am now getting into years, that is to say, I was twenty a month ago, and another year will send me into the world, to run my career of folly with the rest. I was then just fourteen—you were almost the first of my Harrow friends, certainly the first in my esteem, if not in date; but an absence from Harrow for some time shortly after, and new connections on your side, and the difference in our conduct, from that turbulent and riotous disposition of mine which impelled me into every species of mischief, all these circumstances combined to destroy our intimacy, which affection urged me to continue, and Memory compels me to regret. But there is not a circumstance attending that period, hardly a sentence we exchanged, which is not impressed on my mind at this moment.

"There is another circumstance you do not know:—the first lines I ever attempted at Harrow were addressed to you; but as on our return from the holidays we were strangers, the lines were destroyed.

"I have dwelt longer on this theme than I intended, and I shall now conclude with what I ought to have begun. Will you sometimes write to me? I do not ask it often, and, if we meet, let us be what we should be, and what we were."

Young Harness, gifted with a calm and mild temperament, was being educated for the Church. Besides being always at Harrow, and four years younger than Byron, the life which the latter led at Newstead and at Cambridge did not suit one destined to a career which requires greater severity of demeanor. But the two friends corresponded, and Lord Byron sent him one of his early copies of "Hours of Idleness." In the letter which the Rev. W. Harness wrote to Moore, after Byron's death, to tell him the nature of the quarrel which he and Byron had had together, and their subsequent reconciliation, he ends by saying:—

"Our conversation was renewed and continued from that time till his going abroad. Whatever faults Lord Byron may have exhibited toward others, to myself he was always uniformly affectionate. . . . I can not call to mind a single instance of caprice or unkindness in the whole course of our intimacy to allege against him."

The fault to which Harness alludes, and which he acknowledges, was one of the kind to which Byron was most sensitive, namely, coldness. Having lost some of his early and best friends, Edward Long, and all the others being spread far and near, abroad and in England, following out their respective careers and destiny, Harness was about the only early friend he had near him.

The time was approaching when he was going to leave England, to travel and to learn by study the great book of Nature. His heart was wounded by the injustice which had been done him, by the many disenchantments which he had experienced, by the brutal criticism of his "Hours of Idleness" from the pen of his relation Lord Carlisle, and by his money difficulties. Unable as yet to foretell the effects of his satire, which had not yet appeared, and the success of which might have consoled him a little for past mortifications, he found in friendship his sole relief, and particularly in the friendship of Harness. At this very critical time, Harness—(be it either through the influence of his family and relations, or through a notion that his principles were rather unsuited to the heterodox opinions of Lord Byron)—behaved coldly toward Byron. Dallas, however, who from puritanism and family pride, and even from jealousy, was rather an enemy of

Lord Byron's intellectual friends—(contending that it was they who had instilled into Byron all the anti-orthodox views which the poet had adopted)—makes an exception in favor of Harness.

Byron spoke of Harness with an affection which he hoped was repaid to him. I often met him at Newstead, and both he and Byron had had their portraits taken, which they were to make a present of to one another. It was not until some unknown cause sprung up to establish a coldness between the two friends that their intimacy ceased, and at the same time Harness's visits to Newstead. Byron felt it very keenly.

In what degree the conduct of Harness hurt Lord Byron and contributed to those explosions of misanthropy which, slight and passing as they were; have nevertheless been urged as a reproach against his first and second cantos of "Childe Harold," I shall examine later.

Here it is only necessary to say that in a soul such as his, where rancor could never live, such a coldness wounded him without altering his sentiments in any way. After two years' absence he returned to England, and so heartily forgave Harness that he actually wished to dedicate to him the first two cantos of "Childe Harold," and only gave up this idea from a generous fear that its dedication might injure him in his clerical profession, on account of certain stanzas in the poem which were not quite orthodox.

"The letter," says Moore, "in which he expresses these delicate sentiments is, unfortunately, lost."

Some months after his return to England he resumed his correspondence with Harness, and both the friends assembled at Newstead. Harness, however, as a clergyman, was severe in his judgments. Byron wrote to him:—

"You are censorious, child: when you are a little older, you will learn to dislike every body, but abuse nobody. . . . . I thank you most truly for the concluding part of your letter. I have been of late not much accustomed to kindness from any quarter, and I am not the less pleased to meet with it again from one to whom I had known it earliest. I have not changed in all my ramblings; Harrow, and of course yourself, never left me, and the

'Dulces reminiscitur Argos.'

attended me to the very spot to which that sentence alludes in the mind of the fallen Argive. Our intimacy began before we began to date at all, and it rests with you to continue it till the hour which must number it and me with the things that were."

Two days afterward, he writes to him again a letter full of endearing expressions, couched in a friendly tone of interest, of which the following extracts are instances :—

"And now, child, what art thou doing? Reading, I trust. I want to see you take a degree. Remember, this is the most important period of your life; and don't disappoint your papa and your aunt and all your kin, besides myself.

"You see, *mio carissimo*, what a pestilent correspondent I am likely to become; but then you shall be as quiet at Newstead as you please, and I won't disturb your studies as I do now."

On the 11th of December, of the same year, he invites Moore to Newstead and says, "H—— will be here, and a young friend named Harness, the earliest and dearest I ever had from the third form at Harrow to this hour."

And, finally, he wrote to Harness that he had no greater pleasure than to hear from him; indeed, that it was more than a pleasure.

HIS LATER FRIENDS.

When he had reached his nineteenth year, which was the second of his stay at Cambridge, Byron (having lost sight of most of his Harrow friends to whom he dedicated his verses, and having lost both Long and Eddleston) suddenly found himself launched into the vortex of a university life, for which he had no liking. Happily, however, he was thrown among young men of great distinction, whom fate had then gathered at Cambridge.

"It was so brilliant a constellation," says Moore, "that perhaps such a one will never be seen again." Among these he selected his friends from their literary merit. Those he most distinguished were Hobhouse, Matthews, Banks, and Scroope Davies. They formed a coterie at Cambridge, and spent most of their holidays at Newstead.

HOBHOUSE.

Sir John Cam Hobhouse, Bart., since created a peer, under

the name of Lord Broughton, is one of the statesmen and writers the memory of whom England most reveres. It is he whom Byron addresses as Moschus in the "Hints from Horace." After being Byron's friend at college, he became his faithful companion likewise in his travels, and throughout his short-lived but brilliant career. It was he who accompanied Byron in the fatal journey to Seaham, where Byron wedded Miss Milbank. It was he who stood best man on that occasion, and it was he whom Byron selected as his executor.

As soon as Byron became of age in 1809, the two friends left England together to visit Greece, Portugal, Spain, and Turkey. The results of these travels were, Byron's first two cantos of "Childe Harold," and Hobhouse's "Journey across Albania, and other Provinces of Turkey in Europe and in Asia."

On their return to England, their intimacy did not cease. "Hobhouse," Byron was wont to say, "ever gets me out of difficulty;" and in his journal of 1814 he says, "Hobhouse has returned. He is my best friend, the most animated and most amusing, and one whose knowledge is very deep and extensive. Hobhouse told me ten thousand anecdotes of Napoleon, which must be true. Hobhouse is the most interesting of travelling companions, and really excellent."

Lord Byron wished him to be his best man when he married Miss Milbank at Seaham, and after his separation from her Hobhouse joined him in Switzerland. They travelled together through the Oberland, and visited all the scenes which inspired that magnificent poem entitled "Manfred." Thence they left for Italy, and visited it from North to South; from the Alps to Rome. The result of this journey was the fourth canto of "Childe Harold" from Byron, and from Hobhouse a volume of notes, which constitutes a work of very great merit. If such a companion was agreeable to Byron, Byron was not less so to Hobhouse, who deplores a journey he had made without the company of that friend, whose perspicacity of observation and ingenious remarks united in producing that liveliness and good-humor, which take away half the sting of fatigue, and soften the aspect of danger and of difficulties.

During his absence from England Byron always insisted

that all matters relating to the settlement of his affairs should pass through the hands of Hobhouse, his "alter ego" when near or when absent. His highest testimony of regard and friendship for Hobhouse, however, is to be found in the dedication of the fourth canto of "Childe Harold," which was written in Italy in 1815, and which is as follows:—

CANTO THE FOURTH.

To John Hobhouse, Esq., A.M., F.R.S., etc.

Venice, January 2, 1818.

MY DEAR HOBHOUSE,—After an interval of eight years between the composition of the first and last cantos of Childe Harold, the conclusion of the poem is about to be submitted to the public. In parting with so old a friend, it is not extraordinary that I should recur to one still older and better,—to one who has beheld the birth and death of the other, and to whom I am far more indebted for the social advantages of an enlightened friendship, than—though not ungrateful—I can, or could be, to Childe Harold, for any public favor reflected through the poem on the poet,—to one whom I have known long and accompanied far, whom I have found wakeful over my sickness and kind in my sorrow, glad in my prosperity and firm in my adversity, true in counsel and trusty in peril,—to a friend often tried and never found wanting;—to yourself.

In so doing, I recur from fiction to truth; and in dedicating to you, in its complete or at least concluded state, a poetical work which is the longest, the most thoughtful and comprehensive of my compositions, I wish to do honor to myself by the record of many years' intimacy with a man of learning, of talent, of steadiness, and of honor. It is not for minds like ours to give or to receive flattery; yet the praises of sincerity have ever been permitted to the voice of friendship; and it is not for you, nor even for others, but to relieve a heart which has not elsewhere, or lately, been so much accustomed to the encounter of good-will as to withstand the shock firmly, that I thus attempt to commemorate your good qualities, or rather the advantages which I have derived from their exertion. Even the recurrence of the date of this letter, the anniversary of the most unfortunate day of my past existence,* but which can not poison my future while I retain the resource of your friendship, and of my own faculties, will henceforth have a more agreeable recollection for both, inasmuch as it will remind us of this my attempt to thank you for an indefatigable regard, such as few men have experienced, and no one could experience without thinking better of his species and of himself.

It has been our fortune to traverse together, at various periods, the countries of chivalry, history, and fable—Spain, Greece, Asia Minor, and Italy; and what Athens and Constantinople were to us a few years ago, Venice and Rome have been more recently. The poem also, or the pilgrim, or both, have accompanied me from first to last; and perhaps it may be a pardonable vanity which induces me to reflect with complacency on a composition which in some degree connects me with the spot where it was produced, and the objects it would fain describe; and however unworthy it may be deemed of those magical and memorable abodes, however short it may fall of our distant conceptions and immediate impressions, yet as a mark of respect for what is venerable, and of feeling for what is glorious, it has been to me a source of pleasure in the production, and I part with it with a kind of regret, which I hardly suspected that events could have left me for imaginary objects.

---

* His marriage.

With regard to the conduct of the last canto, there will be found less of the pilgrim than in any of the preceding, and that little slightly, if at all, separated from the author speaking in his own person. The fact is, that I had become weary of drawing a line which every one seemed determined not to perceive: like the Chinese in Goldsmith's "Citizen of the World," whom nobody would believe to be a Chinese, it was in vain that I asserted, and imagined that I had drawn, a distinction between the author and the pilgrim; and the very anxiety to preserve this difference, and disappointment at finding it unavailing, so far crushed my efforts in the composition, that I determined to abandon it altogether—and have done so. The opinions which have been, or may be, formed on that subject, are *now* a matter of indifference: the work is to depend on itself and not on the writer; and the author, who has no resources in his own mind beyond the reputation, transient or permanent, which is to arise from his literary efforts, deserves the fate of authors.

In the course of the following canto it was my intention, either in the text or in the notes, to have touched upon the present state of Italian literature, and perhaps of manners. But the text, within the limits I proposed, I soon found hardly sufficient for the labyrinth of external objects, and the consequent reflections; and for the whole of the notes, excepting a few of the shortest, I am indebted to yourself, and these were necessarily limited to the elucidation of the text.

It is also a delicate, and no very grateful task, to dissert upon the literature and manners of a nation so dissimilar; and requires an attention and impartiality which would induce us—though perhaps no inattentive observers, nor ignorant of the language or customs of the people among whom we have recently abode—to distrust, or at least defer our judgment, and more narrowly examine our information. The state of literary as well as political party appears to run, or to *have* run, so high, that for a stranger to steer impartially between them is next to impossible. It may be enough then, at least for my purpose, to quote from their own beautiful language—"Mi pare che in un paese tutto poetico, che vanta la lingua la più nobile ed insieme la più dolce, tutte tutte le vie diverse si possono tentare, e che sinche la patria di Alfieri e di Monti nòn ha perduto l'antico valore, in tutte essa dovrebbe essere la prima." Italy has great names still: Canova, Monti, Ugo Foscolo, Pindemonte, Visconti, Morelli, Cicognara, Albrizzi, Mezzophanti, Mai, Mustoxidi, Aglietti, and Vacca, will secure to the present generation an honorable place in most of the departments of art, sciences, and belles-lettres; and in some the very highest. Europe—the World—has but one Canova.

It has been somewhere said by Alfieri, that "La pianta uomo nasce più robusta in Italia che in qualunque altra terra—e che gli stessi atroci delitti che vi si commettono ne sono una prova." Without subscribing to the latter part of his proposition—a dangerous doctrine, the truth of which may be disputed on better grounds, namely, that the Italians are in no respect more ferocious than their neighbors—that man must be willfully blind, or ignorantly heedless, who is not struck with the extraordinary capacity of this people, or, if such a word be admissible, their *capabilities*, the facility of their acquisitions, the rapidity of their conceptions, the fire of their genius, their sense of beauty, and amid all the disadvantages of repeated revolutions, the desolation of battles, and the despair of ages, their still unquenched "longing after immortality"—the immortality of independence. And when we ourselves, in riding round the walls of Rome, heard the simple lament of the laborers' chorus, "Roma! Roma! Roma! Roma non è più come era prima," it was difficult not to contrast this melancholy dirge with the bacchanal roar of the songs of exultation still yelled from the London taverns, over the carnage of Mont St. Jean, and the betrayal of Genoa, of Italy, of France, and of the world, by men whose conduct you yourself have exposed in a work worthy of the better days of our history. For me,—

"Non movero mai corda
Ove la turba di sue ciance assorda."

What Italy has gained by the late transfer of nations, it were useless for Englishmen to inquire, till it becomes ascertained that England has acquired something more than a permanent army and a suspended Habeas Corpus; it is enough for them to look at home. For what they have done abroad, and especially in the south, "verily they *will have* their reward," and at no very distant period.

Wishing you, my dear Hobhouse, a safe and agreeable return to that country whose real welfare can be dearer to none than to yourself, I dedicate to you this poem in its completed state; and repeat once more how truly I am ever, your obliged and affectionate friend, BYRON.

MATTHEWS.

"Of this remarkable young man, Charles Skinner Matthews," says Moore, "I have already had occasion to speak; but the high station which he held in Lord Byron's affection and admiration may justify a somewhat ampler tribute to his memory.

"There have seldom, perhaps, started together in life so many youths of high promise and hope as were to be found among the society of which Lord Byron formed a part at Cambridge. Among all these young men of learning and talent, the superiority in almost every department of intellect seems to have been, by the ready consent of all, awarded to Matthews. . . . . Young Matthews appears—in spite of some little asperities of temper and manner, which he was already beginning to soften down when snatched away—to have been one of those rare individuals who, while they command deference, can at the same time win regard, and who, as it were, relieve the intense feeling of admiration which they excite by blending it with love."

Matthews died while bathing in the Cam.

On the 7th of September, 1811, Byron wrote to Dallas as follows:—"Matthews, Hobhouse, Davies, and myself, formed a coterie of our own at Cambridge and elsewhere. . . . Davies, who is not a scribbler, has always beaten us all in the war of words. H—— and myself always had the worst of it with the other two, and even M—— yielded to the dashing vivacity of S. D——."

And in another letter:—"You did not know M——: he was a man of the most astonishing powers."

And again, speaking of his death to Mr. Hodgson, he writes:—

"You will feel for poor Hobhouse; Matthews was the god

of his idolatry; and if intellect could exalt a man above his fellows, no one would refuse him pre-eminence."

Matthews died at the time when he was offering himself to compete for a lucrative and honorable position in the University. As soon as his death was known, it was said that if the highest talents could be sure of success, if the strictest principles of honor, and the devotion to him of a multitude of friends could have assured it, his dream would have been realized.

Besides a great superiority of intellect, Matthews was gifted with a very amusing originality of thought, which, joined to a very keen sense of the ridiculous, exercised a kind of irresistible fascination. Lord Byron, who loved a joke better than any one, took great pleasure in all the amusing eccentricities of him who was styled the Dean of Newstead, while Byron had been christened by him the Abbot of that place.

Shortly before his death, in 1821, Byron wrote a very amusing letter from Ravenna to Murray, recalling a host of anecdotes relating to Matthews, and which well set forth the clever eccentricity of the man for whom Byron professed so much esteem and admiration.

SCROOPE DAVIES.

We have already seen what Byron thought of Davies. His cleverness, his great vivacity, and his gayety, were great resources to Byron in his moments of affliction. When, in 1811, Byron experienced the bitterest loss of his life—that of his mother—he wrote from Newstead to beg that Davies would come and console him.

Shortly after, he wrote to Hodgson to say, "Davies has been here. His gayety, which death itself can not change, has been of great service to me: but it must be allowed that our laughter was very false."

We must not forget to mention, among the friends of Byron, William Banks, Mr. Pigott, of Southwell, and Mr. Hodgson, a writer of great merit, who was one of his companions at Newstead, and with whom he corresponded even during his voyage in the East. For all these he maintained throughout life the kindest remembrance, as also for Mr. Beecher, for whom he entertained a regard equal to his affection. Mr.

Beecher having disapproved of the moral tendency of his early poems, Lord Byron destroyed in one night the whole of the first edition of those poems, in order to prove his sense of esteem for Mr. Beecher's opinion. In the same category we should place Lord Byron's friendship for Dr. Drury, his tutor at Harrow; but this latter friendship is so marked with feelings of respect, veneration, and gratitude, that I had rather speak of it later, when I shall treat of the last-named quality, as one of the most noticeable in Lord Byron's character.

GRIEF WHICH HE EXPERIENCED AT THE LOSS OF HIS FRIENDS.

The grief which the loss of his friends occasioned to him was proportioned to the degree of affection which he entertained for them. By a curious fatality he had the misfortune to lose at an early age, almost all those he loved. This grief reached its climax on his return from his first travels.

"If," says Moore, "to be able to depict powerfully the painful emotions it is necessary first to have experienced them, or, in other words, if, for the poet to be great, the man must suffer, Lord Byron, it must be owned, paid early this dear price of mastery. In the short space of one month," he says in a note on Childe Harold, "I have lost her who gave me being, and most of those who made that being tolerable." Of these young Wingfield, whom we have seen high on the list of his Harrow favorites, died of a fever at Coimbra; and Matthews, the idol of his admiration at Cambridge, was drowned while bathing in the Cam. The following letter, written shortly after, shows so powerful a feeling of regret, and displays such real grief, that it is almost painful to peruse it:

"MY DEAREST DAVIES,—Some curse hangs over me and mine. My mother lies a corpse in this house; one of my best friends is drowned in a ditch. What can I say, or think, or do? My dear Scroope, if you can spare a moment, do come down to me; I want a friend. Matthews's last letter was written on Friday; on Saturday he was not. In ability who was like Matthews? Come to me; I am almost desolate; left almost alone in the world. I had but you and H—— and M——, and let me enjoy the survivors while I can."

Writing to Dallas on the first of August, he says:—

"Besides her who gave me being, I have lost more than one who made that being tolerable. Matthews, a man of the first talents, has perished miserably in the muddy waves of the Cam; my poor school-fellow Wingfield, at Coimbra, within a month: and while I had heard from all three, but not seen one. But let this pass; we shall all one day pass along with the rest; the world is too full of such things, and our very sorrow is selfish."

To Hodgson he writes:—

"Indeed, the blows followed each other so rapidly, that I am yet stupid from the shock; and though I do eat, and drink, and talk, and even laugh at times, yet I can hardly persuade myself that I am awake, did not every morning convince me mournfully to the contrary.

"You will write to me? I am solitary, and I never felt solitude irksome before."

Some months later he heard of the death of his friend Eddleston, of which he wrote to Dallas in the following terms:

"I have been again shocked with a death, and have lost one very dear to me in happier times. But 'I have almost forgot the taste of grief,' and 'supped full of horrors' till I have become callous, nor have I a tear left for an event which, five years ago, would have bowed down my head to the earth. It seems as though I were to experience in my youth the greatest misery of age. My friends fall around me, and I shall be left a lonely tree before I am withered."

On that same day, 11th of October, when his mind was a prey to such grief, he received a letter from Hodgson, advising him to banish all cares and to find in pleasure the distraction he needed. Lord Byron replied by some lines which Moore has reproduced; but the last of which he omitted to give, and which were written only to mystify the excellent Mr. Hodgson, who always looked at every thing and every one in a bright light, and whom Byron wished to frighten.

Here are the first lines:—

"Oh! banish care, such ever be
The motto of *thy* revelry!
Perchance of *mine* when wassail nights
Renew those riotous delights,
Wherewith the children of Despair
Lull the lone heart, and 'banish care,'
But not in morn's reflecting hour."

Two days after replying in verse, he answered him in prose.

"I am growing nervous—it is really true—really, wretchedly, ridiculously, fine-ladically, nervous. I can neither read, write, nor amuse myself, or any one else. My days are listless, and my nights restless."

The same day, 11th October, 1811, one of the darkest in his life, he wrote also his first stanza, addressed to Thyrza, of which the pathetic charm seems to rise to the highest pitch.

"To no other but an imaginary being," says Moore, "could he have addressed such tender and melancholy poetical lines."

BYRON'S FRIENDSHIP FOR MOORE.

At this time of his life, whether from the numerous injuries inflicted on him by men and by fate, or from some other circumstance, Byron seemed to be less given to friendships than formerly. He felt the force of friendship as deeply as before, but he became less expansive. Death, in taking so many of his friends away from him, had endeared those who remained still more to his heart, and caused him to seek among these the consolation he wanted. It is not true to say that Lord Byron was left alone entirely, at any time of his life: quite the contrary, he at all times lived in the midst of friends more or less devoted to him. Dallas and Moore pretend that there was a time in his early youth when he had no friends at all; but this time can not be stated, unless one forgets the names of Hobhouse, Hodgson, Harness, Clare, and many others who never lost sight of him, and unless one forgets the life of devotion which he led at Southwell and at Newstead both before and after his travels in the East.

Dallas and Moore, in speaking of this momentary isolation, in all probability adopted a common prejudice which causes them to believe that a lord must ever be lonely unless he is surrounded by a circle of rich and fashionable companions. The truth is that Byron, having left England immediately on quitting college, only had college connections, with all of whom he renewed his friendship on his return to the mother-country. But it is equally true, and this is to his credit, that he long hesitated to replace departed friends by new ones.

To conquer this repugnance he required a very high degree of esteem for the friend he was about to make, a similarity of tastes, and above all a sympathy based upon real goodness. This was the time of his greatest mental depression. It preceded that splendid epoch in his life, when his star shone with such brilliancy in the literary sphere, thanks to "Childe Harold," and in the world of politics through his parliamentary successes, which had earned for him the praises of the whole nation. Then did friends present themselves in scores, but out of these few were chosen.

Among the great men of the day who surrounded him, he took to several, and in particular to Lord Holland, a Whig like himself, and a man equally distinguished for the excellence of his heart as for his rare intellect. Lord Holland's hospitality was the pride of England. Byron also conceived a liking for Lord Lansdowne,—the model of every virtue, social and domestic; for Lord Dudley, whose wit so charmed him; for Mr. Douglas Kinnaird, brother to Lord Kinnaird, whom Byron called his most devoted friend in politics and in literature; for all those first notabilities of the day, Rogers, Sheridan, Curran, Mackintosh, for all of whom he may be said to have entertained a feeling akin to friendship. But all these were friends of the moment; friends whom the relations of every-day life in the world of fashion had brought together, and whose talents exacted admiration, and hence he formed ties which may be styled friendship, provided the strict sense of that word is not understood. Byron felt this more than any one.

One man, however, contrived to get such a hold on his mind and heart, that he became truly his friend, and exercised a salutary influence over him. This man, who contributed to dispel the dark clouds which hung over Byron's mind, and was the first to charm him in his new life of fashion, was no other than Thomas Moore.

This new intimacy had not, it is true, the freshness of his early friendships, formed, as these were, in the freshness of a young heart, and therefore without any worldly calculations. Moore was even ten years his senior. But his affection for Moore, founded as it was upon a similarity of tastes, upon mutual reminiscences, esteem and admiration, soon developed itself into a friendship which never changed. The circumstances under which Byron and Moore became friends speak too highly for the credit of both not to be mentioned here, and we must therefore say a few words on the subject.

Byron, as the reader knows, had in his famous satire of "English Bards," etc., attacked the poems of Moore as having an immoral tendency. Instead of interpreting the beautiful Irish melodies in their figurative sense, Byron had taken the direct sense conveyed in their love-inspiring words, and considered them as likely to produce effeminate and unhealthy impressions.

> "Who in soft guise, surrounded by a choir
> Of virgins melting, not to Vesta's fire,
> With sparkling eyes, and cheek by passion flush'd,
> Strikes his wild lyre, while listening dames are hush'd?
> 'Tis Little! young Catullus of his day,
> As sweet, but as immoral, in his lay!
> *   *   *   *   *   *   *
> Yet kind to youth, ...
> She bids thee 'mend thy line and sin no more.'"

Lord Byron was always of opinion that literature, when it tends to exalt the more tender sentiments of our nature, pure as these may be, is ever injurious to the preservation of those manly and energetic qualities which are so essential for the accomplishment of a noble mission here below. This opinion is illustrated by the occasional extreme energy of his heroes, and by his repugnance to introduce love into his dramas. If this reproach offended Moore a little, Lord Byron's allusion to his duel with Jeffrey at Chalk Farm in 1806, where it was said that the pistols of each were not loaded, must have wounded him still more, and he wrote a letter to Lord Byron which must, it would seem, have brought on a duel.

Lord Byron was then travelling in the Levant, and the letter remained with his agent in London. It was only two years after, on his return from his travels, that he received it. An exchange of letters with Moore took place, and such was the "good sense, self-possession and frankness" of Byron's conduct in the matter, that Moore was quite pacified, and all chances of a duel disappeared with the reconciliation of both, at the request of each.

The reconciliation took place under the auspices of Rogers, and at a dinner given by the latter for that purpose. After speaking of his extraordinary beauty, and of the delicacy and prudence of his conduct, Moore, in referring to this dinner, ends by saying, "Such did I find Lord Byron on my first experience of him, and such, so open and manly-minded did I find him to the last."

Byron, too, was influenced by the charm of Moore's acquaintance, and so dear to him became the latter's society through that kind of electric current which appears to run through some people and forms between them an unbounded sympathy, that it actually succeeded in dispelling the sombre ideas which then possessed his soul.

Their similarity of tastes, and at the same time those differences of character which are so essential to the development of the intellect of two sympathetic minds, were admirably adapted to form the charm which existed in their relations with one another.

This sympathy, however, would never have found a place in the mind of Lord Byron had it not sprung from his heart. Amiability was essential in his friends before he could love them; and though Moore had not that quality in its highest degree, still he had it sufficiently for Lord Byron to say in one of his notes, "I have received the most amiable letter possible from Moore. I really think him the most kind-hearted man I ever met. Besides which, his talents are equal to his sentiments."

His sympathy for Moore was such that the mention of his name was enough to awaken his spirits and give him joy. This is palpable in his letters to Moore, which are masterpieces of talent.

His cordial friendship for Moore was never once affected by the series of triumphs which followed its formation, and which made the whole world bow before his genius. "The new scenes which opened before him with his successes," says Moore, "far from detaching us from one another, multiplied, on the contrary, the opportunities of meeting each other, and thereby strengthening our intimacy."

This excessive liking for Moore was kept up by all the force which constancy lends to affection. One of Byron's most remarkable qualities was great constancy in his likes, tastes, and a particular attachment to the recollections of his childhood. At the age of fifteen, Moore's "Melodies" already delighted him. "I have just been looking over Little Moore's Melodies, which I knew by heart at fifteen." In 1803 he wrote from Ravenna: "Hum! I really believe that all the bad things I ever wrote or did are attributable to that rascally book."

We have seen that at Southwell he used even to ask Miss Chaworth and Miss Pigott to sing him songs of Moore. At Cambridge, what reconciled him to leaving Harrow were the hours which he spent with his beloved Edward Long, with whom he used to read Moore's poetry after having listened to Long's music.

He already then had a sympathy for Moore, and a wish to know him. The latter's place was therefore already marked out in Byron's heart, even before he was fortunate enough to know him.

Moore's straitened means often obliged him to leave London. Then Byron was seized with a fit of melancholy.

"I might be sentimental to-day, but I won't," he said. "The truth is that I have done all I can since I am in this world to harden my heart, and have not yet succeeded, though there is a good chance of my doing so.

"I wish your line and mine were a little less parallel, they might occasionally meet, which they do not now.

"I am sometimes inclined to write that I am ill, so as to see you arrive in London, where no one was ever so happy to see you as I am, and where there is no one I would sooner seek consolation from, were I ill."

Then, according to his habitual custom of ever depreciating himself morally, he writes to Moore, in answer to the latter's compliments about his goodness: "But they say the devil is amusing when pleased, and I must have been more venomous than the old serpent, to have hissed or stung in your company."

His sympathy for Moore went so far as to induce him to believe that he was capable of every thing that is good.

"Moore," says he, in his memoranda of 1813, "has a reunion of exceptional talents—poetry, music, voice, he has all—and an expression of countenance such as no one will ever have.

"What humor in his poet's bag! There is nothing that Moore can not do if he wishes.

"He has but one fault, which I mourn every day—he is not here."

He even liked to attribute to Moore successes which the latter only owed to himself. Byron had, as the reader knows, the most musical of voices. Once heard, it could not be forgotten.* He had never learned music, but his ear was so just, that when he hummed a tune his voice was so touching as to move one to tears.

"Not a day passes," he wrote to Moore, "that I don't think and speak of you. You can not doubt my sincere admiration, waving personal friendship for the present. I have you by rote and by heart, of which *ecce signum*."

He then goes on to tell him his adventure when at Lady O——'s:—

"I have a habit of uttering, to what I think tunes, your 'Oh, breathe not,' and others; they are my matins and vespers. I did not intend them to be overheard, but one morning in comes not la Donna, but il Marita, with a very grave face, and said, 'Byron, I must request you not to sing any more, at least of those songs.'—'Why?'—'They make my wife cry, and so melancholy that I wish her to hear no more of them.'

"Now, my dear Moore, the effect must have been from your words, and certainly not my music."

To give Moore the benefit of effecting a great success with an Oriental poem, Byron gave up his own idea of writing one, and sent him some Turkish books.

"I have been thinking of a story," says he, "grafted on the amours of a Peri and a mortal, something like Cayotte's 'Diable Amoureux.' Tenderness is not my *forte;* for that reason I have given up the idea, but I think it a subject you might make much of."

Moore actually wished to write a poem on an Oriental subject, but dreaded such a rival as Byron, and expressed his fears in writing to him. Byron replied:—

"Your Peri, my dear Moore, is sacred and inviolable. I have no idea of touching the hem of her petticoat. Your affectation of a dislike to encounter me is so flattering that I begin to think myself a very fine fellow. But it really puts me out of humor to hear you talk thus."

* Lord Holland's youngest son, in speaking of Byron, styled him "the gentleman with the beautiful voice."

Not only did Byron encourage Moore in his task, but effaced himself completely in order to make room for him.

When he published the "Bride of Abydos," Moore remarked that there existed some connection in that poem with an incident he had to introduce in his own poem of "Lalla Rookh." He wrote thereupon to Byron to say that he would stop his own work, because to aspire after him to describe the energy of passion would be the work of a Cæsar.

Byron replied:—

"I see in you what I never saw in poet before, a strange diffidence of your own powers, which I can not account for, and which must be unaccountable when a Cossack like me can appall a cuirassier.

"Go on—I shall really be very unhappy if I at all interfere with you. The success of mine is yet problematical. . . Come out, screw your courage to the sticking-place—no man stands higher, whatever you may think on a rainy day in your provincial retreat."

To Moore he dedicated his "Corsair," and to read the preface is to see how sincerely attached Byron was to his friend.

When at Venice he heard of some domestic affliction which had befallen Moore; he wrote to him with that admirable simplicity of style which can not be imitated, because the true accents of the heart defy imitation.

"Your domestic afflictions distress me sincerely; and, as far as you are concerned, my feelings will always reach the furthest limits to which I may still venture. Throughout life your losses shall be mine, your gains mine also, and, however much I may lose in sensibility, there will always remain a drop of it for you."

When Moore obtained his greatest success, and arrived at the summit of popularity, by the publication of "Lalla Rookh," Byron's pleasure was equal to the encouragements he had given him. But of his noble soul, in which no feeling of jealousy could enter, we shall speak elsewhere. Here, in conclusion, I must add that his friendship for Moore remained stanch through time and circumstances, and even notwithstanding Moore's wrongs toward him, of which I shall speak in another chapter.

In treating of Byron's friendships, I have endeavored to in set forth the wrongs which some of his friends, and Moore particular, have committed against him both before and after his death.

If, as Moore observes, it be true that Byron never lost a friend, was their friendship a like friendship with his own? Has it ever gone so far as to make sacrifices for his sake, and has not Lord Byron ever given more as a friend than he ever received in return? Had he found in his friendship among men that reciprocity of feeling which he ever found among women, would so many injuries and calumnies have been heaped upon his head? Would not his friends, had they shown a little more warmth of affection, have been able to silence those numerous rivals who rendered his life a burden to him? Had they been conscientious in their opinions, they would certainly not have drawn upon them the rather bitter lines in "Childe Harold:" —

"I do believe,
Though I have found them not, that there may be
Words which are things, hopes which will not deceive,
And virtues which are merciful, nor weave
Snares for the failing; I would also deem
O'er others' griefs that some sincerely grieve,
That two, or one, are almost what they seem,
That goodness is no name, and happiness no dream."

And later, in "Don Juan," Byron would not have said with a smile, but also with a pain which sprang from the heart:—

"O Job! you had two friends: one's quite enough,
Especially when we are ill at ease;
They are but bad pilots when the weather's rough,
Doctors less famous for their cures than fees.

Let no man grumble when his friends fall off,
As they will do like leaves at the first breeze;
When your affairs come round, one way or t'other,
Go to the coffee-house and take another."

It is, however, also true that he would not have had the opportunity of showing us so perfectly the beauty of his mind, and his admirable constancy, notwithstanding the conduct of those on whom he had bestowed his friendship. This constancy is shown even by his own words, for immediately after the lines quoted above, he adds:—

"But this is not my maxim; had it been,
Some heart-aches had been spared me."

CHAPTER VII.

LORD BYRON CONSIDERED AS A FATHER, AS A BROTHER, AND AS A SON.

HIS GOODNESS SHOWN BY THE STRENGTH OF HIS INSTINCTIVE AFFECTIONS.

LORD BYRON AS A FATHER.

IF, as a great moralist has said, our natural affections have power only upon sensitive and virtuous natures, but are despised by men of corrupt and dissipated habits, then must we find a proof again of Lord Byron's excellence in the influence which his affections exercised over him.

His tenderness for his child, and for his sister, was like a ray of sunshine which lit up his whole heart, and in the moments of greatest depression prevented desolation from completely absorbing his nature.

His thoughts were never far from the objects of his affection.

CXV.

"My daughter! with thy name this song begun;
My daughter! with thy name thus much shall end;
I see thee not, I hear thee not, but none
Can be so wrapt in thee; thou art the friend
To whom the shadows of far years extend:
Albeit my brow thou never shouldst behold,
My voice shall with thy future visions blend,
And reach into thy heart, when mine is cold,
A token and a tone, even from thy father's mould.

CXVI.

"To aid thy mind's development, to watch
Thy dawn of little joys, to sit and see
Almost thy very growth, to view thee catch
Knowledge of objects,—wonders yet to thee!
To hold thee lightly on a gentle knee,
And print on thy soft cheek a parent's kiss,
This, it should seem, was not reserved for me,
Yet this was in my nature: as it is,
I know not what is there, yet something like to this.

CXVIII.

*   *   *   *   *   *

"Sweet be thy cradled slumbers! O'er the sea
And from the mountains where I now respire,
Fain would I waft such blessing upon thee,
As, with a sigh, I deem thou might'st have been to me."

Who ever read "Childe Harold" and was not touched by the delightful stanzas of the third canto, — a perfect *chef-d'œuvre* of tenderness and kindness, inclosed, as it were, in another master-piece, like, were it possible, a jewel found in a diamond?

Those only, however, who lived with him in Greece and in Italy are able to bear witness to his paternal tenderness. This sentiment really developed itself on his leaving England, and only appears from that time forward in his poems. Byron loved all children, but his heart beat really when he met children of Ada's age.

Hearing at Venice that Moore had lost a child, he wrote to him, "I enter fully into your misery, for I feel myself entirely absorbed in my children. I have such tenderness for my little Ada."

Both at Ravenna and at Pisa he was miserable if he did not hear from Ada. Whenever he received any portraits of her or a piece of her hair, these were solemn days of rejoicing for him, but they usually increased his melancholy. When in Greece he heard of Ada's illness, he was seized with such anxiety that he could no longer give his attention to any thing. "His journal (which, by-the-by, was lost or destroyed after his death) was interrupted on account of the news of his child's illness," says Count Gamba, in his narrative of Byron's last voyage to Greece.

The thought of his child was ever present to him when he wrote, and she was the centre of all his hopes and his fears.

The persecution to which he was subjected for having written "Don Juan," having made him fear one day at Pisa that its effect upon his daughter might be to diminish her affection for him, he said:—

"I am so jealous of my daughter's entire sympathy, that, were this work, 'Don Juan'—(written to while away hours of pain and sorrow), — to diminish her affection for me, I would never write a word more; and would to God I had not written a word of it!"

He likewise said that he was often wont to think of the time when his daughter would know her father by his works. "Then," said he, "shall I triumph, and the tears which my daughter will then shed, together with the knowledge that she will share the feelings with which the various allusions to herself and me have been written, will console me in my darkest hours. Ada's mother may have enjoyed the smiles of her youth and childhood, but the tears of her maturer age will be for me."

He distinctly foresaw that his daughter would be brought up to look indifferently upon her father; but he never could have believed that such means would be adopted, as were used, to alienate from him the heart of his own child. We will give one instance only, mentioned by Colonel Wildman, the companion and friend of Byron, who had bought Newstead, of which he took the most religious care. Having in London made the acquaintance of Ada, then Lady Lovelace, the colonel invited her to pay a visit to the late residence of her illustrious father, and she went to see it sixteen months before Byron's death. As Lady Lovelace was looking over the library one morning, the colonel took a book of poems and read out a poem with all the force of the soul and heart. Lady Lovelace, in rapture with this poem, asked the name of its writer. "There he is," said the colonel, pointing to a portrait of Byron, painted by Phillips, which hung over the wall, and he accompanied his gesture by certain remarks which showed what he felt at the ignorance of the daughter. Lady Lovelace remained stupefied, and, from that moment, a kind of revolution took place in her feelings toward her father. "Do not think, colonel," she said, "that it is affectation in me to declare that I have been brought up in complete ignorance of all that concerned my father."

Never had Lady Lovelace seen even the writing of her father; and it was Murray who showed it to her for the first time.

From that moment an enthusiasm for her father filled her whole soul. She shut herself up for hours in the rooms which he had inhabited, and which were still filled with the things which he had used. Here she devoted herself to her favorite studies. She chose to sleep in the apartments which were most particularly hallowed by the reminiscences of her father, and appeared never to have been happier than during this stay at Newstead, absorbed as she had become for the first time in all the glory of him whose tenderness for her had been so carefully concealed from her. From that time all appeared insipid and tasteless to her; existence became a pain. Every thing told her of her father's renown, and nothing could replace it. All these feelings so possessed her that she fell ill, and when she was on the point of death she wrote to Colonel Wildman to beg that she might be buried next to her illustrious father. There, in the modest village church of Hucknell, lie the father and the daughter, who, separated from one another during their lifetime, became united in death, and thus were realized, in a truly prophetic way, the words which close the admirable third canto of "Childe Harold's Pilgrimage." Words of consolation for those who loved Byron, and whom religion and philosophy inspire with hope; for they think that, despite his enemies, this union of their mortal remains must be the symbol of their union above, and that the prophetic sense of the words pronounced in the agony of despair will be realized by an eternal happiness.

CXVII.

"Yet, though dull Hate as duty should be taught,
I know that thou wilt love me; though my name
Should be shut from thee, as a spell still fraught
With desolation, and a broken claim:
Though the grave closed between us,—'twere the same,
I know that thou wilt love me; though to drain
My blood from out thy being were an aim
And an attainment,—all would be in vain,—
Still thou would'st love me, still that more than life retain."

LORD BYRON AS A BROTHER.

Fraternal love was no less conspicuous in him than his paternal affection. It may be easily conceived how great must have been the influence over one who cared so much for friends in general, of that affection which is the perfection of love, and, at the same time, the most delicate, peaceful, and charming of sentiments. Such a love has neither misunderstandings to dread, nor misrepresentations to fear. It is above the caprices, ennui, and changes which often rule the friendships of our choice.

From his return from his first travels in the East, to the time of his publishing the first two cantos of "Childe Harold," Byron may be said not to have known his sister. The daughter of another mother, and older by several years than himself,—living as she did with relations of her mother, brought up as she was by her grandmother, Lady Carmarthen, and married as she had been at an early age to the Hon. Colonel Leigh, Lord Byron had had very few opportunities of seeing her. It was only on his return from the East that he began to have some correspondence with her, on the occasion of his publication of "Childe Harold." Notwithstanding all these circumstances, which might tend to lessen in him his love for his sister, his affection for her on the contrary increased.

The reader has observed that about this time, under the pressure of repeated sorrows, a shade of misanthropy had spread itself over his character, notwithstanding that such a failing was totally contrary to his nature. The acquaintance with his sister helped greatly to dispel this veil, and, thanks to it, he was able to get rid of the first sorrowful impressions of youth.

His dear Augusta became the confidant of his heart; and his pen on the one hand, and his sister on the other, were the means of curing him of all ills. Her influence over him is shown by the love expressed for her in his letters and his notes at that time, and her prudent advice often puts to flight the more unruly dictates of his imagination. Thus, on one occasion, Mrs. Musters (Miss Chaworth) wrote to ask Byron to come and see her. She was miserable that she had preferred her husband to the handsome young man now the celebrated Byron. Byron is tempted to go and see her; he loved her so dearly when a boy. But Augusta thought it dangerous that he should go and see her, and Byron does not.

"Augusta wishes that I should be reconciled with Lord Carlisle," he says. "I have refused this to every body, but I can not to my sister. I shall, therefore, have to do it, though I had as lief 'Drink up Esil,' or 'eat a crocodile.'"

"We will see. Ward, the Hollands, the Lambs, Rogers,

every one has, more or less, tried to settle these matters during the past two years, but unsuccessfully; if Augusta succeeds it will be odd, and I shall laugh."

To refuse his sister any thing was out of the question. He loved her so much that the least likeness to her in any woman was enough to attract his sympathy. If ill, he would not have his sister know it; if she was unwell, he can not rest until he received better accounts of her health. Nothing, however, shows better his love for her than the lines with which she inspired him at the time of his deepest distress; that is, on leaving England for Switzerland. I can not transcribe them altogether, but I can not refuse myself the satisfaction of quoting some extracts from them.

I.

"When all around grew drear and dark,
And reason half withheld her ray—
And hope but shed a dying spark,
Which more misled my lonely way,

* * * * * *

Thou wert the solitary star
Which rose and set not to the last.

IV.

"Oh! blest be thine unbroken light!
That watch'd me as a seraph's eye,
And stood between me and the night,
Forever shining sweetly nigh.

VI.

"Still may the spirit dwell on mine,
And teach it what to brave or brook;
There's more in one soft word of thine
Than in the world's defied rebuke."

Again,

"Though human, thou didst not deceive me,
Though woman, thou didst not forsake,
Though loved, though forborest to grieve me,
Though slandered, thou never couldst shake,
Though trusted, thou didst not disclaim me,
Though parted, it was not to fly,
Though watchful, 'twas not to defame me,
Nor, mute, that the world might belie.

* * * * * *

"From the wreck of the past, which hath perish'd,
Thus much I at least may recall,
It hath taught me that what I most cherish'd
Deserved to be dearest of all."

This deep fraternal affection, assumed at times under the influence of his powerful genius, and under exceptional circumstances an almost too passionate expression, which opened a fresh field to his enemies. But it was to him a consolation and a benefit, which did him good throughout his short career; and even at the times when troubles came pouring down upon him, the love of his sister, though not sufficient to give him courage enough to bear up, still always appeared to him as a hope and an encouragement to do well.

LORD BYRON AS A SON.

The two sentiments of which we have just spoken were so strong and so proved in Lord Byron, that it would be almost useless to speak of them, were it not for the pleasure which there is in recalling them.

But there is another natural affection which, though less manifested, was not less felt by Byron; I mean his filial love.

Many biographers, and Moore at their head, have not, for reasons to which I have alluded in another chapter, been fair to his mother. Besides the motives which seem always to have actuated them in the exaggeration of his faults, and of the smallest particulars of his life, they wished, I believe, to give to their narrative a more amusing character. Moore would seem to say that Byron's childhood was badly directed; but how so? Does he mean that his mother did not justly appreciate the peculiarities of her child's character, or promote the fine dispositions of his nature? But such a discernment in parents is matter of rare occurrence, and can it be said that many known characters have been handled according to the scientific rules here laid down? Those who speak of these fine theories would, we fear, be rather puzzled by their application, were they called to do so.

It is matter of note that Byron was surrounded as a child with the tenderest care. At a very early age he was handed over, by his over-indulgent mother and nurses, to most respectable, intelligent, and devoted masters; and at no time of his youth was either his physical, intellectual, or moral education ever neglected. I may add that Byron's mother was respected, both as a wife and as a mother. She was an heiress belonging to a most ancient Scotch family, and closely allied to the royal house of Stuart, and was the second wife of the youngest son of Admiral Byron,—an unusually handsome man, and father to the poet.

Though this man had been rather spoiled by the world, and had not rendered her life perfectly happy, she loved him passionately, and was most devoted to him. When he died, four years after their marriage, her grief was such that it completely changed her nature.

A widow at twenty-three, she centred in her only child all the depth of her affection, and though her fortune was considerably reduced, she still had enough to render her child's life comfortable, so that his education did not suffer by it. He was scarcely six years of age when he succeeded to the barony of his great-uncle, and this circumstance in a young Englishman's life always means increased prosperity. His childhood was, therefore, most decidedly fortunate in many respects. This is all the more certain that Byron, throughout his life, always spoke of his happy childhood, and that his ideal of human happiness never seems to have been realized except at that time.

But, notwithstanding Moore's exaggerations, and the excessive kindness of his mother, whose whole life was centred in the one thought of amusing her child, it is very likely that Byron's passionate nature may have rendered his relations at home less agreeable than they might have been. However much this may have been the case, it is still more certain that such little family dissensions never produced in his mind the slightest germ of ingratitude toward or want of care for his mother, and that the recollection of his passionate moments only served to make him acquire by his own efforts that wonderful self-possession for which he was afterward remarkable.

His filial sentiments betrayed themselves at every period, and in every circumstance of his life. The reader has seen how, at Harrow, by showing the names of their parents written on the wall, he prevented his comrades from setting fire to the school.

On attaining his majority, his first care was to improve the financial condition of his mother, notwithstanding the shattered state of his fortune, and to prepare a suitable apartment for her at Newstead.

When the cruel criticisms of the "Edinburgh Review"

condemned his first steps in the career of literature, his chief care after the first explosion of his own sorrow, was to allay, as far as he could, the sensitiveness of his mother, who, not having the same motive or power to summon up a spirit of resistance, was, of course, more helplessly alive to this attack upon his fame, and felt it far more than, after the first burst of indignation, he did himself.

During his first travels to the East his affairs were in a very embarrassed state. But, nevertheless, here are the terms in which he wrote to his mother from Constantinople:—

"If you have occasion for any pecuniary supply, pray use my funds as far as they go, without reserve; and, lest this should not be enough, in my next to Mr. H—— I will direct him to advance any sum you may want."

There is a degree of melancholy in the letter which he wrote to his mother on his return to England. He had received most deplorable accounts of his affairs when at Malta, and he applied the terms apathy and indifference to the sentiments with which he approached his native land. He goes on to say, however, that the word apathy is not to be applied to his mother, as he will show; that he wishes her to be the mistress of Newstead, and to consider him only as the visitor. He brings her presents of all kinds, etc. "That notwithstanding this alienation," adds Moore, "which her own unfortunate temper produced, he should have continued to consult her wishes, and minister to her comforts with such unfailing thoughtfulness (as is evinced not only in the frequency of his letters, but in the almost exclusive appropriation of Newstead to her use), redounds in no ordinary degree to his honor."

This want of affection never existed but in the minds of some of Byron's biographers. Lord Byron knew that his mother doted upon him, and that she watched his growing fame with feverish anxiety.

His successes were passionately looked forward to by her. She had collected in one volume all the articles which had appeared upon his first poems and satires, and had written her own remarks in the margin, which showed that she was possessed of great good sense and considerable talent. Could, then, such a heart as Lord Byron's be ungrateful, and not love such a mother? Mr. Galt, a biographer of Byron's, who is certainly not to be suspected of partiality, renders him, however, full justice in regard to his filial devotion during the life of his mother, and to the deep distress which he felt at her death.

"In the mean time, while busily engaged in his literary projects with Mr. Dallas, and in law affairs with his agent, he was suddenly summoned to Newstead by the state of his mother's health. Before he reached the Abbey she had breathed her last. The event deeply affected him. Notwithstanding her violent temper, her affection for him had been so fond and ardent that he undoubtedly returned it with unaffected sincerity; and, from many casual and incidental expressions which I have heard him employ concerning her, I am persuaded that this filial love was not at any time even of an ordinary kind."

On the night after his arrival at the Abbey, the waiting-woman of Mrs. Byron, in passing the door of the room where the corpse lay, heard the sound of some one sighing heavily within, and, on entering, found his lordship sitting in the dark beside the bed. She remonstrated, when he burst into tears, and exclaimed, "I had but one friend in the world, and she is gone!" This same filial devotion often inspired him with beautiful lines, such as those in the third canto of "Childe Harold," when standing before the tomb of Julia Alpinula, he exclaims:

LXVI.

"And there—oh! sweet and sacred be the name!—
Julia—the daughter, the devoted—gave
Her youth to Heaven; her heart, beneath a claim
Nearest to Heaven's, broke o'er a father's grave.
Justice is sworn 'gainst tears, and hers would crave
The life she lived in; but the Judge was just,
And then she died on him she could not save.
Their tomb was simple, and without a bust,
And held within their urn one mind, one heart, one dust.

LXVII.

"But these are deeds which should not pass away,
And names that must not wither, though the earth
Forgets her empires with a just decay,
The enslavers and the enslaved, their death and birth;
The high, the mountain-majesty of worth
Should be, and shall, survivor of its woe,
And from its immortality look forth
In the sun's face, like yonder Alpine snow,
Imperishably pure beyond all things below."

As a note to the above, Byron writes:

"Julia Alpinula, a young Aventian priestess, died soon after a vain attempt to save her father, condemned to death as a traitor by Aulus Cœcina. Her epitaph was discovered many years ago; it is thus:

"JULIA ALPINULA:
HIC JACEO.
INFELICIS PATRIS, INFELIX PROLES.
DEÆ AVENTIÆ SACERDOS.
EXORARE PATRIS NECEM NON POTUI:
MALE MORI IN FATIS ILLE ERAT.
VIXI ANNOS XXIII.

"I know," adds Byron, "of no human composition so affecting as this, nor a history of deeper interest. These are the names and actions which ought not to perish, and to which we turn with a true and healthy tenderness."

His father having died in 1793, when Byron was only four years of age, he could not know him; but to show how keen were his sentiments toward his memory, I must transcribe a note of Murray's after the following lines in "Hours of Idleness:"—

"Stern Death forbade my orphan youth to share
The tender guidance of a father's care;
Can rank, or e'en a guardian's name supply
The love which glistens in a father's eye?"

"In all the biographies which have yet been published of Byron," remarks Murray, "undue severity has been the light by which the character of Byron's father has been judged. Like his son, he was unfortunately brought up by a mother only. Admiral Byron, his father, being compelled by his duties to live away from his family, the son was brought up in a French military academy, which was not likely at that time to do his morals much good. He passed from school into the Coldstream Guards, where he was launched into every species of temptation imaginable, and likely to present themselves to a young man of singular beauty, and heir to a fine name, in the metropolis of England."

The unfortunate intrigue, of which so much has been said, as if it had compromised his reputation as a man of honor, took place when he was just of age, and he died in France at the age of thirty-five. One can hardly understand why the biographers of Byron have insisted upon depreciating the personal qualities of his father, apart from the positively injurious and wicked assertions made against him in memoirs of Lord Byron's life, and in reviews of such memoirs.

Some severe reflections of this kind having found their way into the preface to a French translation of Byron's works, which appeared shortly before the latter's departure for Greece, called for an expostulation by the son himself on behalf of his father, in a letter addressed to Mr. Coulmann, who had been charged to offer to the poet the homage of the French literary men of the day. This letter is interesting in more than one particular, as it re-establishes in their true light several facts wrongly stated with regard to Byron's family, and because it is, perhaps, the last letter which Byron wrote from Italy. It is quoted *in extenso* in the chapter entitled "Byron's Life in Italy."* I can only repeat here the words which apply more particularly to his father:—

"The author of the essay (M. Pichot) has cruelly calumniated my father. Far from being brutal, he was, according to the testimony of all those who knew him, extremely amiable, and of a lively character, though careless and dissipated. He had the reputation of being a good officer, and had proved himself such in America. The facts themselves belie the assertion. It is not by brutal means that a young officer seduces and elopes with a marchioness, and then marries two heiresses in succession. It is true that he was young, and very handsome, which is a great point.

"His first wife, Lady Conyers, Marchioness of Carmarthen, did not die of a broken heart, but of an illness which she contracted because she insisted on following my father out hunting before she had completely recovered from her confinement, immediately after the birth of my sister Augusta. His second wife, my mother, who claims every respect, had, I assure you, far too proud a nature ever to stand ill-treatment from any body, and would have proved it had it been the case. I must add, that my father lived a long time in Paris, where he saw a great deal of the Maréchal de Biron, the commander of the French Guards, who, from the similarity of our

* This chapter is to be published separately, at no very distant period, by the author.—*Note of the translator.*

names, and of our Norman extraction, believed himself to be our cousin. My father died at thirty-seven years of age, and whatever faults he may have had, cruelty was not one of them. If the essay were to be circulated in England, I am sure that the part relating to my father would pain my sister Augusta even more than myself, and she does not deserve it; for there is not a more angelic being on earth. Both Augusta and I have always cherished the memory of our father as much as we cherished one another,—a proof, at least, that we had no recollection of any harsh treatment on his part. If he dissipated his fortune, that concerns us, since we are his heirs; but until we reproach him with the fact, I know of no one who has a right to do so. BYRON."

From all that has been said it will be seen that Byron's sensitive heart was eminently adapted to family affections. Affection alone made him happy, and his nature craved for it. He was often rather influenced by passion than a seeker of its pleasures, and whenever he found relief in the satisfaction of his passions, it was only because there was real affection at the bottom,—an affection which tended to give him those pleasures of intimacy in which he delighted.

CHAPTER VIII.

QUALITIES OF LORD BYRON'S HEART.

GRATITUDE,—that honesty of the soul which is even greater than social honesty, since it is regulated by no express law, and that most uncommon virtue, since it proscribes selfishness,—was pre-eminently conspicuous in Lord Byron.

To forget a kindness done, a service rendered, or a good-natured proceeding, was for him an impossibility. The memories of his heart were even more astonishing than those of his mind.

His affection for his nurses, for his masters, for all those who had taken care of him when a boy, is well known; and how great was his gratitude for all that Doctor Drury had done for him! His early poems are full of it. His grateful affection for Drury he felt until his last hour.

This quality was so strong in him, that it not only permitted him to forget all past offenses, but even rendered him blind to any fresh wrongs. It sufficed to have been kind to him once, to claim his indulgence. The reader remembers that Jeffrey had been the most cruel of the persecutors of his early poems, but that later he had shown more impartiality. This act of justice appeared to Byron a generous act, and one sufficient for him in return to forget all the harm done to him in the past. We accordingly find in his memoranda of 1814:—

"It does honor to the editor (Jeffrey), because he once abused me: many a man will retract praise; none but a high-spirited mind will revoke its censure, or *can* praise the man it has once attacked."

Yet Jeffrey, who was eminently a critic, gave fresh causes of displeasure to Byron at a later period, and then it was that he forgot the present on recalling the past.

In speaking of this Scotch critic, he considered himself quite disarmed. When at Venice, he heard that he had been attacked about Coleridge in the "Edinburgh Review," he wrote as follows to Murray:—

"The article in the 'Edinburgh Review' on Coleridge, I have not seen; but whether I am attacked in it or not, or in any other of the same journal, I shall never think ill of Mr. Jeffrey on that account, nor forget that his conduct toward me has been certainly most handsome during the last four or more years."*

And instead of complaining of this attack, he laughed at it with Moore:—

"The 'Edinburgh Review' had attacked me. . . . Et tu, Jeffrey! 'there is nothing but roguery in villainous man.' But I absolve him of all attacks, present and future; for I think he had already pushed his clemency in my behoof to the utmost, and I shall always think well of him. I only wonder he did not begin before, as my domestic destruction was a fine opening for all who wished to avail themselves of the opportunity."†

His great sympathy for Walter Scott became quite enthusiastic, owing also to a feeling of gratitude for a service rendered to him by Scott. Shortly after his arrival in Italy, and the publication of the third canto of "Childe Harold," public opinion in England went completely against him, and an article appeared in the "Quarterly Review," by an anonymous pen, in his defense. Byron was so touched by this, that he endeavored to find out the name of its writer.

"I can not," he said to Murray, "express myself better than in the words of my sister Augusta, who (speaking of it) says, 'that it is written in a spirit of the most feeling and kind nature.' It is, however, something more: it seems to me (as far as the subject of it may be permitted to judge) to be very well written as a composition, and I think will do the journal no discredit; because, even those who condemn its partiality, must praise its generosity. The temptations to take another and a less favorable view of the question have been so great and numerous, that what with public opinion, politics, etc., he must be a gallant as well as a good man, who has ventured in that place, and at this time, to write such an article even anonymously.

* Moore, Letter 261.

† Venice, 1817.

"Perhaps, some day or other, you will know or tell me the writer's name. Be assured, had the article been a harsh one, I should not have asked it."

He afterward learnt that the article had been written by Walter Scott, and his sympathy was so increased by his gratitude for the service rendered, that he never after seemed happier than when he could extol Scott's talents and kindness.

Gratitude, which often weighs upon one as a duty, so captivated his soul, that the remembrance of the kindness done to him was wont to turn into an affectionate devotion, which time could not change. Long after the appearance of the article, he wrote as follows to Scott from Pisa:—

"I owe to you far more than the usual obligations for the courtesies of literature and common friendship, for you went out of your way in 1817 to do me a service, when it required, not merely kindness, but courage to do so; to have been mentioned by you, in such a manner, would have been a proud memorial at any time, but at such a time, 'when all the world and his wife,' as the proverb goes, were trying to trample upon me, was something still more complimentary to my self-esteem. Had it been a common criticism, however eloquent or panegyrical, I should have felt pleased, undoubtedly, and grateful, but not to the extent which the extraordinary good-heartedness of the whole proceeding must induce in any mind capable of such sensations. The very tardiness of this acknowledgment will, at least, show that I have not forgotten the obligation; and I can assure you, that my sense of it has been out at compound interest during the delay."

Gratitude, with him, was oftentimes a magnifying-glass which he used when he had to appreciate certain merits. No doubt Gifford was a judicious, clear-sighted, and impartial critic, but Byron extolled him as an oracle of good taste, and submitted like a child to his decisions.

Gratitude levelled every social condition in his eyes, as we may see by his correspondence with Murray, where the proud aristocrat considers his publisher on a par with himself. Moore marvelled at this; but Moore forgets that Murray was no ordinary publisher, and that, generous by nature, he made to Byron on one occasion, in 1815, when the noble poet was in great difficulties, the handsomest offers. Lord Byron refused them; but the act was so noble, that its impression was never effaced from Byron's mind, and modified the nature of their relations.

When he had recovered his fortune, he wrote to Murray from Ravenna:—"I only know of three men who would have raised a finger on my behalf; and one of those is yourself. It was in 1815, when I was not even sure of a five-pound note. I refused your offer, but have preserved the recollection of it, though you may have lost it."

To calculate the degree of gratitude due to a service rendered, would have seemed ingratitude in his eyes. He could create beings who were capable of doling it out in that way, but to apply it to himself was an impossibility.

His predilection for the inhabitants of Epirus, of Albania, and for the Suliotes, is known. This predilection originated in the gratitude which he felt for the care taken of him by two Albanian servants who doted on him, during an illness which he had at Patras at the time when he visited that place for the first time. It was also on the Albanian coast that he was wrecked on one occasion, and where he received that hospitality which he has immortalized in Don Juan.

Byron's predilection for this people even overcame the effects which their ingratitude might have produced, for it is matter of history, how badly the barbarous Suliotes behaved to him at Missolonghi a short time before his death; they who had been so benefited by his kindness to them.

The memory of services done to him was not susceptible of change, and neither time nor distance could in the least affect it. The moment he had contracted a debt of gratitude, he believed himself obliged to pay interest upon it all his life, even had he discharged his debt. One single anecdote will serve to illustrate the truth of these remarks. On the eve of his last departure from London in 1816, when the cruelty of his enemies, powerfully seconded by the spite of Lady Byron, had succeeded in so perverting facts as to give their calumnies the color of truth, and to throw upon his conduct as a husband so false a light as to hold him up to universal execration, it required great courage to venture on his defense. Lady Jersey did it. She—who was then quite the mistress of fashion by her beauty, her youth, her rank, her fortune, and her irreproachable conduct—organized a fête in honor of Byron, and invited all that was most distinguished in London to come and wish Byron farewell.

Among those who responded to the noble courage of Lady Jersey was one equally deserving of praise, Miss Mercer, now Lady K——. This conduct of Miss Mercer was all the more creditable that there had been a question of her marriage with Lord Byron, and that Miss Milbank had been preferred to her.

This party gave Byron a great insight into the human heart, and showed him all its beauty and all its baseness. The reflections which it caused him to make, and the frank account he gave of it in his memoirs—(the loss of which can never be too much regretted)—would not have pleased his survivors. This was unquestionably a powerful reason why the memoirs were destroyed. But Byron cared not so much for the painful portion of this recollection, as he loved to remember the noble conduct of these two ladies.

"How often he spoke to me of Lady Jersey, of her beauty and her goodness," says Madame G——. "As to Miss M——," he said, "she was a woman of elevated ideas, who had shown him more friendship than he deserved."

One of the noblest tributes of gratitude and admiration which can be rendered to a woman was paid by Lord Byron to Miss Mercer. As he was embarking at Dover, Byron turned round to Mr. Scroope Davies, who was with him, and giving him a little parcel which he had forgotten to give her when in London, he added: "Tell her that had I been fortunate enough to marry a woman like her, I should not now be obliged to exile myself from my country."

"If," pursues Arthur Dudley (evidently a name adopted by a very distinguished woman biographer), "the rare instances of devotion which he met in life reconciled him to humanity, with what touching glory used he not to repay it. The last accents of the illustrious fugitive will not be forgotten, and history will preserve through centuries the name of her to whom Byron at such a time could send so flattering a message."

But, as if all this were not enough, he actually consecrated in verse, a short time before his death, the memory of his gratitude to the noble women who had done so much honor to their sex:—

"I've also seen some female *friends* ('tis odd,
But true—as, if expedient, I could prove),
That faithful were through thick and thin abroad,
At home, far more than ever yet was Love—
Who did not quit me when Oppression trod
Upon me; whom no scandal could remove;
Who fought, and fight, in absence, too, my battles,
Despite the snake Society's loud rattles."

It was on that occasion that Hobhouse said to Lady Jersey, "Who would not consent to be attacked in this way, to boast such a defense?" To which Lady Jersey might have replied, "But who would not be sufficiently rewarded by such gratitude, preserved in such a heart and immortalized in such verses?"

IMPULSES OF LORD BYRON.

All those who have studied human nature agree that impulses show the natural qualities of the soul. "Beware of your first impulses, they are always true," said a diplomatist, the same who insisted that speech was given us to conceal our thoughts. If such be the case, Lord Byron's goodness of heart is palpable, for all who knew him agree in bearing testimony to the extraordinary goodness of all his impulses. "His lordship," says Parry, "was keenly sensitive at the recital of any case of distress, in the first instance; and advantage being taken of this feeling immediately, he would always relieve it when in his power. If this passion, however, was allowed to cool, he was no longer to be excited. This was a fault of Lord Byron's, as he frequently offered, upon the impulse of a moment, assistance which he would not afterward give, and therefore occasionally compromise his friends."

To multiply quotations would only be to repeat the same proof. I shall therefore merely add that it was often the necessity of modifying the nobility of his first impulses which made him appear inconstant and changeable.

EFFECTS OF HAPPINESS AND MISFORTUNE UPON BYRON.

"The effect of a great success," writes some one, "is ever bad in bad natures, but does good only to such as are really good in themselves."

As the rays of the sun soften the honey and harden the mud, so the rays of happiness soften a good and tender heart, while they harden a base and egotistical nature. This proof has not been wanting in Byron. His wonderful successes, which laid at his feet the homage of nations, and which might easily have made him vain and proud, only rendered him better, more amiable, and brighter.

"I am happy," said Dallas, on the occasion of the great success which greeted the publication of the first canto of "Childe Harold," "to think that his triumph, and the attention which he has attracted, have already produced upon him the soothing effect I had hoped. He was very lively to day."

Moore says the same; and Galt is obliged to grant that, as Byron became the object of public curiosity, his desire to oblige others increased. After giving a personal proof of Byron's goodness to him, he ends by saying:—

"His conversation was then so lively, that gayety seemed to have passed into habit with him." It was also at that time that he wrote in his memoranda:—"I love Ward, I love A——, I love B——," and then, as if afraid of those numerous sympathies, he adds: "oh! shall I begin to love the whole world?" This universal love was only the expression of the want of his soul which had mollified under the rays of that mild sun which is called happiness.

EFFECTS OF MISFORTUNE AND INJUSTICE UPON BYRON.

If his natural goodness had so large a field to develop itself in happiness, it reached a degree of sublimity in misfortune.

That Byron's short life was full of real sorrows, I have shown in another chapter, when I had to prove their reality against those imputations of their being imaginary made by some of his biographers. He required a strength of mind equal to his genius and to his sensibility, to be able to resist the numerous ills with which he was assailed throughout his life:—

> "Have I not had to wrestle with my lot?
> Have I not suffered things to be forgiven?
> Have I not had my brain sear'd, my heart riven,
> Hopes sapp'd, name blighted, Life's life lied away?"

Such beautiful lines speak loudly enough of the intensity of his sufferings. Great as they were, they did not, however, produce in him any feeling of hatred. To forgive was his only revenge; and not only did he forgive, but, the paroxysm of passion over, there was only room in his soul for those nobler feelings of patience, of toleration, of resignation, and of abnegation, of which no one in London can have formed a notion. The storms to which his soul was at times a prey only purified it, and discovered a host of qualities which are kept back often by the more powerful passions of youth. If he never attained that calmness of spirit which is the gift of those who can not feel, or perhaps of the saints, he at any rate, at the age of thirty-two, began to feel a contempt of all worldly and frivolous matters, and came to the resolution of forgiving most generously all offenses against him.

Shelley, who went to see him at Ravenna, wrote to his wife "that if he had mischievous passions he seemed to have subdued them; and that he was becoming, what he should be,—a *virtuous man*."

Mme. de Bury, in her excellent essay upon Byron, expresses herself thus: "Had his natural goodness not been great, the events which compelled him to leave his country, and which followed upon his departure, must have exercised over his mind the effect of drying it up; and, in lessening its power, would have forced him to give full vent to his passions." Instead of producing such a result, they on the contrary purified it, and developed in him the germs of a host of virtues. I shall not tarry any longer, however, on this subject, as in another chapter I intend to consider Byron's kindness of disposition from a far higher point of view. I shall only add his own words, which prove his goodness of character. "I can not," said he, "bear malice to any one, nor can I go to sleep with an ill thought against any body."

ABSENCE OF ALL JEALOUS FEELINGS IN LORD BYRON.

Among the infirmities of human nature, one of the most general, serious, and incurable, is certainly that of jealousy. Being the essence of a disordered self-love, it presents several aspects, according to the different social positions of those whom it afflicts, and the degree of goodness of the people. It might, in my mind, almost be called the thermometer of the heart. But of all the jealousies, that which has done most harm on earth has been the jealousy of artists and of literary men.

This kind of fever has at times risen to a degree inconceivable. It has raged so high as to call poison to its aid, to invoke the help of daggers and create assassins.

But even putting aside these excesses, proper to Southern countries, it is certain that everywhere and at all times jealousy has caused numberless cases of ingratitude, and has set brothers against brothers, friends against friends, and pupils against masters.

Great minds in France have not been altogether free from it. Corneille, Racine, Voltaire, became a prey to its disastrous influences. In England Dryden, Addison, Swift, Shaftesbury, were its victims. So it has been everywhere, and in Italy even Petrarch, the meek and excellent Petrarch, was not exempted from it.

This moral infirmity is of so subtle a nature, that not only does it injure those who are devoted to those works of the mind, which can not be said to establish a solid claim to glory inasmuch as public opinion is judge, but also those whose influence being confined to a more limited sphere, should be less anxious about obtaining it. It finds so easy an access into the souls of men, that it is said that even Plato was jealous of Socrates, Aristotle of Plato, Leibnitz of Locke, and so forth.

When we behold so many great minds at all times unable to avoid this jealousy, and that we see nowadays jealousy animating the pen of some of the best writers, and completely changing their moral sense, must we not admire the great goodness of him whom, though living in such a heated atmosphere of jealous rivalry, contrived wholly to escape its effects?

This right I claim for Lord Byron, that he was the least jealous of any man, as the proofs which I shall bring forward will abundantly attest.

If Byron was jealous of the living, of whom could he have been so? Of course of such who may have become his rivals in the sphere of literature which he had adopted. When Byron appeared in the literary world, those who were most in repute were Sir Walter Scott, Rogers, Moore, Campbell, and the lakers Southey, Wordsworth, Coleridge, and, later, Shelley.

On one occasion, in 1813, Byron amused himself by tracing what he called a "triangular gradus ad Parnassum," in which the names of the principal poets then in renown are thus classified :—

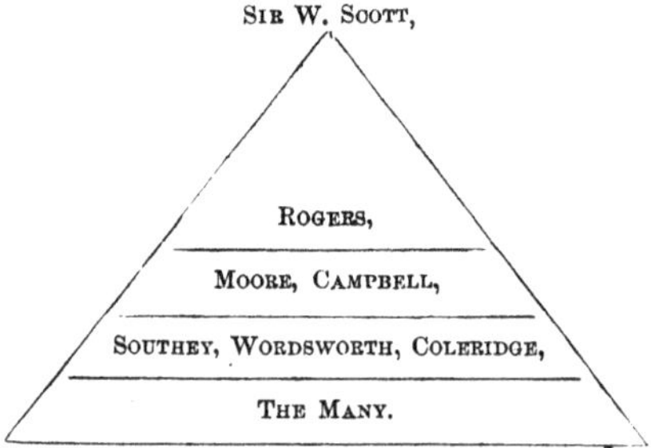

To know best his feelings with respect to his rivals, we must listen to himself; and to preserve the order given in the triangle, let us begin by Walter Scott. We read in Byron's memorandum of the 17th of September, 1813 :—

"George Ellis and Murray have been talking something about Scott and me, George *pro* Scoto—and very right too. If they want to depose him, I only wish they would not set me up as a competitor. Even if I had my choice, I would rather be the Earl of Warwick than all the kings he ever made! Jeffrey and Gifford I take to be the monarch-makers in poetry and prose. I like Scott—and admire his works to what Mr. Braham calls Entusymusy. All such stuff can only vex him, and do me no good."

And elsewhere: "I have not answered W. Scott's last letter, but I will. I regret to hear from others that he has lately been unfortunate in pecuniary involvements. He is undoubtedly the Monarch of Parnassus, and the most English of bards."

When these expressions were written, Byron did not know Scott personally; but notwithstanding his satire, of which he had often made a generous retractation, he had always felt a great sympathy for Scott, who, on the other hand, appeared to have forgotten the wound inflicted by Byron's youthful pen, only to remember the latter's heartfelt praises.

A few years after the publication of "English Bards" and just after that of "Childe Harold," Byron and Sir W. Scott manifested a mutual desire to make each other's acquaintance through the medium of Murray, who was then travelling in Scotland. An exchange of letters full of mutual generosity had taken place, when George IV., then regent, expressed the wish to make Byron's acquaintance.

After speaking to him of "Childe Harold," in terms which Byron was always proud to recall, the prince went on to speak of Walter Scott in the most enthusiastic terms. Byron seemed almost as pleased as if the praise had been addressed to himself, and hastened to make his illustrious rival acquainted with the flattering words used by royalty with regard to him.

It was only in the summer of 1815 that they became personally acquainted. Scott was then passing through London on his way to France. Their sympathy was mutual. Byron, who had been married seven months, already foresaw that a storm was brewing in his domestic affairs, which explains the mysterious melancholy, observed by Scott, upon the countenance of his young friend. Scott's liveliness, however, always brought about a return of Byron's spirits, and their meetings were always very gay, "the gayest even," says Scott, "that I ever spent."

Byron's handsomeness produced a great impression upon Scott. "It is a beauty," said he, "which causes one to reflect and to dream;" as if he wished one to understand that he thought Byron's beauty superhuman.

"Report had prepared me to meet a man of peculiar habits and a quick temper, and I had some doubt whether we were likely to suit each other in society. I was most agreeably disappointed in this respect. I found Lord Byron in the highest degree courteous, and even kind.

"Like the old heroes in Homer, we exchanged gifts: I gave Byron a beautiful dagger mounted with gold, which had been the property of the redoubted Elfi Bey. But I was to play the part of Diomed in the Iliad, for Byron sent me, some time after, a large sepulchral vase of silver. It was full of dead men's bones, and had inscriptions on the sides of the base. One ran thus:—"The bones contained in this urn were found in certain ancient sepulchres within the land walls of Athens in the month of February, 1811. The other face bears the lines of Juvenal—

> 'Expende quot libras in duce summo invenies.
> Mors sola fatetur quantula hominum corpuscula.'

"A letter," adds W. Scott, "accompanied this vase, which was more valuable to me than the gift itself, from the kindness with which the donor expressed himself toward me. I left it, naturally, in the urn with the bones, but it is now missing. As the theft was not of a nature to be practiced by a mere domestic, I am compelled to suspect the inhospitality of some individual of higher station,—most gratuitously exercised certainly, since, after what I have here said, no one will probably choose to boast of possessing this literary curiosity."

Their mutual sympathy increased upon improved acquaintance with one another. When at Venice Byron was informed that Scott was ill, he said that he would not for all the world have him ill. "I suppose it is from sympathy that I have suffered from fever at the same time." At Ravenna a little later, on the 12th of January, 1821, he wrote down in his memoranda:—

Scott is certainly the most wonderful writer of the day. His novels are a new literature in themselves, and his poetry as good as any, if not better (only on an erroneous system), and only ceased to be so popular, because the vulgar learned were tired of hearing Aristides called the Just, and Scott the Best, and ostracized them.

"I like him, too, for his manliness of character, for the extreme pleasantness of his conversation, and his good-nature toward myself personally. May he prosper! for he deserves it.

"I know no reading to which I fall with such alacrity as a work of W. Scott's. I shall give the seal with his bust on it to Mlle. la Comtesse Guiccioli this evening, who will be curious to have the effigies of a man so celebrated."

He did take the seal to the Countess Guiccioli, and she said that Byron's expressions about Scott were always most affectionate. "How I wish you knew him!" he often repeated.

He used to say that it was not the poetry of "Child Harold," but Scott's own superior prose that had done his poetry harm, and that if ever the public could by chance get tired of his novels, Scott might write in verse with equal success. He insisted that Scott had a dramatic talent, "talent," he said, "which people are loth to grant me." He said that the success of Scott's novels was not in the least due to the anonymous character he had adopted, and that he could not understand why he would not sign his name to works of such merit. He likewise asserted that of all the authors of his period, Scott was the least jealous. "He is too sure of his fame to fear any rivals, nor does he think of good works as Tuscans do of fever; that there is only a certain amount of it in the world, and that in communicating it to others, one gets rid of it."

"I never travel without taking Scott's novels with me," said Byron to Medwin, at Pisa; "it is a real library, a literary treasure; I can read them yearly with renewed pleasure."

A few days before his departure for Greece, he learned that M. Stendhall had published an article upon Racine and Shakspeare, wherein there were some unfavorable remarks about Walter Scott.

Notwithstanding his occupations preparatory to departure, he found time to write to Stendhall, and tell him how much he felt the injustice of these remarks, and to request that they should be rectified.

This letter of Byron's to M. Beyle will no doubt be read with universal admiration, as it points out most prominently all the goodness of his character:—

"SIR,—Now that I know to whom I am indebted for a very flattering mention in the 'Rome, Naples, and Florence, in 1817,' by Monsieur Stendhall, it is fit that I should return my thanks (however undesired or undesirable) to Monsieur Beyle, with whom I had the honor of being acquainted at Milan in 1816.* You only did me too much honor in what you were pleased to say in that work, but it has hardly given

* Why has the passage in the first edition of Stendhall's works, which treats in enthusiastic terms of Byron's genius, been cut out of the subsequent editions?

me less pleasure than the praise itself, to become at length aware (which I have done by mere accident) that I am indebted for it to one of whose good opinion I was really ambitious. So many changes have taken place since that period in the Milan circle, that I hardly dare recur to it—some dead, some banished, and some in the Austrian dungeons. Poor Pelico! I trust that in his iron solitude his muse is consoling him in some measure, one day to delight us again, when both she and her poet are restored to freedom.

"There is one part of your observations in the pamphlet, which I shall venture to remark upon: it regards Walter Scott. You say that 'his character is little worthy of enthusiasm, at the same time that you mention his productions in the manner they deserve. I have known Walter Scott long and well, and in occasional situations which call forth the real character, and I can assure you that his character *is* worthy of admiration; that of all men, he is the most open, the most honorable, the most amiable," etc. BYRON."

Even at Missolonghi, where certainly literary thoughts were little in harmony with his occupations, Byron found occasion to speak of his sentiments as regards Scott, since even the simple and anti-poetic Parry tells us, in his interesting narrative of "The Last Days of Lord Byron," of the admiration and affection with which Byron always spoke of Walter Scott. "He never wearied of his praise of 'Waverley,' and continually quoted passages from it."

May we be allowed to observe, in conclusion, that such a generous desire on the part of Byron constantly to put forward the merits of Scott deserved from the latter a warmer acknowledgment. The homage paid to his memory by Scott came late, and is cold. Be it from a Tory or Protestant spirit, Scott in his eulogy of Lord Byron did not disclaim openly the calumnies uttered against the great poet's fame, but almost sided with his hypocritical apologists, by assuming a kind of tone of indulgence in speaking of him.

ROGERS.

Rogers comes next in the triangular order.

Byron's esteem for Rogers was such, that not only did he

spare him in his famous satire, but even addressed him a real compliment in the lines:—

"And thou, melodious Rogers! rise at last,
Recall the pleasing memory of the past;
Arise! let blest remembrance still inspire,
And strike to wonted tones thy hallow'd lyre;
Restore Apollo to his vacant throne,
Assert thy country's honor and thine own."

He equally declared that, after the "Essay on Man" of Pope, the "Pleasures of Memory" constituted the finest English didactic poem. This opinion he maintained always.

"I have read again the 'Pleasures of Memory,'" he wrote in September, 1813. "The elegance of this poem is quite marvellous. Not a vulgar line throughout the whole book."

About the same time he read, in the "Edinburgh Review," a eulogy of Rogers. "He is placed very high," he exclaimed, "but not higher than he has a right to be. There is a summary review of every body. Moore and I included: we were both—he justly—praised; but both very justly ranked under Rogers.

At another time he wrote in his memoranda:

"When he does talk (Rogers), on all subjects of taste, his delicacy of expression is as pure as his poetry. If you enter his house, his drawing-room, his library, you involuntarily say, 'This is not the dwelling of a common mind.' There is not a gem, a coin, a book, thrown aside on his chimney-piece, his sofa, his table, that does not bespeak an almost fastidious elegance in the possessor. But this very delicacy must be the misery of his existence. Oh! the jarrings this disposition must have encountered through life!"

On one occasion he borrows one of Rogers's ideas, to write upon it the "Bride of Abydos;" and in confessing that the "Pleasures of Memory" have suggested his theme, he adds in a note, that "it is useless to say that the idea is taken from a poem so well known, and to which one has such pleasurable recourse."

To Rogers he dedicates the "Giaour," a slight but sincere token of admiration.

When Rogers sent him "Jacqueline," Byron replied that he could not receive a more acceptable gift. "It is grace, delicacy, poetry itself." What astonishes him is that Rogers should not be tempted to write oftener such charming poetry. He sympathized with that kind of soft affection, though he would say that he lacked the talent to express it.

From Venice he wrote to Moore, "I hope Rogers is flourishing. He is the Titan of poetry, already immortal. You and I must wait to become so."

At Pisa he took the part of Rogers against his detractors in the warmest manner. Not only did the "Pleasures of Memory" always enchant him, not only did he insist that the work was immortal, but added that Rogers was kind and good to him. And as people persisted in blaming Rogers for being jealous and susceptible, which Byron knew from experience to be so, he replied, that "these things are, as Lord Kenyon said of Erskine, little spots in the sun. Rogers has qualities which outweigh the little weaknesses of his character."

MOORE.

Moore is third in the order of the triangle. We have seen Byron's sentiments and conduct with regard to this friend. It remains for us to note the feelings of the author for another very popular writer, who was in many respects a worthy rival.

Byron had often recommended Moore to write other poetry than melodies, and to apply his talent to a work of more serious importance. When he learned that he was writing an Oriental poem he was charmed.

"It may be, and would appear to a third person," he wrote to him, "an incredible thing; but I know *you* will believe me, when I say that I am as anxious for your success as one human being can be for another's—as much as if I had never scribbled a line. Surely the field of fame is wide enough for all; and if it were not, I would not willingly rob my neighbor of a rood of it."

And he goes on to praise Moore and to depreciate himself, as was his custom.

After two years' intimacy he dedicated the "Corsair" to Moore, and, in speaking of it to him, he adds:—

"If I can but testify to you and the world how truly I admire and esteem you, I shall be quite satisfied."

And, in dedicating his work to him, he expresses himself thus:—

"My praise could add nothing to your well-earned and firmly-established fame, and with my most hearty admiration of your talents, and delight in your conversation, you are already acquainted."

I have already said that he almost wished to be eclipsed, that Moore might shine the more prominently.

"The best way to make the public 'forget' me is to remind them of yourself. You can not suppose that I would ask you or advise you to publish, if I thought you would *fail.* I really have no literary envy; and I do not believe a friend's success ever sat nearer another's heart, than yours does to the wishes of mine. It is for *elderly gentlemen* to 'bear no brother near,' and can not become our disease for more years than we may perhaps number. I wish you to be out before Eastern subjects are again before the public."

He meanwhile got Murray to use his influence to point out to Moore the best time for appearing.

"I need not say, that I have his success much at heart; not only because he is my friend, but something much better —a man of great talent, of which he is less sensible than, I believe, any even of his enemies. If you can so far oblige me as to step down, do so," etc.

Lord Byron had never ceased to press Moore to publish his poem. When it appeared, he wrote to him from Venice:—

"I am glad that we are to have it at last. Really and truly, I want you to make a great hit, if only out of self-love, because we happen to be old cronies; and I have no doubt you will—I am sure you *can.* But you are, I'll be sworn, in a devil of a pucker, and I am not at your elbow, and Rogers *is.* I envy him; which is not fair, because he does *not envy any body.** Mind you send to me—that is, make Murray send— the moment you are forth."

"I feel as anxious for Moore as I could do for myself, for the soul of me; and I would not have him succeed otherwise than splendidly, which I trust he will do."

* Was this a little irony? I think so, for it was believed that jealousy was the weak point of Rogers.

And then, writing again to Murray, from Venice (June, 1817):—

"It gives me great pleasure to hear of Moore's success, and the more so that I never doubted that it would be complete. Whatever good you can tell me of him and his poem will be most acceptable; I feel very anxious indeed to receive it. I hope that he is as happy in his fame and reward as I wish him to be; for I know no one who deserves both more, if any so much."

A month later he added:—

"I have got the sketch and extracts from 'Lalla Rookh'—which I humbly suspect will knock up . . . ." (he intended himself), "and show young gentlemen that something more than having been across a camel's hump is necessary to write a good Oriental tale. The plan, as well as the extracts I have seen, please me very much indeed, and I feel impatient for the whole."

And, lastly, after he had received it:—

"I have read 'Lalla Rookh.' . . . . I am very glad to hear of his popularity, for Moore is a very noble fellow, in all respects, and will enjoy it without any of the bad feelings which success, good or evil, sometimes engenders in the men of rhyme."

He wrote to Moore from Ravenna, in a sort of jest,—"I am not quite sure that I shall allow the Miss Byrons to read 'Lalla Rookh,'—in the first place, on account of this sad *passion*, and in the second, that they mayn't discover that there was a better poet than Papa."*

To end these quotations, let us add that, shortly before his death, he said to Medwin:—"Moore is one of the small number of writers, who will survive the century which has appreciated his worth. The Irish Melodies will go to posterity with their music, and the poems and the music will last as long as Ireland, or music or poetry."

CAMPBELL.

Campbell, the author of "Pleasures of Hope," and who stands fourth in the triangle, was spared, with Rogers, in the famous satire—

* Moore, Letter 435.

"Come forth, oh! Campbell, give thy talents scope:
Who dare aspire, if thou must cease to hope?"

This homage was strengthened by a note, in which Byron called the "Pleasures of Hope" "one of the finest didactic poems in the English language.

Byron's relations with Campbell were never as intimate as with other poets. Not only because circumstances prevented it, but also in consequence of a fault in Campbell's character, which lessened the sympathy raised by the admiration of his talent and of his worth. This fault consisted in an *excessive* opinion of himself, which prevented his being just toward his rivals, and bearing patiently with their successes, or the criticisms of his own work.

Coleridge at this time was giving lectures upon poetry, in which he taught a new system of poetry.

"He attacks," says Lord Byron, "the 'Pleasures of Hope,' and all other pleasure whatever. . . . Campbell will be desperately annoyed. I never saw a man (and of him I have seen very little) so sensitive. What a happy temperament! I am sorry for it; what can *he* fear from criticism?"

Lord Byron had just published the "Bride of Abydos," when he wrote in his journal, "Campbell last night seemed a little nettled at something or other—I know not what. We were standing in the ante-saloon, when Lord H—— brought out of the other room a vessel of some composition similar to that which is used in Catholic churches for burning incense, and seeing us, he exclaimed, 'Here is some incense for you.' Campbell answered, 'Carry it to Lord Byron; he is used to it.'

"Now this comes of 'bearing no brother near the throne.' I who have no throne am at perfect peace with all the poetical fraternity."

But if this weakness of Campbell lessened Byron's sympathy for him, or rather interfered with his intimacy, it never altered his just appreciation of his merits, or made him less generous to him.

"By-the-by," writes Byron to Moore, "Campbell has a printed poem which is not yet published, the scene of which is laid in Germany. It is perfectly magnificent, and equal to himself. I wonder why he does not publish it."

Later on, in Italy, when in his reply to Blackwood, Byron criticises modern poetry, and gives, without sparing any body, not even himself, his unbiased opinion about the poets of the day, he says: "We are all on a false track, except Rogers, Campbell, and Crabbe."

And in his memoranda in 1821, at Ravenna, we find the following passage:—

"Read Campbell's 'Poets' . . . . justly celebrated. His defense of Pope is glorious. To be sure, it is his own cause too—but no matter, it is very good, and does him great credit . . . If any thing could add to my esteem of this gentleman poet, it would be his classical defense of Pope against the cant of the present day."

On the fifth line of the triangle come the names of Southey, Wordsworth, and Coleridge, commonly called the "Lakers," because they had resided near the Lakes of Cumberland and Westmoreland. He was certainly bitter against these in his satire; but owing simply to their efforts to upset the school of Pope, of which he had made a deep study, and to their endeavors to start an æsthetical school, which he strenuously opposed. As, however, in blaming, he allowed his passion at times to master his opinions and judgments of their merits, he generously made amends and owned his error some years later. He kept to his own notions of poetry and art, but nobly recognized the talent of the Lakers, knowing, however, very well that he would never obtain from them a reciprocity of good feeling.

SOUTHEY.

"Yesterday, at Holland House, I was introduced to Southey,—the best-looking bard I have seen for some time. To have that poet's head and shoulders, I would almost have written his 'Sapphics.' He is certainly a prepossessing person to look on, and a man of talent, and all that—and—there is his eulogy."

"Southey I have not seen much of. His appearance is epic; and he is the only existing entire man of letters. His manners are mild, but not those of a man of the world, and his talents of the first order. His prose is perfect. Of his poetry there are various opinions: there is, perhaps, too much of it for the present generation—posterity will probably select. He has passages equal to any thing. At present he has a party, but no public—except for his prose writings. The 'Life of Nelson' is beautiful."

WORDSWORTH.

Underneath some lines of his satire upon Wordsworth, Byron in 1816 wrote in Switzerland the word "unjust!"

He often praised Wordsworth, even at times when the latter had, for reasons which I will mention hereafter, lost all claims to Byron's indulgence. Even in his poem of the "Island," written shortly before his departure for Greece, where he was to die, Byron found means of inserting a passage from Wordsworth's poem, which he considered exquisite.

COLERIDGE.

Among the three Lakers, Coleridge was the one to whom he showed the most generous feeling. He was poor, and lived by his pen. Lord Byron, putting this consideration above all others, wished to assist at his readings, and praised them warmly. Coleridge having asked him on one occasion to interest himself with the director of Drury-lane Theatre (on the committee of which Byron then stood) the latter did his best to gratify the wishes of Coleridge, and wrote him the most flattering letter, blaming the satire which had been the effect of a youthful ebullition of feeling :—

"P. S.—You mention my 'satire,' lampoon, or whatever you or others please to call it. I can only say that it was written when I was very young and very angry, and has been a thorn in my side ever since; more particularly as almost all the persons animadverted upon became subsequently my acquaintances, and some of them my friends, which is 'heaping fire upon an enemy's head,' and forgiving me too readily to permit me to forgive myself. The part applied to you is pert, and petulant, and shallow enough; but, although I have long done every thing in my power to suppress the circulation of the whole thing, I shall always regret the wantonness or generality of many of its attacks. If Coleridge writes his promised tragedy, Drury Lane will be set up." Though harassed with pecuniary difficulties of all kinds, Byron contrived to help Coleridge, who he had heard was in the greatest distress.

He wrote to Moore :—" By the way, if poor Coleridge—who is a man of wonderful talent, and in distress, and about to publish two volumes of poesy and biography, and who has been worse used by the critics than ever we were—will you, if he comes out, promise me to review him favorably in the E. R.? Praise him I think you must; but will you also praise him well,—of all things the most difficult? It will be the making of him.

"This must be a secret between you and me, as Jeffrey might not like such a project: nor, indeed, might he himself like it. But I do think he only wants a pioneer and a spark or two to explode most gloriously."

He sent Murray a MS. tragedy of Coleridge, begging him to read it and to publish it :—

" When you have been enabled to form an opinion on Mr. Coleridge's MS., you will oblige me by returning it, as, in fact, I have no authority to let it out of my hands. I think most highly of it, and feel anxious that you should be the publisher; but if you are not, I do not despair of finding those who will."

As the reader knows, Byron, while in England, always gave away the produce of his poems. To Coleridge he destined part of the sum offered to him by Murray for " Parisina " and the Siege of Corinth." Some difficulty, however, having arisen, because Murray refused to pay the 100 guineas to any other than Byron himself, he borrowed it himself to give it to Coleridge.

At the same time Byron paid so noble a tribute to Coleridge's talent, and to his poem of " Christabel," by inserting a note on the subject in his preface to the " Siege of Corinth," that Coleridge's editor took this note as the epigraph.

" Christabel!—I won't have any one," he said, " sneer at 'Christabel;' it is a fine wild poem."

In 1816 he wrote from Venice to Moore :—

" I hear that the E. R. has cut up Coleridge's 'Christabel,' and declared against me for praising it. I praised it, firstly, because I thought well of it; secondly, because Coleridge was in great distress, and after doing what little I could for him in essentials, I thought that the public avowal of my good opinion might help him further, at least with the booksellers. I am very sorry that J—— has attacked him, because, poor fellow, it will hurt him in mind and pocket. As for me, he's welcome—I shall never think less of Jeffrey for any thing he may say against me or mine in future."

At Genoa he declared, in a memorandum, that Crabbe and Coleridge were pre-eminent in point of power and talent.

At Pisa he blamed those who refused to see in "Christabel" a work of rare merit, notwithstanding the knowledge which he had of Coleridge's ingratitude to him; and refused to believe that W. Scott did not admire the poem, "for we all owe Coleridge a great deal," said he, "and even Scott himself."

And Medwin adds: "Lord Byron thinks Coleridge's poem very fine. He paraphrased and imitated one passage. He considers the idea excellent, and enters into it."

And speaking of Coleridge's psychological poem, he said: "What perfect harmony! 'Kubla Khan' delights me."

SHELLEY.

If Shelley did not find a place in the triangle, it is only because he was not yet known, except by the eccentricities of his conduct as a boy. But so soon as Byron was able to appreciate his genius, he lavished praises upon the poet and the man, while he blamed his metaphysics.

In all his letters we find proofs of his affectionate regard for Shelley; and during his last days in Greece, he said to Finlay,—"Shelley was really a most extraordinary genius; but those who know him only from his works, know but half his merits: it was from his thoughts and his conversation poor Shelley ought to be judged. He was romance itself in his manners and his style of thinking."

"You were all mistaken," he wrote from Pisa to Murray, "about Shelley, who was, without exception, the best and least selfish man I ever knew."

And when he learned his death, he wrote to Moore:—"There is thus another man gone, about whom the world was ill-naturedly, and ignorantly, and brutally mistaken. It will, perhaps, do him justice now, when he can be no better for it."

Such were Byron's expressions in behalf of poets of whose school he disapproved, before the calumnies spread about, and the perfidious provocations of some, joined to the ingratitude and jealousy of others, obliged him to turn his generosity into bitter retaliation. We will speak elsewhere of this epoch in their mutual relations, and we hope to show, if jealousy caused the change, that it sprang from them and not from him.

To praise was almost a besetting sin in Lord Byron. So amiable a fault was not only committed in favor of his rivals, but also by way of encouragement to young authors. What did he not do to promote the success of M. N. N——, the author of Bertram's dramas, whom Walter Scott had recommended to him?

After reading a tragedy which a young man had submitted to him, Byron wrote in his memoranda:—

"This young man has talent; he has, no doubt, stolen his ideas from another, but I shall not betray him. His critics will be but too prone to proclaim it. I hate to discourage a beginner."

Indulgent to mediocrity, compassionate with the weakness and defects of all, incapable of causing the slightest pain to those who were destitute of talent, even when art required that he should condemn them, his goodness was such, that he almost felt remorse whenever he had been led to criticise a work too severely. He deplored his having dealt too harshly with poor Blackett, as soon as the latter's position became known to him; and also with Keats, whose talent, though great, was raw in many respects, and who had become a follower of the Lakist school, which Byron abhorred.

To praise the humble, however, in order to humble the great, was an action incompatible with his noble character. Great minds constituted his great attractions, and on these he bestowed such praise as could not be deemed too partial or unjust.

Happy in the unqualified praise of Pope, of the classical poets, of the great German and Italian poets, he sometimes made exceptions, and Shakspeare was one. This is not to be wondered at. Lord Byron's mind was as well regulated as it was powerful. His admiration of Pope proves it.

"As to Pope," he writes to Moore from Ravenna, in 1821, "I have always regarded him as the greatest name in our Poetry. Depend upon it, the rest are barbarians. He is a Greek temple, with a Gothic cathedral on one hand, and a Turkish mosque and all sorts of fantastic pagodas and conventicles about him. You may call Shakspeare and Milton pyramids, if you please; but I prefer the Temple of Theseus, or the Parthenon, to a mountain of burnt brick-work."*

Order and proportion were necessities of his nature, so much so that he condemned his writings whenever they departed from his ideal of the beautiful, the essential constituents of which were order and power.

His admiration, therefore, was entirely centred in classical works. But has not Shakspeare a little disregarded the eternal laws of the beautiful observed by Homer, Pindar, and a host of other poets, ancient and modern? .

If Byron, then, did not see in Shakspeare all that perfection which an æsthetical school just sprung from the North attributed to him, was he to be blamed? Has he, on this account, disregarded the great merits of that glorious mind? Even had Byron seen in Shakspeare the founder of a dramatic school, rather than a genius more powerful than orderly, who acted against his will upon certain principles, and who scrutinized the human heart to an almost supernatural depth, was he interdicted from finding fault with that school?

Does Shakspeare so economize both time and mind, as to make the action of his dramas continuous, without fatiguing the mind or weakening the dramatic effect? Are not the unities and the proportions disregarded in his plays? What necessity is there at times to put one piece into another? Are not his discussions and monologues too long? Does not his own exuberant genius become a fatigue to himself and to his readers? Are not, perhaps, his characters too real? and do they not often degenerate, without motive, from the sublime into the ridiculous? Would Hamlet have appeared less interesting or less mad had he not spoken indelicate and cruel words to Ophelia? Would Laertes have seemed less grieved on hearing of the death of his sister had he not made so unnecessary a play on the words?

Was not Byron, therefore, right when he said, with Pope, that Shakspeare was "the worst of models?" And could he

* Moore, Letter 422.

possibly be called jealous, because he added that, "notwithstanding his defects, Shakspeare was still the most extraordinary of men of genius?"

This opinion of Byron was decidedly serious, though his opinions did not always partake of that character. His humor was rather French: he liked to laugh, to joke, to mystify, and astonish people who wished to understand him. He used, then, to employ a particular measure in his praise and his condemnation.

"On one occasion at Missolonghi, and shortly before his death," says Colonel Stanhope, "the drama was mentioned in conversation, and Byron at once attacked Shakspeare by defending the unities. A gentleman present, on hearing his anti-Shakspearean opinions rushed out of the room, and afterward entered his protest most earnestly against such doctrines. Lord Byron was quite delighted with this, and redoubled the severity of his criticism.

"He said once, when we were alone,—'I like to astonish Englishmen; they come abroad full of Shakspeare, and contempt for the dramatic literature of other nations. They think it blasphemy to find a fault in his writings, which are full of them. People talk of my writings, and yet read the sonnets to Master Hughes.'

"And yet," continues Finlay, "he continually had the most melodious lines of Shakspeare in his mouth, as examples of blank verse."

The jealousy of Shakspeare attributed to Byron is, however, nothing when compared to the ridiculous assertion, that he was jealous of Keats, simply because he had repeated in joke what the papers and Shelley himself, a friend of Keats, had said, namely, "that the young poet had been killed by a criticism of the 'Quarterly.'"

But since a French critic, M. Philarète Chasles, has made the same accusation, we must pause and consider it.

At the time when Byron was more than ever penetrated with the perfection of Pope, and opposed to the romantic school,—at the time when he himself wrote his dramas according to all classical rules,—he received at Ravenna the poems of a young disciple of the Lakists, who united in himself all their exaggerated faults. This young man had the audacity—

(which was almost unpardonable in the eyes of Byron)—to despise Pope, and to constitute himself at nineteen a lawgiver of poetical rules in England.

Such ridiculous pride, added to the contempt shown to his idol, incensed Byron and prevented his showing Keats the same indulgence he had shown Maturin and Blackett. He spoke severely of Keats in his famous reply to "Blackwood's Magazine," and to his Cambridge friends—followers of the good old traditions. He quoted some lines of Keats, and remarked that "they were taken from the book of a young man who was learning how to write in verse, but who began by teaching others the art of poetry." Then, after a long quotation, he adds—"What precedes will show the ideas and principles professed by the regenerators of the English lyre in regard to the man who most of any contributed to its harmony, and the progress visible in their innovation."

Let us not forget to add that he styled Keats "the tadpole of the Lakists."

But the following year, when he heard that Keats had died at Rome, the victim of his inordinate self-love, and unable to be consoled for the criticism directed against his poetry, he wrote the following heartfelt, and, as it were, repentant words to Shelley:—

"I am very sorry to hear what you say of Keats—is it *actually* true? I did not think criticism had been so killing. Though I differ from you essentially in your estimate of his performances, I so much abhor all unnecessary pain, that I would rather he had been seated on the highest peak of Parnassus than have perished in such a manner. Poor fellow! though, with such inordinate self-love, he would probably have not been very happy. . . . . Had I known that Keats was dead, or that he was 'alive,' and so 'sensitive,' I should have omitted some remarks upon his poetry, to which I was provoked by his attack upon Pope, and my disapprobation of his own style of writing."

To Murray he wrote the same day:—

"Is it true what Shelley writes me, that poor John Keats died at Rome of the 'Quarterly Review?' I am very sorry for it; though I think he took the wrong line as a poet, and was spoilt by Cockneyfying and suburbing, and versifying

Tooke's 'Pantheon' and Lemprière's 'Dictionary.' I know by experience, that a savage review is hemlock to a sucking author; and the one on me (which produced the 'English Bards,' etc.) knocked me down; but I got up again. Instead of bursting a bloodvessel, I drank three bottles of claret, and began an answer, finding that there was nothing in the article for which I could lawfully knock Jeffrey on the head, in an honorable way. However, I would not be the person who wrote the homicidal article for all the honor and glory in the world, though I by no means approve of that school of scribbling which it treats upon."

Some time after he wrote again to Murray, saying,—"You know very well that I did not approve of Keats's poetry, nor of his poetical principles, nor of his abuse of Pope. But he is dead. I beg that you will therefore omit all I have said of him either in my manuscripts or in my publications. His 'Hyperion' is a fine monument, and will cause his name to last. I do not envy the man who wrote the article against Keats."

Several months later he made complete amends. He added to his severe article in answer to Blackwood, a note in the following terms:

"I have read the article before and since; and although it is bitter, I do not think that a man should permit himself to be killed by it. But a young man little dreams what he must inevitably encounter in the course of a life ambitious of public notice. My indignation at Mr. Keats's depreciation of Pope has hardly permitted me do justice to his own genius, which, *malgré* all the fantastic fopperies of his style, was undoubtedly of great promise. His fragment of 'Hyperion' seems actually inspired by the Titans, and is as sublime as Æschylus. He is a loss to our literature; and the more so, as he himself, before his death, is said to have been persuaded that he had not taken the right line, and was reforming his style upon the more classical models of the language."

Were we wrong in saying that the accusations against Byron, with respect to Keats, did not deserve a notice? If we have noticed them, it has been merely to show, that the French critic should have judged matters in this instance with greater conscientiousness and reflection.

Influenced as Byron always was by his own ideas of beauty, he required in the authors themselves certain moral qualities which would demand for their works the bestowal of his praise. It was not only their talent, but their loyalty, their independence of character, their political consistency, and their perfect honesty, which endeared Walter Scott, Moore, and others, to him.

Byron, on the other hand, had never found these qualities in the Lakists, and especially in the head of their school, whose whole life, on the contrary, bore the marks of quite opposite characteristics. Since Southey's dream of a life of intimacy with other poets of his school, such as Wordsworth and Coleridge, in some blissful remote spot from which they would publish their works in common, and where they would live with their wives and children in community of interests, some change had taken place; for Southey had so far deviated from his purpose as to become Laureate, to write for himself, and to profess ultra-Tory principles, the ultimate objects of which could not but be palpable.

All this called for Byron's contempt. To this contempt, however, he gave no expression, for fear of wounding without reason, until that reason did arise by the Laureate's unforgiving spirit. "The Laureate," says Byron, "is not one of those who can forgive." Incapable of forgetting that Byron's genius had obscured his own reputation, Southey hated Byron with an intensity, such as to make him look out for opportunities of doing him an injury. This opportunity Southey found in Byron's departure for the Continent, subsequently to the unfortunate result of his marriage; and not only did he join in all the calumnies which were set forth against him in England, but actually followed him to Switzerland, there to invent new ones, in the hope of crushing his reputation and ruining the fame of the poet by the depreciation of the man.

Lord Byron for some time was ignorant of the Laureate's baseness, for oftentimes friends deem it prudent to hide the truth which it would perhaps be better to make known. But when he came to know of them, his whole soul revolted, as naturally must be the case with a man of honor, and in "Don Juan" he came down upon Southey with a double-edged sword, throwing ridicule upon the author's writings, and odium upon his conduct as a calumniator.

This revenge was well deserved. It was not only natural but just, and even necessary, for it was requisite to show up the man, to judge of the value to be attached to his calumnies; and later, when he called him out, he did what honor required of him.

We have seen elsewhere how far the Laureate's conduct justified Byron's retaliation. It is enough, therefore, that I should have shown here that Byron's anger was rather the result of Southey's envy than his own, and that his sarcasms were due entirely to the disgust which he felt for such dishonorable proceedings.

From that time his language, when speaking of Wordsworth and Coleridge, always reflected the same disgust. Both had made themselves the echoes of Southey, and both had been inconstant from interested motives, and had solicited favors from the party in power, which they had abused in their writings. "They have each a price," said Byron at Pisa.

On one occasion, as Shelley and Medwin were laughing at some of Wordsworth's last poems, which disgusted them, not only from the subservient spirit to Toryism which pervaded them, but also excited their laughter from their absurdity, Byron, in whose house they were, said to them, "It is satisfactory to see that a man who becomes mercenary, and traffics upon the independence of his character, loses at the same time his talent as a poet."

Byron had such a notion of political consistency, that he ceased having any regard for those who failed in this respect.

"I was at dinner," says Stendhall, "at the Marquis of Breno's at Milan, in 1816, with Byron and the celebrated poet Monti, the author of 'Basvilliana.' The conversation fell upon poetry, and the question was asked which were the twelve most beautiful lines written in a century, either in English, in Italian, or in French. The Italians present agreed in declaring that Monti's first twelve lines in the 'Mascheroniana' were the finest Italian lines written for a century. Monti recited them. I observed Byron. He was in raptures. That kind of haughty look which a man often puts on when he has to get rid of an inopportune question, and which rather took away from the beauty of his magnificent countenance, suddenly disappeared to make way for an expression of happiness. The whole of the first canto to the 'Mascheroniana,' which Conti was made to recite, enchanted all hearers, and caused the liveliest pleasure to the author of 'Childe Harold.' Never shall I forget the sublime expression of his countenance: it was the peaceful look of power united with genius."

He learned, later, that Monti was a man inconsistent in his politics, and that on the sole impulse of his passions he had passed from one party to another, and had called from the pen of another poet the remark that he justified Dante's saying,—

"Il verso si non l' animo costante."

Byron's sympathy for Monti ceased from that time, and he even called him the "Giuda del Parnaso," whereas his esteem and sympathy for Silvio Pellico, for Manzoni, and for many other Italians, remained perfectly unshaken.

His sense of justice extended to all nationalities. He was a cosmopolite, and, provided the elements essential to claim his admiration existed both in the man's work, and in his character, no personal consideration ever came in the way of his bestowing praise,—the most pleasing duty that could befall him. The great minds of antiquity, those of the middle ages—especially the Italians,—all the modern great men, of whatever nation, were all for him of one country, the country of great intellects, and the degree of his sympathy for each was calculated upon the degree of their merit.

We know how ably he defended Dante, the greatest of Italian poets; how ably he translated "Francesca da Rimini," and how he exposed the error of those who did not find that Dante was not sufficiently pathetic.

We know his admiration for Goethe, who was not only his contemporary, but also his rival. Could Goethe see with pleasure another star rise in the horizon, when his own was at its zenith? Some say that he could. Without sharing altogether in this opinion, it is impossible, however, not to find that the first impressions which he gave to the world with respect to Byron do not justify the accusations of those who said he was jealous of him.

While at Ravenna, Byron received several numbers of a German paper edited and written by Goethe. It contained several articles upon English literature, and, among others, upon "Manfred." Curious to know what the patriarch of German literature thought of him, and being unable to read German, Byron sent these articles to Hoppner, at Venice, begging him to translate them.

" . . . If I may judge by two notes of admiration (generally put after something ridiculous by us), and the word '*hypocondrisch*,' they are any thing but favorable. I shall regret this; for I should have been proud of Goethe's good word; but I sha'n't alter my opinion of him, even though he should be (savage). . . . Never mind—soften nothing—I am *literary proof*—as one says of a material object, when he puts it to the proof of fire and water," etc.

The article was any thing but favorable. After recognizing that the author of "Manfred" is gifted with wonderful genius, Goethe pretends that it is an imitation of his "Faust," and thereupon writes a tissue of fanciful notions which he palms off upon the world.

On learning all this, Byron was by no means put out, but laughed heartily at the notion of the author of "Werther" accusing him of inciting others to a disgust of life. He wondered at such a man as Goethe giving credence to such silly fables, and giving out as authentic what were merely suppositions. Instead of being angry at this evident hostility, he declared that the article was intended as favorable to him, and, as an acknowledgment, wished to dedicate to him the tragedy of "Marino Faliero," upon which he was engaged. In the dedication, which was only projected, the reality of his admiration for Goethe soars above some jesting expressions.

To Goethe also he wished to dedicate "Sardanapalus." "I mean," said he, at Pisa, "to dedicate 'Werner' to Goethe. I look upon him as the greatest genius that the age has produced. I desired Murray to inscribe his name to a former work; but he said my letter containing the order came too late. It would have been more worthy of him than this. I have a great curiosity about every thing relating to Goethe, and please myself with thinking there is some analogy between our characters and writings. So much interest do I take in him, that I offered to give £100 to any person who would translate his memoirs for my own reading. Shelley has sometimes explained part of them to me. He seems to be very superstitious, and is a believer in astrology, or rather was, for he was very young when he wrote the first part of his 'Life.' I would give the world to read 'Faust' in the original. I have been urging Shelley to translate it." In comparing 'Cain' to 'Faust,' he said, "'Faust' itself is not so fine a subject as 'Cain,' which is a grand mystery. The mark that was put upon Cain is a sublime and shadowy act; Goethe would have made more of it than I have done."

Not being able to dedicate "Sardanapalus" to him, he dedicated "Werner" "to the illustrious Goethe, by one of his humblest admirers."

All these tokens of sympathy pleased Goethe. Their mutual admiration of one another brought on an exchange of courtesies, which ended by creating on both sides quite a warm feeling. In a letter which Goethe wrote to M. M——, after Byron's death, he speaks of his relation with the noble poet; after saying how "Sardanapalus" appeared without a dedication, of which, however, he was happy to possess a lithographed fac-simile, he adds:—

"It appeared, however, that the noble lord had not renounced his project of showing his contemporary and companion in letters a striking testimony of his friendly intentions, of which the tragedy of 'Werner' contains an extremely precious evidence."

It might naturally be expected that the aged German poet, after receiving from so celebrated a person such an unhoped-for kindness (proof of a disposition so thoroughly amiable, and the more to be prized from its rarity in the world), should also prepare, on his part, to express most clearly and forcibly a sense of the gratitude and esteem with which he was affected:—

"But this undertaking was so great, and every day seemed to make it so much more difficult; for what could be said of an earthly being whose merit could not be exhausted by thought, or comprehended by words?

"But when, in the spring of 1823, a young man of amiable and engaging manners, a M. St. ——, brought direct from Genoa to Weimar, a few words under the hand of this estimable friend, by way of recommendation, and when, shortly after, there was spread a report that the noble lord was about to consecrate his great powers and varied talents to high and perilous enterprise, I had no longer a plea for delay, and addressed to him the stanzas which ends by the lines,—'And he self-known, e'en as to me he's known!'

"These verses," continued Goethe, "arrived at Genoa, but found him not. This excellent friend had already sailed; but being driven back by contrary winds, he landed at Leghorn, where this effusion of my heart reached him. On the era of his departure, July 23, 1823, he found time to send me a reply, full of the most beautiful ideas and the divinest sentiments, which will be treasured as an invaluable testimony of worth and friendship, among the choicest documents which I possess.

"What emotions of joy and hope did not that paper at once excite! but now it has become, by the premature death of its noble writer, an inestimable relic, and a source of unspeakable regret; for it aggravates, to a peculiar degree in me, the mourning and melancholy that pervade the whole moral and poetical world,—in me, who looked forward (after the success of his great efforts) to the prospect of being blessed with the sight of this master-spirit of the age—this friend so fortunately acquired: and of having to welcome, on his return, the most humane of conquerors."

These are, no doubt, most noble words, but they were called forth by the still nobler conduct of Byron toward him. It can not be said that Goethe ever appreciated all that there was of worth in his young rival, and a few words at the end of his letter make one believe that he still credited some of the absurd stories which he had been told about Byron's youth, and whom he still believed to be identified in the person of "Manfred." He entertained a great affection for Byron, no doubt, but he believed, however, that indulgence and forgiveness were not only necessary on his part, but actually generous in him.

Lord Byron's sympathetic admiration had this peculiarity, —that it did not attach to one class of individuals devoted like himself to poetry, but extended to every class of society. The statesman, the orator, the philosopher, the prince, the subject, the learned, women, general, or literary men, all were equally sure of having justice done to them. At every page of his memoranda, we find instances of this. Thus of Mackintosh he says: "He is a rare instance of the union of every transcendent talent and great good-nature."

Of Curran he speaks in the most enthusiastic terms:—

"I have met Curran at Holland House—he beats every body;—his imagination is beyond conception, and his humor (it is difficult to define what is wit) perfect. Then he has fifty faces, and twice as many voices, when he mimics; I never met his equal. Now, were I a woman, and e'en a virgin, that is the man I should make my Scamander. He is quite fascinating. Remember, I have met him only once, and I almost fear to meet him again, lest the impression should be lowered.

"Curran! Curran's the man who struck me most. Such imagination! There never was any thing like it, that ever I saw or heard of. His *published* life—his published speeches—give you no idea of the man, none at all."

In his memoranda there were equally enthusiastic praises of Curran. "The riches," said he, "of his Irish imagination were exhaustless. I have heard that man speak more poetry than I have ever written—though I saw him seldom, and but occasionally."

In speaking of Colman, he said, "He was most agreeable and sociable. He can laugh so well, which Sheridan can not. If I could not have them both together, I should like to begin the evening with Sheridan, and finish it with Colman."

He praised loudly the eloquence of Grattan:—

"I differ with him in politics, but I agree with all those who admire his éloquence."

As to Sheridan, he never ceased his eulogies:—

"At Lord Holland's the other night, we were all delivering our respective and various opinions on him and other *hommes marquants*, and mine was this:—'Whatever Sheridan has done, or chosen to do, has been, *par excellence*, always the *best* of its kind. He has written the *best* comedy ("School for Scandal"), the *best* drama (in my mind, far before that St. Giles's lampoon, the "Beggars' Opera"), the *best* farce (the "Critic,"—it is only too good for a farce), and the *best* address ("Monologue on Garrick"), and, to crown all, delivered the very best oration (the famous "Begum Speech") ever conceived or heard in this country.'"

His enthusiasm for Sheridan partook even of a kind of tender compassion for his great weaknesses and misfortunes. He wrote in his memoranda, on one occasion, when Sheridan had cried with joy on hearing that Byron had warmly praised him:—

"Poor Brinsley, if they were tears of pleasure, I would rather have said those few, but most sincere words, than have written the "Iliad," or made his own celebrated "Philippic." Nay, his own comedy never gratified me more, than to hear that he had derived a moment's gratification from any praise of mine, humble as it must appear to 'my elders, and my betters.'"

And also:—

"Poor, dear Sherry! I shall never forget the day when he, Rogers, Moore, and myself, spent the time from six at night till one o'clock in the morning, without a single yawn; we listening to him, and he talking all the time."

When he speaks of great men recently dead,—of Burke, Pitt, Burns, Goldsmith, and others of his distinguished contemporaries,—he is never-ending in his praise of them. His affectionate admiration for so many went so far, almost, as to frighten him into the belief that it was a weakness: after having said—"I like A——, I like B——. By Mohammed!" he exclaims in his memoranda, "I begin to think I like every body; a disposition not to be encouraged; a sort of social gluttony, that swallows every thing set before it."

Not only was it a pleasure to him to praise those who deserved it, but he would not allow the dead to be blamed, nor the illustrious among the living; we all know how much he admired the talents of Madame de Staël: "Il avait pour elle des admirations *obstinées*." "Campbell abused Corinne," he says in his journal, 1813: "I reverence and admire him; but I won't give up my opinion. Why should I? I read her again and again, and there can be no affectation in this. I can not be mistaken (except in taste) in a book I read and lay down and take up again; and no book can be totally bad, which finds some, even *one* reader, who can say as much sincerely."

And elsewhere:

"H—— laughed, as he does at every thing German, in which, however, I think he goes a little too far. B——, I hear, contemns it too. But there are fine passages; and, after all, what is a work—any or every work—but a desert with fountains, and, perhaps, a grove or two every day's journey? To be sure, in mademoiselle, what we often mistake and 'pant for' as the 'cooling stream,' turns out to be the 'mirage' (*criticè*, verbiage); but we do, at last, get to something like the temple of Jupiter Ammon, and then the waste we have passed is only remembered to gladden the contrast."

He who was so sparing of answers to his own detractors, could not allow a criticism against a friend to be left unanswered. We have seen how he defended Scott, Shelley, Coleridge, and numerous other remarkable persons, whenever they were unjustly attacked, although they were alive to defend themselves. The respect and justice which he claimed for the dead was equally proportioned. "Do not forget," he wrote to Moore on hearing that he was about to write the "Life of Sheridan;" "do not forget *to spare the living without insulting the dead.*"

On reading, at Ravenna, that Schlegel said, that Dante was not popular in Italy, and accused him of want of pathos: "'Tis false," said he, with indignation; "there have been more editors and commentators (and imitators ultimately) of Dante, than of all their poets put together. *Not* a favorite! Why they talk Dante, write Dante, and think and dream Dante at this moment (1821) to an excess which would be ridiculous, but that he deserves it.

"In the same style this German talks of gondolas on the Arno—a precious fellow to dare to speak of Italy!

"He says, also, that Dante's chief defect is a want, in a word, of gentle feelings. Of gentle feelings! and this in the face of 'Francesca of Rimini'—and the father's feelings in 'Ugolino'—and 'Beatrice'—and 'La Pia!' Why, there is a gentleness in Dante beyond all gentleness, when he is tender. It is true, that in treating of the Christian Hades, or Hell, there is not much scope or room for gentleness; but who *but* Dante could have introduced any 'softness' at all into Hell? Is there any in Milton? No—and Dante's heaven is all *love*, and *glory*, and *majesty*."

We have alluded to his admiration for Pope. It was such as to appear almost a kind of filial love. He was sorry, mortified, and humbled, not to find in Westminster Abbey the monument of so great a man:—

"Of all the disgraces that attach to England, the greatest," said he, "is that there should be no place assigned to Pope in Poets' Corner. I have often thought of erecting a monument to him at my own expense in Westminster Abbey; and hope to do so yet."

To add any thing more to show how totally Byron was free from all sentiments of an envious nature, would be to exhaust the subject, and to abuse the reader's patience. This absence of envy in him shows itself so clearly in all his sayings and doings, that it appears to be impossible to doubt it, and yet he has not been spared even such a calumny! I do not allude to the French critics, who neither knew the man nor the author, and whose systematic attacks have no value; but I allude to a certain article in the "London Magazine," which appeared shortly before his death, under the title of "Personal Character of Lord Byron," and which caused some sensation because it appeared to have been written by some one who had known Byron intimately. It was all the more perfidious because it gave an appearance of truth to a great many falsehoods, derived from the truth with which these falsehoods were mixed. It was the work of one who had gone to Greece, there to play a great part, but who, having failed in his attempt and exposed himself to the laughter of his friends, felt a kind of jealousy for Byron's success in that line, and revenged himself by saying, among other things, "that it was dangerous for Byron's friends to rise in the world, if they preferred his friendship to their glory, because, as soon as they arrived at a certain pre-eminence, he was sure to hate them."

Such a calumny exasperated Byron's real friends, and among these Count Gamba, who hastened to reply to it, by publishing an interesting book, precious from its veracity, and which does equal credit to Byron and to the young man honored with his friendship. After analyzing the anonymous article, Count. Gamba goes on to say: "My own opinion is just the contrary to that of the writer in the magazine. I think he prided himself on the successes of his friends, and cited them as a proof of discernment in the choice of some of his companions. This I know, that of envy he had not the least spark in his whole disposition: he had strong antipathies, certainly, to one or two individuals; but I have always understood, from those most likely to know, that he never broke with any of the friends of his youth, and that his earliest attachments were also his last.'

It may be remarked that Byron's popularity made it difficult for him to indulge sentiments of envy. But without referring to the unstable character of popularity, was not his own attacked by the jealousy of those who wished to pull him down from the pedestal of fame, to which they hoped themselves to rise? Did he not think, some years before his death, that his popularity was wavering, and that his rivals would profit by it? Was he less pleased at the success of his friends? Does not all he said, and all he did, prove that where he blamed he did so unwillingly, from a sense of justice and truth; but that when he praised, he did so to satisfy a desire of his heart?

We have dwelt at considerable length upon this subject, because we believe that a total absence of envy is so rare among poets, and so conspicuous in Lord Byron, that we can take it to be the criterion of his nobility of soul. We can sum up, therefore, all we have said, by declaring, that if Byron has been envied by all his enemies, and even his friends, with, perhaps, the exception of Shelley, and has not himself envied one, though he suffered personally from the consequences of their jealousy, it is because the great kindness of his nature made him the least envious of men.

CHAPTER IX.

BENEVOLENCE AND KINDNESS OF LORD BYRON.

BENEVOLENCE.

THE benevolence of Byron's character constitutes the principal characteristic of his nature, and was particularly remarkable from its power. All the good qualities in Byron do not show the same force in the same degree. In all the sentiments which we have analyzed and given in proof of his goodness, though each may be very strong, and even capable of inspiring him with the greatest sacrifice, yet one might find in each that personal element, inherent in different degrees to our purest and most generous affections, since the impulse which dictates them is evidently based upon a desire to be satisfied with ourselves. The same thing might be said of his benevolence, had it been only the result of habit: but if it had been this, if it had been intermittent, and of that kind which does not exclude occasional harshness and even cruelty, I would not venture to present it to the reader as a proof of Byron's goodness.

His benevolence had nothing personal in its elements. It was a kind of universal and habitual charity, which gives without hope of return, which is more occupied with the good of others than with its own, and which is called for only by the instinctive desire to alleviate the sufferings of others. If such a quality has no right to be called a virtue, it nevertheless imprints upon the man who possesses it an ineffaceable character of greatness.

There was not a single moment in his life in which it did not reveal itself in the most touching actions. We have seen how neither happiness nor misfortune could alter it.

As a child, he went one day to bathe with a little schoolfellow in the Don, in Scotland, and having but one very small Shetland pony between them, each one walked and rode alternately. When they reached the bridge, at a point where the river becomes sombre and romantic, Byron, who was on foot, recollected a legendary prophecy, which says:—

"Brig o' Balgounie, black's your wa':
Wi' a wife's ae son and a mare's ae foal
Doun ye shall fa'!"

Little Byron stopped his companion, asked him if he remembered the prediction, and declared that as the pony might very well be "a mare's ae foal," he intended to cross first, for although both only sons, his mother alone would mourn him, while the death of his friend, whose father and mother were both alive, would cause a twofold grief.*

As a stripling, he saw at Southwell a poor woman sally mournfully from a shop, because the Bible she wished to purchase costs more money than she possesses. Byron hastens to buy it, and, full of joy, runs after the poor creature to give it to her. As a young man, at an age when the effervescence and giddiness of youth forget many things, he never forgot that to seduce a young girl is a crime. Then, as ever, he was less the seducer than the seduced.

Moore tells us that Byron was so keenly sensitive to the pleasure or pain of those with whom he lived, that while in his imaginary realms he defied the universe, in real life a frown or a smile could overcome him.

Proud, energetic, independent, intrepid, benevolence alone rendered Lord Byron so flexible, patient, and docile to the remonstrances or reproaches of those who loved him, and to whom he allowed friendly motives, that he often sacrificed his own talent to this genial and kindly sentiment. The Rev. Mr. Beecher, disapproving as too free one of the poems he had just published at the age of seventeen, in his first edition of the "Hours of Idleness," Lord Byron *withdrew* and *burnt* the whole edition. At the solicitation of Dallas and Gifford he suppresses, in the second canto of "Childe Harold," the very stanzas he preferred to all the rest. Madame G——, grieved at the persecution drawn down on him by the first canto of "Don Juan," begs him to discontinue the poem, and he ceased to write it.

* Galt's Life of Byron, p. 329.

At the request of Madame de Staël, he consented, in spite of his great disinclination, to attempt a reconciliation with Lady Byron.

The "Curse of Minerva," a poem written in Greece, while he was still painfully impressed by the artistic piracies of Lord Elgin in the "Parthenon," was in the press and on the eve of publication; but Lord Elgin's friends reminded him of the pain it would inflict on him and on his family, and the poem was sacrificed. No one ever bore more generously than he with reproaches made with good-will and kindness. This amiable disposition, observed in Greece by Mr. Finlay, led him to say that it amazed him. As regards Lord Byron's tenderness toward his friends, it was always so great and constant, that we have thought it right to devote a long article to it. We will, however, quote as another instance of the delicacy of his friendship and his fear of offending his friends, or of giving them pain, a letter which Moore also cites as a proof of his extreme sensitiveness in this respect.

This letter was addressed to Mr. Bankes, his friend and college companion, on one occasion when Byron believed he had offended him involuntarily:—

"MY DEAR BANKES,—My eagerness to come to an explanation has, I trust, convinced you that whatever my unlucky manner might inadvertently be, the change was as unintentional as (if intended) it would have been ungrateful. I really was not aware that, while we were together, I had evinced such caprice. That we were not so much in each other's company as I could have wished, I well know; but I think so astute an observer as yourself must have perceived enough to explain this, without supposing any slight to one in whose society I have pride and pleasure. Recollect that I do not allude here to 'extended' or 'extending' acquaintances, but to circumstances you will understand, I think, on a little reflection.

"And now, my dear Bankes, do not distress me by supposing that I can think of you, or you of me, otherwise than I trust we have long thought. You told me not long ago, that my temper was improved, and I should be sorry that opinion should be revoked. Believe me, your friendship is of more account to me than all those absurd vanities in which, I fear, you conceive me to take too much interest. I have never disputed your superiority, or doubted (seriously) your good-will, and no one shall ever 'make mischief between us' without the sincere regret on the part of your ever affectionate, etc.

"BYRON."

In the midst of the unexampled enthusiasm of a whole nation, Byron is neither touched by the adoration which his genius inspires, nor the endless praises which are bestowed upon him, nor the love declarations which crowd his table, nor the flattering expressions of Lord Holland, who ranks him next to Walter Scott as a poet, and to Burke as an orator; nor indeed by those of Lord Fitzgerald, who, notwithstanding a flogging at Harrow, can not bear malice against the author of "Childe Harold," but desires to forgive. To be the friend of those whom his satire offended, so penetrates him with disgust for that poem, that his dearest wish is to lose every trace of it; and, though the fifth edition is nearly completed, he gives orders to his publisher, Cawthorn, to burn the whole edition.

It is well known that on the occasion of the opening of the new Drury Lane Theatre, the committee called upon all England's poetical talent for an inaugural address. The committee received many, but found none worthy of adoption. It was then that Lord Holland advised that Lord Byron, should be applied to, whose genius and popularity would enhance, he said, the solemnity of the occasion. Lord Byron after a refusal, and much hesitation arising partly from modesty and partly from the knowledge that the rejected authors would make him pay a heavy price for his triumph, at last, with much reluctance, accepted the invitation, merely to oblige Lord Holland. He exchanged with the latter on this topic a long correspondence, revealing so thoroughly his docility and modesty, that Moore declares these letters valuable as an illustration of his character; they show, in truth, the exceeding pliant good-nature with which he listened to the counsel and criticism of his friends. "It can not be questioned," says he, "that this docility, which he invariably showed in matters upon which most authors are generally tenacious and irritable, was a natural essence of his character, and which might have been displayed on much more important occasions had he been so fortunate as to become connected with people capable of understanding and of guiding him."

Another time Moore wrote to him at Pisa:—"Knowing you as I do, Lady Byron ought to have discovered, that you are the most docile and most amiable man that ever existed, for those who live with you."

His hatred of contradiction and petty teasing, his repugnance to annoy or mortify any one, arose from the same cause. Once, after having replied with his usual frankness to an inquiry of Madame de Staël, *that he thought a certain step ill-advised,* he wrote in his memorandum-book:—"I have since reflected that it would be possible for Mrs. B—— to be patroness; and I regret having given my opinion, as I detest getting people into difficulties with themselves or their favorites."

And again:—

"To-day C—— called, and, while sitting here, in came Merivale. During our colloquy, C—— (ignorant that M—— was the writer) abused the mawkishness of the 'Quarterly Review,' on Grimm's correspondence. I (knowing the secret) changed the conversation as soon as I could, and C—— went away quite convinced of having made the most favorable impression on his new acquaintance. . . . . I did not look at him while this was going on, but I felt like a coal; for I like Merivale, as well as the article in question."

HIS INDULGENCE.

His indulgence, so great toward all, was excessive toward his inferiors.

"Lord Byron," says Medwin, "was the best of masters, and it may be asserted that he was beloved by his servants; his goodness even extended to their families. He liked them to have their children with them. I remember, on one occasion, as we entered the hall, coming back from our walk, we met the coachman's son, a boy of three or four years of age. Byron took the child up in his arms and gave him ten pauls."

"His indulgence toward his servants," says Mr. Hoppner, "was almost reprehensible, for even when they neglected their duty, he appeared rather to laugh at than to scold them, and he never could make up his mind to send them away, even after threatening to do so."

Mr. Hoppner quotes several instances of this indulgence, which he frequently witnessed. I will relate one in which his kindness almost amounts to virtue. On the point of leaving for Ravenna, whither his heart passionately summoned him, Tita Falier, his gondolier, is taken for the conscription. To release him it is not only necessary to pay money, but also to take certain measures, and to delay his departure. The money was given, and the much-desired journey postponed.

"The result was," says Hoppner, "that his servants were so attached to him that they would have borne every thing for his sake. His death plunged them into the deepest grief. I have in my possession a letter written to his family by Byron's gondolier, Tita, who followed him from Venice to Greece, and remained with him until his death. The poor fellow speaks of his master in touching terms: he declares that in Byron he has lost rather a father than a master, and he does not cease to dilate upon the goodness with which Byron looked after the interests of all who served him."

Fletcher also wrote to Murray after his master's death:—

"Pray forgive this scribbling, for I scarcely know what I do and say. I have served Lord Byron for twenty years, and his lordship was always to me rather a father than a master. I am too distressed to be able to give you any particulars about his death."

Lord Byron's benevolence also shone forth in his tenderness toward children, in the pleasure he experienced in mingling in their amusements, and in making them presents. In general, to procure a moment's enjoyment to any one was real happiness to him.

Quite as humane as he was benevolent, cruelty or ferocity he could not brook, even in imagination. His genius, although so bold, could not bear too harrowing a plot. "I wanted to write something upon that subject," he told Shelley at Pisa, "as it is extremely tragical, but it was too heartrending for my nerves to cope with."

His works, moreover, from beginning to end, prove this. An analysis of the character of all his heroes will prove that, however daring, they are never ferocious, harsh, nor perverse. Even Conrad the Corsair, whose type is sketched from a ferocious race, and who is placed in circumstances that tempt to inhumanity, — Conrad is yet far removed from cruelty. The drop of blood on Gulnare's fair brow makes him shudder, and almost forget that it was to save him that she became guilty. The cruel deeds of a man not only prevented Lord Byron from feeling the least sympathy for him, but even made gratitude toward him a burden. However much Ali Pasha, the fierce Viceroy of Janina, may overwhelm him with kindness, wish to treat him as a son, address him in writing as "Excellentissime and Carissime," the cruelties of such a friend are too revolting for Byron to profit by his offer of services. He calls him the man of war and calamity, and in immortal verse perpetuates the memory of his crimes, and even *foretells the death he actually died a few years later*. He can forgive him the weakness of the flesh, but not those crimes which are deaf to pity's voice, and which, to be condemned in every man, are still more so in an old man:—

> "Blood follows blood, and through this mortal span
> In bloodier acts conclude those who with blood began."

The recollection of human massacres spoilt in his eyes even a beautiful spot. In exalting the Rhine, the beautiful river he so much admired, the remembrance of all the blood spilt on its banks saddened his heart:—

> "Then to see
> The valley of sweet waters, were to know
> Earth paved like Heaven; and to seem such to me
> Even now what wants thy stream?—that it should Lethe be:
> * * * * * * * *
> But o'er the blacken'd memory's blighting dream
> Thy waves would vainly roll, all sweeping as they seem."

As to being himself a witness and spectator of scenes of violence, it was an effort which exceeded the strength, however great, of his will. Gifted with much psychological curiosity, and holding the theory that every thing should be seen, he was present at Rome at the execution of three murderers, who were to be put to death, on the eve of his departure. This spectacle agitated him to such a degree that it brought on a fever.

In Spain he attended a bull-fight. The painful impression

produced by the barbarous sight is immortalized in verse (*vide* "Childe Harold," 1st canto).

But his actions, above all, testify to his humane disposition. He never heard of the misfortune or suffering of a fellow-creature without endeavoring to relieve it, whether in London, Venice, Ravenna, Pisa, or Greece; he spared neither gold, time, nor labor to achieve this object. At Pisa, hearing that a wretched man, guilty of a sacrilegious theft, was to be condemned to cruel torture, he became ill with dread and anxiety. He wrote to the English ambassador, and to the consuls, begging for their interposition; neglected no chance, and did not rest until he acquired the certainty that the penalty inflicted on the culprit would be more humane.

In Greece, where traits of generous compassion fill the rest of his life, Count Gamba relates that Colonel Napier, then residing in the Island of Cephalonia, one day rode in great haste to Lord Byron, to ask for his assistance, a number of workmen, employed in making a road, having been buried under the crumbling side of a mountain in consequence of an imprudent operation. Lord Byron immediately dispatched his physician, and, although just sitting down to table, had his horses saddled, and galloped off to the scene of the disaster, accompanied by Count Gamba and his suite. Women and children wept and moaned, the crowd each moment increased, lamentations were heard on all sides, but, whether from despair or laziness, none came forward. Generous anger overcame Lord Byron at this scene of woe and shame; he leapt from his horse, and, grasping the necessary implements, began with his own hands the work of setting free the poor creatures, who were there buried alive. His example aroused the courage of the others, and the catastrophe was thus mitigated by the rescue of several victims. Count Gamba, after dwelling on the good Lord Byron did everywhere, and on the admirable life he led in Greece, expresses himself as follows in a letter to Mr. Kennedy:—

"One of his principal objects in Greece was to awaken the Turks as well as the Greeks to more humane sentiments. You know how he hastened, whenever the opportunity arose, to purchase the freedom of woman and children, and to send them back to their homes. He frequently, and not without incurring danger to himself, rescued Turks from the sanguinary grasp of the Greek corsairs. When a Moslem brig drifted ashore near Missolonghi, the Greeks wanted to capture the whole crew; but Lord Byron opposed it, and promised a reward of a crown for each sailor, and of two for each officer rescued."

"Coming to Greece," wrote Lord Byron, "one of my principal objects was to alleviate, as much as possible, the miseries incident to a warfare so cruel as the present. When the dictates of humanity are in question, I know no difference between Turks and Greeks. It is enough that those who want assistance are men, in order to claim the pity and protection of the meanest pretender to humane feelings. I have found here twenty-four Turks, including women and children, who have long pined in distress, far from the means of support and the consolations of their home. The Government has consigned them to me: I transmit them to Prevesa, whither they desire to be sent. I hope you will not object to take care that they may be restored to a place of safety, and that the governor of your town may accept of my present. The best recompense I could hope for would be to find that I had inspired the Ottoman commanders with the same sentiments toward those unhappy Greeks, who may hereafter fall into their hands.

"BYRON."

"Lord Byron," pursues Count Gamba, "never could witness a calamity as an idle spectator. He was so alive to the sufferings of others, that he sometimes allowed himself to be imposed upon too readily by tales of woe. The least semblance of injustice excited his indignation, and led him to intervene without a thought for the consequences to himself of his interposition; and he entertained this feeling not only for his fellow-creatures but even toward animals."

His compassion extended to every living creature, to every thing that could feel. Without alluding to his well-known fondness for dogs, and for the animals of every kind he liked to have about him, and of which he took the greatest care, it will be sufficient to point out the motive which led him to deprive himself of the pleasures of the chase,—a pastime that would have been, from his keen enjoyment of bodily exercises, so congenial to his tastes. The reason is found in his memorandum for 1814 :—

"The last bird I ever fired at was an eaglet, on the shore of the Gulf of Lepanto, near Vostitza. It was only wounded, and I tried to save it, the eye was so bright: but it pined and died in a few days; and I never did since, and never will, attempt the death of another bird."

Angling, as well as shooting, he considered cruel.

"And angling, too, that solitary vice,
Whatever Izaak Walton sings or says:
The quaint, old, cruel coxcomb, in his gullet
Should have a hook, and a small trout to pull it."

And, as if he feared not to have expressed strongly enough his aversion for the cruelties of angling, he adds in a note:—

"It would have taught him humanity at least. This sentimental savage, whom it is a mode to quote (among the novelists) to show their sympathy for innocent sports and old songs, teaches how to sew up frogs, and break their legs by way of experiment, in addition to the art of angling,—the cruelest, the coldest, and the stupidest of pretended sports. They may talk about the beauties of nature, but the angler merely thinks of his dish of fish; he has no leisure to take his eyes from off the streams, and a single bite is worth to him more than all the scenery around. Besides, some fish bite best on a rainy day. The whale, the shark, and the tunny fishery have somewhat of noble and perilous in them; even net-fishing, trawling, etc., are more humane and useful. But angling!—no angler can be a good man."

"One of the best men I ever knew (as humane, delicate-minded, generous, and excellent a creature as any in the world) was an angler; true, he angled with painted flies, and would have been incapable of the extravagances of Izaak Walton."

"The above addition was made by a friend, in reading over the MS.:—'*Audi alteram partem*'—I leave it to counterbalance my own observations."

It is well known that Lord Byron would not deride certain superstitions, and was sometimes tempted to exclaim with Hamlet,—

"There are more things in Heaven and earth, Horatio,
Than are dreamt of in your philosophy."

He, consequently, also conformed to the English superstition, which involves, under pain of an unlucky year, the eating of a goose at Michaelmas. Alas! once only he did not eat one, and that year was his last; but he eat none because, during the journey from Pisa to Genoa, on Michaelmas eve, he saw the two white geese in their cage in the wagon that followed his carriage, and felt so sorry for them that he gave orders they should be spared. After his arrival at Genoa they became such pets that he caressed them constantly. When he left for Greece he recommended them to the care of Mr. Kennedy, who was probably kind to them for the sake of their illustrious protector.

Not only could Lord Byron never contribute voluntarily to the suffering of a living being, but his pity, his commiseration for the sufferings of his fellow-creatures showed itself all his life in such habitual benevolence, in such boundless generosity, that volumes would be necessary to record his noble deeds.

Although, in thus analyzing and enumerating the proofs of his innate goodness, we have declared we did not entertain the pretension of elevating them to the rank of lofty virtues, we are yet compelled to state that if his generosity was too instinctive to be termed a virtue, it was yet too admirable to be considered as an instinct; that while in remaining a quality of his heart, it elevated and transformed itself often through the exertion of his will into an absolute virtue, and through all its phases and in its double nature, it presented in Lord Byron a remarkably rare blending of all that is most lovable and estimable in the human soul.

Here we merely speak of the generosity that showed itself in benefits conferred. As to that which consists rather in self-denial, sacrifice which forgives injuries, and which is the greatest triumph of mortal courage, that, in a word, is indeed a sublime virtue. Such generosity, if he possessed it, we will treat of in another chapter.*

As we here wish to establish by facts that only which appears to have been the impulse of his good heart, the difficulty lies in the choice of proofs, and in the necessity of limiting

* See chapter "Generosity raised to a Virtue."

our narrative. We will, therefore, in order not to convert this chapter into a volume, forbear from quoting more than a few instances; but justice requires us to say, that misfortune or poverty never had recourse to him in vain; that neither the pecuniary embarrassments of his youth, nor the slender merits of the applicants, nor any of the pretexts so convenient to weak or hypocritical* liberality, ever could become a reason with him to refuse those who stretched out their hand to him. The claim of adversity, as adversity, was a sufficient and sacred one to him, and to relieve it an imperious impulse.

An appeal was once made to Lord Byron's generosity by an individual whose bad repute alone might have justified a harsh rebuff. But Lord Byron, whose charity was of a higher order, looked upon it otherwise.

"Why," said Murray, "should you give £150 to this bad writer, to whom nobody would give a penny?" "Precisely because nobody is willing to give him any thing is he the more in need that I should help him," answered Lord Byron.

A certain Mr. Ashe superintended the publication of a paper called "The Book," the readers of which were attracted rather by its ill-nature and scandal, and the revelations it made in lifting the veil that had so far concealed the most delicate mysteries, than by the talent of the author. In a fit of repentance this man wrote to Lord Byron, alleging his great poverty as an apology for having thus prostituted his pen, and imploring from Lord Byron a gift to enable him to live more honorably in future. Lord Byron's answer to this letter is so remarkable for its good sense, kindness, and high tone of honor, that we can not refrain from reproducing it.

"SIR,—I leave town for a few days to-morrow; on my return I will answer your letter more at length. Whatever may be your situation, I can not but commend your resolution to

* When travelling in Greece, he often found himself in straitened circumstances, merely because he had helped a friend.

"It is probable," he wrote to his mother from Athens in 1811, "I may steer homeward in spring: but, to enable me to do that, I must have remittances. My own funds would have lasted me very well: but I was obliged to assist a friend, who I know will pay me, but in the mean time I am out of pocket."

abjure and abandon the publication and composition of works such as those to which you have alluded. Depend upon it they amuse few, disgrace both reader and writer, and benefit none. It will be my wish to assist you, as far as my limited means will admit, to break such a bondage. In your answer inform me what sum you think would enable you to extricate yourself from the hands of your employers, and to regain, at least, temporary independence, and I shall be glad to contribute my mite toward it. At present, I must conclude. Your name is not unknown to me, and I regret, for my own sake, that you have ever lent it to the works you mention. In saying this, I merely repeat your own words in your letter to me, and have no wish whatever to say a single syllable that may appear to insult your misfortunes. If I have, excuse me: it is unintentional. BYRON."

Mr. Ashe replied with a request for a sum of about four thousand francs. Lord Byron having somewhat delayed answering him, Ashe reiterated his request, complaining of the procrastination; whereupon, "with a kindness which few," says Moore, "would imitate in a similar case," Byron wrote to him as follows:—

"SIR,—When you accuse a stranger of neglect, you forget that it is possible business or absence from London may have interfered to delay his answer, as has actually occurred in the present instance. But to the point. I am willing to do what I can to extricate you from your situation. . . . . I will deposit in Mr. Murray's hands (with his consent) the sum you mentioned, to be advanced for the time at ten pounds per month.

"P.S.—I write in the greatest hurry, which may make my letter a little abrupt; but, as I said before, I have no wish to distress your feelings. BYRON."

Ashe, a few months later, asked for the whole amount, to defray his travelling expenses to New South Wales, and Lord Byron again remitted to him the entire amount.

On another occasion, some unhappy person being discussed in harsh terms, the remark was made that he deserved his misery. Lord Byron turned on the accuser, and fired with generous anger, "Well!" exclaimed he, "if it be true that N—— is unfortunate, and that he be so through his own fault, he is doubly to be pitied, because his conscience must poison his grief with remorse. Such are my morals, and that is why I pity error and respect misfortune."

The produce of his poems, as long as he remained in England, he devoted to the relief of his poor relations, or to the assistance of authors in reduced circumstances. I will not speak of certain traits of heroic generosity which averted the disgrace and ruin of families, which robbed vice of many youthful victims, and would cast in the shade many deeds of past and proverbial magnanimity, and deserve the pen of a Plutarch to transmit them to posterity.

When we are told, with such admiring comments, of Alexander's magnanimity in respecting and restoring to freedom the mother and the wife of Darius, we do not learn whether those noble women were beautiful and in love with the Macedonian hero. But Lord Byron succored, and restored to the right path, many girls, young and gifted with every charm, who were so subjugated by the beauty, goodness, and generosity of their benefactor, that they fall at his feet, not to implore that they might be sent back to their homes, but ready to become what he bade them. And yet this young man of six-and-twenty, thinking them fair, was touched, and tempted perhaps, yet sent them home, rescued, and enlightened by the counsels of wisdom.

There is more than generosity in such actions, and we therefore hold back details for another chapter, in which we will examine this quality under various aspects. Here we will content ourselves with stating that these noble traits became known, almost in spite of himself; for his benevolence was also remarkable in this respect, that it was exercised with a truly Christian spirit, and in obedience to the Divine precept that "the left hand shall not know what the right doeth." Having conferred a great favor on one of his friends, Mr. Hodgson, who was about to take orders, he wrote in the evening in his journal:—

"H—— has been telling that I . . . . I am sure, at least, I did not mention it, and I wish he had not. He is a good fellow, and I oblige myself ten times more by being of use than I did him,—and there's an end on't."*

It was said of Chateaubriand that if he wished to do any thing generous, he liked to do so on his balcony; the contrary may be said of Byron, who would have preferred to have his good action hid in the cellars.

"If we wished to dwell," says Count Gamba in a letter to Kennedy, "on his many acts of charity, a volume would not suffice to tell you of those alone to which I have been a witness. I have known in different Italian towns several honorable families, fallen into poverty, with whom Lord Byron had not the slightest acquaintance, and to whom he nevertheless *secretly* sent large sums of money, sometimes 200 dollars and more; and these persons never knew the name of their benefactor."

Count Gamba also tells us that, to his knowledge, in Florence, a respectable mother of a family, being reduced to great penury by the persecution of a malignant and powerful man, from whom she had protected the honor of one of her *protégées*, Lord Byron, to whom the lady and her persecutor were equally unknown, sent her assistance, which was powerful enough to counteract the evil designs of her foes. He adds that, having learnt at Pisa that a great number of vessels had been shipwrecked during a violent storm, in the very harbor of Genoa, and that several respectable families were thereby completely ruined, Lord Byron *secretly* sent them money, and to some more than 300 dollars. Those who received it never knew their benefactor's name. His charity provided above all for absent ones, for the old, infirm, and retiring. At Venice, where it was difficult to elude the influence of the climate, and of the manners of the time, and where he shared for a time the mode of life of its young men, it was still charity, and not pleasure, that absorbed the better part of his income. Not satisfied with his casual or out-of-the-way charities, he granted a large number of small monthly and weekly pensions. On definitely leaving Venice to reside in Ravenna, he decided that,

* It may be observed here, that he was not willing, even to confide to paper, the nature and degree of the act of kindness. Hodgson wanted thirty-five thousand francs to establish himself. Byron actually borrowed this amount, to give it to him, as he had not the sum at his disposal.

in spite of his absence, these pensions should continue until the expiration of his lease of the Palazzo Mocenigo. Venice watched him as jealously as a miser watches his treasure, and when he left it the honest poor were grieved and the dishonest vexed. Listening to these, one might have been led to believe, that Lord Byron had by a vow bound himself and his fortune to the service of Venice, and that his departure was a spoliation of their rights.*

In Ravenna his presence had been such a blessing, that his departure was considered a public calamity, and the poor of the city addressed a petition to the legate, that he might be entreated to remain.

Not a quarter of his fortune, as Shelley said in extolling his munificence, but the half of it, did he expend in alms. In Pisa, in Genoa, in Greece, his purse was ever open to the needy.

"Not a day of his life in Greece," says his physician, Doctor Bruno, "but was marked by some charitable deed: not an instance is there on record of a beggar having knocked at Lord Byron's door who did not go on his way comforted; so prominent among all his noble qualities was the tenderness of his heart, and its boundless sympathy with suffering and affliction. His purse was always opened to the poor." After quoting several traits of benevolence, he goes on to say:—"Whenever it came to the knowledge of Lord Byron that any poor persons were lying ill, whatever the maladies or their cause, without even being asked to do it, my lord immediately sent me to attend to the sufferers. He provided the medicines, and every other means of alleviation. He founded at his own expense a hospital in Missolonghi."†

This noble quality of his heart had the ring of true generosity; that generosity which springs from the desire and pleasure to do good, and which is so admirable, that in his own estimate of benevolence he always linked it with a sense of order. It never had any thing in common with the capricious munificence of a spendthrift. His exceeding delicacy, the loyalty and noble pride of his soul, inspired him with the deepest aversion for that egotism and vanity which alike ignores its own duties and the rights of others.

* See his "Life in Italy."

† Vide Kennedy.

Lord Byron was, therefore, very methodical in his expenditure. Without stooping to details, he was most careful to maintain equilibrium between his outlay and his income. He attended scrupulously to his bills, and said he could not go to sleep without being on good terms with his friends, and having paid all his debts.*

He was often tormented, if his agents were tardy in making remittances, with the dread of not being able to meet his engagements. Of his own gold he was liberal, but he respected the coffers of his creditors.

"I have the greatest respect for money," he often said in jest. He cared for it, indeed, but as a means of obtaining rest for his mind, and especially of helping the poor. Although so generous, he was sometimes annoyed and sorry at the thought of having ill-spent his money, because he had in the same ratio diminished his power of doing good.

We should have given but an unfair idea of the lofty nature of his generosity, if we did not add that it was not sustained by any illusory hopes of gratitude. These illusions his confiding heart had entertained in early manhood, and were those the loss of which he most regretted; but their flight, though causing bitter disappointment, left his conduct uninfluenced. He expected ingratitude, and was prepared for it; he *gave*, he said, and *did not lend;* and preferred to expose himself to ingratitude rather than to forsake the unhappy.

We fain would have concluded this long chapter, devoted to the proofs of his goodness in all its manifestations, by gathering the principal testimonies of that goodness which were received after Byron's death, and show it in its original character and in its modifications through life. But we must confine ourselves to the mention of a few testimonies only, taken from among those borne him at the outset and at the end of his life, so as to extend throughout its course, and to show what those who knew him personally, and well, thought of it.

M. Pigott, a friend and companion of Byron's, who lived

* "Yesterday I paid him (to Scroope Davies) four thousand eight hundred pounds, ... and my mind is much relieved by the removal of that debt," he says in his memorandum of 1813. All his difficulties were inherited from his father, and not contracted by him personally.

at Southwell, in the neighborhood of Newstead, who travelled with Byron during his holidays, told Moore that few people understood Byron; but that he knew well how naturally sensitive and kind-hearted he was, and that there was not the slightest particle of malignity in his whole composition. Mr. Pigott, who thus spoke of Byron, was one of the most revered magistrates of his county, and the head of that family with whom Byron was wont to spend his holidays, and who loved him, both before and after his death, as good people only can love and mourn. "Never," says Moore, "did any member of that family allow that Byron had a single fault."

Mr. Lake, another biographer of Byron, says, "I have frequently asked the country people what sort of a man Lord Byron was. The impression of his eccentric but energetic character was evident in the reply. 'He's the devil of a fellow for comical fancies—He flogs th' oud laird to nothing, but he's a hearty good fellow for all that.' "

Here is Dallas's opinion, which can not be suspected of partiality, for reasons which we have elsewhere given; for he believed himself aggrieved, and considered as a great culprit the man who, ever so slightly, could depart from the orthodox religious teachings; who had not a blind admiration of his country; who could suffer his heart to be possessed by an affection which marriage had not legitimatized; who preferred to family pride the satisfaction of paying the debts bequeathed to him by his ancestors, and who could make use of his right of selling his lands. Yet, notwithstanding all this, Mr. Dallas expresses himself to the following effect:—"At this time (1809), when on the eve of publishing his first satire, and before taking his seat in the House of Lords, I saw Lord Byron every day. (This was the epoch of his misanthropy). Nature had gifted him with most amiable sentiments, which I frequently had occasion to notice, and I have often seen these imprint upon his fine countenance a really sublime expression. His features seemed made expressly to depict the conceptions of genius and the storms of passion. I have often wondered with admiration at these curious effects. I have seen his face lighted up by the fire of poetical inspiration, and, under the influence of strong emotions, sometimes express the highest degree of energy, and at others all the softness and grace of mild and gentle affection. When his soul was a prey to passion and revenge, it was painful to observe the powerful effect upon his features; but when, on the contrary, he was conquered by feelings of tenderness and benevolence (which was the natural tendency of his heart, it was delightful to contemplate his looks. I went to see Lord Byron the day after Lord Falkland's death. He had just seen the inanimate body of the man with whom, a few days before, he had spent such an agreeable time. At intervals, I heard him exclaim to himself, and half aloud, 'Poor Falkland!' His look was even more expressive than were his words. 'But his wife,' added he, 'she is to be pitied!' One could see his soul filled with the most benevolent intentions, which were sterile.* If ever pure action was done, it was that which he then meditated; and the man who conceived it, and who accomplished it, was then progressing through thorns and thistles, toward that free but narrow path which leads to heaven."

Several years later, Mr. Hoppner, English Consul at Venice, and who spent his life with Byron in that city, wrote in a narrative of the causes which created so much disgust in Byron for English travellers, that Byron's affected misanthropy, as observable in his first poems, was by no means natural to him; and he adds, that he is certain that he never met with a man so kind as Byron.

We might stop here, certain as we are that all loyal and reasonable readers are not only convinced of Byron's goodness, but experience a noble pleasure in admiring it. We can not, however, close this chapter, without calling the attention of our readers to the last and painful proofs given of this kindness and goodness of Byron's nature: we allude to the extraordinary grief, caused by his death.

"Never can I forget the stupefaction," says an illustrious writer, "into which we were plunged by the news of his death. So great a part of ourselves died with him, that his death appeared to us almost impossible, and almost not natural. One would have said that a portion of the mechanism of the universe had been stopped. To have questioned him, to have blamed him, became a remorse for us, and all our veneration

* Although not rich, and on the point of undertaking a long and expensive journey, he devoted a large sum to the alleviation of the wants of that family.

for his genius was not half so energetically felt as our tenderness for him.

> "'His last sigh dissolved the charm, the disenchanted earth
> Lost all her lustre. Where her glittering towers?
> Her golden mountains where? All darkened, down
> To naked waste a dreary vale of years!
> The great magician's dead!'"—YOUNG.

Such griefs are certainly reasonable, just, and honorable: for the deaths which bury such treasures of genius are real public calamities. On hearing of Byron's death, one might repeat the beautiful and eloquent words of M. de Saint Victor:

"What a great crime death has committed! It is something like the disappearance of a star, or the extinction of a planet, with all the creation it supposed. When great minds have accomplished their task, like Shakspeare, Dante, Goethe, their departure from the scene of the world leaves in the soul the sublime melancholy which presides over the setting of the sun, after it has poured out all its rays. But when we hear of the death of a Raphael, of a Mozart, and especially of Byron, struck down in their flight, just at the time when they were extending their course, we can not refrain from calling these an eternal cause for mourning, irreparable losses, and inconsolable regrets! A genius who dies prematurely carries treasures away with him! How many ideal existences were linked with his own! What sublime thoughts vanish from his brow! What great and charming characters die with him, even before they are born! How many truths postponed, at least, for humanity!"

And we will add: to how many great and noble actions his death has put an end!

Such regrets do honor as much to those who experience them as to those who give them rise. But it is not to the enthusiasm created by his genius, nor to the grief evinced by the Greek nation, for whom he died, that we will turn for a last proof of the goodness of his nature. Such regrets might almost be called interested,—emanating, as they do, from the knowledge of the loss of a treasure. Of the tears of the heart, which were shed for the man without his genius, shall we ask that last proof.

These are the words by which Count Gamba describes his affliction:—

"In vain should I attempt to describe the deep, the distressing sorrow that overwhelmed us all. I will not speak of myself, but of those who loved him less, because they had seen him less. Not only Mavrocordato and his immediate circle, but the whole city and all its inhabitants were, as it seemed, stunned by the blow—it had been so sudden, so unexpected. His illness, indeed, had been known; and for the three last days, none of us could walk in the streets, without anxious inquiries from every one who met us, of 'How is my lord?' We did not mourn the loss of the great genius,—no, nor that of the supporter of Greece—our first tears were for our father, our patron, our friend. He died in a strange land, and among strangers: but more loved, more sincerely wept, he could never have been, wherever he had breathed his last.

"Such was the attachment, mingled with a sort of reverence and enthusiasm, with which he inspired those around him, that there was not one of us who would not, for his sake, have willingly encountered any danger in the world. The Greeks of every class and every age, from Mavrocordato to the meanest citizen, sympathized with our sorrows. It was in vain that, when we met, we tried to keep up our spirits—our attempts at consolation always ended in mutual tears."

None but beautiful souls, and those who are really thoroughly good, can be thus regretted; and heartfelt tears are only shed for those who have spent their life in drying those of others.

CHAPTER X.

QUALITIES AND VIRTUES OF SOUL.

ANTIMATERIALISM.

AMONG Lord Byron's natural qualities we may rank his antipathy, not only for any thing like low sensuality or gross vice, but even for those follies to which youth and human nature are so prone. Whatever may have been said on this head, and notwithstanding the countenance Lord Byron's own words may have lent to calumnies too widely believed, it will be easy to prove the truth of our assertion. Let us examine his actions, his words (when serious), the testimony of those who knew him through life, and it will soon appear that this natural antipathy with him often attained to the height of rare virtue.

Lord Byron had a passionate nature, a feeling heart, a powerful imagination; and it can not be denied that, after the disappointment he experienced in his ethereal love entertained at fifteen, he fell into the usual round of university life. But as he possessed great refinement of mind, never losing sight of an ideal of moral beauty, such an existence speedily became odious to him. His companions thought it all quite natural and pleasant; but he disapproved of it and blamed himself, feeling ashamed in his own conscience.

It is well known that Lord Byron never spared himself. He invented faults rather than sought to extenuate them. And so he fully merits belief, when he happens to do himself justice. Let us attend to the following:—

"I passed my degrees in vice," he says, "very quickly, *but they were not after my taste.* For my juvenile passions, though most violent, were concentrated, and did not willingly tend to divide and expand on several objects. I could have renounced every thing in the world with those I loved, or lost it all for them; but fiery though my nature was, *I could not share without disgust in the dissipation common to the place and time.*"

This makes Moore say, that even at the period to which we are alluding, his irregularities were much less sensual, much less gross and varied than those of his companions.

Nevertheless it was his boyish university life that caused Lord Byron to be suspected of drawing his own likeness, when two years later, after his return from the East, he brought out "Childe Harold"—an imaginary hero, whom he imprudently surrounded with real circumstances personal to himself.

Moore, with his usual good sense, protests strongly against such injustice, saying that, however dissipated his college and university life might have been during the two or three years previous to his first travels, no foundation exists, except in the imagination of the poet, and the credulity or malice of the world, for such disgraceful scenes as were represented to have taken place at Newstead, by way of inferences drawn from "Childe Harold." "In this poem," adds Moore, "he describes the habitation of his hero as a monastic dwelling—

'Condemn'd to uses vile!
Where Superstition once had made her den
Now Paphian girls were known to sing and smile.'"

These exaggerated, if not imaginary descriptions, were, nevertheless, taken for serious, and literally believed by the greater part of his readers.

Moore continues: "Mr. Dallas, giving way to the same exaggerated tone, says, in speaking of the preparations for departure made by the young lord, 'He was already satiated with pleasure, and disgusted with those comrades who possessed no other resource, so he resolved to overcome his senses, and accordingly dismissed his harem.' The truth is, that Lord Byron did not then even possess sufficient fortune to allow himself this Oriental luxury; his manner of living at Newstead was plain and simple. His companions, without being insensible to the pleasures afforded by liberal hospitality, were all too intellectual in their tastes and habits to give themselves up to vulgar debauchery. As to the allusions regarding his *harem*, it appears certain that one or two women were suspected *subintroductæ*—to use the style of the old monks of the Abbey—but that even these belonged to the servants of the house. This is the utmost that scandal could allege as the groundwork for suspicion and accusation."

These assertions of Moore have been corroborated by many other testimonies. I will only relate that mentioned by Washington Irving, in the account of his visit to Newstead Abbey in 1830. Urged by philosophical curiosity, Washington Irving managed to get into conversation with a certain Nanny Smith, who had passed all her life at Newstead as house-keeper. This old woman, after having chattered a great deal about Lord Byron and the ghosts that haunted the Abbey, asserting that though she had not seen them, she had heard them quite well, was particularly questioned by Mr. Irving as to the mode of life her young master led. She certified to his sobriety, and positively denied that he had led a licentious life at Newstead with his friends, or brought mistresses with him from London.

"Once, it is true," said the old lady, "he had a pretty *youth* for a *page* with him. The maids declared it was a young woman. But as for me, I never could verify the fact, and all these servant-girls were jealous, especially one of them called Lucy. For Lord Byron being kind to her, and a fortune-teller having predicted a high destiny for her, the poor little thing dreamed of nothing else but becoming a great lady, and perhaps of rising to be mistress of the Abbey. Ah, well! but her dreams came to nothing."*

"Lord Byron," added the old lady, "passed the greater part of his time seated on his sofa reading. Sometimes he had young noblemen of his acquaintance with him. Then, it is true, they amused themselves in playing all sorts of tricks—youthful frolics, that was all; they did nothing improper for young gentlemen, nothing that could harm any body."†

"Lord Byron's only amusements at Newstead," says Mr. Irving, "were boating, boxing, fencing, and his dogs."

"His constant occupation was to write, and for that he

* The history of the page is, however, true. Lord Byron was then nineteen years of age. Not to give his mother the grief of seeing that he had made an acquaintance she would have disapproved, he brought Miss —— from Brighton to the Abbey, dressed as a page, that she might pass for her brother Gordon.

† See "Newstead Abbey," by Washington Irving.

had the habit of sitting up till two and three in the morning. Thus his life at Newstead was quite one of seclusion, entirely devoted to poetry."

After having passed a year in this way at Newstead, following on his college and university life, he left England in order to mature his mind under other skies, to forget the injustice of man and the hardships of fortune that had already somewhat tinged his nature with gloom.

Instead of going in quest of emotions, his desire was, on the contrary, to avoid both those of the heart and of the senses. The admiration felt by the young traveller for charming Spanish women and beautiful Greeks did not outstep the limits of the purest poetry. Nevertheless the stoicism of twenty, with a heart, sensibility and imagination like his, could not be very firm, nor always secure from danger. He did actually meet with a formidable enemy at Malta; for he there made acquaintance with Mrs. Spencer Smith, the daughter of one ambassador and the wife of another, a woman most fascinating from her youth, beauty, mind, and character, as well as by her singular position and strange adventures. Did he avoid her so much as the stanzas addressed to the lovely Florence, in the first canto of "Childe Harold," would fain imply? This may be doubted, on account of the ring which they exchanged, and also from several charming pieces of verse that testify to another sentiment.

In any case, he showed strength of mind, and that his senses were under the dominion of reason; for, unable to secure her happiness or his own, he sought a remedy in flight.

When writing "Childe Harold," however, about this period, an evil genius suggested expressions, that if taken seriously and in their literal sense, might some day furnish the weapons of accusation to his enemies. For, while acting thus toward Florence, he introduced the episode into "Childe Harold" in a way that looks calumnious against himself:—

"Little knew she that seeming marble heart,
Now mask'd in silence or withheld by pride,
Was not unskillful in the spoiler's art,
And spreads its snares licentious far and wide;
Nor from the base pursuit had turn'd aside,
As long as aught was worthy to pursue."

"We have here," says Moore, "another instance of his propensity to self-misrepresentation. However great might have been the irregularities of his college life, such phrases as the 'art of the spoiler' and 'spreading snares' were in nowise applicable to them."*

Galt expresses the same certainty on this head. "Notwithstanding," says he, "the unnecessary exposure he makes of his dissipation on his first entrance into society (in the first two cantos of 'Childe Harold'), it is proved beyond *all dispute*, that at no period of his existence did Lord Byron *lead an irregular life.* That on one or two occasions he fell into some excesses, may be true; *but his habits were never those of a libertine.*"†

And after saying that the declaration by which Byron himself acknowledges his antipathy to vice carries more weight than all the rest, and that what he says of it is vague and metaphysical, he adds:—"But that only further corroborates my impression concerning him,—that is to say, that he took a sort of vanity in setting forth his experience in dissipation, but *that this dissipation never became a habit with him.*"

His true sentiments at this time are well portrayed in his letters, and especially in those addressed to his mother from Athens, when she consulted him on the conduct to be observed toward one of his tenants, a young farmer, who had behaved ill to a girl. "My opinion is," answered he, "that Mr. B—— ought to marry Miss K——. *Our first duty is not to do evil* (but, alas! that is not possible); our second duty *is to remedy it, if that be in our power.* The girl is his equal. If she were inferior to him, a sum of money and an allowance for the child might be something,—although, after all, a miserable compensation; but, under the circumstances, he ought to marry her. I will not have *gay seducers* on my estate, nor grant my farmers a privilege *I would not take myself of seducing other people's daughters.* I expect, then, this Lothario to follow my example, and begin by restoring the girl to society, or, by my father's beard, he shall hear of me."

To this letter Moore justly adds:—"The reader must not pass lightly over this letter, for there is a *vigor of moral*

* Moore, vol. i. p. 346.

† See Galt, "Life of Lord Byron."

sentiment in it, expressed in such a plain, sincere manner, that it shows how full of health his heart was at bottom, even though it might have been scorched by passion."

Lord Byron returned to his own country, after having spent two years travelling in Spain, Portugal, and the East, in the study and contemplation requisite for maturing his genius.

His distaste for all material objects of love or passion, and, in general, for sensual pleasures, was then remarked by all those who knew him intimately.

"An anchorite," says Moore, "who knew Lord Byron about this time, could not have desired for himself greater *indifference toward all the attractions of the senses*, than Lord Byron showed at the age of twenty-three."

And as on arriving in London he met with a complication of sorrows, he could, without any great effort, remain on his guard against all seductions. He did so in reality; and Dallas assures us that, even when "Childe Harold" appeared, he still professed positive distaste for the society of women. Whether this disposition arose from regret at the death of one he had loved, or was caused by the light conduct of other women, it is certain that he did not seek their society then; nay, even avoided them.

"I have a favor to ask you," he wrote, during this sad time, to one of his young friends: "never speak to me in your letters of a woman; make no allusion to the sex. I do not even wish to read a word about the feminine gender."

And to this same friend he wrote in verse:—

"If thou would'st hold
Place in a heart that ne'er was cold,
By all the powers that men revere,
By all unto thy bosom dear,
Thy joys below, thy hopes above,
Speak—speak of any thing but love."

Newstead Abbey, October 11, 1811.

But if he did not seek after women, they came in quest of him. When he had achieved celebrity—when fame lit up his noble brow—the sex was dazzled. They did not wait to be sought, but themselves made the first advances. His table was literally strewn with expressions of feminine admiration.

Dallas relates that one day he found Lord Byron so absorbed in answering a letter that he seemed almost to have lost the consciousness of what was passing around him.

"I went to see him again next day," says he, "and Lord Byron named the person to whom he had written.

"While we were together, the page of the lady in question brought him a fresh letter. Apparently it was a young boy of thirteen or fourteen years of age, with a fresh, delicate face, that might have belonged to the *lady herself.* He was dressed in a hussar jacket, and trowsers of scarlet, with silver buttons and embroidery; curls of fair hair clustered over part of the forehead and cheeks, and he held in his hand a little cap with feathers, which completed the theatrical appearance of this childish Pandarus. I could not help suspecting it was a disguise."

The suspicions were well founded, and they caused Dallas's hair to stand on end, for, added to his Puritanism, was the hope of becoming the young nobleman's Mentor, and he fancied he saw him already on the road to perdition. But was it likely that Lord Byron, with all his imagination, sensibility, and warm heart, should remain unmoved—neither touched nor flattered by the advances of persons uniting beauty and wit to the highest rank? The world talked, commented, exaggerated. Whether actuated by jealousy, rancor, noble or despicable sentiments, all took advantage of the occasion afforded for censure.

Feminine overtures still continued to be made to Lord Byron, but the fumes of incense never hid from him the sight of his ideal. And as the comparison was not favorable to realities, disenchantment took place on his side, without a corresponding result on the other. THENCE many heartbreakings. Nevertheless there was no ill-nature, no indelicacy, none of those proceedings that the world readily forgives, but which his feelings as a man of honor would have condemned. Calantha, in despair at being no longer loved, resolved on vengeance. She invented a tale, but what does she say when the truth escapes her?

"If in his manners he (Glenarvon) had shown any of that freedom or wounding familiarity so frequent with men, she might, perhaps, have been alarmed, affrighted. But what was it she would have fled from? Certainly not gross adulation, nor those light, easy protestations to which all women, sooner or later, are accustomed; but, on the contrary, respect at once delicate and flattering; attention that sought to gratify her smallest desires; grace and gentleness that, not descending to be humble, were most fascinating, and such as are rarely to be met with," etc.

Let us now reverse the picture, and pass from shade to light: the difference is striking.

Passing in review his former life, Lord Byron said one day to Mr. Medwin:—"You may not compare me to Scipio, but I can assure you that *I never seduced any woman.*"

No, certainly he did not pretend to rival Scipio; his fault was, on the contrary, that he took pleasure in appearing the reverse. And yet Lord Byron often performed actions during his short life that Scipio himself might have envied. And who knows whether in any case Scipio could have had the same merit?—for, in order to attain that, he would have required to overcome such sensibility, imagination, and heart, as were possessed by Lord Byron.

The single fact of being able to say, "I never seduced any woman," is a very great thing, and we may well doubt whether many of his detractors could say as much. But let us relate facts.

In London the mother of a beautiful girl, hard pressed for money, had recourse to Lord Byron for a large sum, making him an unnatural offer at the same time. The mother's depravity filled him with horror. Many men in his place would have been satisfied with expressing this sentiment either in words or by silence. But that was not enough for his noble heart, and he subtracted from his pleasures or his necessities a sum sufficient to save the honor of the unfortunate girl. At another time, shortly before his marriage, a charming young person, full of talent, requiring help, through some adverse family circumstances, and attracted to Lord Byron by some presentiment of his generosity, became passionately *in love* with him. She could not live without his image before her. The history of her passion is quite a romance. Utterly absorbed by it, she was forever seeking pretexts for seeing him. A word, a sign, was all she required to become any thing he wished. But Lord Byron, aware he could not make her happy and respectable, never allowed that word to pass his lips, and his language breathed only counsels of wisdom and virtue.*

Even at Venice, when his heart had no preference, we find him saving a young girl of noble birth from the danger caused by his involuntary fascinations.† In Romagna, at Pisa, in Greece, he also gave similar proofs of virtue and of his delicate sense of honor.

Let us now examine his words. In 1813, with regard to "The Monk," by Lewis, which he had just read, Lord Byron wrote in his memoranda:—"These descriptions might be written by Tiberius, at Caprera. They are overdrawn; the essence of vicious voluptuousness. As to me, I can not conceive how they could come from the pen of a man of twenty, for Lewis was only that age when he wrote 'The Monk.' These pages are not natural; they distill cantharides.

"I had never read this work, and have just been looking over it out of sheer curiosity, from a remembrance of the noise the book made, and the name it gave Lewis. But really such things can not even be dangerous."

About the same period Mr. Allen, a friend of Lord Holland, very learned—a perfect Magliabecchi—a devourer of books, and an observer of mankind, lent Lord Byron a quantity of unpublished letters by the poet Burns—letters that were very unfit to see the light of day, being full of oaths and obscene songs. After reading them, Lord Byron wrote in his memoranda:—

"What an antithetical intelligence! Tenderness and harshness, refinement and vulgarity, sentiment and sensuality; now soaring up into ether, and then dragging along in mud. Mire and sublimity; all that is strangely blended in this admixture of inspired dust. It may seem strange, but to me it appears that a true voluptuary should never abandon his thought to the coarseness of reality. It is only by exalting whatever terrestrial, material, physical element there is in our pleasures, by veiling these ideas, or forgetting them quite, or, at least, by never boldly naming them to ourselves, only thus can we avoid disgust."

* See chapter on "Generosity." † See "Life in Italy."

This is how Lord Byron understood voluptuousness. We might multiply such quotations without end, taking them from every period of his life; all would prove the same thing.

As to his poetry written at this time, especially the lyrical pieces where he expresses his own sentiments, what can there be more chaste, more ethereal? When a boy, he begins by consigning to the flames a whole edition of his first poems, on account of a single one, which the Rev. Dr. Beecher considered as expressing sentiments too warm for a young man. In his famous satire, written at twenty, he blames Moore's poetry for its effeminate and Epicurean tendencies, and he stigmatized as evil the whole poem of "The Ausonian Nun," and all the sensualities contained in it. In his "Childe Harold," his Eastern tales, his lyric poems above all, where he displays the sentiments of his own heart, every thing is chaste and ethereal. The way in which the public appreciated these poems may be summed up in the words used by the Rev. Mr. Dallas—the living type of Puritanism in its most exaggerated form — at a date when, through many causes, Lord Byron no longer even enjoyed his good graces.

"After 1816," says he (the time at which Lord Byron left England), "I had no more personal intercourse with him, but I continued to read his new poems with the greatest pleasure until he brought out 'Don Juan.' That I perused with a real sorrow that no admiration could overcome. Until then his truly English muse had despised the licentious tone belonging to poets of low degree. But, in writing 'Don Juan,' he allied his *chaste and noble genius* with minds of that stamp."

And then he adds, nevertheless, that into whatsoever error Lord Byron fell, whatsoever his sin (on account of the beginning of "Don Juan"), he did not long continue to mix his pure gold with base metal, but ceased to sully his lyre by degrees as he progressed with the poem.

Whether Dallas be right or not in speaking thus of "Don Juan," we do not wish here to examine. In quoting his words, my sole desire is to declare that, until the appearance of this poem, Lord Byron's muse had been, even for a Dallas, the *chaste muse of Albion*. This avowal from such a man is worthy of note, and renders unnecessary any other quotation.

We must not, however, pass over in silence Mr. Galt's very remarkable opinion on this subject:—

"Certainly," says he, "there are some very fine compositions on love in Lord Byron's works, but there is not a *single line* among the thousand he wrote which shows a *sexual* sentiment. With him, all breathes the *purest* voluptuousness. All is vague as regards love, and *without material passion*, except in the delicious rhythm of his verses."

And elsewhere be says:—

"It is most singular that, with all his tender, passionate apostrophes to love, Lord Byron *should not once have associated it with sensual images.* Not even in 'Don Juan,' where he has described voluptuous beauties with so much elegance."

Then, quoting from "Hebrew Melodies,"—

SHE WALKS IN BEAUTY.

She walks in beauty, like the night
Of cloudless climes and starry skies;
And all that's best of dark and bright
Meet in her aspect and her eyes:
Thus mellow'd to that tender light
Which heaven to gaudy day denies.

One shade the more, one ray the less,
Had half impair'd the nameless grace
Which waves in every raven tress,
Or softly lightens o'er her face;
Where thoughts serenely sweet express
How pure, how dear their dwelling-place.

And on that cheek, and o'er that brow,
So soft, so calm, yet eloquent,
The smiles that win, the tints that glow,
But tell of days in goodness spent,
A mind at peace with all below,
A heart whose love is innocent!

"Behold in these charming lines," continues Galt, "a perfect sample of his *ethereal admiration*, his *immaterial* enthusiasm.

"The sentiment contained in this fine poetry," says he, "beyond all doubt belongs to the highest order of intellectual beauty;" and it seemed proved to him that love, in Lord Byron, was rather a metaphysical conception than a sensual passion. He remarked that even when Lord Byron recalls the precocious feelings of his childhood toward his little cousins—feelings so strong as to make him lose sleep, appetite, peace; when he describes them, still unable to explain them—we feel that they were passions much more ethereal with him than with children in general.

"It should be duly remarked," says Galt, "that there is not a single circumstance in his souvenirs which shows, despite the strength of their natural sympathy, the smallest influence of any particular attraction. He recollects well the color of her hair, the shade of her eyes, even the dress she wore, but he remembers his little Mary as if she were a Peri, a pure spirit; and it does not appear that his torments and his wakefulness haunted with the thought of his little cousin, were in any way produced by jealousy, or doubt, or fears, or any other consequence of passion."

And when Galt speaks of "Tasso's Lament," he expresses the same opinion, namely, that in his writings Lord Byron treats of love as of a metaphysical conception, and that the fine verses he has put into the mouth of Tasso would still better become himself:—

"It is no marvel—from my very birth
My soul was drunk with love, which did pervade
And mingle with whate'er I saw on earth:
Of objects all inanimate I made
Idols, and out of wild and lonely flowers,
And rocks, whereby they grew, a Paradise,
Where I did lay me down within the shade
Of waving trees, and dream'd uncounted hours."

"The truth is," adds Galt, by way of conclusion, "that no poet has ever described love better than Lord Byron in that particular *ethereal* shade:—

"'His love was passion's essence:—as a tree
On fire by lightning, with ethereal flame
Kindled he was, and blasted; for to be
Thus, and enamor'd, were in him the same.
But his was not the love of living dame,
Nor of the dead who rise upon our dreams,
But of ideal beauty, which became
In him existence, and o'erflowing teems
Along his burning page, distemper'd though it seems.'"

"*Childe Harold*," canto iii. stanza 78.

And even if it should be denied that love, in Lord Byron's

writings, as indeed in himself, was purely metaphysical, it must, at least, be acknowledged that it was chaste. This would be more easily recognizable if the letters dictated by his heart, if his *love-letters*, were known. But since we can not open these intimate treasures of his heart to the public, we will speak of those given us in his writings, and we will thence draw our conclusions: firstly, in regard to the characters he gives to all his heroines; secondly, as to the pictures he makes of love in passages where he speaks seriously, and in his own name.

LORD BYRON'S FEMALE CHARACTERS.

What poet of energy has ever painted woman more chaste, more gentle and sweet, than Lord Byron?

"One of the distinguishing excellences of Lord Byron," says one of his best critics, "is that which may be found in all his productions, whether romantic, classical, or fantastical, an intense sentiment of the loveliness of woman, and the faculty, not only of drawing individual forms, but likewise of infusing into the very atmosphere surrounding them, the essence of beauty and love. A soft roseate hue, that seems to penetrate down to the bottom of the soul, is spread over them."

More than any other genius, Lord Byron had the magic power of conjuring up before our imagination the ideal image of his subject. He was not at all perplexed how to clothe his ideas. That quality, so sought after by other writers, and so necessary for hiding faults, was quite natural to him. When he describes women, a few rapid strokes suffice to engrave an indelible image on the mind of the reader. Let us take for examples:—

Leila, in the "Giaour."
Zuleika, in the "Bride of Abydos."
Medora, in the "Corsair."
Theresa, in "Mazeppa."
Haidée, in "Don Juan."
Adah, in "Cain."

The gentle Medora, ensconced within the solitary tower where she awaits her Conrad, is fully portrayed in the melancholy song stealing on the strings of her guitar, and in the tender, chaste words with which she greets her lover.

Zuleika, the lovely, innocent, and pure bride of Selim, has her image graven in the following fine lines:—

"Fair, as the first that fell of womankind,
When on that dread yet lovely serpent smiling,
Whose image then was stamp'd upon her mind—
But once beguiled—and evermore beguiling;
Dazzling, as that, oh! too transcendent vision
To Sorrow's phantom-peopled slumber given,
When heart meets heart again in dreams Elysian,
And paints the lost on Earth revived in Heaven;
Soft as the memory of buried love;
Pure, as the prayer which Childhood wafts above,
Was she—the daughter of that rude old Chief,
Who met the maid with tears—but not of grief.

"Who hath not proved how freely words essay
To fix one spark of Beauty's heavenly ray?
Who doth not feel, until his failing sight
Faints into dimness with its own delight,
His changing cheek, his sinking heart confess
The might, the majesty of Loveliness?
Such was Zuleika, such around her shone
The nameless charms unmark'd by her alone—
The light of love, the purity of grace,
The mind, the Music breathing from her face,
The heart whose softness harmonized the whole,
And, oh! that eye was in itself a Soul!
Her graceful arms in meekness bending
Across her gently-budding breast;
At one kind word those arms extending
To clasp the neck of him who blest
His child, caressing and carest."*

THERESA.

Theresa's form—
Methinks it glides before me now,
Between me and yon chestnut's bough,
The memory is so quick and warm;
And yet I find no words to tell
The shape of her I loved so well;
She had the Asiatic eye,
Such as our Turkish neighborhood
Hath mingled with our Polish blood,
Dark as above us is the sky;

* The heroism of the young Zuleika, says Mr. G. Ellis in his criticism, is full of purity and loveliness. Never was a more perfect character traced with greater delicacy and truth; her piety, intelligence, her exquisite sentiment of duty and her unalterable love of truth seem born in her soul rather than acquired by education. She is ever natural, seductive, affectionate, and we must confess that her affection for Selim is well placed.

But through it stole a tender light,
Like the first moonrise of midnight;
Large, dark, and swimming in the stream,
Which seem'd to melt to its own beam;
All love, half languor, and half fire,
Like saints that at the stake expire,
And lift their raptured looks on high,
As though it were a joy to die.
A brow like a midsummer lake,
  Transparent with the sun therein
When waves no murmur dare to make,
  And heaven beholds her face within.
A cheek and lip—but why proceed?
  I loved her then, I love her still;
And such as I am, love indeed
  In fierce extremes—in good and ill.

LEILA.

Her eye's dark charm 'twere vain to tell,
But gaze on that of the Gazelle,
It will assist thy fancy well;
As large, as languishingly dark,
But Soul beam'd forth in every spark
That darted from beneath the lid,
Bright as the jewel of Giamschid.
Yea, *Soul*, and should our Prophet say
That form was naught but breathing clay,
By Allah! I would answer nay;
Though on Al-Sirat's arch I stood,
Which totters o'er the fiery flood,
With Paradise within my view,
And all his Houris beckoning through.
Oh! who young Leila's glance could read
And keep that portion of his creed
Which saith that woman is but dust,
A soulless toy for tyrant's lust?
On her might Muftis gaze, and own
That through her eye the Immortal shone;
On her fair cheek's unfading hue
The young pomegranate's blossoms strew
Their bloom in blushes ever new;
Her hair in hyacinthine flow,
When left to roll its folds below,
As midst her handmaids in the hall
She stood superior to them all,
Hath swept the marble where her feet
Gleam'd whiter than the mountain sleet
Ere from the cloud that gave it birth
It fell, and caught one stain of earth.
The cygnet nobly walks the water;
So moved on earth Circassia's daughter—

The loveliest bird of Franguestan!
As rears her crest the ruffled Swan,
And spurns the waves with wings of pride,
When pass the steps of stranger man
Along the banks that bound her tide;
Thus rose fair Leila's whiter neck:—
Thus arm'd with beauty would she check
Intrusion's glance, till Folly's gaze
Shrunk from the charms it meant to praise.
Thus high and graceful was her gait;
Her heart as tender to her mate;
Her mate—stern Hassan, who was he?
Alas! that name was not for thee!

ADAH.

Adah is the wife of Cain. It is especially as the drama develops itself that Lord Byron brings out the full charm of Adah's beautiful nature—a nature at once primitive, tender, generous, and Biblical.

CAIN.

Lucifer. Approach the things of earth most beautiful,
And judge their beauty near.
Cain. I have done this—
The loveliest thing I know is loveliest nearest.
Lucifer. What is that?
* * * *
Cain. My sister Adah.—All the stars of heaven,
The deep blue noon of night, lit by an orb
Which looks a spirit, or a spirit's world—
The hues of twilight—the sun's gorgeous coming—
His setting indescribable, which fills
My eyes with pleasant tears as I behold
Him sink, and feel my heart float softly with him
Along that western paradise of clouds—
The forest shade—the green bough—the bird's voice—
The vesper bird's, which seems to sing of love,
And mingles with the song of cherubim,
As the day closes over Eden's walls:—
All these are nothing, to my eyes and heart,
Like Adah's face: I turn from earth and heaven
To gaze on it.

Even those charming children of Nature, Haidée and Dudù, in "Don Juan," and the Neuha, in "The Island," scarcely meant to represent more than the visible material part of the ideal woman he could love if he met with her—even these charming creatures possess not only the pagan beauty of form, but also Christian beauty, that of the soul: goodness, gentleness, tenderness. And it is also to be remarked, that by degrees, as time wore on, Lord Byron's female types rose in the moral scale, while still preserving their adorable charms, and their harmony with the state of civilization wherein he placed them. For instance, his Haidée, in the second canto of "Don Juan," written at Venice in 1818, is not worth, morally, the Haidée of the fourth canto, written at Ravenna in 1820. Beneath his pen at Ravenna, the adorable maiden evidently becomes spiritualized. This may be attributed to the poet's state of mind, for he was quite different at Ravenna to what he had been at Venice. The portrait of this lovely child is certainly very charming in 1818, but, while admiring her spotless Grecian brow, her beautiful hair, large Eastern eyes, and noble mouth, we can not help remarking something vague and undecided about her. And even in those fine verses where he says that Haidée's face belongs to a type inconceivable for human thought, and still more impossible of execution for mortal chisel, it is still the beauty of form that he shows you; while the Haidée of Ravenna is quite spiritualized in all her exquisite beauty.

After having described her as she appeared in her delicious Eastern costume, Lord Byron expresses himself in these terms:—

"Her hair's long auburn waves down to her heel
Flow'd like an alpine torrent, which the sun
Dyes with his morning light,—and would conceal
Her person if allow'd at large to run;
And still they seem'd resentfully to feel
The silken fillet's curb, and sought to shun
Their bonds, whene'er some Zephyr, caught, began
To offer his young pinion as her fan.

"Round her she made an atmosphere of life,
The very air seem'd lighter from her eyes,
They were so soft and beautiful, and rife
With all we can imagine of the skies,
And pure as Psyche ere she grew a wife—
Too pure even for the purest human ties;
Her overpowering presence made you feel
It would not be idolatry to kneel."

And, describing the whiteness of her skin, he says:—

"Day ne'er will break
On mountain-tops more heavenly white than her;
The eye might doubt of it were well awake,
She was so like a vision."

In the sixth canto of "Don Juan"—the hero being in the midst of a harem—all his sympathies are for Dudù, a beautiful Circassian, who unites to all the charms, all the moral qualities that a slave of the harem might possess. This is the portrait which Lord Byron draws:—

XLII.

"A kind of sleepy Venus seem'd Dudù,
Yet very fit to 'murder sleep' in those
Who gazed upon her cheek's transcendent hue,
Her Attic forehead and her Phidian nose.
* * * * * *

XLIII.

"She was not violently lively, but
Stole on your spirit like a May-day breaking.
* * * * * *

LII.

"Dudù, as has been said, was a sweet creature,
Not very dashing, but extremely winning,
With the most regulated charms of feature,
Which painters can not catch like faces sinning
Against proportion—the wild strokes of nature
Which they hit off at once in the beginning,
Full of expression, right or wrong, that strike,
And, pleasing or unpleasing, still are like.

LIII.

"But she was a soft landscape of mild earth,
Where all was harmony, and calm, and quiet,
Luxuriant, budding; cheerful without mirth,
Which, if not happiness, is much more nigh it
Than are your mighty passions and so forth,
Which some call 'the sublime:' I wish they'd try it:
I've seen your stormy seas and stormy women,
And pity lovers rather more than seamen.

LIV.

"But she was pensive more than melancholy,
And serious more than pensive, and serene,
It may be, more than either: not unholy
Her thoughts, at least till now, appear to have been.
The strangest thing was, beauteous, she was wholly
Unconscious, albeit turn'd of quick seventeen,
That she was fair, or dark, or short, or tall;
She never thought about herself at all.

LV.

"And therefore was she kind and gentle as
The Age of Gold (when gold was yet unknown)."

As to Neuha, the daughter of Ocean (in "The Island"), his last creation, she is, indeed, the daughter of Nature also, and no less admirable than her sister Haidée, but she is still more highly endowed in a moral sense:—

> "The infant of an infant world, as pure
> From nature—lovely, warm, and premature;
> Dusky like night, but night with all her stars,
> Or cavern sparkling with its native spars;
> With eyes that were a language and a spell,
> A form like Aphrodite's in her shell,
> With all her loves around her on the deep,
> Voluptuous as the first approach of sleep;
> Yet full of life—for through her tropic cheek
> The blush would make its way, and all but speak:
> The sun-born blood suffused her neck, and threw
> O'er her clear nut-brown skin a lucid hue,
> Like coral reddening through the darken'd wave,
> Which draws the diver to the crimson cave.
> Such was this daughter of the southern seas,
> Herself a billow in her energies,
> To bear the bark of others' happiness,
> Nor feel a sorrow till their joy grew less:
> Her wild and warm yet faithful bosom knew
> No joy like what it gave; her hopes ne'er drew
> Aught from experience, that chill touchstone, whose
> Sad proof reduces all things from their hues:
> She fear'd no ill, because she knew it not."

When, after the combat, she arrives in her bark to save Torquil, the poet exclaims:

> "And who the first that springing on the strand,
> Leap'd like a nereid from her shell to land,
> With dark but brilliant skin, and dewy eye
> Shining with love, and hope, and constancy?
> Neuha—the fond, the faithful, the adored—
> Her heart on Torquil's like a torrent pour'd;
> And smiled, and wept, and near, and nearer clasp'd
> As if to be assured 'twas *him* she grasp'd;
> Shuddered to see his yet warm wound, and then,
> To find it trivial, smiled and wept again.
> She was a warrior's daughter, and could bear
> Such sights, and feel, and mourn, but not despair.
> Her lover lived,—nor foes nor fears could blight,
> That full-blown moment in its all delight:
> Joy trickled in her tears, joy filled the sob
> That rock'd her heart till almost heard to throb;
> And paradise was breathing in the sigh
> Of nature's child in nature's ecstasy."

"All these sweet creations realize the idea, formed from all time, of surpassing loveliness, of gentleness with passion," justly observes Monsieur Nisard—he who, in his very clever sketch of the illustrious poet, so often forms erroneous judgments of Lord Byron. For he also accepted him as he was presented—namely, as the victim of calumny and prejudice; or else he considered him after a system, examining only some *passages and one single period* of the man's and the *poet's* life, instead of taking the whole career and the general spirit of his writings,—a method also perceivable in his appreciation of Lord Byron's female characters.

Indeed Monsieur Nisard evidently only speaks of the Medoras, Zuleikas, Leilas, and in general of all the types in his Eastern poems, and appertaining to his first period: most fascinating beings undoubtedly, true emanations of the purest and most passionate love, but yet as morally inferior to the Angiolinas, Myrrhas, Josephines, Auroras, as his poems of the first period are intellectually inferior to those of the second, beginning with the third canto of "Childe Harold," and as civilized Christian woman is superior to a woman in the harem. But Monsieur Nisard, who has a very systematic way of judging things—wishing to prove that Lord Byron's loves were quite lawless in their ungovernable strength, filling the whole soul to the absorption of every other sentiment and interest (which might, indeed, perhaps he said of the personages in his Eastern poems), and not able, without contradicting himself, to assert the same as regards the love and devotion shown by the heroic Myrrhas and virtuous Angiolinas, and other dramatic types, all so different one from the other—has been obliged to omit all mention of them, thus sharing an error common to vain, ignorant critics. Yet these delightful creatures all resemble each other in the one faculty of *loving passionately and chastely*, for that is a quality which constitutes the very essence of woman, and Lord Byron's own qualities must always have drawn it out in her. But there is something far beyond beauty and passion in these noble and heroic creations of his second manner.

"Where shall we find," says Sir Edward Bulwer Lytton, "a purer, higher character than that of Angiolina, in the 'Doge of Venice?' Among all Shakspeare's female characters there is certainly not one more true, and not only true and natural, which would be slight merit, but true as a type of the highest, rarest order in human nature. Let us stop here for a moment, we are on no common ground; the character of Angiolina has not yet been understood."

Bulwer then quotes the scene between Marian and Angiolina, and after having pointed out its moral beauty, exclaims:—

"What a deep sentiment of the dignity of virtue! Angiolina does not even conceive that she can be suspected, or that the insult offered her required any other justification than the indignation of public opinion."

And Bulwer goes on to quote the verses where Marian asks Angiolina if, when she gave her hand to a man of age so disproportioned, and of a character so opposite to her own, she loved this spouse, this friend of her family; and whether, before marriage, her heart had not beat for some noble youth more worthy to be the husband of beauty like hers; or whether since, she had met with some one who might have aspired to her lovely self. And after Angiolina's admirable reply, Bulwer says:—

"Is not this conception equal at least to that of Desdemona? Is not her heart equally pure, serene, tender, and at the same time passionate, yet with love, not material but *actual*, which, according to Plato, gives a visible form to virtue, and then admits of no other rival. Yet this sublime noble woman had no cold stiffness in her nature; she forgives Steno, but not from the cold height of her chastity.

"'If,' said she to the indignant page, 'oh! if this false and light calumniator were to shed his blood on account of this absurd calumny, never from that moment would my heart experience an hour's happiness, nor enjoy a tranquil slumber.'"

"Here," says Bulwer, "the reader should remark with what delicate artifice the tenderness of sex and charity heighten and warm the snowy coldness of her ethereal superiority. What a union of all woman's finest qualities! Pride that disdains calumny; gentleness that forgives it! Nothing can be more simply grand than the whole of this character, and the story which enhances it. An old man of eighty is the husband of a young woman, whose heart preserves the calmness of purity; no love episode comes to disturb her serene course, no impure, dishonorable jealousy casts a shade on her bright name. She treads her path through a life of difficulties, like some angelic nature, though quite human by the form she wears."

Wishing only to call attention to the beauty of the female characters he created, without reference to the other beauties contained in the work, we shall continue to quote Bulwer for the second of these admirable creations of womankind in his dramas, namely, Myrrha. After having praised that magnificent tragedy "Sardanapalus," he adds:—

"But the principal beauty of this drama is the conception of Myrrha. This young Greek slave, so tender and courageous, in love with her lord and master, yet sighing after her liberty; adoring equally her natal land and the gentle barbarian: what a new and dramatic combination of sentiments! It is in this conflict of emotions that the master's hand shows itself with happiest triumph.

"The heroism of this beautiful Ionian never goes beyond nature, yet stops only at sublimest limits. The proud melancholy that blends with her character, when she thinks of her fatherland; her ardent, generous, *unselfish* love, her passionate desire of elevating the soul of Sardanapalus, so as to justify her devotion to him, the earnest yet sweet severity that reigned over her gentlest qualities, showing her faithful and fearless, capable of sustaining with a firm hand the torch that was to consume on the sacred pile (according to her religion) both Assyrian and Greek; all these combinations are the result of the purest sentiments, the noblest art. The last words of Myrrha on the funereal pyre are in good keeping with the grand conception of her character. With the natural aspirations of a Greek, her thoughts turn at this moment to her distant clime; but still they come back at the same time to her lord, who is beside her, and blending almost in one sigh the two contrary affections of her soul, Myrrha cries:—

"Then farewell, thou earth!
And loveliest spot of earth! farewell, Ionia!
Be thou still free and beautiful, and far
Aloof from desolation! My last prayer
Was for thee, my last thoughts, save *one*, were of thee!
Sar. And that?
Myr. Is yours."

"The principal charm," says Moore, "and the life-giving

angel of this tragedy, is Myrrha, a beautiful, heroic, devoted, ethereal creature, enamored of the generous, infatuated monarch, yet ashamed of loving a barbarian, and using all her influence over him to elevate as well as gild his life, and to arm him against the terror of his end. Her voluptuousness is that of the heart, her heroism that of the affections."

Another admirable character, full of Christian beauty, is that of Josephine in "Werner."

"Josephine," said the "Review," when "Werner" appeared, "is a model of real spotless virtue. A true woman in her perfection, not only does she preserve the character of her sex by her general integrity, but she also possesses a wife's tender, sweet, and constant affection. She cherishes and consoles her afflicted husband through all the adversities of his destiny and the consequences of his faults.

"Italian by birth, the contrast between the beauties and circumstances of her native country compared with the frontiers of Silesia, where a pretty feudal tyranny exists, displays still more the fine sentiments that characterize her."

We shall close this long list of admirable conceptions (which one quits with regret, so great is their charm) by giving some extracts from the portrait he was engaged on, when death, alas! caused the pencil to drop from his fingers: we mean Aurora Raby in "Don Juan:"—

"Aurora Raby, a young star who shone
O'er life, too sweet an image for such glass;
A lovely being, scarcely form'd or moulded,
A rose with all its sweetest leaves yet folded;
* * * * * *
"Early in years, and yet more infantine
In figure, she had something of sublime
In eyes which sadly shone, as seraphs' shine.
All youth—but with an aspect beyond time;
Radiant and grave as pitying man's decline;
Mournful—but mournful of another's crime,
She look'd as if she sat by Eden's door,
And grieved for those who could return no more."

And then:—

"She was a Catholic, too, sincere, austere,
As far as her own gentle heart allow'd."

And again:—

"She gazed upon a world she scarcely knew,
As seeking not to know it; silent, lone,

As grows a flower, thus quietly she grew,
And kept her heart serene within its zone.
There was awe in the homage which she drew:
Her spirit seem'd as seated on a throne
Apart from the surrounding world, and strong
In its own strength—most strange in one so young!"

* * * * * *

"High, yet resembling not his lost Haidée;
Yet each was radiant in her proper sphere."

* * * * * *

"The difference in them
Was such as lies between a flower and gem."
"*Don Juan*," canto XV.

Now that we have seen Lord Byron's ideal of womankind, let us mark with what sentiments they inspired him, and in what way love always presented itself to his heart or his imagination. Ever dealing out toward him the same measure of justice and truth, people have gone on complacently repeating that his love sometimes became a very frenzy, or anon degenerated into a sensation rather than a sentiment. And his poetry has been asserted to contain proof of this in the actions, characters, and words of the persons there portrayed. I think, then, that the best way of ascertaining the degree of truth belonging to these asseverations, is to let him speak himself, on this sentiment, at all the different periods of his life:—

"Yes, Love indeed is light from heaven;
A spark of that immortal fire
With angels shared, by Allah given
To lift from earth our low desire.
Devotion wafts the mind above,
But Heaven itself descends in love;
A feeling from the Godhead caught,
To wean from self each sordid thought;
A Ray of Him who form'd the whole;
A Glory circling round the soul!
I grant *my* love imperfect, all
That mortals by the name miscall;
Then deem it evil, what thou wilt;
But say, oh say, *hers* was not guilt!
She was my life's unerring light:
That quench'd, what beam shall break my night?"
"*The Giaour.*"

In 1817, at Venice, when his heart, at twenty-nine years of age, was devoid of any real love, and had even arrived at never loving, although suffering deeply from the void thus created, Lord Byron giving vent to his feelings wrote thus:—

"Oh! that the Desert were my dwelling-place,
With one fair Spirit for my minister,
That I might all forget the human race,
And, hating no one, love but only her!
Ye elements!—in whose ennobling stir
I feel myself exalted—Can ye not
Accord me such a being? Do I err
In deeming such inhabit many a spot?
Though with them to converse can rarely be our lot."*

At the same period, he also unveils his soul, in guessing that of Tasso:—

"And with my years my soul began to pant
With feelings of strange tumult and soft pain;
And the whole heart exhaled into One Want,
But undefined and wandering, till the day
I found the thing I sought—and that was thee;
And then I lost my being, all to be
Absorb'd in thine; the world was pass'd away;
Thou didst annihilate the earth to me!"

"*The Lament of Tasso.*"

A short time after, having described the charm of the pine forest at Ravenna, seen by twilight, he begins to paint the happiness of two loving hearts—of Juan and Haidée, and says:—

VIII.

"Young Juan and his lady-love were left
To their own hearts' most sweet society;
Even Time the pitiless in sorrow cleft
With his rude scythe such gentle bosoms.
* * * * * *
They could not be
Meant to grow old, but die in happy spring,
Before one charm or hope had taken wing.

IX.

"Their faces were not made for wrinkles, their
Pure blood to stagnate, their great hearts to fail!
The blank gray was not made to blast their hair,
But like the climes that know nor snow nor hail,
They were all summer; lightning might assail
And shiver them to ashes, but to trail
A long and snake-like life of dull decay
Was not for them—they had too little clay.

---

* "Childe Harold," canto iv. stanza 177.

X.

"They were alone once more; for them to be
Thus was another Eden; they were never
Weary, unless when separate: the tree
Cut from its forest root of years—the river
Damn'd from its fountain—the child from the knee
And breast maternal wean'd at once forever,—
Would wither less than these two torn apart;
Alas! there is no instinct like the heart.

XII.

"'Whom the gods love die young,' was said of yore,
And many deaths do they escape by this:
The death of friends, and that which slays even more—
The death of friendship, love, youth, all that is,
Except mere breath;
* * * * * *
Perhaps the early grave
Which men weep over, may be meant to save.

XIII.

"Haidée and Juan thought not of the dead.
The heavens, and earth, and air, seem'd made for them:
They found no fault with Time, save that he fled;
They saw not in themselves aught to condemn;
Each was the other's mirror.

* * * * * *

XVI.

"Moons changing had roll'd on, and changeless found
Those their bright rise had lighted to such joys
As rarely they beheld throughout their round;
And these were not of the vain kind which cloys,
For theirs were buoyant spirits, never bound
By the mere senses; and that which destroys
Most love, possession, unto them appear'd
A thing which each endearment more endear'd.

XVII.

"Oh beautiful! and rare as beautiful!
But theirs was love in which the mind delights
To lose itself, when the old world grows dull,
And we are sick of its hack sounds and sights,
Intrigues, adventures of the common school,
Its petty passions, marriages, and flights,
Where Hymen's torch but brands one strumpet more,
Whose husband only knows her not a wh—re.

XVIII.

"Hard words; harsh truth; a truth which many know.
Enough.—The faithful and the fairy pair,
Who never found a single hour too slow,
What was it made them thus exempt from care?

Young innate feelings all have felt below,
Which perish in the rest, but in them were
Inherent; what we mortals call romantic,
And always envy, though we deem it frantic.

XIX.

"This is in others a factitious state,
* * * * * *
But was in them their nature or their fate.
* * * * * *

XX.

"They gazed upon the sunset: 'tis an hour
Dear unto all, but dearest to *their* eyes,
For it had made them what they were: the power
Of love had first o'erwhelm'd them from such skies,
When happiness had been their only dower,
And twilight saw them link'd in passion's ties;
Charm'd with each other, all things charm'd that brought
The past still welcome as the present thought.
* * * * * *

XXVI.

"Juan and Haidée gazed upon each other
With swimming looks of speechless tenderness,
Which mix'd all feelings, friend, child, lover, brother;
All that the best can mingle and express
When two pure hearts are pour'd in one another,
And love too much, and yet can not love less;
But almost sanctify the sweet excess
By the immortal wish and power to bless.

XXVII.

"Mix'd in each other's arms, and heart in heart,
Why did they not then die?—they had lived too long
Should an hour come to bid them breathe apart;
Years could but bring them cruel things or wrong."
"*Don Juan*," canto iv.

It was this love which caused Campbell the poet to say: "If the love of Juan and Haidée is not pure and innocent, and expressed with delicacy and propriety, then may we at once condemn and blot out this tender passion of the soul from the list of a poet's themes. Then must we shut our eyes and harden our hearts against that passion which sways our whole existence, and quite become mere creatures of hypocrisy and formality, and accuse Milton himself of madness."

At Ravenna, where Lord Byron composed so many sublime works, he also wrote "Sardanapalus" and "Heaven and Earth." He was then thirty-two years of age. The love predominating in these two dramas is that which swayed his own soul, the same sentiment which, a year later, also inspired the beautiful poem composed on his way from Ravenna to Pisa.

No quotation could convey an idea of the noble energetic feeling animating these two dramas, for adequate language is wanting; impervious to words, the sentiment they contain is like a spirit pervading, or a ray of light warming and illuminating them.

They require to be read throughout. I prefer to quote his words on love, in the 16th canto of "Don Juan," and in "The Island," because they are the last traced by his pen. Written a few days previous to his fatal departure for Greece, it can not be doubted that the sentiment which dictated them was the same that accompanied him to his last hour.

CVII.

* * * * * *

"And certainly Aurora had renew'd
In him some feelings he had lately lost,
Or harden'd; feelings which, perhaps ideal,
Are so divine, that I must deem them real:—

CVIII.

"The love of higher things and better days;
The unbounded hope, and heavenly ignorance
Of what is call'd the world, and the world's ways;
The moments when we gather from a glance
More joy than from all future pride or praise,
Which kindle manhood, but can ne'er entrance
The heart in an existence of its own,
Of which another's bosom is the zone."*

And then, in describing the happiness of two lovers, in his poem of "The Island," a few days before setting out for Greece, he says again:—

"Like martyrs revel in their funeral pyre,
With such devotion to their ecstasy,
That life knows no such rapture as to die;
And die they do; for earthly life has naught
Match'd with that burst of nature, even in thought;
And all our dreams of better life above
But close in one eternal gush of love."

After speaking of the religious enthusiast, and saying that his soul preceded his dust to heaven, he adds:—

* See "Don Juan," canto xvi.

> "Is love less potent? No—his path is trod,
> Alike uplifted gloriously to God;
> Or link'd to all we know of heaven below,
> The other better self, whose joy or woe
> Is more than ours."

But enough of quotations; and now what poet has ever written or spoken of love with words and images more chaste, more truly welling from his own heart? We feel that he has given us the key to that. And if, after all these demonstrations, there still remain any readers who continue to accept as true the pleasantries, satires, and mystifications contained in some of his verses, I do not pretend to write for them. They are to be pitied, but there is no hope of convincing them. That depends on their quality of mind. The only thing possible, then, is to recall some of those anecdotes which, while justifying them in a measure, yet at the same time illustrate Lord Byron's way of acting. I will select one. When Lord Byron was at Pisa a friend of Shelley's, whom he sometimes saw, had formed a close intimacy with Lady B——, a woman of middle-age but of high birth. The tie between them was evidently the result of vanity on Mr. M——'s side, and, as she was the mother of a large family, it was doubly imperative on her to be respectable. But that did not prevent Mr. M—— from boasting of his success, and even (that he might be believed) from going into disgusting details in his eagerness for praise.

One day that Mr. M—— was in the same *salon* (at Mrs. Sh——'s house) with Lord Byron and the Countess G——, the conversation turned upon women and love in general, whereupon Mr. M—— lauded to the skies the devotedness, constancy, and truth of the sex. When he had finished his sentimental "tirade," Lord Byron took up the opposite side, going on as Don Juan or Childe Harold might. It was easy to see he was playing a part, and that his words, partly in jest, partly ironical, did not express his thoughts. Nevertheless they gave pain to Mme. G——, and, as soon as they were alone, Lord Byron having asked her why she was sad, she told him the cause.

"I am very sorry to have grieved you," said he, "but how could you think that I was talking seriously?"

"I did not think it," she said, "but those who do not

know you will believe all; M—— will not fail to repeat your words as if they were your real opinions; and the world, knowing neither him nor you, will remain convinced that he is a man full of noble sentiments, and you a real Don Juan, not indeed your own charming youth, but Molière's Don Juan!"

"Very probably," said Lord Byron; "and that will be another true page to add to M——'s note-book. I can't help it. I couldn't resist the temptation of punishing M—— for his vanity. All those eulogiums and sentimentalities about women were to make us believe how charming they had always been toward him, how they had always appreciated his merits, and how passionately in love with him Lady B—— is now. My words were meant to throw water on his imaginary fire."

Alas! it was on such false appearances that they made up, then and since, the Lord Byron still believed in by the generality of persons.

Lord Byron by his marriage gave another pledge of having renounced the foibles of the heart and the allurements of the senses; and it is very certain that he redeemed his word. If, through susceptibility or any other defect, Lady Byron, going back to the past or trusting to vile, revengeful, and interested spies, did not know how to understand him, all Lord Byron's friends did, whether or not they dared to say so. And he himself, who never could tell a lie, has assured us of his married fidelity.* His life in Switzerland was devoted to study, retreat, and even austerity. How little this stood him in stead with his enemies is well known. "I never lived in a more edifying manner than at Geneva," he said to Mr. Medwin. "My reputation has not gained by it. Nevertheless, when there is mortification, there ought to be a reward."†

When he arrived at Milan many ladies belonging to the great world were most anxious to know him; these presentations were proposed to him, and he refused. As to his life at Venice, a wicked sort of romance has been made of it, by exaggerating most ordinary things, and heaping invention upon invention; but this has been explained with sufficient

* See chapter on Marriage. † Medwin, p. 13.

detail in another chapter, where all the different causes of these exaggerations have been shown in their just measure of truth.*

Here, then, I will only say, that if, on arriving at Venice, he relaxed his austerity to lead the life common to young men without legitimate ties: if, under the influence of that lovely sky, he did not remain insensible to the songs of the beautiful Adriatic siren, nor trample under foot the few flowers fate scattered on his path, to make amends perhaps for the thorns that had so long beset it; if he sometimes accepted distractions in the form of light pleasures, as well as in the form of study,† did he not likewise always impose hard laborious occupation upon his mind, thus chaining it to beautiful immaterial things? Did his intellectual activity slacken? Was his soul less energetic, less sublime? The works of genius that issued from his pen at Venice are a sufficient reply. "Manfred," conceived on the summit of the Alps, was written at Venice; the fourth canto of "Childe Harold" was conceived and written at Venice. The "Lament of Tasso," "Mazeppa," the "Ode to Venice," "Beppo" (from his studies of Berni), the first two cantos of "Don Juan," were all written at Venice.

Moreover, it was there he collected materials for his dramas; there he studied the Armenian language, making sufficient progress to translate St. Paul's Epistles into English. And all that, in less than twenty-six months, including his journeys to Rome and to Florence. Let moralists say whether a man steeped in sensual pleasures could have done all that.

"The truth is," says Moore, "that, so far from the strength of his intellect being impaired or dissipated by these irregularities, it never was perhaps at any period of his life more than at Venice in full possession of all its energies."‡

All the concessions Moore was obliged to make, from a sort of weakness, not to compromise his position, to certain extreme opinions in politics or religion, cloaking in reality personal hatred; are they not all destroyed by this single avowal?

Shelley, who came to Venice to see Lord Byron, said that

* See "Life in Italy." † Ibid. ‡ Moore, vol. ii. p. 182.

all he observed of Lord Byron's state during his visit gave him a much higher idea of his intellectual grandeur than what he had noticed before. Then it was, and under this impression, that Shelley sketched almost the whole poem of "Julian and Maddalo." "It is in this latter character," says Moore, "that he has so picturesquely personated his noble friend; his allusions to the 'Swan of Albion,' in the verses written on the Engancennes hills, are also the result of this fit of enthusiastic admiration." At Venice Lord Byron saw few English; but those he did see, and who have spoken of him, have expressed themselves in the same way as Shelley; which caused Galt to say, that even at Venice, with regard to his pleasures, his conduct had been that of most young men! but that the whole difference must have consisted in the extravagant delight he took in exaggerating, through his conversation, not what was conducive to honor, but, on the contrary, what was likely to do him harm. The whole difference, however, does not lie here, but rather in the indiscretion shown by some friends.* Among the best testimonies borne to his way of living at Venice we must not forget that of Hoppner, who bore so high a character, and who was the constant companion of his daily afternoon walks; nor that of the excellent Father Pascal, who shared his morning studies at the Armenian convent.†

But in this united homage to truth I can not pass over in silence nor refrain from quoting the words of a very great mind, who, under the veil of fiction, has written almost a biography of Lord Byron, and who too independent, *though a Tory*, to *wish* to conceal his thought, has declared in the preface to his charming work of "Venetia" that Lord Byron was really his hero.

This writer, after speaking of all the silly calumnies with which Lord Byron was overwhelmed at one time, says of the two more especially calculated to stir up opinion against him, those which accused him of *libertinism* and *atheism*:—

"A calm inquirer might, perhaps, have suspected that abandoned profligacy is not very compatible with severe study, and that an author is seldom loose in his life, even if he be licentious in his writings. A calm inquirer might, per-

* See "Life in Italy," at Venice.

† See "Life in Italy."

haps, have been of opinion that a solitary sage may be the antagonist of a priesthood without absolutely denying the existence of a God; but there never are calm inquirers. The world, on every subject, however unequally, is divided into parties; and even in the case of Herbert (Lord Byron) and his writings, those who admired his genius and the generosity of his soul were not content with advocating, principally out of pique to his adversaries, his extreme opinions on every subject—moral, political, and religious. Besides, it must be confessed, there was another circumstance almost as fatal to Herbert's character in England as his loose and heretical opinions. The travelling English, during their visits to Geneva, found out that their countryman solaced or enlivened his solitude by unhallowed ties. It is a habit to which very young men, who are separated from or deserted by their wives, occasionally have recourse. Wrong, no doubt, as most things are, but, it is to be hoped, venial; at least in the case of any man who is not also an atheist. This unfortunate mistress of Herbert was magnified into a *seraglio;* extraordinary tales of the voluptuous life of one who generally *at his studies outwatched the stars*, were rife in English society; and

'Hoary marquises and stripling dukes,'

who were either *protecting opera-dancers*, or, still worse, *making love to their neighbors' wives*, either looked grave when the name of Herbert (Lord Byron) was mentioned in female society, or affectedly confused, as if they could a tale unfold, if they were not convinced, that the sense of propriety among all present was infinitely superior to their sense of curiosity."

In addition to all the proofs given by the varied uses Lord Byron made of his intellect we must not omit those furnished by the state of his heart. If, too readily yielding at Venice to momentary and fleeting attractions, Lord Byron had been led to squander the powers of youth, to wish to extinguish his senses in order to open out a more vast horizon to his intelligence; if, thus mistaking the means, he had, nevertheless, weakened, enervated, degraded himself, would not his heart have been the first victim sacrificed on the altar of light pleasures?

But, on the contrary, this heart which he had never succeeded in lulling into more than a slumber, when the hour of awakening came, held dominion by its own natural energy over the proud aspirations of his intelligence, and found both his youth and faculty of loving unweakened, and that he had a love capable of every sacrifice, a love as fresh as in his very spring-tide.

Are such metamorphoses possible to withered souls? Moralists have never met with a like phenomenon. On the contrary, they certify that in hearts withered by the enjoyments of sense all generous feelings, all noble aspirations become extinct.

If Lord Byron's anti-sensuality were not sufficiently proved by his actions, words, writings, and by the undeniable testimony of those who knew him, it might still be abundantly proved by his habits of life, and all his tastes; to begin with his sobriety, which really was wonderful. So much so, that if the proverb, *Tell me what you eat, and I will tell you what you are*, be true, and founded on psychological observation, one must admit that Lord Byron was almost an immaterial being.

His fine health, his strong and vigorous constitution, lead to the presumption that, at least in childhood and during his boyish days, his rule of life could not have differed from that of the class to which he belonged. Nevertheless, his sobriety was remarkable even in early youth; at eighteen he went with a friend, Mr. Pigott, to Tunbridge Wells, and this gentleman says, "We retired to our own rooms directly after dinner, for Byron did not care for drinking any more than myself."

But this natural sobriety became soon after the sobriety of an anchorite, which lasted more or less all his life, and was a perfect phenomenon. Not that he was insensible to the pleasures of good living, and still less did he act from any vanity (as has been said by some incapable of sacrificing the bodily appetites to the soul); his conduct proceeded from the desire and resolution of making *matter* subservient to the *spirit*.

His rule of life was already in full force when he left England for the first time. Mr. Galt, whom chance associated with Lord Byron on board the same vessel bound from Gibraltar to Malta, affirms that Lord Byron, during the whole voyage, seldom tasted wine; and that, when he did occasionally take some, it was never more than half a glass mixed with water. He ate but little, and never any meat; only bread and vegetables. He made me think of the ghoul taking rice with a needle."

On board "La Salsette," returning from Constantinople, he himself wrote to his friend and preceptor Drury, that the gnats which devoured the *delicate body* of Hobhouse had not much effect on him, because he lived in a *more sober manner.*

As to his mode of living during his two years' absence from England we can say nothing, except that he lived in climates where sobriety is the rule, and that his letters expressed profound disgust at the complaints, exacting tone, and effeminate tastes of his servants, and his own preference for a monastic mode of life, and very probably also for monastic diet. The testimony to his extraordinary sobriety becomes unanimous as soon as he returns home.

Dallas, who saw him immediately on his landing in 1811, writes:—

"Lord Byron has adopted a mode of diet that any one else would have called dying of hunger, and to which several persons even attributed his lowness of spirits. He lived simply on small sea-biscuits, very thin; only eating two of these, and often but one, a day, with one cup of *green tea*, which he generally drank at one in the afternoon. He assured me that was all the nourishment he took during the twenty-four hours, and that, so far from this régime affecting his spirits, it made him feel lighter and more lively; and, in short, gave him *greater command over himself in all respects. This great abstinence is almost incredible. . . . . . He thought great eaters were generally prone to anger, and stupid.*"*

It was about this time that he made the personal acquaintance of Moore at a dinner given by Rogers for the purpose of bringing them together and of reconciling them.

"As none of us," says Moore, "knew about his singular régime, our host was not a little embarrassed on discovering,

* Dallas, 171.

that there was nothing on the table which his noble guest could eat or drink. Lord Byron did not touch meat, fish, or wine; and as to the biscuits and soda-water he asked for, there were, unfortunately, none in the house. He declared he was equally pleased with potatoes and vinegar, and on this meagre pittance he succeeded in making an agreeable dinner."*

About the same time, being questioned by one of his friends, who liked good living, as to what sort of table they had at the Alfred Club, to which he belonged, "It is not worth much," answered Lord Byron. "I speak from hearsay; for what does cookery signify to a vegetable-eater? But there are books and quiet; so, for what I care, they may serve up their dishes as they like."

"Frequently," says Moore again, "during the first part of our acquaintance we dined together alone, either at St. Alban's, or at his old asylum, Stevens's. Although occasionally he consented to take a little Bordeaux, he *always held to his system of abstaining from meat.* He seemed truly persuaded that animal food must have some particular influence on character. And I remember one day being seated opposite to him, engaged in eating a beefsteak with good appetite, that, after having looked at me attentively for several seconds, he said, gravely, 'Moore, does not this eating beefsteaks make you ferocious?'

"Among the numerous hours we passed together this spring, I remember particularly his extreme gayety one evening on returning from a soirée, when, after having accompanied Rogers home, Lord Byron — who, according to his frequent custom, had not dined the last two days — feeling his appetite no longer governable, asked for something to eat. Our repast, at his choice, consisted only of bread and cheese; but I have rarely made a gayer meal in my life."

In 1814 he relaxed his diet a little, so far as to eat fish now and then; but he considered this an excessive indulgence. "I have made a regular dinner for the first time since Sunday," he writes in his journal. "Every other day tea and six dry biscuits. This dinner makes me heavy, stu-

* Moore, 315.

pid, gives me horrible dreams (nevertheless, it only consisted of a pint of Bucellas and fish; I do not touch meat, and take but little vegetable). I wish I were in the country for exercise, instead of refreshing myself with abstinence. *I am not afraid of a slight addition of flesh; my bones can well support that! but the worst of it is, that the devil arrives with plumpness, and I must drive him away through hunger!* I DO NOT WISH TO BE THE SLAVE OF MY APPETITE. If I fall, my heart at least shall herald the race."*

Except the last phrase, which is more worldly or more human, might not one fancy one's self listening to the confession or soliloquy of some Christian philosopher of the fourth century: one of those who sought the Theban deserts to measure their strength of soul and body in desperate struggles with Nature; the confession of a Hilarion or a Jerome, rather than that of a young man of twenty-three, brought up amid the conveniences and luxuries surrounding the aristocracy of the most aristocratic country in the world, where material comfort is best appreciated?

Thus it was, nevertheless, that Lord Byron practiced epicureanism with regard to his food, making very rare exceptions when he consented to dine out.

If time, change of circumstances, and climate, caused some slight modifications in his manner of living, his mode of life did not vary. At Venice, Ravenna, and Genoa, this epicurean would never suffer meat on his table; and he only made some rare exceptions, to avoid too much singularity, at Pisa, where he invited some friends to dinner. Count Gamba, after having spoken of the sobriety of his regimen on board the vessel that took him to Greece, the Ionian Islands, and finally to Missolonghi, says, "He ate nothing but vegetables and fish, and drank only water. Our fear was," says he, "lest this excessive abstinence should be injurious to his health!"

Alas! we know that it was. It is certain that this debilitating régime, joined to such strong moral impressions, too strongly felt, undermined Lord Byron's fine constitution, which had only resisted so long through its extreme vigor and the rare purity of his blood.

* Moore, first vol.

The bodily exercise he took had the same object, and further added to the injurious effect of his obstinate fasts. "I have not left my room these four days past," he writes in his memorandum, April, 1814, at a moment when his heart was agitated by a passion; "but I have been fencing with Jackson an hour a day by way of exercise, *so as to get matter under, and give sway to the ethereal part of my nature.* The more I fatigue myself, the better my mind is for the rest of the day; and then my evenings acquire that calm, that prostration and languor, that are such a happiness to me. To-day I fenced for an hour, wrote an ode to Napoleon Bonaparte, copied it out, ate six biscuits, drank four bottles of soda-water, read the rest of the time, and then gave a load of advice to poor H—— about his mistress, who torments him intolerably, enough to make him consumptive. Ah! to be sure, it suits me well to be giving lessons to ——; it is true they are thrown to the winds."*

This desire of giving mind dominion over matter is shown equally in all his tastes, all his preferences. Beauty in art consisted wholly for him in the expression of heart and soul. He had a horror of realism in art; the Flemish school inspired him with a sort of nausea. Certain material points of beauty in women, that are generally admired, had no beauty for him. The music he liked, and of which he never grew tired, was not brilliant or difficult, but simple; that which awakens the most delicate sentiments of the soul, which brings tears to the eye.

"I have known few persons," says Moore, "more alive than he to the charms of simple music; and I have often seen tears in his eyes when listening to the Irish Melodies. Among those that caused him these emotions was the one beginning—

"When first I met thee, warm and young."

The words of this melody, besides the moral sentiment they express, also admit a political meaning. Lord Byron rejected this meaning, and delivered his soul over, with the liveliest motion, to the more natural sentiment conveyed in that song."

"Only the fear of seeming to affect sensibility could have

* Moore, 315.

restrained my tears," he said once, on hearing Mrs. D—— sing

"Could'st thou look."

"Very often," said Mme. G——, "I have seen him with tears in his eyes when I was playing favorite airs to him on the piano, of which he never got tired."*

Stendhall also speaks of Lord Byron's emotion while listening to a piece of music by Mayer at Milan, and says that if he lived a hundred years he could never forget the divine expression of his physiognomy while thus engaged.

At most, Lord Byron could only admire for a moment material beauty without expression in women; it might give rise to sensations, but could never inspire him with the slightest sentiment.

We have said enough of the female characters he created: sweet incarnations of the most amiable qualities of heart and soul. Let us add here, that although greatly alive to beauty of form, he could not believe in a fine woman's delicate feeling, unless her beauty were accompanied by expression denoting her qualities of heart and mind. Beauty of form, of feature, and of color were nothing to him, if a woman had not also beauty of expression; if he could not see, he said, beauty of soul in her eyes. "Beauty and goodness have always been associated in my idea," said he, at Genoa, to the Countess B——, "for in my experience I have generally seen them go together. What constitutes true beauty for me," added he, "is the soul looking through the eyes. Sometimes women that were called beautiful have been pointed out to me that could never in the least have excited my feelings, because they wanted physiognomy, or expression, which is the same thing; while others, scarcely noticed, quite struck and attracted me by their expression of face."

He admired Lady C—— very much, because, he said, her beauty expressed purity, peace, dreaminess, giving the idea that she had never inspired or experienced aught but holy emotions. He once thought of marrying another young lady, because she excited the same feelings. All the women who more or less interested him in England were remarkable for their intellect or their education, including her whom he se-

* See "Life in Italy."

lected for his companion through life. Only, with regard to her, he trusted too much to reputation and appearance; he saw what she had, not what was wanting. She was in great part the cause of his deadly antipathy to regular "blue stockings;" but that did not change the necessity of intellect for exciting his interest. It only required, he said, for the *dress to hide the color of the stockings.* The name he gave to his natural daughter belonged to a Venetian lady, whose cleverness he admired, and with whom his acquaintance consisted in a mere exchange of thought. Often he has been heard to say that he could never have loved a silly woman, however beautiful; nor yet a vulgar woman, whether the defect were the result of birth, or education, or tastes. He felt no attraction for that style of woman since called "fast." Even among the light characters whose acquaintance he permitted to himself at Venice, he avoided those who were too bold. There lived then at Venice Mme. V——, a perfect siren. All Venice was at her feet; Lord Byron would not know her, and at Bologna he refused to make acquaintance with a person of still higher rank, Countess M——, who was both charming and estimable, but who had the fault in his eyes of attracting too much general admiration. Her air of modesty and reserve was what principally drew him toward Miss Milbank. At Ferrara, where he met Countess Mosti and thought her most delightful, he did not feel the same sympathy for her sister, who was, however, much more brilliant, and whose singing excited the admiration of every one.

In order to be truly loved by Lord Byron, it was requisite for a woman to live in a sort of illusive atmosphere for him, to appear somewhat like an immaterial being, not subject to vulgar corporeal necessities. Thence arose his antipathy (considered so singular) to see the woman he loved eat. In short, spiritual and manly in his habits, he was equally so with his person.

It sufficed to see his face, upon which there reigned such gentleness allied to so much dignity; and his look, never to be forgotten; and the unrivalled mouth, which seemed incapable of lending itself to any material use; a simple glance enabled one to understand that this privileged being was endowed with all noble passions, joined to an instinctive horror of all that is low and vulgar in human nature. "His beauty was quite independent of his dress," said Lady Blessington.

If, then, his nails were roseate as the shells of the ocean (according to her expression); if his complexion was transparent; his teeth like pearls; his hair glossy and curling; he had only to thank Providence for having lavished on him and preserved to him so many free gifts. But it is not easy to persuade others of such remarkable exceptions to the general rule. Those who do not possess the same advantages are incredulous; and, indeed, there were not wanting persons to deny, at least in part, that he had them.

Soon after his death an account of him was published in the "London Magazine," containing some truths mixed up with a heap of calumnies. Among other things, it was said "that Lord Byron constantly wore gloves." To which Count Pietro Gamba replied, "*That is not true;* Lord Byron wore them less than any other man of his standing."

Another declared that his fingers were loaded with rings; he only wore one, which was a token of affection. In his rooms hardly ordinary comforts could be found. He was not one to carry about with him the habits of his own country. Indeed, his habits consisted in having none. During his travels, the most difficult to please were his valet and other servants. "On his last journey," says Count Gamba, "he passed six days without undressing."

His sole self-indulgence consisted in frequent bathing; for his only craving was for extreme cleanliness. But, just as the disciples of Epicurus would never have adopted his regimen, so would they equally have refused to imitate this last enjoyment; which was a little too manly for them, for his baths were mostly taken on Ocean's back; struggling against the stormy wave, and that in all seasons, up to mid-December. Such was the fastidious delicacy of this epicurean!*

But to acknowledge all these things, or even any thing extraordinarily good in the author of "Don Juan," the "Age

* "He was more a mental being, if I may use this phrase," said Captain Parry, who knew him at Missolonghi, "than any one I ever saw; he lived on thoughts more than on food."

of Bronze," the "Vision;" in a son so *wanting in respect* for the weaknesses of his mother-country; in a poet that had dared to chastise powerful enemies, and the limit of whose audacity was not even yet known, for his death had just condemned, through revelations and imprudent biographies, many persons and things to a sorry kind of immortality; to praise him, declare him guiltless, do him justice,—truly that would have been asking too much from England at that time. England has since made great strides in the path of generous toleration and even toward justice to Lord Byron. For vain is calumny after a time: truth destroys calumny by evoking facts. These form a clear atmosphere, wherein truth becomes luminous, as the sun in its atmosphere: for facts give birth to truth, and are mortal to calumny.

CHAPTER XI.

THE CONSTANCY OF LORD BYRON.

AMONG Lord Byron's moral virtues, may we count that of constancy? Men in general, not finding this virtue in their own lives, refuse to believe in its existence among those who, in exception to the common rule, do possess it. They must be forced to this act of justice as to many others. This is comprehensible; constancy is so rare!

"I less easily believe constancy in men than any thing else," says Montaigne, "and nothing more easily than inconstancy."

Besides the difficulties common to every one, Lord Byron had also to fight against those difficulties peculiar to his sensitive nature and his vast intelligence.

"The largest minds," says Bacon, "are the least constant, because they find reasons for deliberating, where others only see occasion for acting."

But if these difficulties overcame Lord Bacon's constancy, could they have the same power over Lord Byron, who was indeed his equal in mind, but his opposite in conduct and strength of soul? There are three sorts of constancy: that of affection, which has its source in goodness of heart; that of taste, flowing from beauty of soul; that of idea, derived from rectitude of intelligence.

Did Lord Byron possess the whole of these, or only a part? As this may be chiefly proved, not from writings or words, but by conduct, let us ask the question of those who knew him personally and at all periods of his life.

Was he constant in his ideas? Moore, speaking of Lord Byron's intellectual faculties, of his variableness, of which he makes too much, for the reasons I have mentioned,* and of the danger to which it exposed his consistency and oneness of character, says:—

* See chapter on "Mobility."

"The consciousness, indeed, of his own natural tendency to yield thus to every chance impression, and change with every passing impulse, was not only forever present to his mind, but, aware as he was of the suspicion of weakness attached by the world to any retractation or abandonment of long-professed opinions, had the effect of keeping him in that general line of consistency, on certain great subjects, which, notwithstanding occasional fluctuations and contradictions as to the details of these very subjects, he continued to preserve throughout life. A passage from one of his manuscripts will show how sagaciously he saw the necessity of guarding himself against his own instability in this respect:—'The world,' he says, 'visits change of politics or change of religion with a more severe censure than a mere difference of opinion would appear to me to deserve. But there must be some reason for this feeling, and I think it is that this departure from the earliest instilled ideas of our childhood, and from the line of conduct chosen by us when we first enter into public life, have been seen to have more mischievous results for society, and to prove more weakness of mind than other actions, in themselves more immoral.'"

"To superficial observers," says the Hon. Col. Stanhope, "his conduct might appear uncertain; and that was the case sometimes, but only *up to a certain point.* His genius was limitless and versatile, and in conversation he passed boldly from grave to gay, from light to serious topics; but nevertheless, *upon the whole and in reality,* no man was more constant, I might almost say *more obstinate,* than Lord Byron *in the pursuit of great objects.* For instance, in religion and in politics, he seemed as firm as a rock, though, like a rock, he was sometimes subject to great shocks, to the convulsions of nature in commotion. What I affirm is, that Lord Byron had very fixed opinions on important matters. It is not from the opinion he wished to give of himself, nor from what he allowed to escape his lips, that I could have drawn this conclusion; for, in conversing with me on politics or religion, and passing capriciously over this latter subject, sometimes laughing and making strings of jests, he would say, for instance, '*the more I think the more I doubt—I am a thorough skeptic;*' but I find these words contradicted in *all his actions, and in all his sen-*

timents seriously expressed from childhood to death. And I opine that although occasionally he may have appeared changeable, still he always came back to certain fixed ideas in his mind; that he always entertained a constant attachment to liberty, according to his notions of liberty; and that, although not orthodox in religion, he *firmly believed* in the existence of a God. It is then equally false to represent him as an atheist or as an orthodox Christian. Lord Byron was, as he often told me, *a thorough deist.*"*

It would be easy to prove in a thousand ways that, despite the danger of inconstancy resulting from his great sensibility, imagination, and intellect, no one, more than Lord Byron, steadily and firmly adhered *through life* in his actions to the principles which *constitute the man of honor.* Chances, caprices, inequalities of temper, which are to sensitive natures what bubbles are on a lake, all disappeared when these great principles required to be acted upon; and the effects even of his well-nigh inexhaustible benevolence were checked, if he had to struggle against his principles. We find in his memoranda, 1813:—"I like George Byron" (his cousin, the present lord); "I like him much more than one generally does one's heirs. He is a fine fellow. I would do any thing to see him advance in his career as a sailor; *any thing except apostatize!*" (Lord Byron was a *Whig*, and his cousin a *Tory.*)

As it is impossible to quote every thing, I will only say that his passion for firmness and constancy in the principles of honor, went so far as to inspire him with repugnance for those characters lacking the firmness and oneness of action which he considered it a sacred duty to practice. It is even to this sentiment that must be attributed certain antipathies which he expressed, sometimes by words and sometimes by silence, and which have been laid to totally different, and quite impossible motives. For instance, his silence concerning Chateaubriand, expressive of his little sympathy for the individual (a silence so much resented by this proud vindictive poet, and for which he revenged himself in different ways), was not caused solely by the radical antagonism existing between their two natures. Assuredly, the literary affectation, the want of sincerity, the theatrical and declamatory nature of Chateau-

* Stanhope, Parry, 235.

briand's soul, who was positively ill with insatiable pride, innate and incurable ennui, all this could little assimilate with the simplicity, sincerity, passionate tenderness and devotion of Lord Byron. But his repugnance was especially directed against the skeptic, who made himself the champion of catholicism, and the liberal who upheld the divine right of kings.*

A few days before Lord Byron set out for his last journey to Greece, a young man (M. Coullmann) arrived at Genoa, bringing him the admiring homage of many celebrated men in France, who sent him their respective works. Among the number were Delavigne and Lamartine. Chateaubriand, of course, was conspicuous by his absence: but an anecdote Coullmann related, of what had just occurred at Turin, greatly amused Lord Byron. Chateaubriand had lately been presented in his capacity of ambassador, whereupon the queen said to him: "Are you any relation to that Chateaubriand who has written *something?*"

Lord Byron, laughing heartily at the anecdote, hastened to go and repeat it to the Countess G——.

The same sentiment had disenchanted him with Monti, whom he had so much admired at Milan, and with several other rival poets.

When Lord Byron heard it said of any one, "he has changed sides, he has abandoned his party, he has forfeited his word," one might feel sure that all his natural indulgence, generally so great, was gone: he looked upon such a fault as forming only a despicable variety of the vice he never forgave, viz., untruth. At most, he could only make an exception in favor of women.

"I have received a very pretty note from Madame de Staël," we read in his memoranda of 1813; "her works are my delight, and she also (for half an hour). But I do not like her politics, or, at least, *her changes* in politics. If she had been, *æqualis ab incepto,* that would be nothing. But, she is a woman, . . . and, intellectually, she has done more than all the rest of her sex put together."

Nevertheless, constancy in idea being subservient to the consent of the mind, must undoubtedly have undergone oscillations with Lord Byron. That was, however, only the case

* See Sainte-Beuve, vol. i. p. 286.

with regard to ideas which could be discussed, and which required to pass through the ordeal of long reflection and practice, before being fully adopted by him. But religious ideas were not of this number; on the contrary, they held the first place in the order of those to be accepted and raised into principles by every man of honor and good sense. For, whatever may have been his fluctuations with regard to certain points of religious doctrine, sects and modes of worship, it is certain that in great fundamental matters his mind never seriously doubted, and thus escaped the influence of friends less sensible,—of Matthews in his early youth, and of Shelley at a later period.* That touching Prayer to the Divinity, written in boyhood, and which is so full of hope and faith in the soul's immortality, and in the existence of a personal God, he might have signed again when he came to act instead of writing, as also on his death-bed.†

Between the commencement of his career at eighteen and its close at the age of thirty-six, it is easy to see, by his language, correspondence, and works, that his mind had passed successively through different phases before arriving at the last result. The religious idea is more or less clear. Nevertheless, one perceives a golden ray ever present, connecting the different periods of his life, keeping up heat and light in his soul, and giving unity to his whole career. Hope, desire, and I may almost say, a sort of latent faith, always influenced him until they merged into the conviction whose light never more abandoned him.

At fifteen years of age, while at Harrow, he fought with Lord Calthorpe for calling him an *atheist;* at eighteen, he wrote his beautiful profession of faith in the Prayer to the Divinity, and in the touching "Adieu," which he wrote when he thought he would soon die. At nineteen, giving the list in his memoranda of books already read (a list hardly credible), he says: "With regard to books on religion, I have read Blair, Porteous, Tillotson, Hooker,—all very tiresome. I detest books about religion, but I adore and love my God, apart from the blasphemous notions of sectarians, and without believing in their absurd and damnable heresies, mysteries, etc."

* See chapter on "Religion."

† See this prayer in chapter on "Religion."

At twenty-one, when he had passed through the double influence exercised by Pagan classical literature and German philosophies, and was in a transition state, he wrote "Childe Harold;" but the skeptical tendencies to be found in one stanza appear like a bravado, the result of spleen, a feeling that made him suffer, and which he speedily threw aside. For he wrote, at the same time, the stanza upon the death of a friend, whom he *hopes to see again in the land of souls*, and afterward, the elegies to Thyrza, which are full of *faith in immortality*. At thirty, writing some philosophical reflections in his memorandum-book, he says: "One can not doubt the immortality of the soul."

And, elsewhere, he also says that Christianity appears to him essentially founded on the immateriality of the soul, and that, for this reason, the Christian materialism of Priestley had always struck him as being a deadly sort of doctrine. "Believe, if you please," added he, "in the material resurrection of the body, but not without a soul: it would be cruel indeed, if, after having had a soul in this world (and our mind, by whatever name you call it, is really a soul), we were to be separated from it in the other, even for material immortality! I confess my partiality for mind."

Alluding to the systems of philosophy that do not admit creation according to Genesis, he says, that "even if we could get rid of Adam and Eve, of the apple and the serpent, we should not know what to put in their place; that the difficulty would not be overcome; that things must have had a beginning, it matters not when and how; that creation must have had an origin and a Creator. For creation is much more natural and easy to imagine than a concurrence of atoms; that all things may be traced to their sources even though they end by emptying themselves into an ocean."

We have seen what he said to Parry upon religion* and its ministers, upon God Almighty and the hope of enjoying eternal life, only a few weeks before his glorious death.

And when the hand of death was already upon him, a few moments before his agony, did he not say that eternity and space were already before his eyes, but that on this point, thanks to God, *he was happy and tranquil?* that the thought

* See chapter on "Religion."

of living *eternally*, of living another life, was a great consolation to him? that Christianity was the purest and most liberal of all religions (although a little spoiled by the ministers of Christ, often the worst enemies of its liberal and charitable doctrines); but that, as to the questions depending on these doctrines, and which God alone, all powerful, can determine, in Him alone did he wish to rest?

But if Lord Byron was constant to a certain order of ideas, was he equally constant in his affections? Moore again shall answer:—

"The same distrust in his own steadiness, thus keeping alive in him a conscientious self-watchfulness, concurred not a little, I have no doubt, with the innate kindness of his nature, to preserve so constant and unbroken the greater number of his attachments through life—some of them, as in the instance of his mother, owing evidently more to a sense of duty than of real affection, the consistency with which, so creditably to the strength of his character, they were maintained."

But, putting aside family affections, where constancy may appear a duty and a necessity, let us see what Lord Byron was in affections of his own choice,—such as friendship and love, where inconstancy is a sin that the world easily forgives.

We have seen what the friendship of Lord Byron meant. Death destroyed several of the young existences with which his heart was bound up, and his first sorrows sprang from these misfortunes. But *never* by his will, caprice, or fault, did he lose a single friend! Even the wrongs they inflicted, while they weighed upon his mind, altered his opinions sometimes, dispelled some sweet illusions and grieved his heart, yet could not succeed in changing it. He contented himself with judging the individual in such cases, sometimes with philosophical indulgence which he was only too much accustomed to hide under the veil of pleasantry, and sometimes in showing openly how much his heart was wounded.*

This constancy of heart that he showed in friendship, was it equally his in matters of love? By his energy of soul, unable ever to forget any thing, Lord Byron possessed the first condition toward constancy in love. Contrary to those un-

* See octaves 48, 49 and 50, canto xiv. "Don Juan;" and several in "Childe Harold," cantos iii. and iv.

stable persons who say that they cease to love, for the simple reason that they have already loved too much, it might rather be said of Lord Byron that he still loved on only because he had loved. In all his poems, he has idealized fidelity and constancy in love. All the heroes of his poems are faithful and constant, from Conrad, Lara, Selim, all those of the Oriental poems of his youth, up to those of his latter life, to his Biblical mysteries. Even the angels, the seraphim, in that beautiful poem, written shortly before his death, "Heaven and Earth," prefer suffering to inconstancy,—to forfeit heaven rather than return there without their beloved. In vain the archangel Raphael presses the two amorous seraphim to come back to the celestial sphere, to abandon the two sisters, and menaces them. Samiasa replies:—

> "It may not be:
> We have chosen, and will endure."

The poet gives it to be understood that they will be punished; which forms the moral of the piece. Don Juan himself refuses the love of a beautiful sultana, from fidelity to the remembrance of his Haidée; and when, afterward, he does yield, he seems to bear with, rather than to have sought success. One feels that this idealization of fidelity and constancy really has its source in Lord Byron's heart, and not in his imagination. Still, however, the chief and undeniable proof must be drawn from his own life.

The first condition for judging any one impartially with regard to inconstancy in love, is not only to know the facts and real circumstances connected with an intimacy, but especially to know the nature of the sentiment to which the name of love has been applied. We are aware that, at fifteen years of age, Lord Byron's heart was already under the influence of a young girl of eighteen.* The mere disproportion of age prevents such an affection from offering any grounds on which to examine his capability of being constant. It is well known how much suffering this early passion caused him. The object of it, after denying him no token of reciprocal love that was innocent, giving him her picture, agreeing to meetings, receiving all the spontaneous, innocent, confiding tenderness of his young and ardent heart, left him in the lurch one fine day, on

* See chapter on "Generosity."

account of his youth, in order to marry a fashionable, vulgar man. And thus did she destroy the charm which governed his heart. Precocious reflection, with its accompaniment of knowledge, agitating, confusing, throwing young souls on the road to error, succeeded to his enchantment. He then began (at sixteen) to talk of vanished illusions; and, for want of something better, allowed himself to be carried away, and to lead the ordinary university life. He evidently only did what others did; but he was made of different materials; and while they thought this dissipation very natural, and, tranquil in their inferiority, believed themselves innocent, he alone disapproved of his own conduct and blamed it. The better to escape all this, he went in search of forgetfulness amid the fresh breezes of ocean, across the Pyrenees, among the ruins of ancient civilization. Yet, after two years' travelling, on his return to England, his soul all love, his heart burning with an infinite ardor, through that intoxication of success which weakens, through that eagerness for emotion caused by his vivacity of mind, and even by a sort of psychological curiosity, Lord Byron did fall into new attachments. And these attachments, not being of a nature that could stand the trial of reflection, caused him to give up known for unknown objects. But his soul was ever agitated, in commotion, and, even when he changed, it was through necessity rather than caprice. In order to escape once more from himself, from the allurements of the senses, from the effects of the enthusiasm which his personal beauty and his genius excited among women, he resolved to take refuge in an indissoluble tie, in a tie formed by duty, not love. Perhaps he might have found strength for perseverance in the beauty of the sacrifice. His soul was quite capable of it. But destiny pursued him in his choice, and rendered it impossible. To his misfortune, he married Miss Milbank.* Again he drifted away from the right path, but, this time, with the resolution of keeping his heart independent, his soul free and unfettered by any indissoluble tie.† But in coming to this determination at the age of twenty-eight, he had not consulted his heart, ever athirst for infinitude. Vainly he sought to lull it, to keep it earthward, to laugh at his own aspirations—useless labor! One day it broke loose. Nature is like water;

* See chapter on "Marriage." † See "Life at Venice, at Milan."

sooner or later it must find its equilibrium. From that day forth Psyche's lamp had no more light; reflection had no more power; and the love which had taken possession of his soul left him not again, but accompanied him to his last hour, through the modifications inevitable in earthly affections. This constancy maintained thenceforth without a struggle, he understood at once; and felt that the unchanging sentiment belonged equally to his will and to his destiny. "*Cœlum, non animam mutant qui trans mare currunt*," wrote he one day at Ravenna, on the opening page of "Jacopo Ortis," Foscolo's work, that had just fallen into his hands; for he knew that no one could read this avowal of his heart where he had traced it. After having remarked the strange coincidence by which this volume was brought a second time before him, just when he was, as once before, in extreme agitation, he continued thus:—

"Most men bewail not having attained the object of their desires. I had oftener to deplore the obtaining mine, for I can not love moderately, nor quiet my heart with mere fruition. The letters of this Italian Werther are very interesting; at least I think so, but my present feelings hardly render me a competent judge."

Another time, a volume of "Corinne," translated into Italian, fell under his notice at Ravenna. In the same language, which no one then about him could read, he confided to this book the secret of his heart, and, after having poured out its fullness in words of noble melting tenderness, concluded thus: —"Think of me when Alps and sea shall separate us; *but that will never come to pass, unless you so will it.*"

It was not willed, and therefore the separation did not take place. But, alas! the day arrived when he was so entangled in a multiplicity of complications, and honor spoke so loudly, that both sides were forced to will it.

Whoever should consider this departure the result of inconstancy, is incapable to form an estimate of his great soul. His affection, that had lasted for years, admitted no longer of any uneasiness, for it was brought into complete harmony with that of her he loved. Naturally his heart underwent the transformation produced by time. His affection was gradually acquiring the sweetness of unchanging friendship, without losing the charm appertaining to ardor of passion. The sacrifice entailed by this departure was in proportion to these sentiments. "Often," says M——, "during the passage, we saw his eyes filled with tears." The sadness described by Mr. Barry of his last visit to Albano has been seen.* These tears and this sadness betray the extent of his sublime sacrifice! And then, when once arrived in Greece, although determined to brave all the storms gathering above his head, he wrote unceasingly to Madame G——, with that ease and simplicity which not only forbade any exaggeration of sentiment, but even made him restrain its expression; which was also rendered imperative by the circumstances then surrounding her.

"I shall fulfill the object of my mission from the committee, and then . . . return to Italy. . . Pray be as cheerful and tranquil as you can, and be assured that there is nothing here that can excite any thing but a wish to be with you again, though we are very kindly treated by the English here of all descriptions."

"September 11.

"You may be sure that the moment I can join you again will be as welcome to me as at any period of our acquaintance. There is nothing very attractive here to occupy my attention; but both honor and inclination demand that I should serve the Greek cause. I wish that this cause, as well as the affairs of Spain, were favorably settled, that I might return to Italy and relate all my adventures to you."

Thus much for his constancy when he truly loved. It would be worth inquiry how many men and how many writers have carried their ideal of constancy into their own life to a higher degree than Lord Byron? My opinion is that if, the same circumstances given, the number went a little beyond one, we might consider the result very satisfactory.

After having seen that Lord Byron was unchangeable in great principles and ideas, as soon as his mind was convinced, and that he was constant to all the true sentiments of his heart, it still remains to be shown whether he was equally so in his tastes and habits.

* See chapter on "Strength of Soul."

It may be said of most men that they have no character, because they often vary in taste, and without even perceiving it. That could not be asserted of Lord Byron, although sometimes, according to his self-accusing custom, he declared himself to be inconstant.

The truth is that he was, on the contrary, remarkably steadfast in his tastes. The nature of his preferences, and the conclusions to be drawn from them, will form the subject of another chapter. We shall only speak of them here as relating to constancy.

"We shall often have occasion," says Moore, "to remark the fidelity to early habits and tastes which distinguished Lord Byron." Moore then observes the extraordinary constancy Lord Byron showed in clinging to all the impressions of youth; and he adduces as a proof the care with which he preserved the notes and letters written by his favorite comrades at school, even when they were younger than himself. These letters he enriched with dates and notes, after years of long interval, while very few of his childish effusions have been kept by the opposite parties. Moore also notes several other features of this constancy, which he continued to practice throughout life. For instance, his punctuality in answering letters immediately, despite his distaste for epistolary effusions; and his love for simple music, such as that of the ballads that used to attract him at sixteen to Miss Pigott's saloon. It was partly this same taste that made him enjoy so much, at twenty-six, the evenings he passed at his friend Kinnaird's house (some months before his marriage, the last of his London life), when Moore would sing his favorite songs, bringing tears to Byron's eyes. And it was this same taste that subsequently drew him to the piano at which Madame G—— sat, at Ravenna, Pisa, Genoa; and which, when she played or sung Mozart's and Rossini's favorite motets, made him say that he no longer loved any other music but hers.

What he had once loved never tired him. Memory was to him like an enchanter's wand, throwing some charm into objects which in themselves possessed none. He loved the land where he had loved, however naturally unattractive it might be: witness Ravenna, and Italy in general.

"Possession of what I truly love," said he, in the very

rare moments when he did himself justice, "does not cloy me." He loved the mountains of Greece, because they recalled those of Scotland; he would have loved other mountains, because they recalled those of Greece.

A few months before his death, he said in his charming poem "The Island,"—

> "Long have I roam'd through lands which are not mine,
> Adored the Alp, and loved the Apennine,
> Revered Parnassus, and beheld the steep
> Jove's Ida and Olympus crown the deep:
> But 'twas not all long ages' lore, nor all
> *Their* nature held me in their thrilling thrall;
> The infant rapture still survived the boy,
> And Loch-na-gar with Ida look'd o'er Troy,
> Mix'd Celtic memories with the Phrygian mount,
> And Highland linns with Castalie's clear fount.
> Forgive me, Homer's universal shade!
> Forgive me, Phœbus! that my fancy stray'd;
> The north and nature taught me to adore
> Your scenes sublime, from those beloved before."*

He would love a place of abode because he had loved when in it. The same with regard to a dwelling, a walk, a melody, a perfume, a form, and even a dish; he who cared so little for any sort of food. His childish impressions, his readings at that age, had a great deal to do with his choice of poetic subjects afterward; and we find them again reproduced even in his last dramatic work. "Werner," written in such a fine moral sense, is the result of the "Canterbury Tale" read in childhood. Never was man more constant in his habits and tastes than he; and, indeed, it required that indefinable charm of soul he possessed, and which pervaded his whole being, to prevent monotony from perverting this quality into a fault.

Why, then, have his biographers talked so much of his mobility, if it were not to make Lord Byron pass for a creature swayed by every fresh impulse, and incapable of steady feeling? I have given the first reason elsewhere.† But I will add another, namely, that they have transferred the qualities of the *poet to the man* in an erroneous manner; that to the versatility of his genius (one of his great gifts, and which ever belong to him) they have added mobility of character, such as often, too often, perhaps, influenced his conversation, and tinctured his external fictitious nature. But they have

* "The Island," canto ii. stanza 12.

† See chapter on "Mobility."

done so without examining his actions, without reflecting that this mobility vanished as it was written, or in the light play of his witty conversation, or the trivial acts of his life. Otherwise they would have been forced to confess, that it never had any influence on his conduct in matters of moment, that he was persevering and firm to an extremely rare degree in all things *essential* and which constitute *man in his moral and social capacity.*

We may then sum up by saying that Lord Byron generally established on an impregnable rock, guarded by unbending principles, those great virtues to which principles are essential; but that, after making these treasures secure—for treasures they are to the man of honor and worth—once having placed them beyond the reach of sensibility and sentiment, he may sometimes have allowed the *lesser virtues* (within ordinary bonds) such indulgence as flowed from his kindly nature, and such as his youth rendered natural to a feeling heart and ardent imagination. Like all men, he was only truly firm under serious circumstances, when he wished to show energy in fulfilling a duty. Thus Lord Byron allowed his pen to jest, to mark the follies of men: sometimes attacking them boldly in front, sometimes aiming light arrows aslant, ridiculing, chastising, as humor or fancy prompted; and he gave himself the same liberty of language in private conversation, according to the character of those with whom he conversed. On all these occasions his genius undoubtedly gave itself up to versatility. But let us not forget that all that which changes and becomes effaced in hearts of inconstant mood, and which ought not to change in men of honor and worth, never did vary in him. Let us acknowledge, in short, that, if mobility belonged to the *sensitive* parts of his nature, constancy no less characterized his *moral and intellectual* being.

CHAPTER XII.

THE COURAGE AND FORTITUDE OF LORD BYRON.

ALL the moral qualities that flow from energy—courage, intrepidity, fortitude; in a word, self-control—shone with too much lustre in Lord Byron's soul for us to pass them over in silence, or even to call only superficial attention to them.

But, it may be said, Why speak of his courage? No one ever called it in question. Besides, is courage a virtue? It is hardly a quality; in reality it is but a duty. Yes, undoubtedly, that is true, but there are different kinds of courage, and Lord Byron's was of such a peculiar nature, and showed itself under such uncommon circumstances as to justify observation, for it evinces a quality necessary to be noticed by all who seek to portray his great soul with the wish of arriving at a close resemblance.

"Whatever virtue may be allowed to belong to personal courage, it is most assuredly those who are endowed by nature with the liveliest imaginations, and who have, therefore, most vividly and simultaneously before their eyes all the remote and possible consequences of danger, that are most deserving of whatever praise attends the exercise of that virtue."

Certainly Lord Byron made part of the category, so that Moore adds:—

"The courage of Lord Byron, as all his companions in peril testify, was of that noblest kind which rises with the greatness of the occasion, and becomes the more self-collected and resisting the more imminent the danger."

Thus, far from its being the natural impetuosity that causes rash natures to rush into danger, Lord Byron's courage was quite as much the result of reflection as of impulse. *His was courage of the noblest kind*, a quality mixed up with other fine moral faculties, shining with light of its own, yet all combining to lend mutual lustre. This is, indeed, what ought to be called *fortitude* and *self-control*, and this is what we remark in Lord Byron. But, in order not to sin against the scientific classification used by moralists, and which requires subdivisions, we will isolate it for a moment, and examine it under the name of courage, presence of mind, and coolness.

Unaffected in his bravery, as in all things else, Lord.Byron did not seek dangers, but when they presented themselves to him he met them with lofty intrepidity.

To give some examples—and the difficulty is to choose—let us consider him under different circumstances that occurred during his first travels in the East.

While at Malta he was on the point of fighting a duel, through some misunderstanding with an officer on General Oakes's staff. The meeting had been fixed for an early hour, but Lord. Byron slept so soundly that his companion was obliged to awaken him. On arriving at the spot, which was near the shore, his adversary was not yet there; and Lord Byron, although his luggage had already been taken on board the brig that was to convey him to Albania, wished to give him the chance at least of another hour. During all this long interval he amused himself very quietly walking about the beach perfectly unconcerned.

At last an officer, sent by his antagonist, arrived on the ground, bringing not only an explanation of how the delay had arisen, but likewise all the excuses and satisfaction Lord Byron could desire for the supposed offense. Thus the duel did not take place.

The gentleman who was to be his second could not sufficiently praise the coolness and firm courage shown by Lord Byron throughout this affair.

Some time later Lord Byron was on the mountains of Epirus with his friend and fellow-traveller, Mr. Hobhouse (now Lord Broughton). These mountains being then infested with banditti, they were accompanied by a numerous escort, and even by one of the secretaries, as well as several retainers belonging to the famous Ali Pasha of Joannina, whom they had just been visiting. One evening, seeing a storm impending, Mr. Hobhouse hastened on in front with part of their suite, in order sooner to reach a neighboring hamlet, and get shelter prepared. Lord Byron followed with the remainder of the escort. Before he could arrive, however, the storm burst, and soon became terrific. Mr. Hobhouse, who had long been safe under cover in the village, could see nothing of his friend.

"It was seven in the evening," says Mr. Hobhouse, in his account of it, "and the fury of the storm had become quite alarming. Never before or since have I witnessed one so terrible. The roof of the hovel in which we had taken shelter trembled beneath violent gusts of rain and wind, and the thunder kept roaring without intermission, for the echo from one mountain crest had not ceased ere another frightful crash broke above our heads. The plain, and distant hills, visible through the chinks of the hut, seemed on fire. In short, the tempest was terrific; quite worthy of the Jupiter of ancient Greece. The peasants, no less religious than their ancestors, confessed their fears; the women were crying around, and the men, at every new flash of lightning, invoked the name of God, making the sign of the cross."

Meanwhile hours passed, midnight drew near, the storm was far from abating, and Lord Byron had not appeared. Mr. Hobhouse, in great alarm, ordered fires to be lighted on the heights, and guns to be let off in all directions. At length, toward one in the morning, a man, all pale and panic-stricken, soaked through to the skin, suddenly entered the cabin, making loud cries, exclamations, and gestures of despair. He belonged to the escort, and speedily related the danger to which they had been exposed, and in which Lord Byron and his followers still were, and urging the necessity of sending off at once horses, guides, and men with torches, to extricate them from it.

It appears that at the commencement of the storm, when only three miles from the village, Lord Byron, through the fault of his escort, lost the right path. After wandering about as chance directed, in complete ignorance of their whereabouts, and on the brink of precipices, they had stopped at last near a Turkish cemetery and close to a torrent, which they had been enabled to distinguish through the flashes of lightning. Lord Byron was exposed to *all the fury of the storm for nine consecutive hours;* his guides, instead of lending him any assistance, only increased the general confusion, running about on all sides, because they had been menaced with death by the dragoman George, who, in a paroxysm of rage and fear, had fired off his pistols without warning any body, and Lord Byron's English servants, fancying they were attacked by robbers, set up loud cries.

It was three in the morning before the party could reach the shelter where their friends awaited them. During these nine consecutive hours of danger, Lord Byron never once lost his self-possession or serenity, or even that pleasant vein of humor which made him always see the ridiculous side of things.

About the same period Lord Byron and his companion, after having visited Eleusis, were obliged, by stress of weather, to stop some days at Keratea. Having heard of a wonderful cavern situated on Mount Parné, they determined to visit it. On arriving at the entrance they lighted torches of resinous wood, and, preceded by a guide, penetrated through a small aperture, dragging themselves along the ground until they reached a sort of subterranean hall, ornamented with arcades and high cupolas of crystal, supported by columns of shining marcasite; the hall itself opened out into large horizontal chambers, or else conducted to dark, deep yawning abysses toward the centre of the mountain. After having strayed from one grotto to another, the travellers arrived near a fountain of crystal water. There they stopped, till, seeing their torches wane low, they thought of retracing their steps. But, after walking for some minutes in the labyrinth, they again found themselves beside the mysterious fountain. Then they grew alarmed, for their guide acknowledged with *terror that he had forgotten the itinerary of the cavern, and no longer knew where to find the outlet.*

While they were wandering thus from one grotto to another, in a sort of despair, and occasionally dragging themselves along to get through narrow openings, their last torch was consumed. They remained a long time in total darkness, not knowing what to do, when, as if by miracle, a feeble ray of light made itself visible, and, directing their steps toward it, they ended by reaching the mouth of the cavern. Certainly, it would be difficult to meet with a more alarming situation. Mr. Hobhouse, while confessing that for some moments it had been impossible to look forward to any thing else but the chance of a horrible death, declared that, not only Lord Byron's presence of mind and coolness were admirable in the teeth of such a prospect, but also that his playful humor never forsook him, and helped to keep up their spirits during minutes that must have seemed years to all of them.

It was during this same journey that, finding the mountains which separated them from the Morea were infested with banditti, they embarked on board a vessel of war, called the "Turk." A tempest broke out, and its violence, joined to the ignorance betrayed by the captain and sailors, put the vessel in great danger. Shipwreck seemed inevitable, and close at hand. Nothing was heard on board but cries, lamentations, and prayers. Lord Byron alone remained calm, doing every thing in his power to console and encourage the rest; and then at length, when he saw that his efforts were useless, he wrapped himself up in his Albanian cloak, and lay down on the deck, *going tranquilly to sleep until fate should decide his destiny.*

After having given his mother a simple description of this tempest, he adds:—"I have learned to philosophize during my travels, and, if I had not, what use is there in complaining?"

And Moore says:—

"I have heard the poet's fellow-traveller describe this remarkable instance of his coolness and courage even still more strikingly than it is here stated by himself. Finding that he was unable to be of any service in the exertions which their very serious danger called for, after a laugh or two at the panic of his valet, he not only wrapped himself up and lay down, in the manner here mentioned, but, when their difficulties were surmounted, was found fast asleep."

These adventures happened to him when he was only twenty-one years of age, and within the course of a few weeks. But all his life he gave the same proofs of courage when circumstances called for them.

And since we have chosen these examples from his first journey into Greece, at the beginning of his career, let us select some others from the last, which took place near its close.

Mr. H. Brown having been asked by Lord Harrington what his impressions were of Lord Byron, replied, "Lord Byron was extremely calm in presence of danger. Here are two instances that I witnessed myself:—A Greek, named Costantino Zalichi, to whom his lordship had given his passage, once took up one of Manton's pistols, belonging to Lord Byron. It went off by accident, and the ball passed quite close to Lord Byron's temple. Without the least emotion Lord Byron began explaining to the Greek how such accidents could be avoided.

"On another occasion, near the Roman coast, we observed a suspicious-looking little vessel, armed, and apparently full of people. It was toward the end of the last war with Spain, during which many acts of piracy had been committed in the Mediterranean. And our captain was much alarmed. We were followed all day by this vessel, and toward evening, it seemed so ready for action that we no longer doubted being attacked. However a breeze arose, and darkness came on soon after, whereupon we lost sight of it. Lord Byron, while the danger lasted, remained perfectly calm, giving his orders with the greatest tranquility and reflection."*

And Lord Harrington, then Colonel Stanhope, says himself, in his Essay on Lord Byron:—

"Lord Byron was the *beau idéal* of chivalry. It might have lowered him in the esteem of wise men, if he had not given such extraordinary proofs of the noblest courage.

"Even at moments of the greatest danger, Lord Byron *contemplated death with philosophical calm.* For instance, at the moment of returning from the alarming attack which had surprised him in my room (at Missolonghi), he immediately asked, with the most perfect self-possession, whether his life were in danger, as, in that case, he required the doctor to tell him so, *for he was not afraid of death.*

"Shortly after that frightful convulsion, when, weakened by loss of blood, he was lying on his bed of suffering, with his nervous system completely shaken, a band of mutinous Suliotes, in their splendid dirty costumes, burst suddenly into his room, brandishing their weapons, and loudly demanding their savage rights. Lord Byron, as if electrified by the unexpected act, appeared to have recovered his health, and, the more the Suliotes cried out and threatened, the more *his cool courage triumphed. The scene was really sublime.*"†

* Parry, 206. † Essay by Colonel Stanhope.

And Count Gamba, in his interesting narrative of "Lord Byron's Last Journey into Greece," adds:—

"It is impossible to do justice to the coolness and magnanimity Lord Byron showed on all great occasions. Under ordinary circumstances he was irritable, but the sight of danger calmed him instantly, restoring the free exercise of all the faculties of his noble nature. A man *more indomitable, or firmer in the hour of danger than Lord Byron was, never existed.*"*

But enough of these proofs, which, perhaps, say nothing new to the reader. Nevertheless, as they may call up again the pleasure ever afforded by the spectacle of great moral beauty, let us further add—the better to set forth the nature of Lord Byron's wonderful intrepidity in face of danger—that his energetic soul loved to contemplate those sublime things in Nature that are usually endured with terror. Tempests, the thunder's roll, the lightning's flash—any mysterious display of Nature's forces, so that its violence occasioned neither misfortune nor suffering to sensitive beings—aroused in him the keenest sense of enjoyment, which in turn ministered to his genius, incapable of finding complete satisfaction in the beautiful, and ever yearning passionately after the sublime.

As to his fortitude, that self-control which makes one bear affliction with external serenity, Lord Byron possessed it in as high a degree as he did firmness with regard to material obstacles and dangers.

Endowed with exquisite sensibility, the great poet assuredly went through cruel trials during his stormy career; but instead of ostentatiously exhibiting his sorrows, Lord Byron on many occasions rather exaggerated the delicacy that led him to veil them under an appearance of stoicism. Only very rarely did his poetry echo back the sufferings endured within.

Once, nevertheless, he wished, and rightly, to perpetuate in his verses the memory of the indignities heaped upon him by a guilty world. He wished that the great struggle he had been obliged to sustain against his destiny should not be forgotten; he wished to show how much his heart had been torn, his hopes sapped, his name blighted by the deepest injuries, the meanest perfidy. He had seen, he said, of what beings

* "Last Journey to Greece," p. 174.

with a human semblance were capable, from the frightful roar of foaming calumny to the low whisper of vile reptiles, adroitly distilling poison; double-visaged Januses, who supply the place of words by the language of the eyes, who lie without saying a syllable, and, by dint of a shrug or an affected sigh, impose on fools their unspoken calumnies. Yes, he had to undergo all that, and for once he wished it to be known.

He owed it to himself to make this complaint; his total silence would have been wrong; it was necessary once for all to defend his *character* and reputation, and when he ran the risk of losing the esteem of the world his sensibility could not show itself in too lively a manner.

But if he thus raised his voice to immortalize these indignities, it was not because he recoiled from suffering.

"Let him come forward," exclaimed he, "whoever has seen me bow the head, or has remarked my courage wane with suffering."

Already, at the time of the unexampled persecution raised against him in London, when the separation from his wife took place, he wrote to Murray:—

"February 20th, 1816.

"You need not be in any apprehension or grief on my account. Were I to be beaten down by the world and its inheritors, I should have succumbed to many things years ago. You must not mistake my not bullying for dejection; nor imagine that because I feel, I am to faint."*

In all he wrote at this fatal period of his life, one perceives the wide gaping wound, which is however endured with the strength of a Titan, who at twenty-nine is to become quite a philosopher, good, gentle, almost resigned.

"The camel labors with the heaviest load,
And the wolf dies in silence,—not bestow'd
In vain should such example be; if they,
Things of ignoble or of savage mood,
Endure and shrink not, we of nobler clay
May temper it to bear,—it is but for a day."†

Like all those who feel deeply the joys and griefs of their fellow-men, Lord Byron had received from nature all that could render him capable of moderating the external expres-

* Moore, "Letters," p. 241.

† "Childe Harold."

sion of his sensibility, when injustice was personal to himself. Moreover, circumstances, alas! had only too much favored the development of this noble faculty in him. For, very early, he had received severe lessons from those terrible masters who nurture great souls to self-control; from reverses, vanished illusions, perils, wrongs. The storms however it was his destiny to encounter, though violent, not only did not cause him to be shipwrecked, but even helped to encircle his brow with the martyr's halo.

But, we may be asked, whether this great control which Lord Byron exercised over himself, with regard to obstacles, dangers, and human injustice, existed equally with regard to his own passions. To those who should doubt it, and who, forgetting that Lord Byron only lived the age of passions, without taking into consideration all the circumstances that rendered difficult to him what is easier for others, should pretend that Lord Byron gave way to his passions oftener than he warred against them, to such we would say: "What was he doing, then, when, at barely twenty-two years of age, he adopted an anchorite's *régime*, so as to render his soul more *independent* of *matter?* When he shut himself up at home, with the self-imposed task of writing whole poems before he came out, in order to *overcome his thoughts, and maintain them in a line contrary to that which his passions demanded?* When, grieved, calumniated, outraged, he *preferred exile rather than yield to just resentment*, and in order to avoid the danger of finding himself in situations where he *might not have preserved his self-control?*"

Have they forgotten that at Venice he subjected himself to the ungrateful task of learning languages *more than difficult*, and of working at other *dry studies*, in order to *fix his thoughts on them, and divert them from resentment and anger?*

He writes to Murray: "I find the Armenian language, which is double (*the literary and the vulgar tongue*), difficult, but not insuperably so (at least I hope not). I shall continue. I have found it necessary to chain my mind down to very severe studies, and as this is the most difficult I can find here, it will be a *net for the serpent*."

And have we not seen him overcome himself, just as he was setting out to go where his heart called him (for, notwithstanding all his efforts, it had ceased to be independent), and thus defer a journey he sighed for, only to *exercise acts of generosity, and liberate one of his gondoliers from the Austrian conscription?*

If a true biography could be written of Lord Byron we should see a constant struggle going on in this young man against his passions. And can more be asked of men than to fight against them? Victory is the proof and the reward of combat. If sometimes, as with every man, victory failed him, oftener still he did achieve it; and it is certain that his great desire always was to free himself from the tyranny of his passions.

His last triumphs were not only great—they were sublime.

The sadness that overwhelmed him during the latter part of his stay at Genoa is known. The struggles he had to maintain against his own heart may be conceived.

It is also known how, being driven back into port by a storm, he resolved on visiting the palace of Albaro; and it may well be imagined that the hours passed in this dwelling, then silent and deserted, must have seemed like those that count as years of anguish in the life of great and feeling souls, among whom visions of the future float before the over-excited mind. It can not be doubted that he would then willingly have given up his fatal idea of leaving Italy; indeed he declared so to Mr. Barry, who was with him; but the sentiment of his own dignity and of his promise given triumphed over his feelings.

The night which followed this gloomy day again saw Lord Byron struggling against stormy waves, and not only determined on pursuing his voyage, but also on appearing calm and serene to his fellow-travellers.

Could peace, however, have dwelt within his soul? To show it outwardly must he not have struggled?

"I often saw Lord Byron during his last voyage from Genoa to Greece," says Mr. H. Browne, in a letter written to Colonel Stanhope; "I often saw him in the midst of the greatest gayety suddenly become pensive, *and his eyes fill with tears*, doubtless from some painful remembrance. On these occasions he generally got up and retired to the solitude of his cabin."

And Colonel Stanhope, afterward Lord Harrington, who only knew Lord Byron later at Missolonghi, also says: "I have often observed Lord Byron in the middle of some gay animated conversation, stop, meditate, and his eyes to fill with tears."

And all that he did in that fatal Greece, was it not a perpetual triumph over himself, his tastes, his desires, the wants of his nature and his heart?

He saw nothing in Greece, he wrote to Mme. G——, that did not make him wish to return to Italy, and yet he remained in Greece. He would have preferred waiting in the Ionian Islands, and yet he set out for that fatal Missolonghi! Liberal by principle, and aristocratic by birth, taste, and habits, he was condemned to continual intercourse with vulgar, turbulent, barbarous men, to come into contact with things repugnant to his nature and his tastes, and to struggle against a thousand difficulties—a thousand torments, moral and physical; he felt, and knew, that even life would fail him if he did not leave Missolonghi, yet he remained. Every thing, in short, throughout this last stage of the noble pilgrim, proclaims his empire over self. His triumph was always beautiful, and often sublime, but, alas! he paid for it with his life.

CHAPTER XIII.

THE MODESTY OF LORD BYRON.

AMONG the qualities that belong to his genius, the one which formed its chief ornament has been too much forgotten.

Modesty constituted a beautiful quality of his soul. If it has not been formally denied him; if, even among those whom we term his biographers, some have conceded modesty as pertaining to Lord Byron's genius, they have done so timidly; and have at the same time indirectly denied it by accusing him of pride.

Was Lord Byron proud as a poet and as a man? We shall have occasion to answer this question in another chapter. Here we shall only examine his claims to modesty; and we say, without hesitation, that it was as great in him as it has ever been in others. It shines in every line of his poetry and his prose, at every age and in all the circumstances of his life.

"There is no real modesty" (says a great moralist of the present day) "without diffidence of self, inspired by a deep sense of the beautiful and by the fear of not being able to reach the perfection we conceive."

As a poet, Lord Byron always undervalued or despised himself. As a man, he did so still more; he exaggerated this quality so far as to convert it into a fault, for he calumniated himself.

We have seen how unambitious Lord Byron was as a child, and with what facility he allowed his comrades to surpass him in intellectual exercises, reserving for his sole ambition the wish of excelling them in boyish games and in bodily exercises.

As a youth he did nothing but censure his own conduct, which was not at all different from that which his comrades thought allowable in themselves. We have seen with what modest feelings he published his first poems; with what docility he accepted criticisms, and yielded to the advice of friends whom he esteemed.

When cruel criticism showed him neither mercy nor justice, notwithstanding his youthful age, he lost, it is true, serenity and moderation of spirit, but never once put aside his modesty.

Instigated by a passion for truth, he exclaims in his first satire,—

> "Truth! rouse some genuine bard, and guide his hand
> To drive this pestilence from out the land."

Certainly, he does not spare censure in this passionate satire; but, while inflicting it, he questions whether he should be the one to apply the lash:—

> "E'en I, least thinking of a thoughtless throng,
> Just skill'd to know the right and choose the wrong."

It was during the time of his first travels that Lord Byron wrote his first *chef-d'œuvre*:* but so little was he aware of possessing great faculties that, while suffering from the exactions and torments they created within him, he only asked in return some amusement, an occupation for long hours of solitude.

Having begun "Childe Harold" as a memorial of his travelling impressions, he communicated it, on his return to England, to the friend who had been his companion throughout. But, instead of meeting with indulgence and encouragement, this friend only blamed the poem, and called it an extravagant conception.

He was, nevertheless, a competent judge and a poet himself. Why, then, such severity? Did he wish to sacrifice the poet to the man, fearing for his friend lest the allusions therein made should lend further weapons to the malice of his enemies? Did he dread for himself, and for those among their comrades who, two years before, had donned the preacher's garb at Newstead Abbey, lest the voice of public opinion should mix them up in the pretended disorders of which the Abbey had been the theatre, and which the poem either

* The first two cantos of "Childe Harold."

exaggerated or invented? Whatsoever his motive, this friend was not certainly then a John of Bologna for Lord Byron; but the modesty of the poet surpassed the severity of his judge; for, accepting the blame as if it were merited, he restored the poem to its portfolio with such humility that when Mr. Dallas afterward heard of it almost by chance, and, fired with enthusiasm on reading it, pronounced this extravagant thing to be a sublime *chef-d'œuvre*, he had the greatest difficulty in persuading Lord Byron to make it public.

Gifford's criticisms were always received by Lord Byron not only with docility and modesty but even with gratitude.

He never lost an occasion of blaming himself as a poet and of depreciating his genius. Living only for affection, more than once when he feared that the war going on against him might warp feeling, he was on the point of consigning all he had written to the flames; of destroying forever every vestige of it; and only the fear of harming his publisher made him at last withdraw the given order.

He knew only how to praise his rivals, and to assist those requiring help or encouragement.

Notwithstanding the favor shown him by the public, it always appeared to him that he would weary it with any new production.

When about to publish the "Bride of Abydos," he said, "I know what I risk, and with good reason,—losing the small reputation I have gained by putting the public to this new test; but really I have ceased to attach any importance to that. I write and publish solely for the sake of occupation, to draw my thoughts away from reality, and take refuge in imagination, however dreadful."

In 1814, when Murray (who was thinking of establishing a periodical for bringing out the works of living authors) consulted Lord Byron on the subject, he, whose splendid fame had already thrown all his contemporaries into the shade, answered simply, that supported by such poets as Scott, Wordsworth, Southey, and many others, the undertaking would of course succeed; and that for his part, he would unite with Hobhouse and Moore so as to furnish occasionally —a failure! and at the same time he made use of the opportunity to praise Campbell and Canning.

His memorandum-book is one perpetual record of his humility, even at a time when the public, of all classes and sexes, had made him their idol.

After having expressed in his memoranda for 1813 his sublime aspirations after glory—that is to say, the happiness he should experience in being *not a ruler, but a guide and benefactor of humanity, a Washington, a Franklin, a Penn;* "but no," added he; "no, I shall never be any thing: or rather, I shall always be nothing. The most I can hope is that some one may say of me, '*He might, perhaps*, if he would.'"

The low estimation in which he held his poetical genius, to which he preferred action, amounted almost to a fault; for he forgot that grand and beautiful truths, couched in burning words and lighted up by genius, are also actions. He really seemed to have difficulty in forgiving himself for writing at all. Even at the outset of his literary career he was indignant with his publisher for having taken steps with Gifford which looked like asking for praise.

"It is bad enough to be a scribbler," said he, "without having recourse to such subterfuges for extorting praise or warding off criticism."

"I have never contemplated the prospect," wrote he, in 1819, "of occupying a permanent place in the literature of my country. Those who know me best are aware of that; and they also know that I have been considerably astonished at even the transient success of my works, never having flattered any one person or party, and having expressed opinions which are not those of readers in general. If I could have guessed the high degree of attention that has been awarded to them, I should certainly have made all possible efforts to merit it. But I have lived abroad, in distant countries, or else in the midst of worldly dissipation in England: circumstances by no means favorable to study and reflection. So that almost all I have written is but passion; for in me (if it is not Irishism to say so) indifference itself was a *sort of passion*, the result of experience and not the philosophy of nature."

The same contempt, manifested in a thousand ways throughout his life, was again expressed by Lord Byron, a few days before his death, to Lord Harrington, on being told by the latter that, notwithstanding the war he had waged against English prejudices and national susceptibility, he had nevertheless been the pride and even the idol of his country.

"Oh!" exclaimed he, "it would be a stupid race that should adore such an idol. It is true, they laid aside their superstition, as to my divinity, after 'Cain.'"

We find in his memoranda, with regard to a comparison made between himself and Napoleon, these significant words: "I, an *insect*, compared to that creature!"*

Sometimes he ascribes his poetical success to accidental causes, or else to some merit not personal to himself but transmitted by inheritance; that is, to his rank.

The generality of authors, especially poets, love to read their productions over and over again, just as a fine woman likes to admire herself in the glass. He, on the contrary, avoided this reflection of his genius, which seemed to displease him.

"Here are two wretched proof-sheets from the printer. I have looked over one; but, on my soul, I can not read that 'Giaour' again—at least not now and at this hour (midnight); yet there is no moonlight."

He never read his compositions to any one. On inviting Moore to Newstead Abbey, soon after having made his acquaintance, he said, "I can promise you Balnea Vina, and, if you like shooting, a manor of four thousand acres, fire, books, full liberty. H——, I fear, will pester you with verses, but, for my part, I can conclude with Martial, '*nil recitabo tibi;*' and certainly this last promise ought not to be the least tempting for you."

Nevertheless, this was a great moment for a young author, as "Childe Harold" was then going through the press. He never would speak of his works; and when any translation of them was mentioned to him, they were sure to cause annoyance to him. Several times in Italy he paid large sums to prevent his works from being translated, at the same time not to injure the translator; but while refusing these homages for himself he desired them for others, and with that view praised and assisted them. We have already seen all

* Moore, vol. i. p. 512.

he did to magnify Moore, as well as others, both friends and rivals. The Gospel says, "Do unto others as ye would they should do unto you;" but for him the precept should rather have been reversed thus, "Do for yourself what you would do for others."

In the midst of his matrimonial sufferings, at the most cruel moments of his existence, he still found time to write and warmly recommend to his publisher works written by Hunt and Coleridge, who afterward rewarded all his kindness with the most dire ingratitude. And after praising them greatly, he adds, speaking of one of his own works, "And now let us come to the last, my own, of which I am ashamed to speak after the others. Publish it or not, as you like; I don't care a straw about it. If it seems to you that it merits a place in the fourth volume, put it there, or anywhere else; and if not, throw it into the fire." This poem, so despised, was the "Siege of Corinth!"

About the same time, on learning that Jeffrey had lauded "Hebrew Melodies"—poems so much above all praise that one might believe them (said a great mind lately)* thought by Isaiah and written by Shakspeare—Lord Byron considered Jeffrey very kind to have been so indulgent.

With what simplicity or contempt does he always introduce his *chefs-d'œuvre*, either by dedication to his friends, or to his publisher.

"I have put in press a devil of a story or tale, called the 'Corsair.' It is of a pirate island, peopled with my own creatures, and you may easily imagine that they will do a host of wicked things, in the course of three cantos."

And this *devil of a story or tale* had numberless editions. Several thousand copies were sold in one day. We have already seen the modest terms in which he announced to his friend Moore the termination of his poem "Manfred." This is how he mentioned it to his publisher:—

"I forgot to mention to you that a kind of poem in dialogue (in blank verse), or drama, from which the translation is an extract, begun last summer in Switzerland, is finished; it is in three acts, but of a very wild, metaphysical, and inexplicable kind. BYRON."

* The present Dean of Westminster.

He describes to Murray the causes, and adds:—

"You may perceive by this outline that I have no great opinion of this piece of fantasy; but I have at least rendered it *quite impossible* for the stage, for which my intercourse with Drury Lane has given me the greatest contempt.

"I have not even copied it off, and feel too lazy at present to attempt the whole; but when I have, I will send it to you, and you may either throw it into the fire or not.

"I have really and truly no notion whether it is good or bad, and as this was not the case with the principal of my former publications, I am, therefore, inclined to rank it very humbly. You will submit it to Mr. Gifford, and to whomsoever you please besides. With regard to the question of copyright (if it ever comes to publication), I do not know whether you would think *three hundred* guineas an over-estimate, if you do you may diminish it. I do not think it worth more. BYRON.*

"Venice, March 9, 1817."

Lord Byron never protested against or complained of any criticism as to the talent displayed in his works. His protests (much too rare, alas!) never had any other object than to repel some abominable calumny. When they criticised without good faith and without measure his beautiful dramas, saying they were not adapted for the stage, what did he reply?

"It appears that I do not possess dramatic genius."

His observations on that wicked and unmerited article in "Blackwood's Magazine" for 1819, are quite a *chef-d'œuvre* of reasoning and modesty. There again, if he defends the man a little, he condemns the poet.

His modesty was such that he almost went so far as to see, in the enmity stirred up against him during his latter years, a symptom of the decay of his talent. He really seemed to attach value to his genius only when it could be enlisted in the service of his heart.

In 1821, being at Ravenna, and writing his memoranda, he recalls that one day in London (1814), just as he was stepping into a carriage with Moore (whom he calls with all his heart

* Moore, Letter 265.

the poet *par excellence*), he received a Java Gazette, sent by Murray, and that on looking over it, he found a discussion on his merits and those of Moore. And, after some modest amusing sentences, he goes on to say :—

"It was a great fame to be named with Moore; greater to be compared with him; greatest *pleasure*, at least, to be *with* him; and, surely, an odd coincidence, that we should be dining together while they were quarrelling about us beyond the equinoctial line. Well, the same evening, I met Lawrence the painter, and heard one of Lord Grey's daughters (a fine, tall, spirited-looking girl, with much of the patrician thorough-bred look of her father, which I dote upon) play on the harp, so modestly and ingenuously, that she looked music. Well, I would rather have had my talk with Lawrence (who talked delightfully) and heard the girl, than have had all the fame of Moore and me put together. The only pleasure of fame is that it paves the way to pleasure; and the more intellectual our pleasure, the better for the pleasure and for us too."*

This modesty sometimes even carried him so far as to lead him into most extraordinary appreciation of things. For instance, he almost thought it blamable to have one's own bust done in marble, unless it were for the sake of a friend. Apropos of a young American who came to see him at Ravenna, and who told him he was commissioned by Thorwaldsen to have a copy of his bust made and sent to America, Lord Byron wrote in his journal :—

"*I* would not pay the price of a Thorwaldsen bust for any human head and shoulders, except Napoleon's, or my children's or some *absurd womankind's*, as Monkbarns calls them, or my sister's. If asked why, then, I sat for my own? Answer, that it was at the particular request of J. C. Hobhouse, Esq., and for no one else. A picture is a different matter; every body sits for their picture; but a bust looks like putting up *pretensions to permanency*, and smacks something of a *hankering for public fame rather than private remembrance*."

Let us add to all these proofs of Lord Byron's modesty, that his great experience of men and things, the doubts in-

* Moore, vol. v. p. 76.

separable from deep learning, and his indulgence for human weakness, rendered his reason most tolerant in its exigencies, and that he never endeavored to impose his opinions on others. But while remaining essentially a modest genius, Lord Byron did not, however, ignore his own value. If he had doubted himself, if he had wanted a just measure of confidence in his genius, could he have found in his soul the energy necessary for accomplishing in a few years such a marvellous literary career? His modesty did not proceed from conscious inferiority with regard to others.

Could the intellect that caused him to appreciate others so well fail to make him feel his own great superiority? But that *relative superiority* which he felt in himself left him *perfectly modest*, or he knew it was subject to other relations that showed it to him in extreme littleness: that is to say, the relation of the finite with the aspiration toward the infinite. It was the appreciation of the immense distance existing between what we know and what we ignore, between what we are and what we would be; the consciousness, in fact, of the limits imposed by God on man, and which neither study nor excellence of faculties can ever enable us to pass beyond.

Those rare beings, whose greatness of soul equals their penetration of mind, can not themselves feel the fascination they exercise over others; and while performing miracles of genius, devotion, and heroism, remain admirably simple, natural, and modest, believing that they do not outstep the humblest limits.

Such was Lord Byron. We may then sum up by saying that he was not only a modest genius, but also that, instead of being too proud of his genius, he may rather be accused of having too little appreciated this great gift, as well as many others bestowed by Heaven.

CHAPTER XIV.

THE VIRTUES OF HIS SOUL.

HIS GENEROSITY A VIRTUE.

ALL that we have hitherto said, proves that Lord Byron's generosity has never been disputed; but the generosity usually attributed to him was an innate quality, the impulse of a good heart, naturally inclined to bestow benefits.

Certainly, to distribute among the poor our superfluities, and very often more than that, to borrow rather than suffer the unfortunate to wait for assistance; to subtract from our pleasures, and even to bear privations, the better to help all the afflicted, without distinction of opinion, age, or sex; to measure the kindness done rather by their wants, than our own resources, and to do all that, without ostentation, habitually, in secret and unknown, with God and our conscience for sole witnesses: certainly, all that is full of moral beauty; and we know on what a large scale Lord Byron practiced it all his life. We have seen him in childhood, of which we should vainly seek one more amiable and more admirable, wish to take upon himself the punishments destined for his comrades; rescue their hall from the senseless fury of his school-fellows, by showing them the dear names of their parents written on the walls; desire to expose himself to death, to save a comrade, who had two parents to regret his loss, while he himself had only one; and send his good nurse the first watch of which he became possessed,—and we know what a treasure the first watch is to a child. We have followed him later, a youth at college, at the university, and at Newstead, in his devoted passionate affections; a young man on his travels, and in the midst of the great world, and we have seen his compassion for every kind of misfortune, and his mode of assuaging them.

When we perceive, despite the ardor and mobility of his

heart, where so many contrary elements combined, contradicted, jarred against, or succeeded each other, that there never was a single instant in his life when generosity did not reign supreme over every impulse and consideration, not only are we compelled to pronounce him generous, but we are likewise forced to acknowledge that generosity, with a passion for truth, divided the empire of his soul, and formed the two principal features of his character. But if his generosity had ended in only satisfying the fine tendencies of his nature, would it have acquired the right to be called virtuous? We do not think so. For generosity, to merit that sacred epithet, must express sentiments rarer and more elevated, arrive at the highest triumph of moral strength, at the greatest self-abnegation; it must succeed in overcoming appetite, in forgetting the most just resentments, in returning good for evil. Then, alone, can generosity attain that sublime degree which entitles it to be called a virtue.

Did Lord Byron's generosity reach this great moral height? Let us examine facts; they alone can answer.

If a young man lends assistance to a young and beautiful girl, without any interested motive, and with exquisite delicacy, he certainly gives proof that he possesses delicacy of soul. His merit becomes much greater if he acts thus solely to save her honor. But if the young girl, full of gratitude, falls deeply in love with her benefactor; if, unable to hide the impression produced on her heart by his presence and his generosity, she makes him understand that her gratitude would have no limits; and if he, at the age when passion is all awake, though touched by the sentiments this charming person has conceived, nevertheless shuts his senses against all temptations, does not the greatness of his soul then become admirable? Well, this was fully realized in Lord Byron. And not only in a single instance; but often during his life. For, if temptations were numerous, so were victories also. We will only quote one example, with sufficient details to make it justly appreciated.

Miss S——, who had been bred in ease, but who, with her family, had been reduced, through a series of misfortunes, to absolute want, found herself exposed to the greatest evil that can menace a portionless girl. Her mother, whose temper had been soured by reverses which had likewise quite overthrown her sense of morality, had become one of those women who consider poverty the worst of all evils. Unscrupulous as to the means of putting an end to it, she did not think it necessary to fortify her daughter's mind by good counsels. Happily the young girl had lofty sentiments and natural dignity. Secure from vulgar seduction, and guided by wholesome steady principles, she desired to depend only on her talents for gaining a livelihood, and for assisting her parents. Having written a small volume of poetry, she had already got subscriptions from persons of high position; but her great desire was to obtain Lord Byron's name.

An impulse, often recurring, induced her to apply to the young nobleman, who was then still unmarried. She only knew him through his works, and by report, which already associated with admiration for his talents a thousand calumnies concerning his moral character. The skeptical stanzas of "Childe Harold" still troubled orthodox repose; the lines on the tears of the Princess Royal irritated the Tories, and his last success with the "Corsair," added to those he had already gained, further embittered his jealous rivals. Thus calumnies made up from these different elements besieged the poet's house, so as to prevent truth concerning the man from being known. Even in her family, Miss S—— found hostility against him; for her mother, who called herself a Tory, only discovered moral delicacy when she wished to show her repugnance for the Whig party, to which Lord Byron belonged. Miss S——, in a moment of extreme anguish and pressing embarrassment, resolved upon applying to the young nobleman. He received her with respect and consideration, and soon perceived how intimidated she was by the rather bold step she had taken, and also by the cause that prompted it. Lord Byron reassured her, by treating her with peculiar kindness, as he questioned her respecting her circumstances. When she had related the sad reasons that determined her to ask him for a subscription, Lord Byron rang for his valet, and ordered a desk to be brought to him. Then, with that delicacy of heart which formed such a remarkable trait in his character, he wrote down, while still conversing, a few words, which he wrapped up in an envelope, and gave to the young lady. She soon after withdrew, thinking she had obtained the coveted subscription.

When fairly out, all she had seen and heard appeared to her like a dream. The door which had just closed behind her seemed the gate of Eden, opening on a land of exile. Nevertheless, she was to see him again. He had consented to receive her volume. Lord Byron was not for her the angel with the flaming sword, but rather an angel of gentleness, mercy, and love. Never had she seen or imagined such a combination of enchantments; never had she seen so much beauty, nor heard such a voice; never had such a sweet expressive glance met hers. "No;" she repeated to herself, "he is not a man, but some celestial being. *Oh, mamma, Lord Byron is an angel!*" were the first words that escaped her on returning home. The envelope was opened; and a new surprise awaited them. Together with his subscription, she found, wrapped up, fifty pounds. That sum was, indeed, a treasure for her. She fell on her knees with all her family; even her mother forgot for the moment that it was Whig money to which they owed their deliverance, and seemed almost to agree with her eldest daughter, whose enthusiasm communicated itself to the younger one, who never wearied in questioning her sister about Lord Byron's perfections, until the night was far spent.

But if the family was thus relieved, if the young girl's honor was safe, her peace of mind was gone. The contempt and dislike she already felt for several men who were hovering about her with alarming offers of protection, were now further increased by the comparison she was enabled to make between their vulgar and low, basely hypocritical or openly licentious natures, and that of the noble being she had just seen.

Thenceforth Byron's dazzling image never left her mind. It remained fixed there during the day, to reappear at night in her dreams and visions. Such a hold had it gained over her entire being, that Miss S—— seemed from that hour to live heart and soul only in the hope of seeing him again.

When she returned to take him her book, she found that she had to add to all the other charms of this superior being that respect which the wisdom of mature age seems only able to inspire. For he not only spoke to her of what might best suit her position, and disapproved some of her mother's projects, as dangerous for her honor, but even refused to go and see her as she requested; nor would he give her a letter of introduction to the Duke of Devonshire, simply because a handsome girl could not be introduced by a young man without having her reputation compromised.

The more Miss S—— saw of Lord Byron, the more intense her passion for him became. It seemed to her that all to which heart could aspire, all of happiness that heaven could give here below, must be found in the love of such a pre-eminent being. Lord Byron soon perceived the danger of these visits. Miss S—— was beautiful, witty, and charming; Lord Byron was twenty-six years of age. How many young men, in a similar case, would not without a scruple have thought that he had only to cull this flower which seemed voluntarily to tempt him? Lord Byron never entertained such an idea. Innocent of all intentional seduction, unable to render her happy, even if he could have returned her sentiments, instead of being proud of having inspired them, he was distressed at having done so. He did not wish to prove the source of new misfortunes to this young girl, already so tried by fate, and without guide or counsellor. So he resolved to use all his efforts toward restoring her peace. It would be too long to tell the delicate mode he used to attain this end, the generous stratagems he employed to heal this poor wounded heart. He went so far as to try to appear less amiable. For the sake of destroying any hope, he assumed a cold, stern, troubled air; but on perceiving that he had only aggravated the evil, his kindliness of heart could resist no longer, and he hit on other expedients. Finally he succeeded in making her comprehend the necessity of putting an end to her visits. She left his house, having ever been treated with respect, the innocence of their mutual intercourse unstained; and the young man's sacrifice only permitted one kiss imprinted on the lovely brow of her whose strong feelings for himself he well knew.

What this victory, gained by his will and his sentiment as a man of honor over his senses and his heart, cost Lord Byron, has remained his own secret. But those who will imagine themselves in similar circumstances at the age of twenty-six, may conceive it. As to Miss S——, the excess of her emotions made her ill; and she long hung between life and death. Nevertheless, the strength of youth prevailed, and ended by giving her back physical health. But was her mind equally cured? The only light that had brightened her path had gone out, and, plunged in darkness, how did she pursue her course through life? Was her heart henceforth closed to every affection? Or did she chain it down to the fulfillment of some austere duty, that stood her in lieu of happiness? Or, as it sometimes happens to stricken hearts, did a color, a sound, a breeze, one feature in a face, call up hallucinations, give her vain longings, make her build fresh hopes and prepare for her new deceptions? Proof against all meannesses, but young and most unhappy, was she always able to resist the promptings of a warm, feeling, grateful heart? We are ignorant of all this. We only know of her, that never again in her long career did she meet united in one man that profusion of gifts, physical, intellectual, and moral, that made Lord Byron seem like a being above humanity. She tells it to us herself, in letters written at the distance that separates 1814 from 1864, lately published in French, preceding and accompanying a narrative composed in her own language, in which she has related her impressions of Lord Byron, and given the details of all that took place between her and him. It was a duty, she says, that remained for her to accomplish here below.

Her narrative and these letters are charming from their simplicity and naïveté; what she says bears the stamp of plain truth, her admiration has nothing high-flown in it, and her style is never wanting in the sobriety which ought always to accompany truth, in order to make it penetrate into other minds.

We would fain transcribe these pages, that evidently flow from an elevated and sincerely grateful heart. For they reflect great honor on Lord Byron, since, in showing the strength of the impression made on the young girl, they bring out more fully all the self-denial he must have exercised in regard to her; likewise, because, in her letters, this lady, after so long an experience of life, never ceases proclaiming Lord Byron the handsomest, the most generous, and the best of men she ever knew. But though it is impossible for me to reproduce all she says, still I feel it necessary to quote some passages from her book. In the first letter addressed to Mrs. B——, she says:—

"At the moment of the separation between Lord Byron and that woman who caused the misery of his life, I was not in London; and I was so ill, that I could neither go to see him nor write as I wished. For he had shown me so much goodness and generosity that my heart was bursting with gratitude and sorrow; and never have I had any means of expressing either to him, except through my little offering.* Even now my heart is breaking at the thought of the injustice with which he has been treated.

"His friend Moore, to whom he had confided his memoirs, written with his own hand, had not the courage to fulfill faithfully the desire of his generous friend. Lady Blessington made a book upon him very profitable *to herself*, but in which she does not always paint Lord Byron *en beau*, and where she has related a thousand things that Lord Byron only meant in joke, and which ought not to have been either written or published. And when it is remembered that this lady (as I am assured) never saw or conversed with Lord Byron but out of doors, when she happened to meet him on horseback, and very rarely (two or three times) when he consented to dine at her house, in both of these cases, in too numerous a company for the conversation to be of an intimate nature; when it is known (as I am further assured) that Lord Byron was so much on his guard with this lady (aware of her being an authoress), that he never accepted an invitation to dine with her, unless when his friend Count Gamba did: truly, we may then conclude that these conversations were materially impossible, and must have been a clever mystification,—a composition got up on the biographies of Lord Byron that had already appeared, on Moore's works, Medwin's, Lord Byron's correspondence, and, above all, on "Don Juan." She must have made her choice, without any regard to truth or to Lord Byron's honor; rather selecting such facts, expressions, and observations as allowed her to assume the part of a moral,

* She had dedicated to him a small collection of poems, which she sent to Pisa, in 1821, with a letter, *to which she received no answer*.

sensitive woman, to sermonize, by way of gaining favor with the strict set of people in high society, and to be able to bring out her own opinions on a number of things and persons, without fear of compromising herself, since she put them into Lord Byron's mouth.

"Verily these conversations can not be explained in any other way. At any rate, I confess this production of her ladyship so displeased me that I threw it aside, unable to read it without ill-humor and disgust. At that time (1814) he was not married; and I beheld in him a young man of the rarest beauty. Superior intellect shone in his countenance; his manners were at once full of simplicity and dignity; his voice was sweet, rich, and melodious. If Lord Byron had defects (and who has not?) he also possessed very great virtues, with a dignity and sincerity of character seldom to be found. The more I have known the world, the more have I rendered homage to Lord Byron's memory."

Miss S—— wrote thus to a person with whom she was not acquainted; but, encouraged by the answer she received, she dispatched a second letter, opening her heart still further, and sending some details of her intercourse with Lord Byron,—what she had seen and known of him.

"Ah! madam," she exclaims, "if you knew the happiness, the consolation I feel in writing to you, knowing that all I say of him will be well received, and that you believe all these details so creditable to him!"

In the same letter, she declares "that when he was exposed to the attacks of jealousy and a thousand calumnies spread against him, he always said, 'Do not defend me.'

"But, madam, how can we be silent when we hear such infamous things said against one so incapable of them? I have always said frankly what I thought of him, and defended him in such a way as to carry conviction into the minds of those who heard me. But a combat between one person and many is not equal, and I have several times been ill with vexation. Never mind; what I can do, I will."

She announced her intention of communicating the whole history of her acquaintance with Lord Byron.

"I am about to commence, madam, the account of my acquaintance with our great and noble poet. I shall write all concerning him in English, because I can thus make use of his own words, which are graven in my heart, as well as all the circumstances relating to him. I will give you these details, madam, in all their simplicity; but their value consists less in the words he made use of, than in the manner accompanying them, in the sweetness of his voice, his delicacy and politeness at the moment when he was granting a favor, rendering me such a great service. Oh! yes, he was really good and generous; never, in all my long years, have I seen a man *worthy to be compared to him.*"

She wrote again on the 10th of November, 1864:—

"Here, madam, are the details I promised you about my first interview with Lord Byron. I give them to you in all their simplicity. I make no attempt at style; but simply tell unvarnished truth; for, with regard to Lord Byron, I consider truth the most important thing,—his name is the greatest ornament of the page whereon it is inscribed. I will also send you, madam, if you desire, my second and third interview with this noble, admirable man, who was so *misjudged.* To write this history is a great happiness for me; since I know that, in so doing, I render him that justice so often denied him by the envious and the wicked.

"His conduct toward me was always so beautiful and noble, that I would fain make it known to the whole world. I think they are beginning to render him the justice that is his due; everywhere now he is quoted—*Byron said this, Byron thought that*—that is what I hear continually, and many persons who formerly spoke against him, now testify in his favor.

"They say we ought not to speak evil of the dead; that is very well, but as this maxim was not observed toward Lord Byron, I also will repeat what I have heard said of his wife—I mean that the blame was hers—that her temper was so bad, her manners so harsh and disagreeable, that no one could endure her society; that she was avaricious, wicked, scolding; that people hated to wait upon her or live near her. How dared this lady to marry a man so distinguished, and then to treat him ill and tyrannically? Truly it is inconceivable. If she were charitable for the poor (as some one has pretended), she certainly wanted Christian charity. And I also am wanting in it perhaps; but, when I think of her, I lose all patience."

On announcing to Mrs. B—— the sequel of her narrative, she says:—

"It contains the history of the two days that passed after my first interview with him whom I ever found the *noblest and most generous* of men, whose memory lives in my heart like a brilliant star amid the dark and gloomy clouds that have often surrounded me in life; it is the single ray of sunshine illumining my remembrances of the past."

Miss S—— had not forgotten a look, a word, not even the material external part of things; and when Mrs. B—— expressed her astonishment at this lively recollection,—

"All that concerned Lord Byron," said she, "has been retained by my heart. I recall his words, gestures, looks, now, as if it had all taken place yesterday. I believe this is owing to his great and beautiful qualities, such a rare assemblage of which I never saw in any other human being.

"There was so much truth in all he said, so much simplicity in all he did, that every thing became indelibly engraven on heart and memory."

After having said that Lord Byron gave her the best counsels, and among others that of living with her mother ("not knowing," she adds, "to what it would expose me"), she continues:

"You say, madam, there is no cause for astonishment that I so admire and respect Lord Byron. In all he said, or advised, there was so much right reason, goodness and judgment far above his age, that one remained enthralled."

On sending the conclusion of her history to Mrs. B——, she says:—

"You who knew Lord Byron, will not be surprised that I loved him so much. But a woman does not pass through such a trial with impunity. On returning home, I threw myself on my knees and tried to pray, imploring Heaven for strength and patience. But the sound of his voice, his looks, pierced to my very heart, my soul felt torn asunder; I could not even weep. For two years and a half I was no longer myself. A man of high position offered me his hand. He would have placed me in the first society; but he wished for love, and I could only offer him friendship."

And, finally, when the reception of the concluding part of her narrative was acknowledged, she further added:—

"I am very glad that the history of my heart appears to you a precious document for proving the virtues of one whom I have ever looked upon as the *first of men, as well for his qualities as for his genius.*"

Her last letter ends exactly as did her first:—"*Ah! there never was but one Lord Byron!*" In her narrative, which is quite as natural in style as her letters, no detail of her interviews with Lord Byron has escaped her memory.*

We have already seen how, in a moment of despair, the young girl, full of confidence in Lord Byron, whom she considered as one of the noblest characters that ever existed, thought she might go and ask his protection. A fashionable young man, and still unmarried, the reports current about him might well lead to the belief that his house was not quite the temple of order. She was surprised on knocking timidly at his door, on explaining to the *valet-de-chambre* who opened it, her great desire to speak to Lord Byron, to see Fletcher listen to her with a civil, compassionate air, that predisposed her in favor of his master.

He conducted her into a small room, where all Lord Byron's servants were assembled, and there also she was greatly surprised at the order and simplicity in the establishment of the young lord.

"I never saw servants more polite and respectful," says she. "Fletcher and the coachman remained standing, only the old house-keeper kept her seat."

Miss S—— had dried her tears when admitted into Lord Byron's presence.

"Surprise and admiration," says she, "were the first emotions I experienced on seeing him. He was only twenty-six years of age, but he looked still younger. I had been told that he was gloomy, severe, and often out of temper: *I saw, on the contrary, a most attractive physiognomy, wearing a look of charming sweetness.*"

Miss S—— soon found cause to appreciate Lord Byron's delicacy. She began by excusing herself for having come to him, saying she had taken this step in consequence of family misfortunes. She remained standing. After some moments

* "All that," says she, "lives in my heart and soul, as if these things had taken place a few weeks ago, instead of so many years" (1864).

of silence, during which Lord Byron appeared to interrogate memory, he said :—

"Pray be seated; I will not hear another word until you are. You appear to have an independent spirit, and this step must have cost you much."

Having already partly seen the results of this interview, we refrain from giving further details here, although they are full of interest on account of the goodness, generosity, and delicacy they reveal.

Miss S—— endeavored to draw his portrait, but the pencil dropped from her hands :—

"I feel that unless I could portray his look, and repeat his words as pronounced by him, I could not even do justice to his actions."

She does it, however in a few bold touches which, on account of their truth, we have quoted in the chapter entitled *Portrait* of Lord Byron.

After having said that it was impossible to see finer eyes, a more beautiful expression of face, manners more graceful, hands more exquisite, or to hear such a tone of voice, she adds:

"All that formed such an assemblage of seductive qualities, that never before or since have I remarked any man who could be compared to him. What particularly struck me was the serene, gentle dignity of his manner. Lady Blessington says, that she did not find in Lord Byron quite the dignity she had expected; but surely, then, she does not understand what dignity is? Indeed she did not understand Lord Byron at all. With me he was unaffected, amiable, and natural. The hours passed in his society I look upon as the brightest of my life, and even now I think of them with an effusion of gratitude and admiration, rather increased than diminished by time."

Lord Byron saw directly that Miss S—— had a noble nature. It must have been such; it must even have been, so to say, *incorruptible*, since she had been able to preserve her purity of soul and simplicity in the position to which she was, despite her surroundings and with such a mother. Lord Byron, seeing her so unprotected and ill-advised, took an interest in her, and instead of profiting by her isolation, resolved to save her. With virtue superior to his years, he opposed the best counsels to the more than imprudent projects of a mother who thought only of repairing her fortune by whatever means. Miss S——, attracted toward him with her whole heart and soul, begged her young and noble benefactor to come and see her, if it were only once a month. "I should be so happy, my lord, if you would sometimes grant me the favor of a visit, and guide my life," said she to him.

But Lord Byron had perceived the excited state of feeling in which the young girl was. Besides, he was betrothed, and did not wish to expose her and himself to the consequences. Honor and prudence alike counselled a refusal, and he refused.

"My dear child," answered he, "I can not. I will tell you my present position, and you will understand that I ought not: I am going to marry."

"At these words," said she, "my heart sunk within me, as if a piece of lead had fallen on my chest. At the same instant I experienced an acute pain in it. It seemed as if a chilly steel had pierced me. A horrible, indescribable sensation shook my whole frame. For some moments I could not possibly articulate a single word. Lord Byron looked at me with an expression full of interest, for indeed I must have changed countenance."

Lord Byron, already aware that his image was graven on this young heart, and might become dangerous to her, then understood still better the silent ravages that love must be making there. He pitied her more than ever, he felt the necessity of refusal and sacrifice, and, from that moment, all struggle between will and desire ceased.

He also refused, after some hesitation, to recommend her to the Duke of Devonshire.

"You are young and pretty," said he, "and that is sufficient to place any man, wishing to serve you, in a false position. You know how the world understands a young man's friendship and interest for a young woman. No; my name must not appear in a recommendation to the duke. Don't think me disobliging, therefore. On the contrary, I wish you to make an appeal to Devonshire, but without naming me; I have told you my reasons for refusing to be openly your advocate."

"Another time," adds she, "I ventured to express the wish of being presented to the future Lady Byron. But he again answered by a refusal. 'Though amiable and unsuspicious,' said he, 'persons about Lady Byron might put jealous suspicions, devoid of foundation, into her head.' "

Thus equally by what he refused her and what he granted her, he proved his great generosity, the elevation of his character, his virtuous abnegation and self-control.

Although Miss S—— was then in an humble and humiliating position, she had received a fine classical and intellectual education from her uncle, who was a professor at Cambridge. Her natural wit, the *naïveté* and sincerity of her ideas, uncontaminated by worldly knowledge, were appreciated by Lord Byron. He understood her worth, despite the difficulties that made virtue of greater merit in her, and notwithstanding appearances that were against her; and he showed interest in her conversation during the different interviews she obtained from him. He talked to her of literature, the news of the day; and even had the goodness to read with indulgence and approbation the verses she had composed. One day, among others, she had the happiness of remaining with him till a late hour, and when his carriage was announced, to take him to a *soirée*, he had her conducted home in the same carriage.

"Oh! how delightful that evening was to me," says she. "Lord Byron's abode at the Albany recalled some collegiate dwelling, so perfectly quiet was it, though situated at the West End, the noisiest quarter of the metropolis. His conversation so varied and delightful, the purity of his English, his refined pronunciation, all offered such a contrast even with the most distinguished men I had had the good fortune to meet, that I really learned what happiness was."

These conversations afforded her the opportunity of knowing and admiring him still more. In conversing on literature, she was able to appreciate his modesty by the praises he lavished on the talents of others, and by the slight importance he attached to his own; and also his love of truth when, *à propos* of some book of travels she was praising, he told her that he preferred a simple but true tale of voyages to all the pomp of lies. In speaking about an adventure in high life that was then making a great noise in England, she was able to appreciate his high sentiments of delicacy and honor. When the conversation fell on religion, she had the happiness of hearing

ing him declare he abhorred atheism and unbelief; and when his childhood was touched upon, of hearing him say that it had been pleasant and happy. Finally, when she asked his advice with regard to her future conduct, he displayed, at twenty-six years of age, the wisdom that seldom comes before the advent of gray hairs. In short, by word and by action, he manifested that nobleness of soul which always unveiled itself to pure open natures, but which closed against artificial ones; and which makes Miss S—— say at the beginning as well as at the end of her account:—"There has been but one Byron on earth: how could I not love him?"

But it is especially on account of the great love she felt for him, on going over it, reflecting, comparing the depth of feelings she had been unable to hide from him, with the conduct of this young man of twenty-six, who drew from duty alone a degree of strength superior to his age and sex, that she expressed herself thus. She can still see his looks of tenderness; she can judge what the struggle was, the combat that was going on in him as soft and stern glances chased each other; at length she sees honor gain the victory, and remain triumphant.

It is this spectacle of such great moral beauty, still before her eyes, that can be so well appreciated after the lapse of long years, and which justifies the words that begin and close her recital by divesting it of all semblance of exaggeration:—"There has been but one Byron!"

When we have known such beings, admiration and love outlive all else. And while the causes that may have led to transient emotions in a long career—an error, a fault—pass away and are forgotten like some beautiful vision, these glorious remembrances, these more than human images, tower above, living and radiant, in memory, and even come to visit us in our dreams, sometimes to reproach us with our useless and imprudent doubts, ever to sustain us amid the sadnesses of life; and if the love has been reciprocal, then to console us with the prospect of another life, in that blessed abode where we shall meet again forever.

After this long narrative, it would be useless and perhaps wearisome for the reader if we quoted many other similar facts in Lord Byron's life. They might differ in circumstances, but would all wear the same moral character.

CHAPTER XV.

GENEROSITY A HEROISM.

PARDON, MAGNANIMITY.

It remains for us to examine Lord Byron's generosity under another form. I mean that which, after having passed by different degrees of moral beauty, may reach the highest summit of virtue, and become the greatest triumph of moral strength, because it overcomes the most just resentments, forgives, returns good for evil, and constitutes the very heroism of Christian charity.

Did Lord Byron's generosity really attain such a high degree? To convince ourselves of it, we must again examine his life.

Clemency and forgivness showed themselves in Lord Byron at all periods of his life. In childhood, in youth, though so passionate, and so sensitive at school and at college, so soon as the first explosion was over, he was ever ready to make peace.

In the poems composed during his boyhood and early youth, he was always the first to forgive. He even forgave his wicked guardian (Lord Carlisle). Although this latter only evinced indifference, or worse, with regard to his ward, Lord Byron dedicated his first poems to him. The noble earl having further aggravated his faults by behaving in an unjustifiable manner, Lord Byron was of course greatly irritated, since he hurled some satirical lines at him. But soon after, at the intercession of friends, and especially at that of his sister, he showed himself disposed to forget the faults of his bad guardian with all the clemency inherent to his generous nature. He writes to Rogers, 27th June, 1814:—"Are there any chances or possibility of ending this, and making our peace with Carlisle? I am disposed to do all that is reasonable (or unreasonable) to arrive at it. I would even have done so sooner; but the 'Courier' newspaper, and a thousand disagreeable interpretations, have prevented me."

Afterward, he further sealed this generous pardon by those fine verses in the third canto of "Childe Harold," where he laments the death of Major Howard, Lord Carlisle's son, killed at Waterloo.*

He forgave Miss Chaworth; and in this case also there was great generosity. The history of this boyish love is well known. Even if the name of love should be refused to the feeling entertained by a child of fifteen for a girl of eighteen, who only looked upon him, it is said, as a boy, and liked him as a brother, not only on account of the difference of age, but also because she was already attached to the young man whom she afterward married, still it can not be denied that these first awakenings of the heart, though full of illusion, cause great suffering. For if Lord Byron was a child in years, he was already a young man in intellect, soul, imagination, and sensibility. That Miss Chaworth should raise emotion in his heart is very comprehensible, for every girl has good chances of appearing an angel to youths, whose preference invariably falls on women older than themselves. Besides, Miss Chaworth was placed in quite exceptional circumstances with regard to Lord Byron, such as were well calculated to act powerfully on the imagination of a boy, and render the dispelling of his poetic dream a most painful reality.

Miss Chaworth was heiress of the noble family whose name she bore, and her uncle had been killed in a duel by the last Lord Byron, grand-uncle of the poet. She resided with her family at Annesley, a seat two miles distant from Newstead Abbey. Their two properties touched each other; but the slight barrier separating them was marked with blood. The two children then, despite their near vicinity, only saw each other by chance, or by secretly getting over the boundary of their respective grounds. The chief obstacle to the reconciliation of the two families was the young girl's father. But when Lord Byron reached his fourteenth

* "Their praise is hymn'd by loftier hearts than mine,
Yet one I would select from that proud throng,
Partly because they blend me with his line,
And partly that I did his sire some wrong."

year, and, according to custom, came from Harrow to pass his holidays at Newstead, Mr. Chaworth was dead, and the mother of the young heiress received him at Annesley with open arms, for she did not partake her husband's feelings, but, on the contrary, looked forward with pleasure to the possibility of a union with her daughter, despite the difference of age between them. The development of their mutual sympathy was equally encouraged by the professors, governesses, and all surrounding the young lady, for they liked young Byron extremely.

From that time he had his room at Annesley, and was looked upon as one of the family. As to the young lady, she made him the companion of her amusements. In the gardens, parks, on horseback, in all excursions, he was constantly by her side. For him she played, and sang to the piano. What was her love for him? Were there not moments in which she did not look upon him only as a brother, or a child? Did she ever contemplate the possibility of becoming his wife?

Moore does not think so.

"Neither is it, indeed, probable," says he, "had even her affections been disengaged, that Lord Byron would, at this time, have been selected as the object of them. A seniority of two years gives to a girl, 'on the eve of womanhood,' an advance into life with which the boy keeps no proportionate pace. Miss Chaworth looked upon Byron as a mere schoolboy. His manners, too, were not yet formed, and his great beauty was still in its promise and not developed."

Galt is still more explicit in the same sense. Washington Irving appears to think the contrary :—

"Was this love returned?" says he. "Byron sometimes speaks as if it had been; at other times he says, on the contrary, that she never gave him reason to believe so. It is, however, probable, that at the commencement her heart experienced at least fluctuations of feeling: she was at a dangerous age. Though a child in years, Lord Byron was already a man in intelligence, a poet in imagination, and possessed of great beauty."

This opinion is the most probable. We may add that every thing must have contributed to keep up his illusion.

Miss Chaworth gave him her portrait, her hair, and a ring. Mrs. Chaworth, the governess, all the family of the young heiress liked him so much, that after his death, when Washington Irving visited Annesley, he found proofs of this affection in the welcome given to, and the emotion caused even by the presence of a dog that had belonged to Lord Byron. This beautiful waking dream lasted, however, only the space of a dream in sleep.

At the expiration of his six weeks' holidays, young Byron returned to Harrow.

While he was cherishing the sacred flame with his purest energies of soul, what did she? She had forgotten him! The impression made on her heart by the schoolboy's love could not withstand the test of absence. She gave her heart to another.

"I thought myself a man," says he; "I was in earnest, she was fickle."

It was natural, however. She had arrived at the age when girls become women, and leave their childish loves behind them.

While young Byron was pursuing his studies, Miss Chaworth mixed in society. She met with a young man, named Musters, remarkable for his handsome person, and whose property lay contiguous to her own.

She had perceived him one day from her terrace, galloping toward the park followed by his hounds, the horn sounding in front, and he leading a fox hunt; she had been struck with his manly beauty and graceful carriage. From that day his image seated itself in her remembrance, and probably in her heart. It was under these favorable auspices that he made her acquaintance in society. Soon he gained her love. And when young Byron at the next vacation saw her again, she was already the willing betrothed of another.

That was still, however, a secret locked up in her heart. Her parents would not have wished this union. She had not then declared her intentions, and Lord Byron could not of course guess them. He was still welcomed at Annesley, and treated as heretofore. The young lady herself, instead of repelling him, continued to accept his attentions. This lasted until one day when Musters was bathing with Byron in a river that ran through the park he perceived a ring which he recognized as having belonged to Miss Chaworth. This discovery, and the scenes it gave rise to, obliged the lady to declare her preference.

The grief this broken illusion caused Lord Byron is shown by some of his early verses, and by the "Dream," written at Geneva, while musing how different his fate might have been if he had married Miss Chaworth, instead of Miss Milbank. It might be objected that sorrows, the proof of which rests on poetry, are not very authentic, and that it is not quite certain they really did pass through his heart. One might consider with Galt that this childish sentiment was less a real feeling of love than the phantom of an enthusiastic attachment, quite intellectual in its nature, like others that possessed such power over Lord Byron, since Miss Chaworth was not the sole object of his attention, but divided it with study and passionate friendships. One might say, with Moore, that the poetic description given by Lord Byron of this childish love, ought to serve especially to show how genius and sentiment may raise the realities of life, and give an immense lustre to the most ordinary events and objects. In short, one might think that Lord Byron perceived all the poetic advantages accruing from the remembrance of a youthful passion, at once innocent, pure, and unhappy; how it would furnish him with a magic tint to enrich his palette with an inexhaustible fund of sweet, graceful, and pathetic fancies, with delicate, lofty, and noble sentiments, and therefore that he resolved to shut it up in his heart, so as to preserve its freshness amid the withering atmosphere of the world; and in order to draw thence those exquisite images that so often shed ineffable grace and tenderness over his poems. It may, then, be said that, by maintaining alive in his mind scenes passed at Annesley, which recall the chaste, unhappy loves of Romeo and Juliet, and Lucy, he thereby satisfied an intellectual want of the poet that was quite independent of his heart as a man.

But, nevertheless, all those who can feel the heart's beatings through the veil of poetic language will understand that Lord Byron's verses on Mary Chaworth owe their origin to real grief.

Could it be otherwise? The experience resulting from reflection and comparison, which made him afterward say, that the perfections of the girl were the creation of his imagination at fifteen, because he found her in reality quite other than angelic;* that she was fickle, and had deceived him. This experience, I say, was wanting to the child. Thus, then, Miss Chaworth was for him at that period the beau ideal of all his young fancy could paint as best and most charming.

At the same time, this love, notwithstanding the difference of age, was not, on his side, the giddy result of too much ardor. It was composed of a thousand circumstances and feelings,—of practical, wise, and generous thoughts. A far-off prospect of happiness heightened all the noble instincts of the boy, and all the ideas of order that belonged to his fine moral nature.

To reunite two noble families,—to efface the stain of blood and hatred through love,—to revive again the ancient splendor of his ancestral halls,—all these thoughts mingled with the idea of his union with Miss Chaworth, and made his heart beat with hope. If there were excess in such hope,—if there were illusion,—the fault lies with the relatives of the young lady and herself, rather than with him. Generosity was on his side alone, because he alone had a right to feel rancor.

"She jilted me," says he in prose, and in verse we read,—

> "She knew she was by him beloved,—she knew,
> For quickly comes such knowledge, that his heart
> Was darken'd with her shadow, and she saw
> That he was wretched."

If, then, it was natural for a girl to prefer a young man of more suitable age, handsome and fashionable, to a boy whose features were yet undeveloped, and whom she treated as a child and a brother; was it quite as natural to flatter him,—load him with caresses,—with those gifts likely to foster illusion and hope,—pledges considered as love tokens? Was it natural that in order to justify certain coquetries to her affianced, she should make use of insulting expressions with regard to young Byron? But, on the other hand, would it

* See Medwin.

not have been very natural for him, having heard them, to feel a little rancor against her? Surely she was guilty if she had spoken in jest, and more guilty still if she were in earnest.

And yet what was his conduct? In his poem called the "Dream," where he sings this romance of his boyhood, he tells us how he quitted Annesley, after having learned that Miss Chaworth was engaged to Mr. Musters:—

> "He rose, and with a cold and gentle grasp
> He took her hand; a moment o'er his face
> A tablet of unutterable thoughts
> Was traced, and then it faded, as it came;
> He dropped the hand he held, and with slow steps
> Retired, but not as bidding her adieu,
> For they did part with mutual smiles; he pass'd
> From out the massy gate of that old hall,
> And mounting on his steed he went his way;
> And ne'er repass'd that hoary threshold more."

Then he jumped upon his horse, intending to gallop over the distance separating Annesley from Newstead. But when he arrived at the last hill overlooking Annesley, he stopped his horse, and cast a glance of mingled sorrow and tenderness at what he left behind,—the groves, the old house, the lovely one inhabiting there. But then the thought that she could never be his dispelled his reverie, and putting spurs to his horse he set off anew, as if rapid motion could drown reflection. However, instead of the reflections he could not succeed in drowning, *he cast away all rancor.*

When he alludes to her in his early poems it is always with tenderness and respect.* He contents himself with calling her once, *deceitful girl*, and another time, *a false fair face.*

After an interval of some years, when the boy had become a fine young man, before setting out for the East, he accepted the proffered hospitality of Annesley.

> "In the shade of her bower, I remember the hour
> She rewarded those vows with a Tear.
>
> By another possest, may she live ever blest!
> Her name still my heart must revere;
> With a sigh I resign what I once thought was mine,
> And forgive her deceit with a Tear."
>
> "*The Tear*" (October, 1806).

He never ceased to welcome Musters at Newstead, and, lest he should disturb the peace of Mrs. Musters, he had even concealed his agitation on kissing his rival's child. Heretofore she had only seen the boy or youth, now she beheld the young man whose genius and personal attractions lent to each other light and charm.

It was about this time that the bright star of Annesley began to pale. On her brow, formerly so gay, a veil of sadness was overspread. It seemed as if the gardens had lost their charm for her; as if the spreading foliage of Annesley had become dark for her. What caused this change? On seeing again the companion of her childhood, did she contrast her now solitary walks with those of earlier days in his beautiful park, where beside her was the youth who would fain have kissed the ground on which she trod? The sound of that hunting horn, which anon made her thrill with joy, when it announced the approach of her handsome betrothed, and awakened all the illusions of love,—had it now become to her more discordant and painful by its contrast with the harmonious voice and sweet smile of him whom she had just seen again so changed to his advantage?

It was during his travels in the East that Lord Byron heard of this mysterious melancholy. Given the circumstances, such a report would not have displeased, even if it had not pleased, vulgar, rancorous souls. But it produced quite a contrary effect on him. The feeling of his own worth, doubtless, must and ought to have brought certain ideas to his mind; but they saddened his generous nature, and he experienced a desire to drive them away by saying, "Has she not the husband of her choice, and lovely children to caress her?"

"What could her grief be?—she had all she loved.
* * * * * *
What could her grief be?—she had loved him not,
* * * * * *
Nor could he be a part of that which prey'd
Upon her mind—a spectre of the past."

Lord Byron returned from his travels, and by degrees, as he rose in the admiration of England, the melancholy observable in Mrs. Musters deepened.

One day she felt such a longing to see again the companion of her childhood, that she asked for an interview. Could he not desire the meeting? But ought he to grant it? He had had the courage to meet her again when he thought her happy, when sorrow for the past belonged to him alone, when she appeared neither to understand nor to share it. But would his heart be equally strong—would it not yield on seeing her unhappy?* And yet, what could he then do for her happiness? With the same generosity that induced him always to sacrifice his pleasure to the happiness of others, he listened to his reason, his heart, and the prudent counsels of his sister; he refrained from an interview which could only augment the troubles of that devastated soul, soon to become the "*queen of a fantastic kingdom*" in reason's night. But he ever preserved a tender remembrance of Miss Chaworth, only forgetting the wrong she had done him.†

Lord Byron's conduct had been no less generous toward Mr. Musters, his triumphant rival in the affections of Miss Chaworth. Mr. Musters, though several years older than Lord Byron, was, nevertheless, among his early companions. The parents of this young man resided at their country-seat, called Colwich, a few miles distant from Newstead, and Lord Byron often accepted their hospitality. One day the two youths were bathing in the Trent (a river which runs through the grounds of Colwich), when Mr. Musters perceived a ring among Lord Byron's clothes, left on the bank. To see and take possession of it was the affair of a moment. He had recognized it as having belonged to Miss Chaworth. Lord Byron claimed it, but Musters would not restore the ring. High words were exchanged. On returning to the house, Musters jumped on a horse and galloped off to ask an expla-

* She had been obliged to separate from her husband, who returned her sacrifices by bad and even brutal treatment.

† "Oh! she was changed
As by the sickness of the soul; her mind
Had wandered from its dwelling, and her eyes
They had not their own lustre, but the look
Which is not of the earth; she was become
The queen of a fantastic realm; her thoughts
Were combinations of disjointed things;
And forms impalpable and unperceived
Of others' sight familiar were to hers.
And this the world calls frenzy."

nation from Miss Chaworth, who, being forced to confess that Lord Byron wore the ring with her consent, felt obliged to make amends to Musters by promising to declare immediately her engagement with him. Proud of his success, he returned home and acquainted Lord Byron with Miss Chaworth's determination. Dinner was announced. The family sat down, and soon perceived there was something amiss between the two friends, whose gloomy silence spoke more eloquently than words. Before the end of dinner Lord Byron left the table, unable to endure the provocations of his rival.

The parents of Musters, though completely ignorant of what had caused the quarrel, were uneasy for the consequences. After dinner bitter words were again exchanged between the two young men, and Musters used such coarse, insolent language that Lord Byron could ill restrain his indignation. Anger flashing from his eyes expressed itself as warmly in words. In this frame of mind he retired to his room, and remained long shut up there, while Musters believed he was preparing to leave Colwich that very night. But the magnanimous youth, on reflection, understood that at fifteen he ought not to pretend to carry off the fair prize of seventeen from a man nine years his senior; and that it was not generous to grieve his hosts and hurt the reputation of the lady he loved. Accordingly, he suppressed his sorrow, his pride, his anger. Instead of returning to Newstead, he made his appearance as usual in the drawing-room, and to the astonishment of his rival, excused himself for having shown anger, and thus failed in politeness to his hosts. Candidly, and with regret, he acknowledged that the excess of his feelings had caused the outburst. From that day forth he gave up all pretensions to Miss Chaworth's love, and, forgiving them both with equal magnanimity, he even continued inviting his rival to Newstead. "But," said he, "now my heart would hate him if he loved her not."

On declaring to Moore, in a letter written from Pisa, that he would still forgive fresh wrongs, Lord Byron made this avowal:—"The truth is, I can not keep up resentment, however violent may be its explosion."

At all periods of his life, he remained the young man of 1814, saying that he could not go to rest with anger at his heart. In Greece, a few weeks before his glorious death, he gave another proof of it by his conduct toward Colonel Stanhope (afterward Lord Harrington). They had persuaded Lord Byron that the colonel was very jealous of his influence, and of the enthusiasm manifested for him. True or not, Lord Byron could not but believe it. The colonel arrived in Greece (sent by the London committee), for the purpose, it was said, of uniting with Lord Byron, and acting jointly in favor of Greek independence; but in reality, it would have seemed as if he came only to counteract what Byron wished. Their ideas on matters of administration and on political economy, their principles with regard to institutions and means of government, were totally opposed. Bentham was the colonel's idol and model, while Lord Byron particularly disliked the moral and social consequences flowing from Bentham's doctrines. Ever straightforward and practical, Lord Byron thought the Greeks ought to begin by gaining their independence, *and that they had better be taught to read before they were made to buy books, and the liberty of the press were given them.* Good and honorable, but fond of systems, the colonel always wished to begin by the end. Thence resulted long discussions between them, which produced hours of ennui for Lord Byron, and many annoyances, most prejudicial to his health, which was then very delicate. One evening, among others, the colonel grew so excited, that he told him he believed him to be a friend of the Turks. Lord Byron only answered: "Judge me by my actions." Both appeared angry; the colonel got up to leave. Lord Byron, who was the offended party, instead of bearing rancor, rose also, and, going straight to the colonel, said: "Give me your honest hand, and good-night." The night would not have passed tranquilly for Lord Byron without this reconciliation.

Among numerous proofs of this generous spirit of forgiveness,—so numerous that choice is difficult—we shall select his behavior toward a certain Mr. Scott, who, at the time of his separation, had attacked him in a savage, cruel manner,—not only unjustly, but even without any provocation.

"I beg to call particular attention," says Moore, "to the extract about to follow.

"Those who at all remember the peculiar bitterness and

violence, with which Mr. Scott had assailed Lord Byron, at a crisis when both his heart and fame were most vulnerable, will, if I am not mistaken, feel a thrill of pleasurable admiration, in reading these sentences, such as they were penned by Lord Byron, for his own expressions can alone convey any adequate notion of the proud, generous pleasure that must have been felt in writing them:—

"'Poor Scott is no more! In the exercise of his vocation, he contrived, at last, to make himself the subject of a coroner's inquest. But he died like a brave man, and he lived an able one. I knew him personally, though slightly; although several years my senior, we had been school-fellows together, at the grammar-school of Aberdeen. He did not behave to me quite handsomely, in his capacity of editor, a few years ago, but he was under no obligation to behave otherwise. *The moment was too tempting for many friends, and for all enemies.* At a time when all my relations (save one) fell from me, like leaves from the tree in autumn winds, and my few friends became still fewer,—when the whole periodical press (I mean the daily and weekly, not the *literary*, press) was let loose against me, in every shape of reproach, with the two strange exceptions (from their usual opposition) of, "The Courier" and "The Examiner,"—the paper of which Scott had the direction was neither the last nor the least vituperative. Two years ago, I met him at Venice, when he was bowed in grief, by the loss of his son, and had known, by experience, the bitterness of domestic privation. He was then earnest with me to return to England, and on my telling him, with a smile, that he was once of a different opinion, he replied to me, "*that he, and others, had been greatly misled; and that some pains, and rather extraordinary means, had been taken to excite them.*" Scott is no more, but there are more than one living who were present at this dialogue. He was a man of very considerable talents and of great acquirements. He had made his way, as a literary character, with high success, and in a few years. Poor fellow! I recollect his joy, at some appointment, which he had obtained, or was to obtain, through Sir James Mackintosh, and which prevented the further extension (unless by a rapid run to Rome) of his travels in Italy. I little thought to what it would conduct him. *Peace be with him! and may all such other faults as are inevitable to humanity be as readily forgiven him as the little injury which he had done to one who respected his talents and regrets his loss.* BYRON.'"

Nor did his magnanimity stop here. After Scott's death, a subscription for his widow was got up, and Lord Byron was requested to contribute ten pounds.

"You may make my subscription for Mr. Scott's widow thirty pounds, instead of the proposed ten," answered he; "but do not put down *my name.* As I mentioned him in the pamphlet, it would look indelicate."

But this refined generosity was only one of the forms which Lord Byron's kindliness took. To act thus, was a necessity for this privileged nature, that could not endure to hate, and loved to pardon. Still, his generosity had not yet entered on the road of great sacrifices. It had not yet reached the highest degree of power over self. It did attain to that, when it led him to comprise in one general pardon the so-called friends who had abandoned him in his hour of sacrifice, and those bitter enemies who knew no reconciliation, *when he forgave Lady Byron.* Then his generosity merited the name of virtue.

Pusillanimity, which binds with an invisible chain the hearts and tongues of vulgar souls, in unreal exacting society, had carried away some; jealousy of his superiority had rendered others ferocious; and an absolute moral monstrosity—an anomaly in the history of types of female hideousness—had succeeded in showing itself in the light of magnanimity. But false as was this high quality in Lady Byron, so did it shine out in him true and admirable. The position in which Lady Byron had placed him, and where she continued to keep him by her harshness, silence, and strange refusals, was one of those which cause such suffering, that the highest degree of self-control seldom suffices to quiet the promptings of human weakness, and to cause persons of even slight sensibility to preserve moderation. Yet, with his sensibility and the knowledge of his worth, how did he act?—what did he say? I will not speak of his "Farewell," of the care he took to shield her from blame by throwing it on others, by taking much too large a share to himself, when in reality his sole fault lay in having married her; because it might be objected that, when he acted thus, he had *not given up the wish of reunion.*

But at Venice, and more especially at Ravenna and Pisa, this project certainly had ceased to exist; the measure of insult was filled up to overflowing. And yet, in one of those days of exasperation which letters from London never failed to produce, and precisely when he was writing pages on Lady Byron that could scarcely be complimentary, he learned that she had been taken ill. His anger and his pen both fell simultaneously, and he hastened to throw into the fire what he had written. Another time he was told that Lady Byron lived in constant dread of having Ada forcibly taken from her.

"Yes," he replied, "I might claim her in Chancery, without having recourse to any other means; but I would rather be unhappy myself than make Lady Byron so."

And he said this, well knowing how his name was kept from his daughter, like a forbidden thing; and that his picture was hidden from her sight by a curtain.

One day at Rome, while he was walking amid the ruins of the Forum, treading upon those mighty relics that, to him, breathed language and well-nigh sentiments, that seemed like some magic temple of the past, Lord Byron traced back, in thought, his own career. The meannesses of which he had been, and still was, the victim rose up to view. He allowed his thoughts to wander amid the saddest memories. All the wounds of his still bleeding heart opened afresh. The serenity of the starry sky, the silence of that solemn hour, the ideas of order, peace, and justice, which such a scene ever awakens, contrasted strangely with the material devastation around worked by time. The natural effect of a grand spectacle like this, is to render sadder still those moral ruins accumulated within by the wickedness of man.

Then did his past, so recent still, rise up before him in all its bitterness. And, taking earth and heaven to witness, he exclaimed:—

"Have I not had to wrestle with my lot?
Have I not suffered things to be forgiven?
Have I not had my brain sear'd, my heart riven,
Hopes sapp'd, name blighted, Life's life lied away?

And only not to desperation driven,
Because not altogether of such clay
As rots into the souls of those whom I survey.

"From mighty wrongs to petty perfidy,
Have I not seen what human things could do?
From the loud roar of foaming calumny
To the small whisper of the as paltry few,
And subtler venom of the reptile crew,
The Janus glance of whose significant eye,
Learning to lie with silence, would SEEM *true,*
And without utterance, save the shrug or sigh,
Deal round to happy fools its speechless obloquy."

His spirit stirred with excitement, he invoked the aid of the divinity whose shrine these Roman remains appeared to be—

"O Time! the beautifier of the dead,
Adorner of the ruin, comforter
And only healer when the heart hath bled;
Time! the corrector where our judgments err,
The test of truth, love—sole philosopher,
For all beside are sophists—from thy thrift,
Which never loses though it doth defer—
Time, the avenger! unto thee I lift
My hands, and eyes, and heart, and crave of thee a gift."

And what was this gift? Was it vengeance? No! It was the *repentance* of those who had done and were still doing him wrong; that was the prayer he sent up to heaven, so as not to have worn in vain this iron in his soul, and so that, when his earthly life should cease, his spirit,—

"*Like the remember'd tone of a mute lyre,*
Shall on their soften'd spirits sink, and move,
In hearts all rocky now, the late remorse of love."*

Arrived before the temple of Nemesis,—that dread divinity who has never left unpunished human injustice,—Lord Byron evokes her thus:—

"Dost thou not hear my heart?—Awake! thou shalt, and must."

He feels that the guilty will not escape the vengeance of the goddess, since it is *inevitable;* but, as to him, he will not wreak it. Nemesis shall watch; he will sleep. *He reserves to himself, however, one revenge. Which? Ever the same:—Forgiveness!*

"That curse shall be forgiveness."†

---

* "Childe Harold," canto iv.

† Ibid.

Now, we have seen that his generosity did not recoil from any sacrifice of fortune, repose, affection; we have seen it strong against all privations, all instincts, all interests; in short, we have looked at it under all the aspects that constitute great beauty of soul. There remains only one degree more for him to attain—heroism. But the constant exercise of generosity of soul, in inferior degrees, will give him power to reach that sublime height, and, summing up all in one, arrive at *the crowning sacrifice of his life.*

Already more than once, in Italy, and especially in Romagna, when that peninsula was preparing a grand struggle for independence, Lord Byron had shown himself ready to make any sacrifice, to aid in throwing off Austrian chains. But, owing to subsequent events, his extreme devotedness could not then go beyond the offer made. Two years later it was accepted; an enslaved nation, eager for redemption, asked Lord Byron's assistance toward regaining its liberty. In this sacrifice on his part, no single feature of greatness is wanting. Lord Byron would have been great, had he sacrificed himself for his country; but how much greater was he in sacrificing himself for a foreign nation, for the general cause of humanity? He would still have remained great, had he been led into this noble sacrifice by his own enthusiasm, by his illusions, by personal hopes. But no illusion, no enthusiasm, impelled him toward Greece; naught save the satisfaction caused in a noble mind by the performance of a great action. He did not even hope to escape ingratitude or to silence calumny; for, although so young, he had already acquired the experience of mature years. He knew Greece, and was well aware what he should find there, in exchange for his repose and for all dear to him in this world. We know what sadness overwhelmed his soul during the last period of his sojourn at Genoa. The struggles he had with his own heart may be imagined, when we reflect, that despite his self-control, he was more than once surprised with tears in his eyes.

When hardly out of port from Genoa, a tempest cast him back. He landed, and resolved on visiting the abode he had left with such anguish the day before. While climbing the hill of Albano, the darkest presentiments took possession of his soul. "Where shall we be this day next year?" said he to Count Gamba, who was walking by his side. Alas! we know that precisely that day next year, his mortal remains were carried through the streets of London, on their way to repose with his ancestors, near Newstead. His sorrow only increased on arriving at the palace. His friends were gone; all within that dwelling was silent, deserted, solitary. He asked to be left alone; and then shut himself up in his apartments, remaining there for several hours. What was his occupation? What were his thoughts? Through what strange agony did he pass? Who shall tell us (since he concealed it), of that last struggle between the Man and the Hero?

The sadnesses of great souls are *unspeakable*, almost *superhuman.* They are beyond the scales where we would weigh them. But we know that he understood and tasted the bitterness of this chalice,* without drawing back, without failing to drain it to the last.

Night came, and behold him once more on board the vessel. The tempest roared again, then ceased; but the storm within his soul did not cease. Only when a tear sometimes threatened betrayal, did he hasten to the privacy of his cabin.

We will not give here the narrative of this voyage. These pages, we again repeat, are not a biography, but the picture of a soul.

On arriving at the Ionian Islands, he soon understood that his sacrifice, though not beyond what circumstances demanded, certainly far transcended any hope that could exist of regenerating this fallen race, and constituting a nation worthy to bear the glorious name of Greece. But it mattered not: he had given his word, and he was resolved to remain in the country. He even quitted the asylum afforded by the Ionian Islands, and determined to encounter all dangers, the better to accomplish his mission.

Then he went to Missolonghi. The privations he underwent there, the moral and physical fatigue, the effluvia from the adjoining marshes, and the mode of life he was forced to lead, all combined to affect his naturally good health. He was entreated to leave this unhealthy place, and told that his life depended on it. He felt it and knew it. Already

* See his "Life in Italy."

he perceived the spectre of the future, and, at the same time, the image of his beloved Italy floated before his eyes,—all that he had left, and would still find there; he represented to himself the existence he might lead there, quiet and happy, surrounded with love and respect. Still so young, handsome, rich, and almost adored, for whom could life have more value? But, if he left, what would become of Greece? His presence was worth an army to that unhappy country. So, then, he would not desert his post; *he resolved to remain, come what might.* "*No, Tita; no, we will not return to Italy,*" said he sadly to his faithful Venetian follower a few days before he fell ill. *He did remain, and he died.*

By this action, in which he overcame himself, Lord Byron gave one of those rare examples of self-immolation, of virtue, and heroism, which, says a noble mind of our day,* "afford real consolation to the soul, and reflect the greatest honor on the human race."

* M. Janet.

CHAPTER XVI.

FAULTS OF LORD BYRON.

AFTER having shown the virtues Lord Byron possessed, it might seem useless to inquire whether he had not the faults whose absence they prove. Still, however, it is well to look at the subject from anothei point of view, and to offer, so to say, counter-proof. For, in judging him, all rules have been disregarded, not only those of justice and equity, but likewise those of logic. And, as it has been variously asserted of him, that he was constant and inconstant, firm and fickle, guided by principle, yet giving way to every impulse; that he was both chaste and profligate, a sensual man and an anchorite; calumny alone can not be accused of all these contradictions. We must then seek out conscientiously whether there were not other causes for this *inconsistency*, so as to return back within due bounds, and bring contradiction in accord with truth. It is, of course, beyond dispute that the first cause of the unjust verdicts passed upon him lay in the bad passions stirred up by his success, by the independent language he used, and his contempt for a thousand national prejudices. Nevertheless, as the degree of injustice dealt out toward him was quite extraordinary, it may be asked whether some real defects did not lend specious reason to his enemies, and thus we are forced to confess that he had one great fault, which did powerfully aid their wickedness; it consisted in a species of *cruelty* toward himself, *a positive necessity of calumniating himself.*

Although the origin of this fault or defect must have been principally in the greatness of his soul, it certainly had other secondary and lesser causes, and, in common with many other qualities, it was fatal to his happiness; for men accustomed to exaggerate their own virtues only too readily believed him. This mode of doing harm to and *persecuting* himself, of casting shadows over his brilliant destiny, was so strange and so real, that it is necessary to show to what extent he did it, by collecting some of the numerous testimonies given among those who knew him, before we bring out the real cause of his fault, as well as the effect it had on his happiness and his reputation.

In no hands could his character have been less safe than his own, nor any greater wrong offered to his memory than the substitution of what he affected to be, for what he was.

While yet a student at Cambridge, he wrote a letter to Miss Pigott, full of gayety and fun, giving as an excuse for his silence the dissipated life he was leading, and which he calls *a wretched chaos of noise and drunkenness, doing nothing but hunt, drink Burgundy, play, intrigue, libertinize.* Then he exclaims:—

"What misery to have nothing else to do but make love and verses, and create enemies for one's self."

But while avowing this misery, he adds that he has *just written* 214 *pages of prose and* 1200 *verses.*

And Moore remarks, in a note annexed to this curious letter:—

"We observe here, as in other parts of his early letters. that sort of display and boast of *rakishness* which is but too common a folly at this period of life, when the young aspirant to manhood persuades himself that to be profligate is to be manly. Unluckily, this boyish desire to be thought worse than he really was remained with Lord Byron, as did some other failings and foibles, long after the period when, with others, they are past and forgotten; and his mind, indeed, was but beginning to outgrow them when he was snatched away."

When Moore speaks of the letter in which Lord Byron, replying to the praise given by Mr. Dallas, says he did not merit it, and depreciates himself morally in every possible way, Moore adds:—

"Here again, however, we should recollect there must be a considerable share of allowance for the *usual tendency to make the most and the worst of his own obliquities.* There occurs, indeed, in his first letter to Mr. Dallas, an account of this strange ambition, the *very reverse,* it must be allowed, of hypocrisy—which led him to court rather than avoid the reputation of profligacy, and to put, at all times, the worst face on his own character and conduct."

Mr. Dallas, writing for the first time to Lord Byron after having read his early poems, paid him some compliments on the moral beauties and charitable sentiments contained in his verses, remarking that they recalled another noble author, who was not only a poet, an orator, and a distinguished historian, but one of the most vigorous reasoners in England on the truths of that religion of which forgiveness forms the ruling principle, viz., the good and great Lord Lyttelton. Lord Byron answered, depreciating himself in a literary sense, and calumniating himself morally, by the assertion that he resembled Lord Lyttelton's son — a bad, though talented man — rather than the great author.

Dallas had the good sense to take this appreciation for what it was worth, and asked permission to pay the young nobleman a visit. Lord Byron answered politely that he should be happy to make his acquaintance, but continued to paint himself, especially as regarded his opinions, in the most unfavorable colors. Moore gives the whole of this letter, and then adds:—

"It must be recollected, before we attach any particular importance to the details of his creed, that in addition to the temptation—never easily resisted by him—of displaying his wit, at the expense of his character, he was here addressing a person who, though, no doubt, well meaning, was evidently one of those *officious self-satisfied advisers* whom it was the delight of Lord Byron, at all times, to *astonish* and *mystify*.

"The tricks which, when a boy, he played upon the Nottingham quack, Lavander, were but the first of a long series, with which, through life, he amused himself, at the expense of all the numerous quacks whom his celebrity and sociability drew around him."

In the first satire he gave to the world, and which attracted sympathy for his talent as well as for the justice of his cause, the horror he entertained of hypocrisy already made him speak against himself:—

"E'en I—least thinking of a thoughtless throng,
Just skill'd to know the right and choose the wrong."

After having quoted an early poem of Lord Byron, written

in an hour of great depression, and which would seem inspired by momentary madness, Moore makes the following declaration:—

"These concluding lines are of a nature, it must be owned, to awaken more of horror than of interest, were we not prepared, by so many instances of his exaggeration in this respect, not to be startled at any lengths to which the spirit of *self-libelling* would carry him. It seemed as if, with the power of painting fierce and gloomy personages, he had also the ambition to be himself the dark 'sublime he drew,' and that, in his fondness for the delineation of heroic crime, he endeavored to fancy, where he could not find in his own character, fit subjects for his pencil."

Moore, mentioning another article in his memoranda, where Lord Byron accuses himself of irritability of temperament in his early youth, follows up with this reflection:—

"In all his portraits of himself, the pencil he uses is so dark that the picture of his temperament and his self-attempts, covering as they do with *a dark shadow the shade itself*, must be taken with large allowance for exaggeration."

In another passage of his work, Moore further says:—

"To the perverse fancy he had for falsifying his own character, and even imputing to himself faults the most alien to his nature, I have already frequently adverted. I had another striking instance of it one day at La Mira."

Moore then relates that, on leaving Venice, he went to La Mira to bid Lord Byron farewell. Passing through the hall, he saw the little Allegra, who had just returned from a walk. Moore made some remark on the beauty of the child, and Byron answered, "Have you any notion—but I suppose you have—of what they call the parental feeling? For myself, I have not the least." And yet, when that child died, in a year or two afterward, he who had uttered this artificial speech was so overwhelmed by the event, that those who were about him at the time actually trembled for his reason.*

Colonel Stanhope, afterward Lord Harrington, who knew Lord Byron in Greece, shortly before his death, says:—

"Most men affect a virtuous character; Lord Byron's ambition, on the contrary, seemed to be to make the world be-

* Moore's "Life," vol. iv. p. 241.

lieve that he was a sort of *Satan*, though impelled by high sentiments to accomplish great actions. *Happily for his reputation, he possessed another quality that unmasked him completely: he was the most open and most sincere of men, and his nature, inclined to good, ever swayed all his actions.*"*

Mr. Finlay, who knew Lord Byron about the same time, says *that not only he calumniated himself, but that he hid his best sentiments.*

Speaking of the simplicity of his manners, and his repugnance for all *emphasis*:—

"I have always observed," continues Mr. Finlay, "that he adopted a very simple and even monotonous tone, when he had to say any thing not quite in the ordinary style of conversation. Whenever he had begun a sentence which showed that the subject interested him, and which contained sublime thought, he would check himself suddenly, and come to an end without concluding, either with a smile of indifference or in a careless tone. I thought he had adopted this mode *to hide his real sentiments when he feared lest his tongue should be carried away by his heart;* and often he did so evidently to hide the author or rather the poet. But in satire or clever conversation his genius took full flight."†

And Stanhope further adds:—

"I also have observed that Lord Byron acted in this way. He often liked to hide the noble sentiments that filled his soul, and even tried to turn them into ridicule."‡

This was only too true. The spirit of repartee and fun often made him display his intellectual faculties at the expense of his moral nature and his truest sentiments.

Moore says that when Lord Byron went to Ravenna to see Countess G—— again, he wrote to Hoppner, who looked after his affairs, in such a light vein of pleasantry, that it would have been difficult for any one not knowing him thoroughly to conceive the possibility of his expressing himself thus, while under the influence of a passion so sincere:—

"But such is ever the wantonness of the mocking spirit, from which nothing—not even love—remains sacred; and which at last, for want of other food, turns upon self. The same horror, too, of hypocrisy that led Lord Byron to exag-

* Parry, 273. † Letter from Finlay to Stanhope, Parry, 210. ‡ Parry, 210.

gerate his own errors led him also to disguise, under a seemingly heartless ridicule, all those natural and kindly qualities by which they were redeemed."

And by way of contrast with the strange lightness of his letter to Hoppner, as well as to do justice to the reality of his passion, Moore then quotes the whole of those beautiful stanzas, called "The Po," which Lord Byron wrote while crossing that river on his way from Venice to Ravenna.*

We might multiply quotations, in order to prove that all those who knew him have more or less remarked this phenomenon. But no one has well determined its principal cause; or else it has been too much confounded with the strange caprices he showed, especially in early youth; for subsequently, says Moore, "*when he saw that the world gravely believed the opinion he had given of himself, he refused any longer to echo it.*"

There is certainly truth in the judgment passed by Moore and others. It can not be denied that, when as a boy, he boasted of his dissipated life at the University, the chief reason of it lay in the folly common to that period of life, which impels human beings while yet children to seek to appear like men by aping the vices of riper years. It can not be denied, either, that the pleasure of mystifying suggested his answer to Dallas; that an exaggerated horror of hypocrisy taught his pen a thousand censures of himself beginning with his first satire; that a sort of over-excitement and reaction of imagination gave him, at times, the strange ambition of appearing to be one of those dark, proud heroes he loved to paint for the sake of effect. Moreover, we must not forget that witty turn of mind which his extraordinary perception of the ridiculous, and his facility for seeing the two sides of things, often made him to display at the expense of his better nature, by seeming to mock his truest sentiments, as when he wrote to Hoppner: a psychological phenomenon, of which the cause has been more particularly sought elsewhere. Finally, we may also add that he might have believed he was disarming envy and malice by speaking against himself; and that he was to a certain extent escaping from the effects of those evil passions by throwing them something whereon to feed. Who knows

* Moore, 214, vol. ii. in 4to.

whether he also did not—a little through goodness of heart, and greatly through the tactics that make good politicians complain of the unpleasantnesses attached to their greatness —ascribe to himself imaginary defects, so as to let some compassion, under the form of blame, mix with the malice that hemmed him in on all sides; and whether he did not think it well to make use of this means, as of a shield, to ward off their blows? This sort of generous artifice, which I more than once suspected in him, may serve as long as public favor lasts; but when persecution gets the upper hand,—which is the case sooner or later with all greatness and all virtues—when Envy triumphs by means of calumny, she converts into poison, benefits, virtues, gratitude. Thus, if our hypothesis be correct, Lord Byron would have been cruelly punished for his weakness in allowing that to be believed of him which was not true. Still, all we have observed can only furnish, at best, the secondary and evanescent causes of the moral phenomenon described, and those who would fain penetrate the recesses of Lord Byron's soul must search deeper for explanation. Our idea is, the first cause will be found to lie in some sentiment that reigned all powerful in his breast. I mean that he placed *his ideal standard too high*, and the influence it exercised over him was manifest *even to his last moments.*

In the severe judgments which he has pronounced upon himself in the first place, on mankind in general, and on some particular individuals, the ideal model of all the intellectual, moral, and physical beauty which he found in the depth of his own mind, shone with divine lustre before his imagination, by the union of faculties imbued with extraordinary energy.

We see, by a thousand traits, that his ideal was formed much earlier than is common with ordinary children. In his first youthful poems it already displayed itself much developed. Ever attracted toward truth, his first desire was to seek after that; and the better to do so, he searched into himself, analyzed what was passing within and without, and finally proclaimed it without any consideration for himself or others.

At Harrow we see him leaving off play to go and sit down alone and meditate on the stone now called *Byron's tomb.*

At Cambridge afterward, despite the dissipation he shared equally with his comrades, amid games and exercises in which he greatly excelled, we still find him courting meditation under shady trees. On returning to his home, the Abbey, when surrounded with the noise and frolic of boisterous companions, we see him devote himself to study and solitary reflection; finally, during his travels, and after his return, when all England was at his feet, we behold him still and ever experiencing that imperious *want* of scanning himself, of descending into the depths of his own heart, interrogating his conscience, and very often of writing down in his memorandum-books the severe sentences pronounced by that inflexible judge. And, as he could not put away from sight his divine model, he came out from these examinations *humbled, dissatisfied, reproaching and punishing himself for having strayed from it.* For he discovered too many terrestrial elements in all human virtues. For instance, in friendships, though so generous on his side, he found the satisfaction of a personal want, consequently, an egotistical element; the same, and much more strongly, with regard to love. He found something personal in the best instincts, in the passion for glory, in patriotism, even in the sentiment of veneration, since that is an echo of our tastes and personal sympathies. That the high standard of his ideal was the first cause of injustice toward himself, a thousand proofs might be offered. I will choose some only. We read in his memoranda:—

"It has lately been in my power to make two men happy. I am delighted at it, especially as regards the last, for he is excellent. *But I wish there had been a little more sacrifice on my part, and less satisfaction for my self-love in doing that, because then there would have been more merit.*"

Such was this great culprit. He actually felt pleasure in doing good! Another time he was asked to present a petition to Parliament. "I am not in a humor for this business," writes he in the evening journal, where he examined his conscience. He was suffering then from grief, caused by the absence of a person he loved, and he apostrophizes himself in these terms:—"Had —— been here she would have *made* me do it. *There* is a woman who, amid all her fascination, always urged a man to usefulness or glory. Had she remained, she had been my tutelar genius.

"Baldwin is very unfortunate; but, poor fellow, 'I can't get out; I can't get out,' said the starling. *Ah! I am as bad as that dog Sterne, who preferred whining over a dead ass to relieving a living mother. Villain! hypocrite! slave! sycophant! But I am no better. Here I can not stimulate myself to a speech for the sake of these unfortunates, and three words and half a smile of ——, had she been here to urge it (and urge it she infallibly would; at least, she always pressed me on in senatorial duties, and particularly in the cause of weakness), would have made me an advocate, if not an orator. Curse on Rochefoucault for being always right!*"

Another time *he also accused himself of selfishness, because he wrote only for amusement!* He was then but twenty-three years of age:—

"To withdraw myself from myself (*oh, that cursed selfishness!*) has ever been my sole, my entire, my sincere motive in scribbling at all; and publishing is also the continuance of the same object, by the action it affords to the mind, which else recoils upon itself."

This hard opinion of man's virtue, formed by many moralists, and especially by those who see virtue only in pure disinterested benevolence, was an impulse with Lord Byron rather than the result of reason; and I much doubt whether this craving for equity and truth were ever practically combined and harmonized with the faculty of benevolence in any one else as it was with Lord Byron, for this combination evidently formed the most striking part of his character. Montaigne himself,—who, if he did not possess as much innate benevolence, had nevertheless the faculty, and even felt the want of entering into his conscience, and examining it, so as to draw forth general notions,—says, "When I examine myself conscientiously, I find that my best sort of goodness has a *vicious tint.*"

And he fears that even Plato, in his *brightest virtue*, had he analyzed it well, would have found *some human admixture.* And then he sums up by saying, "Man is made up of bits and oddities."*

* Montaigne, vol. iii. p. 87.

But these sincere philosophers are few in number, and their maxims can never be popular. For men in general experience rather the want of magnifying than of depreciating themselves, and, instead of taking their best models from an ideal, they choose them from reality, judge characters, compare themselves to other men, and, living like other people, see no guilt in themselves; while Lord Byron, living as they did, discovered in himself weaknesses, reasons for modesty, regret, repentance. If he could have done as they did, he would have been satisfied, and he would either have escaped or vanquished calumny. But he could not and would not, though conscious of the harm thence resulting to himself.

"You censure my life, Harness. When I compare myself with these men, my elders and my betters, I really begin to conceive myself a monument of prudence,—a walking statue, without feeling or failing; and yet the world in general has given me a proud pre-eminence over them in profligacy. Yet I like the men, and, God knows, ought not to condemn their aberrations; but I own I feel provoked when they dignify all this by the name of love. Romantic attachments for things marketable for a dollar!"

One of his biographers pretends that he rendered himself justice another time, and represents him as saying, speaking of M——:

"See how well he has got on in the world! He is just as little inclined to commit a bad action as incapable of doing a good one; fear keeps him from the former, and wickedness from the latter. The difference between him and me is that I attack a great many people, and truly, with one or two exceptions (and note that they are persons of my own sex), I do not hate one; while he says no harm of any one, but hates a great many, if not every body. Fancy, then, how amusing it would be to see him in the palace of Truth, when he would be thinking he was making the sweetest compliments, while all the time he would be giving vent to the accumulated spite and rancor of years, and then to see the person he had flattered so long listen to his real sentiments for the first time. Oh! that would truly be a comic sight. As to me, I should appear to great advantage in the palace of Truth, for while I should be thinking to vex friends and enemies with harsh speeches, I should be saying pretty things on the contrary; for at bottom, *I have no malice or ill-nature,—at least, not of that kind which lasts more than a moment.*"

"Never," adds the biographer, "was a truer observation made. Lord Byron's nature is *very fine*, despite all the bad weeds that might have attempted to spring up in it; and I am convinced that it is the excellence of the poet, or rather the effect of such excellence, which has caused the faults of the man.

"The severity of censure lavished on the man has increased in proportion to the admiration excited by the poet, and often with the greatest injustice. The world offered up incense to the poet, while heaping ashes on the head of the man. He was indignant at such usage, and wounded pride avenged itself by painting himself in the darkest colors, as if to give a deeper hue than even his enemies had done; all the time forcing them to admiration for his genius, as boundless as was their disapprobation of his supposed character."*

Is this conversation real or imaginary? Doubt is allowable; but, however it may be, the reflections of the biographer in this case are too sensible and too true for us not to quote them with pleasure.

In concluding these remarks, which prove how high was the ideal type that impelled Lord Byron to be unjust to himself, I will further observe, that it was the exaggeration of his great characteristic faculties which made him fail in some little virtue (such as prudence, when it has its source *solely in our personal interest*). For it was only to this degree, and from this point of view, that Lord Byron lacked it. And it appears singular that his great mind should not have made him see, in this very craving after self-examination, caused by his inclination for truth, and in that extraordinary susceptibility of conscience which lead to self-reproach for egotism, only because he *felt pleasure in exercising beneficence and that it did not contain enough sacrifice;* it is singular, I say, that this same spirit of equity did not make him see how he shone in the only two faculties that can have no alloy of egotism, and which were very evidently the most *striking qualities of his character*. But he was, with regard to himself,

* "Journal of Conversation," p. 195.

like the torch which, lighting up distant objects, leaves those near it in obscurity. Lord Byron did not know himself; he had by no means overcome that difficulty which the oracles of Greece pronounced *the greatest.* Only he was sometimes conscious of it. In his memoranda, written at Ravenna, in 1821, after having said that he does not think the world judges him well, he adds:—

"I have seen myself compared, personally or poetically, in English, French, German as (interpreted to me), Italian and Portuguese, within these nine years, to Rousseau, Goethe, Young, Aretin, Timon of Athens, Dante, Petrarch, an Alabaster Vase lighted up within, Satan, Shakspeare, Bonaparte, Tiberius, Æschylus, Sophocles, Euripides, Harlequin the clown, Sternhold and Hopkins, to the Phantasmagoria, to Henry the Eighth, to Chenier, to Mirabeau, to Young, R. Dallas (the schoolboy), to Michael Angelo, to Raphael, to a *petit maître*, to Diogenes, to Childe Harold, to Lara, to the Count in 'Beppo,' to Milton, to Pope, to Dryden, to Burns, to Savage, to Chatterton, to 'oft have I heard of thee, my Lord Byron,' in Shakspeare, to Churchill the poet, to Kean the actor, to Alfieri, etc., etc. The object of so many contradictory comparisons must probably be like something different from them all; but what *that* is is more than I know, or any body else."

But had he known himself, he would have found that he realized one of the finest types of character that humanity can offer; for his two characteristic faculties were, his attraction toward truth and benevolence. And in ceasing to calumniate himself, he would have snatched from the hands of the envious and the enemies of truth, the principal weapon they made use of to defame him.

When one reflects on all this, one questions with astonishment how it is that all his biographers should have remained outside of truth. But it is useless insisting thereupon, for we have given sufficient answer.*

I will, then, confine myself to remarking here that one characteristic peculiar to the biographers of great men in general, is the extreme repugnance they feel toward praising their own subjects. What is the cause? Do they fear being told they have made a panegyric, passing for flatterers, appearing

* See chapter on Lord Byron's biographers.

to get through a task? Do they believe that, in order to show cleverness, perspicacity, and deep knowledge of the human heart, it is necessary to put in place of simple truth a sort of malice, not very intelligible, and often contradictory? All that may well be, but I believe that what they especially feel is, that if their books were only written for noble minds, possessing such qualities as only belong to the minority of the human race, they might run the risk of being less sought after and less bought. Thus they search for faults with ardor, just as miners do for diamonds; and when they think they have discovered a vice in their hero, they look upon it as the "Mogul" of their book. They make it shine, polish it up, show it in a thousand lights, bring it out as the striking part of their work,—the chief quality of their hero, who, unable to defend himself, is handed down, disfigured, to posterity. Such are the strange perils incurred, as regards truth and justice, and the wrong done toward the great departed; and this is why their surviving friends are called on to protest against the false assertions of biographers. Those who have written on Lord Byron, unable to find this great "Mogul" (for Lord Byron had no vices), have all, more or less, sought at least to draw the attention of their readers to a thousand little weaknesses, mostly devoid of reality. Upon what basis, indeed, do they rest?—Almost always on Lord Byron's words. Now we know what account should be made of his testimony when he speaks against himself. For instance, he has called himself irritable and prone to anger, and biographers have found it very convenient to paint him with his own brush. Men never fail to treat those who depreciate themselves with equal injustice. Nor is this surprising. If it be true that we are always judged on our faulty side, even though we endeavor to show the best, what must be the case if our efforts tend only to display our worst? And besides, why should others give themselves the trouble of exonerating a man from blame who depreciated himself? As it requires great discernment, great generosity, and very rare qualities, not to go beyond truth in self-esteem, biographers have not hesitated to declare Lord Byron, on his own testimony, *very irritable*, and even very passionate; but was he really so? This is a question to be examined.

CHAPTER XVII.

IRRITABILITY OF LORD BYRON.

WAS Lord Byron irritable? With his poetic temperament, his exquisite and almost morbid sensibility, so grievously tried by circumstances, it would be equally absurd and untrue to pretend that he was as impassible as a stoic, or phlegmatic as some good citizen who vegetates rather than lives. Did such qualities, or rather faults,—for they betoken a cold nature, — ever belong to Milton, Dante, Alfieri, and those master-spirits whose strength of passion, combined with force of intellect, have merited for them the rank of geniuses?

All more or less were, and could not fail to have been, susceptible of irritation and anger; for such susceptibility was indispensable in the peculiar constitution of their minds. But he who finds sufficient strength of will to control himself, when over-excitement is caused by some wounded feeling, does not that person approach to virtue? Did Lord Byron possess this power? Every thing, even to the testimony of his servants, his masters, his comrades, proves that he did. In childhood he showed that he knew how to conquer himself, and would use his power. He says, himself, that his anger was of a silent nature, and made him grow pale. Now, is not pale and silent anger of the kind that is overcome? We know that Lord Byron's mother, while still young, suffered so cruelly from the simultaneous loss of her fortune and a husband she adored, that her temper became changed and embittered. She gave way to violent bursts of passion, quite at variance with her excellent qualities of heart; thus she loved her son, but being very jealous of his affection, a trifle sufficed to make her launch out into reproaches and disagreeable scenes. This disposition on her part was not calculated to inspire the tenderness which her passionate fondness for him would otherwise have merited. But it was his disapprobation of such scenes that taught him to overcome in himself all outward tokens of anger, and to keep guard over his temper. Thus he opposed to the violence displayed by his poor mother a calm and silent demeanor that provoked her still more, it is true, but which proved great strength of will in him. After a violent scene that took place with her during one of his Cambridge vacations, he even determined on leaving home.

"It was very seldom," says Moore, "that he allowed himself to be so far provoked by her as to come out of his passivity."

And by what he himself declares in his memoranda, written at the age of twenty-two, we see that he did not permit any external demonstration of his temper, and that under this discipline it certainly had already improved. "It is especially when I wish to keep silence, and when I feel my cheeks and brow grow pale," says he, "that it becomes very difficult for me to control myself; but the presence of a woman, though not of all women, suffices to calm me."

To proceed with justice in any psychological study, we should never lose sight of the particular circumstances of the subject under treatment. Now, the circumstances amid which Lord Byron's moral and social life first began to unfold itself were very irritating.

While yet a boy we see his heart expand to love, to tenderness, excited by the way in which the young lady received his attentions, by the gift she made him of her portrait, by meetings, by the encouragement her parents afforded; for, notwithstanding the disproportion of age, they looked favorably on a union that was equal with regard to fortune and position. And while he was thus beguiled, this girl—whom he considered an angel—deemed the timid youth too childish, and entered into a union with a man of fashion.

On the eve of a long farewell to England, a friend whom he loved with all the devotedness that belonged to a heart like his, showed the utmost indifference at his departure. Having attained his majority, he ought to have taken his seat in the House of Peers; but his noble guardian, Lord Carlisle, whom he had always treated with respect, and to whom he had lately shown the attention of dedicating his early poems to him, behaved toward him in an unjustifiable manner. Not only did he refuse to present him to the House of Lords, but he even delayed sending the documents necessary for his admission, because forsooth the noble earl *did not like his ward's mother!* Lord Byron had published a charming collection of poems that won for him equal applause and sympathy; but an all-powerful Review sought to humiliate him and crush his talent in the bud by bringing out a brutal and stupid article against him. Nor was this all; he had likewise the annoyance of money embarrassments inherited from his predecessors in the estate. Leaving England under the sting of all these insults from men and fate, which a phlegmatic temper could alone have borne with patience, would it have been astonishing if his young heart had felt irritation? But could it have existed without being perceived by those who lived with him? Yet they say nothing about it. His fellow-traveller was a friend and comrade of old,—Lord Broughton, then the Hon. Mr. Hobhouse. If Lord Byron had been of an irritable, violent temper, who more than his daily companion would have perceived it, and suffered from it in that constant intercourse which tries the gentlest natures? Mr. Hobhouse had lived with Lord Byron at Cambridge, was one of his inseparable companions of Newstead, and was a member of the confraternity of the chapter. Thus he knew him well, and if Lord Byron's temper had been unamiable, would he have undertaken such a long journey with him? Lord Byron did not then possess even the prestige of celerity to render him desirable as a fellow-traveller. Well, on returning from this journey, Mr. Hobhouse was more attached than ever to Lord Byron, and, speaking of his qualities, expressed himself thus: —"To perspicacity of observation and ingenious remarks, Lord Byron united that gayety and good-humor which keeps attention alive under the pressure of fatigue, smoothing all difficulties and dangers."

Journeys taken together test tempers so much, that a good understanding which has withstood the trial of twenty years, is often compromised in a journey of twenty-four hours. Thus to choose again for our travelling companions those with whom we have already long journeyed, is the best testimony that can be rendered to their amiable disposition. Well, this testimony was given by Mr. Hobhouse; and while proving Lord Byron's excellent temper, it also proves the high character of Mr. Hobhouse. For we must not forget that malice and stupidity were inflicting a real persecution on Lord Byron at the very moment when Mr. Hobhouse hastened to rejoin him at Geneva, so as to travel again in company with his noble friend. They accomplished together an excursion into the Alps, and afterward crossed over them to visit Italy. On arriving at Venice, the two friends separated for several months; but in the spring they met again to visit together Rome and Florence. It was beside Mr. Hobhouse, while scaling the Alps, that the plan of "Manfred" was conceived; and it was on the road from Venice to Rome that the fourth canto of "Childe Harold" was written: it is dedicated to Mr. Hobhouse, and he it was who made the volume of notes, which forms, even independently of the text, a work so well appreciated in England.

Having gathered from Lord Byron's first journey proofs of his good natural disposition, and of the control he exercised over himself, I shall also draw others from his last: that journey from Cephalonia to Missolonghi which proved so fatal, and which alone, from all Lord Byron did, said, and wrote during the time it lasted, would suffice to reveal his fine character, and almost every one of his virtues.

It is well known, that during this journey he underwent still greater annoyances than in the one from Genoa to Cephalonia, which had already tried him so much. On seeing both destiny and the elements so pertinaciously combine against its success, one might really be tempted to embrace superstitious ideas, and see therein the efforts of his good genius raising up all sorts of obstacles in order to save him, and keep him from that fatal shore. I have already given the description of this journey so full of dramatic incidents; and I have related Lord Byron's admirable conduct throughout, in the passages where proofs are adduced of his courage in danger, of his extraordinary coolness and extreme generosity. But that is not enough; we must also examine him with regard to amiability of temper and the self-control he was able to exercise.

We have seen him, when pressed on all sides to quit the Ionian Islands for the continent of Greece, yield to these entreaties, although it was the most severe season of the year (28th December), and, notwithstanding a stormy sea, set out for Missolonghi.

He refused the honor of an escort of Greek vessels, hiring instead a Cephalonian *Mistico*, and a heavy *Bombarda* that waited for him at St. Euphemia. But on arriving near the harbor, he was driven back by contrary winds. Forced to remain on shore and wait, what sort of humor did he display under these annoyances? Mr. Kennedy, who went to wish him a pleasant journey, shall tell us.

"I found him," says he, "quietly reading 'Quentin Durward,' and, as usual, in high spirits."

Meanwhile, the sea grew calm. They set sail, and embarked; Lord Byron on the little *Mistico*, with his doctor, two or three servants, and his dogs; Count Gamba on the *Bombarda*, with the arms, horses, followers, baggage, papers, money, etc. On arriving at Zante, persons came to offer Lord Byron means of amusement, various comforts, etc. To accept might have been very pleasant for him; but he knew that he was wanted at Missolonghi; and not an hour would he lose after having transacted business with his bankers. He believed (for it had been announced) that Greek vessels were coming to meet him; nor did he doubt that the Turkish fleet was still anchored at Lepanto. Sea and wind were favorable, the sky serene, fortune for once seemed to smile; but it was only the better to deceive him. The Turks had been informed of his departure; and hoped to make an easy prey of him and his riches. They left the waters of Lepanto, and heading their course toward Patras, set off in pursuit of Lord Byron and his suite.

At the close of a few hours, the *Mistico*, which was a good sailer, lost sight of the *Bombarda*, of slower motion. They halted opposite the Scrophes (rocks in Roumelia), to wait for it; and meanwhile Lord Byron saw a large vessel bearing down upon him. Could it be the Greek vessel sent to meet him? The *Mistico* fired a pistol at its approach, but the vessel did not answer fire. Was it the enemy, then? On hearing the cries of the sailors on board, the captain could no longer doubt it: it was an Ottoman frigate, calling on them to surrender. Their sole hope of safety lay in the swiftness of their sails. Under cover of the darkness, which left the Turks in fear lest the *Mistico* should be a fire-ship, and aided by the almost miraculous silence that reigned,—for even the dogs, that had been barking all night, now held their peace,—the *Mistico* sped onward rapidly. At dawn of day it had arrived opposite the coast, but, owing to a contrary wind, was unable to get into port. At the same moment, another Turkish vessel, on the watch, closed the passage toward the Gulf. An Ionian boat perceived the danger, and made signals from the shore for the *Mistico* not to approach. They then succeeded, all sails set, in throwing themselves between the rocks of Roumelia, called Scrophes, where the Turkish vessel could not penetrate. It was amid these rocks, where he hardly remained an hour, that Lord Byron wrote Colonel Stanhope a letter, truly admirable for its generosity, patience, courage, coolness, and good temper; a letter which it would seem impossible to pen under such circumstances, and which makes Count Gamba say, when he quotes it in his work entitled "Last Voyage of Lord Byron in Greece:"—

"Such was Lord Byron's style in the midst of great dangers. There was always immense gayety in him, under circumstances that render other men serious and full of care. This disposition of mind gave him an air of frankness and sincerity, quite irresistible, even with persons previously less well disposed toward him."

Having hardly, and as if by a miracle, escaped from this danger, and being exposed every instant to assault from the Turks, having seen the *Bombarda* captured by the Ottoman frigate, did he complain of any thing personal to himself? No. His sole anxiety was for Count Gamba; his uneasiness was the danger to which the Greeks with him were exposed. As to his money losses—"*Never mind*," said he, "*don't think about it, we have some left.* But we have no arms, except two carbines and some pistols; and if our friends, the Turks, took a fancy to send their vessels to attack us, I greatly fear that we should only be four on board to defend ourselves."

Not being able to know that the *unexpected apparition* of the Turkish fleet had put out all their calculations, and prevented the Greek government from collecting the vessels sent from Missolonghi to meet him; not knowing that Missolonghi, in great consternation, on learning the danger to which he was exposed, was about to send other vessels in quest of him, other vessels that would no longer find him near the Scrophes rocks, he necessarily believed that nothing had been done to keep the promises made him. Under such a persuasion, would not some few harsh words have been most natural? And yet this is the language Lord Byron used:—

"But where has it gone to; the fleet that lets us advance without giving the least sign of any Moslems in these latitudes? Present my respects to Mavrocordato, and tell him I am here at his disposal. I am ill at ease here (among the rocks), not so much for myself, as for the Greek child with me; for you know what his destiny would be! We are all in good health."

The *Mistico* had hardly been an hour among these rocks, Lord Byron's letter to Colonel Stanhope was hardly finished, when the Turkish vessel on the lookout made toward them to give chase; and they were obliged to fly without delay. Issuing from the rocks, they directed their course, full sail, toward a little port of Acarnania, called Dragomestri, where they arrived before night.

Lord Byron wished to continue his route by land; but it was impossible. The mountains did not afford him better hospitality than the sea. It was the 1st of January; his sole resting-place was the damp deck of the *Mistico.* There he slept, there he eat the coarse sailors' food; and his fingers were so cramped with cold, that he could scarcely write. If he had complained a little of his hard fate, could one be much astonished? Yet these are the terms in which he wrote to his two correspondents at Cephalonia.—*It was the month of January; he wished every one a happy new year; apparently forgetting only himself. He then entered into some details about his "Odyssey" with so much calmness, that nothing seemed to touch him personally; but his heart protested meanwhile, and he could not help showing uneasiness about the fate of his friend Count Gamba, although persuaded that his detention was only temporary:—*

"I regret the detention of Gamba, etc., but the rest we can make up again, so tell Hancock to set my bills into cash as soon as possible, and Corgialegno to prepare the remainder of my credit with Messrs. Webb to be turned into money. We are here for the *fifth day without taking our clothes off, and sleeping on deck in all weathers, but are all very well and in good spirits.* I shall remain here, unless something extraordinary occurs, till Mavrocordato sends, and then go on, and act according to circumstances. My respects to the two colonels, and remembrances to all friends. Tell *Ultima Analise** that his friend Raids did not make his appearance with the brig, though I think that he might as well have spoken with us in or off Zante, to give us a gentle hint of what we had to expect. Excuse my scrawl, on account of the pen and the frosty morning at daybreak. BYRON."

He writes at the same time to Hancock :—

"Here we are—the *Bombarda* taken—or at least missing, with all the Committee stores, my friend Gamba, the horses, negro, bull-dog, steward, and domestics, with all our implements of peace and war—also 8000 dollars ; but whether she will be a lawful prize or no, is for the decision of the governor of the Seven Islands. We are in good condition, considering wind and weather, being hunted by the Turks, and the difficulty of sleeping on deck ; we are in tolerable seasoning for the country and circumstances. But I foresee that we shall have occasion for all the cash I can muster at Zante and elsewhere. Tell our friends to keep up their spirits—and we may yet do well. I hope that Gamba's detention will only be temporary. As for the effects and money, if we have them, well ; if otherwise, patience ! I disembarked the boy and another Greek, who were in most terrible alarm. As for me and mine, we must stick to our goods. I wish you a happy new year ; and all our friends the same. Yours, BYRON."

Would an impatient, irritable temper have acted thus, and preserved such serenity amid so many annoyances, priva-

* Count Delladecima, to whom he gives this name in consequence of a habit which that gentleman had of using the phrase "in ultima analise" frequently in conversation.

tions, and sufferings, of which one alone might suffice to make a stoic bitter?

But this was not yet all. After six days of this life, hopeless of being able to continue by land, and getting no answer from Missolonghi (from whence, nevertheless, several gun-boats had been dispatched to meet him, and also the brig "Leonidas," which he only fell in with near the Scrophes), he resolved on setting out. But the wind, which had never ceased being contrary, soon changed into a furious tempest. Then Byron was truly sublime. His bark was thrown against enormous rocks; the affrighted sailors, seeing their lives in danger, and excited by fear, abandoned the vessel to seek refuge on the rocks. But he remained there, on board the vessel, which every one saw was sinking.*

Encouraged by such an example, the sailors let go their hold on the rocks to try and free the vessel, which they succeeded in setting afloat again; but it was only for it to be forced back a second time by the angry waves. Then despair seized on them all; they trembled for the general safety, and for the illustrious personage on board. He alone showed no emotion; but calmly said to his doctor, who, in great alarm, was about to swim for the shore: "Do not leave the vessel while we have sufficient strength to guide her; only when the water covers us entirely, then throw yourself into the sea, and I will undertake to save you."

And in the midst of those dangers he not only appeared calm, but his gay, playful humor, and his habit of observing the different aspects of every thing, did not abandon him. After having soothed and consoled those around him, he likewise found means of amusement in the strong traits of individuality which fear brought to light among his followers. The sailors who had remained on board, seeing the danger become so imminent, were about to betake themselves, like the rest, to the rocks; but encouraged by Lord Byron's words and example, they remained at their post, and succeeded in bringing the vessel between two little islands, where they cast anchor. Thus Lord Byron, by his courage, firmness, and his great experience in the art of navigation, overcame this great peril, saving several lives, together with the money and

* See the account given by Mr. Bruno, his physician.

other means of assistance he was conveying to Greece! The sailors esteemed themselves happy to be able to cast anchor between these islands, or rather these rocks, in order to pass the night; but even what appeared fortunate, was destined to turn out the reverse in this fatal journey.

If Lord Byron did not complain of the privation and ennui he experienced, he did not, therefore, feel them less. After so many nights passed on the damp and dirty deck of his *Mistico*, he could not resist the desire of refreshing himself, and seeking amid the waves that cleanliness which was an imperative want for his refined nature. And so, without reflecting on the rigor of the season (it was the month of January), he plunged into the troubled sea, and swam there for half an hour. Imprudence no less fatal to him than to Alexander.* For it was then, undoubtedly, that he contracted the seeds of the malady which showed itself soon after, and under which he succumbed. At last he arrived at Missolonghi, without having ceased for one instant to be threatened by the sea. He was expected there as if he had been the Messiah, says Stanhope; and the consternation caused by the dangers he had gone through, gave place, on his arrival, to the most lively joy. Lord Byron met with a reception worthy of himself.† But this enthusiastic joy, which found expression in songs as well as tears, subjected his patience and good-nature to another sort of trial.

"After eight days of such fatigue," says Count Gamba, "he had scarcely time to refresh himself, and converse with Mavrocordato, and his friends and countrymen, before he was assailed by the tumultuous visits of the primates and chiefs. These latter, not content with coming all together, each had a suite of twenty or thirty, and not unfrequently, fifty soldiers! It was difficult to make them understand that he had fixed certain hours to receive them. Their visits began at seven in the morning, and the greater part of them were without any object." This is one of the most insupportable annoyances to which a man of influence and consideration is exposed in the East.

"*I saw Lord Byron bear all this with the greatest patience.*"

* Alexander the Great imprudently bathed in the Cydnus, etc.

† "Life in Italy." See how he was received at Missolonghi.

Could an irritable temper have done so? For my part, I think that this journey alone, borne, as we have seen, by his letters and the unanimous testimony of his companions, with such perfect good-humor, that he could jest, be quite resigned to unavoidable evils, show indulgence to the faults of others, however great the sufferings entailed thereby on himself; and display great self-denial, strength of mind, and imperturbable serenity, amid frightful dangers; all these qualities, I say, paint the moral nature of the man better than all analyses and commentaries.

But alas! while displaying his virtues, this journey also brings out his faults: since, prudent in behalf of others, he was not at all so for himself; and his want of prudence planted in him the germs of the disease which was so soon to be fatally developed in that stifling atmosphere of Greece, then full of tumult and confusion. If the limits of this chapter allowed, we could multiply proofs of his naturally amiable disposition at all periods of his life; and we would show what he was in Switzerland, at Venice, Ravenna, Pisa, Genoa, and in Greece, up to his last hour, as he has been described by Shelley, Hoppner, M. de G——, Medwin, Lady B——, and so many others. But to those who have said he was irritable because, feeling himself susceptible of irritation and anger, he declared himself to be so, I will content myself with answering simply by a few lines borrowed from the truthful conversations of Mr. Kennedy:—

"Even during his last days on earth, he calumniated himself. For instance, he told me, that at a certain hour, every evening, he had intolerable fits of ill-humor. Well, Mr. Finlay and M—— always went to see him precisely at that fatal hour, and they invariably found him gay, pleasant, and amiable, as usual."

Mr. Finlay, a young English officer of merit and high intelligence, whom Lord Byron thought very like Shelley, which, perhaps, increased his sympathy for him, and who only knew him two months before his death, says, in a letter written on Lord Byron to Colonel Stanhope:—

"What astonished me most was the indifference with which Lord Byron spoke to us of all the lying reports his enemies spread against him. He gave his vindication and explanation with as much calm frankness as if it had concerned another person."

And he declares his astonishment at seeing him submit to the lessons of morality, and the censures on his opinions and principles which Kennedy, in his extreme orthodoxy, made him undergo.*

I will also add, that Lord Byron was often heard to say that he had been in a frightful rage with his servants; but, if they were questioned, *they knew nothing at all about it.* It is known, moreover, that his toleration and gentleness with them almost exceeded due bounds, and that, even when he had serious cause for chiding them, his severest reprimands were conveyed in jests and pleasantries.

Persons who will not change their convictions, go so far as to say,—"Well, be it so. We admit that he may have been calumniated in his private life, and that his strange fancy of speaking against himself may have contributed toward it. But how do you explain the anger expressed by his pen? Do you forget his misanthropical invectives, his personal attacks, his 'Avatar,' his epigrams?"

And I answer them:—"Do you forget that there are different kinds of anger? some that can never be vicious, and others that can never be virtuous? The anger expressed by his pen—the sole kind that was real with him—requires to be explained, not excused or forgotten."

"Let us beware," says a great contemporary philosopher, "of him who is never irritated, and can not understand the existence of a noble anger."†

Be so good as to examine, without preconceived opinions, and without prejudice, the nature of every kind of anger he displayed; see if any were personal, egotistical, or whether they did not rather spring from some noble cause; whether they were not rather the generous explosions of a soul burning with indignation at evil and injustice, because it ever held in view the contrast afforded by an ideal of its own that was only too perfect?

It is impossible, for instance, not to see that his pen was guided by one of these generous impulses when he spoke of Lord Castlereagh. He had no personal, malevolent, interest-

* Parry, 215. † Jules Simon.

ed antipathy toward this gay and fashionable nobleman. His pen was inspired simply by his conscience, that revolted at sight of the evils which he attributed to Lord Castlereagh's policy. It was not the colleague, but the minister, that he wished to stigmatize together with his policy, which appeared to Lord Byron inhuman, selfish, and unjust. It was this same policy that caused Pitt to say:—

"If we were just for one hour, we should not live a day." And again:—"Perish every principle rather than England!"

What other statesman did Lord Byron attack except Castlereagh? But him he did detest with a noble hatred.

"By what right do you attack Lord C——?" he was asked.

"By the right," he replied, "that every honest man has to denounce the minister who ruins his country, and treads under foot every sentiment of equity and humanity."

A few days before setting out on his last journey to Greece, he said to an English lady passing through Genoa:—

"With regard to Lord Castlereagh personally, whom you hear that I have attacked, I can only say that a bad minister's memory is as much an object of investigation as his conduct while alive. He is a matter of history; and wherever I find a tyrant or a *villain*, I will mark him. I attacked him no more than I had the right to do, and than was necessary.

"Do not defend me, you will only make yourself enemies —mine are neither to be diminished nor softened."

When Lord Byron wrote about Lord Castlereagh, imagination beheld in him the author of all the evils inflicted on Ireland, the man who through a selfish feeling of nationality, dangerous even to England, had riveted the chains of all Europe.

"If he spoke and wrote thus of Lord Castlereagh," says Kennedy himself, "the reason was that he really thought him an enemy to the true interests of his country; and this sentiment, carried perhaps to excess, made him consider it just to condemn him to the execration of humanity."*

What I have said with regard to his attacks on Lord Castlereagh, may equally apply to all the satire hurled against other individuals, against governments and nations. His

* Kennedy, 330.

benevolence was so great and universal, that it rendered the idea of the sufferings endured by humanity quite intolerable to him. His love of justice likewise was so great, that he became thoroughly indignant at seeing what he worshiped trampled under foot by individual or national selfishness, while deceit and injustice were reigning triumphant. Lord Byron conceived a sort of hatred and dislike for the wicked, and those who voluntarily prevented the well-being of men. And when thus indignant at some injustice, if he snatched up a pen, he could not help expressing himself with a certain kind of violence, in order to chastise, if he could not change, the guilty men who martyrized Ireland, crushed and degraded Italy, and condemned England to the hatred of the whole world. The sparkling, witty strain, mocking at all human things, which had served as a weapon for his reason while asserting the interests of truth and injustice in Italy, and protesting against folly and evil, no longer sufficed him then. He required to brand with fire the limit where folly stops and crime begins. Thus it was not mocking, joking satire he would inflict on these great culprits; but burning words to mark the limits where this should stop, and stigmatize them by condemning moral deformity. This is what he did, and wished to do, with regard to Castlereagh, and also with regard to the Austrians in Italy. Shall it be said that his language was occasionally too violent; that the punishment went beyond the crime? But, in the first place, condemnation was pronounced in the language of poetry; and then, does not appreciation of the measure kept depend solely on the point of view taken by reason and conscience when they sat in judgment?

Shall it be said that the moral sense of these invectives was not always brought forward with all the clearness desirable? But let them be examined attentively, and then the fine sentiments to which they owe their origin will be understood.

Let us read "Avatar," for instance,—"Avatar," teeming with noble anger,—and say if any poetry exists emitting flame and light purer, and more intense in its moral life, more efficacious for keeping within the boundaries of that humane just policy from which Lord Byron never swerved.

If, in the war he waged against evil and its perpetrators, he did not outstep the limits of merited punishment, nevertheless he often did go beyond the limits of a quality (he possessed not) which is raised to the rank of a virtue, but which applied, despite conscience, to our personal interests, is but selfishness and cowardice. And therein was he truly sublime; for in attacking thus, not only the great men of the day, but likewise the prejudices, idolatries, and passions belonging to such a proud nation, he well knew the harm that would result to himself. But Lord Byron was a real hero. So soon as his conscience spoke, he heard no other voice, but kept his glance fixed on the light of justice and truth beaming at the end of his career. Without looking to the right or to the left, without taking into account the obstacles and dangers which personal prudence counselled him to avoid, he held on his course; exposed his noble breast to British vengeance pursuing him across the Channel and the Alps, and then also to Genevan and Austrian shafts that flew back again across the Alps and the Channel on the wings of dark, fierce calumny.

Still I do not pretend to assert that, on some rare occasions, personal suffering did not give rise to irritation and anger. He belonged to humanity; and if, despite the harsh trials to which his sensibility was exposed, he had escaped entirely from nature's laws, he would have been not only heroic, but superhuman.

It is then very possible that, in the sad days preceding, accompanying, and following on his separation from Lady Byron, he may have been irritable. Such a host of evils overwhelmed him at once! He may have allowed to escape his lips at that time some drops of the ocean of bitterness with which his soul was overflowing. It is certain also that when the Edinburgh critics made such cruel havoc with his heart and mind, the over-excitement caused by this review had likewise for its source the wounds inflicted on his self-love. Can we be astonished at it, when we reflect that this senseless, wicked criticism succeeded to, and contrasted strangely with, the praises awarded by such judges as Mackenzie and Lord Woodhouse? They both had expressed their admiration spontaneously, and without knowing the writer: one of them was the celebrated author of the "Man of Feeling," and the other had brought out many esteemed works, and was considered to be at the head of Scottish literature. Besides, these cutting criticisms followed close on the strong admiration expressed by his friends, by all the society in which he was then moving, and by a mother who idolized him! These verses, though not yet the highest expression of his genius, were certainly full of charming tenderness, grace, and naïve sensibility; moreover, they had been given to the public in such a modest way by a man so young that he might almost be called a child! If he were not conscious of his great superiority, of which he must nevertheless have felt some prophetic presentiment — restrained, doubtless, by modesty and timidity,—he must at least have been conscious that he had not, in any way, merited the brutality displayed in attacks which violated all the laws of just and allowable criticism.

Lord Byron's soul revolted at it, and in his indignation repelling assault by assault, he overstepped his aim; for he certainly went to extremes. And yet, in the very paroxysm of such irritation, was a personal sentiment his first incentive? No! it was a good, generous, affectionate feeling that actuated him: fear lest his mother should be grieved at what had occurred.

He had scarcely been told how biting the criticism was, and he had not read it, when he hastened to write to his friend Beecher:—

"Tell Mrs. Byron not to be out of humor with them, and to prepare her mind for the greatest hostility on their part. It will do no injury whatever, and I trust her mind will not be ruffled. They defeat their object by indiscriminate abuse, and they never praise, except the partisans of Lord Holland and Co. It is nothing to be abused when Southey and Moore share the same fate."

In assuming this philosophical calm, which he really did arrive at later, but which he was very far from possessing at this time,—in forcing this language on his just resentment to console his mother, when his whole being was agitated, he certainly made one of those efforts which betoken a soul as vigorous as it was beautiful. He used his pen as soon as he had satisfied this first want of his heart; but the intensity of passion destroyed his equilibrium.

When at Ravenna he wrote:—

"I recollect well the effect that criticism produced on me; it was rage, and resistance, and redress, but not despondency nor despair. A savage review is hemlock to a sucking author; the one on me knocked me down—but I got up again. This criticism was a master-piece of low jests, a tissue of coarse invectives. It contained many commonplace expressions, lowlived insults; for instance, that one should be grateful for what one got; that a gift horse ought not to be looked at in the mouth, and other stable vocabulary; but that did not frighten me. I resolved on giving the lie to their predictions, and on showing them, that, however discordant my voice, it was not the last time they were to hear it."

But when this heat had passed away, his innate passion for that justice so cruelly violated toward himself, made him quickly recover his self-possession. He repented having written this satire, which he designated as insensate, and wished to suppress it. He even judged it more severely than others.

He wrote to Coleridge in 1815:—

"You mention my satire, lampoon, or whatever you like to call it. I can only say, that it was written when I was very young and very angry, and has been *a thorn in my side ever since:* more particularly as almost all the persons animadverted upon became subsequently my acquaintances, and some of them my friends, which is heaping fire on an enemy's head, and forgiving me too readily to permit me to forgive myself. The part applied to you is pert, and petulant, and shallow enough; but, although I have long done every thing in my power to suppress the circulation of the whole thing, I shall always regret the wantonness or generality of its attempted attacks."*

On examining his conscience with regard to this satire, and passing judgment on himself, he adds, in a note to his own verses, after having given great praise to Jeffrey for his magnanimity, etc.:—

"*I was really too ferocious—this is mere insanity.*—B., 1816."

* Moore, vol. iii. p. 159.

And farther on:—

"*This is bad; because personal.*—B., 1816."

With regard to his verses on his guardian, Lord Carlisle, so culpable toward himself, he generously remarks:

"*Wrong also—the provocation was not sufficient to justify such acerbity.*—B., 1816."

To what he said against Wordsworth he simply adds the word, "*Unjust.*"

And again, with reference to Lord Carlisle:—

"*Much too savage, whatever the foundation may be.*—B., 1816."

And at Geneva, 14th of July, 1816, he writes:—

"*The greater part of this satire I most sincerely wish had never been written:* not only on account of the injustice of much of the critical and some of the personal part of it, but the tone and temper are such as I can not approve.—BYRON, *Villa Diodati*, 1816."

Lastly, from Venice he wrote to Murray, who wished to make a superior edition of his works:—

"With regard to a future large edition, you may print all, or any thing, *except* '*English Bards*,' to the republication of which at no time will I consent. I would not reprint them on any consideration. I don't think them good for much, even in point of poetry; and, as to other things, you are to recollect that I gave up the publication on account of the Hollands, and I do not think that any time or circumstances should cancel the suppression. Add to which, that, after being on terms with almost all the bards and critics of the day, it would be savage at any time, but worst of all *now*,* to revive this foolish lampoon."

"Whatever may have been the faults or indiscretion of this satire," says Moore, "there are few who would now sit in judgment upon it so severely as did the author himself, on reading it over nine years after, when he had quitted England, never to return. The copy which he then perused is now in possession of Mr. Murray, and the remarks which he has scribbled over its pages are well worth transcribing. On the first leaf we find:—

* *Now* alludes to the ungenerous treatment received from many of these persons at the time of his separation.

"The binding of this volume is considerably too valuable for its contents. Nothing but the consideration of its being the property of another prevents me from consigning this miserable record of misplaced anger and indiscriminate acrimony to the flames. BYRON."

To this ample reparation offered on account of his early satire we must add the following paragraph, from the first letter he addressed to Sir Walter Scott, in 1812:—

"I feel sorry that you should have thought it worth while to notice the '*evil works of my nonage*,' as the thing is suppressed voluntarily; and your explanation is too kind not to give me pain. The satire was written when I was very young and very angry, and fully bent on displaying my wrath and my wit, and now I am haunted by the ghosts of my wholesale assertions. I can not sufficiently thank you for your praise."

Thus scrupulously did this conscientious man judge himself. And not only do we find him repeating the same fine sentiment a hundred times, but he caused the whole edition, then still in the hands of the publisher, to be destroyed, which of course entailed a great sacrifice of money. He became intimate with the principal personages whom he had attacked; and even, in order to testify that no resentment continued to exist in his mind against his guardian, Lord Carlisle, he seized the first opportunity that presented itself of writing in "Childe Harold" those pathetic generous lines on the death of his son, Major Howard. He acted just in the same way every time he thought he had any fault to repair. But could this same love of justice, that had guided him through life, have caused him equally to disavow what he said of Lord Castlereagh and of Ireland in "Avatar?" of Southey and the Austrians at Venice? or the greater part of the satirical traits contained in "Don Juan" and the "Age of Bronze?" I do not think so. I believe, even, that if on his death-bed, he had been asked to retract some of his writings, he would have answered as Pascal did. And this because the sentiment which under all circumstances guided his pen did not arise from any personal interest, but was only, to use the beautiful language of a great contemporary philosopher, "the indignation and revolt of the generous faculties of the soul, which, hurt by injustice, rose up proudly, to protest against human dignity, offended in one's own person or in that of others."

This sentiment not being capable of change, neither could its consequences bring any repentance. According to Lord Byron, Castlereagh was a scourge for mankind. Faithful to this opinion, as to all his great principles, he wrote to Moore in 1815:—

"I am sick at heart of politics and slaughters; and the luck which Providence is pleased to lavish on Lord Castlereagh, is only a proof of the little value the gods set upon prosperity, when they permit such rogues as he and that drunken corporal, old Bl——, to bully their betters. From this, however, Wellington should be excepted. He *is* a man, and the Scipio of our Hannibal."

Let people read the "Avatar," the eleventh octave and following of the dedication of "Don Juan," the forty-ninth and fiftieth stanzas of the ninth canto of "Don Juan," as well as the epigrams; and they will have a fair idea of the generous sentiments that provoked his indignation against the inhuman policy of this minister. They will understand why he wished to denounce him to the execration of posterity. As to his satirical verses and anger against the poet laureate, it has already been seen on whose side lay the fault, and how this jealous poet, through a combination of bad feelings, in which envy and revenge predominated, spared no means, no occasion, of doing him harm. Thus Lord Byron saw himself and his friends enveloped in one of those darksome conspiracies, forming a labyrinth of calumny, whence the purest innocence has no escape; and he felt that justice violated in the person of his friends, by a man unworthy of respect, required him, in justice, to brand the individual. And rightly did he so with his words of fire. When Ireland, that he would fain have seen heroic under misfortune, degraded herself by her conduct toward this minister and the king, on the occasion of their visit, he, touched with noble indignation, resolved to punish and warn her; and his "Avatar" expressed these fine sentiments. When the prince regent, after having shown himself a Liberal and a Whig, denied his part, betrayed his party, and leagued with the Tories, Lord Byron's noble indignation burst forth in his verses, and, whenever occasion offered, he stigmatized such unworthy conduct.

And a proof that it was the conduct of the individual, and not personal animosity, that guided his pen, may be found in the fact that a single ray of hope of seeing this moral deformity transformed into beauty, sufficed to make him change his tone immediately. When he learned the pardon that had just been granted by George the Fourth to the guilty Lord Edward Fitzgerald, he forgot all past offenses; his soul expanded to admiration and hope; and he composed that beautiful sonnet, which so well reveals the aspirations of his great heart:—

"To be the father of the fatherless,
To stretch the hand from the throne's height, and raise
His offspring, who expired in other days
To make thy sire's sway by a kingdom less,—
This is to be a monarch, and repress
Envy into unutterable praise.
Dismiss thy guard, and trust thee to such traits,
For who would lift a hand except to bless?
Were it not easy, sir, and is't not sweet
To make thyself beloved? and to be
Omnipotent by mercy's means? for thus
Thy sovereignty would grow but more complete:
A despot thou, and yet thy people free,
And by the heart, not hand, enslaving us."

Bologna, August 12, 1819.

And then, as if poetry did not suffice, he adds these lines in prose:—

"So the prince has annulled Lord E. Fitzgerald's condemnation. He deserves all praise, bad and good: it was truly a princely act."

All Lord Byron's expressions of indignation that have been attributed to anger, belong really to his disinterested, heroic, generous nature. We may convince ourselves of this by following him through life, beginning from childhood, at college, when he would plant himself in front of school tyrants, asking to share the punishments inflicted on his friend Peel, and always taking the part of his weak or oppressed companions; then, during his first youth, when an accumulation of unmerited griefs and injustice cast over him a shade of misanthropy, so contrary to his nature; and, lastly, up to the moment when that noble indignation burst forth which he experienced in Greece, and which hastened his end.*

This is the truth. Nevertheless, if, in early youth, he did sometimes go beyond the limits of what may be fairly conceded to extreme sensibility,—to a certain hypochondriacal tendency of race, and more especially of his intellectual life; if he really was sometimes wearied, fatigued, discouraged, inclined to irritation, and to view things darkly, can it, therefore, be said that he weakly gave way to a morbid disposition? By no means. He always wished to sift his conscience thoroughly,—never ceased analyzing causes and symptoms, proclaiming his state morbid, and blaming himself beyond measure, far beyond what justice warranted, for a single word that had escaped his lips under the pressure of intense suffering. And even in the few moments of impatience occasioned by his last illness, he said, "Do not take the language of a sick man for his real sentiments." Lastly, he never gave over struggling against himself; seeking to acquire dominion over his faculties and passions intellectually by hard study, and materially by the strictest régime. What could he do more? it may be said. But if it be true that he had been irritable in his youth, that would only show how much he achieved; for he must have conquered himself immensely, since at Venice, Ravenna, Pisa, Genoa, and in Greece, he certainly displayed no traces of temper, and all those causes which usually excite irritation and anger in others had quite ceased to produce any in him.

"A mild philosophy," says the Countess G——, "every day more and more took possession of his soul. Adversity and the companionship of great thoughts strengthened him so much, that he was able to cast off the yoke of even ordinary passions, only retaining those among the number which impel to good.†

"I have seen him sometimes at Ravenna, Pisa, Genoa, when receiving news of some stupid, savage attack, from those who, in violating justice, also did him considerable harm. No emotion of anger any longer mixed itself up with his generous indignation. He appeared rather to experience a

* See his "Life in Italy." † Ibid.

mixture of contempt, almost of quiet austere pleasure, in the struggle his great soul sustained against fools."

When Shelley saw him again at Venice, in 1818, and painted him under the name of Count Maddalo, he said:—

"In social life there is not a human being *gentler*, *more patient*, *more natural, and modest*, than Lord Byron. He is gay, open, and witty; his graver conversations steep you in a kind of inebriation. He has travelled a great deal, and possesses ineffable charm when he relates his adventures in the different countries he has visited."

Mr. Hoppner, English consul at Venice, and Lord Byron's friend, who was living constantly with him at this time, sums up his own impressions in these remarkable terms:—

"Of one thing I am certain, that I never met with goodness more real than Lord Byron's."

And some years later, when Shelley saw Lord Byron again at Ravenna, he wrote to Mrs. Shelley:—

"Lord Byron has made great progress in all respects; in genius, *temper*, moral views, health, and happiness. His intimacy with the Countess G—— has been of inestimable benefit to him. A fourth part of his revenue is devoted to beneficence. He has conquered his passions, and become what nature meant him to be, *a virtuous man.*"

In concluding these quotations, no longer requisite, I hope, I will only make one last observation, *that all which infallibly changes in a bad nature never did change in him.* Friendship, real love, all devoted feelings, lived on in him *unchanged* to his last hour. If he had had a bad disposition, been capricious, irritable, or given to anger, would this have been the case?

CHAPTER XVIII.

LORD BYRON'S MOBILITY.

So much has been said of Lord Byron's mobility that it is necessary to analyze it well, and examine it under different aspects, so as to define and bring it within due limits. In the first place, we may ask on what grounds his biographers rested their opinion of this extraordinary mobility, which, according to them, went beyond the scope of intellectual qualities rather into the category of faults of temper? Evidently it was again through accepting a testimony the small value of which we have already shown; namely, Lord Byron's own words at twenty-three years of age—that period when passion is hardly ever a regular wind, simply swelling sails, but rather a gusty tempest, tearing them to pieces; and then again they grounded their opinion on verses in "Don Juan," where he explains the meaning of these expressions,—versatility and mobility. Moore, from motives we shall examine hereafter, found it expedient to take Lord Byron at his word, and to make a great fuss about this quality. In summing up his character, he reasons very cleverly on the unexampled extent, as he calls it, of this faculty, and the consequences to which it led in Lord Byron. Following in Moore's wake, other biographers have proclaimed Lord Byron versatile. Moore exaggerates so far as to pretend that this faculty made it almost impossible to find a dominant characteristic in Lord Byron. As if mobility were not, in reality, a universal quality or defect,—as if men could so govern themselves throughout life as to resemble the hero of a drama, where the action is confined within classical rules.

"A man possessing the highest order of mind is, nevertheless, unequal," says La Bruyère. "He suffers from increase and diminution; he gets into a good train of thought, and falls out of it likewise.

"It is different with an automaton. Such a man is like a machine,—a spring. Weight carries him away, making him move and turn forever in the same direction, and with equal motion. He is uniform, and never changes. Once seen, he appears the same at all times and periods of life. At best, he is but the ox lowing, or the blackbird whistling; he is fixed and stamped by nature, and I may say by species. What shows least in him is his soul; that never acts,—is never brought into play,—perpetually reposes. Such a man will be a gainer by death."

La Bruyère also says, "There is a certain mediocrity that helps to make a man appear wise."

And what says Montaigne, that great connoisseur of the human heart?—

"Our usual custom is to go right or left, over mountains or valleys, just as we are drifted by the wind of opportunity. We change like that animal which assumes the color of the spots where it is placed. All is vacillation and inconstancy. We do not walk of ourselves; we are carried away like unto things that float now gently and now impetuously, according to the uncertain mood of the waters. Every day some new fancy arises, and our tempers vary with the weather. This fluctuation and contradiction ever succeeding in us, has caused it to be imagined by some that we possess two souls; by others, that two faculties are perpetually at work within us, one inclining us toward good, and the other toward evil."

Montaigne also says:—"I give my soul sometimes one appearance, and sometimes another, according to the side on which I look at it; if I speak variously of myself, it is because I look at myself variously: all contrarieties, in one degree or other, are found in me, according to the number of turns given. Thus I am shamefaced, insolent, chaste, sensual, talkative, taciturn, laborious, delicate, ingenious, stupid, sad, good-natured, deceitful, true, learned, ignorant, liberal, avaricious, and prodigal, just according to the way in which I look at myself; and whoever studies himself attentively, will find this *variety and discordancy* even in his judgment.

"We are all *parts of a whole,* and formed of such shapeless, mixed materials, that every part and every moment does its own work."

If, then, we all experience the varied influences of our passions a hundred times in a lifetime, not to say in every twenty-four hours; if we are sensible of a thousand physical and moral causes, perpetually modifying our dispositions, and our words, making us differ to-day from what we were yesterday; if even the coldest and most stoical temperaments do not wholly escape from these influences, how could Moore be surprised that Lord Byron, who was so sensitive and full of passion, so hardly used by men and Providence, that he should not prove invulnerable? Moore was not surprised at it in reality, it is true; he only made-believe to be so, and that because Lord Byron was wanting in some of those virtues called peculiarly English. Lord Byron had no superstitious patriotism; he did not love his country through sentiment or passion, but on duty and principle. He loved her, but justice also! and he loved justice best. And in order to do homage to truth, he had committed the fault of saying a host of irreverential truths concerning that country, and also many individuals belonging to it; consequently he had made many enemies for himself. Indeed, his enemies might be found in every camp: among the orthodox, in the literary world, and the world of fashion, among the fair sex, and in the political world. Moore, for his part, wished to live in peace with all these potentates,—the warm, comfortable, and brilliant atmosphere of their society had become a necessity for him; and wishing also, perhaps, to obtain pardon for his friend's boldness, he probably thought to conciliate all things by sparing the susceptibility of the great. Instead, then, of attributing Lord Byron's severe appreciations to observation, experience, and serious reflection, he preferred declaring them the result of capricious and inconsistent mobility. But more just in the depths of his soul than he was in words, Moore, it is easy to see, felt painfully conscious of the wrong done to his illustrious friend, and ardently wished to make his own weakness tally with truth. What was the result? The brilliant edifice he had raised was so unstable of basis, that it could not stand the logic of facts and conclusions. While appearing to consider the excess of this quality as a defect, and calling it dangerous, he was all the time showing that Lord Byron had strength to overcome any real danger it contained; he was giving it to be understood that this versatility of intellect might exist without the least mobility of principle; he made out that mobility was the ornament of his intelligence, just as he had shown constancy to be the ornament of his soul. Then, after having reasoned cleverly on this quality, yclept versatility when applied to the intelligence, and mobility when applied to conduct; after having shown how predominant it must have been in Lord Byron through his great impressionability; Moore says that Lord Byron did yield to his versatile humor, without scruple or resistance, in all things attracting his mind, in all the excursions of reason or fancy assuming all the forms in which his genius could manifest its power, transporting himself into all the regions of thought where there were any new conquests to make; and that thereby he gave to the world a grand spectacle, displayed a variety of unlimited and almost contradictory powers, and finally achieved a succession of unexampled triumphs in every intellectual field. Then, in order to characterize completely this quality of Lord Byron, Moore further adds:—

"It must be felt, indeed, by all readers of that work, and particularly by those who, being gifted with but a small portion of such ductility themselves, are unable to keep pace with his changes, that the suddenness with which he passes from one strain of sentiment to another, from the gay to the sad, from the cynical to the tender,—begets a distrust in the sincerity of one or both moods of mind which interferes with, if not chills, the sympathy that a more natural transition would inspire. In general, such a suspicion would do him injustice; as among the singular combinations which his mind presented, that of uniting at once versatility and depth of feeling was not the least remarkable."

But, throughout this analysis by Moore, do we see aught save an intellectual quality? Does it not stand out in relief, a pure, high attribute of genius? For this to be a defect, it would be necessary that, leaving the domain of intelligence, it should become mobility, by entering into the course of his daily life in *extraordinary* proportions. And how does it, in reality, enter there? Were his principles in politics, in religion, in all that constitutes the man of honor in the highest acceptation of the term, at all affected by it? Did his true affections, or even his simple tastes, suffer from the varied impresses of his versatile genius? In short, was Lord Byron inconstant? Moore has sufficiently answered, since all he remarked and said oblige us to rank *constancy* among Lord Byron's most shining virtues.* And as a human heart can not at the same time be governed by a virtue and its opposite vice, what must we say to those who should persist (for there are some, doubtless, who will), despite all axioms, in considering Lord Byron as a changeable, capricious, fickle man? I reply, that Lord Byron proved, once more, the truth of the observation made by that moralist, who said: "The most beautiful souls are those possessing the greatest variety and pliancy," and that he realized in himself, after a splendid fashion, the moral phenomenon remarked in *Cato the Elder*, who, according to Livy, possessed a mind at once so versatile and so comprehensive, that whatever he did it might be thought he was born solely for that.

I will acknowledge, then, the intellectual versatility and the mobility of Lord Byron, but on condition of their being reduced to their real proportions; of their being shown as they ever existed in him, that is to say, under subjection to duty, honor, and feeling. Through his extreme impressionability, and his power of combining, in the liveliest manner, the greatest contrasts, through the pleasure he took in exercising such extraordinary faculties, and in manifesting them to others, Lord Byron sometimes assumed such an appearance of skeptical indifference and caprice, that he might almost be said to show a certain intermission of faculties, and even of ideas. But if his words and writings are examined, it will be seen that this mobility was only skin-deep. It might affect his nerves and muscles, but did not penetrate into his system. It animated his writings occasionally, and oftener his words, *but never his actions!* for, if in some rare moments of life, he abandoned his will to the sway of light breezes, that was only for very evanescent fancies of youth, in which neither heart nor honor were at stake. And even then it was rather by word than by deed, as occurred at Newstead, when he was twenty years of age, and at Venice when he was twenty-eight. His energetic soul did not, like feebler natures, require inconstancy to awaken it. As to ideas, they were only change-

* See the chapter on "Constancy."

able in him, when they were by nature open to discussion or *accessory;* and they remained floating, until having been elaborated by his great reason, he could admit them into the small number of such as he considered chosen and indisputable. Then they found a sort of sanctuary in his mind, remaining there sacred and unmoved, just like his true sentiments of heart.

His mobility, thus limited and circumscribed within due bounds by unswerving principles and the dictates of an excellent heart, *was thus shorn of all danger*, and had for its first result to contribute toward producing that amiability and that wonderful fascination which he exercised over all those who came near him. Moore quotes, on this head, the words of Cooper, who, speaking of persons with a changeful intellectual temperament, says, that their society "*ought to be preferred in this world, for, all scenes in life having two sides, one dark and the other brilliant, the mind possessing an equal admixture of melancholy and vivacity, is the one best organized for contemplating both.*" Moore adds :—"It would not be difficult to show that to this readiness in reflecting all hues, whether of the shadows or the lights of our variegated existence, Lord Byron owed not only the great range of his influence as a poet, but those powers of *fascination* which he possessed as a man. This susceptibility, indeed, of immediate impressions, which in him were so active, lent a charm, of all others the most attractive, to his social intercourse, and brought whatever was most agreeable in his nature into play."

All those who knew him have said the same thing. This charm was the immediate consequence of his qualities; but they produced another result, that justice requires to be mentioned. Mobility being united in him with constancy and the most heroic firmness, added lustre to his soul through that great difficulty overcome which amounts to virtue. Moralists of all ages have generally found the virtue of constancy so rare, that they have said,—

"Wait for death to judge a man."

"In all antiquity," says Montaigne, "it would be difficult to find a dozen men who shaped their lives in a certain steady course which is the chief end of wisdom."

This is true as regards the generality of minds; but to overcome this difficulty, when one has a mind eager for emotion, variable, with width and depth capable of discerning simultaneously the for and against of every thing, and thus being necessarily exposed to perplexity of choice, it is surely marvellous if a mind so constituted be also constant. Now, Lord Byron personified this marvel. In him was seen the realization of that rare thing in nature, intellectual versatility combined with unswerving principle; mobility of mind united to a constant heart. In short, to sum up:—He possessed the amount of versatility requisite to manifest his genius under all its aspects; a degree of mobility most charming in social intercourse; and such constancy as is always estimable, always a virtue, and which, united to a temperament like his,* becomes positively wonderful.

* See the chapter on "Constancy."

CHAPTER XIX.

LORD BYRON'S MISANTHROPY AND SOCIABILITY.

LORD BYRON has also been accused of misanthropy. But what is a misanthrope? Since Lucian, this name has been bestowed on the man who owns no friend but himself; who looks upon all others as so many rogues, for whom relatives, friends, country, are but empty names; who despises fame, and aims at no distinction except that conferred by his strange manners, savage anger, and inhumanity.

When those who have known Lord Byron, and studied his life, compare him to this type, it may well be asked whether such persons be in their right understanding. The famous tower of Babel, and all the confusion ensuing, rise up to view.

The excess of absurdity may give way, however, to some little moderation in judgment. It will be said, for instance, that there are different kinds of misanthropy. Lucian's "Timon" does not at all resemble Molière's "Alceste:" Lord Byron's misanthropy was not like either of theirs; his was only of the kind that mars sociability, good temper, and other amiable qualities. In short, we shall be given to understand that Lord Byron is only accused of *having liked solitude too much, of having shunned his fellow-creatures too much, and thought too ill of humanity.*

But these modifications can not satisfy our conscience. Still too many reasons of astonishment may be offered to allow us to resist the desire of adding other facts and indisputable proofs to those already adduced in the chapter where we examined the nature and limits of his melancholy at all periods of life, and throughout all its phases.* This chapter might even suffice as a response to the above strange accusation.

A better answer still would be found in all the proofs we

* See chapter on "Melancholy and Gayety."

have given of his goodness, generosity, and humanity. Nevertheless, we think it right rather to appeal to the patience of our readers; so that they may consider with us, more especially, one of the peculiar aspects of Lord Byron's character; namely, his sociability.

That Lord Byron loved solitude, and that it was a want of his nature who can doubt? As a child, we know, his delight was to wander alone on the sea-shore, on the Scottish strand. At school, he was wont to withdraw from his beloved companions, and the games he liked so well, in order to pass whole hours seated on the solitary stone in the churchyard at Harrow, which has been fitly called *Byron's Tomb.* He himself describes these inclinations of his childhood in the "Lament of Tasso:"—

> "Of objects all inanimate I made
> Idols, and out of wild and lonely flowers,
> And rocks, whereby they grew, a paradise,
> Where I did lay me down within the shade
> Of waving trees, and dream'd uncounted hours,
> Though I was chid for wandering; and the wise
> Shook their white aged heads o'er me, and said,
> Of such materials wretched men were made."

Arrived at adolescence, he showed so little inclination to mix in society that his friends reproached him with his overweening love for solitude. Amid the gay dissipation of university life, he was often a prey to vague disquietude. Like the majority of great spirits that had preceded him at Cambridge,—Milton, Gray, Locke, etc.,—he did not enjoy his stay there. He even made a satire upon it in his early poems. At a later period, when he had acquired fame, at the very height of his triumphs, when he was *the observed of all observers,* he often caught himself dreaming on the happiness of escaping from fashionable society, and getting home; for, like Pope, he greatly preferred quiet reading to the most agreeable conversation.

All his life there were hours and days wherein his mind absolutely required this repose.

It may, then, truly be said that he loved solitude, and felt a real attraction for it. But would it be equally just to attribute this taste to melancholy, and then to call his melancholy *misanthropy?* Those who have deeply studied the nature of a certain order of genius, and the phases of its development, will discover something very different in the impulse that attracted the child Byron to the sea-shore in Scotland, and to the sepulchral stone shaded over by the tall trees of Harrow? They will see therein, not the melancholy apparent to vulgar eyes, but the forecast of genius, to be revealed sooner or later, and with a further promise, in the antipathy shown for the routine of schools, and especially of the University of Cambridge,—a suffocating atmosphere for genius, equally uncongenial to Milton, Dryden, Gray, and Locke, who all, like Lord Byron, and more bitterly than he, exercised their satiric vein on it. As for the slight attraction he sometimes showed for the world in his youth—in his seventeenth year—and which the excellent Mr. Beecher reproached him with, his feelings are too well defined by the noble boy himself for us to dare to substitute any words of ours in lieu of those used by him, in justification to his friend.

Dear Beecher, you tell me to mix with mankind;
  I can not deny such a precept is wise;
But retirement accords with the tone of my mind;
  I will not descend to a world I despise.

Did the senate or camp my exertions require,
  Ambition might prompt me at once to go forth;
And, when infancy's years of probation expire,
  Perchance, I may strive to distinguish my birth.

The fire in the cavern of Etna concealed
  Still mantles unseen in its secret recess:
At length in a volume terrific revealed,
  No torrent can quench it, no bounds can repress.

Oh! thus the desire in my bosom for fame
  Bids me live but to hope for posterity's praise.
Could I soar with the phœnix on pinions of flame,
  With him I would wish to expire in the blaze.

For the life of a Fox, of a Chatham the death,
  What censure, what danger, what woe would I brave!
Their lives did not end when they yielded their breath:
  Their glory illumines the gloom of their grave.

Yet why should I mingle in Fashion's full herd?
  Why crouch to her leaders, or cringe to her rules?
Why bend to the proud, or applaud the absurd,
  Why search for delight in the friendship of fools?

I have tasted the sweets and the bitters of love;
  In friendship I early was taught to believe;
My passion the matrons of prudence reprove;
  I have found that a friend may profess, yet deceive.

To me what is wealth?—it may pass in an hour,
If tyrant's prevail, or if Fortune should frown:
To me what is title? the phantom of power;
To me what is fashion?—I seek but renown.

Deceit is a stranger as yet to my soul:
I still am unpracticed to varnish the truth:
Then why should I live in a hateful control?
Why waste upon folly the days of my youth? 1806.

Thus it was the desire of fame that then engrossed his whole soul; the wish of adding some great action to illustrate a name already ennobled by his ancestors.

Subsequently, this ardent desire may have become weakened. Alas! he had been made to pay so dearly for satisfying it. But at the outset of his career this aspiration after glory, that belongs to the noblest souls, was the strongest impulse he had,—the one that often made him prefer the solitary exercise of intelligence to even the usual dissipation of youth, and when he did yield, like others, he punished himself by self-inflicted blame and contempt, often expressed in an imprudent, exaggerated manner.

Nevertheless, the paths that lead to glory are various, and trod by many; which should he choose? Then did he feel the further torment of uncertainty. His faculties were various, and he was to learn this to his cost. He was to feel, though vaguely, that he might just as well aspire to the civic as to the military crown; be an orator in the senate, or a hero on the field of battle.

Among all the careers presenting themselves before him, the one that flattered him least was to be an author or a literary man. But he was living in the midst of young men well versed in letters. Most of them amused themselves with making verses. To tranquillize his heart, and exercise his activity of mind, he also made some, but without attaching any great importance to them. These verses were charming; the first flower and perfume of a young, pure soul, devoted to friendship and other generous emotions. Nevertheless, a criticism that was at once malignant, unjust, and cruel, fell foul of these delightful, clever inspirations. The injustice committed was great. The modest, gentle, but no less sensitive mind of the youth was both indignant and overwhelmed at it. Other sorrows, other illusions dispelled, further increased his agitation, making a wound that might really have become misanthropy, had his heart been less excellent by nature. But it could not rankle thus in him, and his sufferings only resulted in making him quit England with less regret, and throw into his verses and letters misanthropical expressions, no sooner written than disavowed by the general tone of cordiality and good-humor that reigned throughout them; and, lastly, by suggesting the imprudent idea of choosing a misanthrope as the hero of the poem in which he was to sing his own pilgrimage.

This necessity of essaying and giving expression to his genius also made him desire solitude yet more. He found poetic loneliness beneath the bright skies of the East, where he pitched his tent, slowly to seek the road to that fame for which his soul thirsted. But when he arrived at it,—when he became transformed, so to say, into an idol,—did this necessity for solitude abandon him? By no means.

"*April* 10*th*.—I do not know that I am happiest when alone," he writes in his memoranda; "but this I am sure of, I never am long in the society even of her I love—and God knows how I love her—without a yearning for the company of my lamp and my library. Even in the day, I send away my carriage oftener than I use or abuse it."

This desire, this craving for his lamp and his library,—this absence of taste for certain realities of life,—show affinities between Lord Byron and another great spirit, Montaigne. One might fancy one hears Lord Byron saying, with the other:—

"The continual intercourse I hold with ancient thought, and the ideas caught from those wondrous spirits of by-gone times, disgust me with others and with myself."

He also felt *ennui* at living in an age that *only produced very ordinary things.*

But whether he felt happy or sad, it was always in silence, in retirement, and contemplation of the great visible nature, carrying his thought away to what does not the less exist though veiled from our feeble sight and intellect; it was there, I say, that his mind and heart sought strength, peace, and consolation.

His soul was bursting with mighty griefs when he arrived

in Switzerland, on the borders of Lake Leman. He loved this beautiful spot, but did not deem himself sufficiently alone to enjoy it fully.

> "There is too much of man here, to look through
> With a fit mind the might which I behold,"

said he; and he promised himself soon to arrive at that beloved solitude, so necessary to him for enjoying well the grand spectacle presented by Helvetian nature; but, he added:—

> "To fly from, need not be to hate, mankind:
> * * * * * *
> Nor is it discontent to keep the mind
> Deep in its fountain, lest it over boil
> In the hot throng."

And then he continues:—

> "I live not in myself, but I become
> Portion of that around me; and to me
> High mountains are a feeling."

Thus, even in the midst of the beloved solitude so necessary to him, there was no misanthropy in his thoughts or feelings, but simply the desire of not being disturbed in his studies and reveries. Lord Byron often said, that solitude made him better. He thought, on that head, like La Bruyère:—"*All the evil in us,*" says that great moralist, "*springs from the impossibility of our being alone. Thence we fall into gambling, luxury, dissipation, wine, women, ignorance, slandering, envy, forgetfulness of self, and of God.*" If the satisfaction of this noble want were to be called *misanthropy*, few of our great spirits, whether philosophers, poets, or orators, could escape the accusation. For, with almost all of them, the taste for retirement and solitude has been likewise a necessity: a condition without which we should have lost their greatest *chefs-d'œuvre.* The biography of the noblest minds leaves no doubt on this head. But if Lord Byron did not use solitude like a misanthrope, if he loved it solely as a means, and not as an end, so that we may even say it was with him an antidote to misanthropy, can we equally give proof of his sociability? To clear up this point, we have only to glance at his whole life. For the sake of avoiding repetition, let us pass over his childhood, so full of tenderness, and ardor for youthful pastimes; his boyhood, all devoted to feelings affectionate and passionate; his university life, where sociability seemed to predominate over regular study; the vacations, when it was such pleasure to act plays, and he was the life of amateur theatres,—a time that has left behind it such an enthusiastic memory of him, that when Moore, some years after Lord Byron's death, went to obtain information about it from the amiable Pigott family, not one member could be found to admit that Lord Byron *had the smallest defect.* Let us also pass over his sojourn at Newstead, when his sociability and gayety appear even to have been too noisy; and let us arrive at that period of his life when he began to be called a misanthrope, because he gave himself that appellation, because real sorrows had cast a shade over his life, and because, wishing to devote himself to graver things, his object was to withdraw from the society of gay, noisy companions, and then to mature his mind in distant travel. He left his native land, but in company with his friend Hobhouse, a man distinguished for his intelligence, and who, instead of testifying to his fellow-traveller's misanthropy, bears witness, on the contrary, to his amiable, sociable disposition.

When this friend was obliged to take leave of him in Greece, and return to England, Lord Byron frequented the society of pleasant persons like Lord Sligo, Mr. Bruce, and Lady Hester Stanhope, whom he met at Athens, alleviating his studious solitude by intercourse with them.

When he also returned to England, after two years of absence, great misfortunes overwhelmed him. He lost successively his mother, dear friends, and other loved ones. Not to sink beneath these accumulated blows, and mistrusting his own strength, he called in to aid him the society of his friends.

"My dear Scrope," wrote he, "if you have an instant, come and join me, I entreat you. I want a friend; I am in utter desolation. Come and see me; let me enjoy as long as I can the company of those friends that yet remain."

Some time after, having attained the highest popularity, and his mind being soothed by friendship even more than by fame, he entered into the fashionable society in which his rank entitled him to move.

He frequented the world very much at this period, cultivating it assiduously. A moment even came when he seemed to be completely absorbed by gayety. Sometimes going to as many as fourteen assemblies, balls, etc., in one evening. "He acknowledged to me," says Dallas, "that it amused him." Did not his genius suffer then from the new infatuation? So courted, flattered, and surrounded by temptations, did not this worldly life prove too seductive, hurtful to his mind, heart, and independence of character? Did he draw from the world's votaries his rules of judgment, his ways of thought? Did he yield when brought in contact with that terrible *English law of opinion?* No; Lord Byron was safe from all such dangers. Amid the vortex in which he allowed himself to be whirled along, his mind was never idle. In the drawing-rooms he frequented, his intellectual curiosity found field for exercise. Though so young, he had already reflected much on human nature in general; but he still required to study individuals. It was in society that his extraordinary penetration could find out true character, discover the reality lurking under a borrowed mask. The great world formed an excellent school to discipline his mind. There he found subjects for observation that he afterward put in order, and brought to maturity in retirement.

"Wherever he went," says Moore, "Lord Byron found field for observation and study. To a mind with a glance so deep, lively, and varied, every place, and every occupation, presented some view of interest; and, whether he were at a ball, in the boxing-school, or the senate, a genius like his turned every thing to advantage."

And if *salons* in general were powerless to exercise any bad influence over him, this impossibility was still greater with regard to London *salons*. Without adopting as exact the picture drawn of them by a learned academician,* in a book more witty than true, wherein we read:—"that under pain of passing for eccentric, of giving scandal or exciting alarm, English people are forbidden to speak of others or themselves, of politics, religion, or intellectual things or matters of taste; but only of the environs, the roundabouts, a picnic, a visit to some ruin, a fashionable preacher, a fox-hunt,

* M. Nisard.

and the rain,—that never-ending theme kindly furnished by the inconstant climate;" without, I say, adopting this picture as true, for in England it must be considered a clever caricature, it is nevertheless certain, that the discipline of fashionable London *salons* requires independence of mind to be in a measure sacrificed. The tone reigning in these *salons*, which are only opened during the season, is quite different from that produced by the open-hearted hospitality which renders English country residences so very agreeable. Could Lord Byron long take pleasure in the salons of the metropolis, where every thing is on the surface and noisy, where one may say that people are content with simply showing themselves, intending concealment all the while; or where they show themselves *what they are not;* where set forms, or a vocabulary of their own, so far limits allowable subjects of conversation, that fools may easily have the advantage over clever men (for intellect is looked upon as suspicious, dangerous, bold, and called an eccentricity). Lord Byron, so frank, and open-hearted, loving fame, and having a sort of presentiment that Heaven would not accord him sufficient time to reap his full harvest of genius, consequently regretting the moments he was forced to lose; must he not, after seeking amusement in these assemblies, soon have found that they lasted too long, and were too fatiguing? Must he not often have well-nigh revolted against himself, felt something cold and heavy restraining his outburst of soul, something like a sort of slavery; must he not have understood that it was requisite for him to escape from such useless pastimes in order to re-invigorate himself by study, in the society of his own thoughts, and those of the master-spirits of ages? Yes, Lord Byron did experience all that. *Ennui* of the world called him back to solitude. We can not doubt it, he said so himself:—

"Last night, *party* at Lansdowne House; to-night, party at Lady Charlotte Greville's—*deplorable waste of time*, and loss of *temper*, *nothing imparted*, *nothing acquired—talking without ideas*—if any thing like thought were in my mind, it was not on the subjects on which we were gabbling. Heigho! and in this way half London pass what is called life. To-morrow, there is Lady Heathcote's—shall I go? Yes; to punish myself for not having a pursuit."

And, elsewhere :—

"Shall I go to Lansdowne's? to the Berry's? They are all pleasant; but I don't know, I don't think that *soirées* improve one."

He will not go into the world :—

"I don't believe this worldly life does any good; how could such a world ever be made? Of what use are dandies, for instance, and kings, and fellows at college, and women of a certain age, and many men of my age, myself foremost?"

Having changed his apartments, he had not yet got all his books; was reading without order, composing nothing; and he suffered in consequence. "I must set myself to do something directly; my heart already begins to feed on itself." He accuses himself of not profiting enough by time. "Twenty-six years of age! I might and ought to be a Pasha at that age. '*I 'gin to be weary of the sun.*'" But let him be with a clever friend, like Moore, for instance, and, oh! then the *ennui* of salons becomes metamorphosed into pleasure for him, without taking away his clearsightedness as to the world's worth.

"Are you going this evening," writes he to Moore, "to Lady Cahir's? I will, if you do; and wherever we can unite in follies, let us embark on the *same ship of fools.* I went to bed at five, and got up at nine."

And elsewhere, after having expressed his disappointment at seeing Moore so little during the season, he calls London "a populous desert, where one should be able to keep one's thirst like the camel. *The streams are so few, and for the most part so muddy.*"

And ten years later, in the fourteenth canto of "Don Juan," he said, speaking of fashionable London society :—

"Although it seems both prominent and pleasant,
There is a sameness in its gems and ermine.
A dull and family likeness through all ages,
Of no great promise for poetic pages.

XVI.

"With much to excite, there's little to exalt;
Nothing that speaks to all men and all times;
A sort of varnish over every fault;
A kind of commonplace, even in their crimes;

Factitious passions, wit without much salt,
 A want of that true nature which sublimes
Whate'er it shows with truth; a smooth monotony
Of character, in those at least who have got any.

XVII.

"Sometimes, indeed, like soldiers off parade,
 They break their ranks and gladly leave the drill;
But then the roll-call draws them back afraid,
 And they must be or seem what they were: still
Doubtless it is a brilliant masquerade;
 But when of the first sight you have had your fill,
It palls—at least it did so upon me,
This paradise of *pleasure and ennui.*"

It was thus that he judged what is called the great world, the fashionable crowd. Yet never having ceased to frequent it, he also might have said, with Plutarch:—"My taste leads me to fly the world; but the gentleness of my nature brings me back to it again."

The best proof, however, of his sociable disposition does not lie in this fact of his going much to great assemblies, since he submitted to, rather than sought after that; it consists in the pleasure he always took in the society of friends, and those whom he loved; in the want of *intimacy* which he ever experienced. In such quiet little circles he was truly himself, quite different to what he appeared in salons. Then only could he be really known. His wit, gayety, and simplicity were unveiled solely for friends and intimates. He, so light-hearted, became serious amid the forced laughter of drawing-rooms; he, so witty, waxed silent and gloomy amid unmeaning conventional talkativeness. Those who only saw him in salons, or on fashionable staircases, during the four years he passed in England, did not really know him; is it surprising that he should have been wrongly judged? Moore alone has tolerably well described the agreeable, sociable, gay, kind being Lord Byron was.

When he quitted England, his sociable disposition did not abandon him, though his soul was filled with bitterness. He had scarcely arrived at Geneva, when he became intimate with Shelley. He made him the companion of his walks, passed whole days and evenings in his society, and that of his amiable wife. Several London friends came to join him in Switzerland. In his excursions over the Alps, Lord

Broughton (then Mr. Hobhouse) was always his faithful companion. He frequented and appreciated then, more than he had ever done before in England, the society of Madame de Staël at Coppet, because it was there and not in drawing-rooms that this noble-hearted woman showed herself what she was. Always attracted by high intellect, he became intimate with Count Rossi, entertaining so great a sympathy for him, that often when the count was about to leave him and return to Geneva, Lord Byron retained him by his entreaties. As to the natives of Geneva, as he detested Calvinism, and knew that they believed the calumnies wickedly spread abroad against him by some of his country-people, he did not see them often, for he did not like them. "What are you going to do in that den of honest men," said he one day to Count Rossi, who was preparing to leave. On arriving at Milan; he immediately adopted the style of life usual there. Every evening he went to the theatre, occupying M. de Breme's box, together with a group of young and clever men; among them I may name Silvio Pellico, Abbé de Breme, Monti, Porro, and Stendhal (Beyle), who have all unanimously testified to his amiability, social temper, and fascinating conversation. At Venice, he allowed himself to be presented in the most hospitable mansions of the nobility; particularly distinguishing those where Countess Albruzzi and Countess Benzoni presided, for he always went to one or other of these ladies after leaving the theatre. Nor did he disdain, during the early part of his stay at Venice, even the official salon of the Comtesse de Goetz. But his aversion for Austrian oppression and the perfidy of the official press soon obliged him to withdraw; for the oppressors of Venice, knowing him to be a formidable enemy, sought to discredit him by spreading all sorts of calumnious reports against him and his private character.*

It has been seen in his "Life in Italy" how he divided his time at Venice, and the impression he made wherever there had not been a preconceived purpose of judging him unfavorably. In the morning, his first walk was always directed toward the convent of the Armenian Fathers, in the island of San Lazzaro. He went there to study their lan-

* See his "Life in Italy."

guage; and these good monks conceived an extreme affection for him. Afterward he would cross the Laguna going to the Lido, where his stables were. He was accustomed to ride on horseback with the different friends who chanced to arrive from England: such as Hobhouse, Monk Lewis, Rose, Kinnaird, Shelley, and more particularly still with Mr. Hoppner, Consul-general for England at Venice, a man of the noblest stamp, much beloved by Lord Byron, and who, in the account he has left of this intercourse, can not find words adequate for expressing all he wished to say of the charming social qualities Lord Byron displayed at Venice. "*People have no idea*," says he, "*of Lord Byron's gayety, vivacity, and* amiability." He followed Italian customs, went every evening to the theatre, where his box was always filled with friends and acquaintances; and after that, generally spent the remainder of the evening or night, according to the then custom of Venice, in the most distinguished circles of the town, principally at the houses of Countess Albruzzi and Countess Benzoni, where he was not only welcome, but so much liked, that these salons were voted dull when he did not appear. Lastly, his social qualities and amiability gave so much pleasure at Venice, and the inhabitants were so desirous of keeping him among them, that his departure for Ravenna actually stirred up malice, quite foreign to the usual simplicity characterizing Venetian society.*

The friends who came to see him there,—Hobhouse, Lewis, Kinnaird, Shelley, Rose, etc.,—succeeded each other at short intervals, and their arrivals were so many fêtes for him. But while he was leading this sociable life, vulgar tourists, who had not been able to succeed in getting presented to him, took their revenge, by repeating in every direction fables they had gleaned from the gondoliers for a few pence—viz., that Lord Byron was a misanthrope and hated his countrymen. Mr. Hoppner, who was an ocular witness of the life which Lord Byron led at Venice, and whose testimony is so worthy of respect, told Moore how much annoyance Lord Byron endured from English travellers, bent on following him everywhere, eyeglass in hand, staring at him with impertinence or affectation during his walks, getting into his palace under some pretext, and even penetrating into his bedroom.

* See his "Life in Italy."

"Thence," says he, "his bitterness toward them. The sentiments he has expressed in a note termed cynical, as well as the misanthropical expressions to be found in his first poems, *are not at all his natural sentiments.*"

And then he adds that he is very certain "*never to have met with in his lifetime more real goodness than in Lord Byron.*"

Moore, also, is indignant at all these perfidious inventions:—

"Among those minor misrepresentations," says he, "of which it was Lord Byron's fate to be the victim, advantage was at this time taken of his professed distaste to the English, to accuse him of acts of inhospitality, and even rudeness, toward some of his fellow-countrymen. How far different was his treatment of all who ever visited him, many grateful testimonies might be collected to prove; but I shall here content myself with selecting a few extracts from an account given to me by Mr. Joy, of a visit which, in company with another English gentleman, he paid to the noble poet, during the summer of 1817, at his villa on the banks of the Brenta. After mentioning the various civilities they had experienced from Lord Byron; and, among others, his having requested them to name their own day for dining with him: —'We availed ourselves,' says Mr. Joy, 'of this considerate *courtesy* by naming the day fixed for our return to Padua, when our route would lead us to his door; and we were welcomed with all the cordiality which was to be expected from so friendly an invitation. Such traits of kindness in such a man deserve to be recorded on account of the numerous slanders heaped upon him by some of the tribes of tourists, who resented, as a personal affront, his resolution to avoid their impertinent inroads upon his retirement.

"'So far from any appearance of indiscriminate aversion to his countrymen, his inquiries about his friends in England were most anxious and particular.

"'After regaling us with an excellent dinner (in which, by-the-by, a very English joint of roast-beef showed that he did not extend his antipathies to all John Bullisms), he took us in his carriage some miles on our route toward Padua, after apologizing to my fellow-traveller for the separation, on the score of *his anxiety to hear all he could of his friends in England:* and I quitted him with a confirmed impression of the strong ardor and sincerity of his attachment to those by whom he did not fancy himself slighted or ill-treated!'"

It has been seen elsewhere* that Mr. Rose, speaking of Lord Byron's sociable temper at Venice, said *his presence sufficed to diffuse joy and gayety in the salons he frequented.*"

When any worthy persons among his countrymen arrived, his *house*, his *time*, his *purse* were at *their service.*

For further proof, let people only read the details Captain Basil Hall gave Murray of his intercourse with Byron.

"*His witty, clever conversation,*" says Shelley, who visited him at Venice in 1817, "*enlivened our winter nights and taught me to know my own soul. Day dawned upon us, ere we perceived with surprise that we were still listening to him.*"

When he went from Venice to Romagna, he passed by Ferrara. But though eager to arrive where his heart summoned him, he did not fail delivering the letters of introduction given him by friends. At Ferrara he made the acquaintance of a noble family, and went into society there, speaking of it afterward in the most flattering manner.†

At Ravenna, he frequented all the salons where he was introduced; and at the request of Count G——, became the *cavaliere servente* of the young countess. According to the custom of the country, he accompanied her to assemblies or theatres, or spent his evenings in her family circle. At Pisa, he held aloof from the world, because his friends, the Gambas, who had taken refuge there in consequence of the troubles and political enmities existing in Romagna, did not wish to mix in society. But he passed all his evenings regularly with them, either at their house, or sometimes dispensing hospitality at home with the greatest affability and kindness.

"I believe I can not give a better proof of the sociability of Lord Byron's disposition," says Medwin, "than by speaking of the gayety that prevailed at his Wednesday dinner-parties at Pisa. His table, when alone, was more than frugal; but on these occasions, every sort of wine, and all the delicacies of the season, were served up in grand display, worthy of the best houses. I never knew any one who did

* See chapter on "Gayety and Melancholy." † See his "Life in Italy."

the honors of his house with greater affability and hospitality than Lord Byron.

"The vivacity of his wit, the warmth of his eloquence, are things not to be expressed. Could we forget the tone of his voice, or his gesture, adding charm to all he said?"*

At Pisa he generally received in the morning all those who wished to see him, and among others several of his countrymen, mostly acquaintances or friends of Shelley, who also went to see him every day. In the afternoon he rode out on horseback, still followed by his countrymen, and by the young Count Gamba; amusing himself with them till evening came, in shooting exercises or in long excursions. We have already said how he employed his evenings. In fact, he was so seldom alone that people could not understand how he found time for writing. He did find it, however, and without subtracting from social intercourse. Nor was it solely because he composed so rapidly, but likewise because he gave to occupation the hours that young men are wont to pass in idle, not to say vicious, amusements. When he went from Pisa to a villa situated on the hills that overlook Leghorn and the Mediterranean, in order to pass the great heats of summer there, an American painter, Mr. West, who had been commissioned by an American society, requested him to sit for his picture. Lord Byron could not give him much time, and the portrait was not successful. But Mr. West, who, if not a good artist, possessed a just and cultivated mind, drew a picture of his moral character as true as it was flattering,—his pen doing him better service than his brush:—

"I returned to Leghorn," says he, "hardly able to persuade myself that this was the proud misanthrope whose character had ever appeared shrouded in gloom and mystery. For I never remember having met with *gentler*, *more attractive manners* in my life. When I told him the idea I had previously formed, what I had thought about him, he was extremely amused, laughed a great deal, and said, 'Don't you find that I am like every body else?'"

But Mr. Rogers thought him better than every body else, for he says:—

"From all I had observed, I left him under the impression

* Medwin, vol. ii. p. 138.

that he possessed an excellent heart, which had been *completely misunderstood*, perhaps on account of his mobility and apparent likeness of manner. Indeed he took a capricious pleasure in bringing out this contrast between himself and others."

On quitting Pisa he went to Genoa, and there produced the same impression on all who saw him until he left for Greece.

At this last stage of his life, the testimonies as to his amiable, genial nature are so unanimous, from the time of his arrival to the day of his death, that we can not refrain from quoting the language used by some of those who saw him then.

"When I was presented to him," writes Mr. D—— to Colonel Stanhope, "I was particularly struck with his *extremely graceful and affable manners*, so opposite to what I had expected from the reputation given him, and which painted him as *morose*, *gloomy*, almost *cynical*."*

"I took leave of him," writes Mr. Finlay, who was presented to Lord Byron at Cephalonia, "quite enchanted, charmed to find a great man so agreeable."†

Colonel Stanhope, afterward Lord Harrington, who had been sent to Greece by the committee, and who only knew Lord Byron a few months before his death, notwithstanding great discrepancies of idea and character, says frankly, *that with regard to social relations, no one could ever have been so agreeable;* that there was no pedantry or affectation about him, but, on the contrary, that he was like a child for simplicity and joyousness.

"In the evening all the English, who had not, like Colonel Stanhope, turned Odyssean, assembled at his house, and till late at night enjoyed the charm of his conversation. His character *so much differed from what I had been induced to imagine from the relations of travellers*, that either their reports must have been inaccurate, or his character must have totally changed after his departure from Genoa. It would be difficult, indeed impossible, to convey an idea of the pleasure his conversation afforded. Among his works that which may perhaps be more particularly regarded as exhibiting the mirror of his conversation, and the spirit which

* Appendix to Parry's work. † Ibid. p. 210.

animated it, is 'Don Juan.' The following lines from Shakspeare seem as if prophetically written for him :—

> "'Biron they call him; but a merrier man,
> Within the limits of becoming mirth,
> I never spent an hour's talk withal:
> His eye begets occasion for his wit;
> For every object that the one doth catch,
> The other turns to a mirth-moving jest;
> While his fair tongue (conceit's expositor)
> Delivers in such apt and gracious words,
> That aged ears play truant at his tales,
> And younger, hearing, are quite ravished;
> So sweet and voluble is his discourse.'"

Millingen says :—

"His wonderful mnemonic faculties, the rich and varied store with which he had furnished his mind, his lively, brilliant, and ever-busy imagination, his deep acquaintance with the world, owing to his sagacious penetration, and the advantageous position in which, through his birth and other circumstances, he had been placed, conjoined to the highly mercurial powers of his wit, rendered his conversation peculiarly interesting; enhanced, too, as it was by the charm of his fascinating manners. Far from being the surly, taciturn misanthrope generally imagined, I always found him dwelling on the lightest and merriest subjects; carefully shunning discussions and whatever might give rise to unpleasing reflections. Almost every word with him was a jest; and he possessed the talent of passing from subject to subject with a lightness, an ease, and a grace, that could with difficulty be matched. Communicative to a degree that astonished us, and might not unfrequently be termed indiscretion, he related anecdotes of himself and his friends which he might as well have kept secret."

Several persons, influenced by the stories circulated against Lord Byron, asked Dr. Kennedy whether his manners and exterior did not give the idea of a demon incarnate. "Quite the contrary," replied Kennedy, "*his appearance and manners give the idea of a man with an excellent heart, both benevolent and feeling, and he has an amiable, sympathetic physiognomy.* The impression he made on me was that of a man of refined politeness and great affability, united to much gayety, vivacity, and benevolence. His cordial affability even went so far that one was often obliged to recall his rank and fame, in order not to be involuntarily led away by his manner into too great familiarity with him."*

A short time after Lord Byron's death, one of the first English reviews published an article on him entitled "Personal Character of Lord Byron." It was written by a personage who had had several occasions, during Lord Byron's last sojourn in Greece, of observing his habits, feelings and opinions. Though often jealous of Lord Byron's influence in the country, nevertheless when he could get rid of these bad feelings, he expressed himself with tolerable justice:—

"Lord Byron's demeanor," says he, "was perhaps the most affable and courteous I ever met with."

When he was in a good humor, and desirous to be on fair terms with any one, there was a great charm, an irresistible fascination in his manner. Though very gentle, it was always gay, with an air of great frankness and generosity, qualities most real in him. "Lord Byron," he adds, "was known for a sort of poetic misanthrope; but that existed much more in public imagination than in reality. He liked society, and was extremely kind and amiable, when calm. Instead of being gloomy, he was, on the contrary, of a very gay disposition, and was fond of jesting; it even amused him to witness comic scenes, such as quarrels between vulgar buffoons, to make them drink, or lead them on in any other way to show their drolleries. In his writings, certainly, he loved to paint a character more or less the work of his imagination, and which therefore was assigned to himself by public opinion: that is, a proud, haughty being, despising all men, and disgusted with the human species. His liking for bandits and pirates may have sprung from some tendencies of his nature, some circumstances in his life; *but there was not the smallest resemblance between the poet and the corsair.* Lord Byron's heart was full of kindness and generosity, he took pride in splendid acts of beneficence: to change the position of some among his fellow-men, and make them exchange misery for unexpected good fortune, was for him the dearest exercise of his faculties. No one ever sympathized more deeply with the joys he could create."

* See Kennedy.

The same biographer remarks that one great error of Lord Byron's youth was to count upon gratitude and devotedness proportionate to his own, and that most of his accusations against human nature originated with this mistake. And then he adds:—

"But his sentiments, in accordance with his nature, far from obeying the false direction his prejudices and erroneous opinions would have given, always made him, on the contrary, love his fellow-men with a warmth that quite excluded misanthropy. Still this natural ardor rendered him extremely sensitive to neglect from those he loved, especially in early youth, when he was led by the fault of an individual to generalize blame against mankind. He relates somewhere, with merited contempt, that one of his friends would accompany a female relative to her milliner, instead of coming to take leave of him when he was about to leave England for a long time. The truth is that *no one ever loved his neighbor as much as Lord Byron.* Sympathy, respect, affection, attention, were perpetual wants with him. He was really disgusted and sad when they failed him. But then he did not reason much, he only felt like a poet. It was his business to feed all these discontents, for the public likes nothing so much in poetry as disdain, contempt, derision, indignation, and particularly a kind of proud mockery, which forms the line of transition from or distinguishes a disordered state of imagination from madness. Consequently, seeing that this sort of tone pleased the public, when he began to write again he encouraged that style, his first care being to collect, like Jupiter, the darkest clouds."

The same biographer also tries to insinuate that the romantic interest excited by a handsome young man, full of melancholy and mystery, may have influenced Lord Byron's choice of heroes in his early poems; for, says he, it is not every one who can be weary of the most exquisite enjoyments of society, and to be thus sated a man must have been greatly prized by beauty and wealth. These reflections and explanations are arbitrary, and not impartial. But even if Lord Byron, at twenty-one years of age, did borrow ideas and sentiments not really his, by way of producing poetic effect, we must nevertheless acknowledge that, even in this order of sentiments, part still were genuine and real. Like all young men, Lord Byron had entered the world armed with the notions preceptors deem it necessary to inculcate on their disciples regarding generosity, disinterestedness, liberty, honor, patriotism, etc. When he saw that almost all he had thus been taught was mere illusion, a theme for declamation, and that people in the world very rarely act on such principles; then, no doubt, with his exquisite sensibility, and elevated standard of ideal, he must have felt himself more disgusted than any one else, and must have believed he had a right to despise the human race. Especially would this have been the case after he had personally suffered from cruel satire, from the conduct of his relative and guardian, Lord Carlisle, from the lightness of a few women, and the lukewarmness of some few friends. But, while owing to this fault in education, many young men subjected to like trials become sensualists, and others, convinced of the falsities that have been inculcated on them, conclude there is no better system of morality than to seek after place, power, and profit, and become voluntary instruments in the hands of the world's oppressors, Lord Byron's soul revolted at it. Too noble by nature to stoop, and confiding also in his genius, he became a poet with a slight tinge of misanthropy in his mind, but that could never reach unto his heart, that never modified his amiability in society, and which at a later period, when experience of life made him reflect more on the nature of his own sentiments and the weakness of humanity, became transformed into a sweet philosophy, full of indulgence for every human defect. This generous disposition is to be found at the base of all his poems written in Italy.

Another reproach brought against Lord Byron is that he did not paint the good side of human nature. People showed as much indignation at this as if he had betrayed some secret, or calumniated some innocent person. A wondrous susceptibility, assuredly, with regard to the imperfections of our common nature, as tardy as strange. One would think, in reading the reproaches addressed to Lord Byron, that those who made them had quite forgotten how, from all time and in all languages, since man commented on man, our poor human nature has not generally been treated with much respect. Putting to one side moralists, and still more pessimists, have not the Holy Scriptures and all the Fathers of the Church, used the most mortifying language concerning the perversity and corruption of our species? As regards complaints and avowals humiliating for our nature, could there be any more eloquent than those of St. Augustine? Did not Pascal almost wish man to understand that *he is an incomprehensible monster?* Lord Byron would not have called man a *monster;* but shocked at his pride he would willingly have said with Pascal, "If he raises himself, I will lower him; if he abuses himself, I will raise him up." In his drama of "Cain," where Lucifer is conducting Cain through space and worlds, "Where is earth?" asks Cain. "'Tis now beyond thee, less in the universe than thou in it," answers Lucifer. Byron always wished to make man feel his littleness. It is true that, while saying the same thing, a notable difference exists between Lord Byron's thought and that of great Christian souls, who humble man in order to make him see that his sole hope is in supernatural power. Lord Byron follows the same road, but his starting-point and his goal are not the same. When Lord Byron humbles man, it proceeds from a soul-felt want of truth and justice. He sought truth by a natural law of his mind, expressed it unflinchingly, and thus yielded a pleasure to his heart and understanding. But if the impulse that sometimes provoked his severe or contemptuous words was not the sublime one of Christian orthodoxy, that sees no remedy for human depravity save in God alone, it was still farther off from belonging to the school of the pessimists, of La Rochefoucault in particular, who, content with asserting evil, neither saw nor sought for a remedy anywhere. Lord Byron never despaired of mankind. In early youth, especially, he thought,—not like a Utopist, or even a poet, but like a sensible, humane, generous man, who deems that many of the evils that afflict his species, morally and physically, might be alleviated by better laws, under whose influence more goodness, sincerity, and real virtue might be substituted for the hypocrisy and other vices that now deprave our nature. Lord Byron saw in many vices and littlenesses the work of man rather than of nature. It was man corrupted by society, rather than by nature, that he condemned.

If religious hopes did not furnish him with an escape from the cruel sentence, philosophical hopes saved him from being overwhelmed by it. Was that an error?—an illusion? In any case, it was a noble one; sufficient to raise up an insurmountable barrier between him and La Rochefoucault. For a time, it is true, in his first youth, he also seemed to be under the prestige La Rochefoucault exercised over so many minds, through his "Maxims." The elegant manner in which they were written, the clever tone of observation they displayed, boldly laying down the result in the shape of axioms, was well calculated to lead a youthful mind astray, and make a relative appear an absolute truth. For a while, Lord Byron also seemed to confound the self-love that merges into real hateful egotism, with that which constitutes the principle of life, and which, under the influence of heart and intelligence, claims the high name of virtue. He seemed to doubt of many things, and to be uneasy at the best impulses of his heart. We may remember that he accused himself of selfishness, because he took pleasure in the exercise of amiable virtues. But then that was only the passing error of a youthful mind, filled with an ideal of excellence too high for reality, and therefore coming into rude contact with deceptions and sorrows. In those days, recalling the fine pictures of life and mankind that had been presented to him as realities, especially at his first onset, and perceiving how different things actually were, seeing men pursue their fellow-men, and ascribe vices to the good and virtues to the bad, not even finding in his friends the qualities that distinguished his own heart, indignant at seeing so many persons sought after for their attractions, despite the vices that defaced them, his soul revolted at the sight—saddened too—and he exclaimed, sorrowfully, in his memoranda:—"*Yes, La Rochefoucault is right.*"

An illusion might find place in Lord Byron's mind, but it could not last; and if people will read with attention what he has written, they will soon understand the great difference existing between him and the author of the "Maxims." Without even speaking of that which separates prose from poetry, an axiom from a hasty expression, grave from gay, maxims from satire, the difference is still enormous. Lord Byron had not received from nature, any more than the author of the "Maxims," the gift of seeing things in a roseate hue. On the contrary, from his habit of profound observation, he too often saw them enveloped in sombre colors. But, on the other hand, he had received such a great gift of perspicacity and exactness that things false and fictitious could no more resist his glance than fog can resist the rays of the sun. La Rochefoucault is certainly an admirable painter, but he never takes a likeness otherwise than by profile. Just as our satellite turns round our planet, only showing us its volcanoes and calcined summits, and leaving us in ignorance of the other side; just so did La Rochefoucault turn around human nature. It only showed him one side,—the most barren and most unhealthy, and that alone did he describe. Still, his description is made with such art and nicety, and has so much charm about it, that it appears correct at first sight, and, indeed, so it is relatively; but, nevertheless, by dint of omission and generalization, it is false, since it would fain impose a part upon us for the whole. In his voyage of exploration through the windings of the human heart the author of the "Maxims" stops midway, and comes back over the same ground. It would appear as if his mind lacked strength to go through more than half the circle of truth. But Lord Byron, through the vigor and elasticity of his faculties, after having penetrated into the dark regions where only evil is perceived, and gone through the whole circle, raised himself up into that pure, serene atmosphere where goodness and virtue inhabit, and he also could say, with Dante, coming out of the last infernal circle,—

"Alfin tornammo a riveder le stelle."

La Rochefoucault always rails against mankind, without ever finding out any good. Lord Byron, on the contrary, sees both good and evil. He points out the latter, often sadly, and sometimes with light jests; but he is always happy to acknowledge seriously the existence of good, and to proclaim that, despite all hinderances, beautiful souls do exist, practicing all kinds of virtue; thus proving that, however rare, virtue to him is still a reality, and no illusion. If, in his burlesque, satirical poems, wishing especially to stigmatize vice in high quarters, he has painted wicked women and queens (Catherine and Elizabeth), did he not likewise refresh our souls with the enchanting portraits of Angiolina (the wife of Faliero), and of Josephine (the wife of Werner). If he made merry at the expense of coquettish, weak, hypocritical women (like Adeline, for instance), has he not consoled us by painting, in far greater number, angels of loving devotedness, like Myrrha, Adah, Medora, Haidée, and in general all his delightful female creations? Are not all his heroes even, more or less, constant, devoted, ready to sacrifice every thing to the sincerity of their feelings—devoted love, continued even in the heart of Cain toward his Adah? In "Heaven and Earth" the angels gave up celestial happiness, and exposed themselves to every evil, in order not to abandon those who loved them. Don Juan himself loved unselfishly. Bitter remembrances, reflections arising from the conduct of friends, made him, *it is true*, doubt the existence of friendship, generalize, blame sometimes, and write those fine stanzas in the fourteenth canto of "Don Juan:"—

"Without a friend, what were humanity,
To hunt our errors up with a good grace?
Consoling us with—'Would you had thought twice!
Ah! if you had but follow'd my advice!'

XLVIII.

"O Job! you had two friends: one's quite enough,
Especially when we are ill at ease;
They're but bad pilots when the weather's rough,
Doctors less famous for their cures than fees.
Let no man grumble when his friends fall off,
As they will do like leaves at the first breeze:
When your affairs come round, one way or 'tother,
Go to the coffee-house, and take another.

XLIX.

"But this is not my maxim; had it been,
Some heart-aches had been spared me: yet I care not—
I would not be a tortoise in his screen
Of stubborn shell, which waves and weather wear not;
'Tis better on the whole to have felt and seen
That which humanity may bear, or bear not;
'Twill teach discernment to the sensitive,
And not to pour their ocean in a sieve.

L.

"Of all the horrid, hideous notes of woe,
Sadder than owl-songs or the midnight blast,
Is that portentous phrase, 'I told you so,'
Utter'd by friends, those prophets of the past,
Who, 'stead of saying what you now should do,
Own they foresaw that you would fall at last,
And solace your slight lapse 'gainst '*bonos mores*,'
With a long memorandum of old stories."

On looking into his own heart, Lord Byron no longer doubted the existence of sincere friendships, devoid of all ironical selfishness, since he wrote that forty-ninth stanza, where he says that such is not his maxim, or his heart would have had less to suffer.

Did he not make love of country incarnate in that admirable type (*the young Venetian Foscari*); too fine a type, perhaps, though historical, to be understood by every one. And did he not, through other types, equally prove his belief in all the noblest, most virtuous sentiments of our soul? In fine, if he recognized littleness in man, he recognized greatness likewise. All his writings, as well as his conduct through life, belied continuously and broadly a few poetical expressions and mystifications which drew down upon him, in common with other calumnies, that of having unjustly accused humanity. As to the misanthropy of his early youth, it was of so slight a nature that it only passed through his mind, and occasionally rested on his pen; but it always evaporated in words, and especially in his verses. For his life and actions ever showed that such a sentiment was foreign to his nature.

And since its attacks* always took place under the pressure of some great injustice, some excess of suffering imposed by the strong on the weak and inoffensive, we must also add that there was in this pretended misanthropy more real goodness and humanity than in all the elegies, songs, meditations, Messenian odes, etc., of all those who blamed him.

Having studied Lord Byron at all periods of his life, in his relations with society, and in his love of solitude, we have seen him alternately placed in contact with others, and then more directly with himself; now correcting the inconveniences that flow from solitude, by seeking the amusements of

* See chapter on "Melancholy."

youth and society, and then making solitary meditation follow on the useful field of observation sought in the world, and thus he drew profit from both, without ever suffering himself to be exclusively engrossed by one or the other. The enervating atmosphere of drawing-rooms remained innocuous for him; he came out from them with a mind as virile and independent as if he had never breathed it, keeping all his ideas strong and bold, just and humane, as they were before. But the consequences of this rare equilibrium, which he was enabled to maintain between a worldly and a solitary life, were very great, as regarded his fame, if not his happiness; for he gained thereby an experience and a knowledge of the human heart quite wonderful, at an age when the first pages of the Book of Life have in general scarcely been read, so that, in perusing his writings, one might imagine that he had already gone through a long career. Lastly, as afterward not the least trace of this pretended misanthropy remained, he might have repeated what Bernardin de Saint Pierre said of a certain melancholy that we are scarcely ever free from in youth, and which was compared, in his presence, to the small-pox:—"I also have had that malady, but it left no traces behind it."

CHAPTER XX.

LORD BYRON'S PRIDE.

AMONG Lord Byron's biographers, we remark some who doubtless believed it useless to count on success, if their work did not contain a large tribute to human wickedness, and who, seeing it nevertheless impossible to accuse Lord Byron of any vice emanating from heart or soul, gave themselves the pleasure of imagining a host of defects. Besides the faults produced by impetuosity and irritability of temper,—those we have just explained,—they dwell on I know not what exaggerated esteem of himself, and immoderate desire of esteem from others, so as to insinuate that Lord Byron was a prey to pride, ambition, and even vanity.

Though all we have remarked in a general way, with regard to his modesty, might be considered a sufficient response to these accusations, we are willing to take up the theme again and examine more particularly all these forms of self-love.

To assert that Lord Byron was not at all proud, might cause surprise, so much has been said of his pride confounding the man with the poet, and the poet with the heroes of his creation. But assuredly those who would feel surprise could not have known him or studied his character.

Pride is easily recognized by a thousand traits. It is one of those serious maladies of soul, whose external symptoms can no more be hidden from moral psychologists than the symptoms of serious physical infirmities can be hidden from physiologists. Now, what says the moralist of the proud man? That he never listens to the counsels of friendship; that every reproach irritates him; that a proud man can not be grateful, because the burden is too great for him; that he never forgives, makes excuses, or acknowledges his faults, or that he is to blame; that he is extremely reserved and proud in the habits of social life; that he is envious of the goods enjoyed by others, deeming them so much subtracted from his own merits; that hatred toward his rivals fills his heart; finally, that, satisfied with himself almost to idolatry, he is incapable of any moral improvement.

Now, let it be said in all sincerity, what analogy can there be between the proud man and Lord Byron? By his words, his actions, and the testimony of all those who approached him, was not Lord Byron the reverse of all this? Was it he who would have refused the counsels of friendship? turned aside from admonition? been indignant at blame? Let those who think so, only read the accounts of his childhood, his youth, his life of affection, and they will see whether he was not rather the slave of his loving heart; if he did not always give doubly what he had received.

Without even speaking of his childhood, when he was really so charming, of his docility toward his nurses and preceptors, toward good Dr. Glennie at Dulwich, and afterward at Harrow, toward the excellent Dr. Drury; let us consider him at that solemn moment for a boy of eighteen, when he was about to publish his poetic compositions. Did he not burn the whole edition, because a friend whom he respected, disapproved some parts?* See him again accepting the blame of another friend about "Childe Harold," and when, before publishing it, yielding to the advice of Dallas and Gifford, he suppressed the stanzas that most pleased him. See him also ceasing to write "Don Juan," because the person he loved had expressed disapprobation of it, not even substantiated by reasons.

Was it Lord Byron who would have been incapable of forgiving? Why, the pardon of injuries was, on the contrary, a habit with him, a necessity, his sole vengeance, even when such conduct might appear almost superhuman. It was thus, that when cruelly wounded in his self-love, even more than in his heart, by Lady Byron's behavior, he wrote that touching "Farewell," which might have disarmed the fiercest resentment: and that afterward, yielding to Madame de Staël's entreaties, he consented to propose a reconciliation, which

* See what Moore says of this trait in Lord Byron.

was refused: and not even that aggravation prevented him from often speaking well of Lady Byron.

Gratitude, that proves such an insupportable load to the proud man, did it not rather seem a happiness to him?

When he had done some wrong, far from refusing to make excuses, was he not the first to think of it, saying that he could not go to rest, with resentment in his heart? While a mere boy, and when he had been wounded in his most enthusiastic feelings by a fortunate rival, Mr. Musters, was not Byron the first to hold out his hand and express regret for the bitterness of a few words?

Far from hiding his faults, and not satisfied with avowing them, did he not magnify them, exaggerate them to such a degree that this generous impulse became a real fault in him?

Far from having been too proud and reserved in his habits of life, have we not seen him reproached with being too familiar?

Did envy or rivalry ever enter into his soul?

And lastly, far from conceiving too much self-satisfaction, far from rendering his own mind the homage characteristic of pride, did not Lord Byron, looking at himself through the weaknesses of other men, constantly depreciate himself?

All the ways in which genius is wont to manifest itself were assuredly alike familiar to him; neither philosophy nor art had any secrets for him. But he only made use of them to produce continual acts of humility instead of pride; saying, that if philosophy were blind, art was no less incapable of fulfilling the aspirations of mind, and realizing the ideal beheld in imagination.

His very skepticism, or rather what has been called by this name, affords another great proof of his modesty. "Skepticism," says Bacon, "is the great antagonist of pride."

But, the most striking proof of all, undoubtedly, consists in the improvement of his moral being that was perpetually going on; for, to carry it out, he must have dived into the depths of his secret soul, sternly and conscientiously, undeterred by the great obstacle to all self-amelioration, namely—pride.

So many facts, in support of the same assertions, are to be found spread through the different chapters of this work, that we forbear to lengthen the present view of Lord Byron's character by adducing any more. Let us sum up by saying, that not only was Lord Byron devoid of pride, but that it would be difficult to find in any man more striking examples of the opposite virtues; unless, indeed, we sought them in souls completely swayed by the sublimest teachings of Christianity.

And yet it is easy to understand how he might be accused of pride. His contempt for opinion, augmenting as he further appreciated its little worth; a certain natural timidity, of which Moore, Galt, and Pigott have all spoken, though without drawing thence the logical inferences; his eagerness to put down the unfounded *ridiculous pretensions of human nature;* his own dignity under misfortune; his magnanimity and passion for independence; all these qualities might easily betray those superficial minds into error, who do not study their subjects sufficiently to discover the truth.

CHAPTER XXI.

THE VANITY OF LORD BYRON.

BUT it is incomprehensible that any one should have been found to accuse Lord Byron of vanity. For is not the vain man one who lies in order to appear better and more highly gifted than he really is; who knows full well that the good opinion he so ardently seeks is not what he deserves; who endeavors by every means to attract the attention of others; who flatters in order to be flattered; whose willingness to oblige, whose care and kindness, all flow from interested motives; whose whole character savors of ostentation and show; and who despises humble friends, in order to run after brilliant society and wear borrowed plumes? All these signs indicate vanity. Can a single one be found in Byron's character?

Surely our readers will not have forgotten that, for fear of making himself out better, he always wished to appear worse than he was; that he exaggerated the weaknesses common to most of us, and which every body else hides, magnifying them into serious faults; that he never flattered others, nor wished to be flattered himself; that he concealed the services he rendered, the good he did; and kept aloof from those in power so as to give himself more to true friendship.

We know besides that his love of *meriting*, rather than *obtaining*, admiration, went so far as to make undeserved praise quite offensive to him. If eulogiums did not seem to him duly bestowed, his soul, athirst for justice and truth, repelled them indignantly. Blame, or harsh criticism, annoyed him far less than unmerited praise or suffrages obtained through favor or intrigue. At the moment he was about to publish his first poem, "Childe Harold," which might naturally be expected to prove the making of his literary reputation, Dallas having given him some advice with a view to gaining popularity, Lord Byron answered:—

"My work must make its way as well as it can; I know I have every thing against me, angry poets and prejudices; but if the poem is a *poem*, it will surmount these obstacles, and if *not*, it deserves its fate."

And then, when he discovered that his publisher had been taking steps to obtain the approbation of Gifford, the great critic, he wrote indignantly to Dallas, calling this proceeding of Murray's *a paltry transaction.*

"The more I think, the more it vexes me," said he. "It is bad enough to be a scribbler, without having recourse to such shifts to extort praise or deprecate censure, ... and all without my wish, and contrary to my express desire. . . . .*

"I am angry with Murray: it was a bookselling, back-shop, paltry proceeding. . . . I have written to him as he never was written to before by an author, I'll be sworn."

Why, then, accuse a man of vanity when he never complained of criticism and never solicited praise? Was it on account of some of his tastes, particularly the importance he attached to his superiority in boyish games, in bodily exercises, on those which showed dexterity in swimming, fencing, shooting? But all these tastes were as manly as they were innocent. The really trifling tastes common to the youth of his rank and country Lord Byron did not share.

It has also been said that he attached far too much importance to his noble birth. *Much*, perhaps; *too much*, by no means. His ancestors were all illustrious. They were illustrious for their military exploits, and were already nobles in France when they shared the dangers and successes of William the Conqueror; they had followed their kings to Palestine; seven brothers bearing the name of Byron had fought on the same battle-field, and four fell there in defense of their true sovereign and their new country. By his mother he was descended from the kings of Scotland. "Nothing is nobler," says a moralist of our day, "than to add lustre to a great name by our own deeds."

Many of his early compositions testify to the desire he felt of increasing the fame that belonged to his family. For

* Letter 68, to Dallas, 17th September, 1811.

instance, in the poem written at fourteen, and which is entitled "Verses composed on leaving Newstead Abbey," after having sung the valor of his ancestors displayed on the plains of Palestine, in the valley of Crecy, and at Marston, where four brothers moistened the field with their blood, he exclaims :—

"Shades of heroes, farewell! your descendant, departing
From the seat of his ancestors, bids you adieu!
Abroad, or at home, your remembrance imparting
New courage, he'll think upon glory and you.
* * * * * *
Far distant he goes, with the same emulation,
The fame of his fathers he ne'er can forget.

"That fame and that memory still will he cherish;
He vows that he ne'er will disgrace your renown:
Like you will he live, or like you will he perish." 1803.

The same sentiments appear in other poems, and particularly in the "Elegy on Newstead," written at sixteen. His wish of adding fresh lustre to the family name was all the stronger because the last lord, his great uncle, had somewhat blemished it by his eccentric conduct.

But there is a vast difference between this just feeling of pride and the vanity that leads to exultation in mere titles of nobility, which often owe their origin to the favor of princes. Besides, although Lord Byron was aristocratic by birth, and in his every instinct and taste, he was nevertheless truly liberal on principle and through virtue, in politics as well as in private life; for he always admitted into his affections those who possessed fitting qualities of head and soul, without any consideration of their birth.

After having studied Lord Byron's character under the headings of pride and vanity, we must now examine him with regard to ambition: a third form of self-love, which, though separated from the other two by scarcely perceptible shades, and even being often confounded with them, so as to appear one and the same feeling, does not, however, less retain its permanent and distinguishing traits.

Was Lord Byron ambitious?

"Ambitious men must be divided into three classes," says Bacon; "some seek only to raise themselves, forming a common and despicable species; others, with like intent, make the elevation of country enter into the means they employ; this is a nobler ambition, one more refined, and perhaps more violent; lastly, others embrace the happiness and glory of all men in the immensity of their projects. . . . . Ambition is, then, sometimes a vice, and sometimes a virtue."

That Lord Byron's ambition did not range him among either of the two first classes was abundantly proved by the actions of his whole life; and as to his writings, letters, or poetic works, we should vainly seek a single word in them that could be attributed to any low ambition.

An ambitious man has generally been an ambitious child. Now, according to unanimous and competent testimony, Lord Byron was not an ambitious child. The usual emulation founded on ambition had no effect on his progress. All his advancement proceeded from heart and imagination. It was his heart, as we have seen, that made him take his pen in hand, that dictated his first verses; and he was likewise actuated by the need and the pleasure of trying and exercising the strength of his intellectual faculties, of keeping up the sacred fire that warmed his breast, and appeasing his ardent thirst after truth. We have given too many proofs of all this to require to insist upon it any further.

We have also seen that it was disagreeable to him to be admired and praised without having merited it. He felt the same repugnance to seeking for popularity. When "Childe Harold" appeared, Dallas advised him to alter some passages, because, he said, certain metaphysical ideas expressed in the poem might do him harm in public opinion, and that, at twenty-three years of age, it was well to court in an honorable way the suffrages of his countrymen, and to abstain from wounding their feelings, opinions, and even their prejudices.* Lord Byron replied:—

"I feel that you are right, but I also feel that I am sincere, and that if I am only to write *ad captandum vulgus*, I might as well edit a magazine at once, or concoct songs for Vauxhall."†

And yet when he wrote thus to Dallas he had not arrived at any popularity.

Soon, however, it came to him unsought; but he did not

* Dallas, Letter 45. † Lord Byron to Dallas, Letter 66; Moore, vol. ii.

appreciate it nor flatter it to stay, as an ambitious man would not have failed to do. On the contrary, his noble independence of character and incapacity for flattering the multitude gained strength every day. Proofs of the same abound at every period of his life.

"If I valued fame," he said in his memoranda, 1813, "I should flatter received opinions, which have gathered strength by time, and which will last longer than any living works that are opposed to them. But, for the soul of me, I can not and will not give the lie to my own thoughts and doubts, come what may. If I am a fool, I am, at least, a doubting one; and I envy no one the certainty of his self-approved wisdom."

And then, at the same time, he wrote:—

"If I had any views in this country they would probably be parliamentary. But I have no ambition; at least, if any, it would be '*aut Cæsar aut nihil.*' My hopes are limited to the arrangement of my affairs, and settling either in Italy or in the East (rather the last), and drinking deep of the language and literature of both."

The catastrophe that overtook Napoleon, his hero, and the success of fools, quite overcame him at this time:—

"Past events have unnerved me, and all I can now do is to make life an amusement and look on while others play. After all, even the highest game of crosses and sceptres, what is it? *Vide* Napoleon's last twelvemonth," etc., etc.

The following year (1814), when political feeling ran so high against him as to threaten his popularity on account of the lines addressed to the Princess Charlotte, which had offended the regent, who had just gone over from the Whigs to the Tories, Byron wrote to Rogers:—

"All the sayings and doings in the world shall not make me utter one word of conciliation to any thing that breathes. I shall bear what I can, and what I can not I shall resist. The worst they could do would be to exclude me from society. I have never courted it, nor, I may add, in the general sense of the word, enjoyed it—and 'there is a world elsewhere.'"

When once he had quitted England his indifference to popularity and its results further increased. He wrote from Venice to Murray:—

"I never see a newspaper, and know nothing of England, except in a letter now and then from my sister" (1816).

But that did not at all suit his publisher, who set about sending him reviews, criticisms, and keeping him up to all that was going on in the literary and political world, thinking thus to stimulate and keep alive the passions that kindle genius. Then it was that Lord Byron, considering this intellectual régime unwholesome for mind and heart, signified to Murray that their correspondence could not continue unless he consented to *six* indispensable conditions. We regret not being able to give the whole of this beautiful letter, circumscribed as we are by certain necessary limits. Thus we shall only quote what more particularly relates to our subject:*—

"I have been thinking over our late correspondence, and wish to propose to you the following articles for our future:—

"1st. That you shall write to me of yourself, of the health, wealth, and welfare of all friends; but of *me* (*quoad me*) *little or nothing.*

"2dly. . . . .

"3dly. . . . .

"4thly. That you send me no periodical works whatsoever, no 'Edinburgh,' 'Quarterly,' 'Monthly,' or any review, magazine, or newspaper, English or foreign, of any description.

"5thly. That you send me no opinion whatsoever, either *good, bad,* or *indifferent,* of yourself, or your friends, or others, concerning any work of mine, past, present, or to come.

"6thly. . . . . If any thing occurs so violently gross or personal as requires notice, Mr. Kinnaird will let me know; but of praise I desire to hear nothing.

"You will say, 'To what tends all this?' I will answer—to keep my mind free, and unbiased by all paltry and personal irritabilities of praise or censure; to let my genius take its natural direction. All these reviews, with their praise or their criticism, have bored me to death, and taken off my attention from greater objects."

Byron wished, he said, to place himself in the position of a dead man, knowing nothing and feeling nothing of what is

* See Moore, Letter 456.

done and said about him.* At the same time he gave the greatest proof of the reality of the sentiments expressed in this letter by continuing to stay at Ravenna, where people were ignorant of his language, his genius, and his reputation, and where consequently he could only be remarked and appreciated for his external gifts and his deeds of benevolence. When he went from Ravenna to Pisa, Murray, who had not been discouraged by the six conditions, and who was really attached to Lord Byron more as a friend even than as a publisher, became alarmed at the angry feeling stirred up by "Cain," the "Vision of Judgment," "Don Juan," etc., and feared seeing him lose his popularity. So he wrote begging him to compose something in his first style, which had excited such general enthusiasm. But Lord Byron answered:—

"As to 'a poem in the old way,' I shall attempt of that kind nothing further. I follow the bias of my own mind, without considering whether women or men are or are not to be pleased."

His whole conduct in Greece was one long act of abnegation, of disinterested and sublime self-devotion. Let people read Parry, Gamba, even Stanhope.† He sacrificed for Greece all his revenue, his time, pleasures, comforts, even life itself, if necessary, and at the age of thirty-five; and then, after success, he refused every honor, satisfied with having deserved them.

"My intentions with regard to Greece," said he to Parry, at Missolonghi, "may be explained in a few words. I will remain here until Greece either throws off the Turkish yoke, or again sinks beneath it. All my revenue shall be spent in her service. All that can be done with my resources, and personally, I will do with my whole heart. But as soon as Greece is delivered from her external enemies, I will leave without taking any part in the interior organization of the government. I will go to the United States of America, and there, if requisite and they like it, be the agent for Greece, and endeavor to get that free and enlightened government to recognize the Greek federation as an independent State. England would follow her example, and then the

* See Moore, Letter 456 (Ravenna, 24th September, 1821).

† See his "Life in Italy."

destiny of Greece would be assured. She would take the place that belongs to her as a member of Christendom in Europe."

One day, at Missolonghi, a Prussian officer came to complain to Lord Byron, saying, that his *rank* would not allow him to remain under command of Mr. Parry, who was his inferior both in a civil and military capacity, and consequently that he was going to retire. After having done all he could to bring the German to more reasonable sentiments, after having even joked him on his quarterings of nobility, and the folly of wishing to introduce such prejudices into a country like Greece, Lord Byron did not scruple adding :—

"As to me, I should be quite willing to serve as a simple soldier, in any corps, if that were considered useful to the cause."

But if Lord Byron's absence of ambition under the two first categories, as established by Bacon, is well proved; the same can not be said with regard to the third. To deny it would be not only contrary to truth, but especially would it be contrary to all justice; for the third order of ambition ceases to be a fault; it is the love of glory, and, according to Bacon, that is a virtue. At least it is a quality pertaining to noble minds; and could it, then, be wanting in Lord Byron? He had always had a presentiment that glory would not fail him. But he was not satisfied with obtaining it, his special wish was to *deserve* it with just and undeniable right. While yet a child in his fourteenth year, he wrote, in

A FRAGMENT.

"When to their airy hall my fathers' voice
Shall call my spirit
* * * * * *
Oh! may my shade behold no sculptured urns
To mark the spot where earth to earth returns!
No lengthen'd scroll, no praise-encumber'd stone;
My epitaph shall be my name alone:
If *that* with honor fail to crown my clay,
Oh! may no other fame my deeds repay!
That, only *that*, shall single out the spot;
By that remember'd, or with that forgot."

Another time, replying in verse to a poetic composition of one of his comrades which spoke of *the common lot of mortals as lying in Lethe's wave*, Lord Byron, after some charming couplets, ends thus :—

> "What, though the sculpture be destroy'd,
> From dark oblivion meant to guard;
> A bright renown shall be enjoy'd
> By those whose virtues claim reward.
>
> "Then do not say the common lot
> Of all lies deep in Lethe's wave;
> Some few, who ne'er will be forgot,
> Shall burst the bondage of the grave."

Several other compositions belonging to the same period prove that this child, who was so unambitious, and devoid of the usual sort of emulation, did, however, desire to excel in great and virtuous things. In his adieu to the seat of his ancestors, he says, that,—

> "Far distant he goes, with the same emulation,
> The fame of his fathers he ne'er can forget.
> That fame, and that memory still will he cherish;
> He vows that he ne'er will disgrace your renown;
> Like you will he live, or like you will he perish."

And when the Rev. Mr. Beecher, his friend and guide during the college vacation passed at Southwell, reproached him with not going enough into the world, young Byron answered, that retirement suited him better, but that when his boyhood and years of trial should be over, if the senate or the camp claimed his presence, he should endeavor to render himself worthy of his birth :—

> "Oh! thus, the desire in my bosom for fame
> Bids me live but to hope for posterity's praise;
> Could I soar with the phœnix on pinions of flame,
> With him I could wish to expire in the blaze."

But the fame to which he aspired was not literary fame. Garlands weaved on Mount Parnassus had no perfume for him, and to seek after them would have appeared in his eyes a frivolous, unmeaning pastime. This severe and unjust judgment, this sort of antipathy, could they have been a presentiment of the dangers with which the glory obtained by literary fame threatened his repose? However that may be, it is certain that he endured rather than sought after it; and we may be equally sure that the glory to which his soul aspired was such as could be reaped in the senate, the camp, or amid the difficulties of an active, virtuous life. At sixteen he wrote:—

> "For the life of a Fox, of a Chatham the death,
> What censure, what danger, what woe would I brave!
> Their lives did not end when they yielded their breath;
> Their glory illumines the gloom of their grave." 1806.

We find the following in his examination of conscience, written when he was given up to fashionable London life, and in the heyday of his poetic fame:—

"To be the first man—not the dictator, not the Sylla, but the Washington or the Aristides—the leader in talent and *truth*—is next to the Divinity!" (1813.)

These lines show that he did not feel himself in the position he could have wished to occupy, and that he would fain have achieved other success.

But the destiny that was evidently contrary to his tastes, and which through a thousand circumstances carried him away both from a military and a parliamentary career, to keep him almost perforce in the high walks of literature, was this destiny in accordance at least with his nature? Lord Byron's brilliant début in the senate, and his whole conduct in Greece when that country was one great military camp, prove certainly that he might have reaped full harvest in other fields, if fate had so allowed. But nevertheless when we see how prodigious were his achievements, concentrated within the domain of poetry; when we see that, despite himself, despite the resolution he occasionally took of writing no more, that yet, tortured by the energy of his genius, there was no remedy for him but to seize his pen; that he wrote sometimes under the influence of fever; that sleep did not still his imagination, nor travelling interrupt his works; that sorrow did not damp his ardor, nor amusement and pleasure weaken his wondrous energy. When we think that he united to this formidable vigor of genius such a luxuriant poetic vein; that his poems, unrivalled for depth of thought, conciseness, and magic beauty of style, were composed with all the ease of ordinary prose; that he could write them while conversing, interrupt his thread of ideas, and take it up again without difficulty, carry on his theme without previous preparation, not stay his pen except to turn the leaf, not change a single word in whole pages, generally only correcting when the proof-sheets came. When we know that a poem like the "Bride of Abydos" was written in four nights of a London season, the "Corsair" in ten days, "Lara" in three weeks, his fourth Canto of "Childe Harold" in twenty days, the "Lament of Tasso" in the space of time requisite for going from Ferrara to Florence; the "Prisoner of Chillon" by way of pastime during the day bad weather forced him to spend at a hotel on the borders of the Lake of Geneva; when we know that he wrote the "Siege of Corinth" and "Parisina" amid the torments caused by his separation, and when besieged with creditors; that at Ravenna, in the space of one year, while torn by many sorrows, and annoyed by conspiracies, though he generously aided the conspirators, he yet found leisure to write "Marino Faliero," the "Foscari," "Sardanapalus," "Cain," the "Vision of Judgment," and many other things; that the fifth act of "Sardanapalus" was the work of forty-eight hours, and the fifth act of "Werner" of one night; that during another year passed between Pisa and Genoa, in the midst of annoyances, sorrows, perpetual changes, he wrote ten cantos of "Don Juan," his admirable mystery of "Heaven and Earth," his delightful poem of the "Island," the "Age of Bronze," etc. When we see all that, it must be acknowledged that if Lord Byron, in devoting himself to poetry, took a false step for his own happiness, it did not mar the manifestation of his genius. But if the world had cause to applaud, he did not share this sentiment. It might almost be said that he always wrote unwillingly; and certainly it may be added that fame never inspired him with vanity. That noble desire might, doubtless, have made his heart beat for a while, but it yielded to his philosophical spirit. If at twenty-six, being repelled from public business by the political bias of the day, and from a military career by other circumstances, he could write in his memoranda "I am not ambitious," how much more disposed did he feel to renounce every kind of ambition two years later, when he was leaving England, full of disgust, and having sounded all the depths of the human soul.

"The wise man is cured of ambition by ambition itself,"

says La Bruyère; "he tends toward such great things that he can not confine himself to what are called treasures, high posts, fortune, and favor. He sees nothing in such poor advantages *good* or *solid* enough to fill *his heart*, to deserve his cares and desires; and it even requires strong efforts for him not to disdain them too much. The only good capable of tempting him is that sort of fame which ought to be the meed of pure, simple virtue; but men are not wont to give it, and he is fain to go without it."

The only advantage Lord Byron wished to derive from his reputation was to render it subservient to his heart—the true focus of his noble existence. Even in the first days of youth, when his pulses beat strongly for glory, it is evident that he would make it tributary to heart—a means rather than an end. But this became more and more conspicuous when he had really attained to fame. In Italy especially he had become quite indifferent to the pompous praise accorded by reviews, while a single word emanating from the heart made an impression on him, ofttimes causing tears to start. He wrote to Moore from Ravenna, in 1821:—

"I have had a curious letter to-day from a girl in England (I never saw her), who says she is given over of a decline, but could not go out of the world without thanking me for the delight which my poesy for several years, etc., etc., etc. It is signed simply N. N. A., and has not a word of 'cant' or preachment in it upon my opinions. She merely says that she is dying, and that, as I had contributed so highly to the pleasure of her existence, she thought that she might say so, begging me to *burn* her *letter*—which, by the way, I can *not* do, as I look upon such a letter in such circumstances as better than a diploma from Gottingen.

"I once had a letter from Drontheim, in Norway (but not from a dying woman), in verse, on the same score of gratulation. These are the things which make one at times believe one's self a poet."*

And in "Detached Thoughts," which he wrote at Ravenna, we find:—

"A young American, named Coolidge, called on me not many months ago. He was intelligent, very handsome, and

* Letter 436, Moore.

not more than twenty years old, according to appearance; a little romantic—but that sits well upon youth—and mighty fond of poesy, as may be suspected from his approaching me in my cavern. He brought me a message from an old servant of my family (Joe Murray), and told me that he (Mr. Coolidge) had obtained a copy of my bust from Thorwaldsen at Rome, to send to America. I confess I was more flattered by this young enthusiasm of a solitary trans-Atlantic traveller, than if they had decreed me a statue in the Paris Pantheon (I have seen emperors and demagogues cast down from their pedestals even in my own time, and Grattan's name razed from the street called after him in Dublin); I say that I was more flattered by it, because it was *simple, unpolitical, and was without motive or ostentation*, the pure and warm feeling of a boy for the poet he admired."

The lines written on the road between Ravenna and Pisa, scarcely two years before his death, beginning with—

"Oh, talk not to me of a name great in story,"

would alone suffice to prove that his love of fame had both its source and its sole gratification in his heart. These charming verses end thus:—

III.

"Oh FAME!—if I e'er took delight in thy praises,
'Twas less for the sake of thy high-sounding phrases,
Than to see the bright eyes of the dear one discover
She thought that I was not unworthy to love her.

IV.

"*There*, chiefly I sought thee, *there* only I found thee:
Her glance was the best of the rays that surround thee:
When it sparkled o'er aught that was bright in my story,
I knew it was love, and I felt it was glory."

Some days before setting out for Genoa, while walking in the garden with Countess G——, he went into a retrospective view of his mode of life in England. She, on hearing how he passed his time in London, perceiving what an animated existence it was, so full of variety and occupation, showed some fears lest his stay in Italy, leading such a peaceful, retired, concentrated sort of life, away from the political arena presented by his own country, might entail too great a sacrifice offered on the altar of affection. "Oh no," said he, "I regret nothing belonging to that great world, where all is artificial, where one can not live to one's self, where one is obliged to be too much occupied with what others think, and too little with what we ought to think ourselves. What should I have done there? Made some opposition speeches in the House of Lords, that would not have produced any good, since the prevailing policy is not mine. Been obliged to frequent, without pleasure or profit, society that suits me not. Have had more trouble in keeping and expressing my independent opinions. I should not have met you. . . . Ah, well! I am much better pleased to know you. What is there in the world worth a true affection? Nothing. And if I had to begin over again, I would still do what I have done." When Lord Byron thus unfolded the treasures concealed in his heart, his countenance spoke quite as much as his words.

It was at this same period that he wrote in his drama of "Werner:"—

> "Glory's pillow is but restless,
> If love lay not down his cheek there."

And now to sum up, let us say that, after having considered Lord Byron not only in his actions, and their most apparent motives; not only in the exercise of all his faculties, and in his sentiments sincerely expressed, but that, having likewise confronted him with all the forms of self-love, it is impossible for us to see aught else in him but that legitimate pride belonging to great souls, and the noble passion for glory—sentiments united in him with the peculiar feature of being under control of his affections. Thus, then, when the day came that he was called upon to sacrifice his affections, not only in the name of humanity, but also in the name of his love for glory, which was already a virtue, since he only desired and sought it to become a benefactor of mankind; then, by this new sacrifice, and by that even of life, his noble passion for glory attained to the height of a sublime virtue.

Although our impartial examination of Lord Byron's faults end really in demonstrating their absence, let us beware nevertheless of raising him above humanity by asserting that he had none. La Bruyère thus sums up his portrait of the great Condé:—"*A man who was true, simple, and magnanimous, and in whom only the smallest virtues were wanting.*" This fine sentence may partly apply to Lord Byron also. Only, to be just, we must substitute the singular for the plural. And instead of declaring that the lesser virtues were wanting in him, we must say *one* of the smaller virtues. In truth, he had not that prudence which proposes for our supreme end the preservation of our prosperity, fortune, popularity, tranquillity, health—in a word, of all our goods—and which constitutes Epicurean wisdom. But this virtue is really so mixed up with personality and egotism, that one may hesitate ere granting it the rank of a virtue; and we ought not to be astonished if it were wanting in Lord Byron, for it can with difficulty be found united to great sensibility of heart and great generosity of character. Nevertheless, had he possessed it, his life might have been much happier. Had he possessed it, instead of devoting his revenue and all his literary gains to friends, disappointed authors, and unfortunates of all kinds, he would have kept them for himself; and thus he might have been able to brave almost all the storms of his sad year of married life, when his annoyances were greatly increased by the embarrassed state of his affairs. Had he possessed this prudence, he would not in his boyish satire have attacked so many powerful persons, nor, at a later period, would he have made to himself idols of truth and justice. He would have spared the powers that be, and respected national prejudices, in order not to draw down on his own head so much rancor and calumny; he would not have given a hold to slander, nor suffered himself to be insulted by being identified with the heroes of his poems; he would not have compromised his fine health by an anchorite's regimen; he would not have depreciated himself; he would have extended to himself the indulgence with which he knew so well how to cloak the faults of others, and instead of confiding to indiscreet companions, as subjects for curiosity and study, adventures somewhat strange, and the usual routine of juvenile follies, he would have profited by the system so current in our day of satisfying inclinations silently and covertly; lastly, and above all, he would not have married Miss Milbank.

All these reproaches are well founded. But if we may say with reason that he wanted prudence for his own interests, we ought at the same time to *add that he never wanted it for the interests of others.* Did we not see him, even in earliest youth, burn writings, or abstain from writing, through excess of delicacy and fear of wounding his neighbors?

"I have burned my novel and my comedy," said he in 1813. "After all, I see that the pleasure of burning one's self is as great as that of printing. These two works ought not to have been published. I fell too much into realities; some persons would have been *recognized*, and others *suspected*."

When he sent Murray his stanzas to the Po, he forbade him to print it, because it gave intimate details.

His greatest fear at Pisa and Genoa was lest the newspapers should have spoken of his feelings for the Countess G——.

But without seeking other examples, it suffices to glance at his conduct in Greece, where his prudence formed matter of astonishment to every body. Monsieur Tricoupi, the best historian of the war of Greek independence, has rendered him the most complete justice on this head.

Let us then sum up by saying that, contrary to what is found in most, even virtuous men, Lord Byron possessed great and sublime virtues in the highest degree, and the lesser ones only in a secondary degree. As to his faults, it is evident they all sprang from his excellent qualities. Endowed with all kinds of genius, except the one of calculating his personal interest, he failed in different ways to discharge his duty toward himself; and though he only harmed himself by his want of prudence, yet was he cruelly punished for it by sorrows, regrets, and even by a fatally premature death.

CHAPTER XXII.

LORD BYRON'S MARRIAGE AND ITS CONSEQUENCES.

LORD BYRON'S marriage exercised such a deplorable influence over his destiny, that it is impossible to speak of it succinctly, and without entering into details; for this one great misfortune proved the fruitful source of all others.

If we were permitted to believe that Providence sometimes abandons men here below to the influence of an evil genius, we might well conceive this baneful intervention in the case of Lord Byron's conjugal union, and all the circumstances that led to it.

It was but a few months after having returned from his travels in the East, that Lord Byron published his first cantos of "Childe Harold," and obtained triumphs as an orator in the House of Lords. Presenting himself thus for the first time to the public, surrounded by all the prestige belonging to a handsome person, rank, and youth,—in a word, with such an assemblage of qualities as are seldom if ever found united in one person—he immediately became the idol of England. The enemies created by his boyish satire, and augmented by the jealousy his success could not fail to cause, now hid themselves like those vile insects that slink back into their holes on the first appearance of the sun's rays, ready to creep out again when fogs and darkness return. Living then in the midst of the great world, in the closest intimacy with many of the fair sex, and witnessing the small amount of wedded happiness enjoyed by aristocratic couples within his observation, intending also to wing his flight eventually toward climes more in unison with his tastes, he no longer felt that attraction for marriage which he had experienced in boyhood (like most youths), and he said, quite seriously, that if his cousin, George Byron, would marry, he, on his part, would willingly engage not to enter into wedlock. But his friends saw with regret that his eyes were still seeking through English clouds the blue skies of the East; and that he was kept in perpetual agitation by the fair ones who would cast themselves athwart his path, throwing themselves at his head when not at his feet. Vainly did he distort himself, give himself out to the public as a true "Childe Harold," malign himself; his friends knew that his heart was overflowing with tenderness, and they could not thus be duped. If he had wished to cull some flowers idly, for the sake of scattering their leaves to the breeze, as youth so often does, this sort of amusement would have been difficult for him, for the fine ladies of his choice, if once they succeeded in inspiring him with some kind of tender feeling, fastened themselves upon him in such a passionate way that his freedom became greatly shackled, and they generally ended by making the public the confidante of their secret.

Lord Byron had some adventures that brought him annoyance and grief. They made him fall into low spirits,—a sort of moral apathy and indifference for every thing. His best friends, and the wisest among them, thought that the surest way of settling him in England, and getting him out of the scrapes into which he was being dragged by female enthusiasm, would be for him to marry, and they advised him to it pertinaciously. Lord Byron, ever docile to the voice of affection, did not repel the counsels given, but he made them well understand that he should marry from reason rather than choice; and the letter he wrote, when Moore insisted on his choosing a certain beautiful girl of noble birth,* well explains his whole state of mind at this time:—

"I believe," said he, "that you think I have not been quite fair with that Alpha and Omega of beauty with whom you

* "In none of the persons he admired," says Moore, "did I meet with a union of qualities so well fitted to succeed in the difficult task of winning him into fidelity and happiness as in the lady in question. Combining beauty of the highest order with a mind intelligent and ingenuous, having just learning enough to give refinement to her taste, and far too much taste to make pretensions to learning; with a patrician spirit proud as Lord Byron's, but showing it only in a delicate generosity of spirit, a feminine high-mindedness, which would have led her to tolerate the defects of her husband in consideration of his noble qualities and his glory, and even to sacrifice silently her own happiness rather than violate the responsibility in which she stood pledged to the world for his."

would willingly have united me. Had Lady —— appeared to wish it, I would have gone on, and very possibly married with the same indifference which has frozen over the Black Sea of almost all my passions. It is that very indifference which makes me so uncertain and apparently capricious. It is not eagerness of new pursuits, but that nothing impresses me *sufficiently* to fix. I do not feel disgusted, but simply indifferent to almost all excitements; and the proof of this is that obstacles, the slightest even, stop me. This can hardly be timidity, for I have done some imprudent things, too, in my time; and in almost all cases opposition is a stimulus. In this circumstance it is not; if a straw were in my way I could not stoop to pick it up. I have sent you this long tirade, because I would not have you suppose that I have been trifling designedly with you or others. If you think so, in the name of St. Hubert (the patron of antlers and hunters) *let me be married out of hand, I don't care to whom*, so it amuses any body else, and don't interfere with me much in the daytime."

But that to which Lord Byron most aspired was always to wing his flight to brighter skies.

"Your climate kills me," he wrote to Hodgson, directly after his return from the East. And then again, "My inclinations and my health make me wish to leave England; neither my habits nor constitution are improved by your customs or your climate. I shall find employment in making myself a good Oriental scholar. I shall buy a mansion in one of the fairest islands, and describe, at intervals, the most interesting portions of the East."

Lord Byron wrote this before he had attained great celebrity, but this did not change either his sentiments or his tastes. Notwithstanding the embarrassments arising from the legacy left him by his great uncle, and which were principally caused by the action brought against him on account of the illegal sale of the Rochdale mines (a suit which Lord Byron gained, but the expenses of which were ruinous), he was nevertheless sufficiently rich to live at ease, to let his needy friends enjoy the profits arising from his works, and to allow himself acts of beneficence and generosity that were the joy of his heart. And when he had done all that, he still found that he could not spend the surplus in England according to his tastes. After the death of his mother, no longer bound by his promise to her of not selling Newstead, he resolved on effecting the sale so as to settle his affairs definitively. The sale having failed, the forfeit brought him in £25,000; and he wrote to Moore, in September, 1814:—

"I shall know to-morrow whether a circumstance, of importance enough to change all my plans, will occur or not.* If it does not, I am off for Italy next month.

"I have a few thousand pounds which I can't spend after my own heart in this climate, and so I shall go back to the south. Hobhouse, I think and hope, will go with me; but whether he will or not, I shall. I want to see Venice and the Alps, and Parmesan cheeses, and look at the coasts of Greece, or rather Epirus, from Italy as I once did, or fancied I did, that of Italy, when off Corfu."

A few days before writing this letter, his evil destiny had led him to take a step fatal to all his future happiness.

A person, for whom he entertained both affection and deference, observing one day how unsettled he appeared in his state of mind and projects for the future, again reiterated, with more earnestness than ever, the advice to marry.

After long discussions Lord Byron promised to do so. But who should be the object of his choice? A young lady was named who seemed to possess all the qualities requisite for giving happiness in marriage. Lord Byron, on his side, suggested Miss Milbank, with whom he was then in correspondence. She was a niece of Lady Melbourne, who had thought of this union a year before; a circumstance which probably decided Lord Byron's preference, for he liked Lady Melbourne very much.

On hearing Miss Milbank's name his friend protested with great energy, begging him to remark, among other things, that Miss Milbank had no actual fortune, that his affairs were too much embarrassed for him to be able to marry a woman without money, and moreover that Miss Milbank was a learned lady, a *blue-stocking*, who could not possibly suit him. Ever docile to the voice of friendship, Lord Byron yielded,

* This circumstance was his proposal for Miss Milbank; we shall see presently how it had taken place.

and allowed his friend to write a proposal to the other lady. Soon after a negative answer arrived, one morning, that the two friends were together.

"You see," said Lord Byron, "that after all it is Miss Milbank I am to marry; I shall write to her!" He did so immediately; and when the letter was finished, his friend feeling more and more opposed to such a choice, took it from him. After having read it, he exclaimed:—

"Truly, this letter is so charming that it is a pity for it not to go. I never read a better effusion." "Then go it shall," replied Lord Byron, who sealed and sent it off, thus signing his own misfortune!

We have said that he was in correspondence with Miss Milbank. This is how he had made her acquaintance.

Two years previously, at a London *soirée*, he saw sitting in the corner of a sofa a young girl whose simplicity of dress made her look as if she belonged to a less elevated position than most of the other girls in the room; Moore told him, however, that she was a rich heiress, Miss Milbank, and that if he would marry her she might help him to restore the old Abbey of Newstead. Her modest look, in striking contrast with the stiffness and formality common to the aristocracy, interested Lord Byron. He had himself introduced, and some time after ended by asking her to marry him. His proposal, from motives that could not wound him, was not accepted then. But a year later Miss Milbank testified the desire of entering into correspondence with him. Thus the ground was prepared. When he sent his letter with a fresh proposal, it was accepted all the more eagerly that a report had been spread of his wishing to marry a young and beautiful Irish girl, which did not please Miss Milbank. Her answer was couched in very flattering terms, and the fatal marriage was thus decided on. This was perhaps the only time in his life that Lord Byron did not follow the counsels of friendship. It would indeed seem as if an evil genius had taken possession of his will. Warnings were not wanting; but he refused to listen to them. "If you have any thing to say against my decision," wrote he to Moore, in his usual jesting way, after the marriage had been agreed on, "I beg you to say it. My resolve is taken, so positively, fixed, and irrevocably, that I can very well listen to reason, since now it can do me no more harm."

And so he married Miss Milbank three months afterward. During the interval between the promise exchanged and the ceremony concluded, Lord Byron saw his betrothed frequently. Had he no warning, no inspiration from his good genius during all that time? Had he no fear of such perfection? Did he not feel that a faultless coat of mail, like hers, might so have pressed upon her heart that no pulse would be left giving earnest of life? Might not tenderness, piety, indulgence, forbearance, the most amiable and sublime virtues belonging to a Christian woman, have their place filled in the breast of this perfect creature by another kind of sublimity? and was it not very possible that she would increase by one the number of those chaste wives who judge, condemn, punish, and never forgive any thing that does not enter into the category of their virtues, or rather of the single virtue they practice, and under shadow of which they consider themselves able to dispense with all others? Did he not fear that the profound mathematical knowledge of that learned person might have slightly deadened her heart and given a dogmatic tone to her mind, of which he doubtless with his usual penetration suspected the narrowness, likely to render its science pernicious to the heart? All this is easily to be believed, when we see how preoccupied he was before marriage.

"At the beginning of the month of December, being called up to town by business, I had opportunities, from being a good deal in my noble friend's society, of observing the state of his mind and feelings under the prospect of the important change he was now about to undergo; and it was with pain I found that those sanguine hopes with which I had sometimes looked forward to the happy influence of marriage, in winning him over to the brighter and better side of life, were, by a view of all the circumstances of his present destiny considerably diminished. While, at the same time, not a few doubts and misgivings, which had never before so strongly occurred to me, with regard to his own fitness, under any circumstances, for the matrimonial tie, filled me altogether with a degree of foreboding anxiety as to his fate, which the unfortunate events that followed but too fully justified."

Lord Byron might still have avoided this misfortune by giving up marriage; but the die was cast. His evil genius presented him with no other alternative than to rush on to the catastrophe.

We must add that if, unfortunately, the halo of perfection supposed to encircle the heiress was calculated to make him tremble, it was also of a nature to flatter his self-love. This reputation was, in the eyes of Moore, the principal cause of his preference for Miss Milbank. However that may be, in the last days of December, accompanied by his friend Mr. Hobhouse, he set out for Seaham, the residence of Sir Ralph, Miss Milbank's father. And on the morning of the 2d of January, surrounded by visions of the past, by gloomy forebodings, having in his hand the fatal ring that had been dug up in his garden at the moment when Miss Milbank's consent arrived; with a beating heart, and eyes all dizzy, that would have made him draw back, if his honor had not been too far engaged, Lord Byron advanced toward the altar. From that fatal day, if his star of glory did not cease to shine, or even if it shone more brightly seen through the atmosphere of misfortune, nevertheless repose and lasting happiness were gone for him.

An heiress for a wife, but who had no actual fortune, naturally forced him into great expenses, that soon went beyond his resources. His creditors, lured by the riches said to belong to Miss Milbank, came down upon him, as if the wife's fortune could be used to pay the husband's debts.

His marriage had taken place in January, and already, in October, he was obliged to sell his library. Shortly afterward his furniture was seized, and he had to undergo humiliations, all the more keenly felt, that they were quite unmerited, since his debts were inherited with the property. Lord Byron—who had a real horror of debt—with his spirit of justice, moderate desires, simple tastes, detached as he was from material enjoyments, and even, perhaps, through pride, would never have fallen into such embarrassments if he had remained *unmarried*. Indeed, his creditors were patiently awaiting the sale of some property. Besides, he was rich enough while unmarried; he could exercise hospitality, travel in good style, not even keep for himself the produce of his works, and, above all, never refuse to perform works of charity and benevolence. He wrote to one of his friends before marriage that his affairs were about to be settled, that he could live comfortably in England, and buy a principality, if he wished, in Turkey.

Thus, then, marriage alone drew upon him this new disaster, which he must have felt severely, and which, doubtless, led him to make reflections little favorable to the tie so fatally contracted. Then it was that he would have required to meet with kindness, indulgence, and peace at home; thus supported, his heart would have endured every thing.

Instead of that, what did he find? A woman whose jealousy was extreme, and who had her own settled way of living, and was unflinching in her ideas; who united a conviction of her own wisdom to perfect ignorance of the human heart,* all the while fancying that she knew it so well; who, far from consenting to modify her habits, would fain have imposed them on others. In short, a woman who had nothing in common with him, who was unable to understand him, or to find the road to his heart or mind; finally, one to whom forgiveness seemed a weakness, instead of a virtue. Is it, then, astonishing that he should have suffered in such a depressing atmosphere; that he should sometimes have been irritable, and have even allowed to escape him a few words likely to wound the susceptible self-love of his wife?

Lady Byron possessed one of those minds clever at reasoning, but weak in judgment; that can *reason* much without being *reasonable*, to use the words of a great philosophical moralist of our day; one of those minds that act as if life were a problem in jurisprudence or geometry; who argue, distinguish, and, by dint of syllogisms, *deceive themselves learnedly*. She always deceived herself in this way about Lord Byron.

When she was in the family-way, and her confinement drawing near, the storm continued to gather above her husband's head. He was in correspondence with Moore, then

* "Lady Byron," said Lord Byron at Pisa, "and Mr. Medwin were continually making portraits of me; each one more unlike than the other."

absent from London. Moore's apprehensions with regard to the happiness likely to result from a union that had never appeared suitable in his eyes, had, nevertheless, calmed down on receiving letters from Lord Byron that expressed satisfaction. Yet during the first days of what is vulgarly termed the "honey-moon," Lord Byron sent Moore some very melancholy verses, to be set to music, said he, and which begin thus:—

"There's not a joy the world can give like that it takes away."

Moore had already felt some vague disquietude, and he asked why he allowed his mind to dwell on such sorrowful ideas? Lord Byron replied that he had written these verses on learning the death of a friend of his childhood, the Duke of Dorset, and, as his subsequent letters were full of jests, Moore became reassured. Lord Byron said he was happy, and so he really was; for Lady Byron, not being jealous then, continued to be gentle and amiable.

"But these indications of a contented heart soon ceased. His mention of the partner of his home became more rare and formal, and there was observable, I thought, through some of his letters, a feeling of unquiet and weariness that brought back all those gloomy anticipations which I had, from the first, felt regarding his fate."

Above all, there were expressions in his letters that seemed ot sad augury. For instance, in announcing the birth of his little girl, Lord Byron said that he was absorbed in five hundred contradictory contemplations, although he had only one single object in view, which would probably come to nothing, as it mostly happens with all we desire:—

"But never mind," he said, "as somebody says, '*for the blue sky bends over all.*' I only could be glad if it bent over me where it is a little bluer, like *skyish top of blue Olympus.*"

On reading this letter, dated the 5th of January, full of aspirations after a blue sky, Moore was struck with the tone of melancholy pervading it; and, knowing that it was Lord Byron's habit when under the pressure of sorrow and uneasiness, to seek relief in expressing his yearnings after freedom and after other climes, he wrote to him in these terms:—

"Do you know, my dear Byron, there was something in

your last letter—a sort of mystery, as well as a want of your usual elasticity of spirits—which has hung upon my mind unpleasantly ever since. I long to be near you, that I might know how you really look and feel, for these letters tell nothing, and one word *a quattr' occhi*, is worth whole reams of correspondence. But only do tell me you are happier than that letter has led me to fear, and I shall be satisfied."

"It was," says Moore, "only a few weeks after the exchange of these letters, that Lady Byron took the resolution of separating from him. She had left London at the end of January, on a visit to her parents, in Leicestershire, and Lord Byron was to come and join her there soon after. They had parted with mutual demonstrations of attachment and of good understanding. On the journey Lady Byron wrote a letter to her husband, couched in playful, affectionate language. What, then, must have been his astonishment when, directly after her arrival at Kirby Mallory, her father, Sir Ralph, wrote to tell Lord Byron that his daughter was going to remain with them, and would return to him no more."

This unexpected stroke fell heavily upon him. The pecuniary embarrassments growing up since his marriage (for he had already undergone eight or nine executions in his own house), had then reached their climax. He was then, to use his own energetic expression, *alone at his hearth, his penates transfixed around;* and then was he also condemned to receive the unaccountable intelligence that the wife who had just parted from him in the most affectionate manner, had abandoned him forever.

His state of mind can not be told, nor, perhaps, be imagined. Still he describes it in some passages of his letters, showing at the same time the firmness, dignity, and strength of mind that always distinguished him. For example, he wrote to Rogers, two weeks after this thunderbolt had fallen upon him:—

"I shall be very glad to see you if you like to call, though I am at present contending with the 'slings and arrows of outrageous fortune,' some of which have struck me from a quarter whence I did not, indeed, expect them; but, no matter, there is a 'world elsewhere,' and I will cut my way through this as I can. If you write to Moore, will you tell him that I shall answer his letter the moment I can muster time and spirits. Ever yours, BYRON."

This strength of mind he only found a month afterward, and then he wrote to him:—

"I have not answered your letter for a time, and at present the reply to it might extend to such a length that I shall delay it till it can be made in person, and then I will shorten it as much as I can. I am at war *with all the world and my wife*, or, rather, all the world and my wife are at war with me, and have not yet crushed me, and shall not crush me, whatever they may do. I don't know that in the course of a hair-breadth existence I was ever, at home or abroad, in a situation so completely uprooted of present pleasure, or rational hope for the future, as this time. I say this because I think so, and feel it. But I shall not sink under it the more for that mode of considering the question. I have made up my mind.

"By the way, however, you must not believe all you hear on the subject; but don't attempt to defend me. If you succeeded in that it would be a mortal, or an immortal, offense. Who can bear refutation?"*

And, after having spoken of his wife's family, he concludes in these terms:—

"Those who know what is going on say that the mysterious cause of our domestic misunderstandings is a Mrs. C——, now a kind of house-keeper and spy of Lady N——, who was a washer-woman in former days."

Swayed by this idea, he went so far then in his generosity as to exonerate his wife, and accuse himself; whereupon Moore answered that, "*after all, his misfortunes lay in the choice he had made of a wife, which he* (Moore) *had never approved.*"

Lord Byron hastened to reply that he was wrong, and that Lady Byron's conduct while with him had not deserved the smallest reproach, giving her, at the same time, great praise. But this answer, which, according to Moore, *forces admiration for the generous candor of him who wrote it while adding to the sadness and strangeness of the whole affair*—

* Moore, Letter 233.

this answer, of such extraordinary generosity, will better find its place elsewhere. It contains expressions that show his real state of soul under the cruel circumstances:—

"I have to battle with all kinds of unpleasantness, including private and pecuniary difficulties, etc.

". . . . It is nothing to bear the *privations* of adversity, or, more properly, ill-fortune, but my pride recoils from its *indignities.* However, I have no quarrel with that same pride, which will, I think, be my buckler through every thing. If my heart could have been broken it would have been so years ago, and by events more afflicting than these. . . . Do you remember the lines I sent you early last year? I don't wish to claim the character of 'Vates' the prophet, but were they not a little prophetic? I mean those beginning: 'There's not a joy the world can,' etc. They were the truest, though the most melancholy, I ever wrote."

To this letter Moore answered immediately:—

"I had certainly no right to say any thing about the *unluckiness of your choice*, though I rejoice now that I did, as it has drawn from you a tribute which, however unaccountable and mysterious it renders the whole affair, is highly honorable to both parties. What I meant in hinting a doubt with respect to the object of your selection, did not imply the least impeachment of that perfect amiableness which the world, I find, by common consent, allows to her. I only feared that she might have been too perfect, too *precisely* excellent, *too matter-of-fact a paragon for you to coalesce with comfortably*, ... and that a person whose perfection hung in more easy folds about her, whose brightness was softened down by some of 'those fair defects which best conciliate love,' would, by appealing more dependently to your protection, have stood a much better chance with your good-nature. All these suppositions, however, I have been led into by my intense anxiety to acquit you of any thing like a capricious abandonment of your wife; and, totally in the dark as I am with respect to all but the fact of your separation, you can not conceive the solicitude—the fearful solicitude—with which I look forward to a history of the transaction from your own lips when we meet—a history in which I am sure of at least one virtue, manly candor."

Those who knew Lord Byron, gifted as he was with so much that seemed to render it impossible for any woman to resign herself to the loss of his love; with so much to make a wife proud of bearing his name; may well ask what strange sort of nature Lady Byron could have possessed to act as she did toward him; and whether, if she really married out of vanity (as Lord Byron one day told Medwin, at Pisa), and her heart being full of pride only, she found some greater satisfaction for her vanity in the courage and perseverance she fancied displayed in deserting him. But, in order to view her inexplicable conduct with any sort of indulgence, we must say that Lady Byron was an only and a spoilt child, a slave to rule, to habits and ideas as unchanging and inflexible as the figures she loved to study; that, being accustomed to the comforts of a rich house, where she was idolized, she could not do without her regular comforts, so generally appreciated and considered necessary by English people. But it was no easy matter to satisfy all her tastes with mathematical regularity, to let her keep up all her habits, and, above all, to make Lord Byron share them in their married life. In the first place, Lord Byron, who was naturally un-English in taste, had, moreover, through his long stay abroad, given up the peculiarities of English habits. He did not dine every day, and when he did it was a cenobite's meal, little suited to the taste of a true Englishman. He breakfasted on a cup of green tea, without sugar, and the yolk of an egg, which was swallowed standing. The comfortable fireside, the indispensable roast-beef, and the regular evening tea, were not appreciated by him; and, indeed, it was a real pain to him to see women eat at all. Not one of his young wife's habits was shared by him. He did not think his soul lost by going to bed at dawn, for he liked to write at night; or by doing other things at what she called irregular hours; and he must have been at least astonished on hearing himself asked, three weeks after marriage, *when he intended giving up his versifying habits?*

But he did not give them up; nor could he have done so had he wished it. Lady Byron must have flattered herself with the idea of ruling him, of showing the world her power over her husband. As long as their resources sufficed for a life of luxury, both parties might have cherished illusion, and put off reflection. But when creditors, attracted by the name of the wealthy heiress—who in reality had only brought her expectations with her—began to pour in, and that pecuniary embarrassment and humiliations were added to home incompatibilities, then, perhaps, Lord Byron became irritable sometimes, and Lady Byron must have felt more than ever the painful absence of those comforts whose enjoyment cause many other annoyances to be forgotten. She must often have compared her life then, full of mortifications, and, perhaps, of solitude, with the one so comfortable and agreeable (for her) she formerly led at Kirby Mallory, in the midst of her relatives. Indeed, they had spent two months there, both saying they were happy; for at this period of the honey-moon, Lord Byron, kind as he was, doubtless yielded to all the caprices and habits of his hosts. Nevertheless, through the veil of his customary jests and assurances to Moore that he was quite satisfied, it is easy to see how tired he was, and how little the life at Seaham was suited to him.

"I am in such a state of sameness and stagnation, and so totally occupied in consuming the fruits, and sauntering, and playing dull games at cards, and yawning, and trying to read old 'Annual Registers' and the daily papers, and gathering shells on the shore, and watching the growth of stunted gooseberry bushes in the garden, that I have neither time nor sense to say more than yours ever, BYRON."

And then another time he wrote,—

"I have been very comfortable here, listening to that d—d monologue which elderly gentlemen call conversation, and in which my pious father-in-law repeats himself every evening, except when he plays upon the fiddle. However, they have been very kind and hospitable, and I like them and the place vastly."

Again, feeling his thought in bondage at Seaham, when it would fain have wandered free beneath some sunny sky, he wrote to Moore, "By the way, don't engage yourself in any travelling expedition, as I have a plan of travel into Italy, which we will discuss. And then, think of the poesy wherewithal we should overflow from Venice to Vesuvius, to say nothing of Greece, through all which—God willing—we might perambulate."

But on quitting Seaham to return home, without preventing Lady Byron from continuing to follow her own tastes, it is likely that he wished to resume his old habits: his beloved solitude, so necessary to him, his fasts, his hours for study and rest, very different from those of Seaham. And then she must have found it troublesome to have a husband, who was not only indifferent to English comforts, but who even disliked to see women eat! who, despite his embarrassments, continued to refuse appropriating for his own use the money given and offered by his publisher, making it over instead to the poor, and even borrowing to help his friends and indigent authors.* She could not have known how he would ever get disentangled. Being *extremely jealous*, she became the easy dupe of malicious persons; and under the influence of that wicked woman, Mrs. Claremont, allowed herself to be persuaded that her husband committed grave faults, though in reality they were but slight or even imaginary ones. She forced open his writing-desk, and found in it several proofs of intrigues that had taken place *previous* to his marriage. In the frenzy of her jealousy, Lady Byron sent these letters to the husband of the lady compromised, but he had the good sense to take no notice of them. Such a revolting proceeding on the part of Lady Byron requires no commentary: it can not be justified. Meanwhile the conjugal abode was given up to bailiffs, and desolation reigned in Lord Byron's soul. He had lately become a father. This was the moment that his wife chose for leaving him; and the first proof of love she gave their daughter, as soon as she set foot in her own home, was to abandon that child's father and the house where she could no longer find the mode of life to which she had been accustomed. At Kirby Mallory, the vindictive Lady Noel, who detested Lord Byron, doubtless did the rest, together with the governess. And the young heiress, just enriched by a legacy inherited from an uncle, thus newly restored to wealth, had not courage to leave it and them all again. With the kind of nature she possessed, she must have taken pride in a sort of exaggerated firmness; thus

* At this time of embarrassment he borrowed a large sum to give to Coleridge.

seeking to gain strength for trampling under foot all heart-emotions, as if they were so many weaknesses, incompatible with the stern principles that she considered virtues. By assuming the point of view proper to some minds, it is easy to conceive all this, especially when one knows England.

But was it really for the purpose of allowing her to give such a spectacle to the world, and to secure for herself the comforts of life, that God had given to her keeping Lord Byron's noble spirit? Did she forget that it was not simply a good, honest, ordinary man, like the generality of husbands, that she had married; but that Heaven, having crowned his brow with the rays of genius, imposed far other obligations on his companion? Did she forget that she was responsible before God and before that country whose pride he was about to become? Ought she to have preferred an easy life to the honor of being his wife; of sustaining him in his weaknesses; of consoling and forgiving him, if necessary; in short, of being his guardian angel? If she aspired to the reputation of a virtuous woman, could true virtue have done otherwise? Ere this God has judged her above; but, here below, can those possessing hearts have any indulgence for her?

We hear constantly repeated—because it was once said—that men of great genius are less capable than ordinary individuals of experiencing calm affections and of settling down into those easy habits which help to cement domestic life. By dint of repeating this it has become an axiom. But on what grounds is it founded? Because these privileged beings give themselves to studies requiring solitude, in order to abstract and concentrate their thoughts; because, their mental riches being greater, they are more independent of the outer world and the intellectual resources of their fellow-creatures; because, through the abundance of their own resources, their mind acquires a certain refinement, likely to make them deem the society of ordinary persons tiresome; does it therefore necessarily follow that the goodness and sensibility of their hearts are blunted, and that there may not be, amid the great variety of women, hearts and minds worthy of comprehending them, and of making it their duty to extend a larger amount of forbearance and indulgence in return for the glory and happiness of being the companions of these noble beings? It is remarked, in support of the above theory, that almost all men of genius who have married—Dante, Milton, Shakspeare, Dryden, Byron, and many others—were unhappy. But have these observers examined well on which side lay the cause of unhappiness? Who will say that if Dante, instead of Gemma Donati, "the ferocious wife" (a thought expressed by Lord Byron in his "Prophecy," evidently to appropriate it to himself, speaking of "*the cold companion who brought him ruin for her dowry*);" who will say that if Dante, instead of Gemma Donati, had married his Beatrice Portinari, she would not have been the companion and soother of his exile? that the bread of the foreigner shared with her would not have seemed *less bitter?* and that he would not have found it *less fatiguing to mount, leaning on her, the staircase leading to another's dwelling?*—

"Lo scendere e il salio per l' altrin scale."—DANTE.

And can we doubt that Milton's misfortune was caused by his unhappy choice of a wife, since almost directly after her arrival at their conjugal home she became alarmed at her husband's literary habits and also at the solitude and poverty reigning in the house, and finally abandoned him after a month's trial? To speak only of England, was it not from similar causes, or nearly so, that the amiable Shakspeare's misfortune arose—also that of Dryden, Addison, Steele? And, indeed, the same may be said of all the great men belonging to whatsoever age or country.

If we were to enter into a polemic on this subject, or simply to make conscientious researches, there would be many chances of proving, in opposition to the axiom, that the fault of these great men lay in the bad choice of their helpmates. In truth, if there have been a Gemma Donati and a Milbank, we also find in ancient times a Calpurnia and a Portia among the wives of great men; and, in modern times, wives of poets, who have been the honor of their sex, proud of their husbands, and living only for them. Ought not these examples at least to destroy the absolute nature of the theory, making it at best conditional? The larger number of great men, it is true, did not marry; of this number we find, Michael Angelo, Raphael, Petrarch, Ariosto, Tasso, Cervantes, Voltaire, Pope, Alfieri, and Canova; and many others among the poets and philosophers, Bacon, Newton, Galileo, Descartes, Bayle, and Leibnitz.

What does that prove, if not that they either would not or could not marry, but certainly not that they were incapable of being good husbands? Besides, a thousand causes—apart from the fear of being unhappy in domestic life, considerations of fortune, prior attachments, etc.—may have prevented them. But as to Lord Byron, at least, it is still more certain with regard to him than to any other, that he might have been happy had he made a better choice: if circumstances had only been tolerable, as he himself says. Lord Byron had none of those faults that often disturb harmony, because they put the wife's virtue to too great a trial. If the best disposition, according to a deep moralist, is that which gives much and exacts nothing, then assuredly his deserves to be so characterized. Lord Byron exacted nothing for himself. Moreover, discussion, contradiction, teasing, were insupportable to him; his amiable jesting way even precluded them. In all the circumstances and all the details of his life he displayed that high generosity, that contempt of petty, selfish, material calculations so well adapted for gaining hearts in general, and especially those of women. Add to that the *prestige* belonging to his great beauty, his wit, his grace, and it will be easy to understand the love he must have inspired as soon as he became known.

"Pope remarks," says Moore, "that extraordinary geniuses have the misfortune to be admired rather than loved; but I can say, from my own personal experience, that Lord Byron was an exception to this rule."*

Nevertheless, Lord Byron, though exceptional in so many things, yet belonged to the first order of geniuses. Therefore he could not escape some of the laws belonging to these first-rate natures: certain habits, tendencies, sentiments—I may almost say infirmities—of genius deriving their *origin from the same sympathies, the same wants.*

He required to have certain things granted to him: his hours for solitude, the silence of his library, which he some-

* Moore, p. 389.

times preferred to every thing, even to the society of the woman he loved. It was wrong to wish by force to shut him up to read the Bible, or to make him come to tea and regulate all his hours as a good priest might do. When he was plunged in the delights of Plato's "Banquet," or conversing with his own ideas, it was folly to interrupt him. But this state was exceptional with him. "*One does not have fever habitually*," said he of himself, characterizing this state of excitement that belongs to composition; and as soon as he returned to his usual state, and that his mind, disengaged from itself, came down from the heights to which it had soared, what amiability then, what a charm in all he said and did! Was not one hour passed with him then a payment with rich usury for all the little concessions his genius required? And lastly, if we descend well into the depths of his soul, by all he said and did, by all his sadness, joy, tenderness, we may be well convinced that none more than he was susceptible of domestic happiness.

"If I could have been the husband of the Countess G——," said he to Mrs. B——, a few days only before setting out for Greece, "we should have been cited, I am certain, as samples of conjugal happiness, and our retired domestic life would have made us respectable! But alas! I can not marry her."

It is also by his latest affections that he proved how, if he had been united to a woman after his own heart, he might have enjoyed and given all the domestic happiness that God vouchsafes us here below, and that when love should have undergone the transformations produced by time and custom, he would have known how to replace the poetic enchantments of love's first days, by feelings graver, more unchanging too, and no less tender and sacred.

But we must interrogate those who knew and saw him personally, and in the first place Moore; for not only was Moore acquainted with Lord Byron's secret soul, but to him had the poet confided the treasure of his memoirs, whose principal object was to throw light on the most fatal event of his life, and whose sacrifice, made in deference to the susceptibilities of a few living nullities, will be an eternal remorse for England. Now this is how Moore expresses himself on this subject:—

"With respect to the causes that may be supposed to have led to this separation, it seems needless, with the characters of both parties before our eyes, to go in quest of any very remote or mysterious reasons to account for it."

After observing that men of great genius have never seemed made for domestic happiness, through certain habits, certain wants of their nature, and certain faults, which appear, he says, like the shade thrown by genius in proportion to its greatness, Moore adds that Lord Byron still was, in many respects, *a singular exception to this rule*, for his heart was so sensitive and his passions so ardent, that the world of reality never ceased to hold a large place in his sympathies; that for the rest, his imagination could never usurp the place of reality, neither in his feelings nor in the objects exciting them.

"The poet in Lord Byron," says Moore, "never absorbed the man. From this very mixture has it arisen that his pages bear so deeply the stamp of real life, and that in the works of no poet with the exception of Shakspeare, can every various mood of the mind—whether solemn or gay, whether inclined to the ludicrous or the sublime, whether seeking to divert itself with the follies of society or panting after the grandeur of solitary nature—find so readily a strain of sentiment in accordance with its every passing tone."

Nevertheless he did not completely escape the usual fate of great geniuses, since he also experienced, though rarely, and always with good cause, that sadness which, as Shakspeare says,—

"Sicklies the face of happiness itself."

"To these faults, and sources of faults, inherent in his own sensitive nature, he added also many of those which a long indulgence of self-will generates—the least compatible, of all others, with that system of mutual concession and sacrifice by which the balance of domestic peace is maintained. In him they were softened down by good-nature. When we look back, indeed, to the unbridled career, of which this marriage was meant to be the goal—to the rapid and restless course in which his life had run along, like a burning train, through a series of wanderings, adventures, successes, and passions, the fever of all which was still upon him, when, with the same headlong recklessness, he rushed into this marriage, it can but little surprise us that, in the space of one short year, he should not have been able to recover all at once from his bewilderment, or to settle down into that *tame level* of conduct which the close observers of his every action required. As well might it be expected that a steed like his own Mazeppa's—

'Wild as the wild deer and untaught,
With spur and bridle undefiled,'

should stand still, when reined, without chafing or champing the bit.*

"Even had the new condition of life into which he passed been one of prosperity and smoothness, some time, as well as tolerance, must still have been allowed for the subsiding of so excited a spirit into rest. But, on the contrary, his marriage was at once a signal for all the arrears and claims of a long-accumulating state of embarrassment to explode upon him; his door was almost daily beset by duns, and his house nine times during that year in possession of bailiffs; while, in addition to these anxieties, he had also the pain of fancying that the eyes of enemies and spies were upon him, even under his own roof, and that his every hasty word and look were interpreted in the most perverted light.

"He saw but little society, his only relief from the thoughts which a life of such embarrassment brought with it was in those avocations which his duty, as a member of the Drury Lane Committee, imposed upon him. And here, in this most unlucky connection with the theatre, one of the fatalities of his short year of trial, as husband, lay. From the reputation which he had previously acquired for gallantries, and the sort of reckless and boyish levity to which—often in very bitterness of soul—he gave way, it was not difficult to bring suspicion upon some of those acquaintances which his frequent intercourse with the green-room induced him to form, or even (as in one instance was the case) to connect with his name injuriously that of a person to whom he had scarcely ever addressed a single word.

"Notwithstanding, however, this ill-starred concurrence of circumstances, which might have palliated any excesses

* Moore's Life, vol. iii. p. 209.

either of temper or conduct into which they drove him, it was, after all, I am persuaded, to no such serious causes that the unfortunate alienation, which so soon ended in disunion, is to be traced.

"'In all the unhappy marriages I have ever seen,' says Steele, 'the great cause of evil has proceeded from slight occasions,' and to this remark, I think, the marriage under our consideration would not be found, upon inquiry, to be an exception. Lord Byron himself, indeed, when at Cephalonia, a short time before his death, seems to have expressed, in a few words, the whole pith of the mystery.

"An English gentleman, with whom he was conversing on the subject of Lady Byron, having ventured to enumerate to him the various causes he had heard alleged for the separation, the noble poet, who had seemed much amused with their absurdity and falsehood, said, after listening to them all: 'The causes, my dear sir, were too simple to be easily found out.'

"In truth, the circumstances, so unexampled, that attended their separation, the last words of the wife to the husband being those of the most playful affection, while the language of the husband toward the wife was in a strain, as the world knows, of tenderest eulogy, are in themselves a sufficient proof that, at the time of their parting, there could have been no very deep sense of injury on either side. It was not till afterward that, in both bosoms, the repulsive force came into operation, when, to the party which had taken the first decisive step in the strife, it became naturally a point of pride to persevere in it with dignity, and this unbendingness provoked, as naturally, in the haughty spirit of the other, a strong feeling of resentment which overflowed, at last, in acrimony and scorn. If there be any truth, however, in the principle, that they never pardon who have done the wrong, Lord Byron, who was, to the last, disposed to reconciliation, proved, at least, that his conscience was not troubled by any very guilty recollections.

"But though it would have been difficult perhaps, for the victims of this strife themselves to have pointed out the real cause for their disunion, beyond that general incompatibility which is the canker *of all such marriages*, the public, which seldom allows itself to be at fault on these occasions, was, as usual, ready with an ample supply of reasons for the breach, all tending to blacken the already-darkly painted character of the poet, and representing him, in short, as a finished monster of cruelty and depravity. The reputation of the object of his choice for every possible virtue, was now turned against him by his assailants, as if the excellences of the wife were proof positive of every enormity they chose to charge upon the husband. Meanwhile, the unmoved silence of Lady Byron under the repeated demands made for a specification of her charges against him, left to malice and imagination the fullest range for their combined industry. It was accordingly stated, and almost universally believed, that the noble lord's second proposal to Miss Milbank had been but with a view to revenge himself for the slight inflicted by her refusal of the first, and that he himself had confessed so much to her on their way from the church. At the time when, as the reader has seen from his own honey-moon letters, he in all faith fancied himself happy, and even boasted, in the pride of his imagination, that if marriage were to be upon lease, he would gladly renew his own for a term of ninety-nine years!

"At this very time, according to these veracious chronicles, he was employed in darkly following up the aforesaid scheme of revenge, and tormenting his lady by all sorts of unmanly cruelties—such as firing off pistols, to frighten her as she lay in bed, and other such freaks.* To the falsehoods concerning his green-room intimacies, and particularly with respect to

* It is true that once Lord Byron discharged a pistol, by accident, in Lady Byron's room, when she was *enciente*. This action, coupled with the preoccupations and sadness overwhelming Lord Byron's mind at this time, and further aided by the insinuation of Mrs. Claremont, made Lady Byron begin and continue to suspect that he was mad, and so fully did she believe it, that from that hour, she could never see him come near her without trembling. It was under the influence of this absurd idea that she left him. Lady Byron was not guilty of the reports then current against him. They were spread abroad by her parents: she, on the contrary, as long as she thought him mad, felt great sorrow at it. It was only when she had to persuade herself that he was not mad, that she vowed hatred against him, convinced as she was that he had only married her out of revenge, and not from love. But if an imaginary fear, and even an unreasonable jealousy may be her excuse (just as one excuses a monomania), can one equally forgive her silence? Such a silence is morally what are physically the poisons which kill at once, and defy all remedies, thus insuring the culprit's safety. This silence it is which will ever be her crime, for by it she poisoned the life of her husband.

one beautiful actress, with whom, in reality, he had hardly ever exchanged a single word, I have already adverted; and the extreme confidence with which this tale was circulated and believed affords no unfair specimen of the sort of evidence with which the public, in all such fits of moral wrath, is satisfied. It is, at the same time, very far from my intention to allege that, in the course of the noble poet's intercourse with the theatre, he was not sometimes led into a line of acquaintance and converse, unbefitting, if not dangerous to, the steadiness of married life. But the imputations against him on this head were not the less unfounded, as the sole case in which he afforded any thing like real grounds for such an accusation did not take place till after the period of the separation.

"Not content with such ordinary and tangible charges, the tongue of rumor was emboldened to proceed still further; and, presuming upon the mysterious silence maintained by one of the parties, ventured to throw out dark hints and vague insinuations, of which the fancy of every hearer was left to fill up the outline as he pleased. In consequence of all this exaggeration, such an outcry was now raised against Lord Byron as, in no case of private life, perhaps, was ever before witnessed; nor had the whole amount of fame which he had gathered, in the course of the last four years, much exceeded in proportion the reproach and obloquy that were now, within the space of a few weeks, heaped upon him. In addition to the many who, no doubt, conscientiously believed and reprobated what they had but too much right, whether viewing him as poet or man of fashion, to consider credible excesses, there were also actively on the alert that large class of persons who seem to think that inveighing against the vices of others is equivalent to virtue in themselves, together with all those natural haters of success who, having long been disgusted with the splendor of the poet, were now enabled, in the guise of champions for innocence, to wreak their spite on the man. In every various form of paragraph, pamphlet, and caricature, both his character and person were held up to odium. Hardly a voice was raised, or at least listened to, in his behalf; and though a few faithful friends remained unshaken by his side, the utter hopelessness of stemming the torrent was felt as well by them as by himself, and, after an effort or two to gain a fair hearing, they submitted in silence."

As to Lord Byron, he hardly attempted to defend himself. Among all these slanders, he only wished to repel one that wounded his generous pride beyond endurance; and so he wrote to Rogers:—

"You are of the few persons with whom I have lived in what is called intimacy, and have heard me at times conversing on the untoward topic of my recent family disquietudes. Will you have the goodness to say to me at once, whether you ever heard me speak of her with disrespect, with unkindness, or defending myself at her expense by any serious imputation of any description against her? Did you never hear me say, 'that when there was a right or a wrong, she had the right?' The reason I put these questions to you or others of my friends is, because I am said, by her and hers, to have resorted to such means of exculpation."

It makes one's heart bleed to see this noble intellect forced by the stupid cruel persecution of wicked fools to descend into the arena and justify himself. But he soon ceased all kind of defense. A struggle of this sort was most repugnant to him. At first Lord Byron had counted on his wife's return, which would, indeed, have proved his best justification. When he saw this return deferred, he asked simply for an inquiry, but could not obtain what he solicited. His accusers, unable to state any thing definite against him, naturally preferred calumny and *magnanimous* silence to inquiry! At last, when he felt that reunion had become improbable, and that his friends, for want of moral courage and independence, confined themselves to mere condolence, he sought for strength in the testimony of conscience and in his determination of one day making the whole truth known. And he did so in effect, a year later, while he was in Italy, and when all hope of reunion was over. Then it was that he wrote his memoirs.

Here perhaps I ought to speak of one of England's greatest crimes, or rather, of the crime committed by a few Englishmen: I mean *the destruction of his memoirs*, a deed perpetrated for the sake of screening the self-love and the follies, if not the crimes, of a whole host of insignificant beings.

But, having already spoken of that in another chapter, I will content myself with repeating here that these memoirs were all the more precious, as their principal object was to make known the truth; that the impression they left on the mind was a perfect conviction of the writer's sincerity; that Lord Byron possessed the most generous of souls, and that the separation had no other cause but incompatibility of disposition between the two parties. Had he not given irrefragable proof of the truth of these memoirs, by sending them to be read and *commented on* by Lady Byron? We know with what cruel disdain she met this generous proceeding. As to their morality, I will content myself with quoting the exact expressions used by Lady B——, wife of the then ambassador in Italy, to whom Moore gave them to read, and who had copied them out entirely:—

"*I read these memoirs at Florence*," said she to Countess G——, "*and I assure you that I might have given them to my daughter of fifteen to read, so perfectly free are they from any stain of immorality.*"

Let us then repeat once more, that they, as well as the last cantos of "Don Juan," and the journal he kept in Greece, were sacrificed for the sole purpose of destroying all memento of the guilty weakness of persons calling themselves his friends, and also of hiding the opinions, not always very flattering, entertained by Lord Byron about a number of living persons, who had unfortunately survived him. It is difficult to conceive in any case, how these memoirs written at Venice, when his heart was torn with grief and bitterness, could possibly have been silent as to the injustice and calumny overwhelming him, or even as to the pusillanimous behavior of so-called friends; while even writers generally hostile no longer took part against him.

For example, this is how Macaulay speaks of him,—Macaulay who was not over-lenient toward Lord Byron, whom he never personally knew, and who is seldom just as well from party spirit as from his desire of shining in antithesis and high-sounding phrases:—

"At twenty-four he found himself on the highest pinnacle of literary fame, along with Walter Scott, Wordsworth, Southey, and a crowd of other distinguished writers. There is scarcely an instance in history of so sudden a rise to so dizzy an eminence. Every thing that could stimulate, and every thing that could gratify the strongest propensities of our nature, the gaze of a hundred drawing-rooms, the acclamation of the whole nation, the applause of applauded men, the love of lovely women,—all this world, and all the glory of it, were at once offered to a youth to whom nature had given violent passions, and whom education had never taught to control them. He lived as many men live who have no similar excuse to plead for their faults. But his countrymen and countrywomen would love and admire him. They were resolved to see in his excesses only the flash and outbreak of that same fiery mind which glowed in his poetry. He attacked religion; yet in religious circles his name was mentioned with fondness, and in many religious publications his works were censured with singular tenderness. He lampooned the prince regent, yet he could not alienate the Tories. Every thing, it seemed, was to be forgiven to youth, rank, and genius.*

"Then came the reaction. Society, capricious in its indignation as it had been capricious in its fondness, flew into a rage with its froward and petted darling. He had been worshiped with an irrational idolatry. He was persecuted with an irrational fury. Much has been written about those unhappy domestic occurrences which decided the fate of his life. Yet nothing is, nothing ever was, positively known to the public but this,—that he quarrelled with his lady, and that she refused to live with him. There have been hints in abundance, and shrugs and shakings of the head, and '*Well, well, we know*,' and '*We could if we would*,' and '*If we list to speak*,' and '*There be that might an they list.*' But we are not aware that there is before the world, substantiated by credible, or even by tangible evidence, a single fact indicating that Lord Byron was *more to blame than any other man who is on bad terms with his wife.*"

And after having said how the persons consulted by Lady Byron, and who had advised her to separate from her hus-

* All this is either *false* or *exaggerated.* Religious criticisms were not so mild, though he had not in any way *attacked religion*, and the Tories *never forgave* his attack on the prince regent, which they made a great noise about.

band, formed their opinion without hearing both parties, and that it would be quite unjust and irrational to pronounce, or even to form, an opinion on an affair so imperfectly known, Mr. Macaulay continues in these words:—

"We know no spectacle so ridiculous as the British public in one of its periodical fits of morality. In general, elopements, divorces, and family quarrels, pass with little notice. We read the scandal, talk about it for a day, and forget it. But once in six or seven years our virtue becomes outrageous. We can not suffer the laws of religion and decency to be violated. We must make a stand against vice. We must teach libertines that the English people appreciate the importance of domestic ties. Accordingly some unfortunate man, in no respect more depraved than hundreds whose offenses have been treated with lenity, is singled out as an expiatory sacrifice. If he has children, they are to be taken from him. If he has a profession, he is to be driven from it. He is cut by the higher orders, and hissed by the lower. He is, in truth, a sort of whipping-boy, by whose vicarious agonies all the other transgressors of the same class are, it is supposed, sufficiently chastised. We reflect very complacently on our own severity, and compare with great pride the high standard of morals established in England with the Parisian laxity. At length our anger is satiated. Our victim is ruined and heart-broken, and our virtue goes quietly to sleep for seven years more. It is clear that those vices which destroy domestic happiness ought to be as much as possible repressed. It is equally clear that they can not be repressed by penal legislation. It is therefore right and desirable that public opinion should be directed against them. But it should be directed against them uniformly, steadily, and temperately; not by sudden fits and starts. There should be one weight and one measure. Decimation is always an objectionable mode of punishment. It is the resource of judges too indolent and hasty to investigate facts and to discriminate nicely between shades of guilt. It is an irrational practice, even when adopted by military tribunals. When adopted by the tribunal of public opinion, it is infinitely more irrational. It is good that a certain portion of disgrace should constantly attend on certain bad actions.

But it is not good that the offenders should merely have to stand the risks of a lottery of infamy, that ninety-nine out of every hundred should escape, and that the hundredth, perhaps the most innocent of the hundred, should pay for all. We remember to have seen a mob assembled in Lincoln's Inn to hoot a gentleman against whom the most oppressive proceeding known to the English law was then in progress. He was hooted because he had been an unfaithful husband, as if some of the most popular men of the age, Lord Nelson for example, had not been unfaithful husbands. We remember a still stronger case. Will posterity believe that, in an age in which men whose gallantries were universally known, and had been legally proved, filled some of the highest offices in the state and in the army, presided at the meetings of religious and benevolent institutions, were the delight of every society, and the favorites of the multitude, a crowd of moralists went to the theatre, in order to pelt a poor actor for disturbing the conjugal felicity of an alderman? What there was in the circumstances either of the offender or of the sufferer to vindicate the zeal of the audience we could never conceive. It has never been supposed that the situation of an actor is peculiarly favorable to the rigid virtues, or that an alderman enjoys any special immunity from injuries such as that which on this occasion roused the anger of the public. But such is the justice of mankind. In these cases the punishment was excessive, but the offense was known and proved. The case of Lord Byron was harder. True Jedwood justice was dealt out to him. First came the execution, then the investigation, and last of all, or rather not at all, the accusation. The public, without knowing any thing whatever about the transactions in his family, flew into a violent passion with him, and proceeded to invent stories which might justify its anger. Ten or twenty different accounts of the separation, inconsistent with each other, with themselves, and with common sense, circulated at the same time. What evidence there might be for any one of these the virtuous people who repeated them neither know nor cared. For in fact these stories were not the causes, but the effects of the public indignation. They resembled those loathsome slanders which Lewis Goldsmith, and other abject libellers of the same class, were in the habit of publishing about Bonaparte; such as that he poisoned a girl with arsenic when he was at the military school, that he hired a grenadier to shoot Desaix at Marengo, that he filled St. Cloud with all the pollutions of Capreæ. There was a time when anecdotes like these obtained some credence from persons who, hating the French Emperor without knowing why, were eager to believe any thing which might justify their hatred.

"Lord Byron fared in the same way. His countrymen were in a bad humor with him. His writings and his character had lost the charm of novelty. He had been guilty of the offense which, of all offenses, is punished most severely; he had been overpraised; he had excited too warm an interest; and the public, with its usual justice, chastised him for its own folly. The attachments of the multitude bear no small resemblance to those of the wanton enchantress in the Arabian Tales, who, when the forty days of her fondness were over, was not content with dismissing her lovers, but condemned them to expiate, in loathsome shapes, and under cruel penances, the crime of having once pleased her too well.

"The obloquy which Byron had to endure was such as might well have shaken a more constant mind. The newspapers were filled with lampoons. The theatres shook with execrations. He was excluded from circles where he had lately been the *observed* of all *observers*. All those creeping things that riot in the decay of nobler natures hastened to their repast; and they were right; they did after their kind. It is not every day that the savage envy of aspiring dunces is gratified by the agonies of such a spirit, and the degradation of such a name. The unhappy man left his country forever. The howl of contumely followed him across the sea, up the Rhine, over the Alps; it gradually waxed fainter; it died away; those who had raised it began to ask each other, what, after all, was the matter about which they had been so clamorous, and wished to invite back the criminal whom they had just chased from them. His poetry became more popular than it had ever been; and his complaints were read with tears by thousands and tens of thousands who had never seen his face."

These observations of Macaulay are applied by Mr. Disraeli to Lord Cadurcis, who, in his novel called "Venetia," is no other than Lord Byron:—

"Lord Cadurcis," says he, "was the periodical victim, the scapegoat of English morality, sent into the wilderness with all the crimes and curses of the multitude on his head. Lord Cadurcis had certainly committed a great crime, not his intrigue with Lady Monteagle, for that surely was not an unprecedented offense; nor his duel with her husband, for after all it was a duel in self-defense: and, at all events, divorces and duels, under any circumstances, would scarcely have excited or authorized the storm which was now about to burst over the late spoiled child of society. But Lord Cadurcis had been guilty of the offense which, of all offenses, is punished most severely. Lord Cadurcis had been overpraised. He had excited too warm an interest; and the public, with its usual justice, was resolved to chastise him for its own folly. There are no fits of caprice so hasty and so violent as those of society. Cadurcis, in allusion to his sudden and singular success, had been in the habit of saying to his intimates that he 'woke one morning and found himself famous.' He might now observe, 'I woke one morning and found myself infamous.' Before twenty-four hours had passed over his duel with Lord Monteagle, he found himself branded by every journal in London as an unprincipled and unparalleled reprobate. The public, without waiting to think, or even to inquire after the truth, instantly selected as genuine the most false and the most flagrant of the fifty libellous narratives that were circulated of the transaction. Stories, inconsistent with themselves, were all alike eagerly believed, and what evidence there might be for any one of them, the virtuous people, by whom they were repeated, neither knew nor cared. The public, in short, fell into a passion with their daring, and, ashamed of their past idolatry, nothing would satisfy them but knocking the divinity on the head."

And this same Mr. Disraeli, whose testimony is all the more precious as coming from a Tory celebrity, after having described the shameful reception given by the noble House to Lord Cadurcis, when he presented himself there after the duel, and the atrocious conduct of the stupid populace clamoring against him outside, goes on in these terms:—

"And indeed to witness this young, and noble, and gifted creature, but a few days back the idol of the nation, and from whom a word, a glance even, was deemed the greatest and most gratifying distinction—whom all orders, classes, and conditions of men had combined to stimulate with multiplied adulation, with all the glory and ravishing delights of the world, as it were, forced upon him—to see him thus assailed with the savage execrations of all those vile things who exult in the fall of every thing that is great and the abasement of every thing that is noble, was indeed a spectacle which might have silenced malice and satisfied envy!"

To these just appreciations formed by some of Lord Byron's biographers we might add many more; but the limits we have assigned to this work not admitting of it, we will only add, as a last testimony, the most severe of all; him of whom Moore said, "that, if one wished to speak against Lord Byron, one had only to apply to him," that is, to Lord Byron himself.

In 1820, when Lord Byron was at Ravenna, an article from "Blackwood's Magazine," entitled "Observations on Don Juan," was sent him.

It contained such unfounded strictures on his matrimonial conduct, that, for once, Lord Byron infringed his rule and could not help answering it. The extracts from his defense, "*if defense it can be called*," says Moore, "*where there has never yet been any definite charge, will be read with the liveliest interest.*" Here, then, is a part of these extracts:—

"It is in vain, says my learned brother, that Lord Byron attempts in any way to justify his own behavior with regard to Lady Byron.

"And now that he has so openly and audaciously invited inquiry and reproach, we do not see any good reason why he should not be plainly told so by the voice of his countrymen."

"How far the openness of an anonymous poem, and the audacity of an imaginary character, which the writer supposes to be meant for Lady Byron, may be deemed to merit this formidable denunciation from their most sweet voices, I neither know nor care; but when he tells me that I can not 'in any way justify my own behavior in that affair,' I acquiesce, because no man can justify himself until he knows of what he is accused; and I have never had—and, God knows, my whole desire has ever been to obtain it—any specific charge, in a tangible shape, submitted to me by the adversary, nor by others, unless the atrocities of public rumor and the mysterious silence of the lady's legal advisers may be deemed such.

"But is not the writer content with what has been already said and done? Has not the general voice of his countrymen long ago pronounced upon the subject sentence without trial, and condemnation without a charge? Have I not been exiled by ostracism, except that the shells which proscribed me were anonymous? Is the writer ignorant of the public opinion and the public conduct upon that occasion? If he is, I am not: the public will forget both long before I shall cease to remember either.

"The man who is exiled by a faction has the consolation of thinking that he is a martyr; he is upheld by hope and the dignity of his cause, real or imaginary: he who withdraws from the pressure of debt may indulge in the thought that time and prudence will retrieve his circumstances; he who is condemned by the law as a term to his banishment, or a dream of his abbreviation; or, it may be, the knowledge or the belief of some injustice of the law, or of its administration, in his own particular. But he who is outlawed by general opinion, without the intervention of hostile politics, illegal judgment, or embarrassed circumstances, whether he be innocent or guilty, must undergo all the bitterness of exile, without hope, without pride, without alleviation. This case was mine. Upon what grounds the public founded their opinion I am not aware; but it was general, and it was decisive. Of me or of mine they knew little, except that I had written what is called poetry, was a nobleman, had married, became a father, and was involved in differences with my wife and her relatives, no one knew why, because the persons complaining refused to state their grievances. The fashionable world was divided into parties, mine consisting of a very small minority; the reasonable world was naturally on the stronger side, which happened to be the lady's, as was most proper and polite. The press was active and scurrilous; and such was the rage of the day that the unfortunate publication of two copies of verses rather complimentary than otherwise to the subjects of both, was tortured into a species of crime, or constructive petty treason. I was accused of every monstrous vice by public rumor and private rancor; my name, which had been a knightly or a noble one since my fathers helped to conquer the kingdom for William the Norman, was tainted. I felt that, if what was whispered, and muttered, and murmured, was true, I was unfit for England; if false, England was unfit for me. I withdrew: but this was not enough. In other countries, in Switzerland, in the shadow of the Alps, and by the blue depth of the lakes, I was pursued and breathed upon by the light. I crossed the mountains, but it was the same; so I went a little farther, and settled myself by the waves of the Adriatic, like the stag at bay, who betakes him to the waters.

"If I may judge by the statements of the few friends who gathered round me, the outcry of the period to which I allude was beyond all precedent, all parallel, even in those cases where political motives have sharpened slander and doubled enmity."

One regrets not being able to go on reproducing these fine pages written by Lord Byron, but the limits we have assigned ourselves force the sacrifice.

And now, after all that has been placed before the reader, will he not be curious to learn whether Lord Byron truly loved Lady Byron. The answer admits of no doubt. Could love exist between two natures so widely dissonant? But then it will be said, why did he marry her? This question may be answered by the simple observation that two-thirds of the marriages in high life, and indeed in all classes, are contracted without any love, nor are the parties, therefore, condemned to unhappiness. Still it is as well to recall that not only it did not enter into Lord Byron's views to marry for love and to satisfy passion, but that he married rather for the sake of escaping from the yoke of his passions! "If I were in love I should be jealous," said he, "and then I could not render happy the woman I married." "Let her be happy," added he, "and then, for my part, I shall also be so." Then again we find, "Let them only leave me my mornings free." Lastly, he wrote in his journal, before marrying Miss Milbank, and while in correspondence with her, "It is very singular, but there is not a spark of love between me and Miss Milbank." If, then, Miss Milbank married Lord Byron out of self-love, and to prevent his marrying a young and beautiful Irish girl, Lord Byron, on his part, married Miss Milbank from motives the most honorable to human nature. It was her *simple modest* air that attracted him and caused his delusion, and the fame of her virtues quite decided him. As to interested motives, they were at most but secondary; and his disinterestedness was all the more meritorious, since the embarrassed state of his affairs made him really require money, and Miss Milbank had none at that period. She was an only daughter, it is true; but her parents were still in the prime of life, and her uncle, Lord Wentworth, from whom her mother was to inherit before herself, might yet live many years. His marriage with Miss Milbank was thus not only disinterested as regards fortune, but even *imprudently generous;* for she only brought him a small dowry of £10,000—a mere trifle compared to the life of luxury she was to lead, in accordance with their mutual rank.* And these £10,000 were not only returned by Lord Byron on their separation, but generously doubled.

And now let us hasten to add that although Lord Byron was not in love with Miss Milbank, he had no dislike to her person, for she was rather pretty and pleasing in appearance. Her reputation for moral and intellectual qualities, standing on such a high pedestal, Lord Byron naturally conceived that esteem might well suffice to replace tenderness. It is certain that, if she had lent herself to it more, and if circumstances had only been endurable, their union might have presented the same character common to most aristocratic couples in England, and that even Lord Byron might have been able to act from virtue in default of feeling; but that little requisite for him was wholly wanting.

His celebrated and touching "Farewell" might be brought up as an objection to what we have just advanced. It might be said that the word *sincere* is a proof of love, and *insincere*

* See the description of her life made by him to Medwin during his stay at Pisa.

a proof of *falsehood*. Lastly, that in all cases there was a want of delicacy and refinement in thus confiding his domestic troubles to the public. Well, all that would be ill-founded, unjust, and contrary to truth. This is the truth of the matter. Lord Byron had just been informed that Lady Byron, having sent off by post the letter wherein she confirmed all that her father, Sir Ralph, had written, namely, her resolution of not returning to the conjugal roof, had afterward caused this letter to be sought for, and on its being restored, had given way to almost mad demonstrations of joy. Could he see aught else in this account save a certainty of the evil influences weighing on her, and making her act in contradiction to her real sentiments? He pitied her then as a victim, thought of all the virtues *said* to crown her, the illusive belief in which he was far then from having lost; he forgot the wrongs she had inflicted on him — the spying she had kept up around him—the calumnies spread against him—the use she had made of the letters subtracted from his desk. Yes, all was forgotten by his generous heart; and, according to custom, he even went so far as to accuse himself—to see in the victim only his wife, the mother of his little Ada! Under this excitement he was walking about at night in his solitary apartments, and suddenly chanced to perceive in some corner different things that had belonged to Lady Byron—dresses and other articles of attire. It is well known how much the sight of these inanimate mementoes has power to call up recollections even to ordinary imaginations. What, then, must have been the vividness with which they acted on an imagination like Lord Byron's? His heart softened toward her, and he recollected that one day, under the influence of sorrows which well-nigh robbed him of consciousness, he had answered her harshly. Thinking himself in the wrong, and full of the anguish that all these reflections and objects excited in his breast, he allowed his tears to flow, and, snatching a pen, wrote down that touching effusion, which somewhat eased his suffering.

The next day one of his friends found these beautiful verses on his desk; and, judging of Lady Byron's heart and that of the public according to his own, he imprudently gave them to the world. Thus we can no more doubt Lord Byron's sincerity in writing them than we can accuse him of publishing them. But what may cause astonishment is that they could possibly have been ill-interpreted, as they were; and, above all, that this touching "Farewell"—which made Madame de Staël say she would gladly have been unhappy, like Lady Byron, to draw it forth—that it should not have had power to rescue her heart from its apathy, and bring her to the feet of her husband, or at least into his arms. Let us add, in conclusion, that the most atrocious part of this affair, and doubtless the most wounding for him, was precisely Lady Byron's conduct; and in this conduct the worst was *her cruel silence!*

She has been called, after his words, the moral Clytemnestra* of her husband. Such a surname is severe; but the repugnance we feel to condemning a woman can not prevent our listening to the voice of justice, which tells us that the comparison is still in favor of the guilty one of antiquity. For she, driven to crime by fierce passion overpowering reason, at least only deprived her husband of physical life, and in committing the deed exposed herself to all its consequences; while Lady Byron left her husband at the very moment that she saw him struggling amid a thousand shoals, in the stormy sea of embarrassments created by his marriage, and precisely when he more than ever required a friendly, tender, and indulgent hand to save him from the tempests of life. Besides, she shut herself up in silence a thousand times more cruel than Clytemnestra's poniard, that only killed the body; whereas Lady Byron's silence was destined to kill the soul, and such a soul! leaving the door open to calumny, and making it to be supposed that her silence was magnanimity destined to cover over frightful wrongs, perhaps even depravity. In vain did he, feeling his conscience at ease, implore some inquiry and examination. She refused, and the only favor she granted was to send him, one fine day, two persons to see whether he were not mad. Happily Lord Byron only discovered at a later period the purport of this strange visit.

In vain did Lord Byron's friend, the companion of all his travels, throw himself at Lady Byron's feet, imploring her to

* Lord Byron, in lines wrung from him by anguish and anger, says *the moral Clytemnestra of thy lord.*

give over this fatal silence. The only reply she deigned was, that she had thought him mad!

And why, then, had she believed him mad? Because she, a methodical inflexible woman, with that unbendingness which a profound moralist calls the worship rendered to pride by a feelingless soul; — because she could not understand the possibility of tastes and habits different to those of ordinary routine, or of her own starched life! Not to be hungry when she was—not to sleep at night, but to write while she was sleeping, and to sleep when she was up—in short, to gratify the requirements of material and intellectual life at hours different to hers:—all that was not merely annoying for her, but it must be *madness!* or if not, it betokened depravity that she could neither submit to nor tolerate without perilling her own morality!

Such was the grand secret of the cruel silence which exposed Lord Byron to the most malignant interpretations—to all the calumny and revenge of his enemies.

She was perhaps the only woman in the world so strangely organized—the only one, perhaps, capable of not feeling happy and proud at belonging to a man superior to the rest of humanity! and fatally was it decreed that this woman *alone* of her species should be Lord Byron's wife!

Before closing this chapter it remains for us to examine if it be true, as several of his biographers have pretended, that he wished to be reunited to his wife. We must here declare that Lord Byron's intention, in the last years of his life, was, on the contrary, not to see Lady Byron again. This is what he wrote from Ravenna, to Moore, in June, 1820:—

"I have received a Parisian letter from W. W——, which I prefer answering through you, as that worthy says he is an occasional visitor of yours. In November last he wrote to me a well-meaning letter, stating for some reasons of his own, his belief that a *reunion* might be effected between Lady Byron and myself.

"To this I answered as usual; and he sent me a second letter, repeating his notions, which letter I have never answered, having had a thousand other things to think of. He now writes as if he believed that he had offended me by touching on the topic; and I wish you to assure him that

I am not at all so, but on the contrary, obliged by his good-nature. At the same time *acquaint him the thing is impossible. You know this as well as I, and there let it end.*"

A year later, at Pisa, he again said to M—— "*that he never would have been reunited* to Lady Byron; that the time for such a possibility was passed, and he had made *quite sufficient advances.*"

Let us add likewise that during the last period of his stay at Genoa, a person whose acquaintance he had just made, thought fitting, for several reasons and even by way of winning golden opinions among a certain set in England, to insist on this matter with Lord Byron.

In order to succeed, this person represented Lady Byron as a victim, telling him she was very ill physically and morally, and declaring the secret cause to be, no doubt, grief at her separation from him and dread of his asserting his rights over Ada.

Lord Byron, kind and impressionable as he was, may have been moved at this; but assuredly his resolution of not being reunited to Lady Byron was not shaken. His only reply was to show me a letter he had written some little time before:—

"The letter I inclose," said he, "may help to explain my sentiments. . . . . I was perfectly sincere when I wrote it, and am so still. But it is difficult for me to withstand the thousand provocations on that subject, which both friends and foes have for seven years been throwing in the way of a man whose feelings were once quick, and whose temper was never patient. But 'returning were as tedious as go o'er.' I feel this as much as ever Macbeth did; and it is a dreary sensation, which at least avenges the real or imaginary wrongs of one of the two unfortunate persons whom it concerns."

Here is the letter he wrote from Pisa to Lady Byron:—

"I have to acknowledge the receipt of Ada's hair, which is very soft and pretty, and nearly as dark already as mine was at twelve years old, if I may judge from what I recollect of some in Augusta's possession, taken at that age. But it don't curl, perhaps from its being let grow.

"I also thank you for the inscription of the date and name,

and I will tell you why: I believe that they are the only two or three words of your handwriting in my possession. For your letters I returned, and except the two words, or rather the one word, 'household,' written twice in an old account-book, I have no other. I burnt your last note for two reasons:—firstly, it was written in a style not very agreeable; and, secondly, I wished to take your word without documents, which are the worldly resources of suspicious people.

"I suppose that this note will reach you somewhere about Ada's birthday—the 10th of December, I believe. She will then be six, so that in about twelve more I shall have some chance of meeting her; perhaps sooner, if I am obliged to go to England by business or otherwise. Recollect, however, one thing, either in distance or nearness: every day which keeps us asunder should, after so long a period, rather soften our mutual feelings, which must always have one rallying-point as long as our child exists, which I presume we both hope will be long after either of her parents.

"The time which has elapsed since the separation has been considerably more than the whole brief period of our union, and the not much longer one of our prior acquaintance. We both made a bitter mistake; but now it is over, and irrevocably so. For at thirty-three on my part, and a few years less on yours, though it is no very extended period of life, still it is one when the habits and thoughts are generally so formed as to admit of no modification; and as we could not agree when younger, we should with difficulty do so now.

"I say all this, because I own to you that, notwithstanding every thing, I considered our reunion as not impossible for more than a year after the separation; but then I gave up the hope entirely and forever. But this very impossibility of reunion seems to me, at least, a reason why, on all the few points of discussion which can arise between us, we should preserve the courtesies of life, and as much of its kindness as people who are never to meet may preserve, perhaps more easily than nearer connections. For my own part, I am violent, but not malignant; for only fresh provocations can awaken my resentment. To you, who are colder and more concentrated, I would just hint that you may sometimes mistake the depth of a cold anger for dignity, and a worse feeling for duty. I assure you that I bear you now (whatever I may have done) no resentment whatever. Remember that if you have injured me in aught, this forgiveness is something; and that if I have injured you, it is something more still, if it be true, as moralists say, that the most offending are the least forgiving.

"Whether the offense has been solely on my side or reciprocal, or on yours chiefly, I have ceased to reflect upon any but two things, viz., that you are the mother of my child, and that we shall never meet again. I think if you also consider the two corresponding points with reference to myself, it will be better for all three. Yours ever,

"NOEL BYRON."

This letter, though never sent, requires no further proofs. It can now be understood, although the contrary has been said, that Lord Byron's resolution never again to unite with Lady Byron was irrevocable; but that, however, a reconciliation would have pleased him, on account of his daughter, and because no feeling of hatred could find room in his great *soul.*

CHAPTER XXIII.

LORD BYRON'S GAYETY AND MELANCHOLY.

HIS GAYETY.

A GREAT deal has been said about Byron's melancholy. His gayety has also been spoken of. As usual, all the judgments pronounced have been more or less false. His temperament is just as little known as his disposition, when people affect to judge him in an exclusive way.

Let me, then, be permitted in this instance also to re-establish truth on its only sure basis, namely, facts.

Lord Byron was so often gay that several of his biographers had thought themselves justified in asserting that *gayety* and not *melancholy* predominated in his nature. Even Mr. Galt, who only knew him at that period of his life when melancholy certainly predominated, nevertheless uses these expressions: — "Singular as it may seem, the poem itself ('Beppo,' his first essay of facetious poetry) has a stronger tone of gayety than his graver works have of melancholy, commonly believed to have been (I think unjustly) the predominant trait in his character."*

Many others have said the same thing. The truth is, that if by giving way to reflection—which was a necessity of his genius—and through circumstances—which were a fatality of his destiny—he has shown himself melancholy in his writings and very often in his dispositions, it is no less certain that by temperament and taste, by the activity, penetration, and complex character of his mind, he very often showed himself to be extremely gay. No one better than he seized upon the absurd and ridiculous side of things or more easily found cause for laughter. His gayety—the result of a frank, open, volatile nature, full of varying moods—was easily excited by any absurdities, ridiculous pretensions, or witty sallies; and

* Galt, p. 218.

then he became so expansive and charming, body and soul with him both seemed to laugh in such unison, that it was impossible not to catch the contagion; but his laughter was ever devoid of malice. Slight defects of harmony in things, or proportion, or mutual relation, easily gave rise to mirthful sensations in him. Being full of admiration for the beautiful, and having, moreover, a great sense of mutual fitness, and much activity of mind, it was with extraordinary and instinctive promptitude that he seized upon the contradictory relations existing between objects, and indeed on all showing a voluntary absence of order and beauty in the conduct of free reasonable beings. His laughter was then quite as æsthetical as it was innocent. And even if it were not admitted, as it is by all philosophical moralists, that no sort of personal calculation enters into this entirely spontaneous emotion, no sentiment of superiority over the being we are laughing at—for *selfishness and laughter never coexist*—if it were possible, I say, to doubt all this, even then to see Lord Byron laugh would have sufficed to give the right conviction. For truly his mirth was a charming thing; the very air surrounding him appeared to laugh.

Then would his soul, that often required to emerge from its deep reflections, unbend itself, and alternately disport or repose in utter self-abandonment. It dismissed thought, as it were, in order to become a child again; to deliver itself over to all the caprices of those myriad changeful fugitive impressions that course through the brain at moments of excitement.

Moore often recurs to Byron's liveliness. "Nothing, indeed, could be more amusing and delightful. . . . . It was like the bursting gayety of a boy let loose from school, and seemed as if there was no extent of fun or tricks of which he was not capable." When Moore visited him at Mira, in the autumn of 1812, and accompanied him to Venice, the former expressed himself as follows in his memorandum of that occasion:—

"As we proceeded across the lagoon in his gondola the sun was just setting, and it was an evening such as Romance would have chosen for a first sight of Venice, rising 'with her tiara of bright towers' above the wave; while to complete, as might be imagined, the solemn interest of the scene, I behold it in company with him who had lately given a new life to its glories, and sung of that fair City of the Sea thus grandly:—

'I stood in Venice, on the Bridge of Sighs;
A palace and a prison on each hand:
I saw from out the wave her structures rise
As from the stroke of the enchanter's wand:
A thousand years their cloudy wings expand
Around me, and a dying Glory smiles
O'er the far times, when many a subject land
Look'd to the winged Lion's marble piles,
Where Venice sat in state, throned on her hundred isles!'

"But whatever emotions the first sight of such a scene might, under other circumstances, have inspired me with, the mood of mind in which I now viewed it was altogether the reverse of what might have been expected. The exuberant gayety of my companion, and the recollections—any thing but romantic—into which our conversation wandered, put at once completely to flight all poetical and historical associations; and our course was, I am almost ashamed to say, one of uninterrupted merriment and laughter till we found ourselves at the steps of my friend's palazzo on the Grand Canal. All that ever happened, of gay or ridiculous, during our London life together; his scrapes and my lecturings; our joint adventures with the Bores and Blues, the two great enemies, as he always called them, of London happiness; our joyous nights together at Walter's, Kinnaird's, etc.; and that 'd—d supper of Rancliffe's, which ought to have been a dinner;' all was passed rapidly in review between us, and with a flow of humor and hilarity on his side of which it would have been difficult for persons even far graver than even I can pretend to be, not to have caught the contagion."

Lord Byron was especially prone to mirth and fun in the society of those he liked; to jest and laugh with any one was a great proof of his sympathy for them. When he wrote to absent dear ones, he would constantly say, "I have many things to tell you for us to laugh over together." In several letters addressed from Greece to Madame G——, he informs her of these treasures of mirth, held in reserve for the day of meeting, that they might laugh together. Lord Byron rarely used flattering language to those he loved. It was rather by looks than by words that he expressed his feelings and his approbation. His delight with intimates was to bring out strongly their defects, as well as their qualities and merits, by dint of jests, clever innuendo, and charming sallies of humor. The promptitude with which he discovered the slightest weakness, the faintest symptom of exaggeration or affectation, can hardly be credited. It might almost be said that the persons on whom he bestowed affection became *transparent* for him, that he divėd into their thoughts and feelings.

It was this state of mind especially that gave rise to those sallies of wit which formed such a striking feature of his intelligence. Then his conversation really became quite dazzling. In his glowing language all objects assumed unforeseen and picturesque aspects. New and striking thoughts followed from him in rapid succession, and the flame of his genius lighted up as if winged with wildfire. Those who have not known him at these moments can form no idea of what it was from his works. For, in the silence of his study, when, pen in hand, he was working out his grand conceptions, the lightning strokes lost much of their brilliant intensity; and although we find, especially in "Don Juan" and "Beppo," delightful pages of rich comic humor, only those who knew him can judge how superior still his conversation was. But in this gay exercise of his faculties, which was to him a real enjoyment in all his sallies or even in his railleries, not one iota of malice could be traced—unless we call by that name the amusement springing from mirth and wit indulged. Even if his shafts were finely pointed, they were at the same time so inoffensive that the most susceptible could not be wounded.

The great pleasure he took in jesting appears to have belonged to his organization, for it accompanied him throughout life. We have already seen what his nurses, his preceptors, and the friends of his childhood said on this subject. We have observed his sympathy for the old cup-bearer of his family mansion; the pleasantries expended on the quack Lavander, who was always promising to cure his foot, and never did; the jesting tone of his boyish correspondence; afterward the masqueradings that took place at Newstead Abbey; then again his gay doings with Moore and Rogers in London; the jests pervading the correspondence of his maturer years; then their concentration in "Beppo" and "Don Juan;" and finally, how often, even in Greece, when he was already unwell at Missolonghi, he could not help giving way to pleasantry and childish play to such a degree that good Dr. Kennedy, when he wished to convert him to his somewhat intolerant orthodoxy at Cephalonia, found one of the obstacles to consist in the difficulty of keeping Lord Byron serious.

"He was fond," says the doctor, "of saying smart and witty things, and never allowed an opportunity of punning to escape him. . . . . He generally showed high spirits and hilarity. . . . . I have heard him say several witty things; but as I was always anxious to keep him grave and present important subjects for his consideration, after allowing the laugh to pass I again endeavored to resume the seriousness of the conversation, while his lordship constantly did the same."

And then Kennedy adds:—"My impression from them was, that they were unworthy a man of his accomplishments: I mean the desire of jesting."*

These words well characterize the honest Methodist, who, like many other good and noble minds, yet could not understand fun. This incapability is also sometimes the case with persons of a sour, ill-natured, or susceptible disposition, whose excessive vanity is shocked at all simple, innocent explosions of gayety and pleasantry.† Colonel Stanhope, who knew Lord Byron at the same period, and who was not a Methodist, but who from other causes could not appreciate the poet's vivacious wit, said:—

"The mind of Lord Byron was like a volcano, full of fire and wrath, sometimes calm, often dazzling and playful. . . . As a companion," he adds, "no one could be more amusing than Lord Byron; he had neither pedantry nor affectation about him, but was natural and playful as a boy. His conversation resembled a stream; sometimes smooth, sometimes rapid, and sometimes rushing down in cataracts. It was a mixture of philosophy and slang, of every thing,—like his 'Don Juan.' He was a patient, and in general a very attentive, listener. When, however, he did engage with earnest-

* Kennedy, p. 301.

† See Galt, with regard to Hunt.

ness in conversation, his ideas succeeded each other with such uncommon rapidity that he could not control them. They burst from him impetuously; and although he both attended to and noticed the remarks of others, yet he did not allow these to check his discourse for an instant."

"There was usually," writes Count Gamba, his friend and companion in Greece, in his interesting work, entitled "Last Travels of Lord Byron in Greece," "a liveliness of spirit and a tendency to joke, even at times of great danger, when other men would have become serious and pre-occupied. This disposition of mind gave him a kind of air of frankness and sincerity which was quite irresistible with those persons even who were most prejudiced against him."

This allusion of Count Gamba refers to the letter which Byron wrote in the midst of the Suliotes, among whom he had taken refuge during the storm and to escape the Turks.

"If any thing," writes Lord Byron, on the point of embarking for Missolonghi, and in his last letter to Moore, "if any thing in the way of fever, fatigue, famine, or otherwise, should cut short the middle age of a brother warbler, like Garcilasso de la Vega, I pray you remember me in 'your smiles and wine.'

"I have hopes that the cause will triumph; but, whether it does or no, still 'honor must be minded as strictly as a milk diet.' I trust to observe both. BYRON."

"It is matter of history," continues Count Gamba, "that Lord Byron, in consequence of vexations to which he was ever a victim, added to the rigorous diet which he followed (he only fed upon vegetables and green tea, to show that he could live as frugally as a Greek soldier), and from the impossibility which he found to take any exercise at Missolonghi, had a nervous fit, which deprived him of the power of speech and alarmed all his friends and acquaintances. When the crisis had worn off, he merely laughed over it."

"Even at Missolonghi," says Parry, who knew him there only in the midst of troubles and vexations of every description and quite at the close of his life, "he loved to jest in words and actions. These pleasantries lightened his spirits, and prevented him from dwelling on disagreeable thoughts."

Perhaps this disposition of character was the result of his French origin, for it is scarcely known or even appreciated in England.

"Yet," exclaims the greatest-minded woman of our day (Madame G. Sand), "it is that disposition which forms the charm of every delicate intimacy, and which often prevents our committing many follies and stupidities.

"To look for the ridiculous side of things is to discover their weakness. To laugh at the dangers in the midst of which we find ourselves is to get accustomed to brave them; like the French, who go into action with a laugh and a song. To quiz a friend is often to save him from a weakness in which our pity might perhaps have allowed him to linger. To laugh at one's self is to preserve one's self from the effects of an exaggerated self-love. I have noticed that the people who never joke are gifted with a childish and insupportable vanity."

Nevertheless, there are high and noble natures that never laugh, and are incapable of understanding the pleasures of gayety. But minds like these have some vacuum; they certainly lack what is called wit.

Lord Byron's gayety, full of dazzling wit and varied tints, like his other faculties, never went beyond the limits befitting its exercise in a beautiful soul. As much as the truly ridiculous, that which a great writer has defined, "*the strength, small or great, of a free being, out of proportion with its end,*" —as much, I say, as the truly ridiculous attracted and amused him, just as much did grave, moral, and physical disorders, produced by corruption of body or soul, sadden and repel his nature, so full of harmony. He could never laugh at these latter. The grave disorders of soul that exist in free beings, and that are therefore voluntary, raised sadness, anger, or indignation in him, according to the degree of vice or disorder. We need seek no other origin for his bitterest satires in verse and prose. Great ugliness and physical defects certainly inspired him with great disgust, consequent upon his passion for the beautiful; but, at the same time, involuntary misfortunes excited his liveliest compassion, often testified by the most generous deeds.

We know, for instance, that Lord Byron had a defect in one of his feet, but a defect so slight—although it has been greatly exaggerated—that people have never been able to say in which of the two feet it did exist. Nor did it in any way diminish the grace and activity all his movements displayed. If its existence were painful for him, that must have been because his sense of harmony looked upon this defect as detrimental to the perfection of his physical beauty. But whatever may have been the cause of this sensibility, it sufficed in any case to make him feel a generous compassion for all those afflicted with any defect analogous to his own. Lord Harrington, then Colonel Stanhope, says:—

"Contrary to what we observe in most people, Lord Byron, who was always very sensitive to the sufferings of others, showed greatest sympathy for those who had any imperfection akin to his own." At Ravenna, his favorite beggar limped. And on him Lord Byron bestowed the privilege of picking up all the largest coins struck down by his dexterous pistol-shots in the forest of pines. We have said he never laughed at any involuntary defect, not even at a person falling (as is so often the case), for fear it might have been caused by bodily weakness, neither did he ridicule any of the weaknesses or shortcomings of intelligence.

He did not laugh at a bad poet on account of his bad verses. When he was at Pisa, an Irishman there was engaged in translating the "Divine Comedy." The translation was very heavy and faulty; but the translator was most enthusiastic about the great poet, and absolutely lived on the hope of getting his work published. All the English at Pisa, including the kind Shelley, were turning him into ridicule. Lord Byron alone would not join in the laugh. T——'s sincerity won for him grace and compassion. Indeed Lord Byron did still more; for he wrote and entreated Murray to publish the work, so as to give the poor poet this consolation. Not content with that step, he wrote to Moore to beg Jeffrey not to criticise him, undertaking himself to ask Gifford the same thing, through Murray. "Perhaps they might speak of the commentaries without touching on the text," said he; and then he added with his usual pleasantry, "However, we must not trust to it. *Those dogs! the text is too tempting.*"*

* Moore, Letter 468.

Nor did he laugh at exaggerated devotion, even if it were extravagant or superstitious, provided he thought it sincere. Countess G——, paternal aunt of Countess G——, the greatest beauty of Romagna in 1800, had fallen into such extreme mystical devotion, through the brutal jealousy of her husband, that she died in the odor of sanctity. This lady wrote to her brother, Count G——, at Genoa, saying how happy she was, and giving no end of praise to "the good Jesuit Fathers," and speaking of her devotion to St. Teresa. Madame G——, having sent one of these letters to Lord Byron, he answered: "I consider all that as *very respectable*, and, moreover, *enviable*. The aunt is right; I wish I could love the good fathers and St. Teresa. After all, what does this devotee of St. Teresa, this friend of the good Jesuit Fathers, want? Happiness; and she has found it! What else are we seeking for?"

We have already seen elsewhere* that Lord Byron never, at any period of his life, laughed at religion or its *sincere* votaries, whatever might be their creed of belief. Provided their errors came from the heart, they commanded his respect. Dallas himself, in reference to the skeptical stanzas of his twenty-second year, can not help rendering him justice.

"I have not noticed," says he, "a spirit of mockery in you; and you have the little-known art of not wishing that others should be of your opinion in matters of religious belief. I am less disinterested; I have the greatest desire, nay, even a great hope, to see you some day believe as I do." We have seen, also, what Kennedy said of him in Greece.† Dr. Millingen bears the same testimony:—

"During the whole of the time that I visited him, I never heard him utter a single word of contempt for the Christian religion. On the contrary, he used often to say, that nothing could be more reprehensible than to turn into ridicule those who believed in it, since in this strange world it is equally difficult to arrive at knowing what one is or is not to believe; and since many freethinkers teach doctrines which are as much beyond the reach of human comprehension as the mysteries of the revelation itself."

When, by habit of looking at serious things from their ab-

* See chapter on "Religion." † Ibid.

surd and ridiculous side, he feared he had done the same with regard to some religious ceremony, he at once hastened to explain himself. Thus he writes to Moore from Pisa:—

"I am afraid that this sounds flippant, but I don't mean it to be so; only my turn of mind is so given to taking things in the absurd point of view, that it breaks out in spite of me every now and then. Still, I do assure you that I am a very good Christian. Whether you believe me in this, I do not know."

But much as he respected sincere religious feelings, equally did he detest that hypocrisy which despises in secret the idol it adores in public. Even at the transition period of what has been called his skepticism, it was extremely distasteful to him to speak against religion, to despise and mock even the hollow worship practiced outwardly from human motives and personal interest. In Livadia at this time he met with a Greek bishop, whose actions were quite at variance with his language. How great the antipathy Lord Byron conceived for him, may be seen by the notes appended to the first and second cantos of "Childe Harold." For the Pharisees of our days he felt all the anger due to whited sepulchres. No, certainly, it was not true virtue in general, nor any one virtue in particular, that he laughed at sometimes; nor was it friendship, or love, or religion, or any truly respectable sentiment that ever excited his mirth. He only ridiculed semblances, vain appearances, when those who paraded them did so from *personal interest.* Lord Byron knew too well, by experience, that many virtues admired and set forth as such do but wear a mask in reality; and he thought it useful for society to divest them of it, and show the hidden visage. Why should he have shown any consideration for the virtue that patronizes charity-balls, in order to acquire the right of violating, with impunity, the duties of a Christian wife? or that other female virtue which weighs itself in the balance with the privilege of directing Almacks? or that, wishing to unite the advantages of modesty with the gratification of passion? In short, why should he have shown consideration for persons whose merit consists in never *allowing themselves to be seen as they are?* He was very disrespectful, likewise, toward certain friendships that he knew by experience to be full of wordy counsel, but finding nothing to say in the way of consolation or defense. This peculiar variety of friendship had made him suffer greatly. In his serious poems he calls it "*the loss of his illusions;*" and expresses himself with misanthropical indignation, or with a bleeding heart. But, returning to a milder philosophy, he ended by smiling and jesting at it, in words like these:—

> "Look'd grave and pale to see her friend's fragility,
> For which most friends reserve their sensibility."

Seriously; was he bound to any great tenderness toward such friendship as that? And does it not suffice to set Lord Byron right with *true friendship* to hear him say, after having laughed about false friends:—

> "But this is not my maxim: had it been,
> Some heart-aches had been spared me: yet I care not—
> I would not be a tortoise in his screen
> Of stubborn shell, which waves and weather wear not.
> 'Tis better, on the whole, to have felt and seen
> That which humanity may bear, or bear not:
> 'Twill teach discernment to the sensitive,
> And not to pour their ocean in a sieve."*

Friendship was so necessary to him that he wrote to Moore, on the eve of his marriage, 15th of October, 1814:

"An' there were any thing in marriage that would make a difference between my friends and me, particularly in your case, I would none on't."

People should read all he said of Lord Clare and Moore, and see with what almost jealous susceptibility he guarded the title of friend,† before they can understand the value he attached to true friendship. But among many of the *privileges* he conceded to friendship, *duties* also held their place.

And if we pass from friendship to love, could he really bestow such respect on the loves of a Lady Adeline, or of those who, he said, "embrace you to-day, thinking of the novel they will write to-morrow." His ideal of true love has been noticed; and he became impatient when he saw it confounded with any thing else. At twenty-two years of age he wrote to his young friend, the Rev. Mr. Harness:—

"I told you the fate of B—— and H—— in my last. So

* "Don Juan," canto xiv.

† See Lord Byron's letter to Mrs. Shelley.

much for these sentimentalists, who console themselves in their stews for the loss—the never-to-be-recovered loss—the despair of the refined attachment of a couple of drabs ! You censure my life, Harness: when I compare myself with these men, my elders and my betters, I really begin to conceive myself a monument of prudence—a walking statue—without feeling or failing; and yet the world in general hath given me a proud pre-eminence over them in profligacy. Yet I like the men, and, God knows, ought not to condemn their aberrations. But I own I feel provoked when they dignify all this by the name of love—romantic attachments for things marketable for a dollar !"

Yes, Lord Byron never did respect the love that can be bartered for dollars. And afterward, when irritation had given way to a milder and more tolerant philosophy, he took the liberty of laughing at it, both in prose and verse. It may however, be urged against him, that he sometimes turned into ridicule even his deepest sentiments; and Moore remarks this as a defeat, apropos of the jesting tone he assumed once at Bologna, when writing to Hoppner. But Moore forgets to say, that while his heart called him to Ravenna, he was speaking against the counsels given by Hoppner, who, in order to deter him from this visit, for reasons previously cited,* had made the darkest prognostications regarding its consequence; and though he could not shake Lord Byron's determination, it is very probable that he may have upset his imagination. Thus he was trying to show himself ready for every thing. Such pleasantries are like the song of one who is alarmed in the dark. Moreover, from his manner of judging human nature, and his lively sense of the ridiculous, Lord Byron was well aware that a light tone is alone admissible for speaking to others of a love they do not share, and more especially when they disapprove of it. He felt that the gayety of Ovid and the gallantry of Horace are better suited to indifferent people than Petrarch's high-flown phrases and sentimentalities, or Werther's despair. It was through this same nice perception of the sentiments entertained by indifferent individuals that he sometimes adopted a light, playful tone in conversation, or in his correspondence, when

* See his "Life in Italy."

speaking of friendship, devoted feelings of any kind, and a host of sentiments very serious and deep within his own heart, but which he believed less calculated to interest others. And if sometimes his singular penetration of the human heart called forth mockery, it sprang more frequently from seeing fine sentiments put forth in flagrant contradiction with conduct, or morality looked upon as a mere thing of outward decorum, speedily to be set aside, if once the actors were removed from the eyes of the world. He would not grant his esteem to fine sentiments expressed by writers who could be bribed; to the promises of heroes who noisily enroll combatants, while themselves remaining safe by their fireside; or to the generosity that displays itself from a balcony. And, assuredly, he had a right to be particular in his estimate of this latter virtue, which he himself always practiced secretly, and in the shade. He would not consent to its being bartered, nor that people should have the honor of it without any sacrifice on their part. Thus he replied to Moore, who was in an ecstasy about the generosity of Lord some one:—"I shall believe all that when you prove to me that there is no advantage in openly helping a man like you." With wonderful, and, I might almost say, supernatural perspicacity, Lord Byron penetrated into the arcana of souls, and did not come out thence with a very good opinion of what he had seen. But, kind as he was, he did not like to probe too deeply the motives of others, especially as a rule of action for himself. As he says in his admirable satire of "Don Juan,"—

> "'Tis sad to burrow deep to roots of things,
> So much are they besmeared with earth."

Lastly, his mockeries were all directed against the vice he most abhorred—*hypocrisy;* for he looked upon that as a gangrene to the soul, the cause of most of the evils that afflict society, and certainly of all his own misfortunes. As long as he was obliged to bear it, under the depressing influence of England's misty atmosphere, he felt by turns saddened and indignant. But when he reached Italy, his soul caught the bright rays that emanate from a southern sky, and he preferred to combat hypocrisy with the lighter weapons of pleasantry. But whichsoever arm he wielded, he always pursued the enemy remorselessly, following into every fastness, of which none knew better than himself each winding and each resource. For hypocrisy had been the bane of his life; it had rendered useless for happiness that combination he possessed of Heaven's choicest gifts; the plenitude of affections, numberless qualities most charming in domestic life, for he had been exiled from the family circle. Hypocrisy had *forced* him to despise a country also that could act toward him like an unnatural parent, rather than a true mother, wounding him with calumnies, and obstinately depreciating him, solely because she allowed hypocrisy to reign on her soil. Such, then, were the virtues which he permitted himself to mock at.

"*We must not make out a ridicule where none exists*," says La Bruyère; but it is well to see that which has a being, and to draw it forth gracefully, in a manner that may both please and instruct.

As to true, holy, pure, undeniable virtues, no one more than he admired and respected them. "Any trait of virtue or courage," says one of his biographers, "caused him deep emotion, and would draw tears from his eyes, provided always he were convinced that it had not been actuated by a desire of shining or producing effect."

"A generous action," says another, "the remembrance of patriotism, personal sacrifice, disinterestedness, would cause in him the most sublime emotions, the most brilliant thoughts." The more his opinion as to the rarity of virtue appeared to him well-founded, the more did he render homage when he met with it. The more he felt the difficulty of overcoming pasions, the more did a victory gained over them excite his admiration.

"Pray make my respects to Mrs. Hoppner, and assure her of my unalterable reverence for the singular goodness of her disposition, which is not without its reward even in this world. For those who are no great believers in human virtues would discover enough in her to give them a better opinion of their fellow-creatures, and—what is still more difficult—of themselves, as being of the same species, however inferior in approaching its nobler models."

At Coppet he was more touched by the conjugal affection of the young Duchesse de Broglie for her husband, than he was attracted by the genius even of her mother, Madame de Stäel. "Nothing," says he in his memoranda, "was more agreeable than to see the manifestation of domestic tenderness in this young woman." When he received at Pisa the posthumous message sent by a beautiful, angelic young creature, who had caught a glimpse of him but once, and who, nevertheless, in the solemn hours of her agony, thought of him, and prayed to God for him, it made a deep impression on his mind.

"In the evening," says Madame G——, "he spoke to me at great length of this piety and touching virtue."

Mr. Stendhall, who knew him during his stay at Milan in 1816, says:—"I passed almost all my evenings with Lord B. Whenever this singular man was excited and spoke with enthusiasm, his sentiments were noble, great, and generous; in short, worthy of his genius."

And then when Mr. Stendhall speaks of walking alone with him in the large green-room at La Scala, he adds:—

"Lord Byron made his appearance for half an hour every evening, holding the most delightful conversation it was ever my good-fortune to hear. A volume of new ideas and generous sentiments came pouring out in such novel form, that one fancied one's self enjoying them for the first time. The rest of the evening the great man lapsed into the English noble."

Even biographers most hostile to Lord Byron render justice to his sensibility and respect for real virtue, for all that is true and estimable. And if we seek proofs of the same in his poems and correspondence, we shall find it at every page, not excepting "Don Juan,"—the satire that most exposed him to the anger and calumny of *cant*. This is why I shall confine myself to borrowing quotations from this poem. For instance, in speaking of military glory, he says:—

"The drying up a single tear has more
Of honest fame, than shedding seas of gore.

"And why?—because it brings self-approbation;
Whereas the other, after all its glare,
Shouts, bridges, arches, pensions from a nation,
* * * * * *
Are nothing but a child of Murder's rattles."*

* "Don Juan," canto viii.

And then again:—

> "*One* life saved . . . .
> . . . . is a thing to recollect
> Far sweeter than the greenest laurels sprung
> From the manure of human clay, though deck'd
> With all the praises ever said or sung;
> Though hymn'd by every harp, unless within
> Your heart join chorus, Fame is but a din."*

When he speaks of Souvaroff, who, with a hand still reeking from the massacre of 40,000 combatants, began his dispatch to the Autocrat in these words:—

> "Glory to *God* and to the Empress [Catharine]! Ismail's ours!"

Lord Byron exclaims:—

> "Powers
> Eternal! such names mingled!
>
> "Methinks these are the most tremendous words
> Since 'Mené, Mené, Tekel,' and 'Upharsin,'
> Which hands or pens have ever traced of swords.
> Heaven help me! I'm but little of a parson:
> What Daniel read was short-hand of the Lord's,
> Severe, sublime; the prophet wrote no farce on
> The fate of nations;—but this Russ so witty
> Could ryhme, like Nero, o'er a burning city.
>
> "He wrote this Polar melody, and set it,
> Duly accompanied by shrieks and groans,
> Which few will sing, I trust, but none forget it—
> For I will teach, if possible, the stones
> To rise against earth's tyrant's."†

And then when he speaks of truly virtuous men — the Washingtons and Franklins—those who preferred a quiet, retired life; so as better to walk in the paths of justice and goodness, like the ancient heroes of Sparta, one feels that his words come really from the heart. But if I wished to make extracts of all the proofs contained in his works, of respect and enthusiasm for true virtue, a volume of quotations would be requisite. Thus I have only chosen some at hazard, selecting them principally from that admirable satire of "Don Juan," which combines more deep philosophy and true morality than is to be found in the works of many moralists; and I may likewise say more wit, and knowledge of the human heart, more kindness and indulgence, than ever before were united in a volume of verse or prose, and more, perhaps,

* "Don Juan," canto ix. † Ibid. canto viii.

than ever will be. Yet, despite of all this, the independence, boldness, and above all, the true state of things revealed in "Don Juan," excited great anger throughout the political, religious, and moral world of England; indeed, passion went so far in distorting, that the tendency and moral bearing of the poem were quite misunderstood. With regard to France, where this satire is only known through a prose translation, which mars half its cleverness, "Don Juan" serves, however, the purpose of an inexhaustible reservoir, whence writers unwittingly draw much they deem their own. Besides, from analogy of race, he is, perhaps, better appreciated in France than in his own country; for few English do understand what true justice he rendered himself when he said,—that, in point of fact, his character was far too lenient, the greatest proof of his muse's discontent being a smile.

But if, despite all this evidence, people should still persist, as is very possible, in asserting that Lord Byron ridiculed, satirized, and denied the existence of real virtues, at least we would ask to have these virtues named, so as to be able to answer. What are the virtues so insulted? Is it truth, piety, generosity, firmness, abnegation, devotedness, independence, patriotism, humanity, heroism? But if he denied not one of these, if he only ridiculed and satirized their semblances, their hypocritical shadows, then let critics and envious minds—the ignorant, or the would-be ignorant—let them cease, in the name of justice, thus to offer lying insult to a great spirit no longer able to defend himself.

Perhaps he did not render sufficient homage to that great and respectable virtue of his country—conjugal fidelity; but he has told us why. It appeared to him that this virtue, supposed to stamp society, was, in truth, more a pretense than a reality among the higher classes in England; and, if he examined his own heart, this virtue wore a name for him that had been the martyrdom of his whole life.

I may say, farther, that when he saw a truth shining at the expense of some hypocrisy, he did not *shut it up in his casket of precious things*, to carry them with him to the grave, nor did he only name them in a low voice to his secretaries, because by *speaking aloud he might have done some harm to himself* (as, however, the great Goethe did and *acknowledged*).

Lord Byron, without thinking of the consequences that might ensue to himself, deemed, on the contrary, that truth ought to be courageously unveiled: and to the heroism of deeds he added the heroism of words.

It must not be forgotten, either, that there existed a certain kind of timidity among the other elements of his character, and that jesting often helps to season a tiresome conversation, rendering it less difficult, besides enabling us to hide our real sentiments.

CHAPTER XXIV.

THE MELANCHOLY OF LORD BYRON.

"To know the real cause of our sadness is near akin to knowing what we are worth."—PARADOL, *Study on Moralists.*

FROM all that we have said, and judging from that natural tendency of his mind to look at even serious things on the ridiculous, laughable side, would it be correct to infer that Lord Byron was always gay, and never melancholy? Those maintaining such an opinion, would have to bear too many contradictions. Physiology, psychology, and history, would together protest against such an assertion. We affirm, on the contrary, that Lord Byron was often melancholy; but that, in order to judge well the nature and shades of his melancholy, it is necessary to analyze and observe it, not only in his writings, but also in his conduct through life. Whence arose his melancholy? Was it one of those moral infirmities, incurable and causeless, commencing from the cradle, like that of René, whose childhood was morose, and whose youth disdainful; who, ere he had known life, seemed to bend beneath its mysteries; who knowing not how to be young, will no more know how to be old; who in all things wanted order, proportion, harmony, truth; who had nothing to produce equilibrium between the power of genius and the indolence of will? This kind of melancholy is fatal to the practice of any virtue, and seems like a sacrifice of heart on the altar of pride. Was it a melancholy like Werther's, whose senses, stimulated by passion, of which society opposed the development, carried perturbation also into the moral regions? Was it the deep mysterious ailment of Hamlet, at once both meek and full of logic? or the sickness of that "masculine breast with feeble arms;" "of that philosopher who only wanted strength to become a saint;" "of that bird without wings," said a woman of genius, "that exhales its calm melancholy plaint on the shores whence vessels depart, and where only shivered remnants return;" the melancholy of an Obermann, whose goodness and almost ascetic virtues are palsied for want of equilibrium, and whose discouragement and ennui were only calculated to exercise a baneful influence over the individual, and over humanity? No; the *striking* characteristics that exist in all these sorts of melancholy are utterly wanting to Lord Byron's. His was not a melancholy that had become chronic, like René's, ere arriving at life's maturity. For, whereas, the child René was gloomy and wearied, the child Byron was passionate and sensitive, but gay, amusing, and frolicsome. His fits of melancholy were only developed under the action of thought, reflection, and circumstances. Nor was it Werther's kind of melancholy; for, even at intensest height of passion, reason never abandoned its sway over Lord Byron's energetic soul; with himself, if not with his heroes, personal sacrifice always took, or wished to take, the place of satisfied passion.

It was not that of Hamlet, for a single instant's dissimulation would have been impossible for Lord Byron. It was not that of Obermann, for his energetic nature could not partake the weakness and powerlessness of Oberon; his strength equalled his genius.

It was not, either, that of Childe Harold, for this hero of his first poem is, in the first and second canto, the personification of youthful exquisites, with senses dulled and satiated by excesses to which Lord Byron had never yielded when he composed this type, since he was then only twenty-one years of age, and had hardly quitted the university, where he lived surrounded by intellectual friends, who have all testified to his mode of life there, and then at Newstead Abbey, where he may have become a little dissipated, but still without any excess capable of engendering satiety. Nor was his melancholy that of the darker heroes he has described in "Lara" and "Manfred," for he never knew remorse; and we have already seen to what must be attributed all these identifications between himself and his heroes.*

In general, these kinds of melancholy have other causes, or else they arise from individual organization. With him, on the contrary, melancholy always originated from some moral

* See the Introduction.

external cause, which would tend to show, that without such cause, his melancholy would not have existed, or else might have been quite overcome. But, before arriving at a definition, we must analyze it, after taking a rapid glance at his whole life.

It has even been said, that our conduct in early years offers a sure indication of our future; that the man does but continue the child. Let us then begin by studying Byron during his childhood. We know from the testimony of his nurses and preceptors, both in Scotland and England, that goodness, sensibility, tenderness, and likewise gayety, with a tendency to jesting, formed the basis of his character. Nevertheless, a yearning after solitude led him into solitary distant walks, along the sea-shore when he was living at Aberdeen, or amid the wild poetic mountains of Scotland, near the romantic banks of the Dee, often putting his life in danger, and causing much alarm to his mother. But this sprang simply from his ardent nature, which, far from inclining him to melancholy, made earth seem like a paradise.

Has he not described these ecstasies of his childhood in "Tasso's Lament:"—

"From my very birth my soul was drunk with love," etc.

This want of solitude became still more remarkable as reflection acquired further development. At Harrow, he would leave his favorite games and dear companions to go and sit alone on the stone which bears his name. But this want of living alone sometimes in the fairyland of his imagination, feeding on his own sentiments, and the bright illusions of his youthful soul, was that what is yclept melancholy? No, no; what he experienced was but the harbinger of genius, destined to dazzle the world; Disraeli, that great observer of the race of geniuses, so affirms:—

"Eagles fly alone," exclaims Sydney, "while sheep are ever to be found in flocks."

Almost all men of genius have experienced this precocious desire of solitude. But Lord Byron, who united so many contrasts, and, according to Moore, the faculties of several men, had also much of the child about him. And, while almost all children belonging to the race of great intellects, have neither taste nor aptitude for bodily exercises and games of dexterity, he, by exception to the general rule, on coming out of his reveries, experienced equally the want of giving himself up passionately to the play and stir of companions who were inferior to him in intelligence. Up to this, then, we can discover no symptom in him of that *fatal* kind of melancholy — that which is *hereditary* and *causeless*. But anon, his heart begins to beat high, and the boy already courts aspirations, ardent desires, illusions that may well be destined to agitate, afflict, or even overwhelm him. Meanwhile let us follow him from Harrow to the vacations passed at Nottingham and Southwell. There we shall see him acting plays with enthusiasm, making himself the life of the social circle assembled round the amiable Pigott family, delighting in music, and writing his first effusions in verse. Certainly it was not melancholy that predominated in his early poems, but rather generosity, kindness, sincerity, the ardor of a loving heart, the aspiration after all that is passionate, noble, great, virtuous and heroic; but these verses also make us feel by a thousand delicate shades of sentiment portrayed, and by cherished illusions pertinaciously held, that melancholy may hereafter succeed in making new passage for itself, and finding out the path to that loving, passionate heart. And, in truth, it did more than once penetrate there. For death snatched from him, first, two dear companions of his childhood, and then the young cousin, who beneath an angel's guise on earth, first awakened the fire of love. And afterward Lord Byron gave his heart, of fifteen, to another affection, was deceived, met with no return,* but, on the contrary, was sorely wounded. Yet all the melancholy thus engendered was accidental and factitious, springing from the excessive sensibility of his physical and moral being, as well as from circumstances; his griefs resembled the usual griefs of youth. It was in these dispositions that he quitted Harrow for Cambridge University. There, one of the greatest sorrows of his life overtook him. It was a complex sentiment, made up of regret at having left his beloved Harrow, of grief at the recent loss of a cherished affection, and, lastly, sadness caused by a very modest and very singular feeling for a youth of his age; he regretted no

* See chapter on "Generosity."

longer feeling himself a child, which regret can only be explained by a presentiment of therefore soon being called on to renounce other illusions. This is how he spoke of it still, when at Ravenna, in 1821:—

"It was one of the most fatal and crushing sentiments of my life, to feel that I was no longer a child."

He fell ill from it. But all these sorts of melancholy, arising from *palpable avowed* causes, having their origin in the heart, might equally find their cure in the heart. Already did imagination transport him toward his beloved Ida, and he consoled himself by saying, that if love has wings, friendship ought to have none. If this were an illusion, he completed it by writing that charming poem of his youth, "Friendship is Love without Wings."*

At Cambridge he met again one of his dearest friends from Harrow, Edward Long; he also made acquaintance with the amiable Eddlestone, and his melancholy disappeared in the genial atmosphere of friendship. As long as these dear friends remained near him he was happy, even at Cambridge. But they were called to different careers, and destiny separated them. Long, with whom he had passed such happy days,† left the first to go into the guards. Eddlestone remained, but Lord Byron himself was already about to quit Cambridge. During the vacation, we see him modestly preparing his first poems intended as an offering to Friendship; then going to a watering-place with some respectable friends; devoting himself with ardor to dramatic representations at the amateur theatre at Southwell, where he was more than ever the life of society; and thus he remained a whole year away from Cambridge, often seeing his dear Long again in London, and visiting Harrow with him. When he returned, in 1807, to Cambridge, Long had already left, and Eddlestone was shortly to go; thus, he no longer heard the song of that amiable youth, nor the flute of his dear Long, and melancholy well-nigh seized hold on him. Nevertheless, he consoled himself with projects for the future. Besides, he was already nineteen years of age, had made some progress in the journey of life, probably leaving some illusions behind him on the bushes that lined the roadside, and perhaps his soul had already lost somewhat of its early purity.

* See chapter on "Friendships." † Ibid.

He had certainly seen that many things in the moral world were far removed from the ideal forms with which he had invested them; that love, even friendship, virtue, patriotism, generosity, and goodness, by no means attained the height of his first convictions. A year before, he had said: "I have tasted the joy and the bitterness of love." Willingly again would he have given way to the emotions of the heart; but he too soon perceived that to do so were a useless, dangerous luxury,—a language scarcely understood in the world in which he moved; that the idols he had believed of precious metal, were, in reality, made of vile clay. Then he also resolved on taking his degrees in vice; but, unlike others, he did so *with disgust*, and he called satiety, not the *quantity*, but the *quality* of the aliment. A year before he had also said: "*I have found that a friend may promise and yet deceive.*"

Magnanimous as he was, he made advances to the guilty friend, and took half the blame on himself; but in vain was he generous, saying, with tears that flowed from his heart to his pen:—

"You knew that my soul, that my heart, my existence,
If danger demanded, were wholly your own;
You knew me unalter'd by years or by distance,
Devoted to love and to friendship alone."

And then:—

"Repentance will cancel the vow you have made."

And again:

"With me no corroding resentment shall live:
My bosom is calm'd by the simple reflection,
That both may be wrong, and that both should forgive."

The friend did not return, and Lord Byron's generous, pure, delicate nature—fearful lest he might be in the wrong—could only find peace in trying to offer reparation. He wrote to Lord Clare:—

"I have, therefore, made all the reparation in my power, by apologizing for my mistake, though with very faint hopes of success. His answer has not arrived, and, most probably, never will. However, I have eased my own conscience by the atonement, which is humiliating enough to one of my disposition; yet I could not have slept satisfied with the reflection of having, even unintentionally, injured any individual. I have done all that could be done to repair the injury, and there the affair must rest. Whether we renew our intimacy or not is of very trivial consequence."

But although he could no longer rely entirely upon his heart for defending his loved illusions so cruelly attacked by reality, yet it was not possible for him to put out of sight his ideal of all the beauties of soul whose presence was a condition of his being. And it was this presence that made material dissipated life, and also the intellectual routine existence at Granta, both appear so unattractive to him. He wrote a satire on them, and the blame inflicted shows his fine nature. When evil was thus judged, thus condemned, alike by pen and heart, there could be no real danger; not even had it power to sadden him. A more formidable peril menaced him from another side. Sadness might now reach his heart through his mind. That deep intellect, so given to analyze, meditate, generalize, from childhood upward, according to the relative capacity of age, was ever busy with the great problems of life. It has been seen that he began to worry even his nurses with childish questions, and afterward much more to embarrass his tutors, masters etc., and especially the excellent Dr. Glenny at Dulwich. A natural tendency fortified by early religious education evidently drew his heart to God; but, on the other hand, a logical mind, fond of investigating every thing, made him experience the necessity of examining his grounds of belief. The answers, all ready prepared, made to him on great questions could not satisfy him; he required to discuss their basis. Already the increasing play of his faculties had been revealed in that beautiful Prayer to the Divinity which constitutes his profession of faith and worship, "every line of which," says Moore, "is instinct with fervent sadness, as of a heart that grieves at loss of its illusions."

On arriving this year at Cambridge, he found, amid a circle of intellectual companions which Moore calls "a brilliant pleiad," a young man of genius, an extraordinary thinker, a mind that had, perhaps, some affinity to his own, but which, devoid of his sensibility and logic, surpassed him in hardihood; a bold spirit, striving to scrutinize the inscrutable, and, not content with analysis, desirous to arrive at *conclusions.* Through the natural influence of example, and more especially the irresistible fascination exercised by a great intelligence, uniting also the spirit of fun, so amusing to Lord Byron because so like his own; from all these causes, Matthews exercised an immense influence over him. This young man loved to plunge his head into depths from whence he emerged all dizzy. Lord Byron was guided by too reasonable a mind to arrive at such results. He refused to follow where deformity and evil were to ensue, and persisted still in looking upward. Still, however, he allowed his eyes to wander over the magic glass, where danced a few pretended certainties conjoined with a host of doubts. The first he rejected, as too antipathetic to his soul, but perhaps he did not sufficiently repel all the doubts. And, being no longer alarmed at sounding such depths, he imbibed seeds of doctrine capable of producing incredulity or, at least, skepticism. Happily these seeds required a dry soil to fructify, and his, being so rich, they *perished,* after a short period of wretched existence. All these influences, and this precocious experience, were for him at this time a sort of personification of Mephistopheles, although not entailing serious consequences; for in the main his belief was not deeply shaken. It had no other effect than to throw him, for a time, into uncertainty on points necessary to him, "and to teach him," says Moore, "to feel less embarrassed in a *sort* of skepticism."

This disagreement between his reason and his aspirations becoming deeper and wider, his mind ceased always to follow his heart. But the latter following rather the former, though with sadness and fatigue, and all the problems of life becoming more and more enveloped in darkness, it is possible that he passed through gloomy hours, wherein equivocal expressions escaped his pen. In a word, if he avoided dizziness, he was not equally fortunate with regard to ennui.

"Ennui," says the clever Viscomte D'Yzarn de Freissinet, in his deep and delightful book, "*Les Pensées grises,*" "ennui is felt by ordinary minds because they can not understand earth, and by superior ones because they can not understand heaven."

Let us now observe Byron after he had taken his degrees

at the university, and when about to enter into possession of his estates. On seeing this young nobleman of twenty, almost an orphan, commence his career perfectly independent, call around him at Newstead Abbey his dear companions of Harrow and Cambridge, make up masquerades with them, don the costume of abbots and monks, pass the nights in running about his own parks and the heather of Sherwood Forest, and the days amid youthful eccentricities, amiable hospitality, and London dissipation, it would seem as if this odd, shifting, noisy kind of life, however efficient for developing knowledge of men and things, must inevitably obliterate all trace of melancholy.

But it was not so; the responsibilities of life began too soon for him, and the joyous horizon of his twentieth year was already dotted with black marks indicative of the approaching tempest. In the first place, the cassock of a real priest never reposed on a heart more sensitive, endowed with feelings deeper and less hostile to audacity of mind. Moreover, the griefs of his boyhood had sown seeds of sadness in his heart, and the unjust cruel criticism lavished on his early poems had already inflicted a deep wound. Lord Byron, it is true, thought to heal this by writing a satire; still, despite the vein of pleasantry indulged, he continued to discipline his mind by serious study of the great masters of literature and of the deepest thinkers.

It must be acknowledged that the balm he sought in *satire, was* a dangerous caustic which, while closing one wound, might well cause others to open. At the same time, the money embarrassments inherited from his predecessor in the estate went on accumulating, and the period was approaching when the cassock, donned in boyish fun, was to be exchanged for the grave ermine of a peer of the realm. Who should present him, then, to the noble assembly, if not his guardian, and near relative, the Earl of Carlisle? The young lord had always met his coldness with deference and respect, even dedicating his early poems to him. But the noble earl now still further aggravated his unkind conduct toward his ward by abandoning him at this solemn moment. Not only did he refuse to lend countenance himself, but he even hurt and wounded Lord Byron by interposing delays so as to prevent or put off his reception in the House of Peers, and that *solely because he did not like the young man's mother!* It would be impossible for the most loving heart, the one most susceptible of family affections, not to have felt cruelly, under such circumstances, the absence of near ties, and Lord Byron did not then know his sister. Suffer he did, of course; and, had it not been for a distant relative, despite his high birth and wondrous gifts, he must have entered the august assembly accompanied only by his title. However frivolous the young man might have appeared, he was not so in reality; and he hesitated at this time between a project of travelling for information, and the desire to take part immediately in the labors of the Senate. Some months before attaining his majority, when the wish of travelling predominated, after having informed his mother of a thousand arrangements, all equally affectionate, wise, and generous, that he was about to take for her during his absence, he wrote that he proposed visiting Persia, India, and other countries.

"If I do not travel now," said he, "I never shall, and all men should, one day or other. I have, at present, no connections to keep me at home; no wife, or unprovided sisters, brothers, etc. I shall take care of you, and when I return I may possibly become a politician. A few years' knowledge of other countries than our own will not incapacitate me for that part. If we see no nation but our own, we do not give mankind a fair chance: it is from experience, not books, we ought to judge of them. There is nothing like inspection and trusting to our senses."

But while cherishing these ideas, his mind at the same time wavered between the two projects,—Parliament attracted him greatly. Despite his light words, the love of true and merited glory, of the beautiful and the good, ever inflamed his heart. What he wrote a year or two before, to his counsellor and friend, the Rev. Mr. Beecher, had not ceased to be his programme.* He said to his mother, a short time before his majority, that he thought it indispensable, "as a preparation for the future, to make a speech in the House, as soon as he was admitted." He wrote the same thing still more explicitly to Harness; for he then thought seriously of entering upon

* See chapter on "Love of Fame."

politics without delay, and his rights as a hereditary legislator paved the way for it. Nevertheless, being hurt, disappointed, and indignant at his guardian's conduct, and feeling himself isolated, he not only renounced taking any active part in the debates of his colleagues, but, according to Moore, appeared to consider the obligation of being among them painful and mortifying. Thus, a few days after entering Parliament, he returned disgusted to the solitude of his abbey, there to meditate on the bitterness of precocious experience, or upon scenes that appeared more vast to his independent spirit, than those which his country presented.

The final decision soon came. He resolved on leaving England and taking a long journey with his friend Hobhouse, on seeking sunshine, experience, and forgetfulness for his wounded soul. It seemed really at that moment as if, through an accumulation of disappointment, injustice and grief, the result of lost illusions (he had already written the epitaph on "Boatswain"), as if, I say, some germs of misanthropy were beginning to appear. But his bitterness did not reach, or rather, did not change his heart: every thing proves this. One of his friends, Lord Faulkland, was killed in a duel about this time; and our misanthrope not only was inconsolable, but, despite the embarrassment of his own affairs, generously assisted the family of the deceased, who had been left in distress. Dallas, who, through his prejudices, personal susceptibilities, and exaggerated opinions, shows so little indulgence to Lord Byron, thus describes however the impression made on him, and his conduct under the circumstances:—

"Nature had gifted Lord Byron with most benevolent sentiments, which I had frequent opportunities of perceiving; and I sometimes saw them give to his beautiful countenance an expression truly sublime. I paid him a visit the day after Lord Faulkland's death; he had just seen the lifeless body of one in whose society he had lately passed a pleasant day. He was saying to himself aloud, from time to time—'Poor Faulkland!' His look was more expressive than his words. 'But,' he added, 'his wife! 'tis she that is to be pitied!' I read his soul full of the kindest intentions, nor were they sterile. If ever there were a pure action, it was the one he meditated then; and the man who conceived and accomplished it was at that moment advancing through thorns and briers toward the free but narrow path that leads to heaven."*

He was setting out then on a long journey. And at that period long journeys were serious things. His first desire was to have a farewell meeting at Newstead, of all his old school-fellows. And that not sufficing, he even wished to carry their image away with him, so as to enjoy a sensible means of recalling tender remembrances of the past. But his heart found an aliment for misanthropy in the selfish answer given by one of his comrades, who was alarmed at the expense of getting a portrait taken. We see the impression made by this ungenerous reply, in the letter he addressed to his friend Harness:—

"I am going abroad, if possible, in the spring, and before I depart I am collecting the pictures of my most intimate school-fellows. I want yours; I have commissioned one of the first miniature painters of the day to take them, of course, at my own expense, as I never allow any to incur the least expenditure to gratify a whim of mine. To mention this may seem indelicate; but when I tell you a friend of ours first refused to sit, under the idea that he was to *disburse* on the occasion, you will see that it is *necessary* to state these preliminaries, to prevent the recurrence of any similar mistake. It will be a tax on your patience for a week, but pray excuse it, as it is possible the resemblance may be the sole trace I shall be able to preserve of our past friendship. Just now it seems foolish enough, but in a few years, when some of us are dead, and others are separated by inevitable circumstances, it will be a kind of satisfaction to retain, in these images of the living, the idea of our former selves, and to contemplate, in the resemblances of the dead, all that remains of judgment, feeling, and a host of passions."

If misanthropy had not been an element heterogeneous to his character, it might well have assumed larger proportions at this moment; for, on the very eve of his departure from England, his heart had yet to suffer one of those chilling shocks to which sensitive natures, removed far above the usual temperature of the world, says Moore, are only too much exposed. And this proof of coldness, which he com-

* Dallas, vol. ii.

plains of with indignation in a note to the second canto of "Childe Harold," was given precisely by one of the friends he most loved. Mr. Dallas, who witnessed the immediate effect produced by this mark of coldness, thus describes it:

"I found him bursting with indignation. '*Will you believe it?*' said he, 'I *have just* met —— and asked him to come and sit an hour with me; he excused himself; and what do you think was his excuse? He was engaged with his mother and some ladies to go shopping! And he knows I set out to-morrow to be absent for years, perhaps never to return? Friendship! I do not believe I shall leave behind me, yourself and family excepted, and perhaps my mother, a single being who will care what becomes of me!' "*

The conduct of this friend gave him so much pain, that a year after he wrote again about it, from Constantinople, to Dallas:—

"The only person I counted would feel grieved at my departure took leave of me with such coldness, that if I had not known the heart of man I should have been surprised. I should have attributed it to some offenses on my part, had I ever been guilty of aught save *too much affection* for him."

Dallas thought that some lady, from a spirit of vengeance, had excited this young man to slight Lord Byron.

I will not here seek to discover whether he was right or wrong. It suffices that he could believe it, for me to say, that this singular misanthropy, born of heart-deceptions, was in reality nothing else but grief, the causes of which might each be enumerated, but the intensity of which we do not really know, since that deep capacity is the sad privilege of beings highly endowed.

In any case, it is certain that when he left England the measure of disappointments capable of producing real melancholy in such a sensitive heart was quite filled up. Is it, then, surprising that he, like his hero, "Childe Harold," should see with indifference the shores of his native land recede? But if, unhappily, the gloomy ideas he welcomed for a moment brought about a regrettable habit, no more to be lost, of adopting, in his language spoken and written, expressions and mystifications that too often concealed his real feelings, only letting them be seen through the medium of his mind (a sure

* Moore, vol. i

way of making him misunderstood), he could not long stand against the proofs of real attachment shown him by his fellow-traveller, and, indeed, by all who came near him. Even before setting sail, the influence of this sentiment, combined with his natural disposition to gayety, became visible; all annoyances seemed forgotten in the agreeable sensation of a first voyage that was to bear him away from the country where he had suffered so much, and which would probably show him, in other lands, more favorable specimens of the human race. Indeed, this is quite evident in the letters and gay verses sent off from Falmouth to his friends Drury and Hodgson, as well as in the more serious strain, though still gay and affectionate, in which he, at the same time, addressed his mother.*

Hardly had he landed at Lisbon, when his heart, yearning after the beautiful, expanded into admiration at sight of the Tagus and the beauties of Cintra; displaying alike his high moral sense of things, whether he expressed admiration or inflicted blame.†

We see his whole nature revolt at baseness, ingratitude, cowardice, ferocity, all kinds of moral deformity; just as much as it was attracted and delighted by patriotism, courage, devotion, sacrifice, love carried to heroism, grace, and beauty. We perceive, in the poet's soul, a freshness and a moral vigor, that shine all the more brightly, contrasted with the misanthropical melancholy of the hero of his legend. But this personage had been imprudently chosen to typify a state of mind into which youth often falls, and which, perhaps, Lord Byron himself went through during a few short hours of disenchantment. The impressions thus gathered, were treasured in his memory until they came to maturity some months later; then they issued from his pen in flowing numbers, whose magic power he then ignored: but assuredly the fine sentiments expressed came from the soul of the minstrel, not from the satiated feelingless hero, who was incapable of experiencing them. Let people only make the distinction between the two personages whom malice has taken pleasure in confounding, an error willingly adopted by a certain set and imposed on credulous minds.‡

* See Moore, 35th and 36th letters. † See "Childe Harold."

‡ See Introduction.

The relation between the two is not one of family or race, but a purely accidental external resemblance; the result of some strange fancy and intellectual want in the poet, whose powerful imagination, while having recourse only to his own spontaneity for the creation of ideal beings and types, yet required to rest always on reality, for painting the material world and for embodying his metaphysical conceptions.

Thus these two personages leave the same shore, on the same vessel, to make the same voyage, and meet with the same adventures. Both have the same family relations,—a mother, a sister; yes, but their souls are not in the same state, because not of the same nature. That results clearly from a simple inspection of the poem, for all who read in good faith; since, out of 191 stanzas that make up the first two cantos of "Childe Harold," there are 112 wherein the poet forgets his hero, speaks in his own name, and shows his real soul—a soul full of energy and beauty, becoming enthusiastic at sight of the wonders displayed in creation, of grandeur, virtue, and love.

Moralists of good faith can tell whether a mind that was corrupted, satiated, wearied, could possibly have felt such enthusiasm. In reality, these emotions betokened the future poet, then unknown to the world and to himself. Let us return to the man,—the best justification for the poet. From Lisbon he wrote another letter, full of fun, to his friend Hodgson. Already he found all well; better than in England. Already he declared himself greatly amused with his pilgrimage: the sight of the Tagus pleased him, Cintra delighted him; he talked Latin at the convent, fed on oranges, embraced every body, asked news of every body and every thing; "and we find him," says Moore, "in this charming, gay, sportive, schoolboy humor, just at the very moment that 'Childe Harold' is about to reveal to the world his misanthropy, disgust, and insensibility. Lord Byron went from Lisbon to Seville, going seventy miles a day on horseback in the heat of a Spanish July, always delighted, complaining of nothing (in a country where all was wanting), and he arrived in perfect health. There, in that beautiful city of serenades and love-making courtships, his handsome face and person immediately attracted the attention of the fair sex. He was not insensible to the lively demonstrations of two sisters, and especially of the beauteous Doña Josefa, who declared, with naïve Spanish frankness, how much she liked him. This young girl and her sister, who was equally charming, made him all kinds of offers, saying, when he left:—'Adieu, handsome creature, I like thee much; and Josefa asked to have at least a lock of his beautiful hair. On arriving at Cadiz, the lovely daughter of an admiral of high birth, with whom he was thrown in contact, could not hide from her parents or himself her partiality for him. She wished to teach him Spanish, never thought he could be near enough to her at the theatre, called him to her side in crowds, made him accompany her home, invited him to return to Cadiz, and, in short," Moore says:—

"Knowing the beauties of Cadiz, his imagination, dazzled by the attraction of several, was on the point of being held captive by one."

He escaped this danger from being obliged to set out for Gibraltar, where he also met with many attentions from persons of rank among his countrymen; but he encountered another peril at the island of Calypso (Malta). For he met there a real Calypso,—a young woman of extraordinary beauty (the daughter and the wife of an ambassador), and no less remarkable for her qualities of mind than for her singular position. All his time at Malta was passed between studying a language and the society of this goddess. And the true account of the attraction with which he inspired this beautiful heroine, and which he amply returned, is not certainly to be found in the stanzas of "Childe Harold," but in the verses addressed from the monastery of Zitza to the beautiful Florence, who had carried off at the same time (says he) both the ring he had refused to the Seville beauty and likewise his heart. On arriving in Albania (ancient Epirus), he went to visit Ali Pasha at Tepeleni, his country-seat; and the sight of this beautiful, amiable young man so softened the heart of the ferocious old Moslem, that he wished to be considered as Lord Byron's father, treated him like a son, caused his palaces to be opened to him, surrounding him with the most delicate attentions, sending him fresh drinks and all the delicacies of an Oriental table; he also ordered the Albanian selected to accompany Lord Byron to defend him if requisite at the peril of his life. This Albanian, named Basilius, would not leave Lord Byron afterward. Wherever any English residents, consuls, or ambassadors could be found, Lord Byron was the object of a thousand attentions and kindnesses. At Constantinople, the English ambassador, Adair, wished him to lodge at his palace; Mr. S—— proposed the same thing at Patras. When he fell ill, he was taken care of, most affectionately even, by the Albanese. All the sympathies enlisted during his travels (and those who knew him thought them most natural) must certainly have acted on his loving, grateful heart, banishing misanthropy if he had experienced it. But did it really exist? Must not even his peace of conscience have counterbalanced bitter remembrances?

His conscience was unburdened, for the griefs he had had were not merited by him. If a young girl had deceived him, he on his side had deceived no one; if a guardian had neglected and failed in duties toward him, he had always behaved respectfully toward this bad guardian. If hard-hearted critics had insulted, and tried to stifle his budding genius, modest and timid withal, he had already taken his revenge, sure to repent some day of the harshness and injustice which passion had, perhaps, led him into; if his affairs were embarrassed, they had come to him thus by inheritance. If he had taken a share in some youthful dissipation, disgust had quickly followed; not a tear or a seduction had he wherewith to reproach himself. All these testimonies furnished by his conscience, and so consoling in every case, must have been doubly so to a heart like his, which, by his own avowal, could not *go to rest* with the weight of *any remorse* upon it. And, truly, all his correspondence certifies this.

Already at Gibraltar, Lord Byron began writing letters full of clever pleasantry, either to his mother or his friends, and his correspondence always continued in the same tone, with nothing that betrayed melancholy, far less misanthropy like Childe Harold's, although he was composing that poem at this time.

At Malta, it was impossible to find shelter.* His compan-

* "His lordship was in better spirits when I had met with some adventure, and he chuckled with an inward sense of enjoyment, not altogether without spleen, a kind of malicious satisfaction, as his companions recounted, with all becoming

ions grew impatient, but Lord Byron retained his good-humor, laughing and joking. On the mountains of Epirus, which were infested by brigands, the Albanian escort, given him by Ali Pasha, lost their way in the middle of the night, and were surprised by a terrific storm. For nine hours he advanced on horseback under torrents of rain; and when at last he reached his companions his gayety was still the same. Assailed by a frightful tempest while going by sea from Constantinople to Athens, shipwreck seemed impending. Every one was crying out in despair; Lord Byron alone consoled and encouraged the rest, then he wrapped himself up in his Albanian capote, and went to sleep quietly, until his fate should be decided. On visiting a cavern with his friend Hobhouse, they lost their way, their torch went out, and they had no prospect but to remain there, and perish with hunger. Hobhouse was in despair; but Lord Byron kept up his courage with jests, and presence of mind fit to save them, and which did so in effect. Privations, rigor of seasons, sufferings that drew complaints from the least delicate, and from his own servants, had no effect on his good-humor.*

All this does not simply show his courage and good natural dispositions, it likewise proves that there was not the making of a misanthrope in him. And besides, his fellow-traveller Hobhouse says so positively, in his account of their journey, when relating why Lord Byron could not accompany him in an excursion to Negropont; for he energetically expresses his regret at being obliged to separate, even for so short a time, from a companion, who, according to him, *united to perspicacity of wit and originality of observation, that gay and lively temper which keeps attention awake under the pressure of fatigue, softening every difficulty and every danger.*

Truly it might be said that Lord Byron was superior to the weaknesses of humanity. He was evidently patient and amiable in the highest degree. Greece appeared to him de-

gravity, their woes and sufferings as an apology for begging a bed and a morsel for the night. God forgive! but I partook of Byron's levity at the idea of personages so consequential wandering destitute in the streets, seeking for lodgings from door to door, and rejected at all. Next day, however, they were accommodated by the governor with an agreeable house," etc.—GALT, p. 66.

* See chapter on "Courage, Coolness, and Self-control."

lightful,—an enchanting country with a cloudless sky. He liked Athens so much that, on quitting it for the first time, he was obliged to set off at a gallop to have courage enough to go. And when he returned there, though from the cloister of the Franciscan monastery, where he had fixed his abode, he could no longer even perceive the pretty heads of the three Graces *entre les plantes embaumées de la cour;* he felt himself just as happy, because he devoted his time to study, and mixed with persons of note — such as the celebrated Lady Hester Stanhope, Lord Sligo, and Bruce: souvenirs which he has consecrated in his memoirs, saying Lady Hester's (?) was the most delightful acquaintance he had made in Greece.*

He saw Greeks, Turks, Italians, French, and Germans, and was delighted. Now could he observe the character of persons of all nations, and he became more than ever persuaded that travelling is necessary to complete a man's education; he was happy at being able to verify the superiority of his own country, and to increase his knowledge by finding the contrary. He was never either disappointed or disgusted. He lived with both great and small; passing days in the palaces of pashas, and nights in cow-stables with shepherds; always temperate, he never enjoyed better health. "Truly," said he, "I have no cause to complain of my destiny." At Constantinople he found the inhabitants good and peaceable; the Turks appeared superior to the Greeks, the Greeks to the Spaniards, and the Spaniards to the Portuguese. It was the man wearied of all, the misanthrope, who wrote all this to his mother, concluding thus:—"I have gone through a great deal of fatigue, but have *not felt wearied for one instant!*"

All the letters addressed to his friends Drury and Hodgson, from Greece or Turkey, were equally devoid of misanthropy, and, indeed, generally full of jokes. It was only when too long a silence on their part awakened painful remembrances, causing a sort of nostalgia of friendship, that a cry of pain once escaped him in these words:—"Truly, I have no friends in the world!" But one feels that he did not believe it, and only spoke as coquettish women do, knowing they are beloved, and willing to hear the old tale repeated.

* Moore, vol. i.

Again, it was this same man of worn-out feeling, who, despite the embarrassed state of his affairs, showed such unexampled generosity to his mother, and to friends requiring aid both in England and Greece; who likewise displayed touching solicitude toward servants left behind him at home, or even sent away so as not to over-fatigue their youth or their old age: and, finally, who, on learning that one of his dependents was about to commit a bad action, abandoning a young girl whom he had seduced, wrote to his mother:—

"My opinion is that B—— ought to marry Miss N——; our first duty is not to do evil, our second to repair it. I will have no seducers on my estates, and will not grant my dependents a privilege I would not take myself: namely, of leading astray our neighbors' daughters.

"I hope this Lothario will follow my example, and begin by restoring the girl to society, or by my father's beard he shall hear of me."

And then he also recommends a young servant to her:—

"I pray you to show kindness to Robert, who must miss his master; poor boy! he would scarcely go back."

This letter alone shows a freshness of feeling quite consolatory; certainly "Childe Harold" was not capable of it.

But despite all these proofs of his good-humor, gayety, and antimisanthropical dispositions, we could cite persons who, even at this period, thought him melancholy. Mr. Galt, for instance, whom chance had brought in contact with him, having met on the same vessel going from Gibraltar to Greece; and then the British ambassador at Constantinople, Mr. Adair, and even Mr. Bruce, at Athens. How then shall we reconcile these opposite testimonies? It may be done by analyzing his fits of melancholy, observing the time and places of their manifestation.

I have said that Lord Byron's melancholy had always real or probable causes (only capable of aggravation from his extremely sensitive temperament), and it has been seen that superabundant causes existed when he left England. That during the whole period of his absence, they may, from time to time, have cast some shade over him, notwithstanding his natural gayety and his strength of mind, is at least very probable. But did Mr. Galt, Mr. Adair, and Mr. Bruce, really witness the return of these impressions? or would it not be more natural to believe, since that better agrees with the observations made by those living constantly with him, that, through some resemblance of symptoms, they may have taken for melancholy another psychological phenomenon generally remarked—namely, *the necessity of solitude*, experienced by a high meditative and poetic nature like his? Indeed, what does Galt say?—

"When night arrived and there were lights in the vessel, he held himself aloof, took his station on the rail, between the pegs on which the sheets are belayed and the shrouds, and there, for hours, sat in silence, enamored, as people say, of the moon. He was often strangely absent—it may have been from his genius; and, had its sombre grandeur been then known, this conduct might have been explained; but, at the time, it threw as it were, around him the sackcloth of penitence. Sitting amid the shrouds and rattlings, in the tranquillity of the moonlight, composing melodies scarcely formed in his mind, he seemed almost an apparition, suggesting dim reminiscences of him who shot the albatross. He was as a mystery in a winding-sheet crowned with a halo.

"The influence of the incomprehensible phantasma which hovered about Lord Byron has been more or less felt by all who ever approached him. That he sometimes descended from the clouds, and was familiar and earthly, is true; but his dwelling was amid the murk and the mist, and the home of his spirit in the abyss of the storm and the hiding-places of guilt. He was at the time of which I am speaking scarcely two-and-twenty, and could claim no higher praise than having written a clever satire; and yet it was impossible, even then, to reflect on the bias of his mind, as it was revealed by the casualties of conversation, without experiencing a presentiment, that he was destined to execute extraordinary things. The description he has given of "Manfred" in his youth, was of himself:—

'My spirit walk'd not with the souls of men,
Nor look'd upon the earth with human eyes;
The thirst of their ambition was not mine,
The aim of their existence was not mine;
My joys, my griefs, my passions, and my powers,
Made me a stranger.'"

All that is very well, but the only astonishing part is Mr. Galt's astonishment. The incomprehensible phantom of melancholy and caprice then hanging over Lord Byron, was especially his genius seeking an outlet; it was the melancholy that lays hold of so many great minds, because, having a vision of beauty and fame before their eyes, they fear not attaining to it. That it was which one day led Petrarch, all tearful, to his consoler John of Florence. If almost all great geniuses, ere carving out their path, have experienced this fever of the soul, falling into certain kinds of melancholy, that put on all sorts of forms,—sometimes noisy, sometimes capricious, sometimes misanthropical, was there not greater reason for Lord Byron to undergo such a crisis—at a period when energy of heart and mind was not yet balanced by confidence in his own genius? For he had not met with a John of Florence; he had been so much hurt at the cruel reception given to his first attempts, that it appeared to him he ought to seek another direction for the employment of his energetic faculties, and turn to active life, as many of his tastes invited. But his genius, unknown to the world as to himself, was, however, fermenting within his brain, feeding on dreams; now pacing a deck, now beneath a starry sky, anon by moonlight, and causing him to absorb from every thing all homogeneous to his nature; and thus "Childe Harold" came to light. When Lord Byron took his pen, the mechanical part of the work alone remained to be done. The elaboration and meditation of it had taken place almost unknown to himself, so that his conceptions remained latent, and took their shape by degrees in his brain, before being fixed in his writings. He penned "Childe Harold" at Janina and Athens; but it was on the vessel's deck, in that dreamy attitude just seen by Mr. Galt, that he had moulded the clay of his first statue, and given it an immortal form. Could he have done so, if he had always remained in society on deck, laughing, joking, giving way to all his charming, witty bursts of gayety, as he did while coasting the shores of Sicily, when, from time to time, his playful nature enabled him not only to forget the wounds of his heart, and the disagreeable remembrances left behind, but also to impose silence on the severe requirements of his genius?

The same causes must have produced the same opinions from the British ambassador at Constantinople. Without even speaking of the irksomeness of etiquette, always so distasteful to Lord Byron, that Moore looks upon it as one of the causes of the apparent sadness remarked by Adair, we ought to remember that he left Constantinople on board the same frigate as the ambassador, making a sea-voyage of four days with him. During these four days, it is likely that Lord Byron did not deny himself solitude, and that he also courted the secret influences exercised by starry nights on the Bosphorus as he had done under similar circumstances on the Ægean Sea. But he had yet another motive for sadness during this passage, since he was then about to separate from his friend and fellow-traveller, Hobhouse, who was obliged to go back to England. Thus, for the first time, Lord Byron would soon find himself alone in a foreign land. The effect produced by this situation must have shown itself in his countenance; for he was experiencing beforehand quite a new sensation, wherein any satisfaction at perfect independence and solitude must have been more than counterbalanced in his feeling, grateful, and in reality most sociable nature, by real grief at such a separation. And I doubt not that when setting foot on the barren isle of Chios, with its jutting rocks and tall rugged-looking mountains, just after having bade Hobhouse adieu, I doubt not that his heart experienced one of those burning suffocating feelings that belong equally to intense sorrow and joy. When, then, a few days later, he wrote to his mother for the evident purpose of calming the uneasiness she must have felt at knowing him to be alone, and when he mentioned with indifference the departure of his friend, he was exaggerating, except in what he said of loving solitude. That he did not even sufficiently express, for he might have boldly declared that it was positively requisite to him; and, indeed, his resignation at loss of a friend so thoroughly appreciated is the best proof we could have of it.

In the workings of Lord Byron's intellect, observation, reflection, and solitary meditation were brought into play much more than imagination.* Every thing with him took its

* Galt says that what he relates of his visit to Ali Pasha has all the *freshness and life of a scene going on under one's own eye.*

source from facts; and the vital flame that circulates in every phase of his writings is the very essence of this reality, first elaborated in his brain and then stamped on his verse. As long as this first kind of work of observation was going on, as long as he was only occupied in imbibing truths of the visible world that were sure to strike him, and storing them in his memory, society, and especially intellectual society, suited him. But when he began to shape his observations into form, by dint of reflection and meditation, generalizing and making deductions, then constant society forced upon him fatigued him, and solitude became indispensable. Now it was more particularly at the period of which we are speaking that his mind was in the situation described. He had just visited Albania, whose inhabitants were a violent, turbulent race, animated with a passionate love of independence, who were ever rising in rebellion against authority, and whose every sentiment, passion, and principle, formed a perfect contrast with all existing in his own country. He had become familiar with their usages, and recognized in them the possession of virtues which he loved, though mixed up with vices which he abhorred. He had gone through strange emotions and adventures among them; his life had often been in danger from the elements, from pirates and brigands; on the throne sat a prince who united monstrous vices to a few virtues, who, wearing gentleness on his countenance, was yet so ferocious in soul, that Byron, despite the favors lavished on himself, felt constrained to paint the tyrant in his real colors. He found in these contrasts, in this moral phenomenon, that which made him shudder, and precisely because it did cause shuddering, the source of soul-stirring, most original poetry, the type of his Eastern verses—of "Conrad," "The Giaour," and "Lara"—which, having been admitted into the fertile soil of his brain, were one day to come forth in all their terrible truth, though softened down by some of his own personal qualities; and having gone through, unknown to him, a long process of warm fertilization, while nursed in *solitary* reflection. Thus solitude was necessary to him; and this want, I again repeat, was an intellectual one, and had nothing to do with melancholy. From Chios Lord Byron went to Athens, a residence so sad and monotonous at this period, that it was well calculated to give rather than cure the spleen. But as he had no malady of this kind, after an excursion into the Morea with Lord Sligo,—a college friend and companion to whom nothing could be refused,—he returned to Athens; and here, in order to enjoy his cherished independence, would not even give himself the distraction of seeing those lovely young faces he used to admire behind the geraniums at their windows, and which had charmed him some months before he took up his abode at the Franciscan convent. There, amid the silence of the cloister, he could commune freely with his own mind, allow it full expansion, and revert, at will, from solitary contemplation to the most varied studies, especially to that he always so much appreciated—the study of mankind in general.

"Here," he wrote to his mother, "I see and have conversed with French, Italians, Germans, Danes, Greeks, Turks, Americans, etc.; and, without losing sight of my own, I can judge of the countries and manners of others. When I see the superiority of England (which, by-the-by, we are a great deal mistaken about in many things) I am pleased, and where I find her inferior, I am at least enlightened. Now, I might have staid, smoked in your towns, or fogged in your country a century without being sure of this, and without acquiring any thing more useful or amusing at home."

And then he adds:—

"I hope, on my return, to lead a quiet, recluse life; but God knows and does best for us all; at least so they say, and I have nothing to object, as, on the whole, I have no reason to complain of my lot. I trust this will find you well, and as happy as one can be; you will, at least, be pleased to hear I am so."

It was in this admirable frame of mind that he often went from Athens to Cape Colonna. And amid these ruins, washed by the blue waves of the Ægean Sea, immortalized by Plato, who here taught his half-Christian philosophy, Lord Byron took his seat at the celestial banquet spread by the great master, and entered into full possession of his genius. For, although he ignored its great power and extent, it is impossible that he should not have had in hours like these, some vision of the future, some presentiment of coming glory, which, piercing through the veils that yet shrouded his genius, gave moments of ineffable delight. When he bathed in some solitary spot, he tells us in his memoranda that one of his greatest delights was to sit on a rock overlooking the waves, and to remain there whole hours lost in admiration of sky and sea, "absorbed," says Moore, "in that sort of vague reverie, which, however formless and indistinct at the moment, settled afterward on his pages into those clear, bright pictures which will endure forever."

One day, while he was swimming under the rocks of Cape Colonna, a vessel from the coast of Attica drew near. On board, going from London to Athens, were two celebrated personages—Lady Hester Stanhope and Mr. Bruce. The first object that greeted their eyes, on nearing Sanium, was Lord Byron, playing all alone with his favorite element. Some days after, his friend Lord Sligo wished him to make their acquaintance, and he saw a great deal of them at Athens. In his memoranda the following words are applied to them:—"It was the commencement (their meeting at Cape Colonna) of the most delightful acquaintance I have made in Greece." And he wished to assure Mr. Bruce, in case these lines should ever fall under his notice, of the pleasure he experienced in recalling the time they had passed together at Athens. Now I do not see any symptom of melancholy in all this, nor in all preceding, and yet Bruce thought there was. Did he, then, also consider the joy Lord Byron felt in solitude, and his indifference for the false conventional enthusiasm his countrymen affected to display at sight of the ruins of Greece, as so many other tokens of melancholy? In reality Lord Byron was averse to all kinds of affectation, made no exception in favor of the artistic pretensions which constitute the hypocrisy of taste, and only gave the sincere, ardent homage of his soul to those things of antiquity that recall great names or great actions, and to sublime scenes in nature. Notwithstanding his fine intelligence, it is not impossible that Mr. Bruce also may have shared the errors of superficial minds; and it is likewise possible that Lord Byron may really, during the last period of his sojourn at Athens, have sometimes been melancholy, for causes of grief were certainly not wanting. His man of business wished Lord Byron at this time to sell

Newstead, so as to get his affairs into some definite order. Perhaps it would have been wise, but such a determination was extremely repugnant to him, for he was very fond of Newstead, and had even written to his mother, before leaving, that she might be quite easy on this head, as he would never part with it. However, his agent, wishing to get him back to England, then affected negligence, would not write, and made him wait for money. Lord Byron grew uneasy and alarmed, was out of humor, and often seemed capricious, because these circumstances obliged him to change his travelling plans, and finally left him no other alternative but to return to England, where, as he wrote to a friend, his first interview would be with a lawyer, the second with a creditor; and then would come discussions with miners, farmers, stewards and all the disagreeables consequent on a ruined property and disputed mines.

After having resisted all these fears for some time, he was obliged to decide on returning. Behold him, then, on the road to England.

At Malta he had attacks of fever to which his state of mind was certainly not wholly foreign. "We have seen," says Moore, "from the letters written by him on his passage homeward (on board the 'Volage' frigate) how far from cheerful or happy was the state of mind in which he returned. In truth, even for a disposition of the most sanguine cast, there was quite enough in the discomfort that now awaited him in England to sadden its hopes and check its buoyancy."

And yet in these letters, melancholy at bottom, which he addressed to his mother and friends during this tiresome voyage of more than six weeks, we still perceive, overriding all, his kind, sensitive, playful nature. He told them that if one can not be happy, one must at least try to be a little gay; that if England had ceased to smile on him, there were other skies more serene; that he was coming back shaken by fever morally and physically, but with a firm, intrepid spirit. And, in short, pleasantry never failed him.

Always admirable toward his mother, he spoke of his apathy, but re-assured her directly, adding:—

"Dear mother" (he wrote to her on the 'Volage' frigate), "within that apathy I certainly do not comprise yourself, as I will prove by every means in my power.

"P.S.—You will consider Newstead as your house, not mine, and me only as a visitor."*

He had hardly arrived in London when Mr. Dallas hastened to greet him, and instead of finding him changed, thought he was in excellent health, with a countenance that betrayed neither melancholy nor any trace of discontent at his return. The truth is, that those sorrows which did not reach his heart were never very deep with Lord Byron. But already a most formidable tempest was gathering on the horizon of his fate, for it was one that would cruelly wound his heart. Perhaps it was some vague, inexplicable presentiment of what was threatening him that saddened his return to his native country. The storm burst as soon as he set foot in London; for he was summoned in haste to Newstead, his mother's life being declared in danger. He set out instantaneously, but on arriving found only a corpse! This spectacle was still before his eyes; he had hardly quitted the chamber of death, where, in the obscurity of night and alone, believing himself free from all observation, he had given way in silence and darkness to the real sentiments of his heart, weeping bitterly the loss of a mother who had idolized him, when in rapid succession news arrived of the deaths of his dearest friends. Matthews, his mind's idol, had just been drowned in the river Cam, at Cambridge; Wingfield, one of his heart-idols, was dying of fever at Coimbra; his dear Eddlestone was in the last stage of consumption; and, finally, he learned the death of another loved, mysterious being. Six deaths within a few short weeks!

"If to be able," says Moore, "to depict powerfully the painful emotions it is necessary first to have experienced them, or, in other words, if, for the poet to be great the man must suffer, Lord Byron, it must be owned, paid early this dear price of mastery."

This was certainly a most painful crisis in his existence. What he felt then can not be called melancholy; it was truly *desolation, agony of heart.* Seeing himself alone in his venerable but gloomy abode, beside the dead body of his mother, solitude was for the first time intolerable to him, and, despite his strength of mind, he experienced moments of weakness. In his agony he wrote a letter to his friend Scroope Davies

* See Moore, Letters 52 and 54, to Mrs. Byron.

that is truly painful to read, so much does it bear the impress of intense suffering.

"Some curse hangs over me and mine," says he. "My mother lies a corpse in this house; one of my best friends is drowned in a ditch. What can I say, or think, or do?

"My dear Davies, if you can spare a moment, do come down to me; I want a friend. Come to me, Scroope, I am almost desolate, left almost alone in the world. I must enjoy the survivors while I can. Write or come, but come if you can, or one or both."

Hardly had he allowed himself this heartrending expression of grief, most touching for those who knew his repugnance to showing any sensibility of heart, when a new calamity overtook him. His dear friend, Wingfield, died at Coimbra at the age of twenty-one. Thoughts of death even took possession of Lord Byron's soul, influencing and directing all his actions. Neither self-love, nor the hope of great success with "Childe Harold," which had been announced to him as he passed through London, any longer could charm; tears dimmed the lustre of fame; he could only occupy himself with the fate of the surviving, and resolved on making his will in case of his own death. We find him then at this time solely engaged in making out this new deed. He destroyed the old will, rendered useless by the death of his mother, and took care to forget no one in the new one; all his servants were mentioned with admirable solicitude; and, in short, his last testament fully displayed the beautiful, generous soul that had dictated it.

Some weeks after, he wrote to Dallas:—

"At three-and-twenty I am left alone, and what more can we be at seventy? It is true that I am young to begin again, but with whom can I retrace the laughing part of life?"

"Indeed," writes he at the same time to Hodgson, "the blows followed each other so rapidly, that I am yet stupid from the shock; and though I do eat, and drink, and talk, and even laugh at times, yet I can hardly persuade myself that I am awake did not every morning convince me mournfully to the contrary.

"Davies has been here; his gayety (death can not mar it) has done me service; but, after all, ours was a hollow laughter! You will write to me? I am solitary, and I never felt solitude irksome before."

His moral sufferings had never been so great; and what he said and experienced under these circumstances, amply prove that solitude was good for him, when not unhappy. "I can do nothing," writes he to Dallas, "and my days pass, except for a few bodily exercises, in uniform indolence and idle insipidity."

The task of publishing "Childe Harold" was left to Dallas, and the certainty of its success found him pretty nearly indifferent. When his heart was in pain, Lord Byron's self-love always lay dormant. But destiny was still far from granting him any respite. Eddlestone, that dear friend, on whose true affection he most relied, as well as another beloved one, whose name ever remained locked within his breast, both died about this time; so that, as he says in his preface, during the short space of two months, he lost six persons most dear. In announcing this new misfortune to Dallas, he expresses himself in the following words:—

"I have almost forgot the taste of grief; *and supped full of horrors*, till I have become callous; nor have I a tear left for an event which, five years ago, would have bowed down my head to the earth. It seems to me as though I were to experience in my youth the greatest misery of age. My friends fall round me, and I shall be left a lonely tree before I am withered.

"Other men can always take refuge in their families; I have no resource but my own reflections, and they present no prospect here or hereafter, except the selfish satisfaction of surviving my betters. I am, indeed, very wretched, and you will excuse my saying so, as you know I am not apt to cant of sensibility."

But if tears no longer flowed from his eyes, they did from his pen; for it was then he wrote his elegies to "Thyrza," whose pathetic sublimity is so well characterized by Moore; and that he added those melancholy stanzas in "Childe Harold" on the death of friends, which we find at the end of the second canto.

"Indeed," he wrote again to Hodgson, "I am growing nervous, ridiculously nervous, I can neither read, write, nor amuse myself, or any one else. My days are listless, and my nights restless. I have very seldom any society, and when I have, I run out of it. At this present writing, there are in the next room three ladies, and I have stolen away to write this grumbling letter. I don't know that I sha'n't end with insanity, for I find a want of method in arranging my thoughts that perplexes me strangely; but this looks more like silliness than madness, as Scroope Davies would facetiously remark in his consoling manner. I must try the hartshorn of your company; and a session of Parliament would suit me well, any thing to cure me of conjugating the accursed verb *ennuyer*."

Distractions did come to him, but of a kind to make him conjugate verbs equally disagreeable; for they came caused by grief and irritation. In an infamous, ignoble publication, called "The Scourge," an anonymous author, probably making himself the organ of those who wished to avenge Lord Byron's satires, attacked his birth, and the reputation of his mother, who, despite her faults, was a very respectable, excellent woman.

"During the first winters after Lord Byron had returned to England," says Mr. Galt, "I was frequently with him. At that time, the strongest feeling by which he appeared to be actuated was indignation against a writer in a scurrilous publication, called 'The Scourge,' in which he was not only treated with unjustifiable malignity, but charged with being, as he told me himself, the illegitimate son of a murderer. I had not read the work; but the writer who could make such an absurd accusation, must have been strangely ignorant of the very circumstances from which he derived the materials of his own libel. When Lord Byron mentioned the subject to me, and that he was consulting Sir Vicary Gibbs with the intention of prosecuting the publisher and the author, I advised him, as well as I could, to desist simply because the allegations referred to well-known occurrences. His grand-uncle's duel with Mr. Chaworth, and the order of the House of Peers to produce evidence of his grandfather's marriage with Miss Trevannion, the facts of which being matter of history and public record, superseded the necessity of any proceeding.

"Knowing how deeply this affair agitated him at that time, I was not surprised at the sequestration in which he held himself, and which made those who were not acquainted with his shy and mystical nature apply to him the description of his own 'Lara.' "*

* Galt, p. 105.

Lord Byron's conduct at this period, led those who did not know his timid mystery-loving nature, to fancy that they recognized him in the portrait drawn of "Lara." Probably they were unaware how his hard fate was now not sparing him one single grief or mortification; how he was struggling between the necessity of putting up Newstead for sale and the extreme repugnance he felt to such a step.

"Before his resolve was taken on this head," says Mr. Galt, "he was often so troubled in mind, as to be unable to hide his sadness; and he often spoke of leaving England forever."

Already, long absence had made him lose sight of several early comrades; his mother was dead, and he scarcely saw his sister, who lived in quite another circle; through his antecedents, his youth, and his travels abroad, he was still a stranger among his fellow-peers; the only persons he saw much of were five or six college friends, whom death had spared, and to whom he was extremely attached; but they were his sole affections. His ideal standard of perfection which, being brought in contact with reality, had always a little spoilt women for him, had ended by making them almost disagreeable.

"I have one request to make," wrote he at this time to H——, "never again speak to me in your letters of a woman; do not even allude to the existence of the sex. I will not so much as read a word about them; it must be *propria que maribus.*"

It was in this state of relative isolation that he came to London, about the end of the year, and found Dallas preparing to have "Childe Harold" published; a task in which Lord Byron half unwillingly joined.

"He seemed more inclined," says Dallas, "at that time to seek more solid fame, by endeavoring to become an active, eloquent statesman."

But, notwithstanding this perspective, despite his genius and his youth, Lord Byron often fell into a sort of mental prostration, which was, says Dallas again, "rather the *result of his particular situation, feeling himself out of his sphere, than that of a gloomy disposition* received from nature."

We have seen, in effect, that there were circumstances then existing well calculated to darken his noble brow, and give him those nervous movements that may have seemed like caprice to those who were ignorant of their cause; and I wished to enter into these details so as to characterize well the epoch when his melancholy was greatest, and to show that it had its chief source in the anguish of his heart. It was to this time he alluded, when, in other days of suffering (at the period of his separation from Lady Byron), wherein his heart had smaller share, he wrote to Moore:—"If my heart could have broken, it would have done so years ago, through events more afflicting than this."

I also wished to enter into these details, because, desiring to prove that Lord Byron's melancholy almost always arose from palpable causes, it was necessary to make these causes known; and thus those who have declared his griefs to be rather *imaginary* than *real*, may find in this chapter abundant reason for rectifying their ideas. Among the number of such persons we may rank Mr. Macaulay, the eloquent historian, whose opinion, however, has *no weight*, as regards Lord Byron's character. For it is evident that he made use of this great name by way of choosing a good theme for his eloquence, a sort of mould for fine phrases. Besides, Macaulay did not know Lord Byron personally, nor did he study him impartially; facts which are his *fault* and his *excuse*.

After having paid this great tribute to grief during six months, the storm appeared to subside, and a ray of sunshine penetrated into Lord Byron's mind. It was then that he made Moore's acquaintance, and that of other clever men, among whom we may cite Rogers and Campbell. Moore especially, introduced under circumstances that brought out strongly the most amiable and estimable qualities of heart and mind, was to Lord Byron as a beacon-light amid the clouds external and internal harassing him then; and their sympathy was mutual and instantaneous. Lord Byron wrote directly to Harness:—

"Moore is the epitome of every thing exquisite in poetic and personal perfections."

On his side, Moore, after having praised the *manly, generous, pleasing refinement of his new friend*, sums up by saying: —"*Frank and manly as I found his nature then, so did I ever find it to his latest hour.*" And in describing the effect produced on him by his first meeting with Lord Byron, he says:—

"Among the impressions which this meeting left upon me, what I chiefly remember to have remarked was the nobleness of his air, his beauty, the gentleness of his voice and manners. Being in mourning for his mother, the color, as well of his dress as of his glossy, curling, and picturesque hair, gave more effect to the pure, spiritual paleness of his features, in the expression of which, when he spoke, there was a perpetual play of lively thought, though melancholy was their habitual character when in repose."

But this melancholy, having become habitual to him through accident, began then to disperse, as snow melts beneath the soft and warm breath of spring. The first symptom was that he judged better of himself; for, writing to his friend Harness, to express his general opinion on human selfishness, he said, "But I do not think we are born of this disposition."

"From the time of our first meeting," says Moore, "there seldom elapsed a day that Lord Byron and I did not see each other, and our acquaintance ripened into intimacy and friendship with a rapidity of which I have seldom known an example."*

Moore's company was a great consolation to him then, and Providence willed that the first balsam applied to his wounds, after that of time, should come from the hand of one whom he had lashed in his satire. He passed in this way the last months of 1811, and the first two of the following year. Meanwhile his star was about to rise, soon to transform, without any transition, his misty sky into brightest light, too dazzling, alas! to endure. For the sun, when it shines so radiantly in early morning, absorbs too many bad vapors. But we will not anticipate events which I am not relating here.

The parliamentary session being opened, Lord Byron resumed his seat in the upper House. But he was only known there by the satire that had raised him up such a host of enemies; otherwise, the handsome young man who had come among them three years before, but who had since appeared to disdain their labors, preferring foreign travel in Spain and the East, was scarcely remembered. When they saw him return, still so young and handsome, but with a grave melancholy brow, and that he immediately distinguished himself as

* Moore, Letter 81.

an orator, general admiration was excited. Even those he had offended generously forgot their anger in sympathy for a fellow-countryman, and pride in such a colleague; pride and enthusiasm were so general that both parties, Tories and Whigs, shared it equally. Lord Holland told him that *as an orator he would beat them all, if he persevered.* Lord Grenville remarked that for the construction of his phrases *he already resembled Burke.* Sir Francis Burdett declared that his discourse was the *best* pronounced by a lord in parliamentary memory. Several other noblemen asked to be presented, and even those he had offended came round to shake hands. Generous natures showed themselves on this occasion. The success of the orator heralded that of the poet, for "Childe Harold" appeared a few days after.

"The effect was," said Moore, "accordingly electric; his fame had not to wait for any of the ordinary gradations, but seemed to spring up like the palace of a fairy tale, in a night. As he himself briefly described it in his memoranda:—'I awoke one morning, and found myself famous.'

"The first edition of his work was disposed of instantly; and, as the echoes of its reputation multiplied on all sides, 'Childe Harold' and 'Lord Byron' became the theme of every tongue. At his door most of the leading names of the day presented themselves. From morning till night the most flattering testimonies of his success crowded his table from the grave tributes of the statesman and the philosopher down to (what flattered him still more) the romantic billet of some *incognita*, or the pressing note of invitation from some fair leader of fashion; and, in place of the desert which London had been to him but a few weeks before, he now not only saw the whole splendid interior of high life thrown open to receive him, but found himself among its illustrious crowds the most distinguished object."

I may also mention Dallas, who in speaking of this unexampled success, says:—

"Lord Byron had become the subject of every conversation in town.

"He was surrounded with honors. From the regent and his admirable daughter, down to the editor and his clerk; from Walter Scott and Jeffrey down to the anonymous authors of the 'Satirist' and the 'Scourge,' all and each extolled his merits. He was the admiration of the old, and the marvel of the fashionable circles of which he had become the idol."

This adoration of a whole nation did not turn his head, but it touched and rejoiced his heart. When he knew himself forgiven and loved by those even whom he had most offended in his satire, toward whom he felt most guilty, as, for instance, the excellent Lord Holland, who asked for his friendship, predicting his future fame as an orator, and already placing him beside Walter Scott as a poet; then by Lord Fitzgerald, who declared himself incapable of feeling angry with "Childe Harold," and many, many others; when all this occurred, Lord Byron's heart expanded to the better feelings he had long kept under control and hidden. He gave way to his innate kindness, to generous forgiveness; his own good qualities were stimulated by the kindness and generosity of others; this, rather than any satisfaction of self-love, dispelled the clouds from his soul, changed the sky and atmosphere, and his melancholy of that period, which owed its source to the heart, became neutralized by the heartfelt satisfaction he experienced. His letters, and particularly those to Moore, are full of life and animation at this time; and such as he appeared in his letters, such did Moore describe him in his habitual frame of mind. Dallas, who before had so often seen him melancholy, says:—

"I am happy to think that the success with which he has met, and the object of universal attention which he has become, have already produced upon his soul that softening influence which I had expected and foreseen; and I trust, that all his former grief will now have passed forever."

Galt himself, despite the effort he seems to make in praising him, can not help owning that at this period, when every body was kind to Lord Byron, he, on his side, displayed the utmost gentleness, kindness, amiability, and desire of obliging, combined with habitual gayety and pleasantry. The general tone of his memoranda at this time, particularly in 1813, shows him *pleased with every body and every thing.*

After having praised Moore, he speaks highly of Lord Ward, afterward Lord Dudley:—

"I like Ward," he says, and adds, "by Mohammed! I begin to fear getting to like every body; a disposition not to be encouraged. It is a sort of social gluttony, that makes one swallow all one comes in contact with. But I do like Ward."

Nevertheless, this serenity, by lasting over the interval that elapsed between his twenty-third and twenty-sixth year, at which period his marriage took place, was traversed by many clouds, more or less evanescent, and he still had hours and days of melancholy. Assuredly, Lord Byron could not avoid those oscillations of heart and mind that belong to the very essence of the human heart. But, at least, it is easy to assign a palpable cause for all the fits of ennui or melancholy experienced at this time. All his tendencies then show indifference, if not dislike, to female society. His ideal of perfection had spoilt him for women, in the first instance, and the unfortunate experience he had of them still further lowered his opinion of them. But if he did not care about them, it was presumptuous to think he could put aside the sex altogether.

By adopting an anchorite's regimen, he strengthened, it is true, the spiritual part of his nature; and certainly seemed to believe his heart would be satisfied with friendship. His acquaintance with Moore, especially, gave to his daily existence the intellectual and spiritual aliment so necessary to him. But he reckoned on setting woman aside, and his presumptuous heart numbered only twenty-three summers! Among the letters and tokens of homage that piled his table in those days figured many rose-colored notes, written on gilt-edged perfumed paper. Such incense easily ascends, and it was not surprising that his head should also suffer. "Childe Harold," of course, acted most on the imagination of women of powerful intellect and ardent nature, and thus his own peril grew afresh, involuntarily evoked by himself. For, if the prestige of position and circumstance adding lustre to genius, could act strongly even upon men, what must have been their combined influence when added to his personal beauty, upon women?—

". . . . These personal influences acted with increased force, from the assistance derived from others, which, to female imaginations especially, would have presented a sufficiency of attraction, even without the great qualities joined with them. His youth, the noble beauty of his countenance, and its constant play of light and shadow—the gentleness of his voice and manner to women, and his occasional haughtiness to men,—the alleged singularities of his mode of life, which kept curiosity constantly alive; all these minor traits concurred toward the quick spread of his fame; nor can it be denied that, among many purer sources of interest in his poem, the allusions which he makes to instances of '*successful* passion' in his career, were not without their influence on the fancies of that sex whose weakness it is to be most easily won by those who come recommended by the greatest number of triumphs over others. . . . . Altogether, taking into consideration the various points I have here enumerated, *it may be asserted, that there never before existed, and, it is most probable, there never will exist again, a combination of such vast mental powers and such genius, with so many other of those advantages and attractions by which the world is in general dazzled and captivated.*"

This rare combination of advantages were so many means of seduction on his side, involuntarily exercised, and the sole ones he would have condescended to employ; meanwhile all advances were spared him on the other. There were fine ladies whom nothing daunted, if only they could find favor in his sight; who forgot for him their rank, their duties, their families, braving the whole world, donning strange costumes to get at him, carrying jealousy to the verge of madness, to attempted suicide, or to the conception, at least, of crime. One distinguished herself by excessive daring; another, who had not been happy in married life, but who had tried to make up for want of affection by securing her husband's friendship and esteem, was now willing to sacrifice all to her wild passion for the youthful peer.

Whatever the sentiment which in his breast responded to all the feelings he excited, it is certain that they possessed, at least, the power of disturbing his tranquillity. They were like so many beautiful plants, all showy and perfumed, yet distilling poison. The woman whose passion he bore with, rather than shared, could not fail to compromise him; they had exchanged parts, so to say, and he had to suffer from that jealousy, which more frequently falls to the lot of woman. The ennui he thus experienced was tinctured with irritation, while the emotions to which the other lady gave rise, were softer, truer, and more ardent. If we examine well his memoranda and confidential letters of this time, and confront his expressions with facts, we shall always find therein the cause and palpable explanation of those mysterious though short-lived sadnesses then experienced. We shall find the expression of peace sacrificed, or sadness produced, sometimes couched in language indicative of affection or regret; then, again, in words that betray fear or irritation. For instance, we read in a passage of his memoranda:—

"I wish I could settle to reading again,—my life is monotonous, and yet desultory. I take up books, and fling them down again. I began a comedy, and burnt it, because the scene ran into reality; a novel, for the same reason. In rhyme, I can keep more away from facts; but the thought always runs through, through. . . . . Yes, yes; through."

And we have in these two words the precise explanation of this feeling of *ennui*.

He was at this time contemplating a voyage:—

"Ward talks of going to Holland, and we have partly discussed an expedition together. . . . . And why not? . . . . . is far away. . . . . No one else, except Augusta (his sister), cares for me—no ties—no trammels—*andiamo dunque*—se torniamo bene—se no che importa?"*

He was evidently sad that day; but, is not the nature of his sadness revealed in those words:—"She is far away—?"

According to his memoranda, he again fell into this vein of sadness some months later, in February, 1814; but then, also, its causes are very evident. An accumulation of painful things, united to overwhelm him. He had sought to satisfy the longings of his heart by extraordinary intellectual activity, writing the "Bride of Abydos" in four nights, and the "Corsair" in a few days; he had also fought against them, by endeavoring to make a six months' journey into Holland; but this project failed, from obstacles created by a friend who was to accompany him; and, besides, the plague was then prevalent in the East; he was, moreover, embarrassed with the difficulty of selling Newstead, and the necessity of such a painful measure; all which circumstances united to keep him

* "Jacopo Ortis," Ugo Foscolo.

in England. And a host of other irritating annoyances, the work of irreconcilable enemies, who were jealous of his success and his superiority, then fell upon him, as they could not fail to do; for his sun had risen too brightly not to call forth noxious vapors.

After having passed a month away from London, he wrote in his memoranda:—

"I see all the papers are in a sad commotion with those eight lines. . . . . You have no conception of the ludicrous solemnity with which these two stanzas have been treated, ... of the uproar the lines on the little 'Royalty's Weeping,' in 1812 (now republished) have occasioned. The 'Morning Post' gave notice of an intended motion in the House of my brethren on the subject, and God knows what proceedings besides. . . . . This last piece of intelligence is, I presume, too laughable to be true, etc., etc."*

The first blow to his popularity was now given; and soon the whole nation rose up in arms against him. All jealousies, and all resentments now ranged themselves under one hostile banner, distorting Lord Byron's every word, calumniating his motives, making his most generous and noble actions serve as pretexts for attack; reproaching him with having given up enmities from base reasons (while he had done so in reality from feelings of justice and gratitude), pretending† that he had pocketed large sums for his poems, and rendering him responsible for the follies women chose to commit about him. This war, breaking out against him like an unexpected hurricane amid radiant sunshine, must naturally have caused irritation. And if we add to it the embarrassment of his affairs, the deplorable events in his opinion then going on in the world, the fall of the great Napoleon, whom he admired, the invasion of France by the Allied Powers, which he disapproved of, the policy pursued by his country, and the evils endured by humanity—spectacles that always made his heart bleed,—we may well understand how all these causes may have given rise to some moments of misanthropy, such as are betrayed by a few expressions in his journal; but it was a misanthropy that existed only in words, a plant without roots, of ephemeral growth, and most natural to a fine nature. We feel, notwith-

* Moore, Letter 166. † Ibid.

standing all these real palpable causes of ennui, that his principal sufferings still came from the heart.

"Lady Melbourne," writes Lord Byron in his memoranda, in 1814, "tells me that it is said that I am 'much out of spirits.' I wonder if I am really or not? I have certainly enough of '*that perilous stuff which weighs upon the heart,' and it is better they should believe it to be the result of these attacks than that they should guess the real cause.*"

And this real cause was a grief he wished to keep secret. Separation from friends, their departure, even when he was to meet them again, likewise caused him sadness. Especially was this the case with regard to Moore, whom he loved so much, and whose society had an unspeakable charm for him:—"I can only repeat," he said, "that I wish you would either remain a long time with us, or not come at all, for these snatches of society make the subsequent separations bitterer than ever."*

And in the next letter he says:—"I could be very sentimental now, but I won't. The truth is, that I have been all my life trying to harden my heart, and have not yet quite succeeded—though there are great hopes—and you do not know how it sunk with your departure."

This influence is ever visible. The English climate was always distasteful to him, and its fogs displeased him more since he had revelled in the splendor of Eastern suns; moreover, mists grew darker and colder when his imagination was still more influenced by his heart. At those moments his first thought ever was—"*Let me depart, let me seek* a *bright sun, a blue sky.*" When to his great regret, the East was closed against him by the plague of 1813, in his disdain for northern countries, he exclaimed:—

"Give me a *sun*, I care not how hot, and sherbet, I care not how cool, and my heaven is as easily made as your Persian's." Making allusions to this verse—

"*A Persian's heaven is* easily made,—
'*Tis but black eyes and lemonade.*"

But we know that he was thinking of this voyage, in order to divert his mind from the regret of having been obliged,

* Moore, Letters 183 and 184.

from motives of honor and prudence, to give up accompanying into Sicily a family he liked very much. However, the sight of a camel sufficed to carry him back to Asia and the Euxine Sea, and to make him cry out: "*Quando te aspiciam!*"

It was also at this time that he wrote to Moore, "All convulsions with me end in rhyme." To overcome certain agitations of heart, he wrote the "Bride of Abydos," and directly afterward the "Corsair."

But if the melancholy, more or less deep, that cast its shadows over this brilliant period of his triumphs, wore specially the above character, it changed somewhat after his marriage. Thenceforward his melancholy sprang less from the heart, than from bitter disenchantment; from the suffering of a proud nature, cruelly wounded in its sentiment of justice by indignities, calumnies, persecutions, unexampled under such circumstances. Having already spoken of this marriage, I shall leave to regular biographers the detailed account of this painful period, so as only to consider it here under the sole aspect of the griefs it caused. I will not even stop to mention the unaccountable melancholy occasioned by a presentiment before marriage, nor the mysterious sort of agony that seized upon him just as he was about to kneel for the nuptial ceremony in church, nor even the sadness brought about by his first experience of the disposition of the person with whom he had so imprudently linked his fate. I will say, rather, that the melancholy caused and produced by this marriage was really grief; and of the kind that most harshly tries, not only firmness of soul, but likewise true virtue. For all the baseness, cowardice and spirit of revenge that had lain hidden a moment while his triumphal car passed on, united at this moment to overwhelm and cast him down. And the means employed were instinct with such perversity, that his great moral courage, always so powerful in helping him to bear contradictions, disappointments, and personal misfortunes, were no longer of any assistance, threatened as he was with the greatest calamity that can possibly befall a man of honor—namely, to be misjudged, calumniated, accused, thought capable of deeds quite contrary to his high nature. Neither his courage, firmness, nor even the testimony of conscience could shield him from great unhappiness. And he suffered all the more that the blame incurred proceeded from worthy persons who had been mischievously led into error; nor could he conceal from himself that he had voluntarily contributed to produce this unhappy state of things, by not sufficiently avoiding certain appearances, by not attaching sufficient importance to the opinion of his fellow-men, and having lent himself, too easily, to misinterpretation.

"The thorns which I have reaped," said he later (but he thought it much earlier), "are of the tree I planted,—they have torn me,—and I bled; I should have known what fruit would spring from such a seed."*

In addition to all this, Lord Byron had to experience the effects of a phenomenon of a terrible character, a phenomenon almost peculiar to England, the tyrannical power of its public opinion. This power, that gives form and movement to what is called the great world in England, weighed so heavily on the weak minds of several persons calling themselves friends, that, with few exceptions, and though all the while persuaded of the injustice of such opinion, after a few feeble efforts at changing it, and showing the wrong done to Lord Byron, they lost courage to declare their belief. Not only did they no longer protest, but they even pretended to believe part of the stupid calumnies spread abroad. To a heart firm and devoted as his, which, under similar circumstances, would have fought to the death in defense of outraged justice and a persecuted friend, this was one of the most cruel trials imposed on him by adverse destiny. What he must have suffered at this period has been already spoken of in another chapter. I will only say here, that, despite time, and the philosophy, which, subsequently, restored partial serenity, this wound never quite closed, since, even in the fourteenth canto of "Don Juan," written shortly before his last journey into Greece, he still made allusion to it, saying ironically:—

"Without a friend, what were humanity,
To hunt our errors up with a good grace?
Consoling us with—'Would you had thought twice!
Ah! if you had but followed my advice!'
O Job! you had but two friends: one's quite enough,
Especially when we are ill at ease."

---

* "Childe Harold," canto iv.

Moore adds:—"Lord Byron could not have said, at this time, whether it was the attacks of his enemies, or the condolences of his friends that most lacerated his heart."

It was in this state of mind that he quitted England. He visited Belgium, and its battle-plains, still coming across fields of blood; went up the Rhine, and spent some months in Switzerland, where the glaciers, precipices, and the Alps, presented him with a splendid framework for new poems. All the melancholy to be found in "Childe Harold" (third canto), in "Manfred," and in his memoranda at that time, is evidently caused by grief, either of fresh occurrence or renewed by memory. A smile still sometimes wreathed his lip; but, when the gayety natural to his age and disposition would fain have taken possession of his heart, the remembrance of all the indignities he had undergone, rose up before him as the words *Mené, Mené, Tekel, Upharsin*, did to *Belshazzar*. And often his fit of gayety ended in a sigh, which even became habitual after it had ceased to express sorrow. All those who knew Lord Byron have remarked *this singular and touching sigh*, attributing it to a melancholy temperament. But it was especially produced by a crowd of painful indistinct remembrances, intruding upon him at some moment when he would and could have been happy. So he has told us in those exquisite lines of his fourth canto of "Childe Harold;" and he often repeated the same in prose. Thus, for instance, at the time of his excursions to Mont Blanc and the Glaciers, which, had his heart been lighter, would have made him so happy, he finished his memoranda with these melancholy words:—

"In the weather for this tour (of thirteen days) I have been very fortunate—fortunate in a companion (Hobhouse), fortunate in our prospects, and exempt from even the little petty accidents and delays which often render journeys in a less wild country disappointing. I was disposed to be pleased. I am a lover of nature, and an admirer of beauty. I can bear fatigue, and welcome privation, and have seen some of the noblest views in the world. But, in all this, the recollection of bitterness, and more especially of recent and, more, home desolation—which must accompany me through life—have preyed upon me here; and neither the music of the shepherd, the crashing of the avalanche, nor the torrent, the mountain, the glacier, the forest, nor the cloud, have for one moment lightened the weight upon my heart, nor enabled me to lose my own wretched identity in the majesty and the power and the glory around, above, and beneath me."

After having passed eleven months in Switzerland, in about the same frame of mind, he crossed the Alps, and entered Italy. Who can breathe the soft air of that beautiful land, without feeling a healing balm descend on wounds within? The clear atmosphere, and the serene sky, were to him like the indulgent caresses of a sister, bringing a hope—a promise—that peace, and even happiness were about to visit his stricken soul. His first halt was at Milan. There he met with sympathetic, noble minds, instead of the envious, hypocritical, intolerant spirits that had caused him so much suffering; sweet and pleasant was it for him to live with such. Every evening he took his place in a box at the Scala, where the flower of the young intellects of Milan assembled, and where he met with other persons of note, such as Abbé de Brême and Silvio Pellico: gentle, beautiful souls, burning with love of country, and sighing after its independence. From them he learnt more than ever to detest the humiliating yoke of foreign despotism that weighed on Italy; with the independence and frankness of character that belonged to him, he did not scruple to deplore it openly; and his imprudent generosity became a source of annoyance, persecution and calumny for himself. There he heard that passionate music which appeals so strongly to imagination and heart, because it harmonizes so naturally with all its surroundings in Italy. It was listening to this music, at times so pathetic and sweet, that emotion would often lend almost supernatural beauty to his countenance, so that even Mr. Stendhall, the least enthusiastic of men, was wont to say with enthusiasm, *that never, in his whole life, had he seen any thing so beautiful and expressive as Lord Byron's look, or so sublime as his style of beauty.* There he gave himself freely up to all the fine emotions that art can raise. Stendhall accompanied him to the Brêra Museum, "*and I admired,*" says he, "*the depth of sentiment with which Lord Byron understood painters of most opposite schools, Raphael, Guercino, Luini, Titian. Guercino's picture of Hagar dismissed by Abraham quite electrified him, and, from that moment the admiration he inspired rendered every body mute around him.*"

"He improvised for at least an hour, and even better than Madame de Staël," says Stendhall again. "One day Monti was invited to recite before Lord Byron one of his (Monti's) poems which had met in Italy with most favor,—the first canto of the 'Mascheroniana.'" The reading of these lines gave such intense pleasure to the author of "Childe Harold" that Stendhall adds, he shall never forget the divine expression of his countenance on that occasion. "It was," says he, "the placid air of genius and power."

Thus taking interest and pleasure in all around him, if he did experience hours of melancholy (which is very probable, his wounds being so recent and so deep), he had, at the same time, strength to hide it from the public eye, and to express it only with his pen.

The single symptom that might be considered to betray, at this time, a continual malady of soul, was the indifference he showed toward the fair ladies of Milan, who, on their side, were full of enthusiasm about him, and with whom he refused to become acquainted, despite all their advances. But this reserve (though probably more marked and commented on at this particular moment of which we speak) belonged, nevertheless to his nature. After having visited Lake Garda with that pleasure he always experienced from the beauties of nature, and then the tomb of Juliet at Verona, with the interest excited by a true story even more than by Shakspeare's poetry (since he could only take real interest in what was true), he went from Milan to Venice. I have mentioned in another chapter the impression made on him by Venice in particular, and Italy in general; how, aided by exterior circumstances, by the sympathies growing up around him, the severe studies he underwent, so as to keep his heart calm, and bridle an imagination too liable to be influenced by bitter memories; in a few months he began a new existence there, with a more vigorous and healthy impulse for his genius.

When first victimized by the most senseless persecution, he was so surprised and confounded by the noise and violence of calumny, that his keen sentiment of injustice underwent a sort of numbness. On seeing himself thus brutally attacked on the one hand, and so feebly defended on the other, by lukewarm, pusillanimous friends, he may have questioned if he were not really in fault, and hesitated, perhaps, how to reply; for he almost spoke of himself as guilty in the farewell addressed to his cold-hearted wife, and also in the lines composed for his more deserving sister. This situation of mind shows itself without disguise, sadly depicted in the third canto of "Childe Harold." Manfred himself, that wondrous conception of genius, whose lot was cast amid all the sublimities of nature, despite his pride and his strength of will, yet was made to wear the sackcloth of penance. But, on arriving at Venice when months had rolled on, and the Alps were between him and the injustice undergone,—after Lady Byron's new, incredible, and strange refusal to return,—he felt his conscience disencumbered of all morbid influences. The testimony given, the absolution awarded by this impartial, incorruptible judge, whom he had never ceased to consult, became sufficient for him. And by degrees, as he succeeded in forgetting, so as to have power to forgive, peace and tranquillity revisited his mind. Venice was the city of his dream; he had known her, he said, ere he visited her, and after the East she it was that haunted his imagination. Reality spoiled nothing of his dream; he loved every thing about her,—the solemn gayety of her gondolas, the silence of her canals, the late hours of her theatres and soirées, the movement and animation reigning on St. Mark's, where the gay world nightly assembled. Even the decay of the town (which saddened him later), harmonizing then with the whole scene, was not displeasing. He regretted the old costumes given up; but the Carnival, though waning, still recalled ancient Venice, and rejoiced his heart. Familiar with the Italian language, he took pleasure in studying, also, the Venetian dialect, the naïveté and softness of which charmed him, especially on woman's lips. Stretched in his gondola, he loved to court the breezes of the Adriatic, especially at twilight and moonlit hours, unrivalled for their splendor in Venice. In summer and autumn he delighted to give the rein to his horse along the solitary banks of the Lido, or beside the flower-enamelled borders of the Brenta. He loved the simplicity of the women, the freedom from hypocrisy of the men. Feeling himself liked by those among whom chance or choice had thrown him, frequenting theatres and society that could both amuse and instruct, though powerless to fill his thoughts, for these latter required more substantial food, and some hard difficult study to occupy them, being free from all disquieting passions, and wishing to remain thus, sociable as he was by temperament, though loving solitude for the sake of his genius; under all these circumstances, he could satisfy, in due proportion, the double exigency of his nature; for he lived, as we have seen, amid a small circle of sympathetic acquaintances, and of friends arriving from England, who clustered round him without interfering with the independence he had regained, and which formed the natural necessary element for his mind; though he had been deprived of it in England by the cant and pusillanimity of his friends. If, then, he was not exactly happy at this time, at least he was on the road leading to happiness. For he was beginning to make progress in the path of philosophy,—a gentle, indulgent, generous philosophy, as deep as it was clever and pleasing, and which afterward ruled his life, and inspired his genius. All those who saw him at this period are unanimous in saying that melancholy then held aloof from him. In all his letters we find proof of the same. "Venice and I go on well together," wrote he to Murray.

And elsewhere,—"I go out a great deal, and am very well pleased."

Mr. Rose, who visited him at Venice, in the spring of 1818, began a poem which he addressed to him from Albano, where he was taking baths for his health, by alluding to the gayety which Byron spread around him at the reunions which he liked.

But while those living near him, and at Venice, where his poetry was not known, would never have imagined him to be melancholy, in England and other places where people read the sorrow-breathing creations of his genius, he continued to be considered the very personification of melancholy or misanthropy. He knew, and laughed about it sometimes.

"I suppose now I shall never be able to shake off my sable, in public imagination, more particularly since my moral wife demolished my reputation. However, not that, nor more than that, has yet extinguished my spirit, which always rises with the rebound."

And as he did not wish to be considered a misanthrope, he added to Moore, in the same letter:—

"I wish you would also tell Jeffrey what you know,—that I was not, and indeed, am not, even *now*, the misanthropical and gloomy gentleman for which he takes me, but a facetious companion, getting on well with those with whom I am intimate, and as loquacious and laughing as if I were a much cleverer fellow."

And at the same time, to disabuse the public also, and show that he could write gayly, he set himself to study a kind of poetry thoroughly Italian in its spirit, and of which Berni is the father; poetry replete with wit, and somewhat free, but devoid of malice, even when it merges from gayety into satire; a style unknown to England in its varied shades, and which it was easier for him to introduce than to make popular. "Beppo" was his first essay in this line, and it contains too much genuine fun not to have been a natural product of his humor ere flowing from his pen.

On sending it to Murray as a mere sample of the style he thought it possible to introduce into the literature of his country, he said:—

"At least, this poem will show that I can write gayly, and will repel the accusation of monotony and affectation."*

But the gayety visible at this period in his writings and his conduct was not, however, uninterrupted. For such cheerfulness to be constant, neither a continuation of the causes producing it, nor yet the absence of English papers and reviews could quite suffice. It was necessary that no letters should come, awakening painful remembrances that had slumbered awhile, that there should be no necessity for selling his property in England,—a matter always complicated, and difficult of execution at a distance, and which forced upon him cares and occupations most opposed to his character, while affording sad proof of the negligence, ingratitude, and other faults of those intrusted with the management of his affairs. It would have required that friends who had neglected to prevent his departure, should not, when weary of seeing him no more, have conspired to bring about his return, devising a good means of so doing by obstacles thrown in the way of a

* Letter 312.

successful issue to his affairs, which happy conclusion was absolutely necessary for his peace and independence. We see by his letters, written during the summer of 1818, that he was tormented in a thousand ways; sometimes not receiving any accounts, sometimes being advised to come nearer London, then, again, having no tidings of how several thousands had been disposed of. Besides that, he had constantly before his eyes a spectacle most painful for a generous heart to witness. That was Venice choked and expiring in the grip of her foreign rulers. The humiliation thus inflicted on the city of his dreams, and its noble race of inhabitants, and which was every instant repeated and proclaimed by the brutal voice of drums and cannons, with a thousand added vexations (necessary, perhaps, for keeping up an abhorred sway), caused infinite suffering to his just and liberal nature, raising emotions of anger and pitying regret, that flowed from his pen in sublimely indignant language. Thereupon, the despots, unable to impose silence upon him, revenged themselves in various ways, echoing reports spread in London, and inventing new fables, which the idle people of Venice, more idle than elsewhere, and even the gondoliers repeated in their turn to strangers, to amuse and gain a few pence. We pass over any details of the persecution inflicted on him by English tourists, who, not actuated by sympathy, but out of sheer curiosity and eagerness to pick up all the gossip and idle tales in circulation, were wont to run after Lord Byron, intruding on his private walks, and even pressing into his very palace. Such conduct, of course, displeased him, and accordingly in the summer of 1818 we find traces of ill-humor visible in his correspondence, and even in the first two cantos of "Don Juan." Afterward, when he had been laid hold of and absorbed by a great passion, his irritation merged into sadness, melancholy, disquietude, and irresolution.*

But if all this proves that sadness wearing the garb of melancholy sometimes approached him, even at Venice; we see too clearly its real and accidental causes to be able to ascribe it to a permanent and fatal disposition of temperament.

Many signs of suffering escaped his pen at this time. For instance, writing to Moore from Venice in 1818, and wishing

* See his "Life in Italy."

to give him a picturesque description of a creature full of savage energy, who forced herself upon him in a thousand extravagant ways, refusing to leave his house, he said:—

"I like this kind of animal, and am sure that I should have preferred Medea to any woman that ever breathed. You may, perhaps, wonder at my speaking thus (making allusion to Lady Byron). . . . . I could have forgiven the dagger or the bowl, any thing but the *deliberate desolation* piled upon me when I stood *alone upon my hearth* with my household gods shivered around me. . . . . Do you suppose I have forgotten or forgiven it? It has comparatively swallowed up in me every other feeling, and I shall remain only a spectator upon this earth until some great occasion presents itself, which may come yet. There are others more to be blamed than ——, and it is on these that my eyes are fixed unceasingly."

Meanwhile, until Providence should present him with this opportunity, another feeling took involuntary possession of his whole soul. But would not the sentiment which was about to swallow up or transform all others, and which was at last to bring him some happiness, also destroy the peace so carefully preserved in his heart by indifference since he left London? He seemed at first to have dreaded such a result himself; for, in one of the earliest letters addressed to the person beloved (letters which fully unveil his beautiful soul, and where one would vainly seek an indelicate or sensual expression), he tells her "that he had resolved, on system, to avoid a great passion," but that she had put to flight all his resolutions, that he is wholly hers, and will become all she wishes, happy perhaps in her love, but never more at peace,—"*ma tranquillo mai più.*"

And he ends the letter with a verse quoted from Guarini's "Pastor Fido."*

His heart assuredly was satisfied, but precisely because he truly loved, and felt himself beloved; therefore did he also suffer from the impossibility of reconciling the exigencies of his heart with circumstances. In one of these beautiful letters, so full of simplicity and refinement, he tells her:—

"Che giova a te, cor mio, l' esser amato?
Che giova a me l' aver si cara Amante?
Se tu, crudo Destino, ne dividi
Cio che amor ne stringe!"

"What we shall have to suffer is of common occurrence, and we must bear it like many others, for true love is never happy; but we two shall suffer still more because we are placed in no ordinary circumstances."

His real sentiments of soul are likewise displayed in that beautiful satirical poem, "Don Juan," in the third canto of which he exclaims:—

"Oh, Love! what is it in this world of ours
Which makes it fatal to be loved? Ah, why
With cypress branches hast thou wreathed thy bowers,
And made thy best interpreter a sigh?"

Nevertheless, when he had left Venice, which became altogether distasteful to him, and gone to live at Ravenna, his heart grew calmer. To Murray he writes:—

"You inquire after my health and *spirits* in large letters; my health can't be very bad, for I cured myself of a sharp tertian ague in three weeks, with cold water, which had held my stoutest gondolier for months, notwithstanding all the bark of the apothecary, — a circumstance which surprised D'Aglietti, who said it was a proof of great stamina, particularly in so epidemic a season. I did it out of dislike to the taste of bark (which I can't bear), and succeeded, contrary to the prophecies of every body, by simply taking nothing at all. As to spirits, they are unequal, now high, now low,— like other people's, I suppose, and depending upon circumstances."

Having grown intimate with the Count and Countess G——, he was requested by the former to accompany his young wife into society, to the play, everywhere, in short; soon Lord Byron took up his abode in their palace, and the repose of heart and mind he thus attained was so great, that no sadness seemed able to come near him, as long as this tranquil, regular, pleasing sort of existence lasted, and it seemed destined to endure forever.

But nothing is permanent here below, and especially happiness, be its source regular or irregular; such is the mysterious eternal law of this earthly life, doubtless one of probation. To this period of tranquillity succeeded one of uneasiness and grief, which ended by awakening a little melancholy. Let us examine the causes of it in his position at that time.

The object of Lord Byron's love had obtained from His Holiness Pope Pius VII., at the solicitation of her parents, permission to leave her husband's house, and return home to her family. Consequently she had left in the month of July, and was leading a retired life in a country-house belonging to her parents. Thus Lord Byron, who had been accustomed to feel happy in her society, was now reduced to solitude in the same place her presence had gladdened. In order not to compromise her in her delicate position, he was obliged even to deny himself the gratification of calling upon her in the country. Ravenna, which is always a sad kind of abode, becomes in autumn quite a desert, liable to fever. Every body had gone into the country. Even if taste had not inclined Lord Byron to be alone, necessity would have compelled it; for there was no longer a single being with whom he could exchange a word or a thought. Equinoctial gales again swept the sea; and thus the wholesome exercise of swimming, so useful in restoring equilibrium to the faculties and calming the mind, was forbidden. If at least he could have roamed on horseback through the forest of pines! But no; the autumn rains, even in this lovely climate, last for weeks. In the absolute solitude of a town like Ravenna, imprisoned, so to say, within his own apartment, how could he avoid some emotions of sadness? He was thus assailed; and, as it always happened where he himself was concerned, he mistook its causes. Engrossed by an affection that was amply returned, feeling strong against the injustice of man and the hardships of fate, having become well-nigh inaccessible to *ennui*, he was astonished at the sadness that always seemed to return in autumn, and imagined that it might be from some hereditary malady inherent to his temperament.

"This season kills me with sadness," he wrote to Madame G——, on the 28th of September; "when I have my mental malady, it is well for others that I keep away. I thank thee, from my heart, for the roses. Love me! My soul is like the leaves that fall in autumn, all yellow."

And then, as if he almost reproached himself with being sad without some cause existing in the heart, and, above all, not wishing to pain Madame G——, he wound up with a joke, saying:—"Here is a cantator;" a conventional word recalling some buffooneries in a play, and which signified:—"Here is a fine sentence!"

Certainly, the autumnal season, sad and rainy as it is, must have had great influence over him. Could it be otherwise with an organization like his? From this point of view, his melancholy, like his temperament, might be considered as hereditary. But would it have been developed without the aid of other causes?

Let us observe the date of the letter, wherein he blames the season, and the dates of those received from London, or those he addressed thither. The coincidence between them will show clearly that when he called himself melancholy, and accused the season, it occurred precisely on the day when he was most wearied and overwhelmed by a host of other disagreeable things. For instance, Murray, whose answers on several points he had been impatiently expecting, was seized with a new fit of silence. "There you are at your tricks."*

And then, when the silence was broken, the letters almost always brought him disagreeable accounts. Wishing to disgust him with Italy, they sent him volumes full of unjust, stupid attacks on Italy and the Italians whom he liked.

"These fools," exclaimed he, "will force me to write a book myself on Italy, to tell them broadly *they have lied.*"

Nothing was more disagreeable, and even hurtful to him, at this time, than the report of his return to England; and they wrote him word that his presence in London was asserted on all sides, that many persons declared that they had seen him, and that Lady C. L—— had been to call at his house fully persuaded that he was there.†

"Pray do not let the papers paragraph me back to England. They may say what they please, any loathsome abuse but that. Contradict it."

In consequence of this invention, even his newspapers were no longer sent to him; and when he spoke of the harm and annoyance thus occasioned, annoyance increased by Murray's silence, his displeasure certainly amounted to anger. At this time also he was informed by letter that some English tourists, on returning home, had boasted that they *could* have been presented to him at Venice, but *would not.*

* Letter 386. † Letter 389.

The trial of the unfortunate queen was just coming on at this time, and the whole proceeding, accompanied as it was with so many cruel, indecent circumstances, revolted him in the highest degree.

"No one here," said he, "believes a word of all the infamous depositions made."

The article in "Blackwood's Magazine," which was so abominably libellous as to force him out of the silence *he had adopted for his rule*, was often present to his thought; for he dreaded lest his editor should for the sake of lucre publish "Don Juan" with his name, and lest the Noels and other enemies, out of revenge, should profit thereby to contest his right of guardianship over his child, as had been the case with Shelley.

"Recollect, that if you put my name to 'Don Juan' in these canting days, any lawyer might oppose my guardian-right of my daughter in chancery, on the plea of its containing the parody. Such are the perils of a foolish jest. I was not aware of this at the time, but you will find it correct, I believe; and you may be sure that the Noels would not let it slip. Now, I prefer my child to a poem at any time."

Moreover, amid all these pre-occupations, Hobhouse wrote him word that he should be obliged to go to England for the queen's trial; and we know how repugnant this necessity was to Lord Byron. His little Allegra had just fallen rather dangerously ill; Countess G——, notwithstanding the sentence pronounced by His Holiness, continued to be tormented by her husband, who refused to accept the decision of Rome, because he did not wish for a separation. The Papal Government, pushed on by the Austrian police, had recourse to a thousand small vexatious measures, to make Lord Byron quit Ravenna, where he had given offense by becoming too popular with the liberal party.

Lastly, we may further add that, even in those days, he was suffering from some jealous susceptibility, though knowing well how he was beloved. For in the letter, dated 28th of September, where he says "his soul is sick," he also complains of Madame G——'s having passed some hours at Ravenna *without letting him know, and of her having thought fit to hide from him certain steps taken.*

This autumn was followed by a winter still more disagreeably exceptional than the preceding one. The most inclement weather prevailed during the month of January, and generally throughout the winter.

"Bad weather, this 4th of January," he writes in his memoranda, "as bad as in London itself."

The sirocco, a wind that depresses even people without nerves, was blowing and melting the ice. The streets and roads were transformed into pools of half-congealed mud. He was somewhat "*out of spirits.*" But still he hoped:—

"If the roads and weather allow, I shall go out on horseback to-morrow. It is high time; already we have had a week of this work: snow and sirocco one day, ice and snow the other. A sad climate for Italy; but these two winters have been extraordinary."

The next day, he got up "*dull and drooping.*" The weather had not changed. Lord Byron absolutely required to breathe a little fresh air every day, to take exercise on horseback. His health was excellent, but on these two conditions; otherwise, it failed. His temper clouded over, without air and exercise. During the wretched days he was obliged to remain at home, he had not even the diversion letters and newspapers might have afforded, since no post came in. His sole amusement consisted in stirring the fire, and playing with Lion, his mastiff, or with his little menagerie. So much did he suffer from it all, that his kind heart bestowed pity even on his horses:—

". . . . . Horses must have exercise—get a ride as soon as weather serves; deuced muggy still. An Italian winter is a sad thing, but all the other seasons are charming."

On the 7th of January, he adds:—

"Still rain, mist, snow, drizzle, and all the incalculable combinations of a climate where heat and cold struggle for mastery."

If the weather cleared up one day, it was only to become more inclement the next.

On the 12th he wrote in his journal:—

"The weather still so humid and impracticable, that London, in its most oppressive fogs, were a summer bower to this mist and sirocco, which has now lasted (but with one day's interval), checkered with snow or heavy rain only, since the 30th of December, 1820. It is so far lucky that I have a literary turn; but it is very tiresome not to be able to stir out, in comfort, on any horse but Pegasus, for so many days. The roads are even worse than the weather, by the long splashing, and the heavy soil, and the inundations."

And on the 19th:—

"Winter's wind somewhat more unkind than ingratitude itself, though Shakspeare says otherwise. . . . . Rather low in spirits—certainly hippish—liver touched—will take a dose of salts."

There was, however, too much elasticity of spirits in him, and his melancholy was not sufficiently deep for it to last. His evening visit to Countess G—— at eight o'clock (the day's event consoling for all else), a few simple airs played by her on the piano, some slight diversion, such as a ray of sunshine between two showers, or a star in the heavens raising hopes of a brighter morrow, sufficed to clear up his horizon. What always raised his spirits was the prospect of some good or great and generous action to perform, such, in those days, as contributing to the deliverance of a nation. Then, not only did the sirocco and falling rain cease to act on his nerves, as he himself acknowledged, but his genius would start into fresh life, making him snatch a pen, and write off in a few days admirable poems,* worthy to be the fruit of long years of meditation.

We may, then, believe that if his melancholy had been left solely to the physical and moral influences surrounding him at this time, it would never have become much developed, or at least would have soon passed away, like morning mists that rise in the east to be quickly dissipated by the rays of the sun.

But just as these slight vapors may form into a cloud, if winds arise in another part of the sky, bringing fresh moisture to them, so a slight and fugitive sadness in him might be deepened and prolonged through circumstances. And this was exactly what happened in the year of which we speak, for it was full of disappointments and grief for him. To arrive at this persuasion, it is sufficient to remark the co-

* It was then that "Sardanapalus" came to light.

incidence of dates. For example, we find in his memoranda, under the date of 18th of January, 1821:—

"At eight proposed to go out. Lega came in with a letter about a bill *unpaid* at Venice, which I thought paid months ago. I flew into a paroxysm of rage, which almost made me faint. I have not been well ever since. I deserve it for being such a fool — but it *was* provoking — a set of scoundrels! It is, however, but five-and-twenty pounds."

Then, again, on the 19th we find:—

"Rode. Winter's wind somewhat more unkind than ingratitude itself, though Shakspeare says otherwise. At least I am so much more accustomed to meet with ingratitude than the north wind, that I thought the latter the sharper of the two. I had met with both in the course of twenty-four hours, so could judge."

And on the same day he wrote to Murray a letter, in which, after mentioning a host of vexations and worries, he ends by saying:—

"I am in bad humor—some obstructions in business with those plaguing trustees, who object to an advantageous loan, which I was to furnish to a nobleman (Lord B——) on mortgage, because his property is in Ireland, have shown me how a man is treated in his absence."

Between the 19th and the 22d, his physical and moral indisposition seemed to last; for he makes reflections in his memoranda, upon melancholy bilious people, and says that he has not even sufficient energy to go on with his tragedy of "Sardanapalus," and that he has ceased composing for the last few days. Now, it was precisely the 20th that he was more than ever annoyed by the obstinacy of the London Theatre managers, for, despite his determination and his clear right, his protestations and entreaties, they were resolved, said the newspapers that came to hand, on having "Marino Faliero" acted. He had already written to Murray:—

"I must really and seriously request that you will beg of Messrs. Harris or Elliston to let the Doge alone: it is not an acting play; it will not serve their purpose; it will destroy yours (the sale); and it will distress me. It is not courteous, it is hardly even gentlemanly, to persist in this appropriation of a man's writings to their mountebanks."

He wrote thus, on the 19th; but on the 20th his fears had increased to such a pitch that he also addressed the lord-chamberlain, requesting him to forbid this representation. Indeed, so great was his annoyance, that he wrote to Murray twice in the same day:—

"I wish you would speak to Lord Holland, and to all my friends and yours, to interest themselves in preventing this cursed attempt at representation.

"God help me! at this distance, I am treated like a corpse or a fool by the few people that I thought I could rely upon; and I *was* a fool to think any better of them than of the rest of mankind."

On the 21st his melancholy does not appear to have worn off. This is to be attributed to the additions to all the causes of the previous day; and to the news of the illness of Moore, whom he loved so much, there came, in addition, the following event, which we give in his own words:—

"To-morrow is my birthday—that is to say, at twelve o' the clock, midnight—*i. e.*, in twelve minutes, I shall have completed thirty-three years of age!!! and I go to my bed with a heaviness of heart at having lived so long, and to so little purpose."

Let me be allowed here to make some comment on the beauty of the sentiment causing this sadness; for certainly he was not actuated by a common sensual, selfish regret at youth departing. Beauty, youth, love, fortune, and celebrity, all smiled on him then; he possessed every one of them to a degree capable of satisfying any vanity, or any pride, but they were inadequate, for a modesty so rare and so admirable as his! His regrets certainly did not apply to youth; he was only thirty-three years of age! Nor yet to beauty, for he possessed it in the highest degree; nor to fame, that had only too much been his; nor to love, for he was the object of real idolatry;* nor to any actions that called for repentance. To what, then, did they apply? To his *aspirations* after greater things, after *ideal perfections*, that neither he nor any one else can arrive at here below. It was a soaring after the infinite!

The cause, noble in itself, of this sadness consisted then in a sort of nostalgia for the great, the beautiful, the good. The

* See chapter on "Life in Ravenna."

simple words in which he expressed it enable us to well understand its nature. "I do not regret this year," said he, "*for what I have done, but for what I have not done!*"

I will not further multiply proofs; suffice it to say, that this year having been one of incessant annoyances to him, not only can not we be surprised that he should have experienced moments of sadness, but we might rather be astonished at their being so few, if we did not know that living above all for heart, and his heart being then satisfied, he found therein compensation for all the rest. "Thanks for your compliments of the year. I hope that it will be pleasanter than the last. I speak with reference to England only, as far as regards myself, where I had every kind of disappointment—lost an important lawsuit—and the trustees of Lady Byron refusing to allow of an advantageous loan to be made from my property to Lord Blessington, etc., by way of closing the four seasons. These, and a hundred other such things, made a year of bitter business for me in England. Luckily things were a little pleasanter for me here, else I should have taken the liberty of Hannibal's ring."

The political and revolutionary events then taking place in Romagna and throughout Italy, caused emotions and sentiments of too strong a nature in Lord Byron to be confounded with sadness; but they may well have contributed to develop largely certain melancholy inclinations discoverable toward autumn. By degrees, as the first strength of grief passes away, it leaves behind a sort of melancholy current in the soul, which, without being the sentiment itself, serves as a conductor for it, making it gush forth on occurrence of the smallest cause. Causes with him were not so slight at this period, although he considered them such* out of the superabundance of his philosophical spirit; and the year that began with so many contradictions, ended in the same manner. The hope of seeing the Counts Gamba back again at Ravenna was daily lessening. All the letters Madame G—— wrote to him from Florence and Pisa, penned as they were amid the anguish of fear lest Lord Byron should be assassinated at Ravenna, were necessarily pregnant with alarm and affliction.

* "Many small articles make up a sum,
And hey ho for Caleb Quotem, oh!"

Meanwhile his interests were being neglected in London. Murray irritated him by his inexplicable negligence or worried him with sending foolish publications and provoking reviews. Gifford, a critic he loved and revered, from whom no praise, he said, could compensate for any blame, — Gifford, whose ideas on the drama were quite opposite to his own, had just been censuring his beautiful dramatic compositions.* Moreover, Italy having failed in her attempts at independence, was insulted in her misfortune by that world which smiles only on success, and thus, indirectly, the persons loved and esteemed by Lord Byron came in for their share of outrage. And all these contradictions, *where* and *when* did he experience them? At Ravenna, in a solitude and isolation that would have made the bravest stoic shudder, and that was prejudicial to him without his being aware of it. For there were two distinct temperaments in Lord Byron, that of his genius and that of his humanity, and the wants of one were not always those of the other. The first, from its nature and manifestations, required solitude. The second, eminently sociable, while yielding to the tyranny of the first, or bearing it from force of circumstance, suffered nevertheless when solitude became too complete. It was not the society of the great world, nor what are called its pleasures, that Lord Byron required; but a society of friends and clever persons capable of affording a little diversion to his monotonous life. When this twofold want did not meet with reasonable satisfaction, a certain degree of melancholy necessarily developed itself. "*When he was not thrown into some unbearable sort of solitude, like that in which he found himself at Ravenna*," says Madame G——, "*his good-humor and gayety only varied when letters from England came to move and agitate him, or when he suffered morally.*

"*I must, however, add that all sensitive agents, all atmospherical impressions, acted on him more than on others, and it might almost be said that his sky was mirrored in his soul, the latter often taking its color from the former; and if by that is understood the hereditary malady spoken of by others and himself, then they are right, for he had truly inherited a most impressionable temperament.*"

* See Letter 435.

Moreover, the absolute, inexorable solitude caused by the absence of all his friends from Ravenna, was still further augmented by the occurrence of intermittent marshy fevers, which every body endeavors to avoid by flying from Ravenna at the close of summer, and to which he fell a prey. This fever, that seized hold of him, and even prevented his departure, might alone have sufficed to render him melancholy, for nothing more inclines to sadness. But so intimate was his persuasion that when sadness does not proceed from the heart it has no cause for existence, and so little was he occupied with self, that he would not allow there could be sufficient cause for melancholy in all the sufferings weighing upon him.

"I ride, I am not intemperate in eating or drinking, and my general health is as usual, except a slight ague, which rather does good than not. It must be constitutional; for I know nothing more than usual to depress me to that degree."*

But so little was it the necessary product of his temperament alone, so much, on the contrary, did it result from a host of causes accidentally united, that he had scarcely arrived at Pisa, where most of the causes either ceased or were neutralized, than his mind recovered its serenity, and he could write to Moore:—

"At present, owing to the climate (I can walk down into my garden and pluck my own oranges, indulging in this meridian luxury of proprietorship), my spirits are much better."

Whenever, then, his heart was happy in the happiness of those he loved, wherever he found an intellectual society to animate the mind, diverting and amusing him without imposing the chains of etiquette, we vainly seek the faintest trace of melancholy. But two great griefs soon befell him at Pisa, for sorrow never made long truces with Byron. Truly might we say that fate ceased not from making him pay for the privilege of his great superiority, by all the sufferings he endured. Soon after his arrival at Pisa, his little daughter Allegra, whom he was having educated at a convent in Romagna, died of fever, and shortly afterward Shelley was drowned! About the same time the publication of "Cain," then going on, raised a perfect storm, furnishing his enemies with pretexts for attacking and slandering him more than ever. They

* Moore, Letter 471.

did it in a manner so violent and unjust, bringing in likewise his publisher Murray, that Lord Byron thought it incumbent on him to send a challenge to the poet laureate, the most perfidious among them all. At this same period, Hunt, who had lost all means of existence by the death of Shelley, forced himself on Lord Byron in such a disagreeable way as to become the plague of his life. Lastly, in consequence of a quarrel that arose between Sergeant Masi and Lord Byron's riding companions, an arbitrary measure was taken, which again compelled his friends—the Counts Gamba—to leave Pisa for Genoa; and he, though free to remain, resolved on sharing their fate and quitting Pisa likewise. For the Government, though subservient to Austrian rule, did not dare to apply the same unjust decree to an English subject of such high rank. Nevertheless, if we except the death of his little girl, which caused him profound sorrow—although he bore it with all the fortitude belonging to his great soul—and the death of Shelley, which also afflicted him greatly, none of the other annoyances had power to grieve him or to create melancholy.

"It seems to me," he wrote to Murray, "that what with my own country and other lands, there has been *hot water enough* for some time." This manner of announcing so many disagreeables, shows what self-possession he had arrived at, and how he viewed all things calmly and sagely, as Disraeli portrays him with truth in "Venetia," when he makes him say:—"'*As long as the world leaves us quiet, and does not burn us alive, we ought to be pleased. I have grown callous to all they say,*' observed Herbert. '*And I also,*' replied Lord Cadurcis." Cadurcis and Herbert both represent Lord Byron; for Disraeli, like Moore, having felt that Lord Byron had enough in him to furnish several individualities, all equally powerful, thought it necessary to call in the aid of this double personification, in order to paint his nature in all its richness, with the changes to be wrought by time and events.

If the war waged against Lord Byron by envy, bigotry, and wickedness, had had power to create emotion during youth, and even later, the gentle, wise philosophy he afterward acquired in the school of adversity, so elevated his mind, that he could no longer suffer, except from wounds of heart, provided his conscience were at rest. When the stupid persecution raised against him on the appearance of "Cain" took place, he wrote to Murray from Pisa, on the 8th of February:—

"All the *row* about *me* has no otherwise affected me than by the attack upon yourself, which is ungenerous in Church and State. . . . . I can only say, 'Me, me; en adeum qui feci;' —that any proceedings directed against you, I beg may be transferred to me, who am willing, and *ought*, to endure them all."

And then he ends his letter, saying, "I write to you about all this row of bad passions and absurdities, with the *summer* moon (for here our winter is clearer than your dog-days), lighting the winding Arno, with all her buildings and bridges, —so quiet and still!—*What nothings are we before the least of these stars!*"

Soon after, and while still suffering under the same persecution from his enemies and weak fools, he wrote to Moore from Montenero, recalling in his usual vein of pleasantry, their mutual adventures in fashionable London life, and saying, that he should have done better while listening to Moore as he tuned his harp and sang, *to have thrown himself out of the window, ere marrying a Miss Milbank.*

"I speak merely of my marriage, and its consequences, distresses, and calumnies; for I have been much more happy, on the whole, *since*, than I ever could have been with her."

And some time after, conversing with Madame G——, examining and analyzing all he might have done as an orator and a politician, if he had remained in England, he added:—

"That then he would not have known her, and that no other advantages could have given him the happiness which he found in real affection."

This conversation, interrupted by the unexpected arrival of Mr. Hobhouse, and which, but for the inexplicable sadness arising from presentiments, would have made earth a paradise for the person to whom it was addressed, took place at Pisa, in Lord Byron's garden, a few days before his departure for Genoa. At Genoa he continued to lead the same retired, studious, simple kind of life; and, although the winter was this year again extremely rigorous, and although his health had been slightly affected since the day of Shelley's funeral, and his stay at Genoa made unpleasant by the ennui proceeding from Mr. Hunt's presence there,* still he had no fit of what can be called melancholy until he decided on leaving for Greece. Then the sadness that he would fain have concealed, but could not, which he betrayed in the parting hour, acknowledged while climbing the hill of Albano, and which often brought tears to his eyes on board the vessel—this sadness had its source in the deepest sentiments of his heart. In Greece, we know, by the unanimous and constant testimony of all who saw him there, that the rare fits of melancholy he experienced, all arose from the same cause. During his sojourn in the Ionian Islands, as soon as letters from Italy had calmed his uneasiness, finding himself surrounded by general esteem, affection, and admiration, seeing justice dawn for him, and confusion for his enemies, being consoled also with the prospect of a future, and that, with heart at ease, he might at last shed happiness around him; then he was ever to be found full of serenity and even gayety, *only intent on noble virtuous actions.* One day, however, a great melancholy seized upon him, and all the good around suddenly appeared to vanish. Whence did this arise? His letters tell us:—

"Poor Byron!" wrote Count Gamba, to his sister, on the 14th of October, "he has been much concerned by the news which reached him some fortnight ago about the headache of his dear Ada. You may imagine how *triste* were the workings of his fancy, to which he added the fear of having to spend several months without hearing any further tidings of her; besides the suspicion that the truth was either kept back from him or disguised. Happily, another bulletin has reached him, to say that she is all right again,—and one more, to announce that the child is in good health, with the exception of a slight pain in the eyes. His melancholy is, therefore, a little mitigated, though it has not completely disappeared."

The pre-occupation, disquietude, and anxiety, which he experienced more or less continuously in Greece, and above all, at Missolonghi, and which I have mentioned elsewhere, certainly did agitate, trouble, and even irritate him sometimes; but then it was in such a passing way, on account of the great empire he had acquired over himself, that every one during

* See his "Life at Genoa."

his sojourn in the islands, and often even at Missolonghi, unanimously pronounced gayety to be his predominant disposition. And, truly, it was only to griefs proceeding from the heart that he granted power to cloud his brow with any kind of melancholy.

After this long analysis, and before summing up, it still remains for us to examine a species of melancholy that seems not to come within our limits, but which occasionally seized upon him on his first waking in the morning:—

"I have been considering what can be the reason why I always wake at a certain hour in the morning, and always in very bad spirits—I may say, in actual despair and despondency, in all respects—even of that which pleased me over-night. In about an hour or two, this goes off, and I compose myself either to sleep again, or a least, to quiet. . . . . What is it? —liver? . . . . I suppose that it is all hypochondriasis."

What name shall we give to this physiological phenomenon? Was it hypochondriasis, as he imagined? That Lord Byron's temperament, so sensitive to all moral causes, so vulnerable to all atmospherical influences, should likewise have contained a vein of hypochondriasis, is not only possible, but likely. And were we as partial as we wish to be just, there would certainly be no reason for denying it. Hypochondriasis is an infirmity, not a fault. Lord Byron himself, when informed that such a one complained of being called hypochondriacal, replied somewhat to the following effect: "I can not conceive how a man in perfect good health can feel wounded by being told that he is hypochondriacal, since his face and his conduct refute the accusation. Were this accusation ever to prove correct, to what does it amount, except to say that he has a liver complaint?

"'I shall publish it before the whole world,' said the clever Smelfungus. 'I should prefer telling my doctor,' said I. There is nothing dishonorable in such an illness, which is more especially that of people who are studious. It has been the illness of those who are good, wise, clever, and even light-hearted. Regnard, Molière, Johnson, Gray, Burns, were all more or less given to it. Mendelssohn and Bayle were often so afflicted with it, that they were obliged to have recourse to toys, and to count the slates on the roof of the houses opposite, in order to distract their attention. Johnson says, that oftentimes he would have given a limb to raise his spirits."

But, nevertheless, when we seek truth for itself, and not for its results, nor to make it help out a system, we must go to the bottom of things, and reveal all we discover. Thus, after having spoken of this physiological phenomenon, which he suspects to be hypochondriasis, Byron adds, that he came upon him, accompanied with great thirst, that the London chemist, Mann, had cured him of it in three days, that it always yielded to a few doses of salts, and that the phenomenon always recurred and ended at the same hours. It appears, then, to me, that all these symptoms are far from indicating a serious and incurable hereditary malady, which would not be likely to have yielded to doses of salts, and which his general good health would seem to exclude. I consider them rather to point, for their cause, to his diet, which was *quite insufficient for him, and even hurtful, likely to affect the most robust health, and much more that of a man whose organization was so sensitive and delicate.* And, as this system of denying his body what was necessary for it increased the demands of his mind, which in its turn revenged itself on the body, the result was that Lord Byron voluntarily failed in the duties which every man owes to himself. Therefore, I think it more just to rank the melancholy arising from such causes, among his *faults*, and not among the accidents of life, or his natural disposition.*

Now, having examined his melancholy under all its phases, having proved more what it was not than what it was, we shall sum up with saying, that Lord Byron really experienced, during his short life, every kind of sadness. First, in early youth, he had to encounter disappointments, mortifications, disenchantments, deep moral suffering; then the constant warfare of envy, resulting in cruel, unceasing slanders: then, all the philosophical sadness arising in great minds, the best endowed and the noblest, from the emptiness of earthly things; then that unslakable thirst for the true, the just, the perfect; that sort of nostalgia which the noblest souls experience, because their home is not here, because reality disgusts them, from the striking contrast it presents with the ideal type, in their mind, especially at our epoch, and in our present social condition,

* See chapter on "Faults."

when men can with difficulty preserve interior calm by dint of compulsory occupations requiring much energy. And, lastly, there was the sadness inherent to a physical temperament of such exquisite sensibility. Yet, notwithstanding all the above, and though Lord Byron was condemned to drain the cup of bitterness to its dregs, we think he ought not to be classed among geniuses exclusively swayed by the melancholy in their nature, since almost all his sadness sprang from accident, and from a sort of fictitious temperament produced by circumstances. Thus his melancholy, being fictitious, remained generally subject in real life to his fine natural temperament, only gaining the mastery when he was under the influence of inspiration, and with pen in hand.

"All is strange," says La Bruyère, "in the humor, morals, and manners of most men. . . . . The wants of this life, the situation in which we are, necessity's law, force *nature, and cause great changes in it.* Thus such men can not be defined, thoroughly and in themselves; too many external things affect, change, and overwhelm them; they are not precisely what they are, or rather, what they appear to be."

Thus, then, having a natural disposition for gayety received from God, and which I shall call *interior*, which always had the upper hand in all important actions of his life, but which was only truly known by those who approached him closely, I conclude that gayety often predominated, and ought to have predominated much more, in Lord Byron's life.

But through the fictitious character, which I will call *exterior*, derived from *education, from circumstances of family, country, and association*, which (apparently) modified the first, and gave the world sometimes a reason, and sometimes a pretext for inventing that dark myth called by his name, *and which really only influenced his writings*, melancholy often predominated in his life. However, its sway was less in reality than in the imagination of those who wished to identify the man with the poet, and to find the real Lord Byron in the heroes of his early poems.

CHAPTER XXV.

LOVE OF TRUTH; OR, CONSCIENCE A CHIEF CHARACTERISTIC OF LORD BYRON.

SOME of Lord Byron's biographers, unable to overcome the difficulty of defining so complete a character, or of explaining, by ordinary rules, certain contradictions apparent in his rich nature, think to excuse their own inefficiency and elude the difficulty, by saying that he did not possess one of those striking points, or decided inclinations, that constitute a man's moral physiognomy. They pretend that his qualities of heart and mind, his passions, inclinations, virtues, faults, are so combined in his ardent, mobile nature, as to make him in reality the sport of chance; and that no inclination or passion whatsoever could ever become mistress of his heart or mind, so as to constitute the basis of a character, and render it possible to define it.

Moore himself, for reasons I have mentioned,* and which have been sufficiently spoken of in another chapter, contents himself with saying that Lord Byron's intellectual and moral attributes were so dazzling, contradictory, complicated, and varied, beyond all example, that it may be truly said there was not one man, but several men, in him:—

"So various, indeed, and contradictory, were his attributes, both moral and intellectual, that he may be pronounced to have been, not one, but many; nor would it be any great exaggeration of the truth to say that, out of the mere partition of the properties of his single mind, a plurality of characters, all different and all vigorous, might have been furnished. It was this multiform aspect exhibited by him that led the world, during his short, wondrous career, to compare him with that medley host of personages, almost all differing from each other, which he playfully enumerates in one of his journals."

* See Introduction.

These observations of Moore's are only true from a certain point of view — the richness of Lord Byron's nature. But even if this exuberance of faculties, united in one individual, had not been already in itself a character, and had not constituted a well-marked distinct personality, almost unique in kind, Moore would have been at variance with the most profound moralists, who agree that human nature never has the simplicity of a geometrical figure, and that, in reality, characters always are mixed, complicated, composed of opposite elements of incompatible inclinations and passions. For Moore appears to think that men are almost always swayed by one chief passion, round which, as round a pivot, life unrolls itself, just as we see in theatrical pieces. But even if this system were correct, intimate, as he was with Lord Byron, and so full of perspicacity, could he not have found, towering above the rich profusion of qualities in his friend, one dominant passion? Yes, he ought to have discovered it; but there was a *struggle* in Moore between the love of justice and his friendship for Lord Byron on one side, *and the desire, alas! of keeping fair with a host of prejudices* arrayed against Lord Byron on the other; and on the favor of these persons Moore felt that his own position, or rather his pleasure in society, depended. The master-passion that occupied so great a place in Lord Byron's mind was his *love of truth, with all the qualities flowing from it.*

It may, perhaps, be said that all beautiful souls love truth more or less. Yes; but seldom does this quality acquire such complete development as in Lord Byron. For with him it was a *real passion*, since it gave the law, so to say, to his heart, his mind, and all the actions of his life. This extraordinary attraction, coming in contact with the lies, hypocrisy, baseness, cowardice, and deceitfulness of others, often raised indignation to such a pitch that he could not help showing and expressing it. Thus his love of truth affected his social status in England, doing him immense harm; and, if it contributed to his greatness and his heroism, so it likewise added to his sorrows.

This noble quality showed itself in him, we may say, from his birth, under the form of *sincerity, frankness, a passion for justice, loyalty, delicacy, honor, and likewise in the shape of special hatred for all hypocrisy, and for that shade of it peculiar to England, called cant.*

Amid all the passions and events of life, whatsoever the consequences, Lord Byron always went straight at truth; as the hero marches up under fire, or the saint to martyrdom. A lie was not only a lie to him, it was also an injustice, a cowardice, the mark of a corrupt soul, an inconceivable thing, and not to be forgiven. A child, at Aberdeen, he was taken to the play to see one of Shakspeare's pieces, wherein an actor, showing the sun, says it is the moon. He was a timid child, but (incapable then of understanding Shakspeare's meaning) this outrage on truth excited him so far that he rose from his seat and exclaimed, "*I tell you, my dear sir, that it is the sun.*" With regard to lying, he remained his whole life the child of Aberdeen.

Neither his nurses nor preceptors ever surprised him in a lie. Education, which in England, more than elsewhere, modifies and shapes men according to the requirements of their social position, had no power to affect the fundamental part of his nature. While forming his mind, it did not change his heart. It destroyed some very dear illusions, and made his soul grow sick with disappointment, so that he never ceased regretting his happy childhood. In some respects it even had power to superadd a fictitious character to his real one, but his qualities of soul and his natural character still remained untouched.

The ardent affection he entertained for one of the masters at Harrow—Dr. Drury—made him feel dislike to this gentleman's successor. Having been asked to dinner by him, Lord Byron declined, because, he said, that by accepting, *he should belie his heart.* At the university, he, like his companions, ran after the young girls of Cambridge and its environs, but he never seduced or deceived any. Early in life he adopted the good habit of examining himself most rigidly; and so strict was his conscience, that, where his companions saw reason to excuse him, he, on the contrary, found cause for self-reproach.

It was this same imperious, innate want of his nature, which, combined with certain circumstances, made him ill for a time. The malady was one quite foreign to his temperament, springing from self-depreciation, and because he did not then find sufficient gratification in society. A sort of misanthropy stole over his soul, chaining him to the East for two years, as a land where both soul and heart were less tried.

On his return home, the impressionability belonging to his ardent, enthusiastic nature may have produced undue excitement, but no bad feeling could ever dim the lustre of the nobler passion that held sway over him.

For him truth was more than a virtue, it was an imperative duty. Indulgent as he ever showed himself toward all weaknesses in general, and especially toward the faults committed by his servants, he could not forgive *a lie.*

At Ravenna, a young woman attached to the service of his little Allegra, being unwilling to avow, for fear of dismissal, that Allegra had had a fall, though the child bore the mark of it, told an untruth instead. No intercession could prevail on Lord Byron to pardon her, and she was sent away.*

Though eager for glory—especially at an age when not having yet arrived at it, he ignored the bite of the serpent that often lurks within a garland of roses—he yet repelled all undue praise, and was much more indignant at receiving it, than when unmerited blame was heaped upon him. Once, having been compared to a man of high standing in French literature, he, anxious to prove that there could be no resemblance between him and this great man, replied:—"If the thing were true, it might flatter me; but it is impossible to accept fictions with pleasure."

When Dallas—who only knew him then by his family name—read his early productions, he was enchanted with poetry that often rose to the sublime, and was always chivalrous in feeling, "which denoted," he said, "a heart full of honorable sentiments, and formed for virtue." This is a precious verdict, coming as it does, from a man so bigoted in all respects as the elder Dallas. He adds afterward that the perusal of these verses, and the sentiments contained in them, made him discover great affinity of mind between the young author and another literary man, who was equally remarka-

* See "Life in Italy."

ble as a poet, an orator, and a historian—"*the great and good Lord Lyttelton of immortal fame.*" "And I doubt not," added Dallas, "that one day, like him, he will confer more honor on the peerage than it can ever reflect on him." Such a compliment from a man so rigid and respectable might certainly have tempted the most ordinary self-love, but Lord Byron, applying his magnifying-glass to his conscience, and comparing what he saw there with his ideal, did not conceive he merited such praise. Accordingly he answered with candor that enchanted Dallas himself:—

"Though our periodical censors have been uncommonly lenient, I confess a tribute from a man of acknowledged genius is still more flattering. But I am afraid I should forfeit all claim to candor, if I did not decline such praise as I do not deserve, and this is, I am sorry to say, the case in the present instance. My pretensions to virtue are, unluckily, so few, that, though I should be happy to deserve your praise, I can not accept your applause in that respect."

Thus, from fear of being wanting in truth, he exaggerated his youthful imperfections, nor could find any excuse for them. And in the same way throughout life his dread of making himself out better than he was, led him into the opposite defect of representing himself as far inferior to his real worth.

If from considering of the man, we turn to look at the author, we shall still always find the same passion for truth. By degrees, as he observed society around him, this passion increased, for he found the dominant vice was precisely that one most repugnant to his nature. If Lord Byron ever admitted, with La Rochefoucault, *that hypocrisy is a homage vice renders to virtue*, he did not the less consider this homage as degrading to him who offered it, insulting to those to whom it is addressed, and most corrupting in its effect upon the soul.

Thus, then, he from an early period considered hypocrisy and cant as monsters, in the moral world, to be combated energetically whenever an opportunity should present itself, and he resolved on doing so with all the intrepidity and independence of which his nature was capable. His natural gentleness disappeared in presence of the *whited sepulchres*, the *Pharisees* ot our day. His whole literary life was one struggle against this vice, "the crying sin of the times,"* as he called it.

His conscience was quite as strict with regard to intellectual things as it was in the domain of morals. We might even call it marvellously strict for our epoch, for the decay of truth forms a sadly striking characteristic of the present time. I know not what modern critic it is who says that a general enervation of intelligence and languor of soul now prevail in this respect; that the majesty of truth has been profaned, and the ancient regard in which she was held has been destroyed by religious sects, philosophical systems, the insolent attacks of the press, and by the revolution that has taken place in ideas as well as in deeds. Thence the general tendency to place truth and error on the same footing, in theory and in practice. Thence the equality of rights established between both, and which has become like the normal state of mind general in society.

Certainly, in our day, the love and practice of truth have grown obsolete; dramatic pieces and works of fiction, indeed all kinds of literature, especially biography, and even history, combine to outrage truth with impunity; no compunction is felt in transforming great characters into monsters, and monsters into heroes. People are no longer astonished that travellers' narratives should be like poems, good or bad, works of imagination full of anachronisms, exaggerations, impossibilities, making the sea take the place of mountains, and putting mountains where the sea should be. Truth is hidden as dangerous, not always to humanity, but to private interests to which it might bring smaller gains. Now if, at an epoch like this, we meet with geniuses, or even conscientious talents, sacrificing, both in their works and their actions, every interest or consideration to truth, ought we not to look upon them as real marvels? Undoubtedly we ought, and there can be no question that Lord Byron belonged to the small number of such marvels. Friends and enemies are agreed thereupon.

Galt, who was brought into contact with the poet by chance, at the time of his first journey into Greece, and who travelled with him for several days, when remarking the beauty of Lord Byron's poems on Greece, says, "they possess

* Preface to canto xi. of "Don Juan."

the great and rare quality of being *as true with regard to nature and facts as they are sublime for poetic expression.*"

He quotes those beautiful lines with which the third canto of the "Corsair" opens, wherein Lord Byron describes the lovely scenery that met his eye on ascending the Piræus;* and to the Cape Colonna, and to the so-called Tomb of Themistocles in the "Giaour;" and Galt fancies he can remember by what circumstance and aspect of nature they were inspired.

Lord Byron did not admit the possibility of describing a site that had not been seen, a sentiment that had not been experienced, or at least well known on certain and direct testimony. Never could people say of him, what M. Sainte-Beuve asserted of Chateaubriand, namely, *that he had not visited the places he described, that he lent to some what of right belonged only to others, and that he had not even seen Niagara.*

On the contrary, when Lord Byron was writing, the objects described were really present, so to say, as facts rather than in imagination.

Mr. Galt was so persuaded of this that he almost denied him the possession of imagination, and he says that the stamp of personal experience is so strongly marked in many of Lord Byron's productions, usually considered fancies or inventions, that he deems it impossible not to assign for their basis real facts or events wherein he had been either actor or spectator.

To refuse Lord Byron imagination would be absurd; but it is true that his imagination could only have discovered the elements and materials so wonderfully put together, through a scrupulous and profound observation of reality. And it was only afterward, that superadding sentiment and thought, he wrought out such splendid truths, which, if not precisely combined in the living reality, were so far superior that any absence in the original model appeared like a forgetfulness of nature.

Without, then, admitting Mr. Galt's ideas, in their extreme consequences, it is at least certain that Lord Byron's genius required so much to lean on truth in all things, that it may be said he owed far more to facts than to the power of imagination.

* "Slow sinks, more lovely ere his race be run,
* * * * *
Not as in northern climes." "*Corsair*," canto iii.

Apart from the faculty of combining, which he possessed in a splendid manner, if any one should take the trouble to observe, one by one, the characters he has painted, we should be still more confirmed in the above opinion. For instance, Conrad, that magnificent type of the corsair, that energetic compound of an Albanese warrior and a naval officer, far from being an imaginary character, was entirely drawn from nature and real history. All who have travelled in the Levant, and especially at that period, must have met with personages whose appearance distinctly recalled Conrad.

That peaceful men, leading a regular monotonous life in the midst of civilized Europe, or persons who have only travelled over their maps or their books, quietly seated in their library—that they should find characters like Conrad's eccentric, and the incidents of such a career improbable, may easily be conceived; but it is not the less true that both are in perfect keeping with each other and with truth.

I might say the same thing of "Childe Harold." But having spoken of this character sufficiently elsewhere, in order to repel the unjust identification of the Pilgrim with the author,—for "Childe Harold" appears to me the personification of a moral idea, of the accidental transitory state of a soul placed under certain circumstances, rather than type,—I will only add here, that this unjust identification was also caused by that craving which Lord Byron experienced of leaning, in all things, on reality, on facts acquired through his own experience. For although it is incorrect to imagine that he made use of his looking-glass for drawing the portraits of his heroes, since the glass could not even for a passing moment—such as suffices only for a daguerreotype—have converted his gentle, beautiful expression of face into the dark countenance of a Harold, a Giaour, a Conrad, or a Lara; still it is true that he lent them some of his own noble, fine lineaments, some faint shadow of his beauty, and that more than once he committed the fault of placing them in situations exactly similar to his own, even going so far as to install his heroes within the ancient abbey of Newstead,—a hospitality that cost him dear.

Characters that had produced a strong impression on him easily became models for the personages portrayed in his poems. It was the terrible Ali Pasha of Yanina who furnished the most striking features depicted in the heroes of his Eastern poems. The reports current about Ali Pasha's uncle served to lend their share of truth; and we may say, in general, that those acquainted with Lord Byron and his history possessed the clew to his imaginary personages; they could even recognize his Adelinas, Dudus, Gulbeyazs, Angelinas, Myrrhas, Adahs; and having first taken his stand on earth, it cost his fancy very little to soar and idealize what might else have been too commonplace.

As to the historical characters, we are certain of finding them in the most authentic histories; for it would be impossible to carry scrupulous research further than he did. Some observations on "Marino Faliero," his first historical drama, will suffice for an example.

The impression made on Lord Byron, when he arrived in Venice, by the character of this old man, and the terrible catastrophe that overtook him, first gave rise to his idea of the tragedy. But four years intervened between the project and its execution. During this time he consulted all the histories of Venice, every document and chronicle he could lay his hands on. He passed long hours in the hall of the great council, opposite the gloomy black veil surmounted by that terrible inscription—"*Hic est locus Marino Faliero decapitati pro criminibus suis;*" on the Giants' staircase, where the Doge had been crowned ere he was degraded and beheaded; he had interrogated the stones forming the monuments raised to the Doges; often was he seen in the church of St. John and St. Paul, seeking out the tomb of Faliero and his family: and still he was not satisfied, for the motives of the conspiracy did not yet present themselves so clearly to his mind as the fact of the conspiracy itself. Then he wrote to Murray, to search him out in England other *more authentic* documents concerning this tragical end.

"I want it," he said to him in February, 1817, "and can not find so good an account of that business here. . . . I have searched all their histories; but the policy of the old aristocracy made their writers silent on his motives, which were a private grievance against one of the patricians."

And not only did he seek for truth in books and monuments, but he likewise sought it in the character and manners of all classes inhabiting the lagoons. It was only toward the close of 1820, at Ravenna, that he felt ready to write his magnificent drama.

All the characters in this tragedy, except that admirable one of Angiolina, which he drew from imagination and traced with his heart, were supplied by history. In it Lord Byron has scrupulously respected places, epoch, and the time of duration for the action; points which he considered as elements of truth in art; in short, all essential circumstances were faithfully reproduced in his drama.

Even the faults which critics little versed in psychological science, and obstinately forgetful that this work was *not intended for acting*, pretend to find in it, were but the necessary results of historical accuracy. These critics wished to meet with the love, jealousy, and other passions common to their age and country; but Lord Byron would only give them what he found in history. Thence, no love and no jealousy; but a proud, violent character, coming in collision with a government proud and violent as itself; one of those men that are exceptional but real, in whom extremes of good and evil meet; one of those dramatic natures that fastened strongly on his imagination, producing a shock which kindled the flame of genius:—

"It is now four years that I have meditated this work, and before I had sufficiently examined the records, I was rather disposed to have made it turn on a jealousy in Faliero. But perceiving no foundation for this in historical truth, and aware that jealousy is an exhausted passion in the drama, I have given it a more historical form."*.

As to the motives for the conspiracy, the clearness of certainty only came to him a year after his drama had been published. But there was such an attraction between his mind and truth that his intuition had supplied the want of material certainty. And when a year afterward, at Ravenna, he received the document so long desired, he was happy in sending Murray a copy of this document translated from an ancient chronicle by Sir Francis Palgrave, the learned author of the "History of the Anglo-Saxons," to be able to write:—

* See Preface to Marino Faliero.

"Inclosed is the best account of the 'Doge Faliero,' which was only sent to me from an old MS. the other day. Get it translated, and append it as a note to the next edition. You will perhaps be pleased to see that my conceptions of his character were correct, though I regret not having met with this extract before. You will perceive that he himself said exactly what he is made to say about the Bishop of Treviso. You will also see that 'he spoke very little,' and these only words of rage and disdain, after his arrest, which is the case in the play, except when he breaks out at the close of Act V. But his speech to the conspirators is better in the MS. than in the play. I wish that I had met with it in time."

The historical inaccuracies of authors, their carelessness about truth, whether the result of malice or inattention, revolted Lord Byron, and especially if such untruths tended to asperse a great character. The lies of Dr. Moore about the "Doge Faliero" almost made him angry:—

"Where did Dr. Moore find that Marino Faliero begged his life? I have searched the chroniclers, and find nothing of the kind."

Lord Byron observes at this is not only historically, but also logically false:—

"His having shown a want of firmness," said Byron, "indeed, would be as contrary to his character as a soldier, to the age in which he lived, and at which he died, as it is to the truth of history. I know no justification, at any distance of time, for calumniating a historical character: surely truth belongs to the dead, and to the unfortunate; and they who have died upon a scaffold have generally had faults enough of their own, without attributing to them those which the very incurring of the perils which conducted them to their violent death render, of all others, the most improbable."

We know his consideration and sympathy for Campbell, though Campbell had not always behaved well toward him. He forgave him many things, but he could not pardon the indifference this author often showed for *historical truth!*

At Ravenna he wrote in his journal, on the 10th of January, 1821:—

"Read Campbell's 'Poets.' Marked errors of Tom (the

author) for correction. . . . . Corrected Tom Campbell's 'slips of the pen;' a good work, though."

In his appendix to the first canto of "Don Juan," he says, "Being in the humor of criticism, I shall proceed, after having ventured upon the slips of Bacon, to wind up on one or two as trifling in the edition of the 'British Poets,' by the justly celebrated Campbell. But I do this in good-will, and trust it will be so taken. If any thing could add to my opinion of the talents and true feeling of that gentleman it would be his classical, honest, and triumphant defense of Pope against the vulgar cant of the day, as it exists in Grub Street.

"The inadvertencies to which I allude are . . . ."

And after mentioning a few inadvertencies which are faults against justice and truth, he says:—

"A great poet quoting another should be correct: he should also be accurate when he accuses a Parnassian brother of that dangerous charge, 'borrowing:' a poet had better borrow any thing (excepting money) than the thoughts of another—they are always sure to be reclaimed; but it is very hard, having been the lender, to be denounced as the debtor, as is the case of Anstey *versus* Smollett. As 'there is honor among thieves,' let there be some among poets, and give each his due—none can afford to give it more than Mr. Campbell himself, who, with a high reputation for originality, and a fame which can not be shaken, is the only poet of the times (except Rogers) who can be reproached (and in him it is indeed a reproach) with having written too little."

Hereupon he writes to Murray, half joking, half serious:—

"Murray, my dear, make my respects to Thomas Campbell, and tell him from me, with faith and friendship, three things that he must right in his 'Poets.' First, he says Anstey's 'Bath Guide' characters are taken from Smollett. 'Tis impossible: the 'Guide' was published in 1766, and 'Humphry Clinker' in 1771—*dunque*, 'tis Smollett who has taken from Anstey. Secondly, he does not know to whom Cowper alludes when he says there was one 'who built a church to God, and then blasphemed His name:' it was 'Deo erexit Voltaire' to whom that mad Calvinist and coddled poet alludes. Thirdly, he misquotes and spoils a passage from Shakspeare,—'To gild refined gold, to paint the lily,' etc.; for lily he puts rose, and bedevils in more words than one the whole quotation.

"Now, Tom is a fine fellow; but he should be correct: for the first is an injustice (to Anstey), the second an *ignorance*, and the third a *blunder*. Tell him all this, and let him take it in good part: for I might have chastised him in a review and punished him; instead of which, I act like a Christian. BYRON."

With regard to a quotation, or any circumstance intended to prove a truth, his love of *exactness* amounted to a *scruple*. He would have thought himself wanting in honor if he had made a false or an incomplete quotation. In one of the notes to "Don Juan," speaking of Voltaire, he had quoted those famous words:—"*Zaïre, vous pleurez;*" but being accustomed at that time to make great use of the familiar pronoun *thou*, as in the case in Italy, his quotation ran: "*Zaïre, tu pleures.*" But he hastened to write to Murray, "*Voltaire wrote: Zaïre, vous pleurez;* don't forget."

In his tragedy of "Faliero," Lord Byron had said that the Doges, Faliero's predecessors, were buried in the church of St. John and St. Paul; but he afterward ascertained that it was only on the death of Andrea Dandolo, Faliero's predecessor, that the Council of Ten, by a sort of presentiment perhaps, decreed that the Doges should in future be buried with their families in their own church; previously they had all been interred in the church of St. Mark:—

". . . All that I said of his *ancestral Doges*, as buried at St. John's and Paul's, is a mistake, *they being interred in* St. Mark's. Make a note of this, by the *Editor*, to rectify the fact.

"In the notes to 'Marino Faliero,' it may be as well to say that '*Benintende*' was not really of the *Ten*, but merely *Grand Chancellor*, a separate office (although important); it was an arbitrary alteration of mine.

"As I make such pretentions to accuracy, I should not like to be twitted even with such trifles on that score. Of the play they may say what they please, but not so of my costume and *dram. pers.*,—they having been real existences."*

* Moore, Letter 391.

"As to Sardanapalus," he writes to Murray, "I thought of nothing but Asiatic history. The Venetian play, too, is rigidly historical. My object has been to dramatize, like the Greeks (a *modest* phrase), striking passages of history.

"All I ask is a preference for accuracy as relating to Italy and other places."

In books, monuments, and the fine arts, it was always *truth* that interested him. Except Sir Walter Scott's productions, he gave no place in his library to novels; other works of imagination, especially poetry, were excluded; two-thirds of his books were French works. His reading lay chiefly in history, biography, and politics.

Among the books Murray sent him were some travels: "Send me no more of them," he wrote, "I have travelled enough already; and, besides, *they lie.*"*

Books with effected sentiment of any kind, imaginary itineraries, made him very impatient. High-sounding phrases jarred on his ears; and I thoroughly believe that the *forty centuries' looking down from the Pyramids upon the grand French army* somewhat *spoilt* his hero for him.

What he especially sought for in monuments and among ruins was their authenticity. It was on this sole condition that he took interest in them.

Campbell, in his "Lives of English Poets," had averred that readers cared no more for the truth of the manners portrayed in Collins's "Eclogues" than for the authenticity of the history of Troy:—

"'Tis false," says Lord Byron in his memoranda, after having read Campbell; "we do care about 'the authenticity of the tale of Troy.' I have stood upon that plain daily, for more than a month, in 1810; and if any thing diminished my pleasure, it was that the blackguard Bryant had impugned its veracity. It is true that I read 'Homer Travestied' (the first twelve books), because Hobhouse and others bored me with their learned localities, and I love quizzing. But I still venerated the grand original as the truth of history (in the material facts) and of place: otherwise, it would have given me no delight. Who will persuade me, when I reclined upon a mighty tomb, that it did not contain a hero? Its very

* Letter 391.

magnitude proved this. Men do not labor over the ignoble and petty dead—and why should not the dead be Homer's dead? The secret of Tom Campbell's defense of inaccuracy in costume and description is, that his 'Gertrude,' etc., has no more locality in common with Pennsylvania than with Penmanmawr. It is notoriously full of grossly false scenery, as all Americans declare, though they praise parts of the poem. It is thus that self-love forever creeps out, like a snake, to sting any thing which happens, even accidentally, to stumble upon it."

In order then, that Lord Byron might take an interest in either a place, a monument, or a work of art, he must associate them in his mind with some fact which had really taken place. By what was he most impressed on reaching Venice?

"There is still in the Doge's Palace the black veil painted over Faliero's picture, and the staircase whereon he was first crowned Doge and subsequently decapitated. This was the thing that most struck my imagination in Venice—more than the Rialto, which I visited for the sake of Shylock: and more, too, than Schiller's 'Armenian,' a novel which took a great hold of me when a boy. It is also called the 'Ghost Seer,' and I never walked down St. Mark's by moonlight without thinking of it. And 'at nine o'clock he died.' But I hate things all fiction, and therefore the *Merchant* and *Othello* have no great attractions for me, but *Pierre* has. There should always be some foundation of fact for the most airy fabric, and pure invention is but the talent of a liar."

The little taste which he entertained for painting came from the impression that, of all the arts, it was the most artificial, and the least truthful. In April, 1817, he wrote to Murray as follows, on the subject:—

"Depend upon it, of all the arts it is the most artificial and unnatural, and that by which the folly of mankind is most imposed upon. I never yet saw the picture or the statue which came a league within my conception or expectation: but I have seen many mountains, and seas, and rivers, and views, and two or three women, who went as far beyond it."

But, then, what enthusiasm, whenever he did meet with truth in art! When visiting the Manfrini Gallery at Venice, which is so rich in *chefs-d'œuvre*, he admits the charm of painting, and exclaims:—

"Among them there is a portrait of Ariosto by Titian, surpassing all my anticipation of the power of painting or human expression; it is the poetry of portrait and the portrait of poetry. Here was also a portrait of a lady of the olden times, celebrated for her talents, whose name I forget, but whose features must always be remembered. I never saw greater beauty or sweetness, or wisdom: it is the kind of face to go mad about, because it can not detach itself from its frame."

Our readers are aware with what obstinate determination the public voice proclaimed Lord Byron a skeptic, and still does. Nor will we here examine whether that epithet is merited, because a soul has been sometimes visited by the malady always more or less afflicting great minds; we will not ask if disquietude—which constitutes the dignity of our nature; if the torture caused by doubts and universal uncertainty, by the impossibility of explaining what is, or of comprehending what will be, if all this deserve to be called skepticism. It is not necessary to enter into the subject here, because we have already examined in another chapter* with what foundation such a name was applied to Lord Byron.

Now, we will content ourselves with adding that it was his love of truth and his delicacy of conscience which caused, in a great measure, what has been called his skepticism. For these sentiments would not allow him to affirm things that many others perhaps affirm, without believing more in them. Moreover, he appears sometimes to have been *persuaded that doubt was the feeling least removed from truth.*

THIS QUALITY RISES TO A VIRTUE.

If Lord Byron's passion for truth had simply remained within the limits already described, it would have given earnest of a noble soul, more gifted than others, with instincts of a higher order; it would have lighted up his social character, given the charm of that frankness so delightful in his manners, conversation, style; so attractive in the expression of his fine countenance; but still it would only have been a

* See chapter on "Religion."

natural quality, without any more right to the name of virtue than all the other beautiful instincts he had received from Heaven; but, when ceasing to be purely natural, it became a distinguishing characteristic of the author, then it went far beyond these limits. In his writings it raised him above all calculations of interest, made him despise all considerations of ambition or of ease, exposed him to terrible party warfare, to slander, and revenge; spurred him on to attack the great and powerful whenever they turned aside from the path of virtue, justice, or simplicity, and made him forget his nationality, that he might better remember his humanity.

Meanwhile he never once yielded to any interest; and thus this innate faculty, which might have been a virtue easily practiced, *became one of heroic merit.*

We may safely assert that all his griefs through life owed their origin to this rare quality; for perhaps he did not know sufficiently how to reconcile it with a *certain amount* of that social virtue called prudence; whose office it is to keep silence when advisable, and not to utter dangerous truths.

Certainly Lord Byron never showed that wisdom for himself which he knew well how to practice for others; witness his conduct in Greece, where, according to the account given by all who lived with him there at that time, he displayed the utmost prudence, moderation, and ability.*

* M. Tricoupi, in his interesting "History of the Greek Revolution," ends his fine article upon Lord Byron, and upon his death, in the following words :—

"This man's great name, his noble struggle in the midst of misfortunes, the troubles which he had borne for the sake of Greece, the bright hopes which he was on the point of seeing realized, proved sufficiently what the Greeks lost in losing him, and the misfortune which his death was to them. Each one considered and mourned his loss as a private and as a public calamity. In ordering the funeral, the governor of the town exclaimed, 'This time the beautiful Easter rejoicings have turned for us into hours of bitterness,' and he was right. All forgot Easter in presence of the blow which was dealt them by the loss of such a man.

"Byron, as a poet, was enthusiastic, but his enthusiasm, like his poetry, was deep; his policy in Greece was likewise intelligent and profound. No dreams like those formed by most of the lovers of the Greeks. No Utopian plans, democratic or anti-democratic. Even the press appeared to him as yet uncalled-for. The independence of Greece, that was the essential point at issue, and to obtain this end he counselled the Greeks to be united among themselves, and to respect foreign courts. His principal care was the organization of the army, and the procuring of the funds necessary to maintain it. He loved glory, but only that which is solid. He refused to take the title of Commander-general of Continental Greece, which the Government and the nation offered him in common ac-

That social virtue of prudence, which, to our mind, is somewhat akin to a defect, was wholly wanting in him in private life; yet it is a necessary virtue in his country, and especially was so in his day. England then was, in many respects, far from resembling the England of our time. Liberty of opinion was certainly guaranteed by law; but then there were the drawing-room tribunals; very unforgiving with regard to certain truths, and little disposed to admire that inclination which prompts superior minds not to conceal their real thoughts. The earth or the universe might have been conceded as a field open to criticism, he might express his true opinions on all points, provided only some few books, and one island, called England, were excepted. Under show of respect, absolute silence was required on these heads. They constituted the ark of alliance; to speak ill of them was not permissible, and even to praise was almost dangerous.

In the enchanted palace of "Blue beard" one single chamber was reserved; and woe to him who penetrated therein.

Since then, a period of peace and prosperity, together with the effects of time and travel, have greatly improved the noble character of the English nation. In our day, pens, tongues, and consciences are less strictly bound, and many truths may now be avowed without fear of bringing the flush of anger or of indignant modesty to the cheek.

The present, and, still less, the past, are no more considered as sacred ground. Even the Norman conquest is no longer a seditious subject. The dictionary of society has gained many words; and Englishmen no longer fear to see their children lose that patriotism which for them is almost a religion, because they read books not deifying their own country and full of libels on the rest of the globe.

Historians, novel-writers, poets—even theologians—have vied with each other in tearing away the bandages concealing many old wounds, in order to cure them by contact with the vivifying breezes of heaven; and twenty years after Lord Byron, Macaulay has been able, without losing his popularity, to show less filial piety than he, and to blame the past in

cord. He hated politics as a rule, and avoided parliamentary discussions even in his own country. . . ."

language so beautiful as to obtain forgiveness for the sacrifice even of truth.

But, in Lord Byron's time, England was carrying on her great struggle against the lion of the age. Separated from the Continent by war still more than by the sea, the cannon's roar booming across the waters added venom to her wounds, and pride made her prefer to conceal rather than to heal them.

The echo of this detested cannon was still sounding when Lord Byron returned to England, from his travels in the East, with the same thirst for truth as heretofore, but having gained much from observation, comparison, and reflection. He believed he had the right to make use of faculties with equal independence, whether as regarded his own nation or the rest of humanity. England then seemed to wish to arrogate to herself the monopoly, of morality, wisdom, and greatness, together with the right of despising the rest of the world. Lord Byron considered this pretension as excessive, and he expressed his generous incredulity in lines proudly independent. He refused to see heroism where he did not believe it to exist, and would not accord glory to victories that seemed to him the result of chance. He refused to see virtue and religion in what he considered calculation or hypocrisy. He demanded *justice* for Catholic Ireland, and impartiality for enemies; he even went so far as to show sympathy for Napoleon and deplore his fall. He could not allow party spirit to depreciate the genius of Napoleon. Madame de Staël, who had made Lord Byron's acquaintance in London when he was very young, and had conceived a great liking for him, often wrote to him, and always tried to prove that he was wrong in thinking so highly of Napoleon. But on account of this Lord Byron broke off the correspondence suddenly, which vexed Madame de Staël not a little. The invasion of France, the humiliation of a great nation, was painful to him; and this generous sentiment even caused him to commit a real *fault, which he expressed regret for more than once*, says Madame G——, when conversing with her at Pisa and Genoa. The fault was a certain feeling of hostility indulged toward the illustrious Duke of Wellington, whom he yet confessed to be the glory of his country.

"P.S.—If you hear any news of battle or retreat on the part of the Allies (as they call them), pray send it. He has my best wishes to manure the fields of France with an invading army. I hate invaders of all countries, and have no patience with the cowardly cry of exultation over him at whose name you all turned whiter than the snow to which you are indebted for your triumph."

He was too generous an enemy to echo the Archbishop of Canterbury's prayer.*

As a Whig, he was indignant at the Prince of Wales's conduct in deserting his political banner and passing over to the Tories when he became regent; so he wrote some hard verses against him,—"Lines to a Lady weeping," addressed to the Princess Charlotte.

This poem was the olive-branch that Robert was about to snatch from the tomb. All evil passions were now let loose against Lord Byron.

The Tory party—so influential then, and which saw with displeasure the future promise of a great orator held out in the person of a young Whig peer—gladly seized a pretext for displaying its hostility. The higher clergy naturally clung to the interests of the aristocracy, as identical with their own: moreover, they were vexed with the young lord for attacking intolerancy, hypocrisy, and similar anti-Christian qualities, and consequently espoused with ardor Tory grievances. Pretending even to discover danger to religion in some philosophical verses,† they denounced the young poet as an *atheist* and a *rebel.* At the same time his admiration for foreign beauties wounded feminine self-love at home.

In thus placing the interests of truth above every other consideration, not only from the necessity he experienced of expressing it, but also with the design of serving justice, Lord Byron by no means ignored the formidable amount of burning coals he was piling upon his head. He knew well that the secret war going on against him delighted all his rivals, who, not having dared to show their spite at the time of his triumphs, had bided patiently the day of vengeance.

* This strange prayer ran thus:—"O Lord Almighty, give us strength to destroy the last man of that perfidious nation (the French), which has sworn to devour alive thy faithful servants (the English)."

† Stanzas of second canto of "Childe Harold."

He was aware of it all, but did not therefore draw back; and looking fearlessly at the pile heaped with all these combustible materials intended for his martyrdom, he did not any the more cease from his work. He resisted, and accepted martyrdom like a *hero.*

"You can have no conception of the uproar the eight lines on the little Royalty's weeping in 1812 (now republished) have occasioned. . . . . The 'Morning Post,' 'Sun' 'Herald,' 'Courier,' have all been in hysterics. . . . I am an atheist, a rebel, and at last the devil (*boiteux*, I presume). My demonism seems to be a female's conjecture. . . . . The abuse against me in all directions is vehement, unceasing, loud."*

The editor, alarmed, proposed to have them disavowed.

"Take any course you please to vindicate yourself," Lord Byron answered him; "but leave me to fight my own way, and, as I before said, do not *compromise* me by any thing which may look like *shrinking* on my part; as for your own, make the best of it. . . . . I have already done all in my power by the suppression" (of the satire). "If that is not enough, they must act as they please; but I will not 'teach my tongue a most inherent baseness,' come what may. . . . . I shall bear what I can, and what I can not I shall resist. The worst they could do would be to exclude me from society. I have never courted it, nor, I may add, in the general sense of the word, enjoyed it; and there is a world elsewhere!

"Any thing remarkably injurious I have the same means of repaying as other men, with such interest as circumstances may annex to it."

After this first great explosion, of which the verses addressed to the Princess Charlotte had formed the occasion and the pretext, the commotion appeared to subside. But the fire in the mine had not gone out. It still circulated obscurely, gathering strength in the quiet darkness. Another occasion was alone wanting for a second explosion, and a hand to strike the spark. The circumstance of his unhappy marriage, which had taken place in the interval, presented this occasion; and the hand to strike the spark was the one which had received the nuptial ring a year before. The ex-

* Moore, Letter 162.

plosion was brutal, abominable, insensate—unworthy of the society that tolerated it.

Then came another interval; the good who had been drawn into this stormy current were seized with regret and remorse. "*Why did we thus rise against our spoilt and favorite child?*" The wicked knew well wherefore they had done it, but the good did not. Macaulay told it them one day, twenty years afterward, better than any one else has, in one of those passages where the beauty of his style, far from injuring truth, lends it a double charm, enhancing it just as nature's beauty is set off by a profusion of light.

This good feeling stealing over the public conscience alarmed Lord Byron's deadly enemies. They feared lest sentimental remorse should compromise their victory; and they manœuvred so well, that from that hour persecution took up permanent abode in England, under pretext of offense to religion or morals. It followed him on his heroic journey into Greece, and ceased not with his death. Even after that, the vengeance and rage of his enemies—the indiscretion and timidity of friends—the material or moral speculations of all, together with the assurance of impunity—continued to feed the fire which an end so glorious as his ought to have quenched.*

* The system of depreciating Byron's acts never once ceased. It followed him to Greece and even to the tomb. Count Gamba, his friend and companion, in speaking of the excellent health enjoyed by all during the passage from Genoa to Greece, says:—

"We were in excellent health and spirits during our whole voyage from Italy to Greece, and for this we were partly indebted to our medical man, and partly to that temperance which was observed by every one on board, except at the beginning of the voyage by the captain of our vessel, who, however, ended by adopting our mode of life. I mention this to contradict an idle story told in a magazine ('The London') 'that Lord Byron on this voyage passed the principal part of the day drinking with the captain of the ship.' Lord Byron, as we all did, passed his time chiefly reading. He dined alone on deck; and sometimes in the evening he sat down with us to a glass or two, not more, of light Asti wine. He amused himself in jesting occasionally with the captain, whom he ended, however, by inspiring with a love of reading, such as he thought he had never felt before."

But his enemies were not discouraged. When they saw that Byron landed in one of the Ionian Islands, which was a far wiser and more prudent course to adopt, and one which might prove infinitely more beneficial to Greece than going straight to the Morea, they spread the report that instead of going to Greece, he spent his life in debauchery and in the continuation of his poem of "Don Juan," at rest in a lovely villa situated on one of the islands. Moore informed him rather abruptly of this report, which distressed him greatly.

But if the war against him did not cease, his perseverance and courage in saying what he thought did not cease either. Who more than he despised popularity and literary success, if they were to be purchased at the cost of truth?

"Were I alone against the world," said he, "I would not exchange my freedom of thought for a throne." And again: "He who wishes not to be a despot, or a slave, may speak freely."

That such independence of mind, aided by such high genius, should have alarmed certain coteries—not to speak of certain political and religious sets, who were all powerful—may easily be conceived. We can not feel surprise at the scandals they got up in defense of their privileges, when attacked by a new power who made every species of baseness and hypocrisy tremble; nor can we wonder that, unknowing where it would stop, they should have sought to cast discredit on the oracle by slandering the man. That the bark bearing him to exile should have been pushed on by a wind of angry passions in coalition—by a breeze not winged by conscience—may also be conceived; but to *conceive* is not to absolve, and in using the above expression we only mean to allow due share to human nature in general—to the character, manners, and perhaps to the special requirements of England. And if we ought not to condone party spirit in politics, defending privileges to the death; nor the anti-Christian ferocity displayed by that portion of the clergy who, without reason or sincerity, attacked him from the pulpit; nor yet the malice and revenge displayed in the vile slanders that pursued him to his last hour; we can, on the other hand, comprehend, and even, up to a certain point, excuse this prosperous and noble country of England for not classing her great son among popular poets—for hiding her admiration cautiously: since it must be acknowledged that Lord Byron often acted and wrote rather *as belonging to humanity, than merely as belonging to England.*

But if he were treated with the same injustice by foreigners, could the same excuse be made for them? Would a man be excusable if laziness and carelessness made him accept, without examination, some type set up for Lord Byron by a country wounded in her self-love, as England had been, or the reserves made by hostile biographers, under the weighty influence of a society organized as English society then was? The vile system which consists in seeking to give a good opinion of one's own morality by being severe on the morality of others, is only too well known. Would it be excusable to apply it ruthlessly to Lord Byron?—to pretend to repeat that in attacking prejudice he wounded morals?—that he injured virtue by warring against hypocrisy?—that by using a right inherent to the human mind in some hypothetical lines of a poem, written at twenty-one years of age, and which is beyond the comprehension of the multitude, since the greater number of mankind neither read elevated poetry nor works of high taste; is it not absurd to pretend that he wished to upset them in their religious belief, and deprive them of truths which are at once their consolation, support, and refuge in time of sorrow and suffering?

Nevertheless, *Frenchmen* have spoken thus; and in this way, through these united causes, Lord Byron has remained *unappreciated* as a man and unfairly judged as a poet.

One calls him *the poet of evil;* another *the bard of sorrow.* But no! Lord Byron was not exclusively either one or the other. He was *the poet of the soul,* just as Shakspeare was before him.

Lord Byron, in writing, never had in view virtue rather than vice. To take his stand as a teacher of humanity, at his age, would have seemed ridiculous to him. After having chosen subjects in harmony with his genius, and a point of view favorable to his poetic temperament, which especially required to throw off the yoke of artificial passions and of weak, frivolous sentiments, what he really endeavored was to be powerfully and energetically true. He thought that truth *ought* always to have precedence over every thing else—that it was the source of the *beautiful* in art, as well as of all *good* in souls. To him lies were *evil* and *vice;* truth was *good* and *virtue.* As a poet, then, he was the bard of the soul and of truth; and as a man, all those who knew him, and all who read his works, must proclaim him the poet who has come nearest to the ideal of truth and sincerity.

And now, after having studied this great soul under every aspect, if there were in happy England men who should esteem themselves higher in the scale of virtue than Lord Byron, because having never been troubled in their belief, either through circumstances or the nature of their own mind, they *never admitted or expressed any doubt;* because they are the happy husbands of those charming, indulgent, admirable women to be found in England, who *love and forgive so much;* because, being rich, they have not refused *some trifle* out of their superfluity to the poor; because, proud and happy in privileges bestowed by their constitution, they have never *blamed those in power:* if these prosperous ones deemed themselves superior to their great fellow-citizen, would it be illiberal in them to express now a different opinion? Might we not without rashness affirm, that they should rather hold themselves honored in the virtue and glory of their illustrious countryman, humbly acknowledging that their own greater happiness is not the work of their own hands?

REFLECTIONS UPON MR. DISRAELI'S NOVEL

"VENETIA:"

A SEMI-BIOGRAPHY OF LORD BYRON.

Is Mr. Disraeli to be classed among the biographers of Lord Byron because in his preface to "Venetia" he declares that his object is to portray Lord Byron? We do not think so. Truth and error, romance and history, are too much intermixed, and the author himself confesses this fact in calling his work a novel. But while denying to "Venetia" the right of being styled a biography, we must admit that it is both a deep, true, and at times admirable study of the fine and so ill-judged character of Lord Byron. The extraordinary qualities with which he was gifted, both in heart and in mind, his genius, his amiability, his irresistible attractions, his almost supernatural beauty, are all set forth with consummate ability, and the greatest penetration. He has made all his other characters, which are for the most part imaginary, subservient to this end; and he has created some (such as Lady Annabel) which moralists will not easily admit to be possible, it being granted that all the characters in the book are mentally sane. It is questionable whether the virtues and qualities which adorn Lady Annabel are compatible with the defects of her nature. Mr. Disraeli has acted in the same way as regards the circumstances of Byron's life; he has heaped them together without any regard to what may or may not be true in their supposed occurrence, some of them being founded on reality and others not so.

He has given Byron two individualities. Lord Cadurcis represents Byron from his infancy to the time of his marriage, and Mr. Herbert equally represents Lord Byron from that fatal epoch till his death. The selection of two persons to represent one same character and to allow of Byron's simple yet complex nature being better understood was a very happy philosophical notion.

He portrays Lord Byron as he was, or as he would have been in the given circumstances; and he pictures the others as they should or might have been, not as they were. In reading "Venetia" it is impossible not to like Lord Cadurcis, and to admire him, just as all those who knew Lord Byron loved and esteemed him, or not to respect Mr. Herbert, whom he styles "the best and greatest of men," as he would have been revered had Byron reached a greater age. He depicts Byron at every epoch of his life, and as circumstances develop his latent predispositions.

He first shows him to us as the innocent child, whose heart is full of tenderness, meekness, sensibility, and docility, such as his tutor, Dr. Drury, said he was: "rather easier to be led with a silken string than with a cable;" who is gifted with a noble and proud nature, which is easily moved; who possesses a great sense of justice and an undaunted courage; who scorns excuse and cares not to lessen his fault. He then shows him as the thoughtful boy, both when alone and with others; and as the gayest and wildest of creatures when in the company of the beloved companion of his childish sports; a boy full of kindness, and of the desire to please; whose absence is ever a subject of regret, so great is the love he inspires, both in his master and in his servants, and indeed in all who come near him. At his early age can already be traced the germs of those qualities which foretell that brilliant mind which is to win some day the heart of a nation, and dazzle the fancy of a world of admirers. The sight of the fair hair and of the angelic beauty of the little Venetia is enough to dry his tears; and herein we not only perceive already the extreme impressionable disposition of his nature, but also the power and influence which beauty is destined to exercise over him. The love of solitude and meditation is already traceable in the child. He loves to wander at night among the dark and solitary cloisters of his Abbey; he loves to listen to the whistling of the wind re-echoed by the cloisters; he delights in the murmurs of the waters of his lake when the winter storms disturb their serenity, and uproot the strongest oaks of his park. Proud of his race, his whole nature sympathizes with the glorious deeds of his ancestors, and one feels that he would fain rather die than show himself unworthy of them.

One sees the germs of poetry sown in his mind—but one feels that the heart alone can make them fructify, and give them an outward form. Nothing is more touching than the tenderness which he feels and inspires wherever he goes.

Mr. Disraeli then shows him in his youth, just at the time when he is to leave college for the university, and presents him to the reader as a remarkably well-educated young man, in whom the best principles have been inculcated, and whose conduct and conversation bear evidence of a pure, generous, and energetic soul "that has acquired at a very early age much of the mature and fixed character of manhood without losing any thing of that boyish sincerity and simplicity that are too often the penalty of experience.

"He was indeed sincerely religious, and as he knelt in the old chapel that had been the hallowed scene of his boyish devotions, he offered his ardent thanksgiving to his Creator who had mercifully kept his soul pure and true, and allowed him, after so long an estrangement from the sweet spot of his childhood, once more to mingle his supplications with his kind and virtuous friends."

"He is what I always hoped he would be," says Lady Annabel. "Remember what a change his life had to endure; few, after such an interval, would have returned with feelings so kind and so pure. I always fancied that I observed in him the seeds of great virtues and great talents, but I was not so sanguine that they would have flourished as they appear to have done."

Young as he is, he is already accustomed to reflect; and the result of his dreams is a desire to live away from the world with those he loves. The world as seen by others has no attraction for him. ·What the world covets appears to him paltry and faint. He sympathizes with great deeds, but not with a boisterous existence. He cares not for that which is ordinary. He loves what is rare and out of the common way. He dwells upon the deeds of his ancestors in Palestine and in France, who have left a memorable name in the annals of their country. Cadurcis experiences inwardly a desire, and even the power to imitate their example. He feels that to become the world's wonder no sacrifice is great enough; but in this age of mechanism, what career is left to a chivalrous spirit like his? He then longs for the happiness of private life in the company of so perfect a creature as Venetia; but he is still so young, and Venetia, who loves him like a brother and a friend, can not as yet understand the nature of another kind of love. He then leaves for the university, with grief implanted at the bottom of his heart. Disraeli then shows how, after three years, during which time his genius had been smouldering as it were, it at last appeared in a splendor quite unrivalled and unexampled, like a star equally strange and brilliant, which scarcely has it become visible in the horizon, than it already reaches its zenith. Not only is he distinguished by his writings, but by a thousand other ways, which fill the heart and dazzle the eyes. Where every thing is remarkable he is most noticed; and the most conspicuous where all is brilliant. He is envied by men, praised and sought after by women, admired by all. His life has become a perpetual triumph, a splendid act, which is enthusiastically applauded, and in which he ever plays the best and most heroic part. In the midst of this infatuation of a whole nation, among those handsome and noble women who forget themselves too much since they forget themselves entirely for the honor of a look from him, why is he not happy? What is he craving for? What is his occupation? Why, when envied by all, is he yet to be pitied? It is that his life is still, and will ever be, the life of the heart which finds no satisfaction to its desire in the midst of the world wherein it is doomed to live.

On one occasion he finds himself at the house of the most fashionable woman in London, of the great and beautiful person whose love for him is greater than he would wish. Many people are assembled there; dinner is about to be announced. No one but himself attracts attention or calls for enthusiastic eulogies; yet he is sad, absent, wearied. By his proud, handsome looks, his reserve, and his melancholy attitude, he might be taken for an unearthly being, condemned, as a punishment, to visit our terrestrial orb. All of a sudden his melancholy gives way to the liveliest animation; his cheeks glow, and happiness beams in his beautiful eyes. What has happened? Among the guests arriving he has heard the servant call out the name of his old tutor at Cherbury, the friend of all the friends of his youth. Raised to the dignity of a bishop, the late tutor has arrived in London to take his seat in the House of Lords. Again to see this friend of his youth, who is likely to speak to him of Cherbury, which he loved so dearly, and of Venetia, is a pleasure which his triumphs have never afforded him; and from that moment all is changed in his eyes, every thing is smiling, every thing is bright.

He learns that Lady Annabel and Venetia have left their retreat of Cherbury and have arrived in London. Cadurcis has but one thought, one aspiration, that of seeing them again. He does see Venetia again, and he feels that the world's praises are no longer any thing to him, except to be placed at her feet, and that he would give up all the idolatry of which he is the object for one year of happiness spent at Cherbury. When Venetia sees her ideal realized, and that Lord Cadurcis unites in him all the qualities of her dear Plantagenet with those brilliant and imposing talents which command love and admiration; when she beholds in him the genius of her father linked with the heart of her earliest friend, to whom she is still so deeply attached; when she sees her dear Plantagenet "courted, considered, crowned, incensed—in fact, a great man" living in an atmosphere of glory and in the midst of the applause of his contemporaries, Venetia exchanges her fraternal love, which was so touching, for the most ardent passion which one perfect creature can inspire in one as perfect as itself.

But the obstacle to their happiness now arises, and Lady Annabel it is who becomes metamorphosed into a woman whose judgment is false, whose prejudices are great, whose principles are inexorable; who knows nothing of the world, nothing of her own heart nor of the human heart; who judges all things by certain arbitrary rules, and acts sternly in accordance with her inexplicable judgment. All the love which she would have had for Plantagenet at Cherbury is turned into hatred on learning that he has become a great poet, the admiration of his country, the observed of all observers; that all the world is anxious to see him, that the finest ladies sigh for one of his looks, that he is not insensible to their admiration, that he is a Whig, and not only a Whig, but very nearly a rebel. She reads his poems, and her astonishment is only surpassed by the horror with which they inspire her. She sees Herbert in Cadurcis, and unable as she was to understand the former, so is she unequal to the task of comprehending Cadurcis. An imaginative being makes her tremble; such a creature can only be a monster. The praises bestowed upon Cadurcis do not shake her prejudices. His cousin, a brave sailor—a Tory, whose nature is as noble as it is frank and loyal—in vain tells her that Cadurcis is one of the most generous, most amiable, and most praiseworthy of men. In vain does he assure her that notwithstanding the difference of their political opinions, he can scarcely give her an idea of the delicacy and unbounded goodness which he has shown—that his heart is perfect, that his intellect is the finest that ever existed, and that if his conduct has at times been a little irregular, allowances must be made for the temptations which assailed him at the age of twenty-one, the sole master of his acts, and with all London at his feet. "It is too much for any one's head; but say or think what the world may, I know there is not a finer creature in existence. Venetia, who feels the truth of all this, inwardly exclaims, 'Dear, dear Cadurcis, can one be surprised at your being beloved when you are so generous, so amiable, so noble, so affectionate !' But the poor child in vain recalls to her mother the conduct of Plantagenet, who displays constancy in his true affections. 'No,' exclaims Lady Annabel, 'minds like his have no heart, a different impulse directs their existence—I mean imagination.' "

Lady Annabel tortures her daughter, to extort from her the promise that she will never marry Lord Cadurcis. Her devotion for that daughter, which seemed to be the essence of her life, is no longer in this hard-hearted woman but a form of her egotism; and Venetia, vexed in all her natural sentiments, instead of being the idol of her affections, becomes in reality the martyr of her pride.

After dwelling upon the agony of mind experienced by these two beautiful and loving souls, both victims of Lady Annabel's cruelty, Disraeli shows us Cadurcis a prey to despair; enduring the consequences of the fashionable life which he is compelled to lead, that is, of the dissipated existence which he wades through against his will; the victim, besides, of the jealous and fanatical love of the great lady whose yoke he had not been able as yet to shake off. A duel between him and the lady's husband is the result, and nothing is more admirable than the picture of Lord Byron (or Lord Cadurcis) in all the scenes which precede and follow this duel; his calmness, his courage, the mixture of humor and wit with which he ever was wont to meet the greatest perils, and which was one of the characteristics of his nature, and, above all, that great and noble generosity of which he gave so many proofs in every circumstance and at every period of his life. Then followed the consequences of the duel, and the capital derived from it by the accumulated stupidity and revenge of those inferior persons jealous of his superiority and of his popular fame.

Nothing is so beautiful, however, as the scene which takes place first at the club and then at the House of Lords, where Mr. Disraeli shows this noble and calumniated creature the object of the base and hypocritical jealousy of most of his colleagues, who, notwithstanding their hatred for him, were wont to call themselves his friends; when, exhausted and almost the victim of a ferocious hatred of an excited populace, he stands calm in the midst of these truly English elements in the attitute of an archangel or of a demi-god, opposing them and maintaining his ground until with the aid of a few brave and faithful friends, of the constable's truncheon, and the arrival of the mounted guard, he succeeds in getting rid of them altogether. All this, although not quite true, either as a historical fact or in its details, is, however, so admirably told, that it may be taken as a document well worthy of consideration by the biographer, and of which extracts can not be given without spoiling the whole.

In the midst of the turmoil occasioned by this duel, in which his adversary had been seriously wounded, Cadurcis suddenly finds himself abandoned by those who called themselves his friends, calumniated by the press, who spare no falsehoods to disparage his character, but whose contradictions have no effect in his great successes. Cadurcis, gifted as he is with an extreme sensibility, and accustomed to live in an atmosphere of praise, finds himself suddenly nailed to the pillory of public indignation, sees his writings, his habits, his character, and his person, equally censured, ridiculed, and blemished; in fact, he finds himself the victim of reaction, and yet all this does not affect his mind; his true agony is caused not by the regret at losing his prestige and his popularity, nor by the conduct of those who style themselves his friends, and who now joined his enemies in spreading and believing in the false reports respecting him. His greatness of soul and the purity of his conscience alike help him to endure these misfortunes; but what really does give him pain, is the thought that all these absurd rumors will reach the ears of Venetia. He has lost all hope of obtaining her hand, but he feels the want of her esteem. He wishes her to judge him as he deserves to be judged; and the thought that she likewise may put faith in the infamous and stupid reports which are spread about him, throws him into despair. When his cousin announces to him that he has succeeded in making the truth known to Venetia, how consoled he feels, and how grateful is he to his cousin! To his credit, the cousin did actually, in presence of Lady Annabel, who remained incredulous, endeavor to re-establish facts in their true light; and despite her sullen mood, did he courageously undertake the defense of Cadurcis, accuse the Mounteagles and the world in general, and conclude by declaring that "Cadurcis was the best creature that ever existed, the most unfortunate, the most ill-treated; and that if one should be liable to be pursued for such an affair, over which Cadurcis could have no control, there was not a man in London who could be sheltered from it for ten minutes." When Lord Cadurcis receives Venetia's message, which is to tell him that he remains for her what he has ever been, the announcement acts upon him as a charm, brings calm back to his mind, and renders him indifferent for the future to the opinion of the world. The experience of that day has entirely cured him of his former deference for the opinion of society. The world has outraged him. He no longer owes any thing to the world. His reception in the House of Lords, and the riot outside the house, have severed his ties with all classes, from the highest to the lowest; his grateful heart will ever preserve the remembrance of those who have shown him true affection by displaying moral courage in his defense. But they are few,—some relations, or nearly such by their association with them, and for these his gratitude and his respect are unlimited; but as for the others, he will pay them back by showing them his contempt, by publishing the truth respecting them, their country, their habits, their laws, their customs, their opinions, in order that they may be known and judged by the whole world,—a tribunal far more enlightened than the limited one of his native isle. Henceforth he resolves never again to meet the advances of those civilized "ruffians" who affect to be sociable. He prepares to leave England, with the intention never again to return to it. He shuts himself up in his room for a week, and allowing free scope to his passionate and wounded soul, he writes his adieu to England, and in the task his mind finds relief. In this poem, wherein a few well-merited sarcasms find a place, and wherein there are many allusions to Venetia, there are passages so delicate, so tender, so irresistibly pathetic, that it exercised an extraordinary influence upon public opinion. Again the tide of public sympathy runs high in his favor; it is found that Cadurcis is the most calumniated of mortals, that he is more interesting than ever; and Lady Mounteagle is spoken of as she deserves. Cadurcis is, however, too proud to accept new sympathies likely to make him suffer all that he has already suffered. He quits his native land, surrounded by a halo of glory, but with contempt on his part for that popular favor of which he has too cruelly experienced the worth. He sails for Greece, and here Disraeli shows how he led a life of study, and finally depicts him, under the name of Herbert, as a philosopher and a virtuous man, who, after behaving as a hero, and after abandoning some of the illusions of youth, and principally that of making men wiser and better, aspires only at leading a mild, regular, virtuous, and philosophical existence.

Notwithstanding the great charm of Mr. Disraeli's book, to give extracts from which would only be to spoil it, it must, however, be allowed that the real and the imaginary are too much intermingled. All the fictions of time and place, which only leave the sentiments of the real man untouched, all the double and treble characters which at times quit, and at others resume, their individuality almost as in a dream, tend to create a confusion which is prejudicial to truth. Thus, Lady Annabel has charms and qualities wholly incompatible with her supposed stern severity. Miss Venetia, a perfect emanation of love and beauty, is at times transformed into an imaginary Miss Chaworth, and at others into a beloved sister, and at others again into an adorable Ada——; Lady Mounteagle is sometimes too like, and often too unlike, the real Lady C. L——; the whole is confused, fatiguing to the mind, and too fictitious not to be regretted, since the express intention of the author is to paint a historical character, acting in the midst of circumstances generally founded on reality.

In following out the intention of the author, and his want of respect for truth, it is impossible not to ask ourselves why, while respecting circumstances of such slight import as the preservation of the Christian names of the mother and wife, he has not done the same for more important accidents in the hero's life? Why, for instance, have described his childhood as a painful time? Was not Lord Byron surrounded with the tenderest cares while in Scotland? Had he been unhappy there, would he have transmitted to us in such happy lines his remembrance of the time which he spent in the North? Is it not in Scotland that his heart was nursed with every affection, that his mind drank in the essence of poetry? Why make his mother die when he was only twelve years of age, since she died only on his return from Spain and from Greece, that is, when he was twenty-two? Why make her die of grief at being abandoned by him, in consequence of an imaginary scene which obliges her to take refuge in the midst of a band of Bohemian travellers, when it is known that she died rather by the excess of joy which she experienced at the thought of seeing him again after an absence of nearly two years? Why change the ages, and give Miss Chaworth fifteen when she was eighteen, or himself eighteen when he was fifteen? Why give him such an affectionate guardian instead of Lord Carlisle? It may be argued that in these changes in the actual life of Lord Byron, we must only perceive the genius of the writer, who by making the hero's infancy a sad one, and causing the first glimpse of happiness to dawn upon him at Cherbury, in depriving him of his mother at an early age in order that he may live entirely in the Herbert family, where he finds so much happiness, and repays it so well, Mr. Disraeli believed that he could bring out in better relief all the tenderness, kindness, docility, gratitude, constancy, and those other rare and splendid qualities of his hero's young soul. In reducing Miss Herbert's years, and in increasing those of his hero, the author no doubt wished to render forcible the sentiments which a child of fifteen could not otherwise have inspired in a young girl of eighteen. The imaginary duel was probably conceived to afford the author an opportunity of showing his hero under other admirable aspects, and especially to furnish him with the means of casting blame upon English society, of absolving him, and of showing how he was the victim of inherent national prejudices, which time has not yet succeeded in eradicating.

The exuberance and variety of the gifts which nature had bestowed upon Byron, together with the universality of his genius, which created in him such apparently singular contrasts, no doubt inspired Mr. Disraeli with the idea that to make him better known it was necessary to make two persons of one, each of a different age, so as to be able to divide his qualities according to their suitableness to those ages, and to make him act and speak in accordance with each given character: to show us the man in his moral, social, and intellectual capacity during his transition from early youth to a maturer age, after the experience of those hardships of life which have purified and strengthened his soul. The first period is represented by the ardent and passionate Lord Cadurcis, the other by the wise and philosophical Herbert. In making Herbert live to a mature age, and in centring in him every grace, every quality, every perfection with which a mortal can be gifted, he wished to show to what degree of moral perfection Lord Byron might have attained, and how happy he might have been in the peace and quiet of domestic life had he been joined to another wife in matrimony, since notwithstanding Lady Annabel's faults, happiness was not out of Herbert's reach. The conclusion to which Disraeli no doubt points is the inward avowal by Lady Annabel herself that she, not Herbert, was the cause of their separation, and of their useless misfortunes. Again, when young Lord Cadurcis returns from Greece, and when Disraeli recounts his conversation with Herbert, his intention, no doubt, was to show us the intellectual and moral progress which time has caused him to make,—the transition from the "Childe Harold" of twenty-one to the "Childe Harold" of "Manfred" of twenty-nine; and from the "Childe Harold" of thirty to the "Don Juan" and "Sardanapalus" of thirty-three; he thus was able to put in relief that mobility of character which existed in him as regards a certain order of ideas, and which blended itself so well with the depth and the constancy of other of his views, enabling us to penetrate into the recesses of that beautiful soul, and displaying to our admiring gaze its numberless springs of action,—at times his constant aspiration to come to the aid of humanity, and his little hope of succeeding in modifying our corrupt nature; his love of glory, and how little he cared for the appreciation of the public of which he had experienced the fickle favors; his knowledge of life, his simple tastes, his love of nature, and the greatness of his mind, of which no ambition or worldly feeling could tarnish the simplicity and even sublimity. In giving him two individualities the novelist was better able to combine the passionate sarcasms of Cadurcis with the smiles of goodness and tolerance of Herbert, and to show him to us as he was wont to converse, mixing the wittiest remarks with the most serious reflections. He had made him express a number of opinions apparently contradictory, but which belonged to his peculiar character, which was equally simple and complex, alike sensible and passionate, subject to a thousand influences of weather and seasons; and though inflexible in his principles of honor as in the whole course of his existence, yet changeable in things of minor importance. He loves to mystify, and writes, without reflecting as to the possible consequences, a number of things which cross his mind, and in which he does not believe, but of which his love of humor forces the expression to his lips. Again, Disraeli tells us of a number of his real ideas, initiates us into his literary tastes, his philosophical views, his preferences, his admiration for the great men of antiquity and of modern times; tells us why his favorite philosophers are Plato and Epicurus, his favorite characters in antiquity Alexander and Alcibiades, both young and handsome conquerors; in modern times, Milton and Sir Philip Sydney, Bayle and Montaigne; what his opinions respecting Shakspeare and Pope, what Cadurcis, and what Herbert thinks of these; and finally he gives us his views upon the love which we should have for truth, upon the influence which political situations bear upon the grandeur of country, not only in literature and in arts, but likewise in philosophy, and in a number of other ways.

All these means employed by the great novelist certainly succeed in making of "Venetia" a most delightful book; but notwithstanding its charms, as we read, it is impossible not to ask one's self at times whether a historical novel is thus entitled to encroach upon the biography of great men. Without pretending to settle the question, I own that I rather appreciate the truth of a historical work than all the pleasure which the talent of an author can afford me, and it appears to me that if Mr. Disraeli, with his admirable talent, had chosen to write the life of Lord Byron, he would have done better. We should not, it is true, have had in the biography either the pleasant life at Cherbury, or the scene at Newstead, neither the duel nor its consequences; but we should have had almost a similar Lady Mounteagle, and we should have seen the rise of that same base spirit in his colleague which greeted him at one period of his life, the same wickedness which assailed him, the same jealousy with which he was looked upon, the same cruel persecution to which he was subjected, the same hatred which assailed him on the part of the people who had a little before so idolized him, and, in short, the same reaction in the public mind which actually took place. We should, on the other hand, have equally seen the same noble mind, too proud again to submit to the curb under the yoke of popular public feeling. He would not have shown us a charming Lady Annabel styled a virtuous woman, though she abandons her husband simply because she believes he no longer entertains for her all the ardent love which he had evinced during the honey-moon! —a Lady Annabel, indeed, who constitutes in herself a being morally impossible, who though she does abandon her husband, spends her night in bewailing his loss at the foot of his portrait; who, though she adores her daughter, nearly causes her death with grief from the fear which she has that the child will not marry a man of genius like her father. Instead of such a woman we should have had, if not one more logical in her acts, at least more real and historical, and exemplifying the painful and murderous effects of silence in the condemnation of a man against whom the venom of calumny has been directed—that man being no less a person than her own husband. Instead of a Lady Annabel repentant at last, and self-accusing, truth and reality would have presented us with an insensible, hard-hearted, and inexorable woman, who remains inflexible to the last, and who deserves that the effects should be applied to her of the words which Cadurcis, in a moment of despair, pronounces against Venetia's mother, when the former declares that she is the victim of her mother, but that nevertheless she will do her duty:

"Then my curse upon your mother's head! May Heaven rain all its plagues upon her! The Hecate!"

We should not have had a Venetia who is truly a delicious emanation from a poet's mind, and the only woman worthy of becoming the wife of Lord Byron, who sums up in herself all the tenderness which he must have inspired in or felt for a woman, a sister, or a daughter. But we should have had, instead of her, three persons who really existed, and who exercised a great influence over Lord Byron's life. The one a young lady of eighteen, whom Lord Byron styled light and coquettish, but who really possessed his heart at fifteen years of age; the other his dear Augusta, who was truly a Venetia toward him; and finally, his beloved little Ada, for whom he had such a paternal tenderness. Instead of an elderly Herbert returning to domestic happiness, which would simply have been impossible with the wife whom Fate had chosen for Lord Byron, we should have had a handsome young man who has not waited until he had reached the mature age of Herbert to be adorned with every virtue, in whom reason is not the effect of growing years, whose wisdom is not that of the old; and instead of the pathetic catastrophe which is attributed to Herbert and Cadurcis together, and which really occurred to Shelley, we should have had Lord Byron's real death, which was infinitely more pathetic, and could have been described in equally beautiful and heartrending language. How sublime would have been the history of the death of that young man who at the age of thirty-four heroically sacrifices his life for the independence of a country which is not his own, and whose patriotism is greater than that of his countrymen, since he prefers the cause of humanity to the interests of the little spot on the globe where he was born!

If, then, instead of a novel, Mr. Disraeli had given us a true history, the work would have been an everlasting monument erected to the memory of two noble beings, and would have been transmitted to posterity as a valuable testimony of the virtues of Lord Byron.

As the book stands, and written by such a man as Mr. Disraeli, it will ever remain a study worthy of being quoted among those whose object it is to proclaim the truth respecting Lord Byron.

PARIS, *November*, 1868.

THE END.

LOSSING'S FIELD-BOOK OF THE WAR OF 1812. Pictorial Field-Book of the War of 1812; or, Illustrations, by Pen and Pencil, of the History, Biography, Scenery, Relics, and Traditions of the Last War for American Independence. By BENSON J. LOSSING. With several hundred Engravings on Wood, by Lossing and Barritt, chiefly from Original Sketches by the Author. 1088 pages, 8vo, Cloth. (*Publishing in Numbers.*)

LOSSING'S FIELD-BOOK OF THE REVOLUTION. Pictorial Field-Book of the Revolution; or, Illustrations, by Pen and Pencil, of the History, Biography, Scenery, Relics, and Traditions of the War for Independence. By BENSON J. LOSSING. 2 vols., 8vo, Cloth, $14 00; Sheep, $15 00; Half Calf, $18 00; Full Turkey Morocco, $22 00.

ABBOTT'S HISTORY OF THE FRENCH REVOLUTION. The French Revolution of 1789, as viewed in the Light of Republican Institutions. By JOHN S. C. ABBOTT. With 100 Engravings. 8vo, Cloth, $5 00.

ABBOTT'S NAPOLEON BONAPARTE. The History of Napoleon Bonaparte. By JOHN S. C. ABBOTT. With Maps, Woodcuts, and Portraits on Steel. 2 vols., 8vo, Cloth, $10 00.

ABBOTT'S NAPOLEON AT ST. HELENA; or, Interesting Anecdotes and Remarkable Conversations of the Emperor during the Five and a Half Years of his Captivity. Collected from the Memorials of Las Casas, O'Meara, Montholon, Antommarchi, and others. By JOHN S. C. ABBOTT. With Illustrations. 8vo, Cloth, $5 00.

ADDISON'S COMPLETE WORKS. The Works of Joseph Addison, embracing the whole of the "Spectator." Complete in 3 vols., 8vo, Cloth, $6 00.

ALCOCK'S JAPAN. The Capital of the Tycoon: a Narrative of a Three Years' Residence in Japan. By Sir RUTHERFORD ALCOCK, K.C.B., Her Majesty's Envoy Extraordinary and Minister Plenipotentiary in Japan. With Maps and Engravings. 2 vols., 12mo, Cloth, $3 50.

ALFORD'S GREEK TESTAMENT. The Greek Testament: with a critically-revised Text; a Digest of Various Readings; Marginal References to Verbal and Idiomatic Usage; Prolegomena; and a Critical and Exegetical Commentary. For the Use of Theological Students and Ministers. By HENRY ALFORD, D.D., Dean of Canterbury. Vol. I., containing the Four Gospels. 944 pages, 8vo, Cloth, $6 00; Sheep, $6 50.

BANCROFT'S MISCELLANIES. Literary and Historical Miscellanies. By GEORGE BANCROFT. 8vo, Cloth, $3 00.

BARTH'S NORTH AND CENTRAL AFRICA. Travels and Discoveries in North and Central Africa: being a Journal of an Expedition undertaken under the Auspices of H.B.M.'s Government, in the Years 1849–1855. By HENRY BARTH, Ph.D., D.C.L. Illustrated. Complete in Three Vols., 8vo, Cloth, $12 00.

BELLOWS'S OLD WORLD. The Old World in its New Face: Impressions of Europe in 1867–1868. By HENRY W. BELLOWS. 2 vols., 12mo, Cloth, $3 50.

BOSWELL'S JOHNSON. The Life of Samuel Johnson, LL.D. Including a Journey to the Hebrides. By JAMES BOSWELL, Esq. A New Edition, with numerous Additions and Notes, By JOHN WILSON CROKER, LL.D., F.R.S. Portrait of Boswell. 2 vols., 8vo, Cloth, $4 00.

BRODHEAD'S HISTORY OF NEW YORK. History of the State of New York. By JOHN ROMEYN BRODHEAD. First Period, 1609–1664. 8vo, Cloth, $3 00.

BULWER'S PROSE WORKS. Miscellaneous Prose Works of Edward Bulwer, Lord Lytton. In Two Vols. 12mo, Cloth, $3 50.

BURNS'S LIFE AND WORKS. The Life and Works of Robert Burns. Edited by ROBERT CHAMBERS. 4 vols., 12mo, Cloth, $6 00.

COLERIDGE'S COMPLETE WORKS. The Complete Works of Samuel Taylor Coleridge. With an Introductory Essay upon his Philosophical and Theological Opinions. Edited by Professor SHEDD. Complete in Seven Vols. With a fine Portrait. Small 8vo, Cloth, $10 50.

CURTIS'S HISTORY OF THE CONSTITUTION. History of the Origin, Formation, and Adoption of the Constitution of the United States. By GEORGE TICKNOR CURTIS. Complete in Two large and handsome Octavo Volumes. Cloth, $6 00.

www.ingramcontent.com/pod-product-compliance
Lightning Source LLC
LaVergne TN
LVHW021050110826
845150LV00001B/29

* 9 7 8 1 4 2 5 5 6 7 9 8 9 *